**NEW ARABISM, ISLAMISM AND
THE PALESTINE QUESTION 1908-1941**
A Political History
Basheer M Nafi This book traces the origin, development and
interaction of two major Arab political forces during the interwar period: the Arab-Islamic movement and the Palestine
Question. By highlighting key events in the Arab interwar
movement, such as the Jerusalem Western Wall incident, the
Syrian revolt in the mid-1920s, the 1936-9 Palestinian revolt
and the Iraqi-British military clash of 1941, the study follows
the convergence of the fate of the Palestinians with that of the
Arab movement as a whole. Ithaca 1998 £35.00 HB 459pp
[27504]   **£9.99**

**NEW THE STRUGGLE
FOR POWER IN ARABIA**
Ibn Saud, Hussein and Great Britain, 1914-1924
Haifa Alangari In June 1916, outside the Grand Mosque at
Mecca, the Arab Revolt was proclaimed by the Sharif of
Mecca, Hussein ibn Ali, with Britain's full backing. Ten years
later, on the very same spot, Abdul-Aziz ibn Saud was inaugu-
rated as the Sultan of Najd and King of the Hijaz. In this book, Alangari examines the nature and
foundation of the authority of these two leaders and relates it to Britain's intervention in the region
during the First World War. Ithaca 1998 £35.00 HB 290pp Illus
[27501]   **£9.99**

Arabism,
Islamism
and the
Palestine
Question
1908 – 1941
A Political History

Basheer M. Nafi

CW00828235

Arabism, Islamism
and the
Palestine Question

Arabism, Islamism

and the

Palestine Question

1908 – 1941
A Political History

Basheer M. Nafi

ITHACA

ARABISM, ISLAMISM AND THE PALESTINE
QUESTION, 1908–1941
A Political History

Ithaca Press is an imprint of Garnet Publishing Limited

Published by
Garnet Publishing Limited
8 Southern Court
South Street
Reading
RG1 4QS
UK

First Edition

ISBN 0 86372 235 0

British Library Cataloguing-in-Publication Data
A catalogue record for this book is available from the British Library

Jacket design by Michael Hinks
Typeset by Samantha Abley

Printed in Lebanon

Contents

	Note on Transliteration	vi
	Preface	1
1.	Introduction	5
2.	Arabism, Zionism and Palestinian nationalism	15
3.	In pursuit of a lost ideal: rise and decline of pan-Islamism	89
4.	Arabism reawakening	139
5.	The 1936–9 revolt and the Arabization of the Palestinian question: phase 1	191
6.	The 1936–9 revolt and the Arabization of the Palestinian question: phase 2	249
7.	A defeat in Iraq: the decline of Arab-Islamists	329
8.	Conclusion	395
	Bibliography	401
	Index	445

Note on Transliteration

Familiar Arabic names and terms, which are widely used in literature, have been spelt in the commonly adopted form (e.g. Nasser rather than Nasir). Texts of sources consulted have been preserved in their original forms. No diacritical marks are used. The *'ayn* is indicated by an opening quotation mark and the *hamza* by a closing quotation mark.

"O you free Arabs, yours is
A dawn that breaks with a smile all over the universe"

**From a poem by Shaykh Fu'ad al-Khatib
saluting Faysal's Arab army published
in *al-Qibla* newspaper, Mecca,
15 Shawwal AH 1334 (15 August 1916)**

"The British complained that there is general ill feeling against them
in Iraq. This feeling is common to all Arabs owing to their policy
in Palestine and cannot be checked by any Arab statesman."

**Rashid Ali al-Gaylani to Ibn Saud quoted in a dispatch
from Stonehewer-Bird (Jedda) to Foreign Office,
22 January 1941, FO 371/27061/E 84**

"Nationalism – to change the figure – is like a cinema film; to manifest
itself it must be projected on to a screen; we, the British, were
the only possible screen; no other nation had sufficient
standing to be worth accusing of trying to deprive
the country of independence."

**Message from C. J. Edmonds, The British Advisor
to the Ministry of Interior, Iraq, to Sir Kinahan
Cornwallis, Ambassador, Baghdad, 29 July 1941;
quoted in a dispatch from Cornwallis
to Foreign Office, FO 624/24/448**

Preface

A large corpus of research on Palestinian nationalism and the Palestinian question has been published during the past few decades. In most of these works, the Palestinian question was studied from the perspective of its local context, its impact on the evolution of the Palestinian national entity and on Palestinian society, or of its international context.[1] Fewer studies, and of a less comprehensive nature, have been dedicated to the understanding of the Arab and Islamic framework of the Palestinian question, especially in its early stage, during the interwar period.[2] Such an approach is warranted for two important reasons: firstly, for the central role that Palestine assumed and continues to assume in shaping Arab and Islamic politics and ideologies; and secondly, for the simultaneous emergence of the Palestinian question, Arab nationalism and modern political Islam, and the influence that each of these major movements left on the course of the others.

This study attempts to elucidate the complex set of relations that connected the Arab–Zionist conflict in Palestine with the broader scene of Arabism and Islamism on the eve of the Ottoman collapse and during the colonial era. The emphasis here is principally on the political dimensions of this interconnectedness. At the core of this work is a political and, to a lesser extent, social exposition of two generations of the Arab élite, prior to and after the Ottoman demise. The political behaviour of Arab notables, intelligentsia and ulema, whose views of the world were largely shaped by the Arab-Islamic reformist ideas during the first half of the twentieth century, are presented in relation to the struggle for Palestine and to the projects of Islamic and Arab unity.

Following the end of the Cold War, and particularly in the aftermath of the Gulf War, the failure of Arab nationalism and the demise of political Islam became prominent themes in scholarship focusing on Islam and the Arab world.[3] Coupled with the political and ideological shifts in Palestinian nationalism and the Arab–Israeli conflict in the early 1990s, these themes are bound to influence our view of the historical development of Arabism, Islamism and the Palestine question. Underpinning the susceptibility of our understanding of history to the influences of our present realities, John Luckas has in 1990 written of "the mental intrusion into the structure of events".[4] By this, Luckas meant the inseparability of what happens from "the way people think what happens". Although the Arab world has a habit of defying confident scholarship and "expert" predictions, this study consciously attempts to formulate its main assumptions in terms of the historical period under investigation, rather than the present debate on Arabism and Islamism.

This work evolved from an earlier version prepared during a five-year study for a Ph.D. at the University of Reading, United Kingdom, for which I am deeply indebted to Peter Woodward for his friendship, low-key and invaluable guidance, profound insights and, above all, for making the process of learning highly enjoyable. Eugene L. Rogan, with characteristic kindness, made some attentive comments and critical remarks on the original draft, and encouraged me to rewrite the introductory chapter.

To Ibrahim Abu Rabi', Hibba Abugideiri, Ralph Coury and Yusuf T. Delorenzo, my thanks and gratitude for reading and commenting on one chapter or more. I am grateful to Shihab al-Din al-Sarraf for the hours and days of ongoing lively and invigorating debates. I am also indebted to Samih Hamouda, for his faithful help in obtaining many important documents from the archive of the Arab Studies Society in Jerusalem and for providing me with a copy of the original diaries of Khalil al-Sakakini; to Steven Kennedy, for generously allowing me to share the wealth of documents he obtained from the Central Zionist Archive, and to Adnan Aydan and Lutfi Zaytouni for their invaluable technical support during the last stages of preparation and the struggle with the not always amiable software.

My thanks also go to the staff and librarians of al-Azhar University (Cairo), the Centre for National Documents (Damascus), the Institute for Palestine Studies (Beirut), the University of Durham Library (Durham), the Middle East Centre, St Antony's College (University of Oxford), the University of Exeter Library (Exeter), the Public Record Office and the India Office (London), for their magnificent professionalism and support. Thanks are also due to Dr 'Aziz al-'Azma at the University of Exeter for permitting me to examine the papers of 'Aziz and 'Adil al-'Azma.

When I first began working on this project, I was a father of two. Two more children have since arrived. To Tariq, Iman, Ahmad and Safa, and to my wife, Imelda J. Ryan, I will always be indebted for making life continuously novel and a pleasant experience.

NOTES

1 Porath's two-volume study (1974 and 1977) is now considered to be a classical work on Palestinian nationalism in the interwar period. Similar influential studies of the same period include Kayyali (1978), Lesch (1979) and al-Hout (1986). Muslih (1988) dealt with the origins of Palestinian nationalism from the late nineteenth century to 1920, while Wasserstein (1991; first published in 1978) focused on the British policy in Palestine from 1917 to 1929, prior and after the beginning of the mandate. Khalaf (1991) combined political and sociological approaches to the study of Palestinian history from the beginning of World War II to 1948. Smith (1984) and Smith (1992) are more like textbooks that cover a long period of Palestinian history; the first deals with the period from 1876 to 1983, and the second with the period from 1800 to the early 1980s. The diplomatic history of the Arab–Zionist conflict is the subject of Caplan's two volumes (1983), whereas origins of the conflict during the late Ottoman period were discussed by Mandel (1976). A sociological perspective of the Palestinian national movement and of the people is provided by the two collections edited by Migdal (1980) and Nakhleh and Zuriek (1980). Recently, Kimmerling and Migdal (1993) published an extensive socio-political study of the Palestinians covering the period from the 1830s to the 1980s.

2 Best available sources are Jankowiski's two articles (1980:1–38; 1981:427–53) that were dedicated to the study of Egyptian official and popular responses to the Palestinian question during the 1930s and early 1940s. Mayer (1983) published another study on the Egyptian attitudes to Palestine in the period from 1936 to 1945, in which he largely followed Kedourie's dismissive approach to Arabism. An extensive study of the political course of Arab nationalism between 1930 and 1945 was published by Porath (1986). Porath's work, however, while highly influenced by the British official view of the events, sheds little light on the careers, background and outlook of the key personalities of the Arab interwar drama.

3 On the decline of Arab nationalism, see Lewis (1992:92–119), and on political Islam, see Roy (1994).

4 Luckas (1990:52).

1

Introduction

Islamism is the tendency to underline the world outlook with Islamic perceptions. While one root of Islamism can be traced to the nineteenth-century pan-Islamic movement of Sultan Abd al-Hamid II's and Jamal al-Din al-Afghani's views of Islamic unity, the other is related to the revival of Islamic thought, as was largely reflected in the Islamic reform movement of the late nineteenth century and early twentieth century. As such, Islamism is a term with manifold dimensions: Islamic unity and revival; anti-imperialism, and cultural reconstruction. After the demise of the Ottoman state, the pan-Islamic surge was gradually eclipsed by the emergence of Islamic societies and organizations that tended to emphasize aspects of cultural identity and the Islamization of the nation-state rather than the enterprise of Islamic unity.[1]

Arabism is a term often used to indicate the early period of Arab nationalism. No less often, Arabism appears as an alternative expression to "Arab nationalism", without taking into account its historical evolution. In this study, Arabism denotes a particular form of nationalism that began to arise in the Arabic-speaking provinces of the Ottoman empire in the late nineteenth century, where the Arab entity was largely defined in Islamic terms.[2] This, of course, implies a distinction between Arabism and Arab nationalism. Arab nationalism will be used here to mark the stage in which Arabism became more exclusively outlined by its advocates (in terms of race, language and geography), and in which the constituent elements of nationalism were increasingly stripped of their origins, their Islamic origins.

It was from within the circles of the Arab-Islamic reform movement that Arabism – like Islamism – first emerged, reflecting a cultural expression of an Arab sense of identity and a discourse of political opposition. The relationship between the rise of nationalism and the emergence of the modern intellectual in the "underdeveloped" countries, where there was little sense of nationality among the peoples whose nationality the intellectuals were proclaiming, has been described by Edward Shils. The first impetus to nationalism, Shils wrote,

> seems to have come from a deepening of the feeling of distance between ruler and ruled, arising from the spiritual and ethnic remoteness of the foreign rulers, and the dissolution of the particularistic tie which holds ethnically homogeneous rulers and ruled together. This identification of one self as a subject of an unloved (however feared and respected) ruler with others who shared that subjection was one phase of the process. The discovery of the glories of the past, of cultural traditions, was usually but not always an action, *ex post facto*, which legitimated the claims asserted on behalf of that newly imagined collectivity.[3]

Mainly, it was the invocation of the glorious past which was to provide Arabism with its formative ingredients. This invocation was marked by the interlocking of various elements, genuine and real as well as invented – to use Hobsbawm's term – and assumed: the return to the Qur'an and the Prophet's traditions; the assumption of a continuous interconnectedness between the Arabic language and an Arab Semitic race; an exclusive Arab contribution to the glorious early Islamic period; the Turkish race's responsibility for the declining fortunes of Islam, and so forth. Where the Arabs existed since ancient times, Arabism ordained the invention of their sense of nation-ness by inventing the necessary and particular traditions for this nation-ness. Shils's explanation, however, fails to note that the discovery-invention of the past did not occur in a vacuum, but rather in competition with existing images of the past, and that it occurred at a juncture of man's history when old patterns of social structure ceased to function as they used to, and when cultural and technological changes set the conditions for the idea of the nation to be born.

To be sure, the definition of nationalism has always been problematic.[4] In the closest encounter with the spirit and genealogy of the nation, Benedict Anderson wrote, "the nation is an imagined political community – and imagined as both inherently limited and sovereign".[5] By this Anderson meant that the nation did not come into being until it became possible for its members to imagine their communion, although it is impossible for an individual member to know all of those he regards as his fellow members. The nation is also imagined as limited – beyond its boundaries lie other nations; as sovereign, whose birth followed or accompanied the demise of the divinely ordained hierarchical dynastic empires; and as a community because it is primarily conceived as a communion of equal "citizens". The strength of Anderson's statement lies not only in its encompassing of the dynamics of the nation's formation, but also in its transcending of the sociological bifurcation between the cultural and the structural. It was not only an evolution of the objective social structures, or the impact of a new set of ideas, but a combination of both which led to the emergence of this unique phenomenon which we know as nationalism. But since men, in Durkheim's words, are the only active elements of society, the interaction of cultural and structural constraints through the creative human agency engenders new dimensions of ideas and reality, and rarely in a predetermined fashion.[6] Arabism, in this sense, was a choice not an inevitability, an evolving sociocultural construct, not a constant position.

The most powerful element of Arabism was the Arabic language, the living idiomatic medium of the sacred text and the most distinctive feature of the Arabs, through which they instituted their separation from the Turks and by which they felt themselves endowed with continuity. Like the English in their relations with the Scots, the Ottomans never adopted a policy of linguistic-Ottomanization of the Arabic-speaking provinces, for Arabic was also held sacred by the Ottomans.[7] But, unlike the Scots in relation to England, the Arabs were kept at a distance from the Ottoman centre of power for most of the Ottoman epoch. The policy of non-interference and political insulation contributed to maintaining the Arab linguistic identity and to the preservation of Arabic as both a vernacular and a sacred, salient language.

There seems to be no single interpretive model to explain the relationship between religion, language and nationalism. The process of nation-building in the European context involved the rupture of the salient, sacred language's domination and the embrace of vernaculars in most cases. Irish nationalism was, at least in part, defined and fostered by the Catholic Church, while language played no significant role. On the other hand, the Serbian language (a vernacular rather than a sacred language), as well as the Orthodox Church, were crucial elements in the development of Serbian nationalism. In contrast, Arabic, the sacred and salient language, was reappropriated by the Arab-Islamic reformists and their students and employed to provide the psychological elevation of the Arabs over their political masters. The power generated by the new version of Islamic history and the possession of the salient language enabled the Arab-Islamic reformists to retain the sacred and reaffirm its meaning for the existence of the nation. Conscious of the questions that the new cultural position implied for the future of the Islamic political bond between the Arabs and the Turks, the Arab-Islamic reformists called for the establishment of an Arab Caliphate. The inner contradictions of the Caliphate project precipitated the psychological condition for undermining the imagined sacred community of the empire.

Like all other nationalist movements, Arabism could not come into being without the revolutionary transformation of communication and the rise of the print media. Both made it possible for greater numbers of Arabs to view themselves as a nation, facing the calamities of the Ottoman drive for centralization and the colonial experience. For centuries, limited literacy and the confinement of esoteric Arabic within the ulema institution created a cultural state of stratified intelligibility, which in turn reinforced "the stratified society".[8] But since nations are imagined as egalitarian and communal, the print language, with its mass orientation, rendered Arabic open to the occurrences of everyday life. To invite the masses into history, the Arab-Islamic reformists, who fully embraced the power of the press, had to write the invitation card in a language they understood.[9] While the cohesion of the sacred communities of empires lies outside the domain of the print media, for the assumed nation, print language was to facilitate the standardization of idiom and afford a new solidarity, an imagined solidarity.

Yet, this was not the only way in which the cultural and technological changes of modern times made the nation possible. What Renan called the shared amnesia, or the collective forgetfulness, played as important a role in the making of nations as did the invocation of tradition, common memories and cultural solidarity.[10] Old modes of segmentary solidarity, the tribal, the guild-based, the confessional and sub-confessional and regional solidarities, have to be transcended or at least weakened before a sense of nation-ness can be developed. In the Arab nationalist context, the press and modern communications were essential for the initiation of this process, as also were the Ottoman drive for centralization, the rise of the modern high school and university, and the introduction of the Arab-Islamic reformist vision of Islam. The mass and abstract nature of modern education, the demise of the *waqf* system and of the traditional institutions depending on its revenues, and the undermining of the guild associations (*asnaf*) and the traditional market-place under the impact of the Western economic invasion, obliterated the boundaries between the traditional compartments of society. And like scripturalist Protestantism, the Arab-Islamic reform movement emphasized the primacy of the original texts, the Qur'an and the Prophet's traditions, and their immediate relevance to the living moment of society. In the absence of an Islamic canonical church, the reformists sought to establish a unity of religiosity that would rise above and challenge the factional segmentation of the "popular religion", reflected in the dividing adherence to the *fiqhi* schools and Sufi *tariqas*. Their vision of "high Islam" found a receptive environment in the swelling Arab cities of the interwar period where, for the now mobile population, traditional loyalties seemed too distant to be maintained. The new modes of solidarity were subsequently reinforced by the emergent nationalist clubs, Islamic societies, students' unions and political associations of a public or secretive nature.

Yet, arriving fairly late on the nationalist scene, Arabism owed its existence not only to the realm of invention, but also to the realm of importation. By the early twentieth century, the idea of nationhood had been long established in the European theatre, resonating throughout the world of "nations". As with other aspects of modernity, the early Arabists tended to perceive an association between the rise of nationalism and the invigorating of European nations. Even within the Ottoman empire, the ascendance of nationalist movements in the Balkans was forcing the Ottoman government to cede large territories of its European possessions to the new nations. As the question of decline and revival was precipitating a profound sense of crisis among the Ottoman intellectual and political strata, both Arab and Turkish, the Arab-Islamic reformists saw, in the available, powerful and seemingly adaptable European model of the sovereign nation, an appropriate solution for the crisis and a route for entering the international community of nations.

Ultimately, however, imagined communities do not necessarily evolve into political movements. The quest for national sovereignty is not an inevitable outcome of the developed sense of nation-ness. Largely, the integrationist-separatist political tendencies, which characterized certain drives for nationhood, accompanied patterns of nationalism in which the evolution of the particularistic sense of nation-ness preceded the birth of its nation-state.[11] It is usually the perceived association between the realization of the sovereign nationhood and the individual interests of certain groups in society which ignites the politicization of the cultural national movement. At the heart of this process is what Greenfeld described as the sense of dissatisfaction and resentment.[12] Both are generated by a persistent inconsistency between the definition of existing social order and the experience of the involved actors, reinforced with a combined belief of compatibility, or even self-superiority, between the subject and object of dissatisfaction and resentment and a real or even imagined situation of inequality. But while Greenfeld explained resentment in terms of the assumed nation's view of the imitated external power, it is obvious that as a socio-psychological state it can influence the nationalist perspective of both the imitated "other" and the internal political master. The significance of dissatisfaction and resentment lies in the effect they exercise in the transvaluation of values, that is, the reordering of the dominant scale of values in society, upon which political secession and even wars become justified. In times of crisis and transition, dissatisfaction and resentment become key elements in determining the nationalist reactions and in typifying these reactions.

In the forefront of the Arab political movement during the interwar period were two generations of Arabists whose political and ideological attitudes were largely shaped by the Arab-Islamic reformist world view. The proposition of Arab-Islamism as a tool of analysis for the Arab interwar politics must not, however, be seen in isolation from other frameworks of analysis. Out of Albert Hourani's highly influential study of "Ottoman Reforms and the Politics of Notables",[13] students of the modern Middle East have found an effective "ideal type" against which a wide range of social, ideological and political changes in modern Arab history looked clearer and more comprehensible. Hourani suggested that the urban notables – local ulema, military of the local garrison, family chieftains, *aghas* and *amirs*, land *multazims* (later big landowners) – played, as leaders of the urban population, an important intermediary role between the government and the people.[14] For Hourani, the concept of notables is used as a political and not a sociological one. While Ottoman modernization left a significant impact on the urban notables, it would by no means weaken their political influence. On the contrary, following the collapse of Ottoman rule, the urban notables emerged as a major force in the post-World War I Arab political entities, either as the ruling class of the independent and semi-independent states or as leaders of the nationalist movement.

The concept of the notables will certainly be widely employed throughout this study, but only in connection with the Arab-Islamic frame of reference. A term with ideological connotations, Arab-Islamism will nonetheless be used to signify the ideological as well as the political views and behaviour of the Arab interwar generation. Whereas the urban nobility is a political class of largely wealthy and well-established groups, the Arab-Islamists were socially broad and diverse groupings. Their most illustrious members were undoubtedly of notable background, yet amongst them were also key activists, journalists, ideologues, and political leaders from the middle classes, and even of more humble social origins.

The failure of this broadly-based political class to achieve its ideal of a pan-Arab state is rooted in the political complexity of the Arab post-World War I situation. As the Arabic-speaking provinces of the Ottoman empire were divided into several entities by the imperialist powers (adding to the areas that had already been under imperialist control), these entities began to experience a transformational condition that resembled in many respects the transformation of the Latin American Spanish-speaking colonies into independent states. Instrumental in the development of national consciousness and statehood in the western hemisphere was the influence of what Anderson called the "pilgrim Creole functionaries".[15] By this, Anderson meant the shared experience of local white administrators of the European colonies in the Americas, who were barred from ascending to higher positions in the colonial (mother) country, and from moving freely amongst the administrative hierarchies of the different colonies, even when these colonies belonged to one colonial power (as was the case in Spanish Latin America). The limited geographical outlook of the post-World War I Arab regional state (in contrast with the wider outlook of the Ottoman empire), engendered a limited and constrained experience in the daily life of Arab army officers and state bureaucrats. In other words, ingredients of the daily functions, of the social and political dictionary, of the aspirations and priorities, referred largely to a world of Iraqi, Egyptian and Saudi cities and villages, rather than to an Arab whole. Within each of the different military and civilian hierarchies of the Arab regional state, a local and collective sense of interests and identity began to evolve, underlined by the realities of power between the Arab movement and the imperialist system. The drawing of the Arab regional state's map was followed by the development of a local educational code and institutions, of local press, of local history and museum and of local symbols. The regional state was thus becoming an imagined political community of its own.

Arabism, however, was a condition that preceded the formation of local entities; the regional state, therefore, could frustrate but not obscure the Arab nationalist consciousness. In fact, Arabism was, for different reasons and at different junctures, fostered by the regional state and the local nationalist movement. And as an oppositional movement, Arabism found in the imperialist system a new object for dissatisfaction and resentment. At the heart of the complex and tense relationship between the Arab nationalist movement, the regional state and the imperialist regime, the Palestinian question emerged to play a crucial role in reinforcing the Arab sense of identity, as well as in the convergence and inter-rivalries of the Arab regional states.

NOTES

1 On the origins of pan-Islamism in the late nineteenth century, see Landau, 1990:9–21. Kampffmeyer (1932:99–170), was perhaps the first to observe the increasing emphasis within the Islamic circles of the late 1920s on issues related to social and cultural identity rather than Islamic unity.

2 See, for example, Dawn's analysis of Rashid Rida's, Sharif Husayn's and Amir Abdullah's understanding of Arabism in Dawn, 1973:69–85.

3 Shils, 1960:343. Eric Hobsbawm, describing the process of national formation and its sociocultural imperatives, wrote that "the invention of tradition occurs more frequently when a rapid transformation of society weakens or destroys the social patterns for which 'old' traditions had been designed, producing new ones to which they were not applicable" (Hobsbawm, 1992:5).

4 On the problem of definition in the field of nationalist studies, see, for example, Gellner, 1983:1 and Alter, 1989:4–9. Underlining the problem of definition, Hugh Seton-Watson, the prominent historian of nationalism, wrote, "I am driven to the conclusion that no 'scientific definition' of the nation can be devised; yet the phenomenon existed and exists" (Seton-Watson, 1977:5).

5 Anderson, 1991:6–7.

6 Greenfeld, 1992:19–20.

7 For the Anglo-Scottish case, see Anderson, 1991:89–90.

8 Gellner, 1987:14.
9 Narin, 1977: 340; Anderson, 1991:76–7 and 133.
10 Gellner, 1987:6.
11 German nationalism is, of course, a case in point. No such tendencies were vital for the development of English or French nationalism, where the sense of nationhood evolved after the birth of the nation-state. Until 1863, for example, French was still a foreign language for nearly half of the French schoolchildren (Weber, 1976:66).
12 A concept coined and developed by Nietzsche and Max Scheler, was mainly employed by Greenfeld (1992:14–16) to explain the Russian nationalist impulses.
13 Hourani, 1968:41–68.
14 Ibid., 46–8.
15 Anderson, 1991:47.

2

Arabism, Zionism and Palestinian nationalism

By the end of the nineteenth century, Cairo, Damascus and Baghdad had come to witness the emergence of powerful Islamic-reformist voices, questioning the middle Islamic traditions and the Sufi domination of Islamic thought and society. Shihab al-Din, Nu'man and Mahmud Shukri al-'Alusi, Jamal al-Din al-Afghani, Muhammad 'Abduh and Muhammad Rashid Rida, Abd al-Razzaq al-Bitar, Tahir al-Jaza'iri and Jamal al-Din al-Qasimi, were reformist ulema whose ideas and views evolved out of wide-ranging and interactive developments in the eighteenth- and nineteenth-century Muslim world, including the spread of revivalist *tasawuf*, the Wahhabi resurrection in the Arabian peninsula, the sweeping and unsettling impact of the Ottoman modernization programme, known as the *tanzimat*, and the Western challenge to the validity and sustainability of Islamic social systems and mode of life. Beyond their invocation of *tawhid*, *ijtihad*, reason and their call for the return to the principal Islamic texts, the Qur'an and Sunna (the Prophet's traditions), the Arab-Islamic reformists sought to revitalize the Muslim community and its spirit by incorporating Western concepts and institutions and rendering Islamic thought more receptive to the ideas of progress and change.[1] Although their activities were not particularly organized, the Arab-Islamic reformists were largely aware of each other, fairly interconnected and frequently sought to exchange ideas and views. In addition to their major contribution to the shaping of Arab political and intellectual debates in the first half of the twentieth century, it was from within the Arab-Islamic reformists' circles that Arabism first evolved as a cultural expression, reflecting the inner tension of the reformist project and the reformists' attempt to formulate an answer to the question of Islamic decline.

From its Islamic reformist roots, Arabism grew as an opposition movement to "foreign" forces (first the Ottoman state and then the imperialist powers), failing in the process to achieve a congruity between the Arab nation and an Arab state. Faced with the late Ottoman regime's drive for further centralization and for Turkification, the Arab-Islamic reform movement evolved into political organizations with relatively defined nationalist platforms. While the aims of these organizations were not originally to break with the Ottoman bond, secession became an inevitable demand as a result of the increasing oppression of the Committee of Union and Progress (CUP) and the policies and measures it employed during the war years. But though the war would eventually end with the demise of the Ottoman empire, the Arab movement could establish neither an all-encompassing Arab state nor an Arab Caliphate. Imperialist schemes in the Arab world were the first obstacle in the way of Arab aspirations. The second obstacle arose from the emergence of the Zionist project and its encroachment on Palestine, facilitated by the mighty power of the British empire. Gradually, nonetheless, Arab internal rivalries and local nationalism (*wataniyya*) came to play a drastic role in hampering the Arab pursuit of unity.

The effect of the imperialist and Zionist challenge on the Arab-Islamic movement and on shaping modern Arab and Islamic politics was very pronounced. In many respects, the modern Arab-Islamic experience cannot be understood in isolation from the imperialist and Zionist challenge. But if imperialism was to engender a spontaneous reaction in various parts of the Arab world and was largely a common experience for the Arabs, Zionism would perhaps not have evolved as a central Arab-Islamic question without the growth of its immediate "anti"-Palestinian nationalism. This chapter will attempt to draw the necessary outlines of the conditions within which Arabism, Zionism and Palestinian nationalism simultaneously and collidingly unfolded.

Cultural Arabism

Whether in Baghdad, Damascus, or Cairo, the rise of the Arab-Islamic reformists coincided with the intensified opposition that the Young Ottoman movement posed to the *tanzimat* centralized order of government. Ottoman Turkish intellectuals and statesmen, such as Midhat Pasha, Zia Kukalp, Namik Kamal, Ibrahim Shinasi and Ahmad Riza, expressed strong doubts about the concentration of power and the explicitly Westernized system of the *tanzimat*, which was creating a widening gap between the state and the people.[2] Their views revolved around a programme of gradual transformation of the traditional order, containment of the *tanzimat* excesses, and the implementation of a constitutional and accountable system of governance. During the last decades of the nineteenth century, as Sultan Abd al-Hamid II consolidated his power, suppressed the Young Ottomanist voices and reinforced his authoritarian rule, the Arab-Islamic reformists developed a discourse of anti-despotism. But the origin of the reformists' Arabism was not restricted to the realm of political opposition, for the reformists' invocation of pristine Islam implied a condemnation of the late Islam, the non-Arab Islam.

From 1892 until his death seven years later, the pan-Islamic reformist Jamal al-Din al-Afghani (1838–97) was an advisor of Sultan Abd al-Hamid II in Istanbul. Although his advice was rarely heeded, al-Afghani spelled out his vision for salvaging the empire in a meeting with the sultan. Al-Afghani called on the sultan to withdraw from the Balkans, decentralize the state, transfer the capital to Baghdad, make Arabic the official language, seek unity with the Persian and Indian Muslims, and shut the doors and windows through which European winds were blowing.[3] It was a vision of strategic retreat and restructuring, in which Arabic and the Arab lands were seen as the last refuge, the historical fortress of Islam. The association of the Arabs with the glorious past of Islam was a recurring theme in the reformists' reaction to the Ottoman decline, and their loss of hope in the empire's ability to recover. If this theme was mediated with subtlety during al-Afghani's conversation with Abd al-Hamid, it appeared in no ambiguous terms in the reply of his student, the Egyptian reformist Muhammad 'Abduh (1849–1905) to the Syrian Christian writer Farah Antun. 'Abduh condemned the Abbasid Caliphate's introduction of non-Arab military elements into the Islamic state's machinery, and linked the rise of non-Arab (Turkish) political power to the polytheism and stagnation of the late Islamic experience.[4] Pristine Islam for 'Abduh was essentially Arab Islam.

But the language of the late-nineteenth-century Arab-Islamic reformists did not particularly reflect nationalist tendencies in the modern sense. It is true that the *tanzimat*-Hamidian modernization was sweeping away much of the local cultural autonomy of the Arabs, replacing the traditional and open educational institutions with the centrally controlled Lancasterian school system.[5] It is also true that the challenge to ancient Arab-Islamic culture reached a critical stage when Abd al-Hamid II decreed the universal use of Turkish as the medium of instruction throughout the new schools.[6] However, the Arab-Islamic reformists, aware of the precarious nature of the Ottoman administrative policies, perhaps believed that the use of Turkish was not irreversible. Besides, Arab-Islamic education at the primary level was still available, since the modern school system could not obliterate the traditional schooling entirely and immediately. Al-Afghani, 'Abduh, and their disciple, Muhammad Rashid Rida (1865–1935), the Damascene, and Iraqi reformists were all essentially pan-Islamists who held deep convictions in the Ottoman-Islamic bond.[7] What appears to have motivated the rise of their Arab nationalist feelings was a deepening belief in their right to guide the movement of Islamic revival. As John H. Kautsky has explained:

> the intellectuals assume the leadership of nationalist movement because, unlike the other groups, they have broken out of the rigid class lines of the old society, they have a vision of the future and some ideas, however vague or impractical, of how to attain it and they are almost by definition skilled in the use of written and spoken word.[8]

The late nineteenth century witnessed a remarkable movement of literary and linguistic revival, led by the state functionaries in Egypt and the Christian intellectuals in *Bilad al-Sham*, especially those with a background of foreign missionary schooling.[9] As the modern institutions of journalism, the judiciary and education were dislodging the ulema class from their leading position in society, Arabic, the ulema's language of traditional Islam, was rendered more open to the currents of the time, its ideas and its metaphors. Local cultural and philanthropic societies were being established in many cities of the Ottoman Arabic-speaking provinces,[10] and signs of Arab-nationalist calls were reportedly recorded in Syria and Lebanon. But these early calls were largely associated with the Syrians' increasing fear of European encroachment, particularly that of the French, or were encouraged by the Ottoman reformist and ambitious *walis*, such as Midhat Pasha.[11] The startling reality of the late nineteenth century was that the vast majority of the Arabs, traditional ulema and notables as well as the masses at large, were identifying with Abd al-Hamid's pan-Islamic policy and his confrontational attitudes toward the European imperialists. Relatively, the Arabs were faring better in the state's bureaucracy, and some ulema and notables, including Abu al-Huda al-Sayyadi, Abd al-Qadir al-Qudsi, Salim and Najib Malhama,

Shafiq al-Kurani and 'Izzat al-'Abid, occupied prominent positions in the administration and the inner circle of the sultan himself.[12] At this stage, even Rashid Rida would define his stand from a pro-Ottoman vantage point. Writing in *al-Manar* in 1899, Rida made a fierce attack on the local nationalist tendencies (*wataniyya*) in the Muslim world, and in Egypt in particular, and called for the consolidation of the pan-Islamic league by establishing educational and cooperative projects, and for the dissemination of common values and interests through the print media.[13]

Rida's early writings, however, also reflected signs of doubts over Abd al-Hamid's rule and his enterprise for revival. Implicitly critical of the sultan, Rida emphasized the unifying force of the Arabic language, and the urgent need for "religious freedom" and "political reform".[14] For Rida, religious reform was not the building of mosques and *takiyyas*, or lavishly awarding some shaykhs (Sufis) with medals and stipends, but the uniting of Muslims under one *Shari'a* law and one language. Rida then proposed the scheme that would haunt his career for several years to come. According to this scheme, Islamic reform was seen as attainable through the establishment of an Islamic society, based in Mecca with branches in all Islamic countries, entrusted with confronting unacceptable innovations and harmful teachings, reforming Islamic preaching, and spreading the message of Islam. Although Rida's projected society was assumedly to function under the patronage of the Caliph (the sultan), it betrayed the reformist's urge to appropriate a politically sanctioned role in leading the moral and intellectual regeneration of the *umma*, and his inner struggle between the embryonic future he was beginning to imagine, his long established loyalties and the denied reality of his time. But since Abd al-Hamid saw calls for reforms, from whatever quarter they arose, as European-fomented conspiracies against himself and the empire, he suspected the reformists' activities and ideas, and tended to respond to the deepening Ottoman crisis with more despotic and heavy-handed measures. The rupture between his regime and the reformist circles became inevitable. Increasingly, the reformist discourse turned political, combining a poignant critique of despotism and unconstitutionalism with the message of religious reformation.

Taba'i' al-'Istibdad (or Traits of Despotism) was perhaps the reformists' manifesto *par excellence* against Abd al-Hamid's regime. This book was written by Shaykh Abd al-Rahman al-Kawakibi (1849–1902), an *alim*-journalist from Aleppo who escaped from the Hamidian oppression to Cairo late in the nineteenth century. During his short stay in Egypt, al-Kawakibi was received enthusiastically by the reformist circles and his works, which continued to leave deep imprints on the Arab reformist ideal long after his death, were serialized in *al-Manar*.[15] Al-Kawakibi presented a vision of the state derived mainly from the European democratic and parliamentary system. He held that motion was the primary indicator of a nation's progress, whereas despotism was the greatest impediment to progress and development. If a nation was to accomplish freedom and prosperity, oppression ought to be confronted and resisted even by the least of means, denial by the heart. Despotism was destructive to the national morale and will as well as to religious belief; no glory could be accomplished under the shadows of despotism.[16] Though neither Abd al-Hamid nor his government were explicitly mentioned in *Tabaʾiʿ al-ʾIstibdad*, its implications for the evolving Arab self-view were unmistakable. It was in the early Islamic government of Madina that al-Kawakibi found the Islamic equivalent of his political utopia, where the values of *shura*, justice and equality constituted the distinctive characteristics of the Islamic polity in its pure form, the Arab form. This theme was articulated with more clarity in al-Kawakibi's *Umm al-Qura* or the "Mother of Villages" (i.e. Mecca). Here, al-Kawakibi reiterated his vision of an Arab, democratic Islam and articulated the idea that epitomized the reformists' Arabism – the Arabs are the guardians of correct Islam. The decline of Islam was marked with the demise of the Arab role and the ascendance of the Turks with whom pristine Islam was blemished by foreign customs and innovations.[17] It thus followed that since political reform was contingent upon religious reform, the Arab role in Islam must be restored.[18] The crux of al-Kawakibi's project was the call for Ottoman decentralization and the establishment of an Arab Caliphate in Mecca, the heart of the Arab lands, where Islam first emerged.

Opposition to Istanbul became the dominant theme in Arab reformist political writings during the period prior to the ousting of Abd al-Hamid II.[19] Indeed, in some cases, the oppositional discourse was stretched to its logical conclusion. Since pan-Islamism was Abd al-Hamid's most potent shield, some Arab-Islamists began to challenge the validity of the Ottoman Caliphate, both in Islamic as well as in historical terms. Shaykh Abd al-Hamid al-Zahrawi (1863–1916) and Rafiq al-ʿAzm

(1867–1925),[20] two Syrians who, like Rida and al-Kawakibi, escaped to Cairo from the Ottoman oppression, were perhaps the first Arab-Islamists to envision an Arab political entity without the Caliphate institution. Despite their profound Islamic background and their portrayal of an Arab future based on reformed and progressive Islam, al-Zahrawi and al-'Azm suggested that, historically, the Muslims were united by their belief and not by the political league, and that the Caliphate was not essentially a Qur'an-ordained system.[21] At the heart of this formulation was the search for legitimizing the Arabs' affirmation of their "lost" identity. Yet, the Arab-Islamists were not necessarily intent on breaking the Ottoman bond, a demand that would crystallize only after the CUP's rise to power. Those who came to lead and shape Arabism in its political phase were by and large children of the Arab-Islamic reform movement.

Shaykh Tahir al-Jaza'iri (1852–1920), then inspector of public libraries in Syria, had emerged by the late nineteenth century as the most active figure in the Arab-Islamic reformist circles of Damascus. He was becoming a gravitational point for a group of ulema, students of notable and non-notable backgrounds, including: shaykhs Jamal al-Din al-Qasimi (1866–1914), Abd al-Razzaq al-Bitar (1837–1917), Abd al-Hamid al-Zahrawi and Salim al-Bukhari (1851–1927); the historian and man of letters Rafiq al-'Azm; the journalist Muhammad Kurd-Ali; the army officer Salim al-Jaza'iri (Shaykh Tahir's nephew); Shukri al-'Asali; Abd al-Wahhab al-Mulayhi (al-Inkilizi as he came to be known); Abd al-Rahman al-Shahbandar; Shukri al-Quwwatli and the Syrian Christian, Faris al-Khuri (then a translator at the British Consulate).[22] Known in Arabist quarters of Damascus as the "Senior Circle", this group met regularly on Fridays to discuss religious, social and literary issues. Its aim was to exchange ideas on the revival of education, on societal progress, and on the infusion of Islamic life with modern values. While the goals of this early group did not fall within clear politically nationalist boundaries, it certainly did not lack an oppositional motivation, arising from the group's relations with Young Turk officials in Damascus, such as General Badri and the director of education, Husayn 'Awni. The latter frequently attended the circle's meetings.

Another group, known as the "Junior Circle", was formed under the patronage of Shaykh Tahir al-Jaza'iri, and existed from 1903 until he moved to Cairo in 1905. Members of this circle were mainly students of Maktab 'Anbar, the only modern Ottoman secondary school in Damascus.

Among them were Muhib al-Din al-Khatib, 'Arif al-Shihabi, 'Uthman Mardam, Lutfi al-Haffar, Salih Qumbuz and Salah al-Din al-Qasimi.[23] Al-Jaza'iri imparted the reformist vision of Islam and the Arabs to the young members of the Junior Circle; he introduced them to the works of Ibn Taymiyya, Muhammad 'Abduh, and al-Kawakibi, and fostered their critical view of Hamidian rule. Muhib al-Din al-Khatib, a favourite of al-Jaza'iri, maintained links between his fellow students and the Senior Circle. By 1905, several of the Senior Circle Arabists had already moved to Egypt while members of the Junior Circle dispersed to complete their higher studies in Beirut and Istanbul.

Faced with the Arab students' appalling ignorance of their history, culture and language, Muhib al-Din al-Khatib, 'Arif al-Shihabi, and Abd al-Karim al-Khalil (a Lebanese Shi'i student) organized a secret Arab cultural society in Istanbul. Known as Jam'iyyat al-Nahda al-'Arabiyya (the Arab Renaissance Society), it was headed by al-Khatib, and joined by scores of Arab students living in the imperial capital, such as Riyad al-Sulh, Fa'iz al-'Azm and Shukri al-Jundi.[24] The society's activities focused on the study of Arabic language, history and literature, with a view to current affairs. Egyptian Arab publications like *al-Muqtataf*, *al-Mu'ayyad*, and *al-Muqtabas*, were mailed to the group from Cairo by Muhammad Kurd-Ali. Prompted by the success of his initiative, Muhib al-Din al-Khatib wrote to Salah al-Din al-Qasimi with a proposal to form a branch of the society in Damascus. Since al-Qasimi was then studying medicine at the American University of Beirut (AUB), it is plausible that the Damascus branch included young Arabists from Beirut as well.[25] The Istanbul group members would finally meet with their counterparts of the Syrian branch on the island of Buyuk Ada at a Palace owned by an Iraqi Arab notable in the summer of 1907. This gathering included speeches, debates and poetry reading on "Our Duties" and "We and the Others". But as the news of the society's secret meetings reached the secret police, al-Khatib was forced to leave Istanbul in the same year, before completing his law training. His subsequent departure for Egypt and then for Yemen, where he was employed as a translator for the British Consulate at Hudayda, seems to have put an end to the Istanbul society's activities.

Similar organizational trends with a more conspicuous political outlook were evolving among the Syrian Arabist exiles in Cairo, where some of the most eminent students of the Arab-Islamic reform movement took refuge. Sometime before the overthrow of Abd al-Hamid II, Rashid Rida, Rafiq al-'Azm and Dr Abdullah Jawdat, a Turkish intellectual and opponent of the sultan, formed Jam'iyyat al-Shura al-'Uthmaniyya (the Ottoman Consultative Society), calling for constitutional and parliamentary reformation of the state.[26] The society's aims echoed the political programme of the Young Turks, with a special emphasis on organizing Arab-Ottoman opposition to Hamidian rule. While on his way to Yemen, Muhib al-Din al-Khatib joined Jam'iyyat al-Shura after meeting with Rida and al-'Azm, and subsequently worked to establish a new chapter of the society in Yemen.

Out of these Arabist prototypes came many activists of the Arab political movement. They would become leaders of al-Muntada al-Adabi, al-Fatat, al-'Ahd and the Ottoman Administrative Decentralization Party. Scores of them would be hanged on allegations of treason by Jamal Pasha's military court of 1915–16, while others would re-emerge as key figures in the Arab interwar movement. What was important in the political views of these aggregates was their mainly Ottoman outlook. On the cultural level, they were certainly Arabists as much as the Arab-Islamic reform movement was. Their political vision nonetheless was still to reform rather than break up the empire. Thus, when the oppositional forces to Abd al-Hamid, led by the CUP army officers, succeeded in restoring the constitution and parliamentary life in July 1908, the coup was celebrated by the Arab reformists throughout the Arab lands. At Hudayda, al-Khatib turned al-Shura Society's chapter into a CUP branch, while other Arab activists in Beirut, Jerusalem, Damascus, Baghdad and Istanbul showed no hesitation in joining the emerging clubs of the CUP.[27] Whether in the 1908 coup, or its sequel in 1909, Arab Ottoman officers such as 'Aziz Ali al-Misri and Mahmud Shawkat played important roles in the ascendance of the CUP to power. Yet, the alliance between the Arabists and the CUP was short-lived. With their strong nationalist affinities, the Arab and the Turkish modernist projects were bound to diverge.

The Arab political movement

The CUP coup of 1909 not only put an end to the Hamidian regime but also weakened the spirit and the movement of pan-Islamism which was characteristically linked to, and identified with, the deposed sultan.

Externally, the new rulers sought to accommodate the European powers in order to secure financial loans and economic investment. Internally, they adopted a kind of secular programme that reflected three main and contradictory goals: undermining the influence exerted by various Islamic institutions on the state's affairs; emphasizing the internal unity and cohesion of the various ethnic and confessional elements of the Ottoman peoples; and enhancing the trend towards centralization. With the exception of the ulema and notables who were closely associated with Hamidian policies, Arab élites supported the new regime and moved to contribute to its success. For the majority of the leading Arabs, if Islamism had been tempered and had waned, Ottomanism as a binding framework was still alive. Originally, the opposition CUP, whether through personal contacts or through its associates in exile, had promoted a programme of decentralization and equality for the Ottoman peoples.[28] The abandonment of decentralization promises, the divisive nature of parliamentary life, consecutive political crises and military set-backs, as well as conspicuous policies and measures of Turkification pursued by the CUP, created an unhealthy atmosphere of continuous friction between Arab and Turkish politicians and intellectuals and precipitated a tendency among the Arabs to emphasize their national rights.

Nationalism, none the less, is not always an expression of reality, but rather a composite of realities and perceptions, of bias and objectivity, and of the actual and the imagined. What the Arabs, therefore, opposed in the Ottoman policies between 1908 and 1914, and which came to constitute the foundation of their nationalist political discourse, was not always meant in Istanbul as an anti-Arab policy, nor did it always originate in the new regime. Yet, the inexperience of the Unionist leaders, their hasty drive for reforming the empire at whatever cost, their dubious methods of political control and manipulation, and the organized secrecy and inner incoherence of the CUP, had a great share of responsibility for the deterioration of Arab–Turkish relations.

During the anti-Hamidian struggle, the CUP did not particularly develop a defined organizational structure with marked borders between the political and military wings, or between the core members and their associates of the other opposition groups. Within the CUP itself and amongst those who came to identify with it after the 1908 coup, political and ideological outlooks differed to varying extents. In power, especially during the first four years, the new regime would suffer from continuous tension between the CUP's secretive central committee (not until late 1913 did the CUP turn into a political party; until then it operated as a semi-secret organization of which only a network of clubs was public) and its parliamentary party and between the military and civilian blocs, as well as within each of these different centres of power. Immediately after the constitutional restoration, a number of the Unionist leaders came into prominence, including Tal'at, Enver, Dr Nazim, Dr Baha' al-Din Shukri, Rahmi Bey and Emanuel Karasu.[29] The latter was a Jewish lawyer from Salonika, whose role, amongst other things, in the early stages of the new regime, would contribute to the stigmatizing of the CUP as pro-Zionist, though it is unclear whether Karasu himself was a Zionist. At the first congress of the CUP in October 1908, a body of eight members (Tal'at, Husayn Qadri, Midhat Shukru, Hayri, Ahmad Riza, Enver, Habib and Hafiz Ibrahim) known as the central committee (merkez-i-umumi) was elected in a secret session. The central committee, however, could not maintain its monopoly of power in the organization since competition with the CUP parliamentary bloc led to the establishment of a semi-autonomous parliamentary party.[30] Although Tal'at presided over the parliamentary party for a while, this manœuvre could not secure full control for the central committee in parliament.

There were other challenges that the CUP had to face. One arose from the liberal wing of the pre-1908 opposition forces, inspired by Prince Sabah al-Din. A liberal decentralist with a distinctive predisposition for Western political values, Sabah al-Din and some other like-minded activists maintained a relatively amicable relationship with the CUP when the opposition was united in the struggle for a constitutional change in the empire. This goal achieved, the liberals founded a separate political party (the Liberal Union, or Osmanli Ahrar Firkasi) that contested the 1908 elections in opposition to the CUP though it failed to win more than one seat.[31] Other signs of political dissent began to surface within the ranks of the entrenched Arab notability and conservative elements. These signs of disguised opposition took the form of a society (Jam'iyyat al-'Ikha' al-'Arabi al-'Uthmani; or the Arab–Ottoman Brotherhood Society) established in Istanbul by the Syrians, Shafiq al-Mu'ayyad al-'Azm, Rushdi al-Sham'a, Sadiq al-Mu'ayyad al-'Azam, Shabib al-As'ad, Muhammad al-Makhzumi, the Palestinian, Shukri al-Husayni, Sharif Ja'far (a cousin of the sharif of Mecca), the Iraqi, Shakir al-'Alusi, and

Yusuf Shatwan from Tripolitania.[32] There was nothing explicit about the opposition of this group to the Unionists; their declared aims were to work for consolidation of unity among peoples of the empire, dissemination of knowledge and learning among Arabs, and support for the CUP in preserving and safeguarding the constitution. It is likely that the founding of this society was prompted by the known progressive and anti-notable attitudes of the CUP, and the emerging alliance between Unionist officials and Arab reformists. An immediate purge of pro-Hamidian elements from the provincial administration and local councils precipitated strong resentment among the Syrian Arab notables.[33]

During the interim period between the restoration of the constitution in the summer and the holding of parliamentary elections in the autumn of 1908, the CUP central committee declared a temporary political programme, pending the convening of parliament. Although phrased in general terms, this programme appeared contradictory in substance. It made promises for establishing equality between the citizens, for freedom of the press, for the founding of civil societies, and for providing free education for all. Although the programme promised to expand the local administration, it stressed that Turkish was the official language of the state, of its administration and education, and pointed to the Unionists' intention to create a "unified education" throughout the empire.[34] This contradiction between the policy of strengthening local administration and the pursuit of linguistic and educational uniformity on the one hand, and promises of opening up the political system and increasing moves towards consolidating a centralized order on the other, was to characterize most of the CUP-inspired legislation.

Drawing on its surging popularity and the influence of its military members in local garrisons, as well as its effective penetration of provincial administrations, the CUP swept the board in the parliamentary elections of 1908. Except in a few cases, there seemed to be no serious challenge to the CUP candidates in most of the Arab urban centres.[35] Only in Damascus and Basra were the local notables able to defeat the CUP candidates and send to the parliament Shafiq al-Mu'ayyad al-'Azm and Rushdi al-Sham'a, as well as the Iraqi notable, Talib al-Naqib.[36] These three Arab deputies would soon emerge as outspoken opponents of the Unionists. But this opposition was certainly devoid of any nationalist foundation. Indeed, Arab reformists such as Rafiq al-'Azm and Rashid Rida, who possessed a stronger predisposition to develop an

Arab nationalist outlook, expressed their total support for the CUP and did not hesitate to attack the Arab–Ottoman Brotherhood Society and the challenge of Talib al-Naqib to the CUP, calling for the latter to be given a chance to implement its programme for reform.[37]

During the election campaign, Rida was on a visit to Syria where his speeches evinced a clear pro-CUP attitude, and where he was closely identified with the Syrian supporters of the CUP, such as Shaykh Jamal al-Din al-Qasimi, Shaykh Abd al-Razzaq al-Bitar and 'Uthman al-'Azm – all fellow Arab-Islamic reformists. At the great Umayyid mosque of Damascus, Rida was confronted by angry mobs instigated by conservative ulema and anti-CUP notables. In the event, it was the Arab and Turkish Unionist elements of the military and local administration who provided Rida with protection.[38] The Arabs were, of course, faced with the limitations of the election laws which made knowledge of Turkish a condition for entering the parliamentary contest, and also appeared to have been allocated a smaller number of seats than their share of the population entitled them to. Besides, the CUP secured the election of a number of Turkish candidates to represent some dominantly Arabic-speaking regions, which further reduced the Arab representative power in the assembly. However, these issues were not prominent during or immediately after the elections, and were only raised by the Arabists much later, when Arab relations with the CUP had already been damaged.[39]

In parliament, after some early friction over the approval of the election of Shafiq al-Mu'ayyad al-'Azm and Talib al-Naqib, the Arab deputies threw their weight behind the CUP parliamentary party.[40] The mainly amicable relations with the Unionists became even more visible in April 1909 when the new regime was challenged by a counter coup led by the Islamically conservative Jama'iyya Muhammadiyya (the Muhammadan Society). Rafiq al-'Azm made a fierce attack on the "reactionary" coup and most of the Arab deputies rendered their support to the army-led restoration of the new order, which culminated in the ousting of Abd al-Hamid II.[41] Despite the largely good memory of the deposed sultan in the Arab lands, only in Damascus did the Muhammadan Society establish a mass following, encouraged by the city's conservative ulema.[42] One result of the stormy events of April was the dissolution of the Arab–Ottoman Brotherhood Society, some of whose members were accused of conniving with the reactionary coup.[43] Although its members were exclusively Arab, the dissolution of this society was perhaps received with relief and approval by many of the Arab parliamentarians, as well as in Arab reformist circles. The activities of the society had aroused little enthusiasm among the Arabs, and several of its members proved to be motivated by sheer self-interest rather than by real convictions, turning at a later stage into CUP agents and staunch enemies of the Arab movement.

The second and more important result of the abortive counter-revolution was the diminishing of whatever liberal tendencies might have remained within the CUP. Whether in parliament, in government or in the pro-CUP media, the Unionists were tilting more and more towards limiting freedom of the press and the right of public congregation, and towards curbing nationalist political activities.[44] This shift was undoubtedly bolstered by the presence of Ahmad Riza, the CUP centralist, at the head of parliament. Usage of Turkish became obligatory in local administration;[45] courts were for the first time proscribed from conducting proceedings in Turkish,[46] and Arab merchants were asked to use Turkish or French in their business with the customs and ports authorities.[47] These measures could not pass quietly and evoked popular and press reactions from the Arab quarters.

The question of linguistic rights, which became prominent on the Arab movement's agenda, is more difficult to assess. One of the major Arab demands was the adoption of the Arabic language in schools, government, courts, etc. alongside the Ottoman Turkish language. It must first be remembered that the Ottoman Education Law of 1869, which legislated for the nationwide introduction of modern schooling, did not provide for lower elementary education (the first three to four years of schooling).[48] It was because of the ulema's insistence on preserving the traditional Islamic education (study of the Qur'an and Arabic) at this level that modern education was implemented only at the higher elementary level (the *rushdiyya* schools of three to four years' duration) and above (*i'dadiyya*, the middle school of four years' duration, and the *sultaniyya*, the high school lasting six years divided into two equal terms). The implementation of the 1869 Law was, nonetheless, partial, piecemeal and extremely slow. Only a first-stage *sultaniyya* was established in Beirut in the 1880s; none was available in Damascus before 1912, while Jerusalem and Baghdad each had only one school by 1915.[49] The *i'dadiyya* school, which was intended to serve towns of 1,000 homes, became available in the *wilayat* centres and a few other major cities. The legendary Maktab 'Anbar, which opened in Damascus in 1893 and became a hotbed for young Arabist followers of Tahir al-Jaza'iri, combined a *rushdiyya* and *i'dadiyya* together.[50] Teaching at the few *i'dadiyyas* and at the extremely scarce high schools was conducted in Turkish, while Arabic was studied as a mere curriculum subject.

In becoming more widely available, the *rushdiyya* schools constituted the cornerstone of modern Ottoman education. Indeed, the *rushdiyya* was the first line of contact between the official modernist vision and the young generations, through which values and disciplines of the modern order were expected to be instilled in the young Ottomans. A report, prepared in September 1885 by a British consular officer in Jeddah, who also happened to be an Indian Muslim, drew a detailed picture of the state of education in the Hijaz.[51] It confirmed that the government was not interfering in early elementary schooling which was left largely to the traditional *kuttab* and mosque circles. The advent of modern education in the Hijaz accompanied the establishment of a *rushdiyya* at Jeddah in 1874, of another at Madina two years later, but not of one at the more conservative Mecca until 1884. Specifying Nazarat al-Ma'arif (the ministry of education) as the source of these schools' curriculum, the report elaborated on the subjects studied in each year and on the language of instruction. It seems that throughout the four-year schooling period, Arabic and Turkish were used together for the teaching of different subjects within one year, and sometimes alternatively to teach the same subject in different years. Hence, the belief that it was Shaykh Tahir al-Jaza'iri who influenced Midhat Pasha and his successor Ahmad Hamdi Pasha (governors of Syria between 1878 and 1885) to maintain Arabic as the medium of instruction in the Syrian modern schools appears to be not entirely accurate.[52] Until 1885, at least, Arabic was used in the modern *rushdiyya* school as much as, if not more than, Turkish. The *tanzimat* men could not have challenged the privileged position of Arabic instantaneously and abruptly.

However, as Abd al-Hamid's rule was significantly consolidated by the mid-1880s, he embarked on further measures to bring cohesion and homogeneity into the empire. He made Turkish the sole medium of correspondence between the local and central administrations (though the local bureaucracy in the Arab provinces continued to use Arabic until 1909), and Turkified education in the *rushdiyyas* completely.[53] Arab memoirs speak of the Turkish language's dominant position in the Ottoman schools at the turn of the century, with Arabic relegated to a secondary and insignificant place.[54] This situation was strongly objected to by the Arab-Islamic reformists, not only 'Abduh, Rida and al-Kawakibi, but also pro-Istanbul figures such as Abdullah al-Nadim.[55] In essence, what was left to the Arabic language was the lower elementary education. But here, too, the government began to encroach, two years after it deferred to the ulema's wishes in 1869. Believing that the *kuttab* and mosque circles were not functioning regularly and efficiently, the *tanzimat* officials decided in 1871 to extend the supervision of the ministry of education to this sphere of education as well. The consequences of this decision were mixed and inconsistent. In some government elementary schools, principles of Turkish language were introduced as a subject, in addition to study of the Qur'an and Arabic, but not as the sole medium of instruction. In other schools, the government's role was limited to providing teachers with modern training, and to enhancing the efficiency of administration and finance. By and large, the traditional system of elementary education was preserved in the Arab provinces until 1908, when the new regime accelerated its rate of integration into the government-run system.[56] More *rushdiyya* and *i'dadiyya* schools were, of course, established, and the impact of Turkish education on Arab life became stronger than ever, especially as the traditional careers available to graduates of the ulema institutions became increasingly irrelevant to the modern orientation of society.

The CUP regime was therefore pursuing a policy of Turkification that was initially started by the *tanzimat* and augmented by Abd al-Hamid II; the difference was in the vigour, efficiency and accelerated rate of implementation that characterized the workings of the new regime. Similarly, while Arab opposition to Turkification had its seeds in the Arab-Islamic reformist discourse of the late nineteenth and early twentieth centuries, it was fuelled by disappointment with the new regime, and the rapidly falling foundations of cultural autonomy. Where the Arabs understood "Freedom, Equality and Justice" as the reconstruction of their autonomous status and wider participation in the decision-making process, the Unionists sought homogeneity and more powerful and capable central government – that had always been a Turkish government – in order to fend off separatist trends and European encroachments.

In October 1908, Husayn Jahid, editor of *Tanin*, the pro-CUP Istanbul-based newspaper, and one of the most outspoken Turkish nationalists, wrote an article exalting the superior position of the Turkish people in the empire. By right of conquest, Jahid believed, the Turks should always be the rulers, and the constitution should ultimately reflect this privilege.[57] Jahid's essay created an uproar in Istanbul; it was denounced in non-Turkish circles, while Unionist leaders attempted to dissociate their organization from his ideas. But Jahid continued to be regarded as a spokesman for the CUP and one of its active deputies in the chamber. Other Turkish Unionist elements, such as Yusuf Aqjura and Ahmad Agayev, were no less emphatic in expressing their nationalistic views. It is perhaps difficult to gauge the strength and influence of such elements and ideas within the CUP since Unionist policies and rhetoric were never consistent. Yet, it is fair to assume that such an atmosphere was bound to foster feelings of mistrust and suspicion between the Arabs and the Unionists, however vague these feelings were in the beginning. Hence, when the central government launched a sweeping reorganization of the bureaucracy in late 1909 and 1910, leading to the dismissal of many Arab employees, especially from the ministries of interior and foreign affairs, the Arabs suspected that Istanbul was bent upon Turkifying the government services.[58] Whether or not As'ad Daghir, the Arab nationalist writer and activist, was reflecting the reality when he indicated that the reorganization committees were resolved to lay off as many Arab employees as possible, what mattered was the Arab perception.[59] Returning to their home towns, the Arab bureaucrats made it their mission to explain their dismissal in terms of Turkish bigotry. Similar feelings developed when Arab army officers were removed from units stationed in Syria to what was described by the Arabist circles as insignificant clerical positions in Istanbul.[60]

In the autumn of 1909, the CUP paper *Tanin* launched an attack on the Arab minister of *awqaf*, Khalil Hamada.[61] For the Arabs, Hamada was one of the most efficient ministers. When he was excluded from the newly formed government, following the resignation of Husayn Hilmi in December 1909, many Arabs believed that the Unionists were behind his fall. Since the ministry of *awqaf* was traditionally allocated to an Arab minister, Arab opinion was somewhat placated by the appointment of Sharif Ali Haydar in Hamada's place. But by the end of 1910, Haydar, too, was out of office and the Arabs lost their strong and traditional position in government.[62] An Arab would not occupy a ministerial post again until the Lebanese reputed CUP member, Sulayman al-Bustani, was given the agriculture and trade portfolio after the Italian invasion of Tripolitania.

Tension and mistrust between the Arabs and the CUP regime were fed from other sources as well. From late 1908 to the end of 1911, a series of crises that were played out in the Arab lands made the Arabs lose much of their confidence in the CUP. The first crisis originated from the Unionist backing of a project in late 1909 to amalgamate all river transport in Mesopotamia under the control of Lynch Brothers.[63] Being a British company, Lynch Brothers seemed to be favoured by the CUP in an effort to restore goodwill with Britain. The proposal, which was planned to absorb the government shipping company, faced strong Iraqi national resistance, echoed by the Arab deputies in parliament. After several weeks of squabbling and political manoeuvering, the issue was resolved when Haqqi Pasha, the new Grand Vizier, refused the Lynch Brothers' concession. Realizing the depth of Arab opposition, the Unionists made an about-turn and expressed their support for Haqqi Pasha's decision. But here, too, the lines between bad government and nationalist underpinnings of policies were not particularly defined, for neither were the Unionists less protective of Iraqi interests than the Arabs, nor were they united behind the Lynch Brothers' project.

The Druze revolt on Syria's Houran mountain, which erupted in the summer of 1910 was primarily due to inter-communal conflicts, although the whole of Syria was then suffering from the increasing burdens of the inflationary costs of living. In August, the government decided to send an army expeditionary force to restore order in the Houran region.[64] The military campaign continued until the end of the year, by which time the rebellion areas seemed to have been quelled. Yet, the price of this subjugation was too high to be ignored by Arab opinion. Soldiers and officers, with no sensitivity to local customs and traditions, carried out their orders in a manner that was insulting to local leaders, violated the sanctity of the community and caused widespread destruction.[65] One of the most insulting measures was the conclusion of the campaign with forceful collection of private arms from the Druze, as well as from the Bedouin tribes of the neighbouring Karak. The military actions evoked strong reactions, with Arabs in parliament and in the press protesting the excessive measures employed by the army and the widespread insecurity they had given rise to.

Similar sentiments, though more intense, were evoked as a result of the Yemen campaign. The Ottoman authority in Yemen had last been restored in 1872 but was repeatedly challenged during the following decades by local forces. As tension increased between the government and supporters of Imam Yahya, the government formed a parliamentary committee, composed largely of Arab deputies, to suggest a reform plan for Yemen.[66] Inspired by the new spirit of unity and consolidation, the committee finalized its report, in which the complexity of the Yemeni situation was taken into careful consideration, in August 1909. Although the proposed plan was accepted by the cabinet and passed to the parliament for approval, the process of parliamentary ratification was halted by Tal'at, the new CUP minister of interior, in April 1910. What Tal'at appears to have objected to was the plan's envisioned flexible administrative arrangement. The Yemenis, on the other hand, viewed the central rule with deep suspicion, regarding its modern courts and education system as threats to the *Shari'a*. Supported by al-'Idrisi of 'Asir, Imam Yahya of Yemen drew the army into a protracted and bloody war of attrition. From an early stage of the crisis, coverage by the Istanbul-based Turkish papers of the situation in Yemen developed an anti-Arab undertone and was thus to instigate a bitter Arab–Turkish journalistic exchange.[67]

During 1910–11, the whole of Arabia was on fire. Ibn al-Rashid of Ha'il and Sharif Husayn of Mecca, on the government side, launched an open war against the Saudis of Najd, al-'Idrisi of 'Asir and Imam Yahya of Yemen.[68] The Unionists, who were simultaneously attempting to impose central control in Albania, were in effect fighting on both sides of the empire. Ironically, while the Arab media in Cairo made no attempt to hide their pleasure over the government's military failures and the fierce Yemeni resistance, they tended to overlook the roles played by the ashraf, the rulers of the Hijaz, and Ibn al-Rashid, the ruler of Ha'il, in the Yemen campaign when the former symbolized the enduring legacy of Arab political authority. While the hasty drive to centralization was blemishing the image and integrity of the new regime and precipitating further seeds of disintegration, the Yemeni crisis added a new element of doubt to the Arab view of Istanbul. In the end, Yemen proved to be a damning episode for Tal'at's first term in office. He resigned in February 1911 and was promptly replaced by Khalil Bey, the moderate leader of the CUP parliamentary party. The war in Yemen did not end until 9 October 1911, following the signing of a peace agreement between Imam Yahya and the Ottoman military campaign commander, 'Izzat Pasha.[69]

Peace in Yemen came a few days after the Italian invasion of Tripolitania on 28 September, news of which echoed throughout the Arab world as the desperate resistance of the Libyan Arabs and the small Ottoman garrison failed to check the invading force.[70] Feeling a sense of betrayal, the Arabs blamed the government for its earlier decision to withdraw army units from Tripolitania to Yemen, thereby leaving the Libyan coast insufficiently protected at a time when the Italian designs had been obvious.[71] In many ways, the loss of Tripolitania was devastating for Arab relations with Istanbul. Soon enough, the Ottomans suffered another ignominious defeat in the Balkans, a defeat that reinforced Arab doubts about Istanbul's ability to defend the empire – or what remained of it – against the European powers. While the Zionist influx into Palestine was looking unstoppable, educated Arabs were becoming aware of French imperialist schemes in Syria. Whether in Damascus, Istanbul, or in Cairo, many Arabists came to believe that only by taking control of their own affairs would the Arabs succeed in preserving the integrity of their country.[72] For these Arabists, decentralization of the empire and the emergence of autonomous Arab rule was not only seen as necessary to address the issue of the disparity of their relations with an increasingly Turco-centred regime, but was also believed to provide the moral and political means to challenge the imperialist claims. Yet, this was not necessarily a universal Arab opinion.

While exhibiting an Arabist complexion, the growing Arab dissent from the CUP in 1909–11 was not yet expressed in nationalist political forms. It signified a rupture with the CUP not with the Ottoman bond, and assumed Ottomanist, not Arab-nationalist oppositional voices. Arab alienation from the CUP was further prompted by the secretive, conspiratorial, and sometimes unscrupulous methods employed by the Unionists. Until late 1913, when the CUP was turned into a political party, no Arab – in fact no non-Turk Ottoman – could reach the CUP central committee where most of the power resided, despite the fact that numerous prominent Arabs had joined the organization, many of them known for their strong ties with the anti-Hamidian movement before 1908.[73] In February 1909, the CUP parliamentary party and other branches of the organization exerted tremendous pressure on Kamil Pasha, the independent-minded Grand Vizier, to force him out of office. Although the Arab deputies in the chamber did not oppose the Unionist tactics, forty of them took a neutral position during the vote against Kamil Pasha.[74] The CUP's scheming to dominate the government, without being openly accountable to the people or parliament, was becoming abundantly clear. Moreover, while the Unionists were implicated on more than one occasion in the assassination of prominent opposition journalists, real and fictional conspiracies were appropriately used to suppress the legitimate opposition and silence its vocal figures.[75] A new form of despotic rule seemed to be in the making.

By late 1909, a group of deputies was discussing the idea of establishing an Arab parliamentary party. But whether because of internal differences or in order to form a more effective opposition, they finally agreed to join forces with non-Arab opponents of the CUP. In 1910, the Moderate Liberal Party (this name was perhaps meant to distinguish the party from the defunct Liberal Union) was established under the leadership of Isma'il Kamal, the prominent Albanian deputy and former Liberal Unionist. Nafi' al-Jabiri (Aleppo), Sayyid Mahdi (Karbala) and Rushdi al-Sham'a (Damascus) were on the party's leading committee. The Moderate Liberal Party was supported by several publications run by Rida al-Sulh (in Beirut), Sa'id al-Husayni (in Jerusalem) and Shukri al-'Asali (in Damascus), and also by other liberal parliamentarians such as the Kurdish deputy, Lutfi Fikri.[76] Though it called for the extension of local administrative authorities, just allocation of government posts, and respect of the various Ottoman national entities, the Moderate Liberal Party was an Ottomanist party. But since it lacked strong Turkish roots and had to compete with the preponderant Unionist machine, it was an ineffective political platform.

The Arab mood in Istanbul was best reflected at the time by the founding of al-Muntada al-Adabi (the Literary Forum). It was essentially a club for the Arab students in the capital and its emergence illustrated the mixed feelings of the Arab social and intellectual élites and their desire to emphasize their national entity while remaining loyal to the Ottoman league. At some stage, the forum was believed to have attracted the support of nearly a thousand members, including Rushdi al-Shawwa, 'Asim Bsayso, Mustafa al-Husayni and Muhammad Bsayso (all from Gaza), 'Arif al-'Arif and Ahmad Khalil al-Husayni (of Jerusalem), 'Awni Abd al-Hadi and Rafiq al-Tamimi (of Nablus), 'Izzat al-A'zami (of Baghdad), Yusuf Haydar (of Lebanon), Sayif al-Din al-Khatib and Ahmad Qadri (of Damascus).[77] During its first years, the Literary Forum strictly avoided being directly involved in political activities and chose to become a meeting point for the Arabs in Istanbul, where ideas of social reform and cultural awakening were preached. In most of its activities, Arab–Turkish brotherhood and Ottoman unity were especially reiterated. However, as members of the forum were naturally acquainted with Arab deputies and officials with whom Arab–Turkish relations were bound to be discussed, they were inevitably drawn into political activities. At the outset of Jamal Pasha's crack-down on the Arab nationalists in 1915, Abd al-Karim al-Khalil, chairman of the Literary Forum, was executed. His death marked the end of the forum's existence.

One of the major developments in Arab politics was the election of Shukri al-'Asali, a disciple of Tahir al-Jaza'iri, to the parliament. A former *qa'imaqam* of Nazareth, al-'Asali reached the chamber after winning a by-election for a seat in Damascus in January 1911.[78] His intelligence, sharpness and dedication brought a new impetus to the Arab position in the chamber and to the Arab self-view outside. Two months after becoming a deputy, al-'Asali delivered an uncompromising attack on the government's discrimination against the Arabs. Reminding the chamber that the Arabs constituted half of the empire's population, al-'Asali protested the meagre number of posts occupied by Arabs in the central government. His speech was celebrated by the Arab press from Damascus to Cairo, drawing strong support from the Arab-educated stratum, many of whom had been made unemployed by the reorganization of government a few months earlier.[79] After serving in northern Palestine as a sub-governor, al-'Asali was also deeply aware of the Zionist threat to the Palestinians. In Istanbul, it became his mission to put the government's laxity in dealing with the Zionist encroachment on the parliament's agenda. His anti-Zionist crusade, backed by other Arab deputies, especially the Jerusalemite historian and littérateur Ruhi al-Khalidi,[80] added new fuel to the allegations of Freemasonry and Zionist links that had already been thrown at the CUP.

This deterioration in Arab relations with the Unionists was witnessed by a keen observer of the Arab condition, Rashid Rida. Seeking government support for establishing a school of Islamic learning to train ulema and preachers with reformist ideas and in modern ways, Rida arrived in Istanbul in October 1909, where he stayed until October of the following year. Although he was received warmly by Tal'at, the ministers of education and *awqaf*, and by Shaykh al-Islam, the government's early promised backing to his project never materialized. When CUP officials expressed their desire to place the project under governmental supervision, Rida rejected the idea and returned to Egypt filled with bitterness and a sense of humiliation. Rida's project was subsequently taken up by the khedive of Egypt, Abbas Hilmi II, whose relations with the CUP were becoming increasingly strained.[81] The khedive found in Rida's failure in Istanbul an ideal opportunity to mend fences with the distinguished Islamic reformist and win him over to his side. With Egyptian support, Rida first founded a society for his project (Jam'iyyat al-Da'wa wal-'Irshad, or the Society for Proselytizing and Guidance) and then opened the school in March 1912.

One might always argue that it was this very personal experience which precipitated Rida's disagreement with the Unionists, yet Rida's case was part of a wider pattern. From late 1909 onwards, opposition to the CUP was becoming visible not only amongst the Arab parliamentary deputies but also on the pages of the most influential Arab newspapers in the Ottoman domain, including *al-Mufid* and *al-Muqtabas* (in Damascus), *al-Karmil* (in Haifa) and *al-Ittihad al-'Uthmani* (in Beirut).[82] Considering that Kurd-Ali of *al-Muqtabas*, and Shaykh Ahmad Hasan Tabbara of *al-Ittihad al-'Uthmani*, were initially strong supporters of the Unionists, one may appreciate the depth of Arab alienation. In Cairo, the Arab cause was taken up by *al-Ahram*, *al-Muqattam* and *al-Mu'ayyad*. After returning to Egypt in late 1910, Rida would also turn *al-Manar* into an opposition organ to the CUP and form a secret society (Jam'iyyat al-Jami'a al-'Arabiyya, or the Arab League Society) that aimed at uniting Arabist organizations and various amirs of Arabia, in order to promote and safeguard Arab rights.[83]

With the establishment of the Party of Freedom and Concord, or the Entente Libéral, in November 1911, the CUP faced the strongest challenge yet to its position. Comprising a large segment of the Arab, Albanian, Bulgarian, Greek and Turkish opposition, the Entente Libéral was prompted by the split of Sadiq Bec, a former Unionist leader and senior army officer, from the CUP.[84] The new party inherited the old Moderate Liberal Party almost completely, attracting most of the active Arab deputies, including al-'Asali, Shafiq al-Mu'ayyad al-'Azm, Sa'id al-Husayni, Rushdi al-Sham'a, Amin Arslan, Talib al-Naqib, and others. It was soon to open branches in several Arab cities, leading in many cases to a mass exodus from the CUP clubs. Substantially, the Entente Libéral's programme was a reflection of the Ottoman liberal vision of decentralization, cultural and linguistic autonomy and just allocation of government posts.[85]

Meanwhile, two other Arabist organizations were being formed secretly. The first was al-'Arabiyya al-Fatat (the Young Arabs), which originated in Istanbul with two Arab students, the Palestinian, 'Awni Abd al-Hadi, and the Syrian, Ahmad Qadri.[86] Disenchanted with the Turkish public's anti-Arab utterances after the failed counter-revolution of April 1909, and with the rising Turanian undertone of the CUP supporters, Qadri and Abd al-Hadi turned Arabist. Their idea of forming an Arab society to defend Arab rights was subsequently carried to Beirut, Damascus and Arab student circles in Paris, where it was supported by a few other young Arabists, including Ahmad Rustum Haydar, Tawfiq al-Natur, Abd al-Ghani al-'Uraysi, and Muhammad al-Mahammasani (from Lebanon), Rafiq al-Tamimi (from Palestine), Jamil Mardam (from Syria), and the Iraqi Tawfiq al-Swaydi, sometime in 1911.[87] Primarily a student organization, al-Fatat continued to expand with vigour and determination among the young educated Arabs, even during the war years. Its programme was Arabist with Ottoman orientation, best illustrated in the line adopted by *al-Mufid*, established by al-'Uraysi. Rashid al-Khalidi, who wrote the most extensive study of *al-Mufid*, described al-'Uraysi's writings as a combination of "a lively style with impassioned rhetoric, and a respect for Islamic tradition and for the historic role of the Ottoman Empire with a modern insistence on reforms, equality and national self-expression".[88]

The second important Arabist organization to be formed during the same period was al-'Ahd (the Covenant), established by the illustrious Ottoman Arab officer 'Aziz Ali al-Misri. Al-'Ahd's formation followed the Italian–Ottoman war in Tripolitania, at the end of which al-Misri emerged as an Arab–Ottoman hero. Consisting almost exclusively of Arab army officers, al-'Ahd was joined by Yasin and Taha al-Hashimi, Salim al-Jaza'iri, Ali al-Nashashibi, Salim al-Tabbakh, Mustafa Wasfi, Isma'il al-Saffar, Nuri al-Sa'id and many of the early group of Sharifian officers.[89] Al-Misri's outlook was essentially Ottomanist, but like the rest of the Arabs in the Ottoman officers corps, he was alienated by the Unionist exclusivity and control of the army. Though highly ambiguous in its aims, al-'Ahd envisioned an Ottoman reform, based on the Austro-Hungarian model.[90] In reality, it served as a secret fraternity of the Arab army officers, where nationalist sentiments seemed to have been fostered and diffused. As news of the conspiratorial activities of al-Misri reached the Unionist leaders of the army, he was arrested and brought before a military tribunal in February 1914 where he was presented with a largely concocted list of allegations.[91] Although he was sentenced to death, persistent and widespread Arab pressure secured his release, upon which he was expelled to Egypt. His case marked a low point in Arab–Unionist relations.

Spurned by the widening opposition to its rule, the CUP orchestrated a dissolution of parliament in January 1912. The elections that were held three months later came to be known as the "big stick elections". Prior to and during the election campaign, CUP officials in the Arab provinces, as well as in the rest of the empire, used all possible means of intimidation, coercion and vote rigging to ensure the defeat of their opponents.[92] But these were not the sole determinants of the election result. In an abrasive pragmatic shift, the CUP moved to reconcile some of the most entrenched a'yan figures (notables) who had been earlier regarded as reactionary and unworthy of being identified with the progressive image of the organization. Most prominent in this category of the Unionists' new allies were Muhii al-Din Abd al-Qadir, the son of naqib al-ashraf (head of the association of people claiming descent from the Prophet Muhammad) of Baghdad; Muhammad Fawzi al-'Azm and Abd al-Rahman al-Yusuf, the two most entrenched notables of Damascus, and the alim and notable from Acre, Shaykh As'ad Shuqayri.[93] By using the influence of such notables, the enticing power of the incumbent, and by invoking the Islamic sentiments of the populace, the CUP succeeded in preserving the bulk of its support in most of Palestine, while dividing the electorates in Beirut, Damascus and Baghdad. Apart from in Basra, where Talib al-Naqib forced his re-election despite the CUP's intimidation,[94] the latter's victory was astounding. Shukri al-'Asali, Sa'id al-Husayni, Rushdi al Sham'a, Hafiz al-Sa'id, Rida al-Sulh, Abd al-Hamid al-Zahrawi, Muhammad Arslan, and Nafi' al-Jabiri, who all had been identified with the opposition, along with Shaykh 'Ala' al-Din al-'Alusi of the Baghdadi reformist ulema family, who had been mainly a neutral deputy, lost their seats. Others, such as Kamil al-As'ad of Beirut, were coerced into joining the Unionist side.[95]

The elections of 1912 signified a turning-point in the relations between the Arabs and the CUP government. They marked the culmination of the CUP's transformation into an authoritarian ruling power and its full embrace of the Ottoman regime with the whole package of its failings, shortcomings and traditional social base. Abd al-Wahhab al-Inklizi, an old disciple of the grand circle of al-Jaza'iri and at that time sub-governor in the Ottoman administration of Syria (the Ra's al-'Ayn district), resigned his post after receiving transfer orders to a remote area, which was meant to preclude his possible intervention on behalf of his fellow Arabists.[96] Many of the Syrian losers, together with other Arabist elements, departed to Cairo where they would soon coalesce into an exclusively Arab opposition party. The most apparent Arab rift during the elections was essentially a division of the *a'yan* class, though not entirely limited to it. Even amongst the Arab-Islamic reformists, some preferred to maintain links with the Unionists, partly because they feared that their fellow Arabists' opposition to the CUP was moving rapidly towards a rupture with the Ottoman bond, and partly because they still had faith in the Unionists' ability to accomplish a just reform of the empire. Most prominent among this category of Arabists were Amir Shakib Arslan (then *qa'imaqam* of Shuf), Ruhi al-Khalidi, the Egyptian nationalist writer Shaykh Abd al-'Aziz Jawish, and the new deputy in Parliament, Ma'ruf al-Rasafi, a student of Mahmud Shukri al-'Alusi and a new Iraqi deputy.

During those agonizing times for the Ottoman empire, the CUP's pyrrhic election victory, coming on top of a series of political débâcles, internal crises and the loss of Tripolitania, provoked further opposition rather than consolidation, especially among the army officer corps. Cornered by their failures and forced success, the Unionists relinquished power in July 1912.[97] The new Grand Vizier, Ahmad Mukhtar Pasha, supported by what remained of the Entente Libéral and other opponents of the CUP, brought to his cabinet Kamil Pasha, the first Grand Vizier of the constitutional period, who was also regarded as a menace to the Unionists. Upon the outbreak of the Balkan war in October, Kamil Pasha would take over as the head of government. The newly elected parliament was dissolved and the government embarked on a slow purge of the Unionist elements in the administration. The decline of Unionist influence became obvious during the incomplete elections of October 1912. Though the elections were prematurely terminated because of the outbreak of war in the Balkans, the results of a few contested seats had already been declared before the balloting was stopped. In the southern Iraqi regions of Basra and 'Amara, the CUP's defeat was easily accomplished by Talib al-Naqib and his allies.[98] The fact that the CUP had earlier decided to boycott the contests, and was later to change its position and enter the campaign, seemed to add to the wide confusion in Unionist ranks.

The government(s) of Mukhtar Pasha and Kamil Pasha aroused more expectations, in terms of their reformist intentions, than they could really deliver. Essentially, the Ottoman statesmen of the early twentieth century, Unionist or Ententist, faced a situation in which they were divided over whether to hold on to the remaining glories of the past or respond to the demands of an age they themselves had helped to bring about. During the previous decades, urban populations had been growing at unprecedented rates; at the same time dozens of newspapers and magazines were rolling off the presses every day,[99] feeding an educated stratum that was becoming too visible to be ignored.

The Balkan war erupted in October amid continued pressure on the government from the Arabist circles. In December, the government of Kamil Pasha faced another crisis in Lebanon, caused by the demands of the semi-autonomous *mutasarifiyya* of *Jabal* Lebanon for opening the Lebanese port of Junieh to international navigation. Statements made by French officials, including the prime minister, expressing anxiety over the welfare of the Lebanese Christians, brought the spectre of imperialist conquest to the forefront of the Arabist agenda.[100] Taking the divisive situation in Lebanon seriously, the Grand Vizier responded by giving instructions for the *wilayat* council to convene in order to formulate the people's demands for reform.[101] This initiative opened the door for a wider gathering of local notables, Arab activists and officials, which came to be known as the Beirut Reform Society (Jam'iyyat Beirut al-'Islahiyya).[102] Soon after, similar societies emerged in other major Arab cities. In Damascus, however, inner divisions were too deep for the society to reach consensus,[103] whereas the Basra Reform Society became a powerful instrument for consolidating the position of Talib al-Naqib.[104] In Baghdad, a politico-literary club (al-Nadi al-Watani, or the National Club) was founded with the encouragement of the Arab-Islamic reformist, Shaykh Yusuf al-Swaydi, and moved to establish ties with al-Naqib's group of Basra.[105]

It was against this background that the Ottoman Administrative Decentralization Party, the most important Arab political platform, came into being. The Decentralization Party was declared in Cairo in

December 1912. Exclusively Arab, its founding group included Rashid Rida, Shibli Shmayyil, Haqqi al-'Azm, Iskander 'Amun, Abd al-Hamid al-Zahrawi, Sami Jraydini, Muhib al-Din al-Khatib, and Rafiq al-'Azm as president.[106] Since its founding had been under consideration for some time, the Decentralization Party received prompt support from most of the former Syrian deputies and officials, opponents of the CUP, and from the Reformist Societies of Baghdad and Basra.[107] Its strength was illustrated in its success in attracting active members from various parts of Palestine, where the Arab movement had not been particularly strong, including: Hasan Hammad, a notable from Nablus; Salim al-Ahmad Abd al-Hadi of a powerful notable family from Jenin; Muhammad al-Shanti, a journalist from Jaffa; Hafiz al-Sa'id, the former deputy of Jaffa; and the Azhari shaykh Sa'id al-Karmi. During Jamal Pasha's crack-down on the Arab movement in 1915–16, Hammad narrowly escaped arrest and went underground until the end of the war; Abd al-Hadi was hanged by Jamal Pasha's military tribunal in August 1915, as was al-Shanti in May 1916. Al-Sa'id died in prison, while Shaykh al-Karimi's death sentence was commuted to life imprisonment because of his advanced age.[108]

The programme of the Decentralization Party echoed the reformist outlook of the Entente Libéral but with more emphasis on local administrative autonomy and the explicit demand for making national languages – besides the Turkish language – official in the non-Turkish provinces.[109] But the Decentralization Party was fundamentally an Ottoman party. It was founded at a time when the CUP was actually out of power and seemed to be truly weakened, while the government of Kamil Pasha looked more disposed to political reform, even though it was not moving fast enough in that direction. Equally important in the founding of the Decentralization Party was the deepening Arabist fear of the ominous dangers that were engulfing the empire, and the Arab lands in particular.[110] It was this fear which made the party's leaders see decentralization and reform as prerequisites for "enabling the country to defend itself and avoid the disasters of foreign occupation". Separation was not on the Decentralization Party's agenda. But it is also true that implicit in the founding of the Decentralization Party was the assumption of an existing Arab identity and interests that required to be politically and publicly expressed.

On 23 January 1913 Ottoman politics were shattered once again by a military coup. Returning as a hero from Tripolitania, Enver, the young

Unionist army officer, forced Kamil Pasha out of office at gunpoint. The CUP, exploiting a moment of political confusion in Istanbul, returned to power on the promise of restoring Ottoman dignity and honour.[111] This time the Unionist term in office would continue unchallenged until the end of World War I and the collapse of the empire. The Unionist return, nonetheless, did not prevent the reformist groups of Beirut and Basra from concluding their work and presenting their proposals to the new government. But the Unionists were not in a mood to entertain these proposals, nor those of the Decentralization Party.[112] The Arabists responded by escalating their struggle by holding an Arab congress in Paris.

The idea of holding an Arab congress was initiated by the Paris-based activists of al-Fatat.[113] If Tawfiq al-Swaydi, a participant in the congress and member of al-Fatat, is right, the initial plan envisaged a Syrian, not an Arab, congress,[114] which indicated that the Arabist self-view at that stage was not yet defined in pan-Arab geographical terms. Since Arabism was still an opposition movement, those young students of Greater Syrian origin could think of their movement only as an embodiment of the Syrian-Arab demands *vis-à-vis* the government of Istanbul. Being an Iraqi, al-Swaydi protested and the congress was thus named the First Arab Congress.

Preparations for the congress began with a memorandum that the Paris group sent to the Decentralization Party, urging the Arabist elders in Cairo to become the "guide and source of action for the congress", and to nominate its president. It was certainly an acknowledgment of the rising influence of the Decentralization Party, and of the wide Arabist agreement on the programme of reform. The congress was subsequently held in a hall of the French Geographical Society on 17–23 June 1913, and was attended by a rather small caucus of twenty-five members. Its proceedings reflected the existence of three main trends:[115] one represented by the pro-French Lebanese Christians such as George Samne and Nadra Mutran; the second by the more emphatic Arabists of al-Fatat, most visible amongst them being Abd al-Ghani al-'Uraysi; and the third by the decentralist moderate line of the Cairo group and the Beirut Reform Society. Interestingly, Iskandar 'Amun, the Lebanese Christian member of the Decentralization Party, showed no interest in the Lebanese separatist views and remained faithful to the Ottoman decentralist position.[116] The French, who facilitated the congress, kept a close watch on the proceedings, but made no effort at direct intervention. Despite the relentless pressure of the Lebanese separatist bloc, the congress ended with a decentralist list of resolutions.[117] The Lebanese bloc was accommodated by a resolution accepting the appointment of foreign advisors in the *wilayat* of Beirut, but the congress rejected all attempts at foreign intervention in Ottoman affairs. Other resolutions echoed the basic views of the Ottoman Decentralization Party.

The Arab Congress, held in Paris, received a significant number of supporting telegrams from various parts of Greater Syria. Simultaneously, it invoked strong condemnation from leaders of the pro-Istanbul Arab bloc, notables and Arab-Islamists alike. Opponents of the congress included some illustrious and influential figures, such as Shakib Arslan, Muhammad al-Makhzumi, Abd al-'Aziz Jawish, Ma'ruf al-Rasafi, as well as Shaykh As'ad al-Shuqayri, Muhammad Fawzi al-'Azm, Abd al-Rahman al-Yusuf and Sharif Husayn of Mecca.[118] The lines of demarcation between the two sides of the Arab debate were largely drawn by disagreements over the appropriate methods for the Arabs to adopt in the pursuit of their rights, and over how far the Arabs could go without threatening the integrity of the Ottoman bond. In some other cases, the debate was a mere cover for self-interests and self-promotion. Significantly, the congress was also attacked by the Jaffa-based newspaper, *Filastin*. Maintaining a strong Ottomanist line (though owned by a Christian), *Filastin* asserted that disintegration of the empire would turn Palestine into an easy prey for Zionist encroachment, and rightly observed that the Palestinian question was mysteriously absent from the congress's agenda. Even the mainly Arabist-oriented *al-Karmil* of Haifa could not hide its displeasure over the congress's apparent neglect of the Palestinian situation.[119] Both positions were indicative of a growing local Palestinian nationalist response to the Zionist project. Though the Arabists were the first to turn the Zionist danger into an Arab and Ottoman issue, the Paris congress was held amid a series of meetings between representatives of the Zionist movement and a number of Arabists. The Zionists – as we shall see – were aiming at neutralizing the fierce Arabist opposition to the Jewish immigration into Palestine.

The Unionist leaders in Istanbul took note of the congress and moved promptly to contain its consequences by dispatching Midhat Shukri, the secretary of the CUP, to negotiate with leaders of the congress. Negotiations were then transferred to Istanbul, involving Tal'at and other Unionist leaders, Abd al-Hamid al-Zahrawi, Abd al-Karim al-Khalil and representatives of the Beirut Reform Society.[120] The agreement that was eventually signed by both sides in July accommodated most of the Arab demands, yet a subsequent official proclamation in Istanbul endorsed only part of what was agreed upon. Al-Zahrawi and al-Khalil, followed by other supporters of the Decentralization Party, approached the situation with a pragmatic sense. Aware of the inadequacy of the Unionist government's response they still saw it as a step in the right direction. In contrast, the Cairo-based leaders of the party, as well as al-Fatat's young activists, were dissatisfied with the al-Zahrawi–Khalil achievements, reflecting their opposition in public statements and contacts with al-Zahrawi. Unable to defend his position publicly, al-Zahrawi sent a thoughtful and impassioned letter to Rida.[121] Al-Zahrawi expressed his belief in the beginning of change in the Unionist attitude towards the Arabs and the idea of reform in general. He also indicated that the Arab movement was still too weak to force Istanbul's full compliance with the Arab demands, and that European pressures on the empire would soon bring the desired changes without further escalation of the Arab opposition to the government. If al-Zahrawi's assessment of the European powers' approach to the Ottoman question was not entirely accurate, his views of the Arab–Unionist complex at the time were not far from reality.

The Unionists' return to power in early 1912 marked another shift in their political vocation. In June 1913, Grand Vizier Mahmud Shawkat was assassinated in a plot linked to the Entente Libéral's leader Sadiq Bey. Though Shawkat was never really a Unionist, his assassination provided the CUP with the opportunity to eliminate those Ententists who remained active and assume full and direct control of the government. The next month, Enver led an Ottoman offensive on the faltering Balkan alliance and recaptured Edirne from the Balkan forces, bringing to the demoralized nation a long-awaited taste of victory.[122] Displaying a strong sense of self-confidence, the Unionists moved to repair the early damage that they inflicted on the inner cohesion of the empire and on their political fortunes, at a time when the Ottoman future was becoming increasingly dependent on the Arab–Turkish relationship.

The Unionist political language began to reflect more emphasis on the Ottoman and Islamic bonds of the *umma*.[123] Arab representation in the upper chamber was increased by six members, including Abd al-Hamid al-Zahrawi, while Shukri al-'Asali, Abd al-Wahhab al-Inkilizi, the

Iraqi, Naji al-Swaydi, and the Palestinian, Amin al-Tamimi, were appointed to senior judicial and administrative positions.[124] Two secondary schools were established in Damascus and Beirut (under the administration of the Arabists Rafiq al-Tamimi and Rustum Haydar), and another was planned in Baghdad.[125] Arabic was restored in the judicial court system, approved as the language of instruction in pre-secondary schooling, and declared required for the appointment of all government employees in the Arab provinces, except the *walis*.[126] The Arab–Unionist reconciliation was extended to Basra where Talib al-Naqib was thus accommodated,[127] and would in turn broker a vital Unionist–Saudi agreement in early 1914.[128] Underlining the shift in their attitudes, the Unionists followed a largely non-partisan policy towards the parliamentary elections of April 1914 (the third and last of the Ottoman second constitutional period). Although conducted with no organized challenge to the CUP, these elections returned to parliament some of the Arab deputies who had lost to CUP supporters in the "big stick" elections of 1912, including Tawfiq al-Majali and Sa'id al-Husayni. In Acre, Shaykh As'ad al-Shuqayri, the Unionist strongman, lost to Abd al-Fattah al-Sa'id, and the same fate was suffered by the Nablusite pro-CUP notable, Haydar Tuqan, who was squarely defeated by the Decentralist, Hasan Hammad.[129]

The new positive atmosphere in Arab–Unionist relations became more apparent upon the outbreak of the war in September 1914. In spite of widespread doubts over the Unionist decision to enter the war, Rashid Rida published a call to the Syrian Arabs, urging them to defend their country and commit themselves to the government's policy. He further expressed the view that the war required that demands for reform be halted and obedience to the state become genuinely manifested.[130] Abd al-Karim al-Khalil returned from Istanbul to Lebanon to rally his fellow Shi'i countrymen to the war effort, while the known Arabist papers rose to the occasion with firm support of the state.[131] If the roots of Arabism were of Islamic reformist origin, and if Arabism was mainly promoted by students of the Arab–Islamic reform movement, the war created a situation in which the Islamic aspect of Arabism seemed to prevail over its divisive, nationalist aspect.

With a few insignificant exceptions, the hidden face of the Arab movement was in congruence with its visible embrace of the Ottoman cause. Al-Fatat's leaders in Syria, the most assertive in their Arabist sentiments, continued to expand their organization in spite of the

Arab–Unionist reconciliation in late 1913. Prior to and just after the outbreak of war, al-Fatat tended to succeed in casting off its intellectual shell, and to reach out to young urban notables, tribal chiefs, junior Arab bureaucrats and army officers. Among al-Fatat's new recruits were: Nawwaf al-Sha'lan of the Syrian desert Sha'lan tribe; Nasib al-Atrash, a son of the powerful Druze family in the Houran region; Nasib al-Bakri, a young Damascene notable; Rida Pasha al-Rikabi, a former senior army officer; Amir 'Arif al-Shihabi; 'Izzat Drawaza and Shaykh Kamil al-Qassab. A contact was initiated with Yasin al-Hashimi, the Iraqi chief of staff of the 13th army brigade and member of al-'Ahd, after which al-Hashimi joined al-Fatat and became its liaison with al-'Ahd.[132] Aware of the difficulties that began to arise in the relations between Sharif Husayn of Mecca and the Unionists, al-Fatat approached Husayn through Fawzi al-Bakri, a brother of Nasib. In its overture, made after the outbreak of war but before the Ottoman state became a belligerent party, al-Fatat revealed to the sharif its organization and aims, and called on him to lead the Arab endeavour for preserving their rights and country. The cautious Husayn listened to al-Bakri but gave no response.[133] In the meantime, al-Fatat dispatched Shaykh Kamil al-Qassab to Cairo to discuss with leaders of the Decentralization Party the most appropriate position that the Arabists should take in the circumstances of war. Upon al-Qassab's return, al-Fatat's higher committee decided to render full support to the Ottoman war effort.[134] At this early stage of the war, a consensus seemed to have emerged among the Arabist circles towards giving priority to the defence of the empire over nationalist rights.

Breaking the bond

The focus of the Arab movement was soon to shift to the Hijaz and its ashraf rulers. Sharif Husayn, the incumbent in the Hijaz since 1909, was a typical conservative Arab amir with a traditional Ottoman outlook. He was a loyalist who backed the sometimes brutal measures of the state in Arabia and Yemen.[135] Yet Husayn, with his Hamidian views of Islam and governance, had his own doubts about the Unionists and their sincerity towards Islam. His relations with the government were further strained over the Unionist attempt to boost the authority of the *wali*, representative of the central government, at the expense of the sharif's authority and power. While Husayn seemed to nurture certain ambitions to have the Emirate preserved through his immediate dynasty, which was only a branch of the ashraf of Mecca, the Unionists appeared to favour Ali Haydar, a CUP sympathizer and cousin of Husayn.[136] Plans by the government to extend the Hijaz railway from Madina to Mecca further alarmed Husayn and deepened his suspicion of Istanbul's intentions towards him.

Abdullah, a scheming and highly ambitious son of Husayn, stopped at Cairo on his way to Istanbul in early 1914 and became acquainted there with Rashid Rida. It was a time when Rida was actively trying to promote a vision of a united Arab front embracing various amirs of Arabia and the Arab organizations in Syria and Iraq, embodied in his Jam'iyyat al-Jami'a al-'Arabiyya (the Arab League Society). Abdullah seemed to have accepted Rida's ideas and was thus sworn in as a member of the Arab League Society.[137] Most important amongst Abdullah's contacts in Cairo was his introduction by Khedive Abbas II to Lord Kitchener, the British viceregent in Egypt, and his oriental secretary, Ronald Storrs.[138] Relations between the ashraf and Istanbul were then reaching a low point over the new *wilayat* law and its implementation in the Hijaz, which prompted Abdullah to seek British political backing. During this early phase of contacts between the ashraf and the British, which lasted from February to April 1914, the British showed great interest in maintaining the relationship but were reluctant to interfere in a purely internal Ottoman affair that did not involve one of their recognized spheres of influence.[139] In the second phase, that began with the outbreak of war in September and ended two months later, it was the British who initiated the contact.[140] Seeking to pre-empt the Unionist pan-Islamic war efforts and pacify the millions of Muslims in Egypt and India, the British attempted to dissociate Sharif Husayn from Istanbul and cultivate an Arab revolt against the Ottoman state. In an exchange of correspondence with the British officials in Cairo and the Hijaz, Husayn reiterated his friendly attitude to Britain, demanded that the British naval blockade of the Hijazi ports be lifted, and promised not to support the jihad policy of the Unionist governments. He was, however, unequivocally clear in his unwillingness to secede from the Ottoman bond.[141] Less than a year later, this position would be changed, but by then the entire question of Arab–Turkish relations was entering a new phase.

From the beginning of the war, Syria was the base of the Ottoman fourth army, commanded by Jamal Pasha, a key leader of the CUP.

Charged with the task of liberating Egypt from the British, Jamal Pasha became the undisputed ruler of Syria. But Jamal's hastily prepared attack on the Suez Canal, coupled with the Egyptian pro-Ottoman nationalists' failure to instigate an anti-British revolt in Egypt, brought the Ottoman campaign to a disastrous end. Though facing defeat with a brave face, Jamal Pasha returned to Syria filled with a strong sense of vulnerability.[142] When, in a classic *a'yan* intrigue, he was informed by Kamil al-As'ad, the Lebanese Shi'i notable, of a conspiracy led by Abd al-Karim al-Khalil and Rida al-Sulh to ignite a revolt in Syria, Jamal Pasha ordered the arrest of al-Khalil, al-Sulh and some of their associates.[143] During the following few weeks, in July 1915, the Syrian Arabists came under intense pressure from the Ottoman military authorities. While the first wave of arrests was directed largely at the known Decentralist Arabs, al-'Uraysi, Amir 'Arif al-Shihabi and 'Umar Hamad of al-Fatat attempted to escape Syria for the Hijaz. Their subsequent capture broke the secrecy that had for long wrapped al-Fatat's activities in a protective shield.[144] In the process, further Arab activists were arrested and tortured. From August 1915 to May 1916, one group after another of the most educated and illustrious Arabs was hanged in public in Beirut, Damascus and Jerusalem. A climate of terror reigned throughout Syria, where hundreds of suspects and their families were forced into internal exile, or thrown into prison.[145] Nothing could be more self-incriminating than Jamal Pasha's later attempt to justify the campaign of terror that he had unleashed.[146] Arab allegations that Jamal's crack-down on the Syrians was in reality intended to conceal his treachery and contacts with the allies, seem not to be entirely unfounded.[147] In the end, however, although the Ottoman grip on Syria was maintained until the final defeat in 1918, Jamal Pasha's heavy-handedness irreparably shattered Arab–Turkish relations.

In July 1915, Sharif Husayn started his famous and controversial correspondence with Henry McMahon, the new British High Commissioner in Cairo, which ended with the Sharifian alliance with the British.[148] Faysal, the other calculating son of Husayn, was apparently not in favour of the British option. He was therefore permitted by his father to pay another visit to Istanbul in a bid to resolve the outstanding differences with the government. During his stop in Damascus, Faysal was recruited by the remaining activists of al-Fatat, and became fully acquainted with the Arab grievances under Jamal Pasha's rule.[149] Though Faysal was still reluctant to support an open revolt against Istanbul, he was certainly inspired by his meetings with the Arabists of Damascus. Concurrently, the Arab activists in Cairo intensified their contacts with the British and appeared to throw their weight against the Ottomans. The countdown to the Arab revolt began in earnest.

Sharif Husayn proclaimed his Arab revolt against Istanbul on 10 June 1916 at Madina. The revolt was supported by the Arabists in Cairo and various parts of Syria, and was joined later by scores of Arab activists and military officers, turning Husayn into the leader of the Arab movement. But Arab opposition to the revolt, whether based on Islamic and Ottoman loyalty or motivated by fear of Jamal Pasha's repression, was evidently widespread. The anti-revolt camp was led by almost the same Arab elements as those who had been campaigning against the Decentralization Party, the Paris Arab Congress and other manifestations of the Arab movement, including Arslan, Shaykh Salih al-Sharif al-Tunisi, the Libyan, Yusuf Shatwan (an early opponent of the CUP), al-Shuqayri, M. Fawzi al-'Azm, Abd al-Rahman al-Yusuf, Jawish' and al-Rasafi, together with the Tunisian exiled leader, Abd al-'Aziz al-Tha'alibi, al-Afghani's disciple, Abd al-Qadir al-Maghribi, and the reborn Ottoman loyalist Muhammad Kurd-'Ali.[150]

It was this persistent division in the Arab ranks that seems, *inter alia*, to have generated some theories on the origins of Arabism. Hisham Sharabi, for instance, associated the emergence of the Arab movement with the rise of the Arab bourgeoisie, embodied mainly in the modern-educated stratum of Arab Christian intellectuals.[151] In a broader sense, and to varying degrees, Dawn and Khoury have explained the genesis of the Arab political movement in socio-political terms.[152] From this vantage point, Arabism appeared to evolve as the political ideology of a small group of the Arab urban nobility, whose aspirations for senior government positions and social prominence were blocked chiefly by the CUP's allies amongst the entrenched Arab notables, and perhaps by the Unionist drive for centralization. Arabism was also seen to reflect a generational alternation, where the young Arab élite could no longer abide the values and manners of the elder generation of notables, their mediating role and compromising relations with the state. The younger generation was thus less content and more emphatic in asserting its rights (or imagined rights) and demands, viewing the elder notables as an impediment to change and renewal. Despite his emphasis on the

Islamic reformist roots of the early Arabists, Dawn has nonetheless been consistent in arguing that political Arabism after 1908 was largely a reflection of inter-élite conflict.[153]

The Arab political movement during the fateful years of 1908–20, as well as its opposition, was essentially an urban phenomenon, expressed by the politically and culturally active strata of the urban notables, professionals and government bureaucrats, civil and military. If the Arab revolt is taken as the defining moment of the Arab political map, the social fabric of both sides of the Arab political divide would appear more complex than that which the strictly followed notable theory might suggest. On the Arabist side, there were reformist ulema such as Rida, al-Zahrawi, al-Qassab and al-Karmi, journalists such as Muhib al-Din al-Khatib, al-'Uraysi, Shaykh Hasan Tabbara and Kurd-Ali, bureaucrats such as al-'Asali, al-Inkilizi, Rustum Haydar and Rafiq al-Tamimi, notables such as Rafiq al-'Azm, 'Arif al-Shihabi, the Bakri brothers, Salim al-Ahmad Abd al-Hadi, Rushdi al-Sham'a, 'Adil Arslan (the brother of Shakib) and the illusive Talib al-Naqib, together with a whole range of army officers. The active Arabists can also be divided into two age-groups: the first included those born around or before 1870, when education was still largely traditional, such as Rida, al-Zahrawi, al-'Azm, al-Karmi, Mahmud Shukri al-'Alusi, Jamal al-Din al-Qasimi and Tahir al-Jaza'iri. Members of the second group, born after 1870, were by and large graduates of modern Ottoman or European education and included most members of al-Fatat and al-'Ahd and a few others, such as al-'Asali and al-Inkilizi. The common wisdom is that the second group was more emphatic in its Arabist orientation, while the first was more compromising or reluctant to break with the Ottoman traditions. The truth is not so simple. Rida and Rafiq al-'Azm, for example, were more consistent Arabists than the younger and more worldly al-Khalil, al-'Asali, Kurd-'Ali and most of the Arabist army officers.

The ranks of the anti-Arabist camp were not less colourful. Most illustrious in this camp was the *a'yan* group of Ahmad al-Sham'a (the father of the Arabist, Rushdi al-Sham'a), M. Fawzi al-'Azm, and al-Yusuf. Shaykh As'ad al-Shuqayri was both an Azhari *alim* and a landed notable, whereas Shakib Arslan was a writer, historian and a reluctant amir of a leading Druze family. In this camp there were also less privileged members, but who were none the less vocal in their opposition to the

Arab movement. These included al-Rasafi, Jawish, al-Tha'alibi, and the Palestinian journalists, Ali al-Rimawi and Abu al-Iqbal Salim al-Ya'qubi. The anti-Arabists were also distributed over a wide age range.

It is now generally accepted by scholars of the modern Middle East that Arabism arose from Islamic reformist origins, and that Arab Christians had a less significant role in its evolution than had earlier been argued. But rarely has this fact been taken to its logical conclusions. Arabism and the Arab-Islamic reform movement, as this study demonstrates, were associated not only in the early years of the twentieth century but also throughout the interwar period. The persistent dilemma for the early Arabists was not the development of their self-consciousness as Arabs but rather how to define the line between Islam and the Ottoman bond. It is true that the Arab reformist discourse made a powerful claim for a higher Arab role in the history of Islam, with an attempt to link Islamic decline to the ascendance of Turkish political power, but the perception of the Ottoman bond in terms of Islam and the Caliphate had been too deep-rooted to be cast off easily. Despite their obvious Arab cultural dispositions, the late-nineteenth-century Arab-Islamic reformists were still Ottoman loyalists whose goal was to revive the empire, not to break it up. Until the outbreak of war, the Arab political movement was still revolving around a programme of decentralization, at a time when decentralist ideas were becoming common even amongst the Turkish political élite. The turning-point was, of course, the campaign of repression initiated by Jamal Pasha in mid-1915, coupled with signs of Ottoman military retreat, which prompted the active Arabist elements to go further and seek rupture with Istanbul.

Apart from a group of notables whose position lacked strong ideological conviction, many opponents of the Arab movement (the Ottomanists as described by Dawn) were in fact students of the Islamic reform movement. Arslan, Jawish, al-Maghribi, and al-Tha'alibi, had been strongly influenced by al-Afghani and 'Abduh, while al-Rasafi was a student of Mahmud Shukri al-'Alusi; even al-Shuqayri is believed to have been 'Abduh's student. Were they less Arabist than Rida, Rafiq al-'Azm and Muhib al-Din al-Khatib? It has recently been eloquently demonstrated how much the Ottomanist and Arabist loyalties were intertwined in the views and concerns of politically active Arabs, like Arslan and Ruhi al-Khalidi, and how easily Arslan and Sati' al-Husri would embrace Arabism after 1920.[154] It is also interesting that Mahmud Shukri al-'Alusi, an undisputed Islamic reformist and Arabist, would maintain his Ottoman loyalty to the end, taking the trouble to make a long journey from Baghdad to Najd to enlist Saudi support for the Ottoman war strategy in the Persian Gulf.[155]

Most significant in blurring the imagined line between Arabism and Ottomanism was the case of the Arabist army officers. Nearly all members of al-'Ahd (many of whom were originally of modest social background) preserved their positions in the Ottoman army, and continued to rise in rank. The highly celebrated group of the Arabist military elements were those known as the Sharifian officers, who joined the Arab revolt and came later to dominate Iraqi politics in the interwar period. Apart from 'Aziz al-Misri, who was expelled to Egypt before the outbreak of war, together with Nuri al-Sa'id and Muhammad Sharif al-Faruqi, whose stories of defection to the Arab revolt are highly enigmatic, all the other Arabist officers joined Faysal's army from the British prison camps.[156] Those officers fought dutifully as Ottoman army officers. When they were captured, however, they were offered the choice of joining the Arab revolt where they would fight again with distinction. It is certainly too simplistic to explain this phenomenon in terms of the military mercenary model, since the majority of the Sharifian officers had already been known for their Arabist views and affiliations.[157] Indeed, it is rather more comprehensible to see the political behaviour of these officers against the overlapping loyalties of Arabism and Ottomanism. Yasin al-Hashimi, a senior officer, member of al-Fatat and al-'Ahd, was uncompromising in his support of the idea of an Arab revolt during an encounter with Faysal in September 1915. Sometime later, al-Hashimi would find it difficult to desert his position, and would thus continue to serve the empire until the final defeat in late 1918.[158]

The sway that the Ottoman bond held over the Arab psyche was so profound that even Faysal would sentimentally return to it in the middle of his military campaign in Syria. According to Ahmad Qadri, who was a kind of private secretary to Faysal, the Arabs became aware of the Anglo-French Sykes–Picot agreement after it was revealed by the new communist rulers of Russia in late 1917. Feeling betrayed by the allies, Faysal contacted – or was contacted by – the Ottoman military commander in Syria (the young Jamal Pasha who replaced Ahmad Jamal

Pasha), with a proposal to unite the Arab force with the Ottoman army against the advancing British expedition if the Arabs were presented by Istanbul with the same offer they had been promised by the British.[159]

It is this picture of dual and competing loyalties which makes the game of numbers highly unreliable for measuring the strength of the Arab movement prior to the Ottoman defeat.[160] The strength and spread of the Arab idea could not be measured by the mere number of the Arab organizations' members, firstly because the concept of political party was still as novel as other aspects of modernity, and secondly because politics was still practised by different means within institutions of traditional society that were not yet entirely overtaken by the age of modernization, especially the family networks, the tribe, the local mosque and the ulema class.[161] A three-volume British guide to Palestinian and Transjordanian personalities, prepared by the Arab Bureau in Cairo for the use of the British military, provides a fascinating view of the Arab social structure and political orientations in areas that have been regarded for long by Middle East scholars as not so profoundly Arabist as were Damascus and Beirut during the late Ottoman period.[162] Since the three volumes were printed successively between February and May 1917, the picture they delineate was presumably based on extensive intelligence reports, gathered during the preceding few years. The British rightly identified Tawfiq and Hasan Hammad, Ibrahim, Amin and Abd al-Hadi Qasim Abd al-Hadi (the father of 'Awni), Shaykh Nimr al-Dari, and Shaykh 'Umar Zu'aytir, as the most influential men in Nablus, stating: "All the above persons, except Tawfiq Hammad, were leaders of the Arab Party before the war; and with the exception of Omer ez-Zewaiter, all have suffered much in consequence since the war." It is equally significant that the Nablusite notable Haydar Tuqan, the former parliamentary deputy and a staunch supporter of the CUP, was described as being not very influential.

The British guide presents the four main personalities of the town of Tulkarem as follows: "Abdul Rahman Hanun, 30–35. Rich and influential, Anti-Turk; Abdul Rahim al-Jayyusi, 50–55. Rich. Member of the District Council, Anti-Turk; Abdurrahman Hajj Ibrahim, 40–45. Head of the Municipality. Very pro-Turk. Made Kaimmakam by Jemal, disliked by the people; Ahmad al-Hamdullah, 60. Member of the District Council. Hates the Turks but clever enough to conceal it, and is therefore favoured by Jemal." The intricacy of Arab politics at the time can be discerned in the case of al-Shawwa family, a leading Gazzan notable family. Hajj Saʻid al-Shawwa, a large landowner and president of the municipality, was described as undecided in character, "pretends friendship for Jemal. Has been forced to work for the Turks . . . [but] possibly at heart anti-Turk." His son, Rushdi al-Shawwa, a former member of al-Muntada al-Adabi in Istanbul, was reported to be politically opposed to his father. In Hebron, Shaykh Abd al-Hadi al-Tamimi, head of the influential Tamimi family, who held executive and judicial posts under the government, was deported to Anatolia in the winter of 1916 for his anti-Unionist attitudes, together with Shaykh Muhammad Saʻid Tahbub, a former judge of Gaza and the elected mufti of Hebron.

The same pattern of widespread anti-Turk and Arabist sentiments was also recorded in Jerusalem, seat of the most entrenched Palestinian *a'yans*. Husayn al-Husayni, a leading member of his family, president of the municipality until 1915, and Saʻid al-Husayni, deputy of Jerusalem in parliament, were characterized as "more pro-Arab than pro-Turk". Among the Khalidis, the second most influential family in Jerusalem, Shaykh Musa al-Khalidi, chief of the family, a wealthy merchant and landowner, though regarded as anti-European, was also anti-Turk. Rivalry between the Husaynis and Khalidis was one of the distinctive features of the notable politics of Jerusalem; it appears, however, that they were united in their anti-Turk sentiments during the war years. This anti-Turk stance did not necessarily reflect a developed nationalist conviction, yet at a time when the Arabist opposition to Istanbul was becoming highly visible, for many members of these *a'yan* families Arabism seemed perhaps the only available alternative to the Turks.

It is perhaps possible to conclude that Arabism evolved out of the complicated encounter of Arab-Islamic reformism with the dual impact of Ottoman modernization and the Western encroachment. It involved the revival of Arabic language and literature and the embrace of Western ideas of progress and renewal, turning thereby into a political movement amid repercussions amongst Arabs of the real or perceived Turkish exclusiveness of the CUP regime, the gradual demise of the empire and Jamal Pasha's oppressive war order. By emerging in an era in which the traditional society was breaking up, Arabism grew to shape the political outlook of a wide section of Arab society, including ulema, notables, intellectuals and bureaucrats, whose social boundaries were beginning to be blurred by a common belief in the reconciliation of Islam and the idea of an Arab nation. During the following decades, it was the legitimizing power of the Arab movement and ideology that would, *inter alia*, contribute to breaking the social patterns of Arab leadership, providing members of the less privileged classes with a leading role, side by side with the urban notables.

In the meantime, the war was creating a new and different political order throughout the Arab East. Jerusalem fell to General Allenby's troops (advancing from Egypt and Sinai to Palestine) on 9 December 1917; other major Palestinian cities were occupied the following year, during which Damascus was also entered by Faysal's Arab army and the Australian mounted troops on 1 October. A military administration was set up in Palestine, while Arab nationalists, led by Faysal, established an independent government in Damascus on the basis of their understanding of earlier British agreements with Sharif Husayn. In reality, Britain was from 1914 onwards negotiating and concluding agreements with the sharif of Mecca, who was promised an independent kingdom in the Ottoman Arab provinces, with France and Russia (the Sykes–Picot agreement) to carve up the same provinces between the imperial powers, and with the Zionist movement which was promised a Jewish national homeland in Palestine.[163] At the Paris Peace Conference in 1919, the French objected to Britain's apparent consent to the establishment of an independent Arab government in Damascus. The disagreement between the two powers was eventually resolved as the Allied Supreme Council met in San Remo in Italy on 25 April 1920, and subsequently decided to place Syria and Lebanon under the French mandate, and Palestine and Mesopotamia (Iraq) under the mandate of Britain. French troops marched into Damascus in July 1920, bringing about the collapse of the Arab government and forcing Faysal out of Syria on 28 July. Southern Syria across the Jordan (Transjordan, where there was a power vacuum) was made an Arab Emirate and control of it given to Sharif Abdullah. Since Palestine's boundaries were not defined at San Remo, they were finally drawn by the Anglo-French Boundary Convention of March 1923.[164]

Arab aspirations for the establishment of an Arab state were challenged not only by the imperialist designs, but also by the Zionist project in Palestine. Because of the tremendous bearing it would exercise on Arab-Islamic politics and ideology, and on Arab relations with the Western powers during the interwar period and beyond, it is important that we trace the origin and development of the Arab encounter with the Zionist project and the Palestinian-Arab reactions that it began to elicit.

The Zionist challenge

Jewish immigrants began to trickle into Palestine during the later decades of the nineteenth century. In 1870, an aggregate of small French Jewish organizations, the Alliance Universelle Israélite, established a school for agricultural training in Haifa and a Jewish magazine.[165] Since most of these early Zionist activities originated in Western Europe where Jewish communities were largely integrated into the secular milieu of the modern nation-states, they could not attract European Jews to Zionism nor did they engender any significant Jewish migration to Palestine. In contrast, as a result of the assassination of the Russian tsar Alexander II, and the pogroms committed against the Jews, about 20,000 Jews left Russia during 1881 and in the following year. While most of them went to the United States, only 2 per cent arrived in Palestine.[166] Known in Zionist traditions as the first *aliya*, which implies a disregard for the Sephardic Jews as well as the Palestinian people in general, this movement continued intermittently until 1904. (*Aliya* is a common Zionist term roughly meaning "returning to the holy land".) The newly arrived Jews were known as Ashkenazim, a term that was to connote foreignness and evoke animosity in the Palestinian consciousness. Early Ashkenazim were largely uncommitted Zionists who were encouraged by the Hovever Tsion, one of the first Zionist organizations. Among them was a core of activists known as the *Biluim*, who were motivated by a synthesis of the Zionist ideal of the early Russian Zionist thinkers and a socialist romantic vision.[167] Their precarious agricultural experiment was soon to be confronted by the complicated reality of Palestine, and many of them would subsequently return to Europe.[168]

After the holding of the first Zionist Congress in 1897 which established the Zionist Organization, the Zionists began promoting the idea of turning Palestine into a Jewish state under the protection of a major world power such as Britain, Germany or France. Despite their failure to find an international backer, Jewish immigration to Palestine in its second wave, driven by the abortive 1905 Russian revolution, was broader and more organized.[169] Yet, measured against the growth in the Jewish population in Palestine prior to the British occupation, the success of the Zionist movement was remarkably limited. Estimates of the Jewish population in Palestine in the late nineteenth century vary substantially – the highest figure estimates it at seven per cent of the total population.[170] More striking for a movement that deemed engagement in agricultural development to be its *raison d'être* is the fact that in 1919 there were only forty Zionist settlements in Palestine, where 10,000 people lived and worked.[171] Most Jews there were city dwellers.

Without its strategic alliance with British imperialism and the issuing of the Balfour Declaration in 1917, the Zionist movement would probably have lapsed into oblivion, or simply added to the dozens of Jewish religious and intellectual sects spread all over the world. At the beginning of this century, the most powerful Jewish communities in Western Europe and the United States were more preoccupied with preserving and expanding their acquired national rights than with pursuing the dream of an exclusive Jewish entity. A number of British statesmen, such as Joseph Chamberlain, Arthur Balfour, Lloyd George and Mark Sykes,[172] whose attitudes towards Zionism reflected a complex mixture of imperialist vision and biblical conviction, with a subtle anti-Semitic undertone, exerted their utmost efforts to give the Zionist movement centre stage in British designs towards Palestine and the Near East in general.

From the outset, Zionist encroachment on Palestine encountered Arab resistance, primarily in a disorganized and non-political fashion. Yet, soon, the Palestinians became more conscious of the ominous danger emanating from Jewish immigration, and their reaction evolved thereby into a full-fledged anti-Zionist political movement. The issue that came to generate the earliest and most lasting dispute between Arabs and Zionists was the purchase of Arab land by the Jews, many if not all of whom had little regard for the local traditions of farming and pasturing. This attitude was perhaps the cause of the collision over Petah Tikva, a Jewish colony established in 1878, mostly on land belonging originally to the Palestinian village of al-Yahudiyya.[173] On other occasions, the Jewish purchase of land from absentee landlords led to the dispossession and eviction of hundreds of peasant families, a practice manifested in Tiberias in 1901–2, and repeated in 'Affula ten years later.[174] In the urban centres, the growing number of Jews was viewed with suspicion and alarm by local merchants and craftsmen who began to suffer the consequences of economic competition, which prompted the notables of Jerusalem to send a petition to the Grand Vizier in Istanbul on 24 June 1891 demanding the prohibition of Jewish immigration and of purchase of land by Jews.[175]

The central Ottoman government had earlier established a special policy towards Jerusalem and the Jewish settlement in Palestine as growing foreign interests alerted Istanbul in 1872 to separate the *sanjaq* of Jerusalem from the jurisdiction of Damascus and connect it directly with Istanbul, a situation that continued until World War I.[176] In 1881, the Ottoman government declared: "Jewish immigrants will be able to settle as scattered groups throughout the Ottoman empire, excluding Palestine. They must submit to the law of the Empire and become Ottoman subjects."[177] However, this policy was repeatedly transgressed during the next two decades by corrupt and complacent local officials, cooperating with foreign consuls and Zionist activists. Deeply apprehensive, Sultan Abd al-Hamid re-emphasized the official line in a decree issued in October 1900.[178] More effective than any other measure was the setting up of a commission based in Jerusalem in 1897, headed by the mufti, Muhammad Tahir al-Husayni, to verify land sales to the Jews. The commission succeeded in halting the transfer of land for a few years,[179] but its work was soon overtaken by the second wave of Jewish immigration, the precarious political position of the empire, and the corrupt government administrators.

Arab opposition to Zionism intensified after 1908–9, evolving gradually into a national issue. In the Ottoman parliament, through organs of the press and through the organization of local anti-Zionist parties and associations, the Zionist danger became a central issue of the political concerns of Palestine. Najib Nassar, editor of the Arab nationalist newspaper, *al-Karmil*, published a book in 1911 on the history and goals of the Zionist movement, based on information available in the *Encyclopaedia Judaica*.[180] *Al-Karmil*, along with the pro-Ottomanist *Filastin*, campaigned relentlessly against the Zionist project, and became a major source of material for the Arab press in Damascus and Cairo.[181] Rashid Rida's *al-Manar* presented the Zionists as a group of people equipped with knowledge, financial resources and the means of modern civilization and who were bent on establishing their state in Palestine.[182] Drawing on the reformists' discourse, Rida urged Muslims to embrace science and modern skills, to revive their society and to reaffirm its subordination to the supremacy of Islam in order to overcome the Zionist designs.

In the period prior to the outbreak of war, the anti-Zionist movement in Palestine developed into a more organized form. Mass meetings protesting the sale of land to the Zionists were usually followed by telegrams to the central government, while further pressure was exerted on the Palestinian deputies in parliament to force Istanbul into action.[183] In 1911, Shaykh Sulayman al-Tajj al-Faruqi, a prominent anti-Zionist spokesman, established the Ottoman Patriotic Party to "organize and direct the struggle against Zionists and to raise awareness as to its disastrous outcomes".[184] Similarly, Najib Nassar called for organizing the "Palestinian Arab League" in 1913 in order to enlist Arab and Ottoman support for the Palestinian cause.[185] Such efforts were undertaken in several Palestinian cities, as societies and associations, some of an economic and commercial nature, were formed to consolidate the anti-Zionist stand.

Although the Arab views of Zionism in the pre-war period were generally hostile, a certain degree of fascination with Zionist activities and influence was also apparent in a number of non-Palestinian Arab circles. It was in these circles, particularly among leaders of the Decentralization Party, that some steps to negotiate with the Zionists were reluctantly taken in 1913. These moves were motivated by a concern to stem the rising tide of Zionist encroachment and to avoid the inevitable development of a wider conflict in Palestine.[186] A few Arabist leaders, on the other hand, sought in the Zionists a possible ally against Istanbul, especially when the Arab belief in a Zionist–Unionist collusion began to take root. Ideas of a united *umma* embracing all inhabitants of the Arab lands were shaping a new Arab spirit epitomized by the recruitment of the Palestinian Jew, Nasim Mullul, to the Decentralization Party at the initiative of Muhammad al-Shanti, the Jaffan journalist.[187] Moreover, images of Zionist wealth and knowledge and high expectations of the role that Zionists might play in the revival of Syria and Palestine tempted some Arabists to develop a pragmatic attitude towards Zionism. Persistently, however, curbing Jewish immigration would figure as the central issue on the Arabist agenda.

Concurrently, some Zionists in Palestine began expressing the view that only through Arab–Zionist entente could the Zionist enterprise advance, especially as they came to realize that the good relations they enjoyed with the Unionists could not ease the implementation of the Zionist ideal.[188] The intensifying Palestinian opposition, and its echoes in the surrounding Arab provinces and in the Ottoman parliament, necessitated the undertaking of efforts to change the Arab view of Zionism.

The first initiative came from a rather marginal figure: Salim al-Najjar, the correspondent of *al-Ahram* in Istanbul and a former journalist on *Le Jeune Turc*, a pro-Unionist and Zionist-backed newspaper. A supporter of the Arab cause with access to the Arab deputies as well as to some activists of the Decentralization Party,[189] al-Najjar contacted his former employer, Sami Hochberg, the Jewish editor of *Le Jeune Turc*, in early 1913, offering to mediate between the Zionists and the Arab leaders. Al-Najjar's initiative resulted in the holding of several meetings between Hochberg – who was authorized by Victor Jacobson, the Zionist representative in Istanbul – and leaders of the Arab movement in Cairo and Beirut, including Rafiq and Haqqi al-'Azm, Shaykh Ahmad Tabbara, Iskander 'Amun, and Ahmad Mukhtar Bayham. These preliminary encounters, coming against the background of rising tension in Arab–Unionist relations, seem to have created a better atmosphere between the two sides, though no substantial agreement was reached.[190] Encouraged by the results of these contacts and conscious of the implications of the Arab–Turkish discord, Hochberg moved to attend the Paris Arab Congress in June 1913 as an observer.[191] Most likely, it was Hochberg's presence and interventions with members of the congress which led to the absence of the Palestinian question from the congress's agenda. As has already been mentioned, this state of affairs did not escape the attention of the Palestinian anti-Zionist press. Hochberg hoped to reach a full understanding with the Arabists after the conclusion of the congress; his hopes, however, were dashed by the immediate start of the Arab negotiations with the Unionists and the subsequent signing of an agreement in Istanbul.

By early 1914, the Zionists had renewed contacts with the Palestinian and Arab leaders, but no particular progress was recorded.[192] While the Palestinian opposition to Zionism was developing into a more organized movement, almost all candidates in the spring parliamentary elections made resistance to Zionism the central theme of their campaigns.[193] In April, Nahum Sokolow of the Zionist executive made a visit to several Arab capitals in a further effort to improve the public image of the Zionist movement. An important Arabist response to Sokolow's endeavour appeared in an essay that Rafiq al-'Azm wrote for *al-Muqattam*.[194]

Al-'Azm laid out the main elements at the heart of Arab–Zionist conflict. He noted the arriving Jews' refusal to adopt the Ottoman identity, their separateness and exclusion from the Arabs, the alien nature of the Zionist customs, language and economic activities, and their reliance on foreign consuls for protection. As the Arabs had not yet accomplished their *nahda* (revival) – al-'Azm implied – the perils emanating from the Zionist immigration were real, and were enough of a reason to justify Palestinian resistance to Zionism. But Sokolow was still able to find Arabs more receptive to his reconciliatory schemes, amongst them the Palestinian, Nazif al-Khalidi, son of a Jerusalemite notable family and a renowned engineer who had made a significant contribution to the construction of the Hijaz railway. Though the Zionists were not yet speaking in terms of a Jewish political entity in Palestine, al-Khalidi laboured throughout the summer of 1914 to convene an Arab–Zionist round table, though to no avail.[195] Al-Khalidi's effort was in the end overtaken by the outbreak of war.

The conditions of the conflict were fundamentally altered during the war years. Since Britain and the Ottoman empire were on opposing sides in the war, the Zionists immediately took the British side, working energetically for British official adoption of the Zionist enterprise. Though the British–Zionist alliance and the idea of establishing a Jewish national home in Palestine found strong opponents in the British war cabinet, non-Jewish Zionists in government, including Lloyd George and Lord Balfour, and outside government, succeeded in committing Britain to the Zionist cause.

But the Zionists did not give up the idea of reaching an under-standing with the Arabs. Weizmann, the most prominent of the Zionist leaders and the most trusted by the British, would repeatedly approach Faysal and the Arab leaders in Cairo, sometimes with apparent success. In reality, this success was highly imagined and self-deceptive. As the Zionists presented to the Arabs a softened version of their project and the Arabs, in their time of need, expressed their opposition to Zionism in low-key language, each side was led to form a wrong view of the other. Neither Weizmann's apparent understanding with the Cairo Decentralists in 1918,[196] nor his disputed agreement with Faysal a year later would, therefore, leave any impact on the future of the conflict.[197] It is amazing that the British, who maintained for long that the Balfour Declaration was not intended to establish a Jewish state in Palestine, knew since 1918 that the goal of the Zionist movement was otherwise.[198] In the following decades, Arab opposition to Zionism would turn into a mass pan-Arab movement, fuelled by Arab nationalist and Islamic sentiments and beliefs. This development could not have become possible without the resilient spirit with which Palestinian nationalism confronted the Zionist challenge.

Palestinian nationalism

Political, social and intellectual configurations of post-World War I Palestine were largely shaped during the preceding seventy or more years of Ottoman modernization and Western encroachment. It was a modern Palestine that was not, however, entirely modern; a country where old and new existed together and against each other, and where elements of both could no longer relate to the same frame of reference.

In the traditional Ottoman Fertile Crescent societies, the Ottoman ruling élite and local intermediaries were the most dominant forces. The first included administrators, ulema in senior posts, who were usually dispatched from Istanbul, leaders of the local garrisons and the settled non-Arab *aghas* who gradually came to be integrated into the local society. The second comprised local ulema, amirs or Bedouin and mountain chieftains and urban notables.[199] The influence of the *a'yan* rose from the beginning of the seventeenth century as the Ottoman state entered its long phase of decline, during which its dependence on local forces became increasingly necessary to maintain order and preserve loyalty.[200] This function of the *a'yan* and the power it entailed, earned its legitimacy, as far as the leading families (Khalidi, 'Alami, Husayni, Nusayba, Abd al-Hadi, etc.) were concerned, from two major sources: a tradition of learning that produced an all but uninterrupted line of ulema for several generations; and a tradition of leadership based on a clan and kinship system of values. In some cases, the two elements existed jointly together.

The faulty implementation of the 1858 and subsequent land laws led to the private appropriation of land by a small group of new owners, largely made up of the *a'yan*. More than 4 million donums in Palestine (almost half of all privately-owned land) belonged to 250 families. For example, 25 families in Jerusalem and Hebron, including the Khalidi, Nusayba, al-Husayni, al-Nashashibi, al-'Alami, al-Dajani and 'Amr, possessed 240,000 donums, while 11 families in the Nablus, Tulkarem and Jenin areas, including the Tuqan, Abd al-Hadi, Jarrar, al-Nimr, al-Qasim and Barqawi had 235,000 donums between them.[201] The land possessions of al-Shawwa in Gaza, of al-Shuqayri in Acre, and of al-Sa'id, al-Bitar, or Abu Khadra in Jaffa were no smaller. Landownership provided not only the economic foundation of the *a'yan*, but was also a major source of their power and prominence. Moreover, the evolution of the state apparatus, for which members of notable families were increasingly recruited, consolidated the *a'yan's* position and made their power unrivalled.[202] This position would be largely secured during the mandate period, challenged on a small scale by the newly born intelligentsia.

The ulema arrived at a period of steady decline from the middle of the nineteenth century as a result of the state's encroachment onto the *waqf* and the modernization of the legal, educational and military systems. In many cases, the new requirements of public office precipitated the termination of the old learning traditions of the ulema families, who chose to send their younger members to modern and foreign schools to acquire an appropriate education. By this method, families like al-Khalidi, al-Dajani, and al-'Alami succeeded in preserving their social status and surmounting the cataclysmic changes of the new age.[203] For ulema families like al-Husayni, traditionally established power was enhanced by ownership of large tracts of agricultural land.[204] In both contexts, whether by embracing modern education or by becoming big landholders the traditional societal role of the *alim* was impaired, while the ancient inter-*a'yan* rivalry for power was amplified.

Another development that contributed to further dilution of the ulema's influence and to the decline of traditional societal patterns, was the emergence of a Palestinian intelligentsia. In 1914, there were 95 modern government schools in Palestine, attended by 8,248 pupils, and 379 private schools, whether native, foreign or missionary, especially in the Jerusalem area.[205] The values and standards of the new age fostered a growing disposition amongst young Palestinians to attend Istanbul's high schools and European universities rather than the traditional centres of Islamic learning. What can also be considered a novel development is that many graduates of modern education were of relatively modest social backgrounds.[206] Highly indicative of the relevant power of education were the results of Bayan al-Hout's study of the Palestinian political élite during the mandate period, which showed that Christians represented 21.2 per cent of the leading political group between 1918 and 1934,[207] a disproportionate share compared with their share of the total population.[208] Al-Hout also concluded that only 16.9 per cent of the Palestinian leaders received religious studies during their higher education, an illustration of the changing nature of leadership in the early twentieth century.

Developments in the fields of foreign trade, communications, transport and urbanization substantially afflicted other social classes (the urban merchants, artisans and craftsmen), and further reinforced the social breakup. As the balance of trade was beginning to shift in favour of imported goods, there existed two categories of merchants: the traditional inland merchant, trading in livestock, Egyptian agricultural products, Syrian fabrics, spices, olive oil and soap; and a composite of mainly Christian Palestinians and Lebanese, and European agents, who controlled the increasing overseas trade.[209] The modern merchants on the coasts largely spoke foreign languages; their interests were objectively intertwined with the gains and goals of the European economic centres, and in the course of time, the considerable growth of their wealth enabled them to challenge the inland traders in their own domain.

The burgeoning overseas imports, coupled with a cultural shift, induced changes in clothing styles and fostered a taste for modern furniture, decoration and architecture; all adversely affected the survival of artisans and craftsmen. The cotton-weaving trade and wool-knitting, done mainly by the Bedouin, were depressed, whereas manufacture of handicrafts like religious artifacts encountered better times because of the expansion in tourism.[210] To put an end to a whole way of life, the CUP government of 1912 abolished the guild system that had sustained and dominated the Islamic urban economy for centuries. This measure opened the door for many craftsmen to attempt adapting to the new conditions, while many others fell back on the limited and already strained market of agricultural labour, or joined the ranks of the urban proletariat in the cities' slums.

The changing social conditions accompanied and contributed to the birth of new cultural and intellectual milieux, implying that the traditional culture was no longer self-sufficient. The life of a distinguished Palestinian Ottoman statesman testified to the mutable nature of that era. Born into one of the most prominent Jerusalemite families, with both his father and grandfather being senior ulema, Yusuf Diya Pasha al-Khalidi (1842–1906) was first educated in a small traditional school near al-Aqsa mosque. His wish was to complete his studies in al-Azhar, but on his father's wishes he was sent to a Protestant college in Malta for two years. From there he travelled to Istanbul where he spent a year in a medical college, and one year and a half in the American Robert College for Engineering which was established in the Ottoman capital in 1863.[211] As a mayor of Jerusalem, translator in the Ottoman foreign ministry, deputy in the first Ottoman parliament, traveller in Europe and teacher in the Oriental Academy of Vienna, al-Khalidi developed a vision of reform and came to believe that the strength of the Ottoman society could only be regenerated through a comprehensively modernized education. His defence of political freedom and constitutional life marked him as an opponent of Abd al-Hamid and earned him the animosity of the sultan, leading to the disruption of his career and the decline of his family's position. Patriotism and a sense of duty, as manifested in Bismarck's Germany, were some of the values he struggled to introduce to the political life of Istanbul. Yusuf Diya's type of education and liberal dispositions can also be discerned in the life and works of his nephew and contemporary, Ruhi al-Khalidi (1864–1913), a prominent statesman, diplomat and man of letters,[212] who came under the influence of his uncle and perhaps of al-Afghani.

Side by side with the liberalization of the state apparatus and politics, five other major agents were particularly crucial in shaping the space in which the emerging Palestinian intelligentsia of the late nineteenth and early twentieth centuries breathed new ideas and became acquainted with novel systems of knowledge. The first was the increasing number of European residents, including consuls, missionaries, Jewish immigrants, trade agents or other Christian immigrants.[213] Second was the predominance of a new schooling system based on the Western model, which was becoming the backbone of Ottoman education in Palestine during Abd al-Hamid's era; missionary and other foreign schools (Russian, German, English and American) began to be established in Jerusalem as early as 1848.[214] By the beginning of the twentieth century, it became a wide and normal practice amongst many, if not all, of the leading Muslim families to send their children to foreign schools in Palestine or Lebanon, or for higher education in Istanbul and Europe. Third was the introduction of modern printing either by monasteries and convents, the Jewish settlers, or private enterprises,[215] which subsequently prompted a relatively active movement of translation and publishing. As a result of the restoration of constitutional life in 1908, about thirty Arabic newspapers and magazines appeared in Palestine.[216] Fourth was the improvement in communications (telegraph lines and postal systems) which made the flow of news easier and facilitated the spread of more advanced publications from Cairo and Istanbul. Lastly, the founding of social and cultural societies and clubs in many Palestinian cities made a significant contribution to the dissemination of new ideas amongst the élite and encouraged new modes of association.[217] The Arab-Islamic reformist ideas were propagated by ulema such as As'ad al-Shuqayri and Sa'id al-Karmi.[218] Ruhi al-Khalidi, the most distinguished amongst the Palestinian reformers, wrote on "The Eastern Question", the "History of Zionism" and "Chemistry in the History of Arab Civilization" and made an analysis of the CUP coup. He translated the works of Victor Hugo and lectured on the history of the spread of Islamic religion.[219] A supporter of the CUP, he had a profound conviction in the vital necessity of constitutional life for the survival of the Ottoman state. Virtually all newspapers and publications of the post-1908 period were occupied with issues of reform and renewal. Articles on the need for reformed education, better management of *waqf*, decentralization and distribution of power reflected some of the concerns of the new age.[220] But though local modernists and reformists were highly influenced by 'Abduh and Rida, they were not necessarily of the same intellectual calibre. Hence, the Palestinian writings of the time lacked the engaging vision and synthesis expressed by the grand reformists.

As the new age opened up new political ideas, Arabism emerged to compete with the traditional Palestinian Ottoman loyalty. The political euphoria, generated by the sociocultural changes and constitutional life, was giving rise to an increasing Palestinian consciousness amongst Palestinians of their Arab identity. Neither the Palestinian Arabists nor the vocal opponents of the Arab movement invoked a Palestinian national and exclusive entity in the modern sense. The 'Geographical Palestine', as it came to be known after World War I, had been administratively divided into two major parts during the late Ottoman period. The district of Jerusalem and the south of Palestine constituted the *sanjaq* of Jerusalem, which was linked directly with Istanbul, while northern Palestine was part of *wilayat* Beirut. This division on no occasion represented a source of Palestinian nationalist reaction or protest. A sense of communal identification did certainly exist, and writings that took pride in Palestinian culture and history became more apparent, but Palestinian nationalism in its political form was more a response to the Zionist challenge, an outcome of the Ottoman breakup and the demise of the pan-Arab Damascus government, and the impact of the British occupation.

By concentrating their colonizing and land-purchasing efforts on both parts of Palestine, the Zionists helped to create a unity of danger and destiny throughout Palestine. The British reasserted this unity by defining the borders of the Palestine mandate to embrace the *sanjaq* of Jerusalem, together with the two adjacent southern *mutasarifiyyas* of *wilayat* Beirut (Acre and Nablus). But even before the borders were finally and officially drawn up, the British worked actively to promote the idea of separating Palestine from the pan-Arab Damascus government. This British effort received substantive support through the return of Palestinian Ottoman officials and parliamentary deputies, such as Musa Kazim al-Husayni, 'Arif al-Dajani and Raghib al-Nashashibi. Although most of these Palestinians were not known for their opposition to the Arab movement, they were not known either for their Arabist ties. The precarious conditions that surrounded the Damascus Arab government did not allow for reaching out and accommodating all ex-Ottoman Arab officials. Some elements of this group would consequently become more interested in an autonomous, or even separate, Palestinian entity *vis-à-vis* the Arab government of Damascus.

As the fate of the Ottoman empire was sealed, a movement for political organization was engaged in Palestine. One of the first political organizations to emerge was the Muslim–Christian Association (MCA) of Jaffa in late 1918, followed by similar chapters in other Palestinian cities, including Jerusalem. It has been widely agreed that at least in the case of Jaffa the founding of the MCA was encouraged by officials of the British military administration.[221] Preparing the country for a long British rule, enterprising military and intelligence officers sought to foster and manipulate a national representative body. But since the British were also careful not to interfere directly in the MCAs, they became more representative than the British might have desired. Other sociocultural and political societies and clubs began to appear in 1919. Most important were al-Muntada al-'Adabi (invoking the earlier Literary Forum of Istanbul), and *al-Nadi al-'Arabi* (the Arab Club).[222] Both were established in Jerusalem; the first was dominated by members of the Nashashibi family, and the second by the young Husaynis and their associates. And both were clearly anti-Zionist and supportive of Arab unity. Although the founding of these organizations signalled the beginning of competition between the Nashashibis and the Husaynis, the two leading families of Jerusalem, the Arab Club was in fact linked to other similar clubs established in Syrian cities by al-Fatat's activists.

From 27 January to 9 February 1919, the MCAs held the First Palestinian Arab Congress in Jerusalem. The British, who exercised behind-the-scenes influence on some delegates, classified the political affiliations of the congress's 27 members as follows: 11 Palestinian nationalists; 12 Arab nationalists; 2 French sympathizers and 2 apparently undecided.[223] The resolutions of the congress, however, reflected the decisive ascendance of Arab unity.[224] They spoke of Palestine as a part of southern Syria, declared loyalty to the Damascus Arab government and rejected all ideas of separation from Syria. In a memorandum that the congress sent to the Peace Conference in Paris, the Palestinians presented a detailed refutation of the Balfour Declaration and the Zionist claims in Palestine.[225] Several factors contributed to the prevalence of an Arab nationalist line despite the British effort to guide the congress towards the idea of an autonomous Palestine under British protection.[226] First was the moral influence arising from the very existence of the Damascus Arab government; second was the persistent lobbying of the Arabist members; third, and perhaps just as important, was the growing belief among wide segments of the Palestinians that a strategic depth and backing was urgently needed if they were to overcome the challenges of the Zionist project.

Yet, the congress did not conclude in total agreement. 'Arif al-Dajani, president of the Jerusalem MCA and president of the congress, together with Ya'qub Farraj, representative of the Jerusalem Christian Orthodox community, refused to sign the document calling for pan-Syrian unity. They were soon to succeed in persuading four other delegates (from Gaza and Haifa) to renounce their support for the document, calling instead for an independent Palestine with a constitutional autonomous government. Both al-Dajani and Farraj were unequivocal in their pro-British attitudes.[227] Despite the overwhelming popular support for united Syria, Palestinian separatists continued to promote their views until the fall of the Damascus government.

In the midst of the Anglo-French entanglement at the Peace Conference over the future of the ex-Ottoman Arab provinces, the Americans proposed that an inter-Allied commission be sent to assess the demands and aspirations of the inhabitants of these provinces. The

French insisted that their troops replace those of the British in Syria prior to the appointment of the commission – a demand rejected by the British. After further delays by the two imperialist powers, only the American members of the inquiry group, known as the King–Crane Commission, proceeded to the area. In Palestine, preparations for the arrival of the commission in June 1919 were undertaken by the Palestinian Arabists of al-Fatat, such as 'Izzat Darwaza, Rafiq al-Tamimi and Hafiz Kan'an, together with some newcomers to the Arab nationalist scene, such as Amin al-Husayni and 'Arif al-'Arif. The main goal of these activists was to consolidate Palestinian public opinion behind the idea of a unified Syrian Arab state. In a meeting held in Jerusalem, attended by the Arabist group as well as by the proponents of independent Palestine, it was agreed to present the Palestinian people's wishes to the commission as:

> 1. Syria from the Taurus mountains in the north to Rafah in the south to be entirely independent; 2. Palestine (Southern Syria) which is an inseparable part of Syria to be internally autonomous, electing its leaders from among its nationals and enacting its laws according to the wishes of its people and the country's needs; 3. Rejection of the Zionist immigrants and the plan to render Palestine a homeland for the Jews. Those of the Jews who have lived a long time in our country are considered equal nationals.[228]

While demonstrating a consensus on the Zionist question, this formulation carried a distinctive spirit of compromise regarding the political future of Palestine. Indeed, it represented a noticeable concession on the part of the Arabists for the idea of an independent Palestine. It must be recalled that news of the Faysal–Weizmann agreement reached Damascus and Palestine in the spring of 1920,[229] during the interceding period between the end of the First Palestinian Congress and the beginning of the preparations for the arrival of the King–Crane Commission. Evoking a powerful response from various Palestinian circles, this news seems to have weakened the Arabists' position. Still, Palestinian popular support for a united Syria was more assertive than the resolutions of the Jerusalem meeting.[230] The work of the commission was overtaken by the subsequent British–French agreement to divide the Arab countries. Its recommendations were kept secret by the American government for the next three years, but when published they revealed a powerful Palestinian backing for an integrated Syria.

During 1919 and early 1920, Palestinian petitions and protestations to the British military authorities (the Occupied Enemy Territory Administration or OETA), the British Foreign Office, and Paris Peace Conference, emphasized the Palestinian rejection of the Balfour Declaration and desire to remain united with Syria.[231] A week after the formal communication of the mandate and the Balfour Declaration to the Palestinians by Major-General Bols, chief military administrator of Palestine, on 20 February 1920, demonstrations erupted in Jerusalem, Bethlehem and Jaffa.[232] More serious and foreboding for the future were the disturbances of the following April. It was traditional for the Palestinian Muslims to commemorate in the spring a religious festival (*al-Nabi Musa*) at a site near Jericho, popularly believed to be the shrine of the Prophet Moses. Parades from various cities would first converge in Jerusalem and subsequently proceed to the festival site, led by the mufti of Jerusalem. On 4 April, as the people gathered at Hebron gate of the old city, nationalist speeches were made by the mayor, Musa Kazim al-Husayni, Abd al-Fattah Darwish of the Arab Club, 'Arif al-'Arif, Khalil Baydas and Amin al-Husayni.[233] Feelings were already high when a group of extremist Zionists staged a deliberate intrusion into the gathering, sparking a week-long bloody confrontation between the Arabs and the Jews.

The Palestinian eruption was principally of an anti-Zionist nature, but it also demonstrated a persistent demand for a Syrian Arab unity. But, soon, the Palestinians' debate over their political future would be resolved by the crushing of Faysal's short-lived enterprise by the French in July 1920. It would be several years before the vision of Arab unity would recover from the defeat of the Damascus government. Palestinian nationalism became an enforced and inescapable reality that would, in turn, diverge into two distinctive paths: one embodied in a Palestinian nationalist camp with a firm opposition to Zionism and a view of Arab unity and Islamic solidarity, led by Hajj Amin al-Husayni, and a second represented by a group with a much narrower understanding of Palestinian nationalism and interests, led by Raghib al-Nashashibi. Among members of the second group, the British as well as the Zionists found highly useful allies. But even here the Palestinian and Arab realities were too intractably intertwined to be ignored. Hence, when rivalry and competition between the two Palestinian camps became unbridgeable, even Raghib al-Nashashibi would seek pan-Arabist allies such as Amir Abdullah.

The April riot marked a turning-point in the conditions of postwar Palestine. Musa Kazim al-Husayni, who had been earlier appointed to the mayoralty of Jerusalem by the British, was dismissed and replaced by Raghib al-Nashashibi. The old Husayni would soon re-emerge as president of the Palestinian National Congress, where he worked to assert a Palestinian nationalist line. The young Hajj Amin al-Husayni, along with his associate, 'Arif al-'Arif, were sentenced *in absentia* to ten years' imprisonment with hard labour. Both fled the country to Syria, from which they moved to Transjordan after the collapse of Faysal's government.

Most of the senior officers of the OETA grew to sympathize with the Palestinians' deep hostility towards Zionism, while dutifully warning their government that its support for the Zionist project would result in an outbreak of conflict and sour Anglo-Arab relations.[234] The Zionist Commission in Palestine (officially accepted by the British to represent the Jews) accused the OETA of being biased against its cause and of responsibility for the April riot, a view that the British Foreign Office was inclined to accept. Yet, the British government was set on a long course of backing for the Zionist project. To underline this commitment, Lloyd George and Balfour decided to terminate the OETA and to install a British civil administration, long before the mandate was passed by the League of Nations.[235] Herbert Samuel, a dedicated Zionist Jew, was subsequently appointed as the first High Commissioner (HC) of mandated Palestine. When he arrived on 30 June 1920, one of his early decisions was to respond to popular demands to pardon Hajj Amin al-Husayni.

NOTES

1 On al-Afghani, see Keddie, 1968 and 1972. On al-Afghani and Abduh, see Kedourie, 1966. The Islamic reformist circle of Cairo has been the subject of extensive studies, see, for example: Loust, 1938; Hourani, 1962 and Badawi, 1976. The most insightful study of the Damascus-based reform circle and the rise of Arabism is by Commins (1990). The Baghdad circle is the least investigated; on the 'Alusis, see al-'Athari, AH 1345 and 1958. Recently, Tauber (1993) studied the emergence of Arab nationalism in relation to the Arab-Islamic reformist, as well as other, circles.

2 On the Young Ottomans' opposition to the *tanzimat* regime see Lewis (1961:147–70), and on the emergence of the Young Turks and the Committee of Union and Progress (CUP) from the desperation and defeat of the Young Ottomans see ibid., 190–205. The same period was discussed with varying detail and emphasis by: Ramsour, 1957:3–19; Mardin, 1962:10–80 ff.; Berkes, 1964:201–322; and, most recently, Hanioglu, 1995:7–70.

3 Al-Afghani, 1979–81: vol. 2, 9–20. Al-Afghani, who was a non-Arab, began to underline the Arabs' role in Islam much earlier. In his response to the views of the French philosopher Renan on Islam (1883), al-Afghani defended the Islamic civilization as an Arab civilization (Keddie, 1968:181–7). Keddie (1972:211–12 and 261–2) and Kedourie (1974:108), on the other hand, believed that al-Afghani turned to Abbas Hilmi, the Khedive of Egypt, by the mid-1890s, encouraging him to establish an Arab Caliphate.

4 'Abduh, AH 1320: 90–124; see also: 'Abduh, AH 1327: 26; Rida, 1906–31: vol. 1, 913-4. 'Abduh would also become interested in the study of pre-Islamic Arabian culture (Dawn, 1973:136). Rida's interest echoed the work of his fellow Iraqi reformist Mahmud Shukri al-'Alusi who published *Bulugh al-'Irab fi Ahwal al-'Arab* (AH 1314), a study of the Arab conditions before the advent of Islam.

5 The Law of Public Instruction (*Ma'arif-i-Umumiya Nizamnamesi*) was beginning to be implemented in Syria on a wide scale and in a serious manner in 1881 when a Council of Public Instruction was established in Damascus for this task (Gross, Ph.D. thesis, 1979: vol. 2, 326). On the contribution of the modern school, developed by the Englishman Joseph Lancaster early in the nineteenth century, to the centralization of power in society see Foucault, 1977:193. Messick (1993:101–14) presented an illuminating discussion of the relation between the Lancasterian school and power in the Ottoman-Islamic context.

6 Al-Khatib (1971:42), supported by Haddad (1994:202), indicated that the decree for the use of Turkish was issued in 1887. It is, however, likely that this step accompanied the implementation of the 1869 Law of Public Instruction in Syria in 1881 (see the previous note).

7 On an occasion 'Abduh said, "the preservation of the Ottoman state is the third of creeds (for the Muslim)", see Rida, 1906–31: vol. 1, 909.

8 Kautsky, 1967:81.

9 Sharabi, 1970:53–9 ff.; al-Duri, 1986:136–40; Cachia,1990:31–4.

10 Antonius, 1969:51–4; Gross, Ph.D. thesis, 1979: vol. 1, 273; al-Duri, 1986:149–50.

11 On the appearance of anti-Ottoman Arabist placards in 1880–1, their contents and significance or insignificance for the history of the Arab movement, see: Antonius, 1969:81–6; Gross, Ph.D. thesis, 1979: vol. 1, 311–13; al-Duri, 1986:155–60.

12 Tibawi, 1969:172–84 ff.; Akarali, 1986:74–5.

13 "*Al-Jinsiyya wal-Din al-Islami*", *al-Manar*, vol. 2, 1899, 326–7. In the same vein see also: Muhammad Tawfiq al-Bakri, *al-Manar*, vol. 5, 1902, 601–32; Rida, *al-Manar*, vol. 8, 1905, 786–8. On 'Abduh's similar position see *al-Manar*, vol. 10. 1907, 208.

14 *Al-Manar*, vol. 1, 1898, 765–92; vol. 2, 1899, 109–110.

15 Causing a substantial rise in *al-Manar*'s circulation from 1902 onwards (Rida, 1906–31: vol. 1, 1008). On al-Kawakibi see Kurd-'Ali, 1980:279–84.

16 Al-Kawakibi, 1901:49–52, 93 and 112. According to Haim (1954:231–4) al-Kawakibi's analysis was largely influenced by the Italian thinker, Alfieri.

17 Al-Kawakibi, 1899:164–7.

18 Ibid., 154–8 and 169–71.

19 "We have to remove the despotic government and replace it with a government of *shar'* and *shura*," Rida wrote (*al-Manar*, vol. 7, 1904, 358 and vol. 10, 1907, 282–3).

20 On al-Zahrawi see: *al-Manar*, vol. 19, 1916, 169–78; al-Bitar, 1961–3: vol. 2, 791–6; Tarabein, 1991:97–119. On al-ʿAzm see *al-Manar*, vol. 26, 1926, 288–300 and Kurd-Ali, 1960:224–8.

21 Al-Zahrawi, *al-Manar*, vol. 10, 1907, 586–7; idem, 1962: 17, 30, 61–4. In his treaty on *al-fiqh wal-Tasawuf* (1960), which was first published in 1901, al-Zahrawi launched a stinging attack on Tasawuf (ibid., 10–58), while at the same time attemping to establish that the Islamic political unity had broken up since the early history of Islam (ibid., 15–16 and 30). Similar views were also expressed by al-ʿAzm (AH 1344:14–15, 48–52, 80–2). This radical stand on the part of al-Zahrawi and al-ʿAzm did not, however, mean that they sought the rupture of the Ottoman league. Aware of the imperialist schemes in the Arab East, these two Arab reformists believed in preserving the Ottoman state as long as the Arab rights would be guaranteed and as long as the state was able to defend its territories (al-Zahrawi, 1962: 224–30; alʿAzm, AH 1344:140–2).

22 Al-Shihabi, 1959:51; al-Khatib, 1979:13–14. See also Commins, 1990:92–4 ff.

23 Al-Shihabi, ibid., 53; al-Khatib, ibid., 12.

24 Al-Shihabi, ibid., 54–6; al-Khatib, ibid., 18–23.

25 Al-Khatib, 1959:4–10; idem, 1979:25–6 and 28–9.

26 *Al-Manar*, vol. 11, 1908, 737; vol. 14, 1911, 9. See also al-Khatib, 1979:36.

27 On the initial Arab support for the CUP see: *al-Manar*, vol. 11, 1908, 417 and 868; *al-Ahram*, 3 March 1909; al-Sakakini, 1955:33–4; al-ʿArif, 1943:202; al-Shihabi, 1959:62; al-Khatib, 1979:41–4; Kurd-Ali, 1983: vol. 3, 117; al-Nimr, n.d.: vol. 3, 105–15. Rafiq and Haqqi al-ʿAzm, who were active in the Ottoman Shura Society in Cairo, returned to Damascus and joined the CUP (see Rida's introduction to al-ʿAzm, AH 1344). Many Iraqi and Syrian Arab activists, like Abd al-Rahman al-Shahbandar, Talib al-Naqib, Shukri al-ʿAsali, Ruhi al-Khalidi, Muhsin al-Saʿdun, and the army officers ʿAziz Ali al-Misri, Salim al-Jazaʾiri and Yasin al-Hashimi, also joined the CUP (al-Barudi, 1951: vol. 1, 67; Faydi, 1952:65; Khalidi, 1980:211; Seikaly, 1991:77). On the occasion of constitutional restoration a national anthem was written by Tawfiq Fikrat, a Turkish writer, and musically composed by the Lebanese Arab musician Wadiʿ Sabra. Its Arabic version was written by the Iraqi poet Maʿruf al-Rasafi, a student of the Arab-Islamic reformist Mahmud Shukri al-ʾAlusi (al-Husri, 1960:109).

28 In Cairo, Damascus and Paris the Arabist opponents of Hamidian rule were in close contact and cooperating with the various wings of the Young Turks, sharing in some cases the same organizational platform. For details see: Lewis, 1961:192–203; Kayali, Ph.D. dissertation 1988:47–73; Commins, 1990:94–5; Hanioglu, 1995:44–9; 78–84; 101–9.

29 Ahmad (Feroz), 1969:159.

30 Ibid., 159–60.

31 On the liberal decentralist and Westernized views of Prince Sabah al-Din, see Ramsaur, 1957: 65–93 and Lewis, 1961:197–201. On the establishment of the Osmanli Ahrar Firkasi or the Liberal Union see Ahmad (Feroz), 1969:28.

Although CUP clubs began to emerge in several Arab cities, immediately after the 1908 revolution, the two pro-CUP clubs that were established in Damascus by October 1908 were apparently connected with the Liberals (Devey to Lowther, 1 October 1908, FO 371/560/37930).

32 Al-A'zami, 1931–4: vol. 2, 98–102; Sa'id, 1934: vol. 1, 7–8; Antonius, 1969:102.

33 On the early purge of the pro-Hamidian bureaucracy, which should not be confused with the wider bureaucratic reorganization two years later, see Harran, Ph.D. thesis, 1969:52–9; Ahmad (Feroz), 1969:14–15; Kayal, Ph.D. dissertation, 1988:31–3.

34 Ahmad (Feroz), 1969:23; Birru, 1990:85–6.

35 Harran, Ph.D. thesis, 1969:70; Birru, 1990:105; Kayali, 1995:271.

36 On the situation of Damascus see: Devey to Lowther, 1 October 1908, FO 195/2277/51; Harran, Ph.D. thesis, 1969:71; Kedourie, 1974:148; Khoury, 1983:57. In Baghdad, opposition to the Unionists was led by religious notability (Nazmi, 1984:88), but was too weak to challenge the CUP's popularity. Talib al-Naqib of Basra, who won his seat in spite of the CUP, was Naqib al-Ashraf of his city (al-'Azzawi, 1955–6: vol. 8, 166).

37 Al-'Azm, AH 1344:129–30; *al-Ahram*, 1 January 1909; *al-Manar*, vol. 11, 1908, p. 85.

38 *Al-Manar*, vol. 11, 1909, pp. 936–51; Khoury, 1983:56–7.

39 For example, *al-Mu'ayyad*, 9 July 1911.

40 Birru, 1990:106–7 and 110–11.

41 *Al-Ahram*, 23 April 1909.

42 Harran, Ph.D. thesis, 1969:79–81; Gross, Ph.D. dissertation, 1979:529; Kurd-Ali, 1983: vol. 3, 118.

43 Qadri, 1956:10.

44 Ahmad (Feroz), 1969:57–64. For al-Zahrawi's opposition to the Unionist bloc during the debating of the Public Congregation Law see *al-Mu'ayyad*, 2 August 1909.

45 Al-'Azzawi, 1955–6: vol. 8, 178–9, 201; Khalidi, 1980:204 and 221; Haddad, 1995:209–10.

46 *Al-Ahram*, 19 November 1909.

47 *Al-Manar*, vol. 12, 1909, pp. 509, 917–18.

48 'Awad, 1969:253–9; Davison, 1990:172.

49 On Beirut see: 'Awad, ibid., 261 and al-Tamimi and Bahjat, AH 1335: vol. 1, 290, 307, 322, 580. On Baghdad see: al-'Azzawi, 1955–6: vol. 7, 296 and vol. 8, 104, 245 and al-Husri, 1966–8: vol. 1, 115. On Damascus see al-Khatib, 1979:5–9. Al-Khatib had to finalize his secondary education in Beirut (ibid., 14–15) where he graduated in 1905. On Jerusalem: see al-'Arif, 1961:445 and Tibawi, 1966:20. On Ottoman education in Greater Syria see Buchanan, 1922:395–406.

50 Al-Barudi, 1951: vol. 1, 29–32; al-Khatib, 1979:7–8.

51 Abdur Razzack, Acting Consul, Jeddah, to Sir W. G. White, Consular-General, Constantinople, Report on the Educational Establishment in the Hedjaz, 15 September 1885, FO 195/1514/26.

52 Cf. al-Khatib, 1971:42.

53 *Al-Ahram*, 26 April 1913; Bayham, 1950: vol. 2, 17; Tibawi, 1969:168–70; Gross, Ph.D. dissertation, 1979:337.

54 Al-Hakim, 1966: vol. 1, 98–9; al-Khatib, 1979:8; Kurd-Ali, 1983: vol. 4, 74–5; Darwaza, 1984–6: vol. 1, 137–8.

55 See for example his essay "al-Lughat wa-'Insha'", *al-Ustath*, 11 October 1892, 170–83.

56 Davison, 1990:172. In Nablus of 1895, the elementary school had already been put under government supervision (Darwaza, 1984–6: vol. 1, 128–9). See also: al-Tamimi and Bahjat, AH 1335: vol. 2, 185; Tibawi, 1966:77 and Bayat, 1990:115, 121–6. Three years after the rise of the CUP to power, Shukri al-'Asali was still demanding that Arabic become the language of instruction in the Arab primary schools (*al-Mufid*, 17 May 1911).

57 Birru, 1990:96. On Jahid's Turkish nationalist and anti-Arab tainted view before 1908 see Berkes, 1964:298–9. On expressions of Turkism by other Turkish intellectuals see al-Husri, 1960:121–4. It must be mentioned, however, that even Jahid was not always consistent in his Turkish attitudes. Less than a year after he published his provocative essay on the Turks' privileged position, he wrote in support of the cultural autonomy of the empire's various nationalities and of national equality (*al-Ahram*, 16 June 1909).

58 Sa'id, 1934: vol. 1, 4; Findley, 1980:297.

59 Anonymous (widely known to be As'ad Daghir), 1916:52.

60 *Al-Ahram*, 17 March 1910.

61 *Al-Mu'ayyad*, 9 November 1909 and 2 April 1910; anon. (Daghir), 1916:53.

62 Birru, 1990:138.

63 *Al-Mu'ayyad*, 1, 12 and 28 December 1909; *al-Ahram*, 15, 20, 21 December 1909 and 2 January 1910; al-'Azzawi, 1955–6: vol. 8, 186–7; Ahmad (Feroz), 1969:56–7, 66–7, 81; Khalidi, 1980:213–14.

64 *Al-Ahram*, 11 August 1910; anon. (Daghir), 1916:54.

65 *Al-Ahram*, 16, 24 November 1910, 10 and 18 January 1911; Kurd-Ali, 1983: vol. 3, 110–11.

66 *Al-Mu'ayyad*, 15 August 1909 and 13 April 1910.

67 *Al-Ahram*, 23 March 1910; *al-Manar*, vol. 13, 1910, pp. 219–25; al-A'zami, 1931–4: vol. 1, 105–6.

68 *Al-Ahram*, 8 May 1911; Philby, 1955:257–8; Mousa, 1970:52–4.

69 On Tal'at's resignation on 10 February 1911 see Ahmad (Feroz), 1969:86. On the peace agreement with the Imam Yahya of Yemen, see: *al-Manar*, vol. 15, 1912:138–53 and al-A'zami, 1931–4: vol. 1, 1–13.

70 Shukri, 1957: vol. 2, 426–38; Stoddard, Ph.D. dissertation, 1963:76–9.

71 *Al-Manar*, vol. 14, 1911, pp. 862–7; *al-Mu'ayyad*, 2, 4 and 29 October 1911; *al-Ahram*, 22 and 23 October 1911.

72 *Al-Mufid*, 16 April and 4 August 1912; *al-Mu'ayyad*, 24 October 1912; Arslan, 1937:152–3; al-Husri, 1960:119.

73 Khalidi, 1980:219.

74 Ahmad (Feroz), 1969:30–6; Birru, 1990:114–15.

75 In March 1909 *Serbesti*, the liberal opposition paper, implicated the CUP in blackmail to extract money from corrupt officials of the old regime. A month later, Hasan Fehmi, editor of *Serbesti* was assassinated. Again, on 9 June 1910, Ahmed Samim, editor of the *Sedayn Millet*, another opposition paper, was murdered. In both cases the opposition laid the responsibility on the Unionists (Ahmad, ibid., 39, 82). See also *al-Ahram*, 20 July and 9 August 1910.

76 Kayali, Ph.D. dissertation, 1988:124–8 and Birru, 1990:226–9. Both of these sources provide a view of the Moderate Liberal Party as well as the Peoples Party, another small opposition party that gained the support of a few Arab deputies but was likewise unable to pose a serious challenge to the Unionists.

77 *Al-Mu'ayyad*, 17 February 1910; al-'Azami, 1931–4: vol. 3, 3–8ff.; Sa'id, 1934: vol. 1, 10–11; al-'Arif, 1943:203; al-Shihabi, 1959:70–2.

78 Khalidi, 1980:223; Seikaly, 1991:73–96.

79 *Al-Muqtabas*, 6 April 1911 and *al-Mu'ayyad*, 8 April 1911. Al-'Asali became immediately a target of a fierce campaign by the pro-CUP press and the CUP Selunik Clubs (*al-Mu'ayyad*, 15 April 1911). Al-'Asali himself returned to the main themes of his speech in his impassioned and sharp reply to the campaign against him (*al-Mufid*, 17 May 1911).

80 *Al-Ahram*, 24 and 25 May 1911 and Mandel, 1976:112. Al-'Asali's opposition to the Zionist attempts to acquire land of the 'Afula, a northern Palestinian village, was a major episode of his term as *qa'imaqam* of Nazareth (ibid., 171–2). Al-'Asali's version of the event was told in two articles he published immediately after assuming his parliamentary seat (*al-Mufid*, 11 and 19 February 1911). After his noted speech in the chamber, al-'Asali returned to the subject with more vigour in *al-Muqtabas* (5 June 1911), where he made it absolutely clear that his opposition was to the CUP and not to the "glorious Turkish race".

81 *Al-Manar*, vol.13, 1910, pp. 145–9, 230, 465–8 and 750–2 and Arslan, 1937:148–9.

82 Khalidi, 1981:38–61; Khoury and 1933:60–3. In April 1912 *al-Muqtabas* was banned by the government and its editor Muhammad Kurd-Ali escaped to Egypt.

83 *Al-Manar*, vol. 21, 1919, p. 203; Sa'id, 1934: vol. 1, 49–50 and Bayham, 1950: vol. 2, 23.

84 Al-A'zami, 1931–4: vol. 2, 17–18; Ahmad (Feroz), 1969:98–9.

85 *Al-Ahram*, 29 November 1911; al-'Azm. 1912:73–4; Faydi, 1952:96–100.

86 Qadri, 1956:7 and Qasimiyya (ed.), 1974:9.

87 Sa'id, 1934: vol. 1, 9; Darwaza, 1949–51: vol. 1, 27; Antonius, 1969:111.

88 Khalidi, 1991:56. Also, idem, 1981:38–61.

89 Sa'id, 1934: vol. 1, 46; al-Shihabi, 1959:79.

90 Hardings to Balfour, interview with 'Aziz Ali, 14 January 1918, FO 371/3396/11436; al-A'zami, 1931–4: vol. 4, 53.

91 Anonymous (Daghir), 1916:103–7; Mallet to Grey, 24 February 1914, FO 371/2131/9033.

92 Al-'Azm (1912) is the earliest comprehensive Arabist view of the election campaign and balloting; see for example pp. 15–19, 34–9, 40–1, 52–61 on Greater Syria, and 68–9 on Iraq. Khalidi (1984:461–74) is the most comprehensive recent study of the 1912 elections in the Syrian context. Kayali (1995:273–7) with slight variations, agreed with the established view that the 1912 elections were largely and coercingly manipulated.

93 Both al-Yusuf and al-Shuqayri had been deputies in the 1908 parliament. Al-Yusuf was earlier on the conservative side of the Arab opposition to the CUP in parliament. However, he steered away from the Arab parliamentary opposition and managed to cultivate strong relations with the Unionists. It is not clear when al-Shuqayri began his association with the CUP. Before his election in 1908, he was a judicial functionary and a librarian of Abd al-Hamid's library, a position he

acquired through his relations with Shaykh Abu al-Huda al-Sayyadi in 1905. Sometime later Abd al-Hamid suspected that al-Shuqayri was connected with the Arabist shaykh, Abd al-Hamid al-Zahrawi; he was thus arrested and exiled to Tabnin Castle in South Lebanon. He was released after the 1908 revolution. It is believed that Shaykh As'ad, who arrived at al-Azhar in 1875, was also a student of 'Abduh (al-'Awdat, 1976:318–20). M. Fawzi al-'Azm, on the other hand, had been a declared opponent of the CUP. According to Haqqi al-'Azm, it was Fawzi Pasha's sudden alliance with the CUP which secured its victory in Damascus (al-'Azm, 1912:73–4). See also Harran, Ph.D. thesis, 1969:158. In Baghdad, the early opposition to the CUP was led by the Gaylani Ashraf family, Shaykh Sa'id al-Naqshabandi, 'Ala' al-Na'ib and shaykh Yusuf al-Swaydi (Nazmi, 1984:88,100). The election of Muhi al-Din al-Gaylani (al-'Azzawi, 1955–6: vol. 8, 222), therefore, symbolized a *rapprochement* between the CUP and the most conservative notable family of Baghdad, but not the whole of the opposition team, since Yusuf al-Swaydi continued to support the Arabist line and demands.

94 *Al-Mu'ayyad*, 18 April 1912.
95 Al-'Azm, 1912:60–1. For the new list of deputies in Greater Syria see Khalidi, 1980:258–9. For the Iraqi list see al-'Azzawi, 1955–6: vol. 8, 222.
96 Al-'Azm, ibid., 57.
97 Ahmad (Feroz), 1969:106–13.
98 Al-Adhami, 1990:78; Kayali, 1995:277–8.
99 The population of *wilayat* Beirut, Syria and *sanjaq* Jerusalem grew respectively from 568,014; 400,748 and 234,770 in 1893 to 824,873; 914,409 and 328,168 in 1914 (Karpat, 1985:190). Baghdad was served by sixteen newspapers and magazines in 1908, most of them appearing after the Unionist revolution (al-'Azzawi, 1955–6: vol. 8, 168–9). In Jerusalem, six newspapers and magazines appeared in the same year (Yehoshua', 1974:33–98), while twice that number appeared in Beirut (Daghir, 1978:405–14).
100 The 1912 crisis in Lebanon has been discussed with detail in al-Khalidi, 1980:260–84 and Kawtharani, 1986:213–15. For the Arab press reactions to the threatening French statements on Lebanon see: *al-Ahram*, 9 January 1913 and *al-Mufid*, 11 January 1913. See also Sa'id, 1934: vol. 1, 14.
101 Bayham, 1950: vol. 2, 22.
102 *Al-Mufid*, 30 December 1912, 11, 18, 21, 23 and 25 January 1913. For the programme of the Society as presented to the Ottoman authorities, see ibid., 17 and 18 March 1913. See also *al-Manar*, vol. 16, 1913, p. 275.
103 *Al-Mufid*, 15 January 1913.
104 Sa'id, 1934: vol. 1, 24; Faydi, 1952:130.
105 *Al-Mufid*, 14 and 17 April 1913; Nazmi, 1984:99.
106 *Al-Manar*, vol. 16, 1913, pp. 226, 229 and 231; Sa'id, 1934: vol. 1, 14ff; Harran, Ph.D. thesis, 1969:196–7; al-Khatib, 1979:55.
107 But apparently not in the Beirut Society which was composed of a wide variety of local Muslim and Christian leaders (Salam, 1982:152). On the Iraqi links see Faydi, 1952:98 and 116.
108 Al-Nimr, n.d.: vol. 3, 136–7 and Manna', 1986:200–1, 227, 265–6 and 325–6.
109 *Al-Mufid*, 22 February 1913; anonymous (Daghir), 1916:57.
110 Rafiq al-'Azm in *al-Mufid*, 22 April 1913.
111 Ahmad (Feroz), 1969:119–28.

112 Cumerbatch (Beirut) to Lowther, enclosed in Lowther to Grey, 7 February 1913, FO 371/788/7281. The Beirut Reform Society was shut down (*al-Mufid*, 9 April 1913), and the promised new *Wilayat* Law did not meet the Arab demands.

113 Al-Khatib (ed.), 1913:3–11ff.; Qadri, 1956:14.

114 Al-Swaydi, 1969:26–7.

115 Ibid., 30; al-Khatib (ed.), 1913:14–16, 28–39, 42–50 and 56–8.

116 Al-Khatib, ibid., 103–4.

117 Ibid., 113–21; al-Husri, 1956:219; Khalidi, 1980:311–13.

118 *Al-Mufid*, 24, 27, 28 and 29 May 1913; al-Khatib, ibid., 11–12; anonymous (Daghir), 1916:75; al-Swaydi, 1969:29.

119 *Filastin*, 29 July and 13 August 1913; *al-Karmil*, 4, 8, 11, 15 and 22 July 1913. It is, however, significant that out of 387 telegrams of support for the Congress, 139 were sent from Palestine.

120 *Al-Manar*, vol. 16, 1913, pp. 636–7; anonymous (Daghir), 1916:80–100; Sa'id, 1934: vol. 1, 32–4; al-Husri, 1956:220–3.

121 *Al-Manar*, vol. 19, 1916, pp. 715–18; al-A'zami, 1931–4: vol. 4, 19–30; Qadri, 1956:22–8. For the Decentralization Party's statement see *al-Manar*, vol. 16, 1913, 849–79.

122 Ahmad (Feroz), 1969:129–33.

123 Ibid., 135–7, 141. The appointment of Sa'id Halim Pasha as Grand Vizier after the assassination of Shawkat was perhaps another step in that direction. Halim, a member of the Egyptian Khedive family was regarded as an Arab; he wrote in Arabic and French (Berkes, 1964:349). The Unionist leaders even contemplated the appointment of an Arab as Shaykh al-Islam (Ahmad, ibid., 148).

124 *Al-Ahram*, 21 and 30 January 1914; *al-Manar*, vol. 17, 1914, 235; anonymous (Daghir), 1916:99. By then none of the four *mutasarrifs* in *wilayat* Beirut was a Turk: three were Arabs, and the fourth was a Kurd (Kayali, Ph.D. dissertation, 1988:190).

125 Al-'Azzawi, 1955–6: vol. 8, 250; Qadri, 1956:20.

126 *Al-Ahram*, 26 and 29 December 1913. In fact, the decree sanctioning the use of Arabic in courts and in the pre-*Sultaniyya* schools was issued in April 1913, immediately after the return of the CUP to power; its implementation, however, was slow (Lowther to FO, 21 April 1913, FO 195/2452/1831).

127 Crow to Mallet, 14 February 1914, FO 195/2457/350; Mallet to Grey, 25 March 1914, FO 371/2128/13883; Sa'id, 1934: vol. 1, 24.

128 Philby, 1955:269. The agreement was kept secret from the British until they accidently found a copy of it in the Ottoman papers after the British landing in Basra at the outbreak of World War I (Historical Memorandum on the Relations of the Wahhabi Amirs and Ibn Saud with Eastern Arabia and the British Government, 1800–1934 [Confidential], India Office, 26 September 1934, L/P & S/18/B 437, p. 37, and a full text of the agreement, pp. 51–2).

129 *Al-Ahram*, 19 March and 20 May 1914. A generally positive appraisal of the 1914 elections is in Kayali, 1995:278–80. The Arabist view, however, was still negative, see for example anonymous (Daghir), 1916:109 and Faydi, 1952:140–53. A list of the new deputies for Greater Syria is in Khalidi, 1980:258–9.

130 *Al-Ahram*, 26 September 1914; *al-Manar*, vol. 17, 1914, 955.

131 Anonymous (Daghir), 1916:128–9; Jamal Pasha, 1923:340–3.

132 Darwaza, 1949–51: vol. 1, 33–4; Qadri, 1956:12–13, 37, 39–40 and al-Shihabi, 1959:72–6.
133 Al-Ghusayn, 1956:202–3.
134 Cheetham to Grey, 9 November 1914, FO 371/2141/251; Sa'id, 1934: vol. 1, 108; Qadri, 1956:37–8; Bayham, 1950: vol. 2, 29. In Basra, however, Talib al-Naqib approached the British for recognition as Amir of Basra (Mallet to Grey, 7 October 1914, FO 371/2140/942). The British, of course, were not interested and were soon to capture Basra.
135 Al-Jamil (1989:465–94) presents a brief view of the history of the ashraf in the Hijaz and their relations with the Ottomans since the sixteenth century. The most detailed study of Sharif Husayn and the motives that prompted his turning against the Ottomans is still Dawn's 1960 article, republished in Dawn, 1973:1–53, see especially p. 51. See also, Baker, 1979:17–31; and Kayali, Ph.D. dissertation, 1988:196–249.
136 Dawn, 1973:31–9; Abdullah (King), 1973:111ff. and Kedourie, 1976:130–4.
137 Al-Manar, vol. 24, 1923, p. 607; Sa'id, 1934: vol. 1, 50.
138 Storrs, 1945:122–3. This encounter between Kitchener and Abdullah had been preceded by another introductory meeting in 1912 (Mousa, 1970:67–8).
139 Lord Kitchener to Sir W. Tyrrell (Private Letter), 26 April 1914 (included in Storrs, ibid., 122, n. 2).
140 FO to Cheetham (Cairo), 24 September 1914, FO 371/2139/219.
141 Cheetham to FO, 31 October 1914, FO 371/2139/233; Cheetham to FO, 10 December 1914, FO 371/2139/310 and Storrs, 1945:148–52.
142 Stoddard, Ph.D. dissertation, 1963:102–9ff.; Mousa, 1970:106–7.
143 Sa'id, 1934: vol. 1, 63 and 76; Mousa, 1970:110–11. According to the Ottoman military records, prosecutors were ordered to prepare files of the Arab activists from February 1915, immediately after Jamal Pasha's return from the Egyptian front (Stoddard, Ph.D. dissertation, 1963:149).
144 Qadri, 1956:40–2.
145 Al-A'zami, 1931–4: vol. 5, 71–5; vol. 6, 91–4; al-'Arif, 1943:205; idem, 1961:368; Mousa, 1970:107–8; Antonius, 1969:186–7. On the campaign of deportations see Sa'id, 1934: vol. 1, 73; 'Arif, 1943:205; al-Ghusayn, 1956:50 and al-Nimr, n.d.: vol. 3, 136–7.
146 Jamal Pasha's justification for his measures was included in a book he issued in his status as commander of the Fourth Army in 1916 (Al-Qa'id al-'Am lil-Jaysh al-Rabi', AH 1334), and later in his memoirs (Jamal Pasha, 1923:passim, particularly 380–2. Captured papers of the French consulate in Beirut pointed to certain contacts between a few Arabists (including al-'Asali) and the French. These contacts, however, had occurred long before the outbreak of war, could not justify a sentence of execution, and had nothing to do with the majority who were executed. Anti-Turkish instigations intercepted by the Ottoman authorities or delivered to them by Muhammad al-Shanti (Sa'id, 1934: vol. 1, 65–6) involved only two individuals, Haqqi al-'Azm who was then in Cairo scheming with 'Aziz al-Misri and the British without approval of the Decentralization Party (Qadri, 1956:43), and Muhammad al-Mahmasani, who was supposed to receive the subversive materials. Evidence used by the military court at 'Aleyh, as was presented by Jamal Pasha, could not substantiate the claims of widespread conspiracies for rebellion. In most cases, people were executed for their pre-war background,

their membership in the Decentralization Party or al-Fatat, or even after betraying their comrades as was the case of Muhammad al-Shanti. Kayali (Ph.D. dissertation, 1988:266–7) has produced new evidence indicating that Jamal Pasha, a known Turkist among the CUP leaders, was in fact enforcing a Turkification of public life in Syria.

147 Increasing correspondence between Grey (London) and Buchanan (Petrograd) suggests that Jamal was preparing for revolt with a view to conceding Istanbul and the straits connecting the Black Sea with the Mediterranean to the Allies, in exchange for his independence in the Asian parts of the empire. See Buchanan to Grey, 29 December 1915 and 2 January 1916, FO 371/2492/2007 and 2767/878 respectively and Grey to Buchanan, 29 and 30 December 1915, FO 371/2492/3123 and 2767/3148. See also Kayali, ibid., 268–72.

148 The story of the Husayn–McMahon correspondence has been told repeatedly from different perspectives. See, for example: Storrs, 1945:148–90; Antonius, 1969:164–83; Mousa, 1970:201–57; Dawn, 1973:87–121; Tibawi, 1977:64–100. Texts of the correspondence were officially published by the British government in Cmd. 5957, 1939. For the Arabic texts see Mousa (ed.), 1966:18–47.

149 Arab sources indicate that Faysal's meeting with al-Fatat leaders Yasin al-Hashimi and Shaykh Badr al-Din al-Hasani took place in March 1915. On his way back from Istanbul in late May, Faysal was presented by al-Fatat leaders with the Arab covenant, which outlined the Arabists' vision for the future independent Arab state, as the basis for Sharif Husayn's negotiations with the British. What prompted this step on the part of al-Fatat was Faysal's report to the Syrians of his father's ongoing negotiations with the British (Daghir, n.d.:46; Antonius, 1969:152–8; Mousa, 1970:129–33). This version of events is also accepted by Dawn (1973:28–30). It is interesting that Sa'id (1934: vol. 1, 105–7) indicated that Faysal did not in fact meet the Arabist leaders during his March visit. Furthermore, Qadri (1956:46–8), who was the only party to these meetings to leave memoirs, gave a different itinerary. In Qadri's version the decisive encounter between Faysal and the Arabists of Damascus (including Yasin al-Hashimi) occurred in September and again on his way back from Istanbul two months later. Faysal returned to the Hijaz in December and came back to Damascus a month later as he promised Jamal Pasha. If Qadri is right, it seems that the Syrian Arabists' decision to revolt came after Jamal Pasha's crack-down on the Arab movement and not before. Further doubts are cast over the first version of events from the study of Stoddard (Ph.D. dissertation, 1963:140) where it is indicated that in April 1915 Faysal was in Jeddah (not in Damascus or Istanbul as the first version of events made him to be), and was involved in the controversial rescue of the crew of *Emden*, the German cruiser that was earlier lost near Sumatra. It is also important to recall that al-Fatat's decision to render full support to the Ottoman war effort was taken in a meeting at Shukri al-Ayyubi's house in Damascus in March 1915, according to several Arab sources (n. 134 above). It is, therefore, difficult to comprehend that al-Fatat leadership was pursuing two contradictory policies in the same month, supporting the Ottoman state and planning for independence and revolt at the same time.

150 These are, of course, the most illustrious names which appeared, among many others, in the mission of notables, ulema and journalists, led by Shaykh As'ad al-Shuqayri, to show the Syrian Arab support for the state. The mission arrived

in Istanbul in September 1915, a few months after Jamal Pasha had unleashed his campaign of repression (Al-Baqir and Kurd-Ali, 1916). Between 1916 and 1918 Jamal Pasha supported the publication of *al-Sharq* newspaper in Syria. The paper was an official mouthpiece which was meant to counter the Sharifian and other anti-Ottoman propaganda. Involved in *al-Sharq* were Taj al-Din al-Hasani (son of Shaykh Badr al-Din who encouraged Faysal to revolt in September 1915), Shakib Arslan, Abd al-Qadir al-Maghribi and Muhammad Kurd-Ali (Kurd-Ali, 1948–9: vol. 1, 107–8; Arslan, 1969:169–70; Cleveland, 1985:37–8). For further evidence of the wide support for the Ottoman state during the war years, see: al-Sakakini, 1955:83–4; Zeine, 1973:114; al-Nimr, n.d.: vol. 3, 136, 144, 149, 153; Khoury, 1983:75. This support, however, seems to have waned gradually after 1916 (see below for a discussion of this point). Most of the Arab supporters of the state were originally members of the Benevolent Society (al-Jam'iyya al-Khayriyya), a pan-Islamic organization that was established in Istanbul in January 1913 with the support of the CUP (Arslan, 1969:100–2). For a wider and detailed study of the Ottoman pan-Islamic activities during the war, see Landau, 1990:94–121.

151 Sharabi, 1970:2–3, 8, 57, 59–60.
152 Dawn, 1973:170–2; Khoury, 1983:6–8 and 71–3.
153 Dawn, 1973:143, 173, 195; idem 1991:8–9, 11, 23.
154 Cleveland, 1971 and 1985; Khalidi, 1994:1–18.
155 Al-'Azzawi, 1955–6:267; al-'Athari, 1958:44, 91–5.
156 On the recruitment of the Arab prisoners of war for the Arab revolt's army see: al-'Umari, 1924–5: vol. 1, 278–9, 285–92; vol. 2, 70, 179; al-Ghusayn, 1956:176–82; Antonius, 1969:212–13; Tibawi, 1979:134. Faruqi, who later became the revolt's agent in Cairo, was captured by the British at Gallipoli early in October 1915. In a statement to his British interrogators in Cairo, he claimed that he had purposely deserted for his Arab nationalist convictions (secret memorandum on the testimony of Lieutenant Farugi, Cairo, 12 October 1915, FO 371/2486/157740; al-Khatib, 1979:64–5). Nuri al-Sa'id, who maintained that he deserted the Ottoman army after the arrest and expulsion of his mentor 'Aziz Ali al-Misri (Mousa, 1970:162–3; al-Swaydi, 1987:83–4) was also a prisoner of war. Though the circumstances of his capture by the British at Basra are not entirely clear, his release from the British prison in India came upon the intervention of al-Misri in Cairo (al-Khatib, 1979:65). For biographies of the most illustrious Iraqi Sharifian officers, including al-Sa'id, Mukhlis, al-Ayyubi, al-Madfa'i, al-'Askari, Taha al-Hashimi, and others, see Clark Kerr to Eden, 4 January 1938, FO 371/21853/E 435.
157 According to Sa'id (1934: vol. 1, 46–7), 315 out of 490 Arab officers stationed in Istanbul in 1914 were members of al-'Ahd.
158 Qadri, 1956:46–7, 64,77; al-Hashimi, 1967: vol.1, 43.
159 Hussein to Wingate, 31 December 1917, FO 371/3383/25577; Qadri, 1956:69; Mousa, 1970:367–89.
160 Dawn (1973:152–3) calculated that only 126 men were known to have been public advocates of Arab nationalism, since they were recognized as members of the Arabist societies. The number of adherents to Arabism rose substantially by 1919, after Faysal had already established his Arab government in Damascus (ibid., 158). Recently, however, Dawn (1991:13) seems to put less emphasis on

the significance of those numbers in measuring the influence of Arabism. Khalidi (1980:236–42 and 1984:461–74) used Arab parliamentary opposition to the CUP to illustrate the wider appeal of the Arab idea.

161 In the still closely knit Arab society, one must doubt the gap that separated Shakib Arslan, during the heyday of his Ottomanist activities, from his brother 'Adil, member of al-Fatat, who appears to have narrowly escaped the repression of Jamal Pasha (Qadri, 1956:53), or the Ottoman loyalist Ahmad al-Sham'a from his Arabist son Rushdi (Roded, Ph.D. dissertation, 1984:277–8), or even Sa'id al-Shawwa, the Gazan notable, mayor and confidant of the Ottoman authorities throughout the war, from his son Rushdi, member of *al-Fatat*, whose life was saved by Jamal Pasha only for the sake of his father (Manna', 1986:229; see also the following note.)

162 "Personalities of South Syria, Prepared by the Arab Bureau, Cairo: I South Palestine, February 1917; II Transjordan, April 1917; III North Palestine", May 1917, Cairo, Government Press (Wingate Papers, University of Durham, 206/5).

163 Kedourie, 1956: 29–66; Tibawi, 1977:101–25; Yapp, 1991:275–86.

164 Zeine, 1960:169–89; Kedourie, ibid., 169–74; Hurewitz, 1976:17–18; Tibawi, ibid., 399.

165 Tuchman, 1982:230–1.

166 Laqueur, 1976:77.

167 Ibid., 76. *Biluim* is an acronym from the initial letters of the Hebrew for Isaiah 2:5 (O house of Jacob, come ye, and let us walk in the light of the Lord). The most influential of the nineteenth-century Russian Zionist thinkers was Leo Pinsker (1821–91), who published, in 1870, *Auto-Emancipation*, edited and reprinted in England by A. S. Eban in 1932. On Pinsker see also Ha-Am, 1922:56–90.

168 Sachar, 1982:27–32.

169 Laqueur, 1976:153–4; Sachar, 1982:72ff.

170 Hurewitz, 1956:102; Abu Lughud,1971:140–1. According to Karpat (1985:188–9), the most authoritative source on the Ottoman population, the 1914 census, illustrated that the Jewish population was 21,259 out of 328,168 inhabitants of the *mutasarifiyyat* Jerusalem, and 15,025 out of 824,873 of *wilayat* Beirut which encompassed northern Palestine. In both cases the Jews represented less than 7 per cent of the population. The total number of Jews in Palestine – excluding Jewish inhabitants of *mutasarifiyyat* Beirut – was 31,644 while the total Palestinian population was 616,608 (calculations based on Karpat's figures, with whatever margin of error applied, clearly show that the figures commonly quoted by both Arab and Jewish historians of the modern Middle East were highly exaggerated.

171 Grannott, 1952:254; Owen, 1981:270. In light of the above-mentioned study by Karpat, even this figure was perhaps overestimated.

172 On their life, attitudes towards, and relations with, the Zionist movement see: Leslie, 1923; Dugdale, 1937; Amery, 1951: vol. 4. Lord Curzon, and Edwin Montagu (the Jewish member of the war cabinet) expressed their opposition to the Balfour Declaration during the cabinet deliberations prior to its issuing (Tuchman, 1982:333). For detailed studies of the political process that culminated in the Balfour Declaration see Stein, 1961; Tibawi, 1977:196–239; Vereté, 1992:1–38. The text of Balfour's letter to Rothschild (The Declaration) was published by *The Times* on 9 November 1917 (the letter was dated 2 November).

173 Mandel, 1976:36.
174 Ibid., 84–5; Firestone, 1975:2–23.
175 Ro'i, 1968:201; Porath, 1975:376.
176 Al-'Arif, 1961:27; Abu Mannah, 1978:23.
177 Mandel, 1976:2.
178 The text of the original decree was found by the Palestinian historian Ahmad Sidqi al-Dajani (cited in al-Hout, 1991:392). Cf. Abu Mannah (1978:25) where he interpreted Abd al-Hamid's increasing interest in Palestine against his deepening anxiety towards the policies of the British viceroy in Egypt.
179 Mandel, 1976:21.
180 Nassar, 1911.
181 See, for example: al-Karmil, 27 March 1909; 8, 14 March 1913; 12 August and 19 September 1913; 7 July 1914; Filastin, 16, 20 September 1911; 29 May, 20 November, 22 December 1912; 25 January, 9 February, 9 July and 20 August 1913. On the position of the Arab press towards Zionism in 1908–18, see Khalidi, 1982:105–23.
182 Al-Manar, vol. 17, 1914, 319–20, 385–90. Similar views appeared in al-Hilal, vol. 22, 1913–14, 520–1.
183 Al-Karmil, 12 August 1913. See also the discussion above of the Arab parliamentarian activities during the late Ottoman period.
184 Al-Mufid, 19 August 1911.
185 Al-Karmil, 19 September 1913.
186 Qasimiyya, 1973:218ff.
187 Mousa, 1970:63. The spirit of a united umma of Muslims, Christians and Jews was also evident in al-'Uraysi's last words to the Arabs (Anonymous, (Daghir), 1916:244).
188 Ro'i, 1968:210, 213, 220, 226–34; Mandel, 1965:168.
189 Mandel, ibid., 149ff.
190 Mandel, 1976:154–9.
191 Ibid., 159–62.
192 Ibid., 195, 206.
193 Kayyali, 1978:36–8.
194 Al-Muqattam, 14 April 1914 (also cited by Tibawi, 1977:21–2).
195 Mandel, 1965: 254–5; idem, 1976:202–6; Caplan, 1983: vol. 1, 21–4.
196 Weizmann was introduced in Cairo to Sulayman Nasif (Palestinian), Rafiq al-'Azm, Fawzi al-Bakri and Faris Nimr, the editor of al-Muqattam, al-Shahbandar, al-Qassab and others, by Mark Sykes and Major Ormsby-Gore (acting as a kind of British political attaché to the Zionist Commission; later he would become a Colonial Secretary). Neither during the meeting (27 March 1918), nor in the Arab memorandum presented by Nasif to the British (29 March), did the Arab side understand from the British or the Zionists that a Jewish state was in the making. In fact, the Arabs demanded a cessation of Jewish immigration, the establishment of government based on equality in Palestine and the use of Arabic as the official language (Ormsby-Gore to Balfour, 7 April 1918, FO 371/3394/W44/83691; Tibawi, 1977:265–7). Caplan (1983: vol. 1, 32–3) misleadingly gives the impression that an agreement was reached between the two sides, when the whole affair was meant by the British as a public relations exercise on behalf of the Zionists.

197 A meeting between Weizmann and Faysal, at the latter's camp near Aqaba, was also arranged by the British in early June 1918, two months after the Zionist Commission had arrived in Palestine. Since the Palestinian reaction to Weizmann's Commission was generally hostile, the British attempted to open another channel to the Arabs via Faysal. Here, too, Weizmann concealed the real Zionist aims; he went instead into offering Zionist international support for the Arab cause in Europe and the United States and spoke of Zionist intentions to cooperate with the Arabs for the prosperity of Palestine. Faysal, with his usual courtesy, affirmed that as a soldier he did not discuss politics, which was his father's domain, and that as an Arab he could not discuss the future of Palestine either as a British protectorate or as an area for Jewish colonization (Record of Interview by Lt. Colonel P. C. Joyce, 5 June 1918, FO 882/14; Mousa, 1970:431; Tibawi, 1977:271–2; Westrate, 1992:181). Contacts between Weizmann and Faysal were renewed six months later in London. Faysal was then in a different situation, having realized the magnitude of the Arab loss as a result of the French–British secret agreements to divide the Arab provinces between them. His last hope was to introduce some changes through the Peace Conference. Weizmann, supported by Lawrence, gave Faysal the impression that the Zionists and the Arabs were on one side, against the Sykes–Picot agreement, and that the Zionists would throw all their influence behind the Arab cause. Neither during the discussion, nor in the agreement that was signed later (early January 1919) between Weizmann and Faysal, did the latter understand that the Zionists aimed to establish a political entity in Palestine. Weizmann, however, scored two important points as Faysal signed a document that provided for wide-scale Jewish immigration to Palestine and consented to the Balfour Declaration. Nonetheless, before signing the agreement, Faysal added to the English text a paragraph in Arabic, stating that he would be committed to the agreement only if the Arabs gained their independent state (which included from Faysal's perspective, Palestine). If the Arabs failed to do so, Faysal added, they would be no longer bound by the agreement. A draft copy of the agreement, unsigned, can be found in the Clayton Papers, 694/6/39–4, University of Durham Library. It was also published by Weizmann (1949:306–9); and by Antonius (1969:437–9). For a discussion of this episode in the Arab–Zionist entanglement see: Kedourie, 1956:151–2; Mousa, 1970:432–9; Caplan. 1983: vol. 1, 36–46. For a detailed view of Faysal's understanding of Arab independence and the Zionist position in Palestine see his statement to the *Jewish Chronicle*, 3 October 1919.

198 On 16 January 1919, Lord Curzon (Foreign Office) wrote to Lord Balfour (Peace Delegation) expressing anxiety over developments in Palestine and stressing that "A Jewish Government in any form would mean an Arab rising." Balfour replied on 20 January 1919, stating that "As far as I know, Weizmann has never put forward a claim for the Jewish *Government* of Palestine. Such a claim is in my opinion certainly inadmissible and personally I do not think we should go further than the original declaration which I made to Lord Rothschild". Curzon again wrote, on 26 January 1919, that "As to Weizmann and Palestine, I entertain no doubt that he is out for a Jewish Government, if not at the moment then in the near future . . .". Balfour never replied to this letter. (This correspondence was reproduced by the FO on 23 December 1940, FO 371/24565/E 3124.) Moreover, in a collection of reports prepared between 1 February 1918 and 6

February 1919 under the title "Notes on Zionism, Secret and Confidential, . . . written . . . for the information of the General Staff", it was stated in a report concerning the Zionist Commission's activities in Palestine in 1918 (p. 16) that Dr Weizmann (speaking at a meeting with General Allenby in Jerusalem on 24 May) "made no effort to conceal the fact that his ultimate object was the establishment of a Jewish Commonwealth, and that a British Protectorate was the means by which this result was to be brought about". At the second meeting of the Commission he stated "Zionism had as its ultimate political objective the creation of a Jewish commonwealth. The method by which such a political state was to be evolved would be clear to us on our return from Palestine" (Clayton Papers, 694/6/43–53, University of Durham Library).

199 Hourani, 1968:41–68, and 1981:48–9; Lapidus, 1988:362ff.

200 On the ascendance of the *a'yan* in seventeenth- and eighteenth-century Palestine see: al-Muhibi, n.d.: vol. 4, 108; al-'Arif, 1943:176–8, 182ff.; al-Nimr,1975: vol. 1, 107ff.; Rafeq, 1975:277–307; al-'Asali, 1989:215–17.

201 Granott, 1952:36, 81; Shimoni, 1956:344ff.; Khalidi, 1984:73–4; Muslih, 1988:25ff.

202 Al-Nimr, n.d.: vol. 3, 26–7; al-Asad, 1970:38–9; Khoury. 1983:5; Stein, 1984:10; Scholch, 1989:239–40.

203 On the successful adaptation of several ulema families to the new age see Furlonge, 1969:3–28; al-'Awdat, 1976:146–50; Manna', 1986:344–7.

204 According to Granott (1952:81) five thousand donums were owned by the Husayni family.

205 Al-Sakakini, 1955:51–2; Tibawi, 1956:20, 95.

206 'Izzat Darwaza and Abdullah Mukhlis are but two examples (al-'Awdat, 1976:212–16, 574–5; al-'Asali, 1986:11–22).

207 Al-Hout, 1979:92.

208 Only 11 per cent of the population according to the 1922 census (*Report and General Abstracts of the Census of 1922*, Palestine, 1923).

209 Scholch, 1981:36–58; Smith, 1984:25–9; Muslih, 1988:37–44; Cohen, 1989:6, 35–6, 86–7, 90, 110.

210 Bonne, 1948:264, 300; Badran, 1969:47; al-Buhayri, 1980:9.

211 Al-'Arif, 1961; 297ff.; Mandel, 1976:47; Scholch, 1989:241–3; al-Zirkli, 1989: vol. 8, 235; Khalidi, 1994:6–11.

212 *Al-Hilal*, vol. 22, 1913, pp. 15–153; Kahala, 1957: vol. 4, 174–5; al-Asad, 1970; Khalidi, 1994:11–15.

213 Tibawi, 1961:31–80; idem, 1966:73–92; Farah, 1976:321–44; Hopwood, 1969:68–71.

214 *Al-Muqtataf*, vol. 7, 1883. pp. 471–2; *al-Hilal*, vol. 23, 1914, pp. 604–6; al-Sakakini, 1955:72ff.; Tibawi, 1956:20–77ff.

215 *Al-Muqtataf*, ibid., 473; Yehosha'a, 1974:7–13.

216 Yehosha'a, ibid., 31–132.

217 Al-Sakakini, 1955:4; Tibawi, 1961:125; Yaghi, 1968:95–8.

218 Al-Muhafiza, 1987:96–9.

219 Al-Khalidi, 1912, idem, AH 1326.

220 *Filastin*, 15 July 1911; 20 March 1912, 17, 25 and 29 January 1913; Shamir, 1975:507–14.

221 Porath, 1974: vol. 1, 32; Yasin, 1981:35–40; Muslih, 1988:160.

222 Al-Hout, 1986:86–9; Muslih, 1988:9. There were some attempts in March 1919 at uniting these two organizations but without result. According to al-Sakakini, the British had supporters even inside the Arab Club. (Al-Sakakini diaries, entries of 15 March and 2 June 1919. A copy of the diaries is in my possession.)

223 Muslih, 1988:179.

224 Zu'aytir Papers, I/16 (Institute of Palestine Studies, Beirut).

225 Ibid., I/15.

226 Memorandum by G. F. Clayton to FO, 15 November 1918 (Clayton Papers, 694/6/32–4); al-Sakakini, 1925: vol. 1, 16–17.

227 Porath, 1974: vol. 1, 83. A few months later, Farraj, who became a deputy of Jerusalem (representing the Christian Orthodox community) in the Syrian Congress of Damascus (the parliament of Faysal's Arab government), refused to sign the Congress resolutions calling for pan-Syrian unity (al-Sakakini diaries, entry of 11 July 1919). What Farraj was willing to discuss in Damascus was only the choosing of a mandatory power.

228 Zu'aytir Papers, II/4; al-Sakakini, 1955:175–6.

229 Porath, 1974: vol. 1, 89.

230 Howard, 1963:98, 102. On the trends of popular demands see also: Zu'aytir Papers, II/8–14 and al-Sakakini, 1955:186ff. According to al-Sakakini (diaries, entry of 16 June 1919) when a group of Jerusalemite notables, including Raghib al-Nashashibi, Faydi al-'Alami, Zaki Nusayba and Sa'id al Husayni, met with the Commission they spoke with little enthusiasm about Faysal and described relations with the Hijaz as merely religious.

231 Al-Hout (ed.), 1984:18–41.

232 *Al-Karmil*, 28 February 1920; al-Sifri, 1937: vol. 1, 29–30.

233 GHQ (Cairo) to WO, 7 April 1920, FO 371/5117/99; al-Sifri, 1937: vol. 1, 47–8; A Survey of Palestine (Official Publication), 1946: vol. 1, 17; al-Dabbagh, 1965: vol. 1, part 1, 549.

234 See, for example, Clayton to Sykes, 15 December 1917 (Wingate Papers, 147/1); Clayton to FO, 18 April 1918, FO 371/3394/573; Mony to General Staff, 20 November 1918, FO 371/3386/260; Minutes by Sir John Tilly, 15 April 1920, FO 371/5117/130; Curzon to Allenby, 15 April 1920, FO 371/5117/117.

235 With apparent reluctance, Curzon agreed with them (Minutes by Curzon, 29 April 1920, FO 371/5139/82). See also Storrs (1945:331–7) on the passing of the OETA.

3

In pursuit of a lost ideal: rise and decline of pan-Islamism

The collapse of the Arab project in the First World War followed by the abolition of the Caliphate in 1924 unleashed two contrasting forces in the Arab East. One was motivated by either ideological convictions of certain groups or by the personal ambitions of certain rulers to revive the Islamic ideal and the Arab movement, whereas the other was engendered by the strengthening local nationalist tendencies that were largely content with the postwar national entities of Iraq, Syria, Lebanon and Palestine. The great majority of the ex-Ottoman Palestinian officials such as Musa Kazim al-Husayni, Raghib al-Dajani and Raghib al-Nashashibi, who led the Palestinian Executive and dominated Palestinian politics during the 1920s, were less interested in pan-Arab and Islamic politics than in reaching an understanding with the British. Loyal to the traditional mediating role of the *a'yan*, they saw in this understanding the most convenient way of preserving the Arabness of Palestine and achieving its independence. But though the Executive Committee maintained a show of unity for a few years, it was soon to be paralysed by inner divisions and rivalries. By the end of the 1920s, the breakup of the Palestinian national movement into Husayni and Nashashibi camps and the failure of the Palestinian national leadership to extract any real concession from the British government sealed the fate of the Palestinian Arab Executive. It was mainly the demise of the Executive Committee which paved the way for the rise of Hajj Amin al-Husayni, the young mufti of Jerusalem, to a leading national position. Perhaps more than any other Palestinian leader, Amin al-Husayni came to recognize the tremendous challenge that the Palestinians faced in the British commitment to the Zionist project. Widely connected with the Arab-Islamic circles, he capitalized on the Islamic symbolism of Palestine and moved to turn Jerusalem into a centre for the pan-Islamic movement.

A mufti and national leader

Muhammad Amin al-Husayni was born in Jerusalem in 1895 (AH 1313) to one of the most prominent Muslim families of Palestine.[1] His education began in a traditional Islamic *kuttab* and a modern Ottoman *rushdiyya*, followed by two years in the French De La Salle School (Les Frères school) of Jerusalem. In 1912, Amin al-Husayni was sent to al-Azhar to receive formal higher Islamic education, but unsatisfied with al-Azhar's deeply traditional milieu, he complemented his Azhari schedule by joining Rashid Rida's Dar al-Da'wa wal-Irshad institute.[2] This was the time when Rida's rupture with Unionist-dominated Istanbul was almost complete and his Arabist views were becoming highly manifest. In Rida's circle, therefore, Amin al-Husayni encountered the first Arabist and Islamic-reformist influences which came to shape his outlook and relations for most of his long career. It is also believed that Amin al-Husayni became involved with a short-lived Palestinian anti-Zionist society in Cairo,[3] showing early signs of his Palestinian nationalist awareness.

In the summer of 1913, Amin al-Husayni accompanied his mother on the pilgrimage to the Hijaz, after which, for unclear reasons, he prematurely terminated his Azhari studies. He took up a part-time teaching position in Jerusalem, but was soon to join the Ottoman Military Academy in Istanbul. Upon the outbreak of World War I, he was recruited into the Ottoman army, where he rose to officer ranks in August 1916.[4] His military service took him to the war fronts of Macedonia, the Dardanelles and the Black Sea. But following a short illness Amin al-Husayni was granted three-months' leave to spend in Jerusalem where he arrived in December 1917, perhaps after the capture of the city by the British army.[5] The fall of Jerusalem marked another turning-point in the life of the young Husayni. Although his name did not appear amongst lists of members of the main Arab nationalist organizations of the war period, he shifted sides after his return to Jerusalem. While Faysal's Arab army was still advancing along the Hijaz railway northwards to Damascus, Amin al-Husayni cooperated with the British captain C. D. Brunton, in recruiting volunteers from Palestine for the Arab army.[6] This experience of overlapping and shifting loyalties reflected the dilemma of many other Arabists of the late Ottoman period.

Amin al-Husayni's association with the Arab movement continued through his involvement with the Arab Club of Jerusalem, which was affiliated to al-Fatat organization. Following the riots of April 1920, he escaped to Damascus where he stayed until the fall of the Arab government. He was later pardoned by Herbert Samuel, the first High Commissioner in Palestine, and allowed to return to Jerusalem, beginning a period of friendly and cooperative relations with the British administration. Besides having growing Arab and Palestinian nationalist commitments, he was also a notable who understood the ancient game of power. On 21 March 1921, Shaykh Kamil al-Husayni, the mufti of Jerusalem and Amin's elder brother, died after a short illness. In electing his successor, the British followed the Ottoman Order of 1910, according to which the new mufti was to be chosen by the government from among three ulema with the highest votes of an electorate college consisting of the city's ulema and members of the local administrative council.[7] Since Kamil al-Husayni had been pro-British,[8] and the muftiship of Jerusalem was emerging in post-Ottoman Palestine to be a highly prestigious and sensitive position, the British were keen to see the post occupied by another cooperative figure. The Husaynis, who had maintained their monopoly of the post for most of the previous one hundred and fifty years, placed Hajj Amin al-Husayni on the list of candidates. He was a popular figure and his supporters in the Palestinian Muslim and Christian communities, as well as in Transjordan, inundated the mandate government with petitions on his behalf. Although the election results showed that Amin al-Husayni came fourth on the list of six candidates, Shaykh Husam al-Jarallah who held the first position, was compelled to withdraw under popular pressure, thus admitting al-Husayni to the winning bracket. Subsequently, Amin al-Husayni was chosen by Samuel as the new mufti of Jerusalem.[9] Samuel was certainly aware of the wide support for Amin al-Husayni and of the traditional position of his family, but his decision was also precipitated by the obvious shift in Amin's attitudes towards the government as well as the need to balance the power of various rival notable families in the city.

There is little doubt that the post of mufti conferred on Hajj Amin al-Husayni immense prestige and moral authority, but it was another institution, the Supreme Muslim Council (SMC), that came to provide him with a real power base – financial, organizational and subsequently political. The establishment of the SMC at the end of 1921 was a result of the Palestinian Muslim anxiety over the maintenance and control of the *waqf* and *Shari'a* courts under a non-Muslim government, coupled with the British liberal policy of "non-interference" in religious affairs.[10]

In January 1922, elections were held to select the leading committee of the SMC; in these elections the mufti achieved an overwhelming victory and became president of the SMC and head of the Palestinian ulema.[11] Throughout the 1920s, the mufti worked energetically to consolidate his position by expanding the SMC's activities and building a massive network of patronage. With a total revenue of 65,056 Palestinian pounds in 1922/23, and 56,833 Palestinian pounds in 1936, the SMC was effectively the largest single employer after the mandate government.[12] For the mufti, this budget provided a wide opportunity to embark upon intensive projects of renovating old *waqfs*, constructing new schools, establishing orphanages and orphan funds, offering grants for students, entrepreneurs and small industries, and opening new clinics.[13] One of the SMC's most impressive undertakings was the restoration of al-Haram al-Sharif, a project that was initiated by the mufti in the early 1920s. Funds for the project were raised from Egypt, Syria, Iraq, India, the Hijaz, Kuwait, Bahrain and Iran by Palestinian delegations, headed in most cases by the mufti himself.[14] Inaugurated with a pan-Islamic gathering on 30 August 1928, this project contributed to the revival of the Islamic symbolism of Jerusalem and widened Arab and Islamic support for the Palestinians.

Until 1929, Amin al-Husayni concentrated on his functions as a mufti and president of the SMC, avoiding direct involvement in Palestinian political affairs. The Palestinian Arab Executive had been led since 1920 by Musa Kazim al-Husayni, an elder and highly respected figure of the Husayni family, thus blocking any chance the mufti might have had to compete for the leading political role. In its dealings with the British government and in its effort to preserve national unity, the Palestinian Arab Executive seemed to pass from one failure to another. While the British recognized the Zionist Commission as the representative body of the Jewish community and interests, they never extended a similar recognition to the Palestinian Arab Executive.[15] By relying mainly on the means of negotiation and petition, the Palestinian leadership failed to influence the British Jewish National Home (JNH) policy, or to stop the League of Nations from ratifying the terms of the British mandate, including the Balfour Declaration. One of the major set-backs in the fortunes of the Palestinian Arab Executive was its inability to extract from the British a constitution that would grant the Palestinian people a representative government.[16] Throughout a long course of negotiation that extended from 1920 to 1923, various British constitutional schemes denied the Palestinians recognition of their demographic weight and insisted on linking the constitution to the acceptance of the mandate and the JNH policy. When the mandate government attempted to enforce its version of the constitution and hold general elections for a representative council, the Palestinians declared their boycott of the elections. Until the end of the mandate in 1948, the Palestinians were never to enjoy the right of self-government.

The failure of the Palestinian Arab Executive in its relations with the British was compounded by the intensifying rivalry within the Palestinian *a'yan* class. Though each of the Palestinian notable families was in itself a centre of power, the main feature of this rivalry was the Husayni–Nashashibi divide. Both were Jerusalemite families and the role that the Nashashibis and the Husaynis came to play in Palestinian politics reflected the dominant position of Jerusalem over other Palestinian cities, a development that had its origins in the political, social, and administrative transformation of Palestine in the nineteenth century.[17] Like the Husaynis, the Nashashibis had lived in Jerusalem since the late fifteenth century.[18] Their rise to prominence, however, began with Sulayman al-Nashashibi (d.1866), who accumulated considerable wealth from trade and soap manufacture. At the end of the Ottoman period, the Nashashibis were led by Raghib al-Nashashibi, an Ottoman member of parliament with cosmopolitan affinities, a strong sense of pragmatism and worldly manners.[19]

One of the first signs of competition between the Husaynis and the Nashashibis in the post-Ottoman era was the latter's establishment of *al-Muntada al-Adabi* to counterbalance the Husaynis' influence in *al-Nadi al-'Arabi*. The British military officials were, of course, fully aware of the rivalry between the two leading families of the city. When Musa Kazim al-Husayni was implicated in the April 1920 riots, Ronald Storrs, the military governor of Jerusalem, dismissed the elder Husayni from the mayoralty and replaced him with Raghib al-Nashashibi.[20] This episode exacerbated the differences between the two families and marked the Nashashibis as non-patriotic, pro-British, and too soft in their attitudes towards the Zionist enemies. During the next few years, whether in the elections for the muftiship, for the presidency of the SMC, or the municipal elections, the competition for power between the two families would further reinforce their political differences, dividing the country's political arena into two distinctive camps. The Zionists in Palestine found the Nashashibis and other opponents of the Husaynis more amiable to deal with, and Zionist financial support was, thus, conveniently extended to the anti-Husayni activities of the opposition.[21] This state of continuous *a'yan* rivalry undermined the cohesiveness of the Executive Committee and brought activities of the Palestinian National Congress to a standstill. The congress met only twice between June 1923 and June 1928, ending on both occasions with feeble and highly ambiguous resolutions.[22] Not surprisingly, by the end of the 1920s, the Palestinian political scene was ripe for the emergence of new leadership.

Since his ascendance to the muftiship of Jerusalem, Amin al-Husayni had maintained amicable relations with the mandate administration. Largely engaged with his religious duties and with running the SMC, he had little cause for dispute with the British.[23] In the Palestinian context, however, engagement in religion was bound to lead to engagement in politics. The first occasion on which the mufti's position seemed to raise concern among the mandate officials came when he led the popular protest againstst the Second International Missionary Conference in August 1928.[24] Yet, recognizing the religious sensitivity of the issue, Lord Plumer, the High Commissioner at the time, relented to Palestinian pressure and decided to ban the conference from being held again in Palestine. A few months later, a more serious crisis of a religious and political nature erupted in Jerusalem. From 1922 onwards, Palestinian–Jewish relations in the city were frequently strained by Jewish attempts to infringe on Muslim rights at the Western Wall of al-Aqsa mosque, known by the Muslims as al-Buraq and by the Jews as the Wailing Wall, and regarded as sacred by both. Jewish attempts to establish a new status quo at al-Buraq intensified in October 1928 in the face of rising protests from the mufti and the SMC.[25] On 1 November, the SMC called for an unprecedented Arab-Islamic conference in Jerusalem, in order to discuss the Buraq question. Though the majority of the 700 participants were Palestinians, three delegates from Lebanon, two from Syria and seven from Transjordan also joined the conference,[26] marking the beginning of a long association between the Arab-Islamic forces and Palestine. After a day of deliberation, the conference issued a statement asserting the Muslim rights at al-Buraq, and established the Society for Guarding al-Aqsa and the Sacred Islamic Places, chaired by the mufti. The British authorities did move to investigate the dispute, but throughout the first half of 1929 they seemed reluctant to enforce the *status quo ante* on the

Jewish zealot elements, ignoring their own findings on the problem that had already been published as a White Paper in November 1928.[27]

The situation reached a climax on 15 August 1929, following two Jewish demonstrations in Tel-Aviv and Jerusalem. On Friday, the next day, a Muslim counter-demonstration was organized by the Society for Guarding al-Aqsa, which ended with a mass outbreak of anger.[28] During the bloody disturbances that continued for two weeks, Arab–Jewish confrontations in various parts of the country led to the deaths of 133 Jews and 116 Arabs.[29] It was an episode that would mark a turning-point in Palestinian–British relations and in the course of the Palestinian and Arab movement as a whole. A British Commission of Inquiry exonerated the mufti from inciting the disturbances; yet, as president of the SMC, the mufti was from the very beginning at the forefront of the Palestinian protest. Though he certainly did not anticipate or desire to see the dispute escalate to the point it eventually reached, he emerged from the *Buraq* episode as the people's hero, a position that none of the other Palestinian leaders could really fill. A notable of Sharifian descent, an energetic and charming person, he was above all an *alim* who could easily be identified by the ordinary people.

But while the Western Wall dispute created a new leader for the Palestinian national movement, it also awakened Palestinian needs for Muslim and Arab support. Perhaps because of the religious dimension of the dispute, the first idea to surface in the mufti's circles was of an Islamic framework of action. This idea would evolve into the General Islamic Congress of Jerusalem. To be sure, the holding of the congress was also the culmination of a series of important events that marked the course of the pan-Islamic movement in the 1920s.

Pan-Islamism reborn

The first signs of pan-Islamic reawakening in post-Ottoman Palestine appear to have been recorded in 1922–3. In a memorandum prepared on 31 August 1923 the governor of Jerusalem observed that the Palestinians were stirred by the victories of Mustafa Kamal in Turkey and looked towards him for leadership.[30] The newly appointed Caliph in Istanbul was thus recognized by the Palestinians and his name was duly mentioned in mosques throughout the country. If the Ottoman bond could no longer be invoked, the Caliphate was still seen as alive and binding. During the same period, Colonial Office officials in London were baffled over intelligence reports from the Secret Intelligence Service (S.I.S.) indicating the "extent and intensity of pan-Islamic propaganda in Palestine". But Whitehall's apprehensions were finally calmed when Major I. G. Clayton, commenting on these reports, explained that although some Palestinian Arab nationalists "may doubtless be to some extent sympathetic to the Pan-Islamic ideas propagated by Turkish agents for their own purpose", no pan-Islamic body existed in organized form. The SMC, Clayton continued, was distinctly pro-Arab, and the *raison d'être* of political activity in the country was opposition to Zionist policy.[31] An intimate observer of the Arab East, Clayton was more often than not right. In Palestine, as well as in the rest of the Arab world, pan-Islamism of the early 1920s was rather an expression of desperate hopes that the Turkish triumphs in Anatolia might help to reverse the postwar situation in Palestine. Expectations of salvation at the hands of Kamal were, however, soon to fade as pleas to the Turks to take up the question of Palestine in the peace negotiations with the Allies met with utter disregard. Increasingly, the Kamalist movement was taking Turkey into a nationalist path, underlining the new direction by the abolition of the Caliphate on 3 March 1924.

While the end of the Ottoman Caliphate was being received with shocked disbelief by Muslims worldwide, King Husayn of the Hijaz was the guest of his son Abdullah in Transjordan. An aspirant to the prestigious seat for years,[32] Husayn was encouraged by Abdullah to declare himself a Caliph. Abdullah's role in Husayn's hasty move can perhaps be inferred from an early telegram that Abdullah sent to the High Commissioner in Jerusalem on 5 March. Abdullah wrote:

> In consequence of the abolition of Caliphate by the Turkish govern-
> ment, leaders of Moslem religious opinion have been obliged to
> come to a decision regarding the Caliphate. Numerous telegrams of
> allegiance to King Hussein as Emir el Muminin have been received
> from the Holy places of Mecca and Medina, universally recognising
> him as Caliph. King Hussein has therefore accepted the position of
> Caliph.[33]

Two days were, of course, hardly adequate for "leaders of Moslem religious opinion" to deliberate this highly sensitive issue and reach a decision, but Abdullah's propensity for self-delusion was irrepressible. Telegrams of support, largely contrived by pro-Hashemite elements, were subsequently received from various parts of Greater Syria.[34] In the Hijaz, the Hashemite traditional power base, after a request that Husayn should accept the Caliphate had first been stage-managed in Amman, the king telegraphed Mecca ordering his prime minister to work up a similar demand there. According to the British Consulate in Jedda, the Hijazis "were taken completely by surprise by summons to the government building and the announcement by Quaimaqam that his Majesty king Hussein had accepted the Caliphate".[35] In Iraq, recognition was delayed until 14 March on the orders of the circumspect King Faysal, while the issue was being discussed in religious circles.[36] Husayn, however, had no real chance of acquiring the prestigious seat. With his image gravely tarnished after the failure of his anti-Turk revolt and the Western occupation of most Arab countries, he needed more than the sporadic support which he mastered in the Arab *mashriq* to establish the pan-Islamic moral authority of the Caliphate.

The Palestinian reactions to Husayn's Caliphate were mixed. For most of the Palestinian leaders, who were anxiously following the negotiations of the Anglo-Hijazi treaty, the immediate task was to draw the king closer to the Palestine side. It was, therefore, decided by a majority vote in a joint meeting of the Palestinian Executive and the SMC to recognize Husayn's claim, on condition that he should not settle questions concerning Palestine with the British without consulting its people.[37] A delegation, led by Shaykh al-Muzaffar, was subsequently dispatched to present the Palestinian support to Husayn at his residence in the Jordanian village of Shuna. At the popular level, however, Palestinian hostility to Husayn's Caliphate was evidently widespread. When his name was first mentioned as a Caliph during a Friday sermon in Gaza, the mufti of the city was threatened with a beating by members of the congregation.[38] In India and Egypt, where the Hashemites had long been viewed with suspicion, criticisms of Husayn's move were universal.[39] Indeed, Husayn's Caliphate appeared from the outset to be too controversial an issue to take root. Against him were not only other contenders for the seat but also the heavy burden of his alliance with the British against the Ottoman state.

Upon his return to the Hijaz, Husayn scrambled hurriedly to legitimize his precarious position by establishing a 31-member Caliphate advisory council and calling for an Islamic congress. The Hajj Congress of July 1924 was the first in a series of pan-Islamic conventions to be held after the abolition of the Ottoman Caliphate. Though they largely failed to achieve their primary objectives, these conventions served as vital venues for strengthening communications between leaders of Muslim opinion worldwide and for deepening feelings of solidarity among Muslim peoples.

During the Hajj Congress, opposition to Husayn's quest for the Caliphate found in the Tunisian leader, Shaykh Abd al-'Aziz al-Tha'alibi (1875–1944), an eloquent voice to formulate its viewpoint. Al-Tha'alibi argued that the congress was not representative of Muslim world opinion, and thus lacked the authority to resolve the Caliphate issue. Reflecting the declining fortunes of Sharif Husayn, the congress ended with a declaration that avoided the mere mention of the Caliphate.[40] Three months later, Husayn abdicated the Hijazi throne and abandoned his bid for the prestigious seat.

The figure who attracted most attention in the Hajj Congress was Shaykh al-Tha'alibi, whose name would continuously surface throughout the Arab East for more than a decade to come. Al-Tha'alibi was a founder of the old Tunisian Dustur Party and a Muslim reformist with a strong belief in the institution of modern Muslim society on a reconstructed vision of Islam.[41] Like most North African nationalist leaders, he was an Ottomanist who took the side of Istanbul during the war years, developing a close and profound friendship with Shakib Arslan and other Arab-Islamic supporters of Istanbul.[42] It was perhaps this complex background which contributed to defining al-Tha'alibi's antipathy towards Sharif Husayn and other claimants of the Caliphate. His prominent and ubiquitous involvement in pan-Arab and pan-Islamic politics occurred largely during the period of his exile between 1923 and 1937. Two years after the Hajj Congress, al-Tha'alibi would again stand firmly against King Fu'ad's Caliphate ambitions.

Egypt opposed Husayn's bid for the Caliphate in uncompromising terms.[43] Spearheaded by the ulema establishment of al-Azhar, this opposition reflected two principal motivations: the Azharis' belief that they were more entitled than any other Islamic body to resolve the Caliphate issue; and al-Azhar's implicit association with King Fu'ad's quest for the Caliphate seat.[44] But since al-Azhar could not impose its will on the Muslim world by decree, the leading Azhari ulema sought the convening of a pan-Islamic congress in Cairo. To pave the way for such a congress, al-Azhar established a preparatory committee and launched a journal specialised in the congress's affairs in October 1923, which carried a lead article by Rashid Rida.[45] Rida's opposition to Sharif Husayn and the influence of his reformist friend, Shaykh Muhammad Mustafa al-Maraghi, were perhaps the principle motives behind his support for the Azhari project. Initially, al-Azhar's preparatory committee scheduled the congress to meet in March 1925. However, rising opposition to the project and al-Azhar's undeniable collusion with King Fu'ad proved to be more serious than had been anticipated, and the congress was thereby postponed. When it was ultimately convened, the results were spectacularly disappointing.

Dissension over the congress project was first expressed by Prince 'Umar Tusun (1872–1944), a member of the Egyptian royal family. With strong and wide ties in Arab and Islamic circles, Tusun saw himself more appropriately positioned to organize the congress. But since Tusun was not particularly sympathetic to Fu'ad's ambitions, the Azharis excluded him from their preparatory committee. Consequently, Tusun and the Sufi, Shaykh Muhammad Madi Abu al-'Azayim (1869–1937), joined forces in an attempt to organize a rival congress. The rivalry between the two groups shattered the image of Egypt's unity on the issue, which was so essential to bringing about a successful congress. Sa'd Zaghlul, the prime minister at the time, and his Wafd Party, as well as the secularly oriented Egyptian media, were equally opposed to the Azhari-inspired congress.[46] In the midst of this contentious atmosphere, Shaykh Ali Abd al-Raziq, a young Azhari judge of a landed ulema family who had strong connections with the Liberal Constitutionalist Party, published his controversial book *al-Islam wa 'usul al-hukm*.[47] Abd al-Raziq denied that the Caliphate was an Islamic-religious institution and argued that neither the historical model nor the *Shari'a* precluded the Muslims from developing other forms of government. His ideas aroused a passionate and wide debate within Egyptian political and intellectual circles, and led subsequently to his exclusion from the ulema's ranks by an Azhari tribunal.[48] Notwithstanding its long-lasting impact on modern Islamic political thought, this inflammatory episode could only exacerbate the congress's situation. Most of the Egyptian opposition to al-Azhar's project was not directed at the Caliphate institution *per se*, but rather at the king. With the substantial powers afforded to him by the constitution, and the obvious British backing, many Egyptians believed that the Caliphate would turn Fu'ad into an ultimate despot.

Unable to dispel intensifying suspicions of its connection with the Palace, the Azhari preparatory committee encountered hostilities from other parts of the Muslim world. The fact that Egypt was powerful, wealthy and the most advanced of all Muslim countries was not a matter of dispute, but Egypt was also seen as an occupied country whose freedom of action was highly limited. Hence, the vociferous Caliphate Committee of India, led by the brothers Muhammad (1878–1931) and Shawkat Ali (1873–1938), urged the Egyptians to hold more deliberations before denying the Ottoman dynasty its historical rights in the Caliphate. Similar opinions were expressed by the Muslim communities of Bosnia and Singapore.[49] More important was the Saudi reaction. Since the Hijaz had fallen to the Saudis, Ibn Sa'ud did not conceal his intention of holding a pan-Islamic meeting to discuss the maintenance of the holy places. Writing to Shaykh al-Azhar, Ibn Sa'ud asserted that the meeting he was planning would not attend to the Caliphate question, and that he would pledge his allegiance to, and cooperate with, whoever was chosen by the Muslim world as a Caliph.[50] In reality, Ibn Sa'ud had more to fear from the Cairo congress than any other Muslim ruler, for a new Caliph would certainly aspire to extend his control over the holy places in the Hijaz and consequently undercut the Saudi influence in Arabia. It was not surprising, therefore, that no Saudi delegation would participate in the Cairo congress.

When the congress was finally assembled on 13 May 1926, two years of preparations and hundreds of invitations could not attract more than 39 delegates, most of whom were Egyptians.[51] With such an extremely narrow representation of the Muslim world, it was almost impossible for the congress to attempt electing a Caliph. In a primary discussion of the Caliphate question, participants widely disagreed on the essential attributes of a Caliphate candidate, while others argued that, considering the Muslim divisions, it was doubtful if revival of the Caliphate institution would ever be attainable.[52] The delegates' agreement to reconvene a more representative congress the following year was obviously cosmetic, since no such congress would ever be held again. Rather than affirming al-Azhar's role, the congress illustrated the large erosion in the position and influence of the ulema institution. As with the SMC's failure to achieve a Palestinian consensus over the Caliphate of Sharif Husayn, the ulema of Egypt were not only challenged from various Islamic as well as liberal quarters, but were themselves divided on many aspects of the Caliphate question.

Compared with the overall participation in the Cairo congress, the Palestinians were obviously over-represented. The Palestinian delegation consisted of eight members, including Shaykh As'ad al-Shuqayri, Shaykh Khalil al-Khalidi, Shaykh Muhammad Murad, and Jamal al-Husayni, secretary of the SMC.[53] Although some members of the delegation were from among the most senior ulema of Palestine, curiously absent was Hajj Amin al-Husayni. The mufti, a strong believer in the Egyptian Arab and Islamic role, was a frequent visitor to Cairo during the 1920s. Upon the recommendation of Herbert Samuel, General Allenby introduced the mufti to King Fu'ad and the minister of *awqaf*, who both contributed to the Restoration of al-Aqsa Mosque Fund.[54] Yet, in a visit to Egypt prior to the holding of the congress, the mufti was denied a reception by the king or his pro-British prime minister, Ahmad Ziwar.[55] In fact, Ziwar's government had earlier responded positively to a British request for recognition of the mandates of Iraq and Palestine.[56] Ziwar's disregard for Palestinian, as well as Egyptian, public opinion, became more apparent when he dispatched the rector of the Egyptian University, Ahmad Lutfi al-Sayyid, to participate in the inauguration of the Hebrew University in Jerusalem in April 1925.[57] To a considerable extent, the Palestinian nationalists' relations with the Egyptian Palace circles were made even worse by the strong ties that the mufti cultivated in the Egyptian opposition and popular quarters. Prince 'Umar Tusun, the main figure in the anti-Azhari congress movement, was also president of the Egyptian Committee for the Restoration of al-Aqsa Mosque.[58] Yet, there seemed to have been another factor in determining the mufti's position, namely the less than favourable Saudi attitudes towards the congress. Only a few weeks after the end of the Cairo congress, Amin al-Husayni personally led a Palestinian delegation to the Saudi hajj assembly, reflecting the strengthening ties between the Arab-Islamic circles of the interwar period and the Saudis. The deterioration in the mufti's relations with the Egyptian Palace and al-Azhar would reach its lowest point during the preparations for the General Islamic Congress of Jerusalem in 1931.

The third major event on the pan-Islamic calendar of the 1920s was the Saudi congress of the Muslim world. From the outset, this gathering was not intended to deal with the Caliphate question. Even if willing,

Ibn Saʻud was realistic enough to see the complexities surrounding the Caliphate, as well as the controversial image that the Saudi Wahhabi movement elicited throughout the Muslim world. Yet, the congress was not devoid of an implicit search for power and influence. The idea of holding a pan-Islamic assembly in the Hijaz originated in Ibn Saʻud's declaration to the Muslim world in September 1925, just prior to his final prevailing over the Hashemites.[59] Anticipating victory, Ibn Saʻud expressed his gratitude to the Muslims who backed his cause, and sought to alleviate possible concerns over the status of the holy places and the hajj by calling for a Muslim conference.

The Muslim World Congress was held in Mecca between 7 June and 5 July 1926, during the hajj season. Well attended by nearly seventy representatives of various parts of the Muslim world, the congress was also joined by official delegations from Egypt and Turkey. For political and perhaps sectarians reasons, however, no representatives arrived from Iran or Iraq.[60] Most prominent among the participants were Rashid Rida, Muhammad and Shawkat Ali, the pro-Palace and future rector of al-Azhar, Shaykh Muhammad al-Zawahiri, as well as Hajj Amin al-Husayni, Shaykh Ismaʻil al-Hafiz, and ʻAjaj Nwayhid from Palestine. The mufti was apparently given special treatment by the Saudi king, with whom he had several confidential meetings concerning the situation in Palestine and the Syrian revolt.[61] While the congress made no attempt to discuss the Palestinian problem, the mufti's contribution focused on advocating the formation of a technical committee for restoring the Hijaz railway, and on proposing a declaration forbidding Muslims from fighting other Muslims.[62] The first issue reflected a Palestinian economic concern, since a branch of the Hijaz railway originated in Haifa, while the second was intended to encourage West and North African Muslim soldiers of the French army in Syria to desert, at a time when the Syrian revolt was reaching a high point.

The deliberations of the congress could not avoid differences of opinions on several important issues. In his speech to the congress, Ibn Saʻud asserted that domestic or international affairs of other states should not be the subject of discussion, a matter that caused some unease amongst many delegates.[63] Drawing the line between what might be of pan-Islamic concern and what belonged to the newly born nation-state in a wide variety of issues was not an easy task. While Ibn Saʻud was trying not to strain his relations with the imperialist powers, the question of the European occupation of Muslim countries cast heavy shadows on the congress' deliberations. In the event, proposals for a pledge by the congress to rid the whole of Arabia of foreign influence, or for an Islamic pact to refer all inter-Islamic disputes to the congress for arbitration, proved to be particularly thorny to deal with. Equally divisive was the Saudi resistance to allowing a pan-Islamic role in regulating the Hijazi affairs, and the delegates' reciprocal decline to commit themselves to financial support of the Saudi hajj projects.[64]

Yet, the congress did agree on convening annually during the pilgrimage season, on establishing a permanent office of which the absent Shakib Arslan was appointed general secretary, and on calling for the "promotion of mutual understanding and unity among Muslims and for the improvement of security and other means to facilitate the hajj".[65] But Arslan was reluctant to move to the Hijaz, apparently for health reasons. Though he did perform hajj in 1929, and was given an exceptional reception by the Saudis, Arslan never actually assumed the responsibility of the congress's permanent office.[66] Leaders of the Indian Caliphate Committee left dissatisfied, and moved subsequently to publish critical accounts of the congress and Saudi Islamic policy, prompting a strong rejoinder from Rashid Rida.[67] For Ibn Sa'ud, the congress was an occasion to underscore the legitimacy of his rule in the Hijaz, as well as to strengthen his position as a main contender in the Islamic arena. But in contrast to the sense of optimism which surrounded the holding of the congress and the establishment of its permanent office, the financial costs incurred by the Saudis and the political risks emanating from the debates made 1926 the first and last occasion of its convening.

The Islamic gatherings of the 1920s, regardless of their declared aims and immediate outcome, made a significant contribution to the short revival of the pan-Islamic movement. While politics in the Muslim world, including the Arab countries, was becoming increasingly contingent upon a nationalist agenda, this revival helped to provide an Islamic idiom and dimension to the nationalist discourse. Repeatedly, the congress model would be invoked whenever the need was to arise for expressing the collective will of Arab and Islamic forces. Hence, as Palestine was turning into a major Arab and Islamic cause towards the end of the 1920s, the idea of holding a pan-Islamic congress for and in Palestine was born.

The idea of a congress in Jerusalem

By the beginning of the 1930s, the mufti of Jerusalem, Hajj Amin al-Husayni, was already acknowledged as a national, Arab and Islamic leader. His sustained efforts to raise funds for the restoration of *al-Haram al-Sharif*, his support of the Syrian revolt and his active participation in the Mecca Muslim Congress strengthened both his Arab and his Islamic credentials. He occupied a distinguished place amongst that active association of Arab and Islamic reformists, dignitaries and politicians, which connected people such as Rida and Abd al-Hamid Sa'id in Cairo, Arslan in Geneva, Muhammad and Shawkat 'Ali in India, al-Tha'alibi in his exile between Cairo and Baghdad, and al-Quwwatli in Damascus.

The inauguration of *al-Haram al-Sharif*'s restoration, which was organized by the SMC in Jerusalem on 29 August 1928, was attended by many distinguished guests, including Amir Abdullah of Transjordan, Abd al-Hamid Sa'id, the Egyptian president of the Young Muslim Men Society (YMMS), and the Arab-Islamic reformist, Muhib al-Din al-Khatib.[68] It was not, therefore, surprising that in the wake of the 1929 disturbances, the mufti would succeed in turning the hearings of the Western Wall Commission into a demonstration of Muslim and Arab support for the Palestinian cause.[69] The rise of Hajj Amin al-Husayni was immediately noted by the declining Palestinian Executive. Encouraged by the serious investigation of the Western Wall Commission, by the personal dispositions of the High Commissioner, John Chancellor, and the emergence of a new British Labour government under Ramsay MacDonald,[70] the Palestinian Executive elected a delegation to open a new round of negotiations with the British government in London. This delegation was headed by Musa Kazim al-Husayni, and included Raghib al-Nashashibi, 'Awni Abd al-Hadi, Jamal al-Husayni, Alfred Rock and, for the first time, Hajj Amin al-Husayni.

The Palestinian delegates were received by the prime minister and the colonial secretary on 31 March 1930. Negotiations ensued but were utterly inconclusive, both on the issue of Jewish immigration and on the institution of a national parliamentary government. However, the British promised to investigate Palestinian complaints concerning the sale of Arab land to the Jews. In October 1930, the British government published the report of Sir John Hope-Simpson, its appointed land expert on immigration and land settlement.[71] The report became the basis for the Statement of Policy by HM Government on Palestine, known as the

Passfield White Paper.[72] Hope-Simpson concluded in his report that if all the cultivable land in Palestine were divided up among the Arab agricultural population, there would not be enough to provide every family with a decent livelihood. He, therefore, recommended that until further development of land and irrigation had taken place, there was "no room for a single additional settler if the standard of life of the [Arab] fellaheen" was to remain "at its present level". While upholding the principle of "dual obligation" under the mandate (towards the Arabs and Jews), the White Paper adopted Hope-Simpson's estimates and promised to implement his recommendations. It also declared that the time had come to establish a legislative council on the lines indicated in Churchill's White Paper of 1922.

The Zionist reaction to the Hope-Simpson report and the White Paper was vehement. Demonstrations of protest were staged in several Western countries, supported by many leading British politicians. In the words of the Peel Commission report of 1937 (see below Chapters Five and Six), British public reaction to the Passfield White Paper was "an impressive demonstration of the political power the Zionists could mobilise in England".[73] Subsequently, talks began between British officials in London and the Zionist side in order to reach an acceptable reinterpretation of the White Paper. In January 1931, the colonial secretary wrote to the High Commissioner informing him of the necessity of finding a "*modus co-operandi*" with the Jewish organization in the wake of the outcry against the White Paper. The government, Passfield confirmed, "seems to have no alternative to writing and publishing, or allowing to be published, a letter to Dr Weizmann, President of the World Zionist Movement, defining our policy in Palestine in terms more precise and more acceptable to the Jews than those of the White Paper".[74] Indeed, a letter from the prime minister to Weizmann was published shortly afterwards,[75] in which MacDonald assured the world Jewry of the British government's obligation to uphold the terms of the mandate, the JNH policy, and the furtherment of Jewish settlement and immigration. The Palestinians received MacDonald's statement with dismay and anger, calling it the "Black Letter"; Weizmann, however, regarded MacDonald's statement as the major factor in enabling the Zionist enterprise "to make the magnificent gains of the ensuing years".[76] The British turn-round of policy was followed by the replacement of Sir John Chancellor, the accommodating High Commissioner, with Sir

Arthur Wauchope, who opened the doors to mass Jewish immigration. Thus, the post-1929 cautious developments in British policy towards Palestine, which were received with guarded optimism by the Palestinians, came to a disappointing end. Once again, the Palestinians were reminded of their urgent need for Arab and Muslim backing.

In January 1931, mawlana Muhammad Ali, the Indian Muslim leader of the Caliphate Movement, died in London while attending the Round-Table talks. He and his brother Shawkat were well-known pan-Islamic leaders who were particularly supportive of the Palestinians. It was Muhammad Ali who delivered one of the three closing Muslim speeches before the International Commission of the Western Wall. On the arrival of the news of Muhammad Ali's death, the mufti, Hajj Amin al-Husayni, moved to secure his burial in Jerusalem at the sanctuary of *al-Haram al-Sharif*.[77] The mufti's overture was in a sense an acknowledgment of the Indian leader's long support of the Palestinian cause, but it also had the appearance of a calculated measure towards turning Jerusalem into a pan-Islamic capital. Studies of the Jerusalem General Islamic Congress seem to agree that the idea of holding an Islamic congress in Palestine was first suggested by Shawkat Ali during the funeral of his brother on 24 January 1931.[78] However, the Palestinian historian 'Izzat Darwaza, who was known for his close relations with the mufti at the time and was an active member of the congress, related the idea to the Tunisian leader, Abd al-'Aziz al-Tha'alibi.[79] A few months after the congress had been held, *al-Jami'a al-'Arabiyya*,[80] the pro-mufti Jerusalem-based newspaper, wrote that the permanent secretariat of the congress was planning to publish a book on the history, background and works of the congress. The promised book was never officially printed. What appears to have been a draft manuscript of the above-mentioned book has been found among the papers of al-Tha'alibi and subsequently published by a Tunisian publisher known for his interest in al-Tha'alibi's works.[81] Valuable as it is, this book, apart from the texts of letters included, should be considered only as al-Tha'alibi's version rather than the congress's official view of events. Predictably, in various parts of the book, implicitly and explicitly, especially in a letter to the mufti, dated 21 October 1931, al-Tha'alibi left a clear impression that the idea of a congress was his, not Shawkat Ali's.[82]

The importance of determining the roles of Shawkat Ali and al-Tha'alibi is relevant to the verification of the controversy that surrounded the Caliphate question, which was rumoured to have been on the congress agenda, and which became a major obstacle in the way of attracting official representation in the congress, especially from Egypt, Turkey and Saudi Arabia. Shawkat Ali's (and his brother's) interest in the Caliphate was widely known. The Caliphate Movement of India, in which they were prominent figures, had reached its apogee in the mid-1920s.[83] During the following years, the Ali brothers were conspicuously active on the Islamic scene outside India, seeking a pan-Islamic role and advocating their vision of the Caliphate. In contrast, al-Tha'alibi was not particularly concerned about the Caliphate and its restoration to a particular ruler. He played a subversive part in the Hajj and the Cairo Islamic congresses, and had apparently expressed some liberal opinions on the future of the Caliphate, calling for a pope-like role for the Caliph.[84] Al-Tha'alibi was also a close associate of Rida and Arslan and actively cooperated with them during his long exile in the Arab East. He visited Jerusalem as early as 1924 in a mission of mediation between the mufti and his opponents, returned repeatedly, and met with the mufti during the latter's visits to Mecca and Cairo.[85] His pan-Islamic and Arab status as well as his familiarity with the Palestinian scene made him the most suitable candidate for chairing the congress's preparatory committee. Available sources are not decisive in confirming al-Tha'alabi's principal role, although they cast strong doubts on the significance of Shawkat Ali's contribution to conceiving and preparing for the congress. Moreover, when the Caliphate controversy erupted and began to jeopardize the course of preparations, both al-Tha'alibi and the mufti went out of their way to deny the existence of a hidden agenda for the congress and to dislodge Shawkat Ali from his self-assumed role of leadership in the planning effort.

Following the burial of Muhammad Ali, Shawkat embarked on a speech-making tour in Palestine. The tour attracted the attention of the Criminal Investigation Department (CID) in Palestine, which was involved in monitoring the political situation in the country. The CID considered the tour as a sign of pan-Islamic revival, and alleged that the Arab-Islamists were working to run pan-Islamism "on parallel lines with the pan-Arab movement . . . to give it an additional impetus in the Arab countries".[86] Besides the pan-Islamic element, the CID report focused on Shawkat Ali's appeal to the Palestinians to boycott European products. The call for boycotting European products had been gathering momentum since early 1931, but it was not until 18 September, when a conference was held in Nablus, that a national declaration for that purpose was publicly announced.[87] As for the revival of pan-Islamism, Shawkat Ali's speeches included only one concrete proposition, the establishment of an Islamic university in Jerusalem.[88] No specific remark, on the part of Shawkat Ali, pointed to a project for holding a congress, or to the call for the restoration of the Caliphate in Jerusalem. If a project for holding a congress in Jerusalem did exist at the time, it seems not to have been on Ali's agenda. Shawkat Ali's next stop was in Baghdad, from where he travelled to other Arab cities, seeking to raise funds for the proposed Islamic university. Shawkat envisioned the proposed university in Jerusalem to be modelled on the Aligarh Islamic University of India, from which he had graduated. For the Palestinians, the university project was perceived as a Palestinian-Islamic response to the Hebrew University.[89]

At the end of June, as the Palestinians were preparing for the funeral of King Husayn bin Ali, Hasan Hassuna, secretary of the YMMS of Ludd, published an open letter to the mufti, calling for the holding of a pan-Islamic conference in Jerusalem to discuss the question of al-Buraq.[90] Hassuna suggested that the conference be held on the Fortieth Day of King Husayn's death, a traditional mourning day in some Arab regions. On 27 July, the SMC agreed in a meeting presided over by Hajj Amin to hold a Muslim world congress in Jerusalem and decided to send letters of invitation to Muslim rulers, to ulema, and to political and religious bodies in the Muslim world.[91] By this time, the Palestinians had already been aware of the two major developments of the year, the "Black Letter" of February, and the Report of the International Committee on the Western Wall of June. Both developments intensified Palestinian suspicions of British policies and justified a firm Palestinian stand on the question of the Western Wall. Both of these developments also weakened the Palestinian opposition's prestige, as the CID report specifically noted.

Significantly, British intelligence reports on pan-Islamic activities in the Arab world during the spring of 1931 were devoid of all reference to any kind of Islamic congress in Jerusalem. The Residency in Cairo saw in the Palestine CID report an exaggeration of the dangers of pan-Islamism and indicated that in the "Arabic-speaking countries there is a movement towards cultural unity, and . . . the desire for political unity is still strong".[92] The intelligence departments, however, were adamant that a "strong pan-Islamic Society" was being formed which included Shawkat Ali, Abd al-'Aziz al-Tha'alibi, and the Egyptians, Shaykh al-Taftazani, Shaykh Abd al-Wahhab al-Najjar, Abd al-Hamid Sa'id and Muhammad Ali. (As Muhammad Ali is not a known activist, I believe that the report referred to Muhammad Ali 'Alluba.)[93] Hajj Amin al-Husayni, according to the report, was to head the Palestinian branch of the society, which was supported by the Hashemite family. The report added, "Jerusalem is chosen to be the centre of this movement with an Islamic University to which all Moslem countries will contribute." In May, Palestine police reports extended the scope of this revolutionary pan-Islamic society even further as they indicated that Shakib Arslan (not Shawkat Ali) was the leader of the pan-Islamic organisation and that Arslan was maintaining contacts with Arab nationalists in various parts of the Arab world and with activists in Islamic countries. Hajj Amin and Shawkat Ali were regarded as prime associates in the scheme which seemed to be involved in organising gangs for guerrilla operations in Syria and Palestine.[94] Notwithstanding the credibility of these reports, none made any allusion to an Islamic congress in Jerusalem, to a plan to restore the Caliphate, or to bringing the exiled Ottoman Caliph into Jerusalem, although the project for establishing an Islamic university was by then a matter of public record.

Preparations and opposition

The preparatory committee had apparently first decided on an early convening of the congress. Thus, first invitations,[95] issued on 12 Rabi' al-Awwal AH 1350 (28 July 1931), specified the beginning of October for holding the congress. However, it was the second invitation, issued on 22 Rabi' al-Thani AH 1350 (5 September 1931) and indicating 7 December as the start of the congress, which was widely circulated.[96] Texts of both invitations were exactly similar and written in general terms, stating the need to convene an Islamic congress in Jerusalem, "in order to deliberate the present conditions of Muslims, to secure the safety of the holy places . . . and [to discuss] other affairs concerning all Muslims". This generality and vagueness was to contribute to the opponents' efforts to encourage speculation over the nature and aims of the congress. Most likely, the decision to postpone the congress to December was taken at the end of August, during Shawkat Ali's stop in

Palestine on his way to the Round-Table Conference in London. It seems that this was the only occasion when Ali attended the preparatory committee meetings.[97] But once again it was Shawkat Ali who conveyed the new schedule to the public during the Friday *khutba* at al-Aqsa mosque on 11 September.[98] Ali's consistent determination to be identified with the congress project would be another weak spot for the opponents to exploit.

The preparatory committee of the congress was composed of sixteen members; Abd al-'Aziz al-Tha'alibi was its chairman, and Amin al-Husayni his deputy. Other members, included Amin al-Tamimi (member of the SMC), 'Ajaj Nwayhid, Shaykh Isma'il al-Hafiz, Shaykh al-Muzaffar, and Shaykh Hasan Abu al-Sa'ud (the Shafi'i mufti of Jerusalem), who were all known to be supporters of the mufti.[99] The committee did not really engage itself in preparing for the congress, the specific issues to be discussed in its meetings, and its basic document, until 18 September (6 Jamadi al-Awwal), when it was decided that the congress agenda would focus on the Western Wall question, the general Islamic situation in Palestine and issues of Islamic culture.[100] The plan to establish an Islamic university in Jerusalem was considered a part of the last item. Yet, since letters of invitation had been already sent out, they did not include such details, a situation that further contributed to the speculation over the congress. Sometime later, the basic document of the congress was also completed. This document, which dealt with the congress's organisational structure, finance, aims, name, centre etc., was prepared by al-Tha'alibi.[101]

Opposition to the congress began in earnest by mid-September 1931, and arose from various quarters, each with its own reasons.[102] The Zionists in Palestine saw in the congress a dangerous escalation in the Muslims' support for the Palestinians. They first hoped that the British government would ban the congress, but when the British took a detached attitude, they began conspiring to diminish participation in it.[103] On 2 September, the Jewish Telegraphic Agency distributed a report from London, which was perhaps the spark that ignited the Caliphate controversy.[104] The report, entitled "the Caliphate to be re-established with Seat in Jerusalem", said: "Shawkat Ali . . . is putting forward a scheme for the restoration of the Caliphate under the ex-Sultan of Turkey, with its seat in Jerusalem, it is stated here (London) in Moslem circles." The report was of course fabricated; Ali was by then in Palestine not in London, and though his position in the Caliphate Committee of India, and his sympathy with the exiled Ottoman Caliph, were well-known, he made no attempt to use the proposed congress to revive the debate over the Caliphate question.[105] In fact, the whole question of the Caliphate's future was by the late 1920s dying out, while most of the pan-Islamic leaders in various parts of the world were becoming more and more engaged in a different set of preoccupations altogether. For the Zionists, however, Ali and the Indian Muslims in general were seen as a source of too much support for the Palestinians and the mufti. Attempts to win the Ali brothers over to the Zionist side were unrelenting.[106] As Zionist apprehensions over the holding of the congress intensified, Dr Brodetsky of the Jewish Agency confessed during a conversation with a British official that one of the Zionist aims was to "detach Shawkat Ali from the movement".[107]

Until the autumn of 1931 and the distribution of the Jewish Agency's report, no opposition to the congress was recorded in Egypt.[108] The weight of Egypt, being the centre of Arab and Islamic cultural life and the most powerful of Palestine's neighbouring countries, made it a very important target on the mufti's list of participants. Invitations to the congress were sent to many non-official, as well as official and semi-official, figures in Egypt. When the Egyptian official circles expressed their unease over the projected congress, the organizers in Jerusalem had to take notice.[109] The contentious issues on which Cairo apparently focused were: (a) the Caliphate question and whether the congress would discuss restoring the Caliphate to the deposed Ottoman sultan, a matter that was of major concern to King Fu'ad; (b) whether the projected university in Jerusalem was planned to compete with al-Azhar, and (c) the extent to which the congress would become a stage for the Egyptian opposition's anti-government propaganda. Those who would express disapproval of the congress were, therefore, Sidqi's government, the Palace, and Shaykh al-Azhar. To assess the nature of the Egyptian reaction to the congress, it is not enough to refer to the Zionist hostile activities, however serious they were. One should also examine the political situation in Egypt at that particular juncture.

The Egypt of 1931 lived under the heavy-handed policies of Sidqi's pro-Palace and pro-British government which replaced the Wafd's short rule of 1930, following the failure of the Egyptian–British negotiations. Sidqi dissolved the parliament and abrogated the constitution of 1923. His term in office, which lasted until the autumn of 1933, was characterized by an open confrontation with the Wafd and the Liberal Constitutionalist Party,[110] reaching one of its high points in 1931. Sidqi's appointment came in the wake of another conservative and pro-Palace coup in Egyptian public life, namely the replacement of Shaykh al-Azhar, Muhammad Mustafa al-Maraghi (1881–1945), with the conservative al-Ahmadi al-Zawahiri in October 1929.[111] Al-Maraghi, who would make a powerful comeback during Faruq's reign and reoccupy the rectorship of al-Azhar, was a reformist and a student of 'Abduh, who enjoyed good relations with the Liberal Constitutionalist Party. Al-Zawahiri, in contrast, was the Palace nominee, to whom Fu'ad gave the task of abolishing al-Maraghi's sponsored bill to reform the organization and system of teaching at al-Azhar. Not surprisingly, therefore, the king, the prime minister and Shaykh al-Azhar were virtually in alliance.

On 19 October, the mufti denied, in a statement to *al-Ahram*, that the congress would deliberate the Caliphate question, describing such rumours as "Zionist propaganda". Nevertheless, the Egyptian pro-British *al-Muqattam*, whose correspondent in Jerusalem was Shakib al-Nashashibi, a member of the family that rivalled the Husaynis, ignored the mufti's statement and insisted that the Caliphate was central to the congress plan.[112] Al-Tha'alibi was, therefore, dispatched to Cairo in late October, in an attempt to assess and contain the damage that had been inflicted on the project in Egypt. In Cairo, al-Tha'alibi used *al-Muqattam* itself to elaborate the main themes of the congress, and to underscore the minimal role that Shawkat Ali played in its preparations.[113] The preparatory committee followed by issuing an official statement to clarify its position,[114] and supporters of the congress in Egypt began to fight back.[115] More important were the two meetings that al-Tha'alibi held with Shaykh al-Azhar and the prime minister only a few days before the arrival of Amin al-Husayni in Cairo.[116] Shaykh al-Ahmadi al-Zawahiri raised two major complaints – that the preparatory committee did not invite al-Azhar to participate in the planning for the congress, and that the Caliphate issue, "which is of deep concern to higher people [i.e. the king]", had been scheduled to be discussed. Al-Tha'alibi vigorously denied the second charge, and explained the simple nature of the preparatory committee's work, for which no external assistance was needed. He further attacked al-Azhar's unjustified campaign against the congress. Al-Zawahiri, showing a degree of understanding, promised to call off the campaign and asked for a new start in the relations between the two sides.

The meeting with the prime minister was stormy and confrontational. Organized and witnessed by Abd al-Hamid Saʿid, it began with Ismaʿil Sidqi describing the plan to establish an Islamic university in Jerusalem as a challenge to al-Azhar's authority. But realizing the organizers' determination to hold the congress on time, he put forward four conditions for the participation of the Egyptian government: (a) an absolute denial from the organizers that the Caliphate question would be discussed; (b) the avoidance of any criticism of al-Azhar; (c) the avoidance of any involvement in the present Egyptian political affairs; and (d) the appointment of two Egyptian members to the preparatory committee (presumably nominated by the government). The meeting ended with al-Thaʿalibi promising to discuss these demands with the mufti upon the latter's arrival in Egypt on the same evening. Sidqi's real concern, however, was the use which the Egyptian opposition could make of the congress as an arena in which to voice their opposition to his government and not of any other issues raised by Sidqi. Amin al-Husayni's strong relations with opposition circles in Egypt were welcomed neither by the Palace nor by the prime minister. It is also pertinent that it was the Palestinian opposition, not the mufti, which was strongly represented in the Cairo Caliphate Congress of 1926. The dilemma of the mufti's and al-Thaʿalibi's approach to Egypt was in their attempt to win both the government and the opposition to their side without conceding a proper role to the government or al-Azhar in planing the congress, an attempt which proved to be highly unrealistic. If they were both aware of the weight of Egypt and the need for Egyptian support, they failed to express this awareness in a careful approach to the complex Egyptian situation.

The mufti's arrival in Cairo occasioned his immediate and wide access to the Egyptian media by means of which he was able to dispel the rumours and misunderstandings that engulfed the congress idea.[117] He met with Ismaʿil Sidqi and gave assurances with regard to Sidqi's major concerns (except on the demand for including two Egyptians in the preparatory committee); these assurances were later confirmed in a letter to the prime minister.[118] Subsequently, the mufti was received by Shaykh al-Azhar and the anti-congress campaign seemed to subside.[119] But as the opening date approached, Sidqi ordered that Egyptian civil servants should not be permitted to attend, and al-Zawahiri's camp of ulema did not participate either.[120] The damage to the relations between official Egypt and the congress organizers had already been done, and the rift between them was further deepened by the warm reception that the mufti was granted by the Wafd's leadership, headed by al-Nahhas.[121] But although al-Nahhas made the second largest donation to the congress, the Wafdi leader did not participate in the congress nor did most of the other top leaders of the Liberal Constitutionalist Party.[122] The Wafd was represented by Abd al-Rahman 'Azzam, and the Liberal Constitutionalists by Muhammad 'Ali 'Alluba Pasha, a former minister of *awqaf*; along with them was a large delegation from the YMMS, led by Abd al-Hamid Sa'id (who was considered a government and Palace loyalist).[123] It seems that the Egyptian opposition either chose to be circumspect after the protracted controversy over the congress, or was taken aback by another letter that the mufti had sent to no avail to Isma'il Sidqi.[124] At any rate, as non-official Egypt was impressively represented, the political conflict ensuing in Egypt was soon to spill over to the congress sessions.

The third quarter against which the congress had to struggle was the Palestinian opposition, including the Nashashibis and their allies in the SMC, Shaykh Muhii al-Din Abd al-Shafi and Abd al-Rahman al-Taji al-Faruqi. During the 1920s, members of the Nashashibi family established a friendly working, though secretive, relationship with the Zionist Jewish Agency in Palestine. Increasingly, the two parties became deeply involved in their opposition to, and apprehension over, the rise of Amin al-Husayni. For both (the Nashashibis and the Zionists), the holding of an Islamic congress in Jerusalem was seen as a furtherment of the mufti's prestige and a serious addition to his base of leadership. Hence, Fakhri al-Nashashibi, a cousin and right-hand man of Raghib, encouraged by the Zionist hostility to the congress and the widening controversy over its agenda, travelled to Egypt on 20 October in an attempt to harden the position of the congress's opponents. According to al-Tha'alibi, Fakhri unsuccessfully tried to organize an anti-congress working group and made contact with Zionist circles in Egypt.[125] Fakhri returned to Cairo on a similar mission on 13 November, just as the mufti was preparing to head back to Jerusalem.

Although the pro-mufti Egyptian press published some highly discrediting material on Fakhri's Zionist links,[126] Fakhri eventually succeeded in impressing upon 'Alluba and Abd al-Hamid Sa'id the view that the mufti had premeditatedly excluded the Palestinian opposition from the preparatory committee. Sa'id subsequently travelled to Jerusalem but failed to achieve a satisfactory solution.[127] Palestinian opponents of the mufti succeeded in holding a meeting on 13 November, which concluded with the issuing of a statement which criticized the mufti for not consulting "figures of opinion and stature", or inviting them to participate in the preparations for the congress.[128] The preparatory committee, responding to the pressure, deliberated the Palestinian participation in the congress on 26 November and announced a list that included representatives of various social and political forces, including Raghib al-Nashashibi.[129] The list, however, was still dominated by the mufti's supporters and members of the nationalist side. By the standards of the Palestinian political balance of the time, in which the pro-Nashashibi camp was the less influential, the list was perhaps a fair reflection of reality.

Further attempts by Abd al-Hamid Sa'id, Shawkat 'Ali and Rashid Rida to reconcile the two Palestinian sides completely failed.[130] Raghib al-Nashashibi and his group boycotted the congress and went as far as to convene a rival meeting under his presidency. This meeting was designated the "Congress of the Palestine Muslim Nation",[131] and was largely composed of the Nashashibi supporters. Its major aims were to divert attention from the main event, to display the strength of the Nashashibis, and to express lack of confidence in the mufti. To all intents and purposes it failed, and may well have further deepened the isolation of the opposition and the belief in their identification with Zionist circles.[132] On the other hand, the Palestinian delegation to the congress, which included at least 35 members, was joined by Is'af al-Nashashibi, the distinguished man of letters and a cousin of Raghib, as well as Ahmad Hilmi, Amin Abd al-Hadi, Raghib Pasha al-Dajani, and many of the future founders of the Istiqlal Party; none of whom could possibly be considered "yes-men" of the mufti.

Yet, obstacles on the road to the congress arose not only from the familiar quarters of the Jewish Agency or the Palestinian opposition, but also from the Hashemites in Amman and Baghdad. As the Caliphate controversy was blown out of proportion in Egypt, the Hashemites also required some assurances. This task was undertaken by a visit the mufti made to Amman.[133] The Saudis' suspicions, however, were more difficult to assuage, for rumours of Shawkat 'Ali's overestimated role left a negative impact on the Saudi view of the congress. The Saudis' encounter with the Indian Muslim delegation at the Congress of Mecca in 1926 marked relations between the two sides with mistrust and reproach from then onwards. To cause those relations to deteriorate even further, Shawkat Ali repeatedly attacked the Saudi monarch during 1931 as a result of a deal he had apparently struck with the Egyptians.[134] Ibn Sa'ud claimed, belatedly, that the invitation to the congress had not been received in time for him to join, and though news was circulated that he appointed an official representative to the congress, no such representative would turn up.[135] If the mufti had really hoped for the participation of a Muslim ruler, it would have been Ibn Sa'ud. The Saudi king had emerged since the mid-1920s as a powerful ally of the Arab-Islamists, from al-Quwwatli to Rida, and from al-Husayni to Arslan, for whom the Jerusalem congress was, after all, a manifestation of the power and influence they came to possess in the Arab-Islamic arena.

International responses to the congress were properly directed at the British authorities. Turkey was alarmed about the possibility of the ex-Caliph being invited to Jerusalem from his exile in France, while the Italians, whose atrocities in Tripoli inflamed Muslim public opinion, threw their weight with Britain against the congress.[136] Yugoslavia, several of whose Bosnian nationals were expected to attend the congress, expressed concern through its embassy in London. The Egyptians, too, were knocking on British doors, exploring British attitudes and whether the British officials in Palestine were rendering any support to the congress.[137] While the Colonial Office's first response to this wide international reaction was of one of "complete detachment", it sought to ensure that the "Congress activities" were "subject to international relations of the Mandatory".[138] In contrast, the Foreign Office, fearful of any disruption on the international front, was pressing to ban the congress altogether. Eventually, the Foreign Office had to accept the line adopted by the Colonial Office, and its officials in Palestine, that a British decision to stop the congress would "precipitate disorder [in Palestine] possibly even on the scale of an Arab rebellion".[139] The High Commissioner in Palestine, who was not in favour of prohibiting the meeting, maintained constant contact with the mufti to ensure that the congress would not be turned into an inflammatory political occasion. Given the very nature of the Palestinian problem, this, of course, was an impossible task to accomplish.

Participants and proceedings

Considering the immense tribulations, postponement and uncertainty that the project had to face during the preparatory period, the representativeness, number, and stature of participants was undoubtedly impressive. The attendance of 145 personalities from various parts of the Muslim world was far more than the Cairo and Mecca congresses put together.[140] The Egyptian delegation included 25 members (amongst whom were Muhammad Ali al-Tahir, who was a Palestinian living in Cairo, and Rashid Rida). The one who would be long remembered for his role in the congress was the Wafdi representative Abd al-Rahman 'Azzam, who was later to become the first secretary-general of the Arab League. Arriving in Palestine, 'Azzam had already behind him a distinguished career in Arab-Islamic politics, the Ottoman war effort, and the Libyan anti-Italian struggle during and after the end of World War I.[141] After the fall of the Ottoman empire and the subsequent defeat of the Libyan resistance, 'Azzam returned as a hero to Egypt in 1922, where he joined the Wafd shortly afterwards. 'Azzam's association with the Wafd provided him with a great opportunity to defend Arab and Islamic causes in Egypt. He became an advocate of the Libyan refugees, contributed to placing the Syrian revolt on the Wafd's agenda, and maintained firm links with Arab-Islamic circles in Egypt and abroad.[142]

The opening session of the congress was perhaps purposefully held at al-Aqsa mosque. After Amin al-Husayni's welcoming speech, other speakers of different nationalities were given the minbar, and since the Egyptian delegation was obviously divided, both Abd al-Hamid Sa'id and 'Azzam were introduced to speak. While 'Azzam was extending the greetings of al-Nahhas – Egypt's leader of the Opposition at that time – to the congress and his prayers for its success, he was shouted at by Sulayman Fawzi, the pro-Sidqi editor of *al-Kashkul*.[143] 'Azzam was again interrupted by Muhammad al-Subahi, a reporter for the pro-Egyptian government newspaper, *al-Sha'b*. The two incidents secured 'Azzam's position in the congress, and highlighted the split in the Egyptian camp.

Despite the mediatory role that Abd al-Hamid Sa'id played between the mufti and Isma'il Sidqi throughout the confrontation in Egypt between supporters and opponents of the congress, he was more eager to protect Sidqi's interests than to stand by the congress.[144] Even after the opening of the congress, Sa'id, as well as Shawkat 'Ali, were ardently insisting on the participation of the Palestinian opposition, blaming the mufti's intransigence for the Palestinian rift. During most of the proceedings, Sa'id, many of the YMMS's delegation, al-Taftazani, and al-Subahi, sat together and voted as one bloc, supported by Shawkat 'Ali. Other Egyptian participants were more relaxed and associated freely with other delegates, and for the most part sided with the mufti.[145] If Sa'id's position is understood in the light of his commitment to Sidqi and the warm reception afforded to 'Azzam, 'Ali seems to have been overshadowed and marginalized by the many eminent figures at the congress.

The second session, where nominations for the presidency and special committee were conducted, decided the direction of the congress and the weakness of Shawkat 'Ali and the Egyptian pro-government bloc. Hajj Amin al-Husayni was elected president, and subsequently appointed four deputies, including the distinguished Indian poet and Islamic reformist, Muhammad Iqbal, the representative of the Yemeni ruler (the only official representative), Muhammad Zubara, the former Iranian prime minister, Diya al-Din al-Tabatba'i and the Egyptian, M. A. 'Alluba.[146] Amid the wide approval of the participants, protestations from Shawkat 'Ali and Sa'id went largely unnoticed. 'Azzam was elected a member of the fundamental law committee, which was entrusted with drafting a constitution for the permanent congress. In the concluding session, an executive committee for the permanent congress was elected. Although 'Ali was among its list of 25 members, Sa'id and his associates were conspicuously absent.[147] Expectedly, Egypt's representation in the executive committee went to 'Azzam, who had earlier been deported from Palestine.

There were strong and large delegations from Transjordan, Lebanon, and Syria, including mayors, tribal shaykhs and community leaders from various Jordanian cities. Among them were Riyad al-Sulh, the Istiqlalist and future prime minister of Lebanon, Shukri al-Quwwatli, another influential Istiqlalist and a future president of Syria, and Nabih al-'Azma, the staunch Syrian Arabist who was still living in exile. Shakib Arslan, the godfather of many young Arab-Islamists, was still under a ban from entering areas ruled by British or French authorities.[148] Amir Muhammad Sa'id al-Jaza'iri (1881–1970),[149] the grandson of the great Algerian resistance leader and head of the Society for the Defence of the Hijaz Railway, was a member of the Syrian delegation. His attendance was a sign of reconciliation, since his anti-Faysal activities in 1919–20 in

Damascus had made him a rival of the Arabist camp which constituted the backbone of the congress. The influence of the Syrian delegation, coupled with the recent provocative step by the French in seizing the Damascus railway station, added the Hijaz railway issue to the congress's agenda. 'Azzam, Shaykh Abd al-Qadir al-Muzaffar, and M. A. al-Tahir, were the most outspoken in condemning the French measure, indicating that the railway was essentially a Muslim *waqf*, constructed with funds collected from Muslims worldwide.[150] Al-Jaza'iri was elected chairman of the railway committee and Ahmad Hilmi his deputy. Their report recommended to the congress that active steps should be taken to restore the Hijaz railway to the Muslims and place it under the supervision of an Islamic commission.[151] This recommendation was subsequently included in the congress's final resolutions.

The Iraqi delegation, which included ten members, attracted the attention of a discerning observer of the event.[152] Of particular importance in the Iraqi group was the participation of the distinguished Shi'i *mujtahid*, Muhammad Husayn al-Kashif al-Ghita' (1878–1954).[153] His invitation represented a significant leap in the Arab-Islamic effort to re-establish the concept of one Muslim *umma*. Kashif al-Ghita''s credentials made him the best candidate for such an Arab and Islamic gathering. Like his father, also a distinguished *alim*, he was a traveller who visited many Arab countries, including Egypt where he spoke at al-Azhar. On the eve of World War I, he became involved with the Arab movement and had contacts with Abd al-Ghani al-'Uraysi of al-Fatat and Abd al-Karim al-Khalil of the Arab Forum. During the war years, he fought against the British army in Iraq and became active in the Iraqi national movement for independence, to which the Shi'i ulema made a substantial contribution. The day of Kashif al-Ghita''s departure for Palestine was celebrated in al-Najaf as a great occasion, during which a motorcade of more than thirty cars accompanied him to Baghdad on his way to Jerusalem.[154] Kashif al-Ghita' was one of the speakers in the opening session; he spoke again in the twelfth session where he emphasized the central place of Jerusalem in the Muslim consciousness, and called for Islamic unity. It was decided by the congress to print his speech in several languages and distribute it worldwide.[155] The significance of Kashif al-Ghita''s participation was reinforced on 11 December when the congress agreed that the Shi'i *alim* should lead the Friday mass prayer at al-Aqsa, in order to underline the *umma*'s belief in its unity.[156]

The other two Iraqi members of particular significance were Shaykh Muhammad Bahjat al-'Athari, and Sa'id Thabit. Al-'Athari (b.1902) was a teacher, historian, poet, Muslim scholar and the mantle holder of the Iraqi Islamic reform school. He was a disciple of the influential Iraqi Islamic reformist Mahmud Shukri al-'Alusi,[157] in whom al-'Alusi found a committed student who would rise to become a member of the three major Arab academies of Damascus, Cairo and Baghdad.[158] After visiting Cairo in 1928, al-'Athari participated in establishing the YMMS branch of Baghdad and founded the *Magazine of the Muslim World*. He was associated with al-Tha'alibi, who frequented Baghdad during his years of exile, and was perhaps one of the youngest members of the Jerusalem Congress.

Sa'id Thabit (originally Muhammad S. al-Hajj Thabit al-Nu'man, 1883–1941) was born in Mosul and educated in traditional Islamic and modern Ottoman schools.[159] In 1919, he became active in the resistance against the British forces in his city, which subsequently led to his escape to Syria. Back in Iraq two years later, he participated in the movement for preserving Mosul's status as part of Iraq (rather than Turkey). In 1925, Thabit joined the People's Party of Yasin al-Hashimi, the Arabist and powerful Iraqi nationalist. Thabit was elected a member of the Iraqi parliament for several terms, and rose to prominence there in 1926 after standing against the Iraqi–British treaty. His participation in the Jerusalem Congress was an indication of his commitment to Palestine and the Arab-Islamic cause, a commitment that would mark his political career to the end.

The report of the committee of the holy places and the *Buraq* was submitted by its chairman, M. A. 'Alluba, in the afternoon session on 12 December. This was obviously the central theme of the meeting, where the participants' reactions showed the impossibility of separating the religious from the political in the Palestinian question. While the Zionist encroachment on Palestine was being uncompromisingly condemned, Sa'id Thabit gave a fiery speech calling for the observance of a two-minutes silence in memory of the Palestinian martyrs.[160] It was perhaps 'Awni Abd al-Hadi, the Palestinian Arabist lawyer, who provided the most substantial input to the debate on the holy places. He explained the religious ambitions of the Zionist Jews in Jerusalem and described the mandate system as the principal source of the increasing Zionist strength in Palestine.[161] Abd al-Hadi's proposal to reject the mandate was received with supportive contribution by Riyad al-Sulh. Shawkat Ali, however, raised his objection to the proposal on the basis that "discussion on the Mandate was extraneous",[162] and asked Abd al-Hadi to withdraw his motion. In a confrontational turn, Riyad al-Sulh accused Ali of extending no serious assistance to the Arabs or Islam and urged him to recognize that the Arab Muslims demanded the full independence of their countries. Although Ali was soon to be defended by other members, this exchange was obviously injurious to his reputation and position in the congress.[163] In the end, however, the final resolutions made no allusion to Abd al-Hadi's proposal. It seems that the mufti, who promised the High Commissioner to avoid matters political, did not wish to be driven into a confrontational course with the British, a course which he believed would be detrimental to the future of the congress. A five-point programme was agreed upon calling for the boycott of Zionist products, establishing an agricultural company in Palestine, bringing the attention of Muslim ulema and rulers to the Zionist threat, and condemning the report of the International Committee on *al-Buraq* and the activities of land-sale middlemen.[164]

Although the mufti's undertaking to the High Commissioner was an open secret, it could not stop many delegates, especially in the closing session, from launching a furious attack on the colonizers of the Muslim world. Among the speakers were Sa'id Shamil, the grandson of the Caucasian resistance leader, M. A. al-Tahir, Rashid Rida and Riyad al-Sulh.[165] This explosion of anger was not only an expression of the historic reality of "Islam on the defence", but was also a direct reaction to the government's decision to deport Abd al-Rahman 'Azzam before the end of the congress.

'Azzam gave a fiery and emotional speech on 15 December in support of a proposal condemning Italian atrocities in Libya, where he also called on the delegates to raise their voices in protest against the Italian policies.[166] His speech was loudly applauded as Ibrahim al-Wa'iz, the Iraqi delegate, proposed a moment of prayer.[167] 'Azzam and a group of other delegates spent the next day in Nablus where they, and 'Azzam in particular, were received enthusiastically in this very nationalistic Palestinian city.[168] On 17 December, 'Azzam was served in Jerusalem with a deportation order issued by the High Commissioner; he was subsequently driven to Gaza with a police escort, and two days later was taken to the Egyptian border. But his mark on the congress had already been made, since even in Gaza, at the very southern end of Palestine, people gathered *en masse* at his hotel to pay their respects.[169]

The report of the committee for religious propagation and guidance proved to be equally controversial. Chaired and deeply influenced by Rashid Rida, the committee's report was debated on 13 December. At this stage of his life, Rida was becoming less flexible in his religious convictions as his links with the Saudis and his admiration of their rapid rise imprinted his Salafi outlook with rigid Wahhabi streaks. Although many members of the congress maintained good relations with the Saudi government, and some others, like Shaykh Kamil al-Qassab (the Syrian who attended the congress as a Hijazi delegate) held much stricter Wahhabi views, the report was openly challenged on the ground of its "clear tendency towards Wahhabite religious practice".[170] The majority of delegates were ardently determined to preserve a sense of unity, symbolized and expressed in their meeting, and perhaps to keep a distance between the flexibility and openness which characterized the Islamic outlook of many of them and the Wahhabi view of Islam. Thus, when Mustafa al-Ghalayini, president of the Lebanese Muslim Council, condemned sectarianism and urged Muslims to free themselves from religious discord, his contribution was received with wide approval. In this spirit, the congress agreed on a set of resolutions with a specific set of functions (central information office and branches, journal, films, schools etc.),[171] avoiding the controversial parts of Rida's recommendations.

Another committee, chaired by al-Ghalayini, dealt with the important scheme of establishing a university in Jerusalem. The project encountered various degrees of dissension from three quarters. With a rationalist and calculating approach, Sir Muhammad Iqbal argued that the project was difficult to accomplish because of the lack of necessary funds and capable men. Shawkat 'Ali's main concern was the medium of instruction at the university which he envisioned as a culturally unifying centre for all Muslims, and which therefore must adopt all Islamic languages. His standpoint was perhaps embedded in the historical sensitivity which periodically coloured the relations between the non-Arab and the Arab Muslims. Both opinions were overruled by the majority. The Egyptian delegates adopted a more defiant and obstructive attitude towards the university proposal. This was particularly true of Abd al-Hamid Sa'id and al-Taftazani, whose stand outraged other delegates, including al-Hihyawi, editor of the Egyptian newspaper *al-Thaghir*.[172] Finally, in order to accommodate different sensibilities, it was agreed that the scheme should be undertaken in two steps, organizational and financial; it should be entrusted to the executive committee to study its technicalities and report to the next Islamic congress.

All in all, the congress was conducted in a proper and orderly manner, for which the credit was attributed to the efforts of the Lebanese, Riyad al-Sulh, and the Iranian, al-Tabatba'i. Although deprived of the participation of many influential figures, the congress was, by and large, a worthy achievement of the mufti and his determination. It elevated him to the most senior ranks of pan-Islamism and provided a Muslim world dimension to his national leadership. But while the impact of the congress deserves to be seen from a wider perspective, a question must be asked about the efforts to maintain its permanent organization and to actually implement its stated agenda.

Impact and fate

While tending to denote the strength of participation in the Jerusalem congress, recent studies are largely dismissive of its impact.[173] The congress, of course, could neither survive as a permanent effective body nor pursue the tasks it set out to accomplish. However, analysed in a historical context, the impact of this meeting reached far beyond its immediate effect on the local Palestinian rivalry for leadership, or Amin al-Husayni's status. In 1931, the Palestinian question was not yet regarded as a problem of international dimensions. For most Arabs and Muslims, a proper understanding of the situation was still lacking, let alone a clear assessment of the ominous dangers to the very existence of the Palestinian people. In terms of the imperialist *modus operandi*, the interwar period was mainly a continuation of the nineteenth century. As long as the process of imperialism did not seriously affect the balance of power in Europe, the imperialist powers were largely free to conduct their appropriate policies in the territories they possessed. Most Muslim nations had already been subjected to various systems of colonial rule and thereby engaged in addressing their own national question. The important achievement of the Jerusalem congress was to help transform Palestine into a pan-Arab and pan-Islamic problem. Scores of distinguished Arabs and Muslims were made familiar with the Palestinian situation; most of them would become founders or active members in many popular committees and organizations that were to spring up in the Arab and Muslim world in support of the Palestinians.[174] Indeed, the congress not only served the purpose of its predecessors in providing an Arab and Islamic arena, but also strengthened the Palestinians' belief in being part of an extended *umma* in the absence of a pivotal Islamic capital such as Istanbul.[175]

Evidently, however, the congress could not survive as a viable modern organization. The reasons behind its demise were manifold. The first and most damaging drawback was the congress's failure to raise the necessary funds for its projects and organizational structure. During its proceedings, responses from the Palestinian public, and many other sympathizers of the university project, were overwhelming.[176] Yet, ensuing attempts by the mufti, al-Tabatba'i, and M. A. 'Alluba, failed to raise the required money. Even after the relations between the mufti and Shawkat Ali had recovered, a tour in India, Persia, Afghanistan, and Iraq in 1933 was to fall short of expectations.[177] It is interesting that the financial position of the congress was earlier identified by the High Commissioner as the rock on which the congress would stumble. In the aftermath of the congress, the Colonial Office expressed deep apprehension over the possible impact of the congress's permanent office's activities in the Muslim world. Writing to the HC in Palestine, Sir Philip Cunliffe-Lister, the Colonial Secretary, stated that if "the result of the congress as now constituted, is to excite opposition in Moslem countries to the policy of establishing a Jewish National Home in Palestine, this, in effect, would be a challenge to the fundamental policy which His Majesty's Government are pledged to carry out under their international obligations".[178] The British government was obviously beginning to contemplate the policy it should adopt towards the proposed second convention of the congress in 1933, and the possible emergence of a sustainable pan-Islamic solidarity with the Palestinians. In response, the High Commissioner tentatively agreed that unforeseen conditions in Palestine might condone a pro-hibition of the congress, indicating, "The permanent effectiveness of the congress will depend in a large measure upon its financial resources."[179] In the event, a prohibition order was never actually needed.

The congress succeeded in establishing approximately twenty branches in Palestine, while others were also beginning to function in Egypt, Iraq, Jordan, Syria and Lebanon.[180] Even in many African, Far Asian and European countries, efforts were under way in 1932 to establish offices and chapters. Although the congress was severely impaired by its lack of funds and inability to reconvene in 1933, morale was boosted after the mufti, Shakib Arslan, M. A. 'Alluba, and Hashim al-Atasi succeeded on behalf of the congress in bringing peace and reconciliation between Yemen and Saudi Arabia in 1934.[181] Yet, by the next year, the congress's office in Jerusalem was showing no sign of activity, prompting the return of al-Tabatba'i from Europe with the intention of reviving it "in whatsoever channels may be found to be most useful".[182] He would obviously fail.

Besides the lack of finance, sources indicate that the demise of the congress was perhaps precipitated by some other factors, one of which was the lack of cohesion between members of the executive committee and the Jerusalem main office. According to the congress's resolutions, Diya' al-Din al-Tabatba'i was elected a secretary-general, 'Alluba a treasurer, Riyad al-Sulh, assistant to the secretary-general, and Sa'id Shamil, al-Tha'alibi, Amin al-Husayni and Nabih al-'Azma, members of the executive committee.[183] Apart from the last two, none of the others was resident in Jerusalem, a situation which made their regular meetings almost impossible.

Al-Tabatba'i was elected on the merit of his distinguished contribution to the success of the congress. He was regarded as a man of integrity, able, enlightened and a sincere Muslim.[184] In the early 1920s, he was instrumental in ending the state of anarchy in Iran, became a prime minister and helped Rida Shah, the founder of the Pahlavi's short dynasty, to take power. His pursuit of reform policies led him into a course of collision with the newly installed Shah and consequently to leaving Iran for exile in Switzerland. Though non-Arab, and not a Sunni, he was a pan-Islamist with profound convictions, which made him a valuable asset to the congress and the mufti. Before attending the congress, al-Tabatba'i was associated in Switzerland with Abbas Hilmi II, the exiled khedive of Egypt, and his Alliance Musulmane Internationale, a pan-Islamic project through which the former khedive was trying to perpetuate his influence and elevate his prestige in the Muslim world.[185] Unfortunate as it was, Hilmi's everlasting quest for power led him in the early 1930s to a complex entanglement with Mustafa Kamal in Turkey, and the Zionist circles in Palestine and Europe, with whose assistance he hoped to acquire the throne of (Greater) Syria.[186] Shakib Arslan, who had cooperated with the khedive during the 1920s, suspected his contacts and plans, and wrote of his apprehensions to Rashid Rida.[187] For Arslan and Rida, Syria's future was particularly a major concern. In the light of recurrent leaks of his Zionist connections, Abbas Hilmi became a dangerous liability with which to be identified.

In April 1932, as al-Tabatba'i arrived in Jerusalem to assume his responsibilities, Rashid Rida wrote to Nabih al-'Azma of the developments on the khedivial front, demanding that al-Tabatba'i be asked about his relations with the khedive.[188] Al-'Azma, a member of the executive committee, was also chosen to assist al-Tabatba'i in directing the permanent office. Realizing his critical position, al-Tabatba'i ended his relationship with Abbas Hilmi and settled in Palestine for most of 1932. His purchase of a large citrus grove near Gaza, coupled with his persistent efforts to revive the congress's office, were clear indicators of his commitment.[189] But the failure of the fund-raising tour of 1933 and the disagreements over the organizational rules of the permanent office took him back to Switzerland, where he started a carpet business. Subsequently, his visits to Palestine would become shorter and less frequent.

From the very beginning, the task of holding regular meetings of the executive committee emerged as a serious handicap of the permanent office. The mufti, taking into consideration the political and moral impact of the congress, worked to keep its office in Jerusalem. Others were apparently more disposed to meet in Cairo where many members of the executive committee were residing.[190] But even after reaching an agreement on Jerusalem, the majority of members failed to meet and did not easily accept the regulations and other necessary documents prepared by al-Tabatba'i and his team.[191] Feelings of frustration finally culminated in an atmosphere of rivalry and disagreement: first between Nabih al-'Azma and al-Tabatba'i, and then, as the mufti tilted towards the latter, between al-'Azma and the mufti.[192] Later, the energetic Riyad al-Sulh, recognizing the difficulties surrounding the congress's permanent office, submitted his resignation as the assistant secretary-general and called upon 'Izzat Darwaza to replace him.[193] By the end of 1932, the congress's office was not entirely functioning as it should have been, and further attempts to revive it in 1933 were seemingly too little, too late. But though personal rivalry may have played some role in the congress's decline, more important were the formidable tasks that the congress set out to accomplish. A grand vision of pan-Islamic organization could not materialize without the support of a powerful government, and Muslim governments of the 1930s were either unwilling or unable to support such a vision.

In 1937, the mufti left Palestine, fleeing a British order for arrest, and the congress's office in Jerusalem entered a terminal phase. The idea itself survived and was re-launched in Pakistan in the form of the Muslim World Congress in 1949 by Amin al-Husayni, and the Pakistani pan-Islamists, A. B. A. Haleem and Inamullah Khan, supported by Muslim Brotherhood elements.[194] This organization, which still exists with an office in Karachi, was among a few other similar bodies that paved the way for the establishment of the Organization of the Islamic Conference in 1969, the only formal body that coordinates relations between Muslim states.

NOTES

1 The Husaynis' ancestor Muhammad al-Badri was the first to move to Jerusalem in AH 782 (1380) from Wadi al-Nusur on the Jerusalem–Jaffa road, where the Husaynis settled for 200 years. It is generally believed that the Husaynis were of Sharifian descent, and that they originated from the Hijaz. The modern Husaynis, nevertheless, regard Sayyid Abd al-Latif bin Abdullah bin Abd al-Latif (d.1775) as the founding father of their house. His father, grandfather, and many of his descendants, occupied senior positions in the religious hierarchy of the local ulema, including mufti, *naqib al-ashraf* and Shaykh al-Haram. By the end of the nineteenth century, the Husaynis were also becoming one of the major landed families of Palestine. Besides traditional influence, younger members of the family also moved to the Ottoman modern bureaucracy. On the Husaynis, see: al-Jabarti, 1904–5: vol. 1, 374–5; al-Muhibi, n.d.: vol. 4, 313; al-Muradi, 1874–83: vol. 3, 124ff. and Abu Manneh, 1986:93–108. The date of Amin al-Husayni's birth has never been identified with certainty. For a lively discussion of this issue see Khadduri, 1973:68–9; Mattar, 1988:7–8.

2 Al-'Awdat, 1976:109; Mattar, 1988:8–9.

3 Cmd. 5479. Palestine Royal Commission Report (The Peel Commission Report), London, 1937, p.117.

4 Mattar, 1988:10–11.

5 High Commissioner to H. F. Downie, 5 December 1933, CO 733/248/22.

6 Khadduri, 1973:70–1; Mattar, 1988:11–12.

7 Kedourie, 1970:60.

8 Porath, 1971:125–6; and 1974: vol. 1, 188.

9 Bentwich and Bentwich, 1965:191; Kedourie, 1970:64–70; Porath, 1974: vol. 1, 192; Jbara, 1985:43–5; Mattar, 1988:26.

10 The most authoritative work on the SMC is Kupferschmidt, 1987. On the Palestinian Muslims' anxiety over the status of their *waqfs* and other religious properties see High Commissioner to Secretary of State for Colonies, 29 November 1920, FO 371/5262/E14815.

11 High Commissioner to Secretary of State for Colonies, 20 January 1922, CO 733/18/22/4590.

12 Kupferschmidt, 1987:174. Cf. Jbara, 1985:49.

13 *Bayan* of the SMC, 1925 and 1931 (both are official publications of the SMC), Archive of the Arab Studies Society, Jerusalem. See also various reports on the activities of the SMC during 1922–3 in CO 733/45/26756.

14 Tegart Papers, St Antony's Middle East Centre, Oxford University, Box 1, file 3/A; al-'Arif, 1961:87–8.

15 On the British recognition of the Zionist Commission and other local Jewish institutions of Palestine see Minutes of Meeting of Middle East Committee of the War Cabinet, 1 February 1918, FO 371/3394/13; FO to Sir Reginald Wingate, 13 February 1918, FO 371/3392/419; Samuel to Curzon, 8 November 1920, FO 371/5124/101. On the British position regarding the Palestinian National Executive see Samuel to Curzon, 1 January 1921, FO 371/6374/132.

16 The initiative for issuing a constitution for Palestine and establishing a limited constitutional life came from Samuel after the Palestinian riots of May 1921 (Samuel to Churchill, 13 June 1921, CO 733/3/153; Minutes of Conference at Colonial Office on Palestine Constitution, 12–13 August 1921, CO 733/14/168). After the British had formulated their proposal, they failed to bring the Palestinians to accept it (Arab Delegation to Churchill, 1 September 1921, CO 733/16/419; Memorandum by Shuckburgh, 7 November 1921, CO 733/15/268). In September 1922, the Fifth Palestinian Arab Congress rejected the draft constitution offered by the British (Kayyali (ed.), 1988:55–6). The British attempts in February-March 1923 to enforce the constitution by holding general elections in Palestine also failed as a result of a wide Palestinian boycott (al-Hout, 1986:167).

17 Abu Manneh, 1978:21–32.

18 Al-'Arif, 1961: 211. Cf. Nashashibi, 1990:2–3. See also Lindman, 1984:40–5; Manna', 1986:349–51.

19 "Personalities of South Syria", Arab Bureau, Cairo, February 1917 (Wingate Papers, University of Durham Library, file 206/5/1).

20 Storrs, 1945:33–4.

21 Kalvaryski to the Zionist Organisation, 24, 26 and 31 August 1923, CZA-S25/4379; Kisch, 1938:29, 47, 50, 52, 87, 134.

22 On the Seventh Palestinian National Congress see *al-Jami'a al-'Arabiyya*, 21, 25 and 28 June 1928.

23 Luke (chief secretary of the Palestine government) to High Commissioner, 14 January 1929, CO 733/172/1/67296. Under pressure from members of the Palestinian Executive, the mufti reluctantly supported the nationalist campaign against the British-proposed constitution (High Commissioner to Secretary of State for Colonies, 9 March 1923, CO 733/43/133).

24 *A-Jami'a al-'Arabiyya*, 22 March, 2, 9 and 19 April 1928; High Commissioner to Secretary of State for Colonies, 11 and 26 April 1928, CO 733/155/15; Bentwich and Bentwich, 1965:115.

25 Cmd. 3530. Palestine Commission on the Disturbances of August 1929: Report (Shaw Commission Report), London, March 1930, p. 31. On the escalating tension between the Palestinians and Jews, and the increasing involvement of the

mufti, see: *al-Jami'a al-'Arabiyya*, 1 and 25 October 1928; the mufti to Shawkat Ali, 17 October 1928, included in CO 733/173/67314; Meeting of Jewish Delegates with Government Officials, 25 September 1928, CZA-S25/2939; Luke to Secretary of State for Colonies, 3 November 1928, CO 733/160/57540.

26 *Al-Jami'a al-'Arabiyya*, 5 and 15 November 1928.

27 Cmd. 3229. The Western or Wailing Wall in Jerusalem. Memorandum by the Secretary of State. Great Britain, Parliamentary Papers (The White Paper of 1928), London, November 1928. This memorandum supported the Palestinian claim over the *Buraq* and recommended the observance of the status quo.

28 Shaw Commission Report, 46–57; Luke to Secretary of State for Colonies, 17 August 1929, CO 733/163/4/67013; Wasserstein, 1991:230–1.

29 Shaw Commission Report, 66–5. The mufti, who was implicated in instigating the riots by the chief secretary of the Palestine government (Luke Diaries, entry of 23 August 1929, St Antony's Middle East Centre, Oxford University), was exonerated by the Shaw Commission Report (pp. 76 and 82). On the severe and broad punishments that the British authorities inflicted on the Palestinians after the riots see Kayyali, 1978:145.

30 Ronald Storrs, secret memorandum, 31 August 1923, FO 371/9136/45180.

31 Major Young to G. Clayton, 14 September 1923; Clayton to Young, 5 October 1923, CO 537/859/50469.

32 See, for example: Note on the Caliphate, Intelligence Department of the War Office, Cairo, 24 July 1915; Memorandum on the Peril of Pan-Islamism, Investigation Bureau, Cairo, 14 February 1916; Memorandum on the Caliphate and the Future of Islam, signed by G. S. S., 24 December 1915, Wingate Papers, 135/1/53, 136/2/70 and 135/2/35 respectively. Also Kedourie, 1956:53–7.

33 Telegram from Abdullah to High Commissioner, 5 March 1924; Abdullah to the Foreign Minister of the Hijaz, 7 March 1924, FO 371/10217/2187 and 2188 respectively. Also *al-Manar*, vol. 25, 1924, pp. 463–71.

34 Smart to FO, 15, 20 March and 22 April 1924, FO 684/111/98, 121 and 208 respectively; Smart to FO, 28 April 1924, FO 371/10164/4141.

35 British Consul, Jeddah, to FO, 7 March 1924, FO 371/10218/2862.

36 Baghdad to London, 1 March 1924, FO 371/10217/11939. One of the rare telegrams of support from the Shi'i ulema was sent by the Iraqi shaykh Abd al-Karim al-Zinjani (*al-Qibla*, 27 July 1924).

37 The Nablus delegation, however, dissented (High Commissioner to CO, 13 March 1924, FO 371/10217/12314). On the Palestinian delegation to Husayn see *al-Ahram*, 14 March 1924.

38 Similar reactions were also recorded in Jaffa. See Political Reports of Northern and Southern Districts of Palestine, 28 and 29 March 1924, FO 371/10102/3865 and 3866 respectively.

39 The most comprehensive account of the Muslim responses to Husayn's Caliphate appeared in *al-Manar*, vol. 25, 1924, pp. 390–400. Rida himself was bitterly opposed to Husayn.

40 *Al-Qibla*, 7 July 1924.

41 Brown, 1964:38–56; al-Zirikli, 1989: vol. 4, 12–13.

42 Arslan, 1937:343 and 349; Cleveland, 1985:109–10.

43 Allenby to FO, 11 March 1924, FO 371/10217/2230; *al-Ahram*, 10 March 1924.

44 *Al-Ahram*, 27 March 1924; *al-Manar*, vol. 25, 1924, pp. 316–70. *Al-Ahram* (19 November 1924) echoed the widening belief in Egypt that al-Azhar Committee was actually under the government's influence. In his assessment of this episode, Kedourie (1970:183) argued that the Egyptian ulema were from the outset working on behalf of King Fu'ad.

45 *Al-Manar*, vol. 25, 1925, pp. 525–34; Husayn, 1970: vol. 2, 50–1. Rida would later write to Arslan that it was the pressure of his friend and student of 'Abduh, Shaykh Mustafa al-Maraghi, which made him join the Azhari committee for the congress (Arslan, 1937:335).

46 Toynbee, 1927: vol. 1, 81–91; Husayn, 1970: vol. 2, 51–4; Kedourie, 1970:189–92; Kramer, 1986:89–92.

47 Abd al-Raziq, 1925. See also a deeply hostile review of the book in *al-Manar*, vol. 26, 1926, pp. 230–2.

48 *Al-Manar*, ibid., 391–3.

49 Al-Azhar File of the Caliphate Congress, documents 9, 13, 33, 79, 117, and 129.

50 Ibid., document 111. See also documents 16 and 17.

51 Landau, 1990:237.

52 A full account of the Congress proceedings was published by Rida in *al-Manar*, vol. 27, 1926–7, pp. 138–43, 208–32, 280–4, 354–5, 270–6, 449–58.

53 *Revue du Monde Musulman*, vol. 64, 1926, p.48. Other delegates included Shaykh Hasan Abu al Sa'ud, 'Arif al-Dajani, 'Isa Mannun, and Isma'il al-Khatib.

54 Shafiq, n.d.: vol. 3, 305–7.

55 Lord Lloyd to Chamberlain, 30 April 1926, FO 371/11582/J 1144.

56 Henderson to Chamberlain, 7 February 1926, FO 371/11605/J 397. The Egyptians' only reservation concerned the British confirmation of the Egypt–Palestine Borders Agreement of 1906.

57 *Al-Muqattam*, 31 March 1925; *Kawkab al Sharq*, 4 April 1925. For al-Sayyid's defence and apology see *Kawkab al-Sharq*, 5 May 1925.

58 *Al-Balagh*, 28 November 1929; *al-Shura*, 18 December 1929.

59 Nwayhid, 1981:357–8.

60 Sources of Mecca Congress proceedings include: *Umm al-Qura* (the Mecca-based semi-official Saudi paper), June–July 1926; *Revue du Monde Musulman*, vol. 64, 1926, pp. 11–26 and 123–219; Toynbee, 1927:308–19; Nwayhid, 1981:557–71; Kramer, 1986:106–22. Kramer, however, drew heavily on Shaykh al-Zawahiri's prejudiced account of the Congress.

61 Nwayhid, 1981:368–9. Yusuf Yasin, a former colleague of the mufti in Rashid Rida's Islamic school and now a senior aide of Ibn Sa'ud, was instrumental in organizing these meetings.

62 Ibid., 365; *Revue du Monde Musulman*, vol. 64, 1926, pp. 16–18.

63 Ibid., 128–31.

64 Ibid., 16–24; Jeddah to FO, 20 July 1926, FO 371/11446/E4678.

65 The election of Arslan was initiated by Amin al-Husayni and Rashid Rida (Arslan, 1937:446–9). English text of the Congress Constitution was published by Kramer, 1986:186–91.

66 Arslan, 1937:163.

67 *Al-Manar*, vol. 27, 1927, pp. 548–55; vol. 29, 1928, pp. 162–80.

68 *Al-Manar*, vol. 29, 1928, pp. 384–90; SMC, *Bayan* of 1928, 12–13; Nwayhid, 1981:344–55.

69 Great Britain, Colonial Office: Report of the Commission Appointed by His Majesty's Government with the Approval of the Council of the League of Nations to Determine the Rights and Claims of Moslems and Jews in Connection with the Western or Wailing Wall at Jerusalem, London, 1930, pp. 62 ff.
70 Al-Kayyali, 1978:157.
71 Cmd. 3686. Palestine: Report on Immigration, Land Settlement and Development by Sir John Hope-Simpson, London, 1930.
72 Cmd. 3692. Palestine: Statement of Policy by His Majesty's Government in the United Kingdom, London, 1930.
73 Cmd. 5479. Report of the Palestine Royal Commission (Peel Commission Report), London, 1937, p. 74.
74 Passfield to Chancellor, 9 January 1931, CO 733/197/87050.
75 Colonial Office, Middle East No. 39, Palestine: Letter from the Prime Minister to Dr Ch. Weizmann, 13th February 1931. (A copy is found in I. Clayton Papers, St Antony's College Library, Oxford University, Box II).
76 Weizmann, 1949:415.
77 Chancellor to Passfield, 17 January 1931, FO 371/15330/E 259; Kupferschmidt, 1987:194–5; Gibb, 1934:100. At the funeral, which was attended by thousands of Palestinians and many Arab and Muslim dignitaries, Egypt's most distinguished poet Ahmad Shawqi immortalised the occasion with a classic Arabic poem (Nwayhid, 1988:369). See also on the funeral, Chancellor to Passfield, 28 January 1931, FO 371/15332/E 999.
78 Wauchope to Cunliffe-Lister, 24 December 1931, FO 371/16009/E 753; Gibb, 1934:100; Nelson, 1932:342; Ghunaym, 1973:119; Kramer, 1986:125. Nwayhid (1981:371), who accompanied Hajj Amin al-Husayni to the Mecca Congress of 1926, stated that the idea of a Muslim Congress in Jerusalem was first discussed between the mufti and the Indian leader Muhammad Ali in Mecca. Al-Tha'alibi (1988:46–8) claimed that the congress was being thought of for the last two years, i.e., since after the riots of 1929. However, an early mention of the projected congress in Jerusalem can be found in a British Police Report from Cairo entitled "Pan-Islamic and pan-Arab Activities" concerning a private conversation between the mufti and a Muslim friend in Cairo on 18 March 1931, where the mufti indicated that the aim of his visit to Egypt was "to discuss with Moslem leaders of all parties in Egypt details concerning the proposed Islamic Congress which was projected to take place in June of this year", see the Report in McSweeney (CO) to Mr Selby, 30 March 1931, FO 371/15326/E 1713.
79 Darwaza, 1949–51; vol. 1, 79. The idea of holding of a congress in Jerusalem seems to have been circulating among Arab-Islamists, since the Libyan leader Bashir al-Sa'dawi also claimed that he was the first to propose it to the mufti (Shukri, 1957: vol. 2, 870).
80 Al-Jami'a al-'Arabiyya, 3 July 1932.
81 Al-Tha'alibi, 1988 (edited and prepared for publication by Ahmad bin Milad and Hamadi al-Sahili).
82 Ibid., 154; see also pp. 37–8.
83 Landau, 1990:203–15.
84 In a letter from Muhib al-Din al-Khatib, 14 October 1931, to Hajj Amin al-Husayni, included in al-Tha'alibi, ibid., 219.
85 Letters from Rida to Arslan dated 8 March Dhu al-Qa'dah AH 1342 (1924), 14

Rabiʿ al-Awwal AH 1342 (1923), 22 Shaʿban AH 1342 (1924), in Arslan, 1937:333, 343 and 349 respectively. ʿAjaj Nwayhid to Nabih al-ʿAzma, 9 July 1924, al-ʿAzma Papers, University of Exeter Library, Arab Files, 509/9.

86 Deputy Commandant, CID to the Chief Secretary, Weekly Appreciation Summary, 18 February 1931, FO 141/763/495. See also Shawkat Ali to Lord Passfield, 14 February 1931, FO 371/15332/E 1514; *Filastin*, 14 and 21 February 1931.

87 Al-Kayyali, 1978:164–5.

88 CID report of 18 February 1931 (note 87) did not even mention this proposal. However, it was clearly mentioned in *al-Jamiʿa al-ʿArabiyya* of 13 February 1931, which also indicated that funds were being raised for the university.

89 *Al-Jamiʿa al-ʿArabiyya*, 13 February and 9 November 1931.

90 Ibid. 28 June 1931. King Husayn's body was laid in *al-Haram*, next to Muhammad Ali's tomb, on 4 July 1931 (Randall, 1978:232).

91 *Al-Jamiʿa al-ʿArabiyya*, 7 September 1931. H. A. R. Gibb, in his study of the congress (1934:100), wrote that the decision to hold the Jerusalem Congress was actually taken after June 1931.

92 R. H. Hoare to S. of S., 27 February 1931, FO 141/763/495.

93 Extract from Port Police, Port Said, No. COM/P/1(2), 14 February 1931, FO 141/763/495.

94 CID, Palestine, report on "The pan-Islamic Arab Revolutionary Movement", 21 May 1931, CO 733/204/87156; CO to FO, 11 June 1931, FO 371/15282/E 1205; Note on the Present Situation in Palestine, 18 June 1931, CO 733/204/87156.

95 A copy of which is in al-Thaʿalibi 1988:143.

96 See, for example, a copy with a private cover letter (dated 10 October 1931) in ʿAbbas Hilmi Papers, Sudan Archive, Durham University, 125/14 and 125/15. The same version, sent to Rashid Rida, was published in *al-Manar*, vol. 32, 1932, pp. 117–18. Another identical copy is in Nabih al-ʿAzma Papers, Palestinian files, 23/4.

97 Nielsen, 1932:342; al-Thaʿalibi, 1988:38 and 83.

98 *Al-Jamiʿa al-ʿArabiyya*, 6 September 1931.

99 Al-Thaʿalibi, 1988:263.

100 Minutes of the preparatory committee meetings of 18 and 20 September 1931, al-Thaʿalibi, ibid., pp. 256–65. Cf. Kupferschmidt, 1987:199–200.

101 This was unequivocally stated in a letter from Amin al-Husayni to Shawkat Ali (London) on 31 October 1931 (Al-ʿAzma Papers, Palestine Files, 25/4). An English version of the Draft Organic Law is included in CO to FO, 5 January 1932, FO 371/16009/E 87 (Enclosure to Secret B dated 11 December 1931).

102 Kupferschmidt (1987:198) wrongly stated: "The Caliphate question, together with the project to found a Muslim University in Jerusalem compelled Hajj Amin to pay an urgent visit to Egypt in order to soothe high-running feeling." It is understood from Kupferschmidt's reference to this passage (note 48 of the same page) that he meant the mufti's visit to Cairo of March 1931. In fact at that time of 1931, and for several months to come, there was no negative reaction in Cairo to the projected congress, or the plan to establish an Islamic university in Jerusalem. Moreover, neither was the Caliphate issue raised nor was it mentioned in connection with the congress. The British Intelligence Report from Cairo

entitled "Pan-Islamic and pan-Arab Activities", McSweeny (CO) to Mr Selby, 30 March 1931, FO 371/15326/E 1713, concerning a private conversation between the mufti and a friend in Cairo on 18 March (which was cited by Kupferschmidt) made no reference whatsoever to an Egyptian opposition to the university or the congress, or to the restoration of the Caliphate.

103 Jbara 1985:108; Kramer, 1986:126. Both of these authors relied on the Zionist Archive materials to document their conclusions.

104 Jewish Telegraphic Agency, 2 September 1931, London, "Caliphate to be re-established with Seat in Jerusalem", FO 371/15332/E 4757.

105 Mayer's (1982:311) statement that "Shawkat hoped to turn Jerusalem into the new Islamic centre where the future Caliph would be nominated" is misleading. Mayer cited only one reference (note 3, p. 320) related to events of 1931 to support his statement (Note of the Interview of Shawkat Ali with High Commissioner, 10 February 1931, FO 371/15332/E 1514). The fact is that during this interview with the High Commissioner, Shawkat Ali mentioned neither the congress nor the Caliphate question. This also goes for Ali's interview with the High Commissioner on 28 January 1931, a report of which is included in the above-mentioned FO's files. Ali in fact denied the Jewish Agency's report in an interview with Reuters in Jerusalem (see al-Tha'alibi, 1988:34).

106 See, for example, Shawkat Ali's side of the story of the Zionist attempts in his interviews with the High Commissioner in the FO's file indicated above (note 105). See also Ali's interview with Munif al-Husayni, the editor, *al-Jami'a al-'Arabiyya*, 6 December 1931.

107 Mr Rendel's report on the effort of Dr Brodetsky against the congress, 17 September 1931, FO 371/15332/E 4757. This continuous effort on the part of the Zionist elements to impair the preparations for the congress might justify the mufti's and al-Tha'alibi's claims that Zionist hostilities were the main source of the troubles that the congress project encountered (*al-Jami'a al-'Arabiyya*, 6 November 1931; al-Husayni, 1954:183; al-Tha'alibi, 1988:32).

108 Actually, until June 1931 not even an Egyptian opposition to the university project was reported. Sir P. Loraine, writing from Cairo to L. Oliphant in London on 12 June 1931 (FO 371/15282/E 3355) stated that Rashid Rida was attempting to recruit Egyptian Azhari ulema for the planned university in Jerusalem. He also expressed the belief that Rida would succeed, since the Azharis were beginning to suffer an increasing rate of unemployment.

109 On the beginning of opposition to the congress in Cairo see for example: *al-Muqattam*, 18, 23 October 1931; *al-Ahram*, 20, 23 October 1931; *Nur al-Islam*, vol. 2, October–November 1931, p. 464; al-Tha'alibi's letter from Cairo to Amin al-Husayni, 21 October 1931; Mirza Mahdi Rafi' Mashki's letter from Cairo to Amin al-Husayni, 17 October 1931; Muhammad Ali 'Alluba's letter from Cairo to Amin al-Husayni, 18 October 1931 (all in al-Tha'alibi, 1988:154–83).

110 For intimate details of the period see Haykal 1951: vol. 1, 259–91.

111 Kedourie, 1970:178.

112 *Al-Muqattam*, 23 October 1931.

113 Ibid., 24 October 1931. Al-Tha'alibi, of course, was to be followed with the mufti and shaykh, Abd al-Qadir al-Muzaffar, *al-Jami'a al-'Arabiyya*, 5 November 1931.

114 The preparatory committee's statement of 27 October 1931 was published in *al-Jami'a al-'Arabiyya*, 29 October 1931.

115 See, for example: Ali Abd al-Raziq in *al-Siyasa*, 26 October 1931; Muhammad Ali al-Tahir, *al-Muqattam*, 25 November 1931. Others included 'Abbas al-'Aqqad, Muhib al-Din al-Khatib, Muhammad Tawfiq Dyab and Sami al-Sarraj, see *al-Jami'a al-'Arabiyya*, 11 November 1931; al-Tha'alibi, 1988:49–62, 125–34.

116 Al-Tha'alibi's version of the two meetings is in ibid., 68–72 and 73–9.

117 See, for example: *al-Ahram* and *al-Muqattam*, 6,7 and 8 November 1931; *al-Jami'a al-'Arabiyya*, 9 and 11 November 1931; al-Tha'alibi, 1988:81–8.

118 *Al-Ahram*, 9 November 1931; al-Tha'alibi, 1988:88–9.

119 *Al-Jami'a al-'Arabiyya*, 11 and 12 November 1931; Mayer, 1982:314; al-Tha'alibi, 1988:89; Coury, 1992:39. Shaykh al-Muzaffar, who arrived with the mufti, remained in Egypt until 20 November to secure further support, see *al-Jami'a al-'Arabiyya*, 22 November 1931.

120 *Al-Ahram*, 2 December 1931. Other ulema, however, participated, including Shaykh Abd al-Latif Draz, Shaykh Abd al-Wahhab al-Najjar, and Shaykh Muhammad al-Makki, who were all associated with the YMMS, together with Shaykh Muhammad Sa'id Darwish, and Shaykh of the Ghunaymiyya Sufi Order, Muhammad al-Ghunaymi al-Taftazani (Kupferschmidt, 1987:269).

121 A distinguished Wafdi delegation led by al-Nahhas visited the mufti in Cairo and assured him of their full support, *al-Jami'a al-'Arabiyya*, 8 and 9 November 1931.

122 Al-Nahhas made a donation of £E204; the largest donation was also made by an Egyptian from Suez (Tha'alibi, 1988:333–4).

123 *Al-Jami'a al-'Arabiyya*, 7, 9, 10, 13, 15, and 18 December 1931.

124 Mayer, 1982:315.

125 Al-Tha'alibi, 1988:90–1. Al-Nashashibi's machinations in Egypt were supported by other opponents of the mufti, most notably Shaykh As'ad al-Shuqayri (*al-Jami'a al-'Arabiyya*, 8 November 1931.)

126 *Al-Jihad*, 17 November 1931.

127 *Filastin*, 19, 22, 24, 25, and 26 November 1931.

128 Al-Tha'alibi, 1988:112–13. The anti-congress proclamation was published in the oppositions paper, *al-Sirat al-Mustaqim*, 23 November 1931. A copy of that proclamation entitled "Hawl al-Mu'tamar fi Laylat al-Mi'raj" is in the SMC file, Archive of the Arab Studies Society, Jerusalem. This copy, though undated, was presumably prepared some time between 13 and 23 November 1931.

129 *Al-Jami'a al-'Arabiyya*, 4 December 1931.

130 *Al-Muqattam*, 18 December 1931; *al-Manar*, vol. 32, 1932, pp. 128–32; Nielsen, 1932.

131 *Al-Jami'a al-'Arabiyya*, 13 December 1931.

132 Darwaza, 1949–51, vol. 1, 81. On the other hand, pro-mufti circles across the country inundated the newspapers with their telegrams of support, see for instance *al-Jami'a al-'Arabiyya*, 6 and 7 December 1931.

133 Kramer, 1986:129.

134 The Residency, Cairo, to FO, 27 February 1931, FO 141/763/495.

135 *Al-Jami'a al-'Arabiyya*, 26 November 1931; Gibb, 1934:103.

136 Ibid., 102; Kupferschmidt, 1987:200–1; Kramer, 1986:130–1.

137 Mr Campbell, Cairo, to FO, 28 October 1931, FO 371/15282/E 5382; Report from Mr Rendel on a conversation with an Egyptian minister, 4 November 1931, FO 371/15282/E 5495.

138 CO to Cairo, 3 November 1931, FO 371/15282/E 5489.

139 On the FO's views see Minute of the 16 November 1931 meeting, FO 371/15282/E 5711. On the CO's assessment of the situation in Palestine see O. G. R. Williams' note, 17 November 1931, CO 732/51/89205.

140 High Commissioner to Secretary of State for Colonies, 24 December 1931, FO 371/16009/E 753. Kupferschmidt (1987:205), quoting Dutch sources, put the number at 133; Nwayhid (1981:375) mentioned the figure of 150 participants coming from 22 countries.

141 On his early life see Abd al-Rahman 'Azzam, "Abd al-Rahman 'Azzam and the Formation of the Arab League", Ph.D. thesis, Oxford University, 1995. On his political life after returning to Egypt in 1922 see Ralph Moses Coury, "Abd al-Rahman 'Azzam and the Development of Egyptian Arab Nationalism", Ph.D. dissertation, Princeton University, 1984. A sketchy and fragmented biography of 'Azzam is in 'Arif: 1977.

142 Arslan, 1937:591; al-Tahir, 1950:573–98.

143 Al-Tahir, 1950:582; Coury, 1992:42–3; FO 371/16009/E 753 (*op. cit.*).

144 Mayer (1982:315, and 317) stated that Sa'id and his associates were paid by Sidqi for their defence of the government during the congress.

145 Al-Tahir, 1932:191; Coury, 1992:41.

146 Al-Tahir, ibid. 190–2; FO (371/16009/E753) reported that elections for office holders were apparently arranged between the mufti's followers and his supporters among the Syrian Istiqlalists.

147 *Muqararat al-Mu'tamar al-Islami al-'Am*, Jerusalem, (1932), Abbas Hilmi Papers, no. 125; *al-Jami'a al-'Arabiyya*, 18 December 1931; al-Tha'alibi, 1988:360–3.

148 Al-Tahir (1950:553) stated that he, Arslan, al-Quwwatli, and al-Tha'alibi, played the major role in bringing the congress about.

149 For his biography, see al-Farfur, 1987:268.

150 FO 371/16009/E753 (*op. cit.*); *al-Jami'a al-'Arabiyya*, 9 and 10 December 1931; Nielsen, 1932:347.

151 *Muqararat . . .*, p. 17.

152 Gibb, 1934:101–2.

153 On his life, see Basri, 1971:110–16 and al-Mahbuba, 1986: vol. 2, 182–9.

154 Kramer, 1986:133.

155 The speech was published by the Congress Office in Jerusalem the following year (1932) at Dar al-'Aiytam al-Islamiyya Printing House (which belonged to the SMC) under the title: *Al-Khutba al-Tarikhiyya Allati Alqaha fi al-Jalsa al-Thaniya 'Ashra min Jalasat al-Mu'tamar al-Islami al-'Am Samahat al-'Allama al-Jalil al-Imam al-Hujja al-Mujtahid al-Shaykh Muhammad al-Husayn Al Khashif al-Ghita' Yawm al-Ithnayn 4 Sha'ban Sanat 1350*.

156 Zu'aytir memoirs, *al-Hayat*, 20 June 1994.

157 Al-'Alusi's biography was written by al-'Athari in his (AH 1345: 86–239) and (1958).

158 On al-'Athari's life, see al-Samara'i, 1982:113–18; al-Matba'i, 1988. The first, however, stated that al-'Athari was born in 1904 while the latter referred to 1902.

159 For his biography, private papers of the Iraqi historians Mir Basri and Najdat Fathi Safwat, London, were consulted. See also Sir A. Clark Kerr to Mr Eden, 4 January 1938, FO 371/21853/E 435.

160 For more details, see *al-Jami'a al-'Arabiyya*, 13, 14, 15, and 16 December 1931.

161 Abd al-Hadi's speech was translated in full in FO 371/16009/E 753 (*op. cit.*), Enclosure II, based on the Arabic text that appeared in *Filastin*, 15 December 1931.

162 See FO 371/16009/E753, Enclosure IV.

163 Shawkat was received by the High Commissioner on 8 December (FO 371/16009/E87). This, coupled with his recent rift with Ghandi in India, deepened the belief among radical delegates that he had been compromised by the British.

164 *Muqararat . . .*, pp. 18–19.

165 FO 371/16009/E753 (*op. cit.*), Enclosure IV.

166 *Filastin*, 17 December 1931; Coury, 1992:44–5.

167 Al-Wa'iz's suggestion became a point of dispute between the mufti and the High Commissioner on whether the congress approved of 'Azzam's attack on the Italians or not. The mufti indicated that he had attempted to stop 'Azzam several times but failed. See "Note of an interview with the Mufti on Thursday, 17 December 1931", FO 371/16009/1657/E 87.

168 Zu'aytir memoirs, *al-Hayat*, 20 June 1994.

169 *Al-Jami'a al-'Arabiyya*, 18 and 20 December 1931; *al-Ahram*, 18 December 1931; Coury, 1992:45.

170 FO 371/16009/E753 (*op. cit.*), Enclosure IV; *al-Jami'a al-'Arabiyya*, 14 and 15 December 1931. See also on the proposal and its opponents, *al-Manar*, vol. 32, 1931–2, pp. 193–212 and 284–92.

171 *Muqararat . . .*, pp. 11–12.

172 FO 371/16009/E753 (*op. cit.*), Enclosure IV; *al-Jami'a al-'Arabiyya*, 9 and 11 December 1931.

173 For example, Mayer, 1982:311–22; Kupferschmidt, 1987:192–220; and Kramer, 1986:123–41. For a counter argument see the penetrating analysis of Coury, 1992:37–54.

174 On Kashif al-Ghita's long association with the Palestinian question see his *fatwas* in *Hukm al-Islam fi Qadiyat Filastin*, 1979. On Bahjat al-'Athari's involvement see al-Matba'i, 1988:34–5 and 84–8. On the Iraqi, Egyptian, Syrian and Indian responses to the Palestinian revolt of 1936–9, see next chapters.

175 A fact that can easily be ascertained in Palestinian political memoirs; see, for example: Darwaza, 1949–51: vol. 1, 79–86; Nwayhid, 1993:151–8; Zu'aytir, *al-Hayat*, 20 June 1994.

176 *Al-Jami'a al-'Arabiyya*, 7, 10, 12, 15 and 17 December 1931; al-Tha'alibi, 1988:333–4.

177 High Commissioner to Downie, 5 December 1933, CO 733/248/22; *Filastin*, 4 December 1932; *al-Fath*, 21 and 28 June 1933; George Antonius, Annual Report to the Institute of Current World Affairs, New York city, New York, 1933–4 (G. Antonius Private Papers, St Antony's College, Oxford University); Darwaza, 1949–51:86; al-Husayni, 1954:142–3.

178 P. Cunliffe-Lister (London), to High Commissioner 18 February 1932, FO 371/16009/E 753. See also a long letter of protestation from the Jewish Agency to High Commissioner 24 December 1931, FO 371/16009/E 2508.

179 High Commissioner to Secretary of State for Colonies, 26 March 1932, FO 371/16009/E 2508.

180 Gibb, 1934:108; al-Tha'alibi, 1988:302–21; al-Matba'i, 1988:87–8.

181 Arslan, 1937:164 and 330–2; al-Sharabasi, 1978:46; Lesch, 1979:140–1.

182 G. Antonius Annual Report, 1935, Antonius Papers.
183 *Muqararat . . .,* p. 27.
184 High Commissioner to Downie, 5 December 1933, CO 733/248/22; G. Antonius Report of 23 April 1932, Antonius Papers.
185 *Al-Manar,* vol. 32, 1932, pp. 209–12; Arslan, 1937:641–2; 'Abbas Hilmi Papers, files 36 and 37.
186 Mayer, 1984:284–98.
187 Rida (Cairo) to Nabih al-'Azma (Jerusalem), 9 February 1932, al-'Azma Papers, Arab files, 8/410; Arslan, 1937:739; Nwayhid, 1993:223–8.
188 Rida to Nabih al-Azma, 17 April 1932, al-'Azma Papers, Palestine files, 5/44 and 45. See also al-Husayni to al-Tha'alibi, 30 Ramadan AH 1350, in al-Tha'alibi, 1988:298–9, which implied a disagreement on the person who would run the Permanent Office.
189 'Abbas Hilmi Papers, 125/16, 125/17 and 125/18; al-'Azma Papers, Palestine files, no. 4; al-Tha'alibi, 1988:306 ff.; Nwayhid, 1993:157–8.
190 Ibid. 286–92; Sami al-Sarraj (Cairo) to Nabih al-'Azma (Jerusalem), 19 January 1932, al-'Azma Papers, Palestine files, 5/35.
191 'Alluba to Amin al-Husayni, n.d. (1932); Sa'id Thabit (Baghdad) to al-'Azma (Jerusalem), 10 March 1932 (where he described the decision to involve non-residents in Palestine in the Executive Committee as a reckless decision); Tabatba'i to al-'Azma, 7 May 1932, al-'Azma Papers, Palestine files, no. 4.
192 Al-'Azma's memorandum to the Jerusalem Office Staff, 13 July 1932; an undated note by Nabih al-'Azma, al-'Azma Papers, Palestine files, no. 4; Sa'id Thabit (Baghdad) to Nabih al-'Azma (Jerusalem), 8 December 1934, al-'Azma Papers, Palestine files, 7/84.
193 Riyad al-Sulh (Beirut) to Nabih al-'Azma (Jerusalem), 15 October 1932, al-'Azma Papers, Palestine files, 5/60; Riyad al-Sulh to Izzat Darwaza, 15 October 1932, ibid., 5/59.
194 Landau, 1990; 280–3.

4

Arabism reawakening

The struggle against the occupying powers was perhaps the most important feature of the Arab movement during the interwar period. Under the pressure of this struggle and in the heat of its crucible, Arabism would gain new ground, while visions of Arab unity were being born, colliding and re-emerging anew. Because of the strategic position that Palestine occupied, the unique situation that the Arab movement confronted in Palestine and the extensive ties that connected the Palestinian interwar generation of leaders and activists with their Arab counterparts, the Palestinian question was to rise rapidly into the forefront of the Arab agenda. Arabism, on the other hand, was an inevitable choice for the Palestinians, a choice that was not only driven by the strength of the cultural and historical forces of the Arab enterprise, but also by the realities of power in the conflict for Palestine.

The advent of the Palestinian question, Egypt's embrace of Arabism, the reconciliation of the Arabist ranks after the demise of the Damascus Arab government, and the deepening belief among the Arab-Islamists that Arab unity was more realizable than the Caliphate institution, were important factors in augmenting the idea of Arab unity. Yet, if the Arabist–Ottomanist divisions of the war years were finally transcended, the new age carried with it new sources of division and rivalry: some related to the complex and unresolved question of Arab relations with the Western imperialist powers, and some related to the conflicting interests of the newly emerging Arab regional states. Indeed, obstacles on the road to Arab unity would arise not only from the European capitals but also from within the Arab ranks and the Arab ruling élite.

This chapter will focus on three major developments in the course of the Arab movement between 1920 and 1933: first, the changing relations within the Arab-Islamic movement in the period after the end of the war and during the 1920s; second, the origins of Egypt's growing identification with Arabism; and third, the Arabist attempts to formulate a new strategy for Arab unity.

[139]

Changing alliances

Following the forceful French occupation of Damascus in the summer of 1920, Arab leaders, activists and functionaries of Faysal's government dispersed into various parts of the Arab world.[1] Ex-Ottoman Iraqi officers and bureaucrats returned to Iraq where they would soon emerge as the main ruling group of the monarchic era. Only a few Syrians – most notably Sati' al-Husri and Muhammad Rustum Haydar – chose to follow King Faysal and pursue their careers in Iraq, motivated by deep loyalty to Faysal or the belief that the new kingdom of Iraq would soon turn into the centre of the Arab movement. The majority of Palestinians returned home; others, along with a group of Syrian Arab nationalists, moved to Transjordan, where for a short period they took part in establishing Amir Abdullah's government in Amman. As for the Cairo group of Arabists, their option was to head back to their original place of exile. These dispersed men of two generations and different social backgrounds would constitute the driving force for the second phase of the Arab movement, the interwar phase. Before tracing the course of their activities and the development of their relationships, it is important that we glance at their experience prior to, and particularly during, the short life of the Damascus government, where many future political currents originated.

Al-Fatat was for the large part of Faysal's rule in Damascus the most influential Arabist organisation.[2] Faysal himself had been sworn in as a member of al-Fatat in 1915 and his nationalist contacts in Syria, before the declaration of the Arab revolt, were mainly within its circles. Many of al-Fatat's members managed to survive the repressive measures of the Ottoman Unionist policies, thus becoming the first group to seize the opportunity when Faysal's troops entered Damascus in late 1918. In contrast, the Decentralization Party leaders were becoming increasingly hostile towards the ashraf of Mecca, and being Cairo-based were considerably slower in moving to Damascus where events were taking shape. Founders of al-Fatat, who gathered in Damascus, elected the two senior ex-Ottoman officers, Ali Rida al-Rikabi (Syrian), Yasin al-Hashimi (Iraqi), along with Tawfiq al-Natur, Ahmad Qadri, Nasib al-Bakri (Syrians) and Rafiq al-Tamimi (Palestinian), as its first leading bureau. In the period from August 1919 to March 1920, al-Fatat was controlled by al-Hashimi, Qadri, al-Tamimi, Ahmad Mariyud, Shukri al-Quwwatli, Sa'id Haydar and 'Izzat Darwaza (who also served as secretary).[3] To consolidate its grip on the administration, al-Fatat launched a speedy and wide-ranging recruitment drive, which reached all but a few of the distinguished members of the government and its nascent army.[4] This overreaching step of al-Fatat was, therefore, bound to inflate its rank with young opportunists, previously entrenched Ottomanists, and social climbers, with little or no nationalist convictions.

Al-'Ahd, dominated by ex-Ottoman army officers, was another active nationalist organization in Damascus. Under the stress of the postwar situation, where Iraq was occupied by the British and Syria ominously threatened by the French, coupled with the Iraqi–Syrian competition for position and influence, al-'Ahd was soon to split into Syrian and Iraqi groups.[5] The Syrian group, in particular, committed itself to opposing al-Fatat and the government, yet its influence was noticeably limited. A more serious challenge to al-Fatat came from within circles of the Damascene notables who resented the ascendance of many Iraqis and Palestinians to the most senior posts of a government that was born, and being reared, in their own city. Thus, after al-Fatat (which was still a secret organization) had launched Hizb al-Istiqlal (the Independence Party) as a public mass organization in early 1920, some influential notables established the Syrian National Party (al-Hizb al-Watani al-Suri).[6] This party, though supporting a similar nationalist programme, became a vehicle for the local opposition to al-Fatat, and was more prepared to compromise with the French (stationed on the Syrian coast and in Lebanon). To be sure, Faysal was not particularly displeased to see the emergence of a Damascene *a'yan* challenge to al-Fatat. It was to this moderate group of notables, imbued with the *a'yan* traditions, that he would turn for support when he began contemplating an understanding with the French.

By early 1920, a congress, consisting of Greater Syrian representatives, selected by different methods in the different parts of the territory, met in Damascus (the congress was to act as the parliament of the pan-Arab Damascus government). The exclusion of Iraq from participation in what was meant to be the parliamentary body of the Arab government implied perhaps an Arab desire to avoid a confrontation with the British whom Faysal and many of his men were still hoping to come to their aid against the obvious French schemes in Syria. On 8 March 1920, when the congress declared independence and crowned Faysal as king of the Syrian Arab state, it was clear that the Arab government had conceded Iraq to the British and was content to see the Arab ideal materializing in

Greater Syria only. Two parliamentary parties would subsequently emerge from within the congress, al-Taqadum (the Progress), dominated by al-Fatat, and the Democratic Party, which embodied the opposition. Another important organization of the Arabist political scene was the Arab Club (al-Nadi al-'Arabi), which was ostensibly set up in Damascus, with branches in Aleppo and Jerusalem, for cultural activities. Disseminating a radical Arabist message, the club was an offshoot of al-Fatat.[7] This crowded scene of political forces and organizations was largely the outcome of the considerably short evolutionary period during which the Arab idea developed from a political movement to a state. Neither the Unionist repression nor the conditions of war were conducive to the emergence of a stable Arabist political configuration. Even the rise of Sharif Husayn, with his limited political outlook and late arrival in the Arabist arena, could not provide a unifying framework for the Arab movement.

The political chart of Damascus was complicated by the arrival of the Cairo group of Arabists. Most prominent in this group were Iskandar 'Amun, Rashid Rida, Amir Michel Lutfallah, As'ad Daghir, Muhib al-Din al-Khatib, Rafiq al-'Azm, Shaykh Kamil al-Qassab and Abd al-Rahman al-Shahbandar. Largely of Arab-Islamic reformist background, this group was originally active in the Ottoman Decentralization Party. With its reformist rather than secessionist message, the Decentralization Party lost its *raison d'être* after the outbreak of the Arab revolt in 1916. In late 1918, therefore, al-'Azm, al-Shahbandar, al-Qassab, Khalid al-Hakim and Salim Sarkis, together with some other Arab activists, established the Syrian Union Party (Hizb al-Ittihad al-Suri) in Cairo. Michel Lutfallah was the party's president while Rashid Rida was his deputy. From the date of its inception, this party was riddled with political and ideological differences. Compounded with contradictory reactions to the fall of the Damascus Arab government, these differences would give rise to a split in the Arab political movement and underline the internal divisions of the Arab political scene in the 1920s.[8]

The development of Rida's political outlook would perhaps provide a fitting perspective to the Arab movement's tumultuous transition from the war years to the imperialist age. Rida declared his support for the Ottoman war effort immediately after the Unionist government joined the war in November 1914. His strong Arabist feeling and his suspicion of the Unionist policies, however, would soon prevail over his Ottoman loyalties. Hence, in February 1915, Rida endeavoured to impress upon

British officials in Cairo his vision of establishing an Arab decentralized state, consisting of Yemen, Greater Syria, Iraq and the Arabian Peninsula, where the Sharif of Mecca would assume the Caliphate seat.[9] The British, having their own agenda and not yet having confronted any major setbacks in the war, did not take Rida's proposal seriously, thus reinforcing his misgivings about their intentions towards the Arabs. Rida made a second bid for his scheme in a meeting with Sharif Husayn during the hajj season of October 1916, in which, despite Rida's support of Husayn's crowning as king of the Arab countries, the two differed on several important issues.[10] Husayn objected to Rida's anti-European propaganda during the hajj, and refused to adopt his proposal for seeking an alliance with other emirates in Arabia (Najd, 'Asir and Yemen). In Rida's scheme of things, this alliance was seen as the first step towards establishing an independent pan-Arab union. Rida, on the other hand, disapproved of Husayn's immature plan to claim the Caliphate seat before securing the support of a substantial number of influential Muslims (ahl al-hal wal-'aqd). While Rida adhered to the classical Islamic view of political legitimacy, Husayn understood the Caliphate in terms of power. Further contacts between Kamil al-Qassab, al-Shahbandar, and Khalid al-Hakim, of the Cairo Arabists, with Husayn and his son Faysal, raised more suspicions of the ashraf's Arabist policies and their authoritarian conduct of the Arab revolt.[11] Al-Manar turned critical of Sharif Husayn and was consequently banned from distribution in the Hijaz.[12]

Following the disclosure, by the Bolsheviks of Russia, of the existence of a secret Anglo-French agreement to divide the Ottoman Arab provinces, seven Arabist leaders in Cairo presented a memorandum to the British foreign secretary on 26 April 1918. The memorandum outlined the Arab demands for a united state and inquired about the reality of the secret Anglo-French schemes. The British response, delivered by Hogarth to two representatives of the Syrian Arabists in Cairo, promised the independence of the Hijaz and of southern Transjordan, but was vaguely phrased with regard to Iraq, Palestine and Syria.[13] Lack of confidence in the ashraf and the Allied powers and uncertainty about the Arab future led the Cairo Arabist group to embrace the idea of Syrian unity. The establishment of the Syrian Union Party on 19 December 1918, after lengthy deliberations within the group, was an expression of this political and ideological shift.[14] Central to the party's programme was the assertion of the unity and independence of Greater Syria, governed by a decentralized administration. Rida, realising the contradiction between this programme and his pan-Arabist beliefs and aspirations, justified his joining of the Syrian Union in terms of his devotion to the unity of the Syrians in Cairo, both Muslims and Christians. It is more likely, however, that Rida saw in the Greater Syrian project the only possible outcome of a war he was not part of, and of an Arab revolt he could not influence. The key to the rise of the Greater Syria idea was the wealthy Lebanese Christian, Amir Michel Lutfallah, who was the main, if not the only, financier of the new party.

Michel was the eldest son of Habib Lutfallah, a Lebanese emigrant in Cairo of modest extraction, who made considerable wealth in the early twentieth century through moneylending and landownership. His close ties with Sharif Husayn, for whom he served as banker, bought him the title of amir, which was subsequently inherited by his two sons, Michel and Habib junior.[15] Michel, despite maintaining his father's connections with the ashraf of Mecca, appeared to have held some illusions about becoming king of Syria. Like the rest of the Cairo Arabist group, Lutfallah moved to Damascus in 1919, but once he became aware of Faysal's powerful position, he returned to Cairo.[16]

At the beginning of their arrival in Damascus, members of the Cairo Arabist group advocated the establishment of a Syrian republic and expressed their opposition to Faysal and al-Fatat. This opposition, viewed in the context of the partisan politics of Damascus in 1919–20, should not, however, be exaggerated.[17] In the fluid political environment of Damascus, the demarcations between the parties were not so distinctive, nor was the inner cohesion of each party ensured. As a result of al-Fatat's ambitious recruitment drive, almost all members of the Iraqi al-'Ahd group, two of their Syrian counterparts, and Rida, al-Shahbandar, al-Khatib, Daghir and al-Qassab of the Cairo Arabists, became members of al-Fatat.[18] The concept of a political party was still relatively novel to the Arab experience, where the Arab nationalist organizations reflected personal ties, broad and transient political agreements or social coalitions, rather than exclusive ideological convictions or tight class divisions. But if parties' loyalties could not define political attitudes, the fate of Syria and the search for an Arab response to imperialism would.

From early 1920 until its collapse in July, the Damascus government entered into a stage of debilitating and divisive political tension, precipitated by imperialist power politics and the peace settlement.[19] The return of Faysal from his negotiations with the French, with a draft treaty (the Faysal–Clemenceau treaty), generated the first major rift among his men. With the British tight control of Palestine and Iraq, the French occupation of Lebanon and most of the Syrian coast, the pan-Arab project was reduced to an administration in interior Syria, depending largely on the goodwill of the British. Even this precarious and limited sovereignty now appeared threatened by French military might and British complacency. Inspired by the idea of national self-determination, the radical elements in Damascus pushed for the declaration of independence on 7 March, which they naively believed would deter the French. The Allied powers, however, did not recognise Syrian independence, and Faysal was soon to receive a warning from General Henri Gouraud, the French commander in the Levant. Hopes pinned on the Arab–British alliance were finally blown away when the Supreme Allies Council approved the carving up of the Arab East and the implementation of the mandate system, during its meeting in San Remo on 25 April. Under the mounting pressure, the Damascus Arabists were divided between a radical group, calling for a tougher response to the French, and a more accommodating group. Rida al-Rikabi, the prime minister, became a target of the radicals' dissatisfaction with the government's handling of the situation, and was thus forced to resign. A new government, headed by Hashim al-Atasi, was sworn in on 3 May, in which al-Shahbandar, until then considered a radical element, was appointed minister of foreign affairs.[20] Al-Atasi's position as president of the Syrian Congress was taken over by Rashid Rida. But what appeared as a victory for the radical camp would not last for long.

By late June, the French had amassed 90,000 of their troops in eastern Lebanon. The Arab government, whose military power was no match for the French, attempted to avoid the imminent confrontation by peaceful negotiations. On 14 July, Gouraud sent Faysal a letter in which he demanded, inter alia, the abolition of military service in Syria and Arab consent to the French mandate. Although the Syrian Congress rejected Gouraud's conditions, Faysal, supported by a group of moderates, was disposed to yield. When a congressional delegation, headed by Rida, received an audience with the king, the meeting developed into a heated argument.[21]

In the event, while the government's acquiescence with Gouraud's ultimatum made no difference to the French intentions towards Syria, it deepened the rift within the Arab ranks. Shaykh Kamil al-Qassab, the prominent member of al-Fatat and the Syrian Union Party, initiated a wide campaign to mobilize the Damascene populace in an effort to force the government to stand up to the French threats and defend the country. Within al-Fatat, al-Rikabi succeeded in ousting the radically dominated leading bureau of the organization (consisting of Darwaza, Qadri, al-Quwwatli, Rafiq al-Tamimi, Sa'id Haydar and Ahmad Mariyud), replacing it with a moderate group consisting of himself, Jamil Mardam, Nasib al-Bakri, Ahmad al-Hasibi and Muhammad al-Shariqi.[22] The major surprise of the last days of the Damascus government was the unexpected shift in the position of Abd al-Rahman al-Shahbandar, the energetic Syrian Arabist. Although his appointment to the ministry of foreign affairs was principally meant to soothe feelings in the radicals' camp, al-Shahbandar emerged as an outspoken supporter of Faysal and the policy of compromise. When Faysal left Damascus after the collapse of his government, al-Shahbandar was among the small entourage which accompanied the king in his railway carriage.[23] A pragmatist with a strong affinity to modern Western culture, al-Shahbandar would henceforth be identified as a pro-Hashemite Arabist. The lines of demarcation were thus drawn, not between al-Fatat, al-'Ahd, or the Syrian Union Party, but rather between those who saw themselves as defenders of Arab independence and unity, and those who were regarded as being prepared to compromise with the imperialist powers. But although drawn, the lines were not yet sharp.

One of the early refuges of the exiled Arabists after the French occupation of Damascus was Amman. This small Jordanian town became the centre of Amir Abdullah's government in March 1921, following the new British arrangements for the Arab East, agreed upon in the Colonial Office Cairo Conference.[24] Chaired by Winston Churchill, the Colonial Secretary, the conference decided to placate the Hashemites by allocating Transjordan to Abdullah and Iraq to Faysal. Abdullah arrived in the southern Jordanian town of Ma'an (which was still under the Hijazi jurisdiction) on 21 September 1920, leading a small force of 300 men, in a futile attempt to support the Syrian resistance to the French. Abdullah's inflammatory proclamations of his determination to liberate Syria from the French secured him an invitation to Amman by the local notables and the rallying of scores of Arab nationalists.[25] But since Amman lay within the region of the British mandate, the British ensured that

Abdullah would soon abandon his liberation mission. After the declaration of Syrian independence, most of the Iraqi Arabists in Damascus were inclined to offer Abdullah the throne of Iraq, if their country was granted its independence. Now feeling deeply bitter and betrayed over the loss of Iraq to his brother Faysal, Abdullah set out to establish his conditional rule in Transjordan. Serving him were men like Rashid Tlay', a Lebanese Druze Arabist and Abdullah's first prime minister, the Palestinians Amin al-Tamimi and 'Awni Abd al-Hadi, and the Syrians Hasan al-Hakim, Kamil al-Qassab, Yusuf Yasin, Khayr al-Din al-Zirikli and Nabih al-'Azma. At a certain stage of the short tempestuous association between this group of Arabists and Abdullah, the amir invited them to re-establish the Arab Istiqlal Party.[26] Having been the main political force behind the Damascus government, the Istiqlal Party became a symbol of Arabism and Arab unity. Abdullah's proposal marked the beginning of a long search for Arab legitimacy, and for expanding his rule beyond the emirate which he would always hold with contempt. The Istiqlalists, who viewed his adherence to the British line with equal contempt, and who were now aware of his ambitions in Syria and Palestine, ignored his offer.

This conspicuous gathering of Arab activists in Transjordan drew the attention of both the French and the British mandate authorities. In the event, a few Istiqlalists were implicated in anti-French attacks that seem to have originated in Jordan.[27] Under combined pressure from the French and British authorities, Abdullah decided to ban the active Arabist elements from the emirate.[28] But even before their expulsion, the great majority of the Arabists in Transjordan were becoming increasingly alienated by Abdullah's personal and erratic style of government and his utter dependence on the British.[29] At any rate, the Jordanian experience would further reinforce the rift that began to separate a wide segment of the Arab activists from the Hashemite house. Whether in the Hijaz, Transjordan or Iraq, the Hashemites seemed too submissive to the imperialist powers, especially to Britain, too autocratic and unable to lead the Arab revival. Despite Sharif Husayn's refusal to recognize the mandate system, and the consolidation of Faysal's position after Iraqi independence, the Hashemite Arabist image would never completely recover.[30]

It was against this background that, shortly before the collapse of the Sharifian Hijazi kingdom to the Saudi onslaught, the Syrians Kamil al-Qassab, Shukri al-Quwwatli and Yusuf Yasin succeeded in cultivating strong relations with the triumphant Ibn Sa'ud. During the period of uncertainty which followed the fall of Syria, the Syrian Arabists saw the Saudis as the ideal allies of the Arab movement. Yasin, a former student of Rida, was to settle in Saudi Arabia and rise to become its acting foreign minister, while al-Quwwatli turned into a close confidant of Ibn Sa'ud.[30] Yet, this was not the only channel that would connect the Arab interwar movement with the Saudi state which grew in a few decades from an isolated emirate in the Najdi desert of Arabia to become a major participant in Arab and Islamic politics. The other channel originated in Cairo.

Cairo of the 1920s turned into a vital centre for the interwar Arab movement, where leaders of the Syrian Union Party and other former activists and functionaries of the Damascus government resided. The Cairo Arabist group was frequented by Shukri al-Quwwatli, who played a crucial role in maintaining links amongst the Arabist groupings of Cairo, Jerusalem and Damascus. Beside the ambitious and wealthy Michel Lutfallah, and the grand figure of the Arab-Islamic reform movement, Rashid Rida, the Cairo group included the young Arab-Islamist Muhib al-Din al-Khatib. Following a long involvement in the pre-war Arab movement, the Arab revolt, and the Damascus enterprise, al-Khatib settled in Cairo, beginning a career in journalism which culminated in the launching of the weekly *al-Fath* and the monthly *al-Zahra'* in 1926.[31] Al-Khatib's disillusion with the Hashemites turned his Arab-reformist roots into radical *Salafi* convictions and made him a staunch supporter of the Saudi-Wahhabi Islamic outlook. This ideological transformation was not, none the less, limited to al-Khatib. By 1925, Rida, too, was throwing his weight behind Ibn Sa'ud and Saudi expansion in the Arabian Peninsula.[32] Although aware of the Saudi–British ties, what seemed to matter for the growing number of pro-Saudi Arab-Islamists was the Saudi commitment to the *Salafi* school and the independence of the Saudi state, when the Arab countries were almost entirely under Western domination. Against the more worldly Sharifian style of government, the Saudis adopted an ascetic mode of life and were closely associated with the ulema. Indeed, amid the Arab frustration of the early 1920s, the distant Wahhabi roots of the Arab-Islamic reform movement seemed to provide an ideological justification for the Arab-Islamic embrace of the Saudi state.

Another variant amongst the Cairo Arabist gathering was represented by the Palestinian journalist, Muhammad Ali al-Tahir (1896–1974).

Al-Tahir moved from his home town of Nablus to Cairo prior to the outbreak of World War I. During the war years, when his Syrian counterparts were rubbing shoulders with British officials in Egypt, he was suspected of Ottoman loyalties and detained in the prison camp of Jiza until the end of the war.[33] After his release, he returned to Palestine, but British hostility and harassment were again to force him back to Egypt. In Cairo, he established the Palestinian Committee and launched *al-Shura* newspaper, becoming in effect the Palestinian spokesman in Egypt. Al-Tahir was an uncompromising Arabist with radical anti-imperialist views that earned him the trust of Shakib Arslan, one of the most radical figures of the Arab movement.[34] He considered himself a "son" to Arslan and dedicated front-page space in *al-Shura* to his mentor's views and writings.[35]

Yet, Cairo received Syrian Arabists of different attitudes and outlook, most prominent amongst whom was Abd al-Rahman al-Shahbandar (1879–1940). The young Shahbandar was a member of Shaykh Tahir al-Jaza'iri's reformist circle in late nineteenth-century Damascus. In 1896, he joined the Syrian Protestant College (later the American University in Beirut) as a medical student, where he came under Anglo-American liberal influences.[36] His liberal roots would later develop into more radical secular views and Fabian socialist tendencies. Politically, he was a composite of an Arab Anglophile, a populist and highly ambitious Arab nationalist with strong connections with the Hashemites, Faysal in Iraq and then Abdullah in Transjordan.

Early in 1921, members of the Syrian Union Party in Cairo agreed to call for a pan-Syrian congress to discuss methods of organizing the struggle for independence and the Syrian representation in the international arena. After some delay, the Syro-Palestinian Congress was eventually held in Geneva between 25 August and 21 September 1921. The congress was attended by representatives of the Syrian Union party, the Istiqlal Party, the Palestinian Arab Executive, the Palestinian Committee in Cairo and a few Syrian immigrants from north and south America.[37] It ended with a list of resolutions demanding the independence and unity of Syria, Lebanon and Palestine, the abrogation of the mandate system, and the annulment of the Balfour Declaration. A permanent executive was elected, of which Michel Lutfallah, financier of the meeting, was the president, while Rashid Rida and the Palestinian, Tawfiq Hammad, were vice-presidents, and Amir Shakib Arslan secretary-general.

The Palestinian Arab Executive was evidently reluctant to join the Geneva Syro-Palestinian Congress, or to participate in the subsequent meetings of its Syro-Palestinian executive.[38] This position can be attributed to two major factors. First, since the Palestinian Executive had been dominated by a moderate leadership with a Palestinian nationalist agenda, it was becoming less interested in adopting a pan-Syrian or Arabist radical approach to the Palestinian question. When the Geneva congress was convened, a Palestinian delegation, headed by Musa Kazim al-Husayni, was already in London preparing to negotiate the Palestinian future with the British government. Representing the fourth Palestinian National Congress, the delegation decided not to raise the mandate issue and to focus instead on demanding the annulment of the Balfour Declaration and the JNH policy, and the stopping of Jewish immigration to Palestine.[39] Still, the Palestinian Executive did send representatives to the Syro-Palestinian Congress. But when these representatives telegraphed their counterparts in London with the resolutions of the congress, Musa Kazim al-Husayni unequivocally objected to the article concerning the rejection of all mandates in Greater Syria, regarding it as a statement of "overenthusiastic patriotism".[40] Moreover, al-Husayni deemed it unsatisfactory for the Palestinians to be represented by only one member in the Syro-Palestinian executive who could be easily outvoted in case of disagreement. Obstructively, the old Husayni would reject making any financial commitment towards covering the Syro-Palestinian executive's expenses. The second factor related to a leak in July 1922 of a meeting between Zionist officials and a group of Syrian Arab nationalists in Cairo.[41] This Arab–Zionist encounter was first initiated in November 1921; failing to bridge the wide gap between the two sides, it was terminated a few months later.[42] For the Palestinian nationalists, however, it was seen as an unjustified interference in Palestinian affairs on the part of the Cairo Arabist group.

After the end of the congress, Arslan and the Istiqlalist, Ihsan al-Jabri, decided to reside in Geneva to represent the congress before the League of Nations. The congress left no impact on the League's decision to rectify the mandate system on 24 July 1922, but Arslan and al-Jabri continued their activities in Switzerland for many years to come. Arslan had been a vocal pan-Islamist who vigorously opposed the Arab separatist trends in the Ottoman Arab provinces; winning him to the Arab cause was thus a symbol of reconciliation which put an end to the

Arabist–Ottomanist schism of the war years. Shakib Arslan was born in Shuwayfat in 1869 to a family of Lebanese Druze amirs.[43] He studied in Beirut where he was widely believed to have espoused the Sunni faith. During the early 1880s, Arslan met Muhammad 'Abduh in Beirut, and some years later he established a profound friendship with Rashid Rida. Common to both Rida and Arslan was a search for Islamic reform and revival and a legendary fondness for the Arabic language and heritage. By 1912, when Rida's Arabist and anti-CUP attitudes were becoming more evident, Arslan's strong belief in the Ottoman bond turned him into a close associate of the Unionists. After a stormy encounter in Cairo, their irreconcilable political positions led to a nine-year rupture in their relationship.[44] In 1920, while helplessly witnessing the demise of the Damascus Arab government, Rida initiated a reconciliation with his old friend.[45] Throughout the interwar period, Arslan would adhere to an unwavering anti-imperialist line and, despite his advocacy of Syrian independence, his vision was continuously in pursuit of grand designs of pan-Arab unity and Islamic awakening.

To all intents and purposes, Arslan had a certain dislike of Lutfallah, his pretentious aristocracy, his self-centred ambitions and his wealth-based political influence. Nor would Arslan be able to reconcile himself with Lutfallah's unceasing association with the British, his anti-Ottoman background and his secular outlook.[46] The tense relationship between Arslan and Lutfallah, coupled with the growing polarization between the "moderate" and "radical" approaches to the Arab question, led to the emergence of two major camps within the Syrian Arabist ranks. Most of the young Syrian Istiqlalists, including al-Quwwatli, 'Adil Arslan, Nabih and 'Adil al-'Azma and the Cairo-based Arabists, such as Muhib al-Din al-Khatib and Muhammad Ali al-Tahir, identified with Rida and Arslan, while al-Shahbandar, his brother-in-law Nazih al-Mu'ayyad al-'Azm, and his close associate Hasan al-Hakim, took the side of Lutfallah. As'ad Daghir (1886–1958),[47] the Lebanese Christian Arabist, journalist and representative of al-Istiqlal Party in Cairo, sided with Arslan and Rida. The outbreak of the Syrian revolt in 1925, and its ramifications, reinforced this schism and brought the Palestinians into the midst of its complications.

Led by the Druze sultan, Pasha al-Atrash, the Syrian revolt erupted in the Druze mountains in July 1925 and lasted until June 1927.[48] Abd al-Rahman al-Shahbandar, who returned to Damascus in 1924 upon a

French partial amnesty, was the first Damascene political leader to join the rebels. Although many Istiqlalists would soon follow suit, it was al-Shahbandar – and his People's Party – who gained most from the legendary impact of the revolt. In November 1925, the Istiqlalists called upon Hajj Amin al-Husayni to organize support for the revolt. The mufti promptly responded with the establishment of the Palestinian Relief Committee for Syrian Aid, which was dominated by Syrian Istiqlalists, their Palestinian counterparts and supporters of the mufti.[49] During the next two years, the committee became the principal device by which the Istiqlalists would counterbalance the rising fortunes of al-Shahbandar.

Financial aid to the rebels was increasingly channelled through Jerusalem rather than via Cairo where Lutfallah held sway over the finances of the Syro-Palestinian executive. The mufti, Rashid Tlay', Shukri al-Quwwatli and Shakib Arslan were instrumental in raising funds for the Jerusalem committee from the Syrian immigrant communities in the Americas, from the Saudis, from inside Palestine and from other parts of the Arab Muslim world.[50] Infuriated with the Istiqlalists' hold on the revolt's funds, al-Shahbandar complained to Hajj Amin al-Husayni, striving to win him over.[51] But the mufti was clearly intent on taking sides from the moment he established the committee and placed it under the full control of the Istiqlalists. During the recriminations which followed the end of the revolt, the Istiqlalists accused al-Shahbandar of betraying the revolt, while the latter charged his opponents with appropriating the revolt's funds for their own purposes.[52] When these charges were levelled at Amin al-Husayni,[53] the Palestinian opposition found a rare opportunity to question his integrity. A long-lasting alliance was thus forged between al-Shahbandar and his followers in Damascus and the Nashashibis in Jerusalem.

The split within the Syrian Arabist ranks echoed the political rivalry between the Saudis and the Hashemites, as the most influential Arab-Islamic figures seemed to identify with the Saudis. In the Palestinian context, however, the Hashemite–Saudi divide was never absolute. When Sharif Husayn appeared to take a firm stand against the Balfour Declaration during the negotiations for the Anglo-Hijazi treaty, the Palestinian leaders, including the mufti, rendered their support to Husayn's short-lived claim for the Caliphate.[54] The Palestinian relations with Amir Abdullah, however, were shrouded with suspicion and mistrust. Abdullah's ambitions in Palestine made him highly susceptible to Zionist overtures, and led him to establish political and economic ties with Zionist leaders and companies from the early 1920s onwards.[55] To the disadvantage of the amir, these ties would subsequently surface in the Palestinian Arab press.[56] With his total dependence on the British, and his pragmatic attitude to the Zionist project, it was in the Nashashibis, rather than the Husaynis, that Abdullah would find his Palestinian political allies.[57] So that when 'Arif al-'Arif, the newly appointed government secretary of Transjordan, arrived in Amman in 1926, the Jordanian capital was alive with rumours to the effect that Amin al-Husayni was plotting to oust Abdullah from his throne.[58] Mainly because of Abdullah's persistent attempts to extend his rule beyond Transjordan, his relations with the Palestinian nationalist movement would be permanently marked by antagonism and conflict.

In contrast, the Palestinians' realization of Iraq's political and strategic weight helped to maintain their amicable relations with the Hashemites of Iraq for the larger part of the interwar period. Yet, Iraq of the 1920s was not an independent country; it had thus no significant role to play in Arab and Islamic politics. This situation would certainly change after the signing of the Anglo-Iraqi treaty in 1930, and Iraq's joining of the League of Nations two years later. The emergence of an active Iraqi Arab role in the early 1930s occasioned the recovery of the Arab movement from the calamities of the postwar defeat. One of the vital contributory factors to this recovery was the increasing identification of Egypt with the Arab enterprise.

Egypt's embrace of Arabism

Extensive scholarly studies have been dedicated to the examination of Egypt's political and intellectual orientations in the interwar period and to its interest in the Palestinian question.[59] Most have projected the 1920s as a decade marked by Egyptian detachment from Arab and Palestinian affairs, the decline in pan-Islamism and the rise in Egyptian nationalism (of Pharaonism and liberal nationalist intellectualism). Gershoni and Jankowski, who published a detailed and profound study of Egypt's modern intellectual evolution, have emphatically concluded that the 1920s represented the "Triumph of Egyptianism".[60] If this were true, Egypt's embrace of Arabism in the 1930s, its rising interest in the Palestinian question and its subsequent emergence as the leader and centre of the Arab League in 1945, would appear as incomprehensible mutational shifts.[61] In reality, the 1920s saw the engendering of most, if not all, political and intellectual developments that defined Egypt's identity for the next few decades.

Multiple factors contributed to shaping the debate of identity and orientation in post-World War I Egypt. First was the impact of the nineteenth-century modernization drive which, as in other parts of the Ottoman realm, gave rise to a more culturally and politically diverse Egypt. Second was the Egyptian traditional loyalty to the Ottomans before the war, as a result of which Egyptian nationalist aspirations were largely expressed in anti-British pro-Ottoman terms. During the war years, Muhammad Farid, Abd al-'Aziz Jawish and many others of the National Party were natural allies of the Arab Ottomanists and the CUP government rather than the Decentralization Party or the Sharifian revolt.[62] To be sure, the Arab revolt and the Arabist alliance with Britain were viewed from Egypt with a sense of astonishment and disbelief. Third was, of course, the complex issue of Egyptian–British relations. Britain was able to contain the Egyptian revolt of 1919 and depress the Egyptian nationalist thrust. By offering Egypt limited and formal independence, the British succeeded in weakening the Egyptian anti-imperialist movement and introduced a divisive element in Egyptian party politics. The Egyptian ruling élite thus became susceptible to British demands and influences, since the British had now become the chief arbitrators of political power in the country.

During the 1920s, the Palace showed little interest in Arab and Palestinian affairs. The ministry of *awqaf* and King Fu'ad did make donations to the Palestinian-Islamic fund for the restoration of al-Aqsa mosque in 1923, on which occasion the king received the mufti of Jerusalem. It appears, none the less, that the British recommendation was perhaps more instrumental in arranging the meeting than the king's genuine interest.[63] The Palace, where the British influence was more visible than in any other centre of political life, was highly sensitive to British opinions and wishes. In becoming king of Egypt, Fu'ad felt deeply indebted to the British who could have easily picked one of the many other available contenders for the throne.[64] Fu'ad also relied on the British to counterbalance the Egyptian ruling parties' continuous attempts to limit the monarch's role. On the other hand, as the Ottoman empire was divided and Istanbul abdicated its traditional leading Islamic role,

Egypt emerged as the most powerful and advanced country in the *mashriq*. After 1923, despite Egypt's limited independence, and King Fu'ad's restricted room for manœuvre, he eagerly sought the Caliphate with its pan-Islamic influence and prestige. On this occasion, it was essentially Egypt's perception of its weight and position which prompted the move by the king and his supporters.

Though opposition to Fu'ad's and al-Azhar's Caliphate enterprise was as powerful in Egypt as it was outside it, not all of the opposition stemmed from liberal and anti-Islamic Egyptian circles. Prince 'Umar Tusun, for example, was widely known for his Arab and Islamic ties and could not be described as an isolationist; and only a few ulema opposed Fu'ad. Largely, Egyptian resistance to Fu'ad's Caliphate project originated from a wide contention that the Caliphate seat, added to British support, would provide more leverage for the king against the people and the constitutional machinery.[65] Equally indicative of the Palace's rising ambitions in the Arab world was Shaykh Mustafa al-Maraghi's mission to the Hijaz in September 1925.[66] Al-Maraghi was dispatched by King Fu'ad to Jeddah, prior to the ashraf's capitulation to the Saudi siege, to establish an Egyptian foothold in the Hijaz. However, Fu'ad's scheme in the Hijaz was soon to be overtaken by events. The Palestinian postwar situation added a new element to the complexity of Egypt's view of its role in the area. The more Egypt demanded and edged towards independence the more it would see the dangers emanating from the Zionist encroachment in Palestine. What would eventually develop was a historical dialectic between Egypt's interest in Palestine and its identification with the Arab cause.

The Arab attitudes of the main Egyptian political parties were equally complex and manifold, varying between the periods during which these parties were in power and those during which they were in opposition. *Al-Siyasa*, the paper of the Liberal Constitutionalist Party, known for its Egyptian nationalist orientation, paid fair attention to the Palestinian question during the 1920s.[67] It was, none the less, more disposed towards the Palestinian opposition and policy of moderation than to the Husayni-nationalist camp.[68] The Liberal Constitutionalists were, meanwhile, visibly supportive of the emerging Egyptian bourgeois attempts to extend their economic activities into the Arab East, attempts which aimed at establishing new markets for Egyptian cotton and manufactured goods.[69] In 1928, when Tal'at Harb, the founder of Misr

Bank, embarked on a visit to several Arab countries, *al-Siyasa* dispatched Abdullah 'Anan in Harb's footsteps to write a series of articles on these countries. But, following the rise of the Liberal Constitutionalists to power in the late 1920s, *al-Siyasa* and its editor, Dr Muhammad Husayn Haykal, attacked the Palestinians' resort to violence in 1929, called for peaceful negotiations to solve the Arab–Zionist disagreement over the Western Wall, and threatened Palestinian activists in Cairo with deportation.[70] Yet, despite the lack of consistency in the Liberal Constitutionalist Arab and Palestinian policy, some of the ardent supporters of Palestine and Arabism in Egypt came from the party's circles.

The Wafd was even more complex a phenomenon; its foundation was rather spontaneous and it never exhibited a clear distinctive ideology. Within the Wafd of the 1920s, trends of Egyptianism and Arab-Islamism existed side by side. The first significant response from the Wafd to an Arab issue was evoked by the Syrian revolt of the mid-1920s, when the Wafdis were out of power. Encouraged by the Ottomanist reborn Arabist Abd al-Rahman 'Azzam, as well as by Bahii al-Din Barakat and Hamid al-Basil, Sa'd Zaghlul led a national campaign for the political and financial support of the Syrians.[71] Although the activities of the Syro-Palestinian executive in Cairo made an important contribution to nurturing Wafdi interest in the Syrian revolt, equally important was the Wafd's determination to reaffirm its anti-imperialist image. The Wafd's anti-imperialist tendencies, together with its loose ideological parameters, were perhaps the main factors behind the emergence of the pro-Wafdi newspapers, such as *al-Balagh* and *Kawkab al-Sharq*, as powerful advocates of Arab-Islamic and Palestinian causes.[72]

Both papers paid noticeable attention to the Palestinian question, focusing on the dangers of land sales to the Jews and other aspects of the Arab–Zionist conflict.[73] Both viewed the British JNH policy as the principal cause of the Palestinian problem and saw Zionism as a threat to the very existence of the Arab Muslim people of Palestine. Closely associated with the Arab-Islamic circles of Arslan, al-Tahir, 'Azzam and Amin Sa'id, *al-Balagh* and *Kawkab al-Sharq* followed a pro-Palestinian nationalist line and supported the Husayni camp.

Yet, Egypt's coming to Arabism and Palestine was not the work of the Palace or the outcome of the premeditated policy of any political party. It was rather a more subtle process that fermented in the midst of the newly born Islamic societies and the growing cultural and political influence of Arab-Islamic circles. Egypt's embrace of Arabism originated from Egypt's belief in her pan-Islamic identity as the pan-Islamic ideal began to look remote and unattainable. The emergence of Arabism from its pan-Islamic roots was enhanced by the articles in *al-Manar*, *al-Fath*, *al-Shura* and the activities of the Eastern Bond Society, the Young Muslim Men's Society, al-Hidaya Society, the Muslim Brotherhood, and latterly the Young Egypt Society.

In February 1922 a group of Egyptian and Muslim ulema, intellectuals and publicists founded the Eastern Bond Society (Jam'iyyat al-Rabita al-Sharqiyya).[74] The founders represented a mix of ex-Ottomanists, Egyptian liberals, reformists, Sufis, conservative ulema and even non-Muslims. Of this broad coalition, al-Sayyid Abd al-Hamid al-Bakri, shaykh of all-Sufi *tariqas*, became president of the society; his two deputies were Ahmad Shafiq Pasha, head of the court of the former khedive, Abbas II, and Rashid Rida. Other prominent members included: the Azhari shaykhs, Muhammad al-Ghanimi al-Taftazani, Mustafa and Ali Abd al-Raziq, and Muhammad al-Bakhit; the known Arabists, 'Aziz al-Misri and Ahmad Zaki Pasha; and Emile Zaydan of *al-Hilal*, Mansur Fahmi, Habib Lutfallah, Salih Jawdat and Mahjub Thabit. This group was also joined by the Iraqi poet Abd al-Muhsin al-Kazimi, Mirza Mahdi Rafi', a pan-Islamist Iranian merchant resident in Cairo, and the Turk, Nur al-Din Mustafa. Financial support for the society was apparently secured by princes 'Umar Tusun and Yusuf Kamal of the Egyptian royal family.[75]

In its charter, the Eastern Bond Society presented itself as a "scientific social" organization whose concern for the progress and revival of the Eastern nations was envisioned in terms of "acquiring from the Western civilization what is commendable that is not averse to the Eastern spirit". It also aimed at deepening solidarity between Eastern peoples, regardless of race or religion, and set itself an ambitious goal of holding a "general Eastern congress" every three years. The scope of the society's vision was so broad that it encompassed an East extending from Egypt to Japan, which was soon to prove impractical and highly imaginative. Ideologically, many of its founders and proponents expressed their belief in a civilizational conflict between East and West,[76] a theme that was soon to be incorporated by the Islamic revivalists of the Muslim Brotherhood.[77] Yet, both in outlook and composition, the Eastern Bond was a reflection of Egypt's search for a supranational identity in the wake of the Ottoman demise. By the end of the 1920s, even Muhammad Husayn Haykal, who had earlier expressed some doubts over the society's programme,[78] was won over and *al-Siyasa* subsequently turned to support Easternism.[79] In October 1928, however, as the society launched its journal *Majallat al-Rabita al-Sharqiyya*, the deepening rift between its liberal-secular and its Islamic-conservative wings became apparent. The appointment of the controversial Azhari shaykh, Ali Abd al-Raziq, as the editor of the journal caused the departure of Rida and other ulema from the society, while *al-Manar* launched a scathing campaign against Abd al-Raziq.[80] This divisive episode, added to the lack of funds and the ageing of its most active members, pushed the society on to a road of decline, as the Egyptian intellectual scene was becoming more polarized by the beginning of the 1930s.

The Eastern Bond's vision of Eastern solidarity made it a centre to which the mufti of Jerusalem would turn during his frequent visits to Cairo. In 1923, the society led the fund-raising campaign for the restoration of al-Aqsa mosque.[81] Five years later, Ahmad Zaki Pasha was a prominent participant in the Palestinian ceremonies for the completion of the restoration project.[82] Ahmad Zaki, a widely respected historian of Islam, did also give evidence in defence of the Palestinian case before the Wailing Wall Commission of the League of Nations in 1930.[83] It was Zaki, together with Abd al-Hamid Sa'id of the YMMS and the Palestinian shaykh, al-Muzaffar, who played the main role in persuading Muhammad Ali 'Alluba, the lawyer and the Liberal Constitutionalist leader, to participate in the Arab-Islamic effort before the commission.[84] This introduction to Palestine was to convert 'Alluba into an ardent supporter of the Arab and the Palestinian cause for the rest of his long political career.

The Eastern Bond became similarly active in backing other Arab causes, most notably the Syrian revolt, the Libyan struggle against the Italian occupation, as well as the Tunisian and Moroccan national movements.[85] In the summer of 1926, the Syrian Istiqlalists dispatched Nabih al-'Azma to accompany Ahmad Zaki in a mission of mediation between Ibn Sa'ud and the Imam of Yemen, following the eruption of the Saudi–Yemeni dispute over the 'Asir province.[86] The mission illustrated an important aspect of the strength and scope of the Arab-Islamic network that was beginning to extend from Egypt eastwards amid the evolving events of the 1920s. Yet, despite its marked contribution to the

Egyptian search for identity and to placing Palestinian and Arab causes in the stream of Egyptian intellectual and political life, the Eastern Bond Society was not a mass organization. To be sure, the distinguished figures of its founding group never really sought a mass following. In contrast, a significantly more open organizational approach was to be adopted by the YMMS, which was founded in Cairo in 1927.

The YMMS was the brainchild of the Syrian Arab-Islamist Muhib al-Din al-Khatib and a group of prominent members of the National Party.[87] Many Egyptian founders of the YMMS, such as Shaykh Abd al-'Aziz Jawish, and its president, Abd al-Hamid Sa'id, had been strong Ottomanists who spent the war years in exile, and were known for their association with Shakib Arslan and Anwar Pasha.[88] Al-Khatib's partnership with Jawish and Sa'id was another indication of the Arab-Islamists' determination to transcend the legacy of the Arabist–Ottomanist rift of World War I. Other founders included the distinguished figure of Arab historiography and literature, Ahmad Taymur Pasha, Shaykh Muhammad al-Khadr Husayn, as well as Rashid Rida.

In setting its agenda, the YMMS focused on the general themes of spreading Islamic humanist values and morals, educating Muslims in a manner adapted to modern times, working against dissension amongst the Islamic parties and groups, and adopting from the Eastern and Western cultures all that is good and rejecting all that is bad.[89] This agenda was largely a reflection of cultural preoccupation, in which the early reformists' synthesis of Islam and the West was being reproduced. It was also about formulating an Islamic framework for the advance and revival of society.[90] With this emphasis on Islamic identity, the YMMS became exclusively a Muslim organization, inaugurating its engagement in public life with a campaign against missionary activities and foreign education in Egypt. No single feature of the YMMS could better illustrate its orientation than its organizational drive outside Egypt. Expanding in the Arab world, with no serious effort to reach other Islamic countries, the YMMS spread within a short period of its founding into Palestine, Syria and Iraq.[91] Chapters and branches of the YMMS were largely autonomous, though they were expected to keep in contact with the central office in Cairo where a congress of the boards of directors of all branches would normally be held.

YMMS branches in Palestine began to appear from as early as 1928, at the initiative of Abd al-Hamid Sa'id who was a frequent visitor to Palestine. The first general congress of the Palestinian YMMS was held in Jaffa on 18 April 1928.[92] From the list of clubs and organizations which participated in the congress, it seems that some branches were actually set up as a result of the conversion of already existing social, religious or sporting organizations. The constitution of the Nablus branch echoed, in many respects, the mother society's moral, educational and cultural aims, emphazising likewise the religious non-political nature of its activities.[93] But neither in Egypt nor in Palestine could the YMMS commit itself to a total avoidance of matters political. By 1930, therefore, the Jerusalem and Jaffa branches were ordered to be closed, while the mandate government banned all its employees from joining the Nablus branch.[94] Attracting to its ranks a group of the most politically active Palestinian Arab-Islamists, including 'Izzat Darwaza, Shaykh Abd al-Hamid al-Sa'ih, Hamdi al-Husayni, 'Awni Abd al-Hadi, Jamal al-Husayni, Rashid al-Hajj Ibrahim, and Shaykh 'Izz al-Din al-Qassam,[95] the YMMS provided another vehicle for the Palestinian national movement and reinforced its association with the wider Arab-Islamic scene.

The organizational expansion of the YMMS was not the only element of its Arab-Islamic commitment. From its founding, the YMMS's centre in Cairo became an important arena where Egyptian Arab-Islamists, like Mahmud 'Azmi, the poet Ahmad Shawqi and Prince 'Umar Tusun, would associate with young members of the society and get acquainted with pan-Islamic leaders such as Shawkat Ali, or other Arab-Islamists such as Abd al-'Aziz al-Tha'alibi.[96] Besides backing the Libyan and Tunisian causes, the Egyptian YMMS rendered vigorous support to the Palestinians after the outbreak of the Western Wall dispute, and funds were raised for those affected by its consequences.[97] In 1933, during its celebration of Salah al-Din's victory over the crusaders, the YMMS took a decisive step in its identification with Arabism by calling for Arab unity.[98] This bold, though natural, development in the YMMS orientation, was certainly indicative of the rapid evolution of the Egyptian mood at the time.

Yet, Egypt of the late 1920s was to witness the birth of another important organization that came to be closely associated with the Arab and Palestinian question and influence the shaping of Egypt's post-Ottoman identity. The Society of the Muslim Brothers (al-Ikhwan al-Muslimun) was founded in the Suez Canal city of Isma'iliyya in 1928

by the young Hasan al-Banna (1906–49),[99] the society's principal
ideologue and strategist and the embodiment of its spirit. He was born
in the Egyptian Delta village of al-Mahmudiyya, where he received a
traditional primary education, moving soon afterwards to a modern
formal school, and then to the teachers' college of Damanhur city. In
1923, al-Banna arrived in Cairo for the first time, where he joined Dar
al-'Ulum. Graduating in June 1927, he was appointed to a teaching post
at a primary school in Isma'iliyya where the Muslim Brothers Society
would be born a few months later. For the first five years of its founding,
the Ikhwan Society was rather a provincial phenomenon that did not
enjoy a national platform until its headquarters was transferred to Cairo
in 1932, and its weekly review launched the following year.[100]

Before his arrival in Cairo, it was the teachings of al-Husafiyya Sufi
tariqa which constituted the main source of al-Banna's understanding
of Islam. His Sufi dispositions, however, were soon to be confronted
by the modern educational approach of Dar al-'Ulum. This school
was originally conceived in the late nineteenth century to innovate on
al-Azhar's traditional methods of learning by combining instruction in
history and philosophy with Islamic and Arabic disciplines. During his
student years, al-Banna was also a keen observer of the heated debates
that swept the Egyptian capital over the Caliphate question, government
and constitution and the role of Islam in society and in shaping the
national identity.[101] Most crucially in the evolution of al-Banna's political
and intellectual orientations was his association with the Arab-Islamic
reformist circles. He became a regular reader of *al-Manar*, frequented the
office of Rashid Rida at Dar al-Manar, and developed a deep attachment
to Muhib al-Din al-Khatib, which lasted until al-Banna's assassination
in 1949.[102] At al-Khatib's *al-Maktaba al Salafiyya*, al-Banna would meet
the prominent figures of Arab-Islamism, such as Shaykh Muhammad
al-Khadr Husayn and Ahmad Taymur, and would also cooperate in
launching al-Khatib's influential weekly, *al-Fath*.

It was during this period that the pan-Islamic and pro-Arabist
views of the Ikhwani leader were garnered, whereby Arabism would be
expressed in an Islamic framework, or as a step towards Islamic unity.
In Isma'iliyya, the city divided between the British military camp and
the Suez Canal company on one side and the Egyptian quarters on
the other, al-Banna saw the city's division in Arab and foreign terms.[103]
He saw Egypt as both Arab and Islamic: Egyptian, Arab and Islamic

became synonymous. Indicative of al-Banna's intellectual evolution was a newspaper cutting that he kept from the Isma'iliyya days concerning the establishment of a society for Arab unity by Arab immigrants in the United States which proclaimed 17 June (the date on which the British executed three Palestinians in 1930, following the Western Wall disturbances) its memorial day.[104] With the issuing of *al-Ikhwan* weekly review, al-Banna would embark on outlining his vision of Arab unity.[105]

For al-Banna, the primary definition of identity was certainly based on Islam, with the unity of the Muslim *umma* as a fundamental belief. But he also saw the distinctive features that denoted the existence of the people dwelling in the area between the Persian Gulf and Tangier, that is, the Arabic language and the open unhindered geography. In his view Islam in the Arab lands is the sacred religion of the Muslims, and for non-Muslims the *Shari'a* is just. Muslims and non-Muslims are thus united and this unity is reinforced by common customs and traditions. According to al-Banna, Arab unity was also warranted by the political advantages that it would bring about, in an age where only united and integrated nations could survive. It was in a sense a post-Ottoman version of the Arab-Islamic reformist formulation of Arabism, with all of its inner tension and contradictions, on which the imprints of Rashid Rida and Muhib al-Din al-Khatib were evidently clear. But it was also a vision which would underline the future expansion of the Ikhwan and define its list of priorities.

Al-Banna's deep-rooted sense of mission and dedication to the restoration of Islamic moral values and the reconstruction of individual character on the basis of Islam were unparalleled. This religious and cultural orientation persisted as a distinctive element of the Ikhwani programme and was perhaps the principal factor that differentiated and justified the establishment of the Muslim Brotherhood alongside the more liberal and less organizationally integrated YMMS.[106] But the cultural-educational orientation of the Ikhwan was soon to be combined with a powerful Arab-Islamic drive, in which Palestine would feature prominently. In 1933, the Ikhwan initiated the first attempt to spread its message to Palestine, Syria and other Arab countries, manifesting a great interest in the Palestinian question. One of the earliest articles that al-Banna published was, in fact, an essay on the Zionist danger in Palestine, where he expressed deep concern about the future of Palestine, and demonstrated a broad knowledge of its affairs.[107] In a few years,

Palestine would provide the bridge for the Ikwani entry into the heat of the political arena.

By the end of the 1920s, seeds of Arabism were widely sown in Egyptian political and intellectual circles, bringing the most active figures of Egypt's public life to the heart of the Arab-Islamic network of the interwar period. Egypt would be represented in major Arab gatherings of the 1930s, and would subsequently turn into a main centre for the Arab and Palestinian movement.

Revival of the pan-Arab ideal

On 13 December 1931, during the sitting of the General Islamic Congress of Jerusalem, 'Awni Abd al-Hadi, the Palestinian lawyer and Arab nationalist, invited around forty members of the congress to a reception at his home. Many attendees of Abd al-Hadi's reception were former functionaries of the Damascus Arab government and activists of al-Fatat and the old Istiqlal Party, while others were newcomers to the Arabist scene.[108] During this gathering, they agreed on drafting a covenant for the revival of the Arab movement, calling for a pan-Arab congress and naming a committee to prepare for its convention.[109]

Amongst those who participated in Abd al-Hadi's reception and agreed to its three main conclusions were Rashid Rida, the Iraqi, Muhammad Bahjat al-'Athari, the Lebanese, Mustafa al-Ghalayini, Shukri al-Quwwatli, Nabih and 'Adil al-'Azma, Abd al-Rahman 'Azzam, the Moroccans, Muhammad Bannuna and Muhammad Makki al-Nasiri, the Libyan, Bashir al-Sa'dawi and a group of Palestinian Arabists.[110] They were roughly representing two generations of the Arab-Islamic reform movement, with different positions on the Arabist–Ottomanist divide of the war years. For them, however, this divide was no longer an issue as the Arabs were left after the end of the war with the occupation of most of their land by foreign powers. The presence of the Egyptian and North African group was particularly significant, implying that the Arab idea was finally taking roots in the *maghrib*. From Egypt westwards, identity and resistance to colonialism, well until the end of World War I, had largely been expressed in Islamic terms. Political Arabism of the *mashriq* neither sought to reach out to North African Arabs nor was it perceived by the latter with sympathy. While political Arabism signified the Arab-Islamic reformist reaction to the Turkification policies of Istanbul, the priority of the North Africans was the liberation from French occupation. In the post-Ottoman era, both wings of the Arab world came to face similar conditions.

For those who met at Abd al-Hadi's reception, Arab unity was to be pursued, not in opposition to Islamic unity, but rather as a more realistic and viable project to seek. The Syrian and Palestinian Istiqlalists amongst them, who were the driving force behind the Arabist meeting, were instrumental in organizing the Islamic Congress and concluding its works with a high degree of success.[111] Unmistakably therefore, dispatches of the British intelligence at the time spoke of Arab-Islamic activities in reporting what appeared to be a rise in the anti-colonialist movement in the early 1930s.[112]

Some other significant developments at the Arab states' level seem to have added a new stimulus to the Arab movement. While the Saudi state appeared firmly established, Iraq gained independence – however formal – after the signing of the Anglo-Iraqi treaty of 1930. In the same year, Faysal and Ibn Sa'ud held a meeting which, though it could not fully transcend historical and geopolitical realities, markedly eased the tension between Iraq and Saudi Arabia. Even Shakib Arslan, the staunch pan-Islamist and opponent of the Hashemites, moved towards mending fences with Hashemite Baghdad. Grasping the opportunity for an Arab reconciliation, Arslan arranged for Nuri al-Sa'id, the influential Iraqi official, to meet Hafiz Wahba, Ibn Sa'ud's main representative in Europe.[113] There is little doubt that Arslan, too, was coming to the conclusion that the Arab salvation was now in Arab unity rather than in the elusive vision of one Caliphate-one Caliph.

Conspicuously absent from the Arabist meeting at Abd al-Hadi's house was the mufti of Jerusalem, Hajj Amin al-Husayni. His standing as an Arab-Islamic leader was certainly beyond doubt; his attitudes towards Arab radical expressions in the Islamic Congress, however, raised a few questions. Following the passionate attack that Abd al-Rahman 'Azzam launched on the Italian policies in Libya, the mufti terminated the session in order to avoid further pursuit of the same theme. The mufti was aware of the British commitment to preclude the congress from offending other international powers and was, therefore, keen to avoid British reactions. On another occasion, the mufti appeared not to be in favour of a proposal, presented to the congress by 'Awni Abd al-Hadi, to condemn British interference in Muslim religious affairs and to denounce the mandate system.[114] Despite the bloody events of 1929, the mufti's amicable relations with the High Commissioner, John Chancellor, survived, and he seemed eager to maintain a similar rapport with his successor, Arthur G. Wauchope. In a letter he wrote to Rashid Rida after the conclusion of the Islamic Congress, Amin al-Husayni appeared to defend himself against earlier charges from his mentor of being too lenient in dealing with the British.[115] Yet, increasingly, the mufti's anti-imperialist image and his commitment to the Arab cause would come under scrutiny. For many of the Palestinian Arabists, Palestinian politics in general, and the mufti's position in particular, were viewed with pessimism. As the Palestinian desperation over British policies deepened, the Palestinian Arabists came to see the mufti in the light of his family's interests and his official position in the SMC.[116] They felt, therefore, justified in aspiring to establish a third political force, and equally justified in distancing themselves from the mufti.

Participants at the meeting agreed to delegate 'Izzat Darwaza, 'Awni Abd al-Hadi, Subhi al-Khadra, Khayr al-Din al-Zirikli, 'Ajaj Nwayhid and As'ad Daghir as an executive committee, charged with preparing for the Arab congress. By the end of February 1932, the executive committee had finalized its first proposal which included background information about the projected congress, a call for suggestions on the most suitable place and time for its convention, and a draft agenda.[117] This document was sent to a specific list of personalities in various parts of the Arab world, from Tunisia and Libya to Egypt and Iraq. The only official figures in the list were the Saudi monarch and the Imam of Yemen, who were both regarded as independent rulers and viewed positively by the Arab activists. Shakib and 'Adil Arslan, as well as Ihsan al-Jabiri, who were all in Europe, were also contacted.[118] Considered by Rida as "cumbersome",[119] the proposal detailed twenty-four items for the congress to discuss, but was highly modest in its scope. It was devoid of anti-imperialist rhetoric and was characteristically confined to a vision of confederate and gradually evolving Arab unity. It appears that as they approached the specifics, members of the committee came to recognize the difficulties surrounding their mission. What seemed not to figure in the committee's order of things at that early stage of its working was the role of King Faysal and his reawakening ambitions in Syria.

The Iraqi entry

The Arab congress was initially set to convene in the spring of 1932, but because of the slow process of preparations it was postponed to the autumn. There was as yet no agreement on the place, although some Arabists proposed the holding of an initial smaller meeting in Jerusalem, while others recommended Cairo or San'a.[120] Sometime after news of the congress became public, 'Awni Abd al-Hadi received a letter from Faysal offering to receive the congress in Baghdad.[121] Sources are not particularly clear on the date of Faysal's letter, what is clear, none the less, is that Faysal and the Iraqi ruling circles became highly interested in the congress project after the arrival of As'ad Daghir in Baghdad in April 1932.[122] Daghir, who went to Iraq on a journalistic mission (being one of al-Ahram's Cairo-based editors), approached King Faysal for support and conferred with his Iraqi Arabist colleagues. The result of Daghir's contacts in Baghdad was an agreement with Nuri al-Sa'id, the prime minister, and Yasin al-Hashimi, leader of the opposition, on the establishment of an Iraqi committee for the congress project. This course of events is borne out by a letter from the Iraqi, Sa'id Thabit, on 10 March 1932, in which there was no mention of Baghdad as a possible venue for the congress.[123] Thabit was close to al-Hashimi, and near enough to the ruling circles to know of the king's planning for the congress, if there was any. The question of Syria's future was certainly beginning to feature on Faysal's agenda, but what had emerged in Jerusalem was a different project, initiated by the Arab activists, not the Iraqi officials. Not surprisingly, the proposal of the Arab congress executive committee spoke of a pan-Arab confederacy without alluding to the Syrian question. It is highly likely that during Daghir's visit to Baghdad Faysal and the Iraqi ruling circles came to see the favourable conditions that the congress project may create for the Iraqi Arab role. This, of course, did not mean that the congress initiative and the Syrian question would not eventually converge.

Daghir's most important meeting in Baghdad was with Yasin al-Hashimi, Nuri al-Sa'id, Jamil al-Madfa'i, Mawlud Mukhlis and Ali Jawdat al-Ayubi. This group of Iraqi Arabists represented the leading personalities amongst the ex-Ottoman officers who emerged, by the merit of their contribution to the Arab revolt, to dominate Iraqi interwar political life. Their modern Ottoman experience, coupled with their distinguished ability to satisfy the demands of the various segments of the Iraqi people as well as those of the British, were the source of both their survival and eventual demise. Aware of the weight and needs of their newly independent country, their aspirations for a wider role in Arab affairs began to grow. Together, they dictated to Daghir a short message to his colleagues in Jerusalem and Cairo. It read:

> We in our personal capacity and as Arabs don't believe that engaging in local politics did not succeed, on the contrary [it did]. Circumstances have led to our partition and forced each part [of the Arab world] to focus on its own affairs. However, to continue functioning on a regional basis, though necessary for most men in each country, is not adequate to realize the goals for which our brothers had struggled. We, in Iraq, believe that it has become a duty of each country to single out some of its sons for the sake of the common [Arab] cause.[124]

There was a cool, calculating mind behind this text, the political mind of the interwar ruling élite, who had fully grasped the realities of power and had been reconciled with it. It was the mind of the Arab rebel turned statesman, beginning the long balancing act between the interests of the regional state and the pan-Arab ideal.

This group of Iraqi statesmen constituted the core of the Baghdad congress committee. They were also joined by Sa'id Thabit and Ja'afar Abu al-Timman, the two radical Iraqi nationalists and allies of Yasin al-Hashimi.[125] Although the committee embraced some of the best known Iraqi Arabists, it was riddled with personal disagreements and rival political interests. For the Arabists outside Iraq, it was al-Hashimi, more than any other of his colleagues, who was seen as the guardian of the Arab cause in Baghdad. Yasin al-Hashimi (1882–1937) was born to a modest Iraqi Sunni family which claimed Sharifian descent.[126] He first received a traditional religious education and then joined the Ottoman preparatory military school of Baghdad. Opting for a military career, he proceeded to Istanbul Military College, from which he graduated as an army officer in 1902. Stationed in Mosul in 1913, al-Hashimi joined the Arabist al-'Ahd organization, of which he became the most senior leader after 'Aziz al-Misri. While in Syria, two years later, he was also involved with al-Fatat and Faysal's early Arabist activities.[127] His Ottoman loyalties were, however, too profound for him to desert his position and join the Arab revolt. During the war, al-Hashimi was decorated for his accomplishment at the Austrian front, and fought with distinction against the British on the Palestinian front.[128]

At the end of the war, al-Hashimi was reconciled with his Arab nationalist comrades, and was subsequently commissioned to establish the first units of the Damascus Arab army. In November 1919, as the British troops began evacuation from Damascus, he was kidnapped by the withdrawing army and detained in Palestine until May of the next year, two months before the fall of Damascus to the French.[129] The causes behind this flagrant act on part of the British were perhaps related to al-Hashimi's support of the Iraqi tribal anti-British activities, the resistance against the French on the Syrian coast and his apparent contact with the Turkish nationalist army of Kemal Atatürk in Anatolia. Radical politics became a distinctive mark of al-Hashimi's career after his return to Iraq, though he was not denied the gift of compromise when necessary. His reputation as an anti-imperialist, a tough and insubordinate leader, of whom even Faysal had to take account, did not deprive him of a fair share of power. He served repeatedly as a cabinet minister, became a spokesman for parliament, and headed the Iraqi government for the first time from August 1924 to June 1925.[130] When he reached the premiership for his second and last term in March 1935, his Arabist credentials had been so strongly established that he was known within Arab nationalist circles as the Arab Bismarck.

Yet, the key figure behind Iraq's entry into the Arab arena was King Faysal, the leader who, despite many shortcomings, still epitomized the pan-Arab endeavour for unity. From the end of the 1920s, as Faysal's position in Iraq became firmly secured, his pan-Arabist vision oscillated between seeking a united Fertile Crescent or a Syrian–Iraqi merger. In both cases, Faysal envisioned a future in which the whole Arab East could be united, especially if the Saudi state was to collapse after the death of its founder, Abd al-'Aziz al-Sa'ud.[131] The irony, of course, was that Ibn Sa'ud would outlive Faysal by more than two decades. Faysal's attachment to Syria was motivated by a strong element of nostalgia, coupled with a deep belief in his historical rights as a Hashemite and Arab nationalist. More important were the geopolitical realities which deprived Iraq from a safe and adequate outlet to the sea, an outlet which Syria was naturally apt to provide.[132]

Following the eruption of the Palestinian–Zionist confrontation of 1929, Faysal proposed to the British a plan for solving the Palestinian question within a framework of Arab unity. Underestimating the British commitment to the Zionist project, Faysal believed that Jewish immigration would cease to pose a threat to the Palestinians if Palestine was joined to a larger Arab entity: a Syrian–Iraqi–Palestinian unity. But the British rejected Faysal's proposal.[133] It is not clear whether Faysal was influenced by the similar scheme of Sir Herbert Samuel that had been in circulation since 1920. What is clear, however, is that the JNH policy was left highly undefined by its British sponsors and that various concerned parties were creating their own and different interpretations of its implications. For Faysal, the JNH was perceived as a mere Jewish communal existence that could be safely incorporated within a united Arab state.

The situation in Syria, where the French were seemingly unable to manage the country's affairs, provided further reason for Faysal's Arab moves. The French, on the other hand, appeared increasingly interested in adopting the British model of indirect rule, as they compared their failure in Syria to the relative smoothness with which the British administered Iraq. Between the outbreak of the Syrian revolt in 1925 and 1932, official French circles were giving contradictory signals over a possible change in the Syrian system of government. The names of former King 'Ali, Amir Abdullah, and Abbas Hilmi were repeatedly mentioned and discussed with respective mediators in relation to the Syrian throne.[134] In this regard, Faysal himself was twice approached through the French ambassador in Baghdad and during his visit to Paris in September 1931.

Faysal took the French hints seriously and began soliciting support for his candidature, winning to his side Shakib Arslan.[135] Using his subtle influence by highlighting the strength that a united Syrian–Iraqi monarchy might add to the Arab cause, Arslan in turn enlisted the backing of Rashid Rida.[136] But Faysal's chances in Syria were doomed, firstly because of the lack of clarity and the incohesiveness that underlined French policy in Syria, and secondly because of the rising ambitions of the younger generation of Syrian Arab activists. If the support of a staunch pro-Hashemite like Abd al-Rahman al-Shahbandar was almost guaranteed, leaders of the National Bloc, the most powerful political force in Syria, such as al-Quwwatli, Jamil Mardam and Ibrahim Hananu, showed no interest in a Hashemite throne. They had not only been witnesses to Faysal's poor quality of leadership in 1920, but were also now glimpsing at power of their own in their own country. Their strengthening relations with Ibn Sa'ud were also giving them a sense of security, if a counterbalance to the Hashemites was ever needed.[137] Following the first Syrian elections of 1927 and the convening of the National Bloc-dominated assembly, a draft constitution was drawn up in August 1928. The draft constitution asserted the unity of Greater Syria and declared Syria a parliamentary republic.[138] Monarchist factions were clearly too marginal a force to exert any influence on the orientation of Syrian politics, and Faysal's emissaries to Syria, including al-Hashimi and Rustum Haydar, were unable to change the situation. But Faysal was not discouraged. Though he would not mention the Syrian question to the congress executive committee until much later, he undoubtedly saw in the Arab congress an excellent opportunity to consolidate his claim.

During the summer of 1932, new impetus was infused into the congress project. Al-Hashimi travelled to Cairo and Jerusalem to discuss preparations for the congress with Arabist groups and to attract Egyptian support.[139] Warmly received by Rida in Cairo and the Arab activists in Jerusalem, al-Hashimi's mission resulted in expansion of the congress's preparatory committee and in the agreement to convene the congress in Baghdad in the autumn of the same year. Local committees were also established in various Arab countries. The British intelligence list of principal members of the Arab movement at the time seems to have been based on the expanded, rather than the original, December 1931 group.[140] Describing Palestine as the most influential branch of the Arab movement and the centre of its operations, the British list depicted a wide network of Arabists in Iraq, Syria, Transjordan, Saudi Arabia and Egypt. 'Azzam and Hamid al-Basil, who both left the Wafd in 1932, were identified as the Egyptian members.

The Palestinian Istiqlal Party

The Palestinian Arabist group, encouraged by the centre stage it now occupied in the Arab movement, and by the prospects of Iraqi support, decided to re-establish the Arab Istiqlal Party. By the early 1930s, the Palestinian Executive, which led the national movement in the 1920s, was effectively dead, and though the mufti seemed to have assumed the national leading role, *a'yan* rivalry was still too manifest for a national consensus to emerge. In the background, there was also the thorny

Palestinian disagreements on how to conduct relations with the mandate government. Throughout the 1920s, the Palestinian leadership took extreme precautions not to equate the British government with the Zionist project, hoping to attract the British to its side. Among the Istiqlalists, however, the trend was growing for a change in the national agenda.[141] This trend found a strong justification in the policies followed by the new High Commissioner, Arthur Wauchope, which intensified pressure on the Palestinians and left the door wide open to Jewish immigration.[142]

Although increasingly critical of the mufti, the Istiqlalists were fully aware that there was no ideological basis for a rift with his camp. While both sides were connected with the same Arab networks and groupings outside Palestine, they aimed at the same national constituency inside. Before launching the party, therefore, the Istiqlalists proposed to the mufti to resign from the presidency of the SMC (in order to end his official relations with the British), offering to give him full backing in leading the national movement. If he did not resign, they wanted him to declare his support of the new party's agenda, or else to define the lines between his camp and the new party so that both sides would refrain from any form of recrimination.[143] The mufti, who regarded his position in the SMC as vital to the interests of the national movement, rejected the Istiqlalists' proposal. Viewing the new party as a serious challenge to his leadership, he exerted all possible effort to impair its emergence.

There is little doubt that the Palestinian Arabists were inspired in their initiative to re-launch the Istiqlal Party by Nabih al-'Azma, the Syrian exiled Arab nationalist.[144] Al-'Azma (1886–1972) was born in Damascus to a prominent Syrian family of Ottoman officers and bureaucrats.[145] A graduate of Istanbul Military College, al-'Azma, like al-Hashimi, maintained his loyalty to the Ottoman army until the end of the war. Under Faysal's rule in Damascus, he joined the Istiqlal Party and was involved with organizing guerrilla attacks against the French on the Syrian coast. Following the French occupation, he fled from a French execution order to Transjordan where he served in Abdullah's administration until 1925. But like many other Arab nationalists in Amman, he was soon to be expelled from trans-Jordan. A disappointing sojourn in Saudi Arabia, the failure of the Syrian revolt, and an unfruitful stay in Cairo, led him to Palestine, where he directed the permanent office of the General Islamic Congress. Though al-'Azma was not a member of the first preparatory committee of the Arab congress, his distinguished position in the Arab movement made him an active figure in its operation. His impeccable Arabist commitments invited profound respect from his contemporaries, including Rida, al-Hashimi and al-Quwwatli, as well as the Palestinian Istiqlalists.

On 22 August 1932, nine Palestinian Arabists signed the declaration of the Arab Istiqlal Party.[146] The three principal goals of the party were stated as the full independence of all Arab countries, their complete unity, and the assertion of Palestine Arab identity and its belonging to Greater Syria.[147] Two of the founders, 'Awni Abd al-Hadi and Mu'in al-Madi, were of powerful Nablusite and Haifan landed families, but both were well educated and largely detached from family politics.[148] Abd al-Hadi, who was chosen as president of the new party, was an early member of al-Fatat and personal secretary to Faysal in the Peace Conference. His Paris law education made him fluent in French, though appropriately for the party's anti-British attitudes, he spoke no English. Other founders included: Rashid al-Hajj Ibrahim, the merchant and active leader of the Haifan YMMS; Akram Zu'aytir, the young teacher from Nablus; 'Izzat Darwaza, then director of *awqaf* in the SMC; 'Ajaj Nwayhid, the Lebanese of Druze origin who had been settled in Palestine since 1920; and Subhi al-Khadra, another official in the *Awqaf* Department of the SMC and an ex-Sharifian officer.[149] Some of the main supporters of the Istiqlal Party included Ahmad Hilmi Pasha and his son-in-law, Abd al-Hamid Shuman, the legendary founder of the Arab Bank.[150]

The Istiqlalists' agenda was essentially Arabist; yet their continuous attempt to underline their independence from the Palestinian *a'yan* entanglement incurred the wrath of both Palestinian factions. Becoming a target for a fierce Nashashibist attack, they were also confronted with a relentless campaign by the mufti, inside and outside Palestine. After receiving complaints from the mufti, Faysal, who was now seen as a patron of the Istiqlalists, expressed his dismay over their rift with the mufti.[151] Aware of the mufti's standing inside and outside Palestine, Faysal was keen not to see his allies in Palestine in confrontation with him. And as the dispute reverberated throughout the Arab arena, the Istiqlalists were also condemned by al-Hashimi and Rida. In the event, while the Istiqlal Party proved to be one of the most serious challenges to the mufti's bid for leadership, it was mainly this challenge which precipitated the party's decline. Despite its vibrant contribution to Palestinian political life, the Istiqlal Party remained a kind of élitist organization with limited mass support.[152] Its birth from the womb of the Arab congress project was ultimately to determine its fate.

Decline of the congress project

In September 1932, Faysal paid a visit to Amman where he met the Istiqlalist leaders of Palestine, joined by Daghir, Riyad al-Sulh and 'Adil al-'Azma. With an apparent sense of urgency, Faysal requested that the Syrian–Iraqi union be "the principal item on the congress agenda".[153] Faysal's move to disclose his plan was perhaps motivated by recent developments in Syria. A few months earlier, Syria elected its second House of Representatives after the dissolution of the first upon disagreement with the French High Commissioner over the draft constitution. The new assembly sat in June amid increasing signs of an approaching round of negotiations for a Franco-Syrian treaty. Yasin al-Hashimi travelled to Damascus in a second attempt to enlist Syrian nationalist support for the union project,[154] returning with a full view of the Syrians' strong feeling for independence. He, however, refrained from criticizing the Syrian National Bloc and called for a balanced approach to the Syrian question, in which the Arab priority should be the strengthening of the Bloc's position *vis-à-vis* the French government.[155] Al-Hashimi's independent mind and his suspicion of Faysal's qualities of leadership led him to develop his own approach to the issues of Arab unity.

The question of Syrian–Iraqi unity had been under discussion within Arabist circles even before the Amman meeting with Faysal. Rida, Arslan and many Palestinian Arabists were obviously supportive.[156] With a pragmatic view of the Arab situation, they found a convergence between the Arab national interests and the king's personal ambitions. Others, including a wide range of Syrian Arab nationalists, disagreed.[157] The opposition camp was hardened by the Saudi stand, following the revolt of Ibn Rifada in the autumn of 1932. Ibn Rifada, a north Arabian Bedouin chieftain, led an insurgency against the Saudi government that took some bloody confrontations to be suppressed. Although Faysal had nothing to do with Ibn Rifada, Amir Abdullah was widely believed to be his main backer.[158] Abdullah's involvement infuriated the whole Arab-Islamic scene and awakened Saudi fears of a Hashemite Fertile

Crescent closing in on their northern borders. Answering a letter concerning the proposed Arab congress, Ibn Sa'ud reminded Nabih al-'Azma that the Arabs had first to censure the conspirators who encouraged Ibn Rifada to revolt.[159] While still seemingly committed to Arab unity, the Saudi monarch refrained from extending his approval to the holding of the congress in Baghdad.

Since many in the Arab-Islamic movement could not afford a rift with the Saudis, it was agreed that a delegation, headed by Shaykh Kamil al-Qassab, would be dispatched to Saudi Arabia in order to allay the Saudi objections.[160] At the same time, 'Adil Arslan, a strong supporter of holding the congress in Baghdad, arrived in Jerusalem in November 1932 in an attempt to win over the sceptics amongst his Arabist comrades. Proceeding to Baghdad, Arslan made a public statement in which he attacked opponents of the congress project, especially "those entertaining personal animosity towards Baghdad".[161] A month later, al-Hashimi embarked on another journey to Cairo, Jerusalem and Damascus. In Cairo he continued deliberations with Rida and met with al-Nahhas Pasha.[162] Due to the recent departure of 'Azzam and al-Basil from the Wafd, al-Hashimi sought to ensure the Wafd's representation in the congress. In Damascus, al-Hashimi was again confronted with solid Syrian opposition to the union idea, as well as to the holding of the congress in Baghdad.[163] The Saudi objection, coupled with the Syrian nationalist disapproval of Faysal, seemed for the moment to be insurmountable. The return of al-Qassab from his mission in Saudi Arabia brought no good news either.[164]

Political memoirs of the Arab Istiqlalists, as well as some recent studies of the period, have stressed the Saudi role in impeding the Arab congress project.[165] Important and powerful as it was, the Saudi opposition did not seem to have stopped preparations for the congress, which were still in full swing several weeks after the return of al-Qassab from Saudi Arabia. The Syrian executive in Cairo (Rida and Daghir) informed the congress's Jerusalem committee on 28 March 1933 that an agreement had finally been reached with the Baghdad committee for holding the congress in the Iraqi capital during the coming autumn.[166] Significant changes were also beginning to develop on the Syrian nationalist side. Under the influence of Rida, Nabih al-'Azma declared his support for the congress and was followed by Faris al-Khuri. Even Jamil Mardam, the staunch believer in republican and independent Syria, would relent to the strengthening unionist trend, amid the renewed popular opposition to the draft proposal of the Franco-Syrian treaty. In June 1933, Mardam led a delegation to meet Faysal in Amman, which carried a mass petition entrusting the king to represent Syria in the international forums.[167] In contrast with the evolving favourable climate, it was Faysal who was beginning to display signs of indifference. Faysal's apparent withdrawal, coupled with the sudden resignation of al-Hashimi from the Baghdad committee in May, sealed the fate of the congress project.[168] Quite apart from the Saudi role in undermining the congress idea, its decline must be seen from a different perspective.

The question of Arab unity in the interwar period was as pertinent to British policy as it was to Arab interests. For the majority of Arab activists and politicians at the time, Arab unity meant primarily unity of the Arab countries east of Suez. Britain was, of course, the dominant power in most of the area extending from Egypt to the Arabian sea. In the aftermath of the Sharifian defeat in the Hijaz, the question of Arab unity all but disappeared from British concerns in the Middle East. Faysal's attempt in 1929 to link the Palestinian question to Arab unity confronted the British with the whole legacy of their World War I diplomacy.

British officials did see some merits in Faysal's proposal for solving the Palestinian problem in a wider framework of an Arab union.[169] However, the lack of clarity that enveloped London's view of the ultimate form of the JNH, and the increasing strategic importance of Palestine, led to the rejection of Faysal's proposal. Yet, when Faysal's chances of regaining Syria looked more plausible in 1931, the British government took the issue seriously and dealt with it with the utmost care. A Syrian–Iraqi union under one monarch was seen by the Foreign Office as detrimental to British interests in Iraq.[170] Officials of the Foreign Office believed that the best deal available to the Syrians was conditional independence on the lines of the Anglo-Iraqi treaty, leaving Syria politically and culturally linked with France. A union under such circumstances would thus lead to a direct French–British conflict of interest. Since the union would oblige Faysal to reside half of the year in Syria, the union would possibly result in the neglect of Iraqi affairs. Unable to foresee the impact of oil on the Iraqi economy, the Foreign Office predicted that more "virile" (a term that was to be used, less than two years later, to describe the Iraqis) Syrians would gradually overwhelm the less developed Iraqis, and that this would be followed by French influence.

The same issue was then discussed by the Standing Official Sub-Committee on the Middle East of the Committee of Imperial Defence during its meeting of 20 October 1931. The Middle East Affairs Sub-Committee reached similar conclusions to those of the Foreign Office, recommending that Britain should support the establishment of a Syrian republic, ruled by a Syrian president. However, should the crown of Syria be offered to the ex-king, Ali (not Faysal), no grounds existed for opposing the candidature.[171] These recommendations were subsequently endorsed by the Standing Ministerial Sub-Committee for Questions Concerning the Middle East of the Committee of Imperial Defence on 17 November. Although Sir Francis Humphrys, the British ambassador in Baghdad, would have been informed of his government's views on the Iraqi–Syrian union, never were these views communicated to the principal Arab players at the scene.

Faysal of the early 1930s was a king divided between ambitions and aspirations on the one hand, and the calamities of his career in Arab politics on the other. During the 1920s, he developed a twofold approach to his position in occupied Iraq as the obedient ally of the British and the supporter of Iraqi nationalists at the same time.[172] Iraq was, of course, granted a kind of independence after the signing of the 1930 treaty, but not much was changed in terms of British influence in the country. In vital military, strategic and foreign policy spheres, Iraq was still tightly linked to Britain through several provisions of the treaty. British influence in Iraq was still too powerful to be ignored or to be openly challenged by Faysal. He died suddenly in September 1933 and to the very end Faysal never abandoned his dual role of obedient follower and ambitious pan-Arabist.

In September 1932, Nuri al-Sa'id, unaware of the tightly defined British position, sought to reopen the discussion over Faysal's 1929 proposal for Arab unity. During an unofficial conversation at the Colonial Office, Nuri outlined a scheme for an Arab confederation embracing Iraq, Syria, Transjordan, Palestine and the Hijaz.[173] Faysal envisioned, in Nuri's words, a gradually developed confederation, starting with an Iraqi–Syrian union and culminating after twenty years in an Arab–Jewish settlement, whereby both the Palestinian Arabs and Jews would be satisfied with the existence of the JNH on the corner of the Arab confederation. British interests in Palestine would be safeguarded by a treaty similar to the Anglo-Iraqi treaty. This was certainly a more detailed version of the Iraqi Arabist line of thinking, in which the British were again faced with the association between Arab unity and the Palestinian question. Yet, since Nuri's presentation was unofficial, the British were not bound to give a prompt response.

By the end of the year, Faysal was confident of holding the Arab congress in Baghdad in the spring of 1933. He had earlier secured the organizers' agreement to place the Iraqi–Syrian union on the congress's agenda, and a successful visit to Iraq by Amir Faysal of Saudi Arabia gave him reason not to be inhibited by Saudi objections. What was left to attain was the British agreement. Towards this end, Faysal approached Sir Francis Humphrys during a meeting on 20 December 1932. Faysal presented his case for the congress in terms of the pressing reality of a "growing movement among the Arab intelligentsia towards a closer union among all Arab people, and for the future strategic needs of Iraq, being overshadowed by powerful neighbours".[174] Humphrys' response, on the other hand, was subtle and intricate. He could see the implications of holding a pan-Arab congress in Baghdad, but chose not to offend the king by directly rejecting his plan. Instead, he implicitly invoked the Anglo-Iraqi treaty and advised the king to transfer the congress to Mecca, or to restrict it to a cultural and economic agenda. If it were held in Baghdad, Humphrys pointed out, "the Iraqi government would necessarily become responsible if anything were said or done to give offence to their neighbours". This was only the beginning.

In the course of the British deliberations of the matter, Sir Percy Lorraine, High Commissioner in Egypt, wrote to Lancelot Oliphant, assistant under-secretary at the Foreign Office, summarizing opinions of the principal concerned British officials in the Middle East.[175] According to Lorraine, Humphrys was not happy about the idea of holding the congress in Baghdad, but felt it was not for him to take up a definitely hostile attitude towards it. Wauchope, the High Commissioner in Palestine, was more decisive, as indeed was the Colonial Office. Lorraine further noted that a successful issue of the pan-Arab congress movement would be detrimental to British positions throughout the Middle East. In a particular mention of Egypt, he explained, with a sense of relief, that King Fu'ad, as well as Sidqi, "would no doubt be anti-Arab congress as they were anti-Islamic congress". 'Azzam and al-Basil were no longer in the Wafd proper, while "Egyptian extremism" was at that moment "ill-prepared" to challenge the government and go all the way in fighting for the congress.

British concerns about the Arab congress were perhaps divided into three major categories: first, concerns about the prospect of regenerating the Arab movement for unity, which might entail disturbing the status quo in the region; second, concerns about the disagreeable question of Iraqi–Syrian union; and finally, concerns about the future of the JNH and the Zionist position in Palestine. Faysal did recognize the sensitivity of the JNH issue to the British, and attempted therefore to impress Humphrys with what the congress could achieve in terms of alleviating Arab fears once the Palestinian leaders had been received in Iraq with British blessings. But the Zionist role in the congress affair was more than Faysal could handle. At the end of January 1933, as the holding of the congress looked imminent, Professor Brodetsky of the London Zionist Executive called on Mr Williams at the Colonial Office. Referring to attacks made on Zionism during the General Islamic Congress, Brodetsky raised questions regarding the British response in the event of a similar situation arising at the projected Arab congress.[176] In the light of Zionist influence in London, Brodetsky's representation was received with wide attention, leading to exchanges of correspondence between the Colonial Office and Foreign Office, Humphrys in Baghdad and J. H. Hall, chief secretary of the Palestine government.[177] Humphrys' convincing words eventually assured the Zionists that the British government would not tolerate any attempt by members of the Arab congress to stir up racial antagonism in Palestine, and that the congress would be restricted to cultural and economic issues in any case.

Humphrys was not given a specific direction from London about how to deal with the congress project. Matters were left to his good sense, his understanding of British policies and interests, and his experience in handling Faysal and Iraqi affairs. His subtlety and skill, contrasted with Faysal's divided inner self, proved to be highly successful. During a meeting between the two on 2 January 1933, Faysal apologetically attempted to convince the ambassador that holding the congress in Baghdad would make the Arab leaders realize that "co-operation with England was the only method whereby they could achieve the freedom and unity to which they aspired".[178] But Humphrys was far from being impressed with the king's deplorable reasoning. He referred to his earlier warnings, indicating the serious consequences for Iraq if the congress were "to indulge in abusive polemics about the position of the Arabs in either Syria or Palestine".

Towards the end of February, as pressure on Faysal mounted, Colonial Office officials, as well as their men in Palestine, were becoming deeply apprehensive about the prospect of the congress's transfer to Jerusalem. Although Wauchope was deeply hostile to the Istiqlalists and to the congress regardless of its venue, he also believed that its effect would be worse and more far-reaching in Palestine than in any other country. Though it was not yet admitted in London, Palestine was increasingly appearing as the key to the British position in the whole area. Wauchope's views were subsequently augmented with other arguments in London, prompting G. W. Rendel, head of the Foreign Office Eastern Department, to recommend that Humphrys should discourage the holding of the congress altogether.[179] What was absent from Rendel's assessment was the simple fact that if the congress were not held in Baghdad, it was most unlikely to be transferred to Jerusalem. The project of the Arab congress, in its new agenda, required an anchorage, and Baghdad was at the time its natural one. A vision of Arab unity, unleashed by an Iraqi–Syrian union, that would encompass the Arab East and contain the Zionist challenge, was not possible without the involvement of the Iraqi state.

Faysal, finally relenting to Humphrys' pressure, told him sometime in early March 1933 that he had carefully studied his warning and decided that the congress should be postponed to the autumn.[180] In September, Faysal died prematurely, leaving the Arab congress project to another time and place. Faysal, however, had made a reluctant enquiry about the prevailing British views concerning Arab unity. To this, Humphrys replied that the issue could be discussed when the king arrived in London in the summer, while in a quick response Rendel remarked that the British attitudes towards the idea of Arab unity certainly had changed since 1921. While the Hashemites were the only serious candidates for sovereignty over the Arab countries during the war, many others had emerged in the following decade. But as the question of Arab unity had not been properly addressed by the British government since the termination of the Anglo-Hijazi negotiations in the early 1920s, Rendel took the initiative to prepare a detailed memorandum on the "Attitudes of His Majesty's Government towards the question of Arab unity".

In this important document that was to set the limits for the British official political thinking towards Arab unity for more than a decade, British positivism was in full display. Highly efficient, but rather detached from considerations of history and lacking the vision necessary to discern the forces evolving in the Arab world, Rendel argued against the very existence of one Arab nation. Arab unity, in Rendel's view, seemed a phrase of extreme vagueness.[181] It might be akin to pan-Arabism but had no more practical significance than the shadowy pan-Islamic movement. Surviving members of the Hashemite family who were unwilling to abandon Sharif Husayn's dream of a united Arab state were overtaken by developments in the Arabian Peninsula, Syria and Palestine. (What is obvious here is Rendel's employment of post-World War I realities to justify his thesis of the impracticability of Arab unity. Entirely missing was the fact that the new system was originally imposed by the imperialist powers, not freely elected by the peoples of the area.) The impracticality thesis was then taken to its logical conclusions. Rendel unequivocally ruled out any possibility of including Palestine in a united Arab entity, since Britain was precluded "from allowing Palestine to be absorbed in any way in any kind of predominantly Arab union, if only in view of their [the British] deep commitment to the policy of the Jewish national home". Saudi Arabia was also excluded because the concept of unity was presupposed to be Hashemite-linked rather than pan-Arab. Transjordan, on the other hand, was to all intents and purposes unfit to be released from the mandate. Yet, if underdevelopment of Transjordan was the reason for its exclusion, Rendel regarded Syria as more developed then Iraq (indicating, however, that the Syrians were less virile than the Iraqis!) and that an Iraqi–Syrian union would thereby generate a conflict of interests between Britain and France. Rendel seemed to imply – without good reason – that an Iraqi–Syrian union would lead to Syrian domination of Iraqi affairs.

Rendel then moved to the second pillar of his thesis, declaring that even if dynastic and political obstacles were surmounted the possibility of achieving Arab unity would still be doubtful. The reasoning behind this ultimate judgement was that "notwithstanding its apparent homogeneity and compactness, there is no geographical unity in Arabia . . . any idea of unity or confederation based on ordinary European conceptions which such words suggest seems hopelessly inapplicable to an area of this type." In conclusion, Rendel stressed that only from the point of view of general cooperation and understanding, of cultural development, and of economic prosperity, could Britain view with general sympathy any movement which tended to bring the peoples of Arab countries into closer and more friendly relations with each other. To this end, if the question was raised during Faysal's visit to London, British attitudes towards Arab unity must be explained in general terms.

Despite purporting to formulate an objective analysis, Rendel's memorandum was in fact about why Britain should object to the emergence of a united Arab state rather than about why Arab unity was impractical. Real obstacles did, of course, exist, but the British negative attitude towards Arab unity was largely a reflection of what seemed to be an absolute belief that a united Arab state was a threat to British interests in the region, as well as of the deep British commitment to the JNH policy. So entrenched was this outlook that Whitehall continued to view projects of Arab unity with suspicion even when presented by Arab leaders of long-standing loyalty to Britain. The Arab aspirations for unity would later gain the support of some distinguished orientalists and Arabists in London, most notable amongst whom was H. A. R. Gibb, and sometimes even of official figures. Their efforts to render Arab unity acceptable to Whitehall would make little difference to British official policy. Not even the obvious links between responding to Arab aspirations and preserving the British position in the Middle East were seriously considered in London. Until the founding of the Arab League, and even beyond, the British government would adhere to the basic assumptions of Rendel's memorandum.

NOTES

1 The French authorities not only excluded Faysal from Damascus, but also declared death sentences on several dozen Arab activists and Damascus government functionaries (Darwaza, 1984–6: vol. 2, 217).

2 Darwaza, ibid., vol. 2; Qadri, 1956; Mousa, 1970: ch. 8.

3 Darwaza (1984–6: vol. 2, 112–13) is the most reliable source. See also Qadri, 1956:115–16; Qassimiyya, 1982:66–7.

4 Qassimiyya, ibid.,; Darwaza (1949–51: vol. 1, 86–7, and 1984–6: vol. 2, 115) lists the most important new members.

5 Scott to FO, 10 September 1920, FO 371/12237/5040.

6 Darwaza, 1949–51: vol. 1, 86.
7 Darwaza (1984–6: vol. 2, 72) explicitly confirmed this fact, which was also implicitly mentioned by Qadri, 1956:117. Khoury (1983:84), drawing on Porath (1974: vol. 1, 77), identified the club as independent from al-Fatat, dominated by Palestinian members, and dedicated to anti-Zionist activities. The confusion over the real identity of the club has apparently arisen from the presence of the Palestinians shaykh, Abd al-Qadir al-Muzaffar, and Salim Abd al-Rahman, at the head of the Damascus branch. Abd al-Rahman was, in fact, an active member of al-Fatat. The Nablus branch was established by Dr Hafiz Kan'an, a founder of al-Fatat, while the Husayni-led Jerusalem branch was, according to Darwaza (ibid., 25), financed and directed by Kan'an.
8 The following analysis of the Cairo Arabist group's divisions draws, with some modification, on Khoury's (1981:441–69) illuminating paper.
9 A memorandum by Rashid Rida, 12 February 1915, FO 882/2/AP/15/2; Mark Sykes (Cairo) to Major General Calwell (London), 14 July 1915, FO 371/2490/108253; Rashid Rida, Cairo, to Ibrahim Bey (Dimitry), Khartoum, 25 and 28 February 1916, Wingate Papers, 136/2/92 and 136/2/104 respectively (I. Dimitry was an agent for Sir R. Wingate); Ronald Storrs to G. Clayton, 5 December 1915, FO 882/15/PNA/15/10.
10 *Al-Manar*, vol. 20, 1918, 285; vol. 22, 1921, 447–8; vol. 24, 1923, 607. See also Tauber, 1995:107–21.
11 Darwaza, 1984–6: vol. 2, 130.
12 *Al-Qibla*, 14 May 1917.
13 The seven were: Rafiq al-'Azm; Kamil al-Qassab; Mukhtar al-Sulh; Abd al-Rahman al-Shahbandar; Khalid al-Hakim; Fawzi al-Bakri, and Hasan Hamada. Hogarth's reply to the seven was delivered on 21 June 1918. (Details of this episode in the Arab–British entanglement are published in Cmd. 5964, London 1939.)
14 *Al-Manar*, vol. 21, 1919, 202–3.
15 Khoury, 1981:445.
16 Darwaza, 1984–6: vol. 2, 131.
17 Cf. Porath, 1974: vol. 1, 77–8; Khoury, 1983:82–6.
18 Darwaza, 1984–6: vol. 2, 70, 89, 90–2, 115, 132, 136, 139.
19 The most detached accounts of the last months of the Damascus government are in Tibawi, 1978:387–406; Qasimiyya, 1982:171–211 and Khoury, 1983:89–93.
20 Darwaza, 1984–6: vol. 2, 196.
21 "Faysal, in a moment of temper, said to the delegates 'who are you? I created Syria.' Rida promptly retorted 'did you really create Syria? Syria had existed long before you were born' " (Qasimiyya, 1982:202).
22 Darwaza, 1984–6: vol. 2, 99.
23 Ibid., 215.
24 On the Cairo conference in which Churchill drew up the new map of the British Middle East see the *Times*, 26 March 1921. See also Kleiman, 1970:105–38.
25 Al-Zirikli, 1925:9–28.
26 Ibid., 108.
27 Ibid., 187–90.
28 Jarvis, 1946:107–9. A copy of a letter from Amman administrative governor, dated 21 August 1924, considering Nabih al-'Azma and 'Adil Arslan as *persona non grata*, is in al-'Azma Papers, Palestine files, 1/4 (University of Exeter Library).

29 'Arif al-'Arif, Amman Diaries (St Antony's College Middle East Centre, University of Oxford), and al-Zirikli, 1925, are examples of the Arabists' indictment of Abdullah's rule in Jordan during the 1920s. He was depicted as tempestuous, mean, and subdued to British officials, senior and junior. For a more objective approach, but with essentially similar conclusions, see Wilson, 1987.

30 Yusuf Yasin was born in Ladhiqiyya and studied at Rida's School of al-Da'wa wal-Irshad in Cairo before the outbreak of the war (al-Zirikli, 1989: vol. 8, 253). He was introduced to Ibn Sa'ud by al-Quwwatli, the urbane and soft-mannered Syria Arabist, who was admired and trusted by the Saudi monarch (Arab Personalities, al-'Azma Papers, Syrian files, no. 2; Darwaza, 1984–6: vol. 2, 84).

31 Al-Hayat, 10 January 1970; al-Khatib, 1978:1–2; al-Zirikli, 1989: vol. 5, 28.

32 Al-Manar, vol. 20, 1918, 280–8; vol. 26, 1925, 454–77.

33 Al-Hayat, 23 August 1974; Qasimiyya, 1974:150–63; al-Zirikli, 1989: vol. 6, 310.

34 During a meeting of the Palestinian Arab Executive on 26 October 1923, al-Tahir called for a general revolt against the British as the only means of attaining Palestinian rights (Monthly Political Report of October 1923, Samuel to Devonshire, 16 November 1923, CO 733/51/57864). On the establishment of the Palestinian Committee of Cairo and its relations with the Syrian community in Egypt, see Department of Public Security (Cairo) to HC (Palestine), 39 May 1921, FO 141/585/13089.

35 Cleveland, 1985:60–1.

36 Khoury, 1981:445–7. A Marxist analysis of al-Shahbandar's life and ideas was published by Hanna (1989), while al-Shahbandar's memoirs were published in Beirut in 1967.

37 Details of the congress workings were published in al-Mu'tamar al-Suri al-Filastini, Misr, Matba'at al-Manar, 1922. A recent study of the congress is Mouton, 1979:313–28.

38 Porath, 1974: vol. 1, 116–22.

39 Minutes of the Palestinian delegation's eighth meeting, Hotel Cecil, London, 9 August 1920, Zu'aytir Papers, A/129.

40 Telegram from Kazim al-Husayni, Hotel Cecil, London, to the Palestinian delegation, Geneva, 10 September 1921, Zu'aytir Papers, ibid.

41 Al-Karmil, 5 July 1922.

42 Caplan, 1983: vol. 1, 58–60.

43 The most illuminating biography of Arslan is of Cleveland, 1985. Another short study of his life and politics is in Khoury, 1981:447–8. Arslan's autobiography was published in 1969.

44 Arslan, 1937:153–6. For an example of Arslan's anti-Decentralization Party's activities see Arslan, 1913.

45 Arslan, 1937:160.

46 Ibid., 340; Khoury, 1981:448.

47 Al-Zirikli, 1989: vol. 1, 301.

48 For different views of the Syrian revolt see: Miller, 1977:545–63; Burke III, 1973:175–86; al-Mu'alim, 1988:185–98.

49 Al-Shura, 26 November 1925; Nwayhid, 1981:354.

50 Al-Karmil, 7 November 1925; Nwayhid, 1981:354; Khoury, 1981:458–60.

51 Al-Shahbandar to Hajj Amin Effendi al-Husayni, 16 August 1927, Nazih

al-Mu'ayyad al-'Azm Papers, no. 196, Centre for National Historical Documents, Special Section, Damascus.

52 See, for example, accusations directed at al-Quwwatli in an undated leaflet, ibid. no. 302; al-Shahbandar to Hasan al-Hakim, 22 April 1927, Abd al-Rahman al-Shahbandar Papers, 10/26, Centre for National Historical Documents, Special Section, Damascus; Khoury, 1981:406–11.

53 *Filastin*, 22 July and 26 August 1927; Porath, 1974: vol. 1, 203; Jbara, 1985:69. The mufti on his part offered to finance the Syrian Arabist activities if they split with Lutfallah (Arslan, 1937:466–73).

54 On the Anglo-Hijazi negotiations of the early 1920s and their impact on the Palestinian view of Sharif Husayn, see Porath, 1972:20–48; Mousa, 1978:183–94.

55 Caplan, 1983: vol. 1, 51–4 and vol. 2, 11–14; Wilson, 1987:103–5.

56 *Filastin*, 13 February 1923.

57 In 1922, Abdullah and Raghib al-Nashashibi were the only prominent Arabs to attend Samuel's swearing-in ceremony as HC of Palestine (Deeds to Shuckburgh, 15 September 1922, CO 733/38/48206/151).

58 'Arif al-'Arif, Amman Diaries, entry of 9 December 1926.

59 See, for example: Chejne, 1957; Sayigh, 1959; Safran, 1961; 'Amara, 1967; Mustafa, 1973; Abd al-Rahman, 1980; Jankowski, 1981; Coury, 1982; Ramadan, n.d.

60 Gershoni and Jankowski, 1986:270–4.

61 Kedourie (1970:213–35) attributed the rise of the Arab interwar movement, as well as Egypt's embrace of Arabism, to pro-Arab British officials and to King Faruq's dynastic ambitions. While Kedourie's theme is also embraced by Mayer (1983), the latter explained Egypt's involvement with Palestine in terms of political rivalry and intrigue within the ranks of the Egyptian political élite.

62 On the origins and politics of the Egyptian National Party see Goldschmidt, 1968:308–33.

63 In another meeting, the king was reportedly lukewarm to the mufti's offers of rallying Palestinian support to Fu'ad's Caliphate claim (Chancellor to Shuckburgh, 15 May 1929, CO 733/173/3/26).

64 Mayer, 1984:285–6.

65 Ali Abd al-Raziq, writing in *al-Siyasa* (30 October 1922), saw the Caliphate question as a game in the hands of foreign powers.

66 Kramer, 1982:121–36.

67 See, for example: *al-Siyasa*, 10 and 30 August and 3 and 23 September 1923; 13 January and 3, 12 and 18 November 1926; 16 August 1927.

68 Ibid., 18 May 1927.

69 Ibid., 30 June 1928; Tignor, 1977:161–81; Coury, 1982:459–79; Ramadan, n. d.: 344.

70 *Al-Siyasa*, 1, 7 and 28 September 1929; 24 June 1930.

71 *Al-Balagh*, 6 and 8 November 1925; Sayigh, 1959:190. 'Azzam's Arab-Islamic credentials were impeccable. He was a member of the National Party during the war years, participated in the Ottoman war effort and joined the Libyan anti-British and anti-Italian fronts. Returning to Egypt, he joined the Wafd where he emerged as a vocal pan-Islamist and Arabist (Coury, Ph.D. dissertation,

1984:134–325; 'Arif, 1977:39–246). 'Azzam became a frequent contributor to the Egyptian Arab Islamic press such as *al-Balagh*, *Kawkab al-Sharq* and *al-Fath* (see, for example, his famous article "al-'Arab Ummat al-Mustaqbal" or "The Arabs, a nation of the future", *al-Fath*, 8 October 1932; also al-Tahir's tribute to him in *al-Shura*, 20 October 1927).

72 *Al-Balagh*, launched on 28 January 1923, was edited by Abd al-Qadir Hamza. It continued as a pro-Wafdi paper until 1932 and was known for its manifest interest in Arab and Islamic affairs (al-Jundi, 1962:261). *Kawkab al-Sharq* was a daily evening paper which appeared on 12 September 1924. It maintained its support for the Wafd until it ceased publication in 1939. Edited by Ahmad Hafiz 'Awad, a veteran journalist who worked with Shaykh Ali Yusuf at *al-Mu'ayyad*, it established a special section for Eastern affairs, covering Arab and Islamic events. One of its many Arab-Islamist contributors was Shakib Arslan (al-Jundi, ibid., 279–87).

73 *Kawkab al-Sharq*, 14 December 1924; 4 and 22 May and 8 October 1925; 12 August 1926; 7 December 1929; *al-Balagh*, 22 November, 3 December 1926; 9 January, 21 August 1927; 22 January, 14 March 1928; 9 April, 20 May, 9, 11 and 16 September 1929.

74 On the founding of the Eastern Bond Society see Department of Public Security to The Residency, 25 February 1922, FO 141/585/13089; *al-Hilal*, vol. 30, March 1922, 569–70; *al-Manar*, vol. 26, 1925–6, 220–2; *al-Rabita al-Sharqiyya*, October 1928, 3–11; Shafiq, n.d.: vol. 3, 217–333.

75 *Al-Fath*, 17 May 1928.

76 See, for example, Shaykh al-Bakri, writing in *al-Rabita al-Sharqiyya* (February 1929, 1–11) of Egypt's language, culture, history, customs, religion and race that determine its identity as Eastern; and Prince 'Umar Tusun, writing in *al-Hilal* (vol. 38, July 1930, 1037) of "East is East and West is West".

77 Writing in *al-Fath* (7 February 1929), Hasan al-Banna spoke of an "original Eastern road" which leads to "greatness and revival". He attacked imitation of Europe, and called for a thoughtful and "original" modernization in agreement with the Eastern spirit.

78 Haykal, 1951: vol. 1, 104.

79 *Al-Siyasa*, 14 October 1932.

80 *Al-Manar*, vol. 27, 1926–7, 715–18; vol. 29, 1929, 718–20.

81 Shafiq, n.d.: vol. 3, 305–7.

82 *Al-Rabita al-Sharqiyya*, October 1928.

83 Ibid., December 1929 and April and July 1930.

84 *Al-Siyasa*, 2 and 9 August 1930; 'Alluba, 1964:37.

85 *Kawkab al-Sharq*, 31 October 1925; *al-Rabita al-Sharqiyya*, October and December 1928, and February 1929.

86 Qasimiyya (ed.), 1991:38, 186–8.

87 The most detailed account of the founding and early activities of the YMMS is in Kampffmeyer, 1932:101–70. See also *al-Manar*, vol. 28, 1927, 788–92.

88 Director of Special Section, Public Security Department, 21 December 1921, FO 141/650/232. See also Abbas Hilmi II Papers, file 120 (University of Durham Library).

89 Kampffmeyer, 1932:103–4.

90 Ibid., 136.
91 Ibid., 109–12.
92 *Al-Jami'a al-'Arabiyya*, 24 and 26 April 1928.
93 The constitution of the YMMS Nablus branch is included in Kayyali (ed.), 1988:101–11.
94 Nwayhid, 1981:226; al-Hout, 1986:160.
95 Al-Hout, ibid., 861–4.
96 Kampffmeyer, 1932:113, 118, 128; Arslan, 1937:574–6 and 591–3.
97 Kampffmeyer, ibid., 122–3; *Majallat al-Shubban al-Muslimin*, no. 1, October 1929, 73–9; no. 2, November 1929, 211–13 and 224.
98 Sayigh, 1959:198.
99 On the early history of al-Ikhwan al-Muslimin and its founder see al-Banna, n.d: 1–145. This book, *Mudhakkirat al-Da'wa wal-Da'iyya*, was originally published in Beirut in 1951, based apparently on papers left by al-Banna, covering his early life and the organization's history until 1933. For the following period, reports from the Ikhwan's various organs were used. The reference here is to the Cairo edition, published by Dar al-Tawzi' wal-Nashr al-Islamiyya, most probably in 1986, although numerous other editions had appeared in Cairo before that. Other sources on the Ikhwan's early history include Husaini, 1956:1–38 and Mitchell, 1969:1–11.
100 Al-Banna, ibid., 145, 155 and 160–1.
101 Ibid., 57–9 ff.
102 Ibid., 39, 59 and 67.
103 Ibid., 82.
104 Ibid., 159–1.
105 *Jaridat al-Ikhwan al-Muslimin*, 8 and 22 Dhu al-Qa'da, AH 1352 (1933).
106 Al-Banna's address to the fifth congress of the Muslim Brotherhood in 1938, in al-Banna, 1979:115–53, especially 145–6. This address is perhaps one of the most important documents of al-Banna's heritage, in which he outlined a matured vision of Islam, politics, Arabism, etc.
107 *Al-Fath*, 24 January 1929.
108 Gibb, 1935:107; Darwaza, 1949–51: vol. 3, 87; Nwayhid, 1981:159–60, Zu'aytir Diaries, *al-Hayat*, 20 July 1994 (it is the latter which specify the exact date of the meeting).
109 The draft covenant was quietly published in *al-Karmil*, 27 January 1932. A copy with 55 signatures is in al-'Azma Papers, Palestine files, 22/A.
110 Nwayhid, 1993:159–60; Zu'aytir, *al-Hayat*, 20 July 1994.
111 High Commissioner to Secretary of State for Colonies, 24 December 1931, FO 371/16009/E753.
112 Extract from Port Police Report, Port Said, No. COMP 1(2), 14 February 1931, FO 141/763/495; R. H. Hoare to FO, 27 February 1931, FO 141/763/495; CID-Palestine, report on the pan-Islamic Arab revolutionary movement, 21 May 1931, CO 733/204/87156; CO to FO, 11 June 1931, FO 371/ 15282/E1205.
113 Arslan, 1937:610; Husry, 1975:324.
114 Note of an interview between the mufti and the High Commissioner on 17 December 1931, FO 371/16009/E87; High Commissioner to Secretary of State for Colonies, 24 December 1931, FO 371/16009/E753.
115 Text is in al-Tha'alibi, 1988: 295–7.

116 This view is clearly expressed in the political memoirs of several Palestinian Istiqlalists. See, for example: Darwaza, 1949–51: vol. 3, 90–103; idem 1984–6: vol. 2, 31; Nwayhid, 1993:164–9; Zu'aytir, *al-Hayat*, 21 June 1994.

117 A copy, dated 26 February 1932, is in al-'Azma Papers, Palestine files, 5/43.

118 Arslan, 1937:645.

119 Rida to Arslan, 30 June 1932, ibid., 655.

120 Probably Nabih al-'Azma to the Executive Committee of the Arab Congress, 16 February 1932, al-'Azma Papers, Palestine files, 5/42; Arslan, 1937:645.

121 Memorandum on the proposed Arab Congress, Lorraine to Oliphant, 20 January 1933, FO 371/16854/E955.

122 Daghir to Nabih al-'Azma, 8 and 11 April 1932, al-'Azma Papers, Palestine files, 4/155 and 4/157 respectively; Rida to al-'Azma *et al.*, 15 April 1932, ibid., 5/47; Rida to Arslan, 2 May 1932 (Arslan, 1937:649–51).

123 Sa'id Thabit to Nabih al-'Azma, 10 March, 1932, al-'Azma Papers, Palestine files, 4/154.

124 Daghir to al-'Azma, 8 April 1932, al-'Azma Papers, Palestine files, 4/155.

125 It was the wish of Thabit and al-Hashimi to include Abu al-Timman (Thabit to al-'Azma, 13 April 1932, ibid., 4/158). On Abu al-Timman's political life and his association with al-Hashimi, see al-Swaydi, 1987:113–15.

126 Basri, 1987:94–103; al-Swaydi, 1987:71–82. The most comprehensive studies of al-Hashimi's life and political career are: Marr, Ph.D. dissertation, 1967 and al-Qaysi, 1975, 2 vols.

127 Al-A'zami, 1931–4: vol. 4, 99–100; Faydi, 1952:121–5; Qadri, 1956:46.

128 Al-Qaysi, 1975: vol. 1, 50–4.

129 Ibid.

130 Basri, 1987:95.

131 Rendel to Young, 2 November 1932, FO 371/16011/E5752.

132 Record of conservation between King Feisal and Sir John Simon, 22 June 1933, FO 371/16855/E3828; Note of conversation with Sir Humphrys, 13 July 1933, FO 371/16855/E6221.

133 Feisal to Young, 8 December 1929, FO 371/14485/E444.

134 Sir Humphrys to Sir John Simon, 17 January 1933, FO 371/16854/E347; Rida to al-'Azma, 17 April 1932, al-'Azma Papers, Palestine files, 5/44 and 45; Arslan, 1937: 639, 641–2.

135 Arslan to Rida, 17 Rabi' al-Thani AH 1350 (in Sharabasi, 1963: vol. 2, 782–90).

136 Rida to Arslan, 28 October 1931, 21 January 1932 and 24 and 29 March 1932 (Arslan, 1937:628–49); Rida to al-'Azma, 19 February and 15 April 1932, al-'Azma Papers, Arab files, 8/411 and 5/47 respectively.

137 Rida to al-'Azma, 19 February and 6 May 1932, al-'Azma Papers, Arab files, 8/411 and 5/46; Daghir to al-'Azma, 11 April and 3 May 1932, ibid. Palestine files, 4/157 and Arab files, 4/159 respectively. Sharabasi, 1963:788; al-Hashimi, 1967: vol. 1, 358.

138 Lapierre, 1936:133–4; al-Hakim, 1983:214.

139 Rida to al-'Azma, 26 June 1932, al-'Azma Papers, Arab files, 8/413; Lorraine to Oliphant, 20 January 1933, FO 371/16854/E955; Arslan, 1937:665–6.

140 "List of the principle members of the Istiqlal Party in the East", Appendix to Lorraine to Oliphant, 20 January 1933, FO 371/16854/E955. 'Azzam was

originally a member of the December 1931 committee, while Hamid al-Basil was suggested by Daghir (Daghir to al-'Azma, 1 October 1932, al-'Azma Papers, Palestine files, 5/57). Daghir, in fact, sought to involve more Egyptians, even those known for their support for King Fu'ad, in order to avoid eliciting Egyptian official opposition similar to their opposition to the Islamic Congress.

141 See, for example, Subhi al-Khadra's article "Britain is the origin of the disease and head of the affliction", *al-Jami'a al-'Arabiyya*, 13 August 1930.

142 Darwaza, 1949–51: vol. 3, 92–9; Kayyali, 1978:171–2.

143 Darwaza, ibid., 109–10; al-Hout, 1986:270; Nwayhid, 1993:167–8.

144 Subhi al-Khadra to Nabih al-'Azma, 5 July 1932, al-'Azma Papers, Palestine files, 5/50; Zu'aytir, *al-Hayat*, 21 June 1994.

145 On the stormy life of Nabih al-'Azma see High Commissioner to H. F. Downie, 5 December 1933, CO 733/248/22; Qasimiyya (ed.), 1991:17–154; Nwayhid, 1993:46, 71, 156, 161,175 and 232.

146 *Hizb al-Istiqlal al-'Arabi: Bayanuh wa Qanunuh, al-Quds al-Sharif* (Jerusalem), Matba'at al-'Arab, 1932. Darwaza, 1949–51: vol. 3, 104; Zu'aytir, *al-Hayat*, 21 June 1994. The party was declared in July, but the government's official permission was not issued until 13 August 1932.

147 An early draft of the party's principles, found in al-'Azma Papers (Palestine files, 3/18), included rejection of the Balfour Declaration. The omission of this item from the official statement was perhaps calculated to facilitate the issuing of the official permit.

148 A British assessment of both is in High Commissioner to Downie, 5 December 1933, CO 733/248/22. See also Nwayhid, 1981:150, and 280–3.

149 The other two founders were Fahmi al-'Abbushi and Dr Salim Salam. At a later stage, both Hamdi al-Husayni and Harbi al-Aiyubi joined the leading group of the party (Darwaza, 1949–51: vol. 3, 105). for a vivid description of the Istiqlalist group see Nwayhid, 1993:175–9 and *passim*.

150 Al-Hout, 1986:271.

151 Rida to Arslan, 20 July 1932 (in Arslan, 1937:678–80); Sa'id Thabit to al-'Azma, 11 September 1932, al-'Azma Papers, Arab files, 4/167; Darwaza, 1949–51: vol. 3, 110. For the Istiqlalist attack on the Palestinian *a'yan* politics see *al-'Arab* (the Istiqlalist mouthpiece, edited by 'Ajaj Nwayhid), 27 August, 17 and 30 September 1932.

152 According to al-Hout (1986:271), the party's membership did not exceed 60 persons, most of whom were of the Palestinian intelligentsia. The other important factor in the party's decline might have been the interruption of Iraqi financial aid following the death of Faysal. On the Iraqi financing of Istiqlalist activities, see al-'Umar (1983:508–9), quoting Iraqi consulate papers.

153 Lorraine to Oliphant, 20 January 1933, FO 371/16854/E955.

154 Husry, 1975:327.

155 Yasin al-Hashimi to Nabih al-'Azma, 8 May 1932, al-'Azma Papers, Arab files, 8/441.

156 Rida to Arslan, 2 May 1932 (in Arslan, 1937:653–4).

157 In addition to leaders of the National Bloc, Nabih al-'Azma was also doubtful about Faysal's leadership abilities (al-'Azma to Yasin al-Hashimi, 20 September 1932, al-'Azma Papers, Palestine files, 5/55).

158 Sa'id Thabit to al-'Azma, 11 and 18 September 1932, al-'Azma Papers, Arab files,

4/167 and 4/169 respectively; Intelligence Report by L. F. Pendred, 22 October 1932, FO 371/16017/E6355; Arslan, 1937: 671, 680–1.

159 Abd al-'Aziz bin Abd al-Rahman al-Faysal (King Ibn Sa'ud) to Nabih al-'Azma 28 September 1932, al-'Azma Papers, Arab files, 3/134.

160 Al-Quwwatli to Nabih al-'Azma, 13 September 1932; al-Qassab to al-'Azma, 10 October 1932; Riyad al-Sulh to al-'Azma, 15 October 1932, al-'Azma Papers, Palestine files, 5/52, Syrian files 3/75, and Palestine files 5/60 respectively.

161 A translation of an interview that took place between Emir Adil Arslan and a correspondent of a Baghdad newspaper, 8 December 1932, enclosed in Ambassador (Baghdad) to High Commissioner (Cairo), 22 December 1932, FO 141/768/1190.

162 Lorraine to Oliphant, 20 January 1933, FO 371/16854/E955; Arslan, 1937:693.

163 Al-Hashimi to al-'Azma, 16 December 1932, al-'Azma Papers, Arab files, 168 (no file number), al-Quwwatli to Nabih al-'Azma, ibid. appendix to Palestine files, 1/72.

164 Rida to Arslan, 2 February 1933 (Arslan, 1937:695–8).

165 Porath, 1986:16–20; Nwayhid, 1993:160–1. Cf. Darwaza, 1949–51: vol. 3, 3 and 8–9.

166 Rida to Arslan, 28 March 1933 (Arslan, 1937:702).

167 British Consulate (Beirut) to FO, 27 May 1933, FO 371/16976/E2965; Damascus Consulate to FO, 7 June 1933, FO 371/16976/E3195.

168 Darwaza, 1949–51: vol. 3, 88; Rida to Arslan, 25 May 1933 (Arslan, 1937:708).

169 Passfield to Humphrys, 22 January 1930; FO 371/14485/E 444.

170 See notes by head of Middle East Department, assistant foreign under-secretary, and permanent under-secretary, 29 and 30 September 1931, FO 371/15364/E4784.

171 ME (O) 11th meeting, 20 October 1931, CAB 51/2 (quoted in Husry, 1975:330, and in Porath, 1986:200).

172 Basri, 1987:15–22; al-Swaydi, 1987:19–25.

173 Husry, 1975:331–2.

174 Humphrys to Simon, 21 December 1932, FO 371/16011/E6888 (a copy in FO 141/768/1190).

175 Lorraine to Oliphant, 20 January 1933, FO 371/16854/E955.

176 K. W. Baxter to J. H. Hall, 28 January 1933, FO 371/16854/E578.

177 Hall to Baxter, 31 January 1933, ibid.; Humphrys to FO, 14 February 1933, FO 371/16854/E905.

178 Humphrys to Oliphant, 23 January 1933, FO 371/16854/E773. A third conversation on the subject, on 2 February, followed a similar course (Humphrys to Simon, 13 February 1933, FO 371/16854/E863).

179 Arthur Wauchope to Sir Philip Cunliffe-Lister, 1 March 1933; Williams (The Colonial Office) to foreign under-secretary, 22 March 1933; CO to FO, 24 March 1933; minute by Hall, 29 March 1933; minute by G. W. Rendel, 29 March 1933, FO 371/16854/E1544. Also, CO to FO, 24 February 1933, ibid. E 1084.

180 Humphrys to FO, 9 March 1933, and minute by Rendel, FO 371/16854/E1469.

181 Attitude of His Majesty's Government towards question of Arab unity – Discussing meaning of phrase "Arab unity" and attitudes of His Majesty's Government on matter, Foreign Office Memorandum (Mr Rendel), 27 March 1933, FO 371/16854/E1732.

5

The 1936–9 revolt and the Arabization of the Palestinian question: phase 1

The 1936–9 revolt is one of the most important landmarks of modern Palestinian history. Its long, convoluted and violent course as well as its involvement of wide segments of society were instrumental in shaping the Palestinian national consciousness. The revolt, moreover, created an unprecedented opportunity for the Palestinian struggle and the Arab movement to converge and interact as never before. If Arabization of the Palestinian question reached its first climax in the late 1940s, it was the 1936–9 revolt which had laid the foundations. Yet, the revolt revealed many features of the strength, weakness, complexity and fragility of both the Palestinian national movement and the Arab project for unity. This chapter and the following one will attempt to reconstruct the Arab responses to the revolt and study the impact it left on the interwar Arab-Islamic movement.

In considering the evolving interaction between the Arab movement and the Palestinian struggle, it is crucial that the regional and international realities of the post-World War I situation are not overlooked. Understanding the Arab inter-state rivalries, as well as the Anglo-French influence in the Arab East, is essential for establishing a sensible analysis of the period. However, since the conflicting interests of the Arab states have been repeatedly underscored in recent scholarship, it will be the purpose of this study to differentiate between two levels of Arab involvement in Palestine – the state level and the unofficial, popular level. Two other important qualifications have also to be made. The first is that, by the mid-1930s, pan-Islamism as was manifested in the 1920s (i.e. the search for the Caliphate) was largely non-existent. Though Islamic solidarity was still invoked and employed the only viable political enterprise in the Arab East was the idea of Arab unity. The second is that this chapter will be limited to the political ramifications of the revolt, for it was mainly against the background of these ramifications that the Palestinian–Arab interaction was to develop. This should not, however, be seen in any way as an underestimation of the military, or the socio-economic, impact of this intractable and resounding episode of modern Palestinian history.

The strike

The incident that unleashed the first stage of the 1936–9 revolt occurred on the evening of 15 April 1936, when a Palestinian armed band intercepted several cars travelling between Bal'a and 'Anabta in the Tulkaram region, killing one Jewish passenger and seriously injuring two others.[1] In a reprisal, Jewish settlers from the northern colony of Petah Tikva killed two Arab farmers on the following night while they were sleeping in their hut. Several other Jewish assaults and Jewish–Arab clashes ensued, especially as rumours spread of the killing of more Arabs after the funeral of the first murdered Jew on 17 April. The government's first response was to impose a curfew on Tel-Aviv and Jaffa, where most of the clashes were reported, and to declare a state of emergency throughout Palestine. The progression of events, however, proved that the situation was uncontainable.

A tense atmosphere had engulfed the country ever since the killing of the rebel leader Shaykh Izz al-Din al-Qassam and his companions by the British forces in November 1935.[2] Aware of the rising tension in Palestine, the British government authorized the High Commissioner to make an announcement resurrecting the protracted affair of the Legislative Council.[3] But confronted with Jewish rejection in Palestine, Zionist pressure in London, and other objections from the pro-mufti Palestine Arab Party, the Legislative Council's proposal was once again struck down.[4] While the Palestinians would not consider a scheme that did not take their demographic superiority into account, the Zionists feared a British concession to the Palestinians. All that remained of the High Commissioner's plans for offsetting the political tension was to invite a Palestinian delegation to London to resume discussions on the issue. This invitation would similarly soon be overtaken by events.

The precarious situation in Palestine was also echoing developments in neighbouring Arab countries, especially in Egypt and Syria.[5] Week-long anti-British demonstrations in Cairo in November 1935 led to the restoration of the constitution, and the resumption of negotiations between Egypt and Britain for a treaty of independence. In Syria, agitation by the National Bloc developed into the declaration of a national strike that lasted for fifty days during January and February 1936. A Syrian delegation was invited to Paris to begin discussions on a treaty along the lines of the Anglo-Iraqi treaty. The Palestinians were not only watching the developments in Syria, but also became actively involved in supporting the Syrian movement.[6] For many Palestinians, Syria's edging towards independence awakened hopes of a restoration of the Arab state and reversal of the Arab misfortunes. More important, perhaps, was the subtle growing belief in the power of the masses.

The first response to the Jewish attacks and Jewish–Arab clashes in Jaffa came from Nablus, where Ahmad al-Shak'a and Akram Zu'aytir took the initiative to organize a local nationalist meeting on 19 April. Participants in the Nablus meeting included local notables and activists of various inclinations: the mayor, Sulayman Tuqan (a pro-Nashashibi notable), Abd al-Latif Salah (the leader of the National Bloc Party), the young Arab nationalists, Wasif Kamal and Akram Zu'aytir, the local notable, Ahmad al-Shak'a, and a few others.[7] Intent on turning Nablus into a centre for the new wave of the national movement, the meeting decided to establish a local national committee (lajna qawmiyya), declared a general strike in Nablus and called for other Palestinian cities to follow suit. A demand for the termination of Jewish immigration to Palestine was to serve as the litmus test for the British attitude towards Palestine. By 23 April, national committees had already been established in most of the major Palestinian cities, and a Palestinian national strike was in effect implemented.[8]

The spontaneity with which the movement for national disobedience developed in the wake of the Jaffa clashes was a testimony to the depth of the frustration of the Palestinians and the degree of their politicization. Yet, it was not until the end of the first week of the strike that a national leadership was formed to lead the movement. Upon the arrival of a Haifan delegation (led by Rashid al-Hajj Ibrahim) in Jerusalem, speedy negotiations were launched with the mufti, Raghib al-Nashashibi, and Husayn al-Khalidi, the mayor of Jerusalem, which aimed at establishing a national leading body.[9] The main thrust of the Haifan group's proposal was to give the overall leadership to the mufti in a committee that would include leaders of the six major political parties. The mufti, fearing a quick disintegration of such an inherently divided leadership, did not accept the offer until the Istiqlalists pledged their full support to him.[10] Bringing Raghib al-Nashashibi to join a national committee under the leadership of Hajj Amin al-Husayni was not an easy task, though it was finally achieved.[11] On 25 April, the Higher Arab Committee (HAC) was, consequently, established. It consisted of Hajj Amin al-Husayni as president, the Istiqlalist leader 'Awni Abd al-Hadi as secretary, and Jamal al-Husayni, Husayn al-Khalidi, Ya'qub al-Ghusayn, Raghib al-Nashashibi, and Abd al-Latif Salah (all party leaders) as members. Alfred Rock, a supporter of the Husaynis, and Ya'qub Farraj, a supporter of the Nashashibis, represented the Palestinian Catholic and Orthodox Christians. Ahmad Hilmi Abd al-Baqi, though known for his sympathies with the Istiqlalists, was considered a representative of non-partisan political opinion.[12] However precarious, national unity behind the strike was thus secured.

The first major political action taken by the HAC was to call for a congress of the local national committees to be held in Jerusalem on 7 May 1936. A few days before the congress convened, 150 personalities of the district of Jerusalem distributed a statement in which they openly urged the adoption of civil disobedience against the British authorities.[13] Non-cooperation with the government and abstention from paying taxes were seen as the first step towards the escalation of the Palestinian protest and giving teeth to the general strike. Coming from a wide range of personalities, and not from the HAC, the call indicated that the people were more radical in their response to British policies and more defiant to the British authorities than their leaders in the HAC. In this atmosphere, when the congress of the national committees was convened (with 150 participants), the call for the people to stop paying taxes was upheld.[14] The stopping of tax payments was to start on 15 May 1936, pending a change in British policy towards Palestine, especially with regard to Jewish immigration. The congress also decided to continue the strike as well as to boycott the Jews. Complete Palestinian independence within a framework of Arab unity was declared as the ultimate aim of the strike.

At this early stage of the general strike, there were two main developments which need to be highlighted. The first was that the mufti, who seemed in the first days of the strike to be overtaken by events and unsure of their significance or of his own role in their course,[15] had now moved a noticeable distance towards a more radical position. In his speech to the national committees, the mufti neither endorsed a military struggle nor formulated a specific programme for the general strike. However, grounding his argument in the historical experience of Arab–British relations, he was emphatic in condemning Britain's unfulfilled promises to the Arabs in general and to the Palestinians in particular.[16] Calling for a "steadfastness and holding out to the end", he never lost sight of the strategic imperative of soliciting Arab and Muslim support.[17] Against the increasing radicalization of the Palestinian masses and the emerging national consensus, the mufti perhaps reckoned that the general strike would prove to be a defining moment in the Palestinian struggle. This does not mean, however, that the mufti reached a point of rupture with the British government. The second important development was the high regard in which the Palestinians held the HAC. The implication of this development for the future was that the HAC would evolve into a centre of power, holding and extending legitimacy after it itself had been legitimized by the early national consensus of the revolt.

The 1936 general strike was a manifold phenomenon. Since it lasted from April until October, a period of plenty in the Palestinian villages, the fellahin were able to provide for the armed groups scattered over the northern and central hills. In contrast, city dwellers, including merchants, government employees, and labourers, were to feel the impact of the strike rather quickly. In the major Palestinian urban centres, the strike was to cause considerable stagnation of the economy, trade and employment growth.

The first service group to join the strike was the Association of Car Owners and Drivers, after a meeting of its leading committee in Jerusalem on 24 April;[18] this was followed by the entire labour force of Jaffa port.[19] In Haifa, however, the government succeeded in maintaining the port's activity, with the help of the pro-Zionist Palestinian mayor, Hasan Shukri.[20] The few Arab dockers who opted to leave their positions were replaced with British soldiers, Jews, or Arab workers from the southern Syrian Huran region. From the outset, calls for government Arab officials and employees to join the strike were strident.[21] While these calls were met with disdain by the mufti (who was also president of the SMC, an official body) as well as by Husayn Fakhri al-Khalidi (mayor of Jerusalem since 1934), they were, ironically, encouraged by the leaders of the opposition, Raghib al-Nashashibi and his supporter, Hasan Sidqi al-Dajani.[22] Using his influence in the HAC, the mufti succeeded in sparing the government employees. Instead of striking, high-ranking officials were to submit a memorandum to the High Commissioner, protesting the harsh British measures and backing the national demand for the cessation of Jewish immigration.[23] Government officials were also expected to donate at least one-tenth of their salaries to the national fund for sustaining the needy strikers' families. It was another gesture on the part of the mufti to keep the confrontation with the mandate authority within certain limits.

After the mayors had been banned by the government from meeting in Jaffa, they convened secretly in the house of the mayor of Ramallah on 31 May. The most radical anti-strike mayor, the Haifan, Hasan Shukri, did not attend. Under pressure from the Nashashibi camp, only the mayors of Nablus, Ramlah, Hebron, Tulkarem, Lydda, and Jaffa decided to declare the strike of their municipalities. Workers in water, electricity, and rubbish collection services were excluded. Meanwhile, the majority of village mukhtars (head of villages), who were also regarded as government officials, declared their resignation.[24]

The mufti, unable to forsake his power base in the SMC, walked a thin line between popular pressure and his perception of his own interests and those of the nation. On 11 June, he closed down the main offices of the SMC in Jerusalem, but left many of its premises in the rest of the country functioning, including the *Shari'a* courts, the *waqf* administrative offices, and services of the central relief committees.[25] The mufti's attempt to chart a middle course between the British authorities and the Palestinian radical calls for revolt was very much in evidence during the first two or three months of the strike. Although he was thoroughly convinced that the Zionist scheme would never be able to materialize without the backing of Britain,[26] he perhaps still believed in the possibility of bringing about a change in British policy. His background, his position, and his realization of the utter imbalance of power, had all contributed to his clinging to the last strands of hope in dealings with the British government. On 24 April, only one day before he assumed the leadership of the HAC, the mufti assured the High Commissioner that the Friday sermon at al-Aqsa mosque would be moderate. Subsequently, he not only kept his word but also instructed his aides to quell young radicals' calls for protests.[27] The Palestinian political circles that primarily identified with the spirit of the masses were mainly the Istiqlalists and the Nashashibist cynics. The latter, in particular, were motivated by a wild desire to embarrass the mufti. Not surprisingly, the first group of political activists to be detained in late May 1936 included the Istiqlalist, Akram Zu'aytir, Shaykh Sabri 'Abdin, the militant *alim* from Hebron, and the Nashashibist, Hasan Sidqi al-Dajani.[28] It was not until June that a member of the HAC was detained, namely the Istiqlalist leader, 'Awni Abd al-Hadi.[29]

The mufti's circumscribed style of leadership during the first few months of the revolt did not, however, preclude him from using religio-political means to further the Palestinian national cause. Either in response to increasing pressure emanating from his own constituency, or in the hope of effecting a change in British policy, the mufti encouraged protests from religious circles and the ulema. On 1 June, a delegation of ulema and *Shari'a* court judges presented the High Commissioner with a memorandum protesting incidents in which British soldiers violated the sanctity of Muslim women and desecrated the Qur'an.[30] Another protest from the ulema was staged in mid-July.[31] The mufti himself, in an exchange of letters with the High Commissioner on 22 June wrote: "[the SMC] believe that the principal motive which moved the Jews to think of making of Palestine a national home for them is a religious one".[32] Pointing to Zionist threats to the Islamic holy places in Jerusalem, the mufti requested that London respect Muslim religious feelings. Yet, all in all, the mufti's moves were still largely measured and reserved.

In the harsh midsummer of 1936, while the general strike was looming large and the political solution was still looking as far off as ever, the mufti's position seemed to change. His anti-British attitudes became more manifest and his close aides began establishing relations with armed groups. In September 1936, the High Commissioner wrote of the mufti: "There are many factors that weigh with that astute mind but his chief fear is to be left alone in the open, liable to be accused by friend and foe of treachery to the Arab cause."[33] Two major factors seem to have contributed to changing the mufti's approach. First, and contrary to Porath's explanation, was the mufti's realization that the Arab governments' support was not solid enough to counterbalance the uncompromising British stance.[34] This point will be dealt with later. Second was the gloomy impact of the punitive British measures. For the mufti and many of his Palestinian colleagues, notables and students of the Arab-Islamic reform movement, Britain was still perceived in terms of the just and civilized West. In the course of the revolt, this perception was shattered.

Following the established traditions of the British colonial adminis-tration, the mandate government confronted the revolt with both a carrot and a stick. In the Palestinian case, however, the carrot was not particularly sweet and the stick was too heavy. Immediately upon the onset of the strike on 19 April, the government invoked the Palestine Defence Order-in-Council and declared the Emergency Regulations.[35] The extraordinary powers granted to the authorities by this step were further expanded on 22 May and 1 June. The security forces were granted almost absolute freedom to deal with the populace in terms of individual or collective punishment. Widely enforced and extended curfews, blowing up of houses sheltering rebels, and the passing of prison sentences for the mere possession of a weapon (five years for possessing a pistol containing twelve bullets and two years for a knife), all became common measures.[36] Attacks on railways or telephone lines were punished with life imprisonment, while powers to order the detention of persons in internment camps for up to a year were granted to the police as well as the army. Whenever necessary, schools, churches and mosques were used as detention centres.[37] In the British 1936 annual report of the Palestine mandate to the League of Nations, a clear reference was made to "the establishment of a concentration camp by Government".[38]

Homes were destroyed in the cities of Lydda, Hebron, Nablus, Safad, Majdal, Baithlahm, Qalqilia, Khan-Unis, and in 35 villages. In other cases, collective fines were imposed on 250 villages.[39] The most flagrant abuse of power occurred between 19 and 30 June 1936 in the old quarter of Jaffa city, where 237 houses inhabited by 450 families were destroyed.[40] The principal reason for this measure was to facilitate the movement of military patrols in the narrow alleys of the old city. In a case related to this episode, the chief justice, Sir Michael McDonnell passed a judgment in favour of the government, though he duly criticized official policies dealing with the revolt. McDonnell's recurrent attempts to ascertain the superiority and independence of the judiciary would ultimately cost him his post, as the colonial secretary induced the cabinet to force his retirement.[41] It is true that until the end of the strike not a single death sentence was passed; however, the number of Palestinians killed without being involved in "terrorist acts" was still markedly high.[42]

In an analytical memorandum written a decade later, the British authorities in Palestine vindicated the treatment of the Palestinians during the revolt in a novel discourse of colonial anthropology! The memorandum stated that "To combat the mass insurgency which characterized the Arab disturbance the Palestine Government was driven to adopt the principle of collective responsibility and to make use of collective penalties. The principle of collective responsibility was one to which the Arab community had been accustomed from ancient times."[43] Whatever the British justification was, the impact of the anti-strike measures was to be felt drastically by the Palestinians in general, and the mufti in particular. Witnessing the destruction and suffering during his travels in the country, the mufti was astounded with what he called the "cruelty of the English".[44] The harshness of British policies and the radicalization of the attitude of both the mufti and the HAC notwithstanding, both sides left channels of communications open. Taking into consideration the rapidly changing climate of world politics, the British sought a quick end to the strike, political or otherwise, that would not compel them to give substantial concessions to the Palestinians. The latter, on the other hand, assumed that their only chance of defeating the Zionist project was by reaching a political understanding with the British. To bring such an agreement into being, other means of pressure were to be employed, namely Arab and Muslim power.

Arab-Islamic response

From its early days, the general strike generated a wave of moral Arab support. Prior to the establishment of the HAC, the Istiqlalist, Akram Zuʻaytir, received a telegram of solidarity from his Syrian counterpart Shukri al-Quwwatli.[45] Similar responses followed from other Syrian and Iraqi leaders.[46] By the beginning of May, there were increasing signs of a more organized Palestinian effort to enlist popular and official Arab and Islamic backing. In India, an Islamic conference, led by the reformist *alim*, Sulayman al-Nadwi, was held between 29 June and 1 July, threatening a boycott of British goods and a campaign for civil disobedience unless the British policy in Palestine was changed.[47] In Tunisia, the local YMMS, encouraged by the elder Desturian, Shaykh Abd al-ʻAziz al-Thaʻalabi, established a Tunisian Committee for the Defence and Aid of Palestine.[48] Even in such a distant country as Morocco, the National Action Bloc spurred a series of popular protests against the British that would turn into Muslim–Jewish strife on some occasions.[49] Yet, it was mainly in Egypt and the Arab *mashriq* that the strike elicited the most powerful responses, for it was here that the Arab-Islamic networking was more extensive. The support that the Arab masses showed to the Palestinians was not always, if ever, matched by the ruling élite.

Egypt

Egypt of 1936, to which the Palestinians were keenly looking, was passing through a transitional period. The independence of Egypt was still formal rather than real. It was not until 26 August 1936 that an Egyptian–British treaty was signed by the Wafdi government (less than two months before the end of the strike), whereby Egypt gained a somewhat larger degree of freedom of action in its foreign affairs. But the influence of the Egyptian Arab-Islamic forces had been steadily growing in the preceding years. The Muslim Brothers' headquarters was transferred from Isma'iliyya to Cairo in October 1932, giving the organization wider exposure and an opportunity to influence national public opinion.[50] To this end, the Ikhwan began issuing a weekly organ, *Jaridat al-Ikhwan al-Muslimin,* in May 1933. Together with *al-Fath* of Muhib al-Din al-Khatib, *al-Manar* of Rashid Rida, *Majallat al-Hidaiya al-Islamiyya,* and *Majallat al-Shubban al-Muslimin* of the YMMS, the Ikhwan's weekly not only emphasized the Arab-Islamic identity and responsibility of Egypt, but also adopted the idea of Arab unity.[51]

In 1931, the journalist Amin Sa'id established in Cairo Jam'iyyat al-Rabita al-'Arabiyya (the Arab Bond Society), and in May 1936 it began publishing a journal, *al-Rabita al-'Arabiyya.*[52] Although Sa'id was a Syrian, his journal attracted a variety of Syrian and Egyptian Arabists and became an important source of news and analyses of Arab political events and trends. More influential was *al-Risala* of Ahmad Hasan al-Zayyat, which first appeared in January 1933 as a fortnightly journal, and was later turned into a weekly publication.[53] Al-Zayyat's career in Egypt as a liberal writer (strongly associated with Taha Husayn) was interrupted in 1929 when he accepted a teaching post in the Iraqi High School of Education.[54] After his return to Egypt, his writings began to reflect a distinct Arabist conviction based on a strong belief in Arab cultural and linguistic unity.

The deepening identification of Egypt with its Arab surrounding was by no means solely linked to the emergence of new political and intellectual forces, since even within the established political parties of the Wafd and the Liberal Constitutionalists, Arabism was making headway. Either as a result of the intensive Arab-Islamic activities in Egypt (i.e. of the increasing movement of ideas and people, and of economic imperatives), or of the strategic danger implicit in the Zionist encroachment on Palestine, many Egyptian politicians "began to perceive the possibility of a larger ensemble within which Egypt might take leadership and gain political advantage".[55] In 1933, another Egyptian political force was born, evolving subsequently to pose a serious challenge to the liberal establishment on the one side and the reformist Islamic organizations on the other. The founding of Misr al-Fatat (Young Egypt), first as a society and after 1937 as a political party, introduced to Egyptian public life a new political discourse blended with an intense sense of populism.[56] Deeply influenced by the rise of the European Fascist youth movements, Ahmad Husayn, leader of Young Egypt, created a fiery synthesis of Egyptian nationalism, Islamism and Arabism.

Radicalization of political life and the increasing appeal of Arabism made the Egyptian environment highly receptive to the demands of the Palestinian strike. Although Egypt was still occupied by the developments of the treaty negotiations with Britain, *al-Ahram* presented detailed daily coverage of the Palestinian strike.[57] With the Syrian Istiqlalist As'ad Daghir in charge of its foreign affairs desk, and the Istiqlalist 'Ajaj Nwayhid as its correspondent in Jerusalem, *al-Ahram* was well disposed towards the Palestinian national movement and anti-British. In contrast, *al-Muqattam*, the other influential daily, which had always maintained a pro-British line, refrained from publishing the statements of the Palestine Committee in Egypt. The Palestinian Arabist, Muhammad 'Ali al-Tahir, whose newspaper *al-Shura* had been closed by Sidqi's government, was presented with the licence of *al-shabab* (of the Egyptian Arabist, Mahmud 'Azmi) to re-publish.[58] *Al-Shabab* became subsequently an important source of information on Palestinian affairs throughout the revolt. Even *al-Risala*, which was mainly a journal of arts and literature, opened its pages for several supportive features on the Palestinian struggle.[59] This sympathetic attitude of the Egyptian media was reinforced by Palestinian activities in Cairo. One of the earliest arrivals in Egypt after the outbreak of the strike was the Christian Emile al-Ghuri, a close aide of the mufti. His visit to Cairo in mid-May included intensive contacts with Egyptian politicians, journalists, and ulema.[60] The mufti, who had an unwavering belief in the ultimate necessity of winning Egypt, wrote personally to

Egyptian journalists and editors, urging their support. At a certain stage, the prime minister, Mustafa al-Nahhas, anxious to bring the Egyptian–British negotiations to a successful conclusion, had to intervene with the proprietors of *al-Jihad*, *Kawkab al-Sharq*, and *al-Balagh*, in order to restrain and temper their coverage of the situation in Palestine.[61] A long-repressed Egyptian search for a wider and leading supranational role that would reflect Egypt's weight and history seemed to find in the Palestinian situation the most appropriate means of expression.

The YMMS and the Ikhwan spearheaded a far-reaching movement of popular protest, fund-raising and the establishment of support committees, that touched large sections of society. While the YMMS had maintained relations with Palestine since the end of the 1920s, the Ikhwan initiated their first contacts with the Palestinians in August 1935. Increasing self-confidence among the Ikhwan leaders prompted the dispatch of al-Banna's brother, Abd al-Rahman al-Banna, together with the Ikhwan's general secretary, Muhammad As'ad al-Hakim, to Palestine and Syria.[62] The mission was warmly received in Jerusalem by the mufti who subsequently provided the Ikhwani representatives with letters of introduction to Syrian ulema and to Jam'iyyat al-Hidaiya in Damascus. Upon their return to Egypt, the Ikhwan's weekly devoted several articles to the support of the Palestinians, with emphasis on the mufti's role and his dedication to Islam and his people.[63] Relations between the Ikhwan and the mufti would endure for decades to come and would consequently carry some serious implications for the political future of both sides. But whether for the Ikhwan or the YMMS, solidarity with the Palestinians was not only motivated by old relations and acquaintance with the Palestinian situation, but also by the search for legitimacy and the enforcement of this legitimacy in Egypt itself.

Only a few weeks after the outbreak of the Palestinian strike, Hasan al-Banna called on members of the Ikhwan to meet in the society's headquarters to discuss the situation in Palestine. Al-Banna spoke of the religious, linguistic, and Arab ties that united the Egyptians and the Palestinians, and proposed a four-point programme of action in support of the Palestinian struggle, including the formation of an aid- and fund-raising committee as well as the organization of a protest campaign aimed at the British representatives in Egypt and Palestine.[64] After the passing of the proposal, al-Banna wrote to Prince 'Umar Tusun, urging him to transfer unused funds from the Abyssinian aid campaign to the

Palestinians. Another appeal to the same effect was sent to the Coptic Patriarch.[65] The Ikhwani initiative was subsequently adopted by the YMMS which organized a large meeting of politicians and public figures of various political dispositions, at which a higher committee for aiding Palestine (al-Lajna al-'Uliya li-Ighathat Mankubi Filastin) was established. Abd al-Hamid Sa'id was elected president of the committee, and Hasan al-Banna, the Wafdi, Hamad al-Basil, Mahmud Basyuni, president of the Senate House and president of al-Rabita al-'Arabiyya Society, and the Liberal Constitutionalist leader, Muhammad Husayn Haykal, were members.[66]

The activities of the YMMS and the Ikhwan were augmented with similar undertakings by al-Hidaiya Society and the Ulema Solidarity Society.[67] By mid-June, the Egyptian Women's Union and students of al-Azhar and the Egyptian University entered the fray by organizing demonstrations and local support committees throughout Egypt, and sending letters of protests to the British embassy.[68] An indication of the effectiveness and high emotions that were aroused by such a campaign was an article written by Muhammad Husayn Haykal at the end of the strike, in which this highly cultured and respected figure of Egyptian political life responded to the critics of his radical approach to the Palestinian question by saying

> They [the critics] might believe that we rather break the pens that defend Palestine and other [countries] against England. Let them do that if they wish, as for me, I don't believe that a man who witnesses injustice and does not denounce it, is entitled to be a man.[69]

The rising pro-Palestinian sentiment in Egypt and the possibility of its turning into an anti-British movement were viewed with deep apprehension by the prime minister and the acting High Commissioner in Cairo, David Kelly.[70] Both men were invariably conscious of the sensitive stage through which British–Egyptian relations were passing and seemed equally keen to avoid any disruption of these relations. But reverberations from the Palestinian strike were too strong and widespread for al-Nahhas and Kelly to contain. Embraced by the Islamic mass organizations and their chapters nationwide, Palestine was no longer a limited concern of the Cairene politico-cultural dignitaries. Equally significant was the impact that the Palestinian question would leave on the political configuration of Egypt itself. While marking a turning-point in the course of the Palestinian conflict, the strike was introduced to Egypt at a moment of great change. In the mid-1930s, the Ikhwan began moving cautiously from their earlier adherence to a programme of a religio-cultural nature towards a more politicized mode, encouraged by the changing scene of Egyptian politics. As King Fu'ad entered the twilight of his reign, he was forced to bring Shaykh Muhammad Mustafa al-Maraghi back to al-Azhar's shaykhdom in April 1935.[71] This highly politicized Azhari and student of 'Abduh had for years been closely associated with 'Ali Mahir, the chief royal chamberlain at the time.[72] Both were highly ambitious men with grand visions, and not particularly keen on democratic systems.

Prior to his death in April 1936, Fu'ad appointed 'Ali Mahir as premier of a caretaker government to supervise the transition from the unconstitutional period to the holding of the first general elections since 1930. Indicating the future direction of his political alliances, 'Ali Mahir chose the Arab-Islamists Muhammad 'Ali 'Alluba and Abd al-Rahman 'Azzam respectively as minister of education and envoy extraordinary and minister plenipotentiary in Tehran and Baghdad.[73] Both had been out of partisan politics for several years, were close to the Mahir–Maraghi axis and were ardent supporters of the Palestinian cause. Hasan al-Banna had been close to this circle. When the family of the late Rashid Rida handed al-Manar over to the Ikhwani leader to resume its publication, it was al-Maraghi who wrote the prologue for the re-launch, praising the memory of his late friend Rashid Rida, as well as the new editor, Hasan al-Banna.[74] And since the idea of involvement in political life had matured within the Ikhwan, al-Banna opened a line of contact with 'Ali Mahir.[75] In contrast with the Wafd and the Liberal Constitutionalists, which were both natural competitors of the Ikhwan, Mahir had no political party and was thus less threatening as an ally. When Faruq (still a minor) replaced his father under the regency of Prince Muhammad 'Ali, the positions of Mahir and al-Maraghi were strengthened. Mahir emerged in the royal diwan as a counterbalance to al-Nahhas, following the latter's electoral triumph in May 1936, while Shaykh al-Azhar, who had been one of Faruq's mentors, became an important source of guidance for the young king.[76] The stage was thus set for the rise of Arab-Islamic forces in Egypt of the late 1930s.

The challenge posed by the radical populism of Young Egypt and the desire to acquire a similar Arab-Islamic prestige to that of the YMMS, were perhaps amongst the worldly motivations that attracted the Ikhwan to political activism and the Palestinian question. But, eventually, the three organizations would become equally associated with Mahir, the Palace, and Shaykh al-Azhar, especially after Mahir formed his second cabinet in 1939–40. The Palestinian strike of 1936 was the first occasion on which the Ikhwan emerged on to the political arena. Their highly successful performance made them worthy allies and emboldened their approach to what they came to see as their destined role. In June 1936, the Ikhwan protested al-Nahhas's public praise of Atatürk, and in August they called on him to implement the *Shari'a*.[77] Yet, this dialectical exchange between the espousal of the Palestinian cause and the internal political field of the Arab state was not limited to Egypt. Although in different versions and contexts, the Palestinian question and internal political concerns would become equally intertwined in Syria and in Iraq.

Syria

Syria of the 1930s was still directly ruled by the French mandate government, whose officials in Damascus were engaged in persistent attempts to perpetuate the mandate and preserve peace and tranquillity. The Syrian national movement was dominated by the National Bloc which did not take a distinct shape as a political organization until four years after its establishment in 1928. The National Bloc was, in essence, a loose confederation of urban notables, students of the Arab-Islamic reform movement and ex-functionaries of Faysal's government.[78] Having emerged in the wake of the defeat of the Syrian revolt, the National Bloc reflected a Syrian nationalist attitude towards the espousal of what Jamil Mardam called the policy of "honourable cooperation" with the French. But the moderation of the National Bloc and its compliance with the geo-political realities of the newly established regional entities was not universal.

In 1932, Hashim al-'Atasi, president of the National Bloc, attracted Shukri al-Quwwatli, the radical Damascene Istiqlalist and pan-Arabist, to the Bloc.[79] Al-Quwwatli was followed by many other Istiqlalists, a development that would soon reassert the pan-Arabist orientations of the Bloc and the Syrian national movement. After the death of Ibrahim Hananu (1869–1935), the most eminent of the Syrian leaders, al-Quwwatli, emerged as one of the three main figures at the National Bloc's helm. The other two were al-'Atasi, the elderly and accommodating president of the Bloc, and Jamil Mardam, the dynamic rival of the Istiqlalists. Soft-spoken, pragmatic, and highly practical, Mardam was the Syrian leader most favoured to negotiate with the French.[80] His skills in adapting to changing times and realities had been apparent from the early days of his involvement with the Arab movement. A member of al-Fatat and of the Paris Arab Congress, Mardam accepted the French invitation to propagate the Allies' cause against the Ottomans within the Arab immigrant communities of the Americas during World War I.[81] Yet, despite his strong Syrian nationalist and republican beliefs,[82] Mardam would also see the necessity of incorporating a pan-Arabist dimension in his political agenda.[83] Either as a means of asserting his position, or in a genuine response to the Arab political entanglement and interdependence, Mardam would sometimes rival even the radical Istiqlalists in his embrace of the pan-Arab cause.

In October 1934, the National Bloc supported a project proposed by Fakhri al-Barudi to establish the Bureau for National Propaganda (Maktab al-Di'aya wal-Nashr).[84] Later, al-Barudi's office was turned into the Arab Bureau for Research and Information (commonly known as the Arab Bureau, or al-Maktab al-'Arabi), employing a staff of sixteen full-time young Arabists. With a long history of involvement in the Arab movement and the Syrian anti-French resistance, al-Barudi succeeded in attracting the exiled Libyan leader Bashir al-Sa'dawi to the Bureau.[85] Widely connected with the Arab-Islamic circles worldwide, al-Sa'dawi helped to augment the Bureau's pan-Arabist outlook. Until its closure after the outbreak of World War II, the Arab Bureau was a vital centre of propaganda, coordination, and source materials for various Arab liberation movements, especially the Palestinian revolt.

Although cultural and socio-economic ties between Palestine and Syria were of ancient origin, they were reinforced under the Ottomans, as Damascus was the administrative capital of a large part of modern Palestine. The establishment of the Arab government in Damascus at the end of World War I marked a new stage in the Palestinians' view of their association with Syria. For several decades afterwards, the Palestinians in general, and the Istiqlalists in particular, were still speaking of Palestine and Syria in terms of Southern and Mother Syria.[86] Whether in the Syrian revolt of 1925–7, in the Western Wall dispute, in the Islamic Congress of Jerusalem, in support of the Palestinian drive for Arab unity in the early 1930s, or in the Qassami movement, the Palestinian–Syrian association was affirmed repeatedly. No single Arab figure would embody this association as much as Nabih al-'Azma whose involvement in the Palestinian struggle was as extensive as his involvement in Syrian affairs. In July 1936, the Palestinian detainees of Sarafand prison were unsurprisingly joined by al-'Azma, the second Syrian Istiqlalist after Sami al-Sarraj to be arrested for participating in the Palestinian strike.[87] In Syria itself, the strike generated a phenomenal reaction.

The movement between Damascus and Jerusalem intensified from January 1936, when widespread disturbances erupted in Syria and a general strike took place after years of French ambivalence towards the national movement. Solidly supported by the Palestinians, Syrian leaders would travel to Palestine to participate in rallies and fund-raising activities, as well as in order to further the Syrian cause internationally, since communications from Damascus were becoming increasingly difficult.[88] At the beginning of March, the French relented and a Syrian delegation, led by Hashim al-'Atasi and Jamil Mardam, was thus invited to Paris to negotiate a Franco-Syrian treaty.[89] After six months of negotiations, during which the Syrian leaders were keen to avoid committing any blunder that might jeopardize their chances, a treaty was initialled on 8 September 1930.[90] However, since Shukri al-Quwwatli was left in Syria to supervise the National Bloc, he and his radical pan-Arabist friends in the Nationalist Action League (NAL) ensured that the Palestinian strike received the full support of Syria.

Syrian anti-Zionist protests, letters, and petitions inundated the British Consulate in Damascus, the High Commission in Palestine as well as the League of Nations. Although many of the Syrian nationalist and Islamic organizations participated in this campaign, the Arab Bureau was the most active. On 24 and 25 April, only a few days after the beginning of the Palestinian strike, several Syrian cities went on strike too.[91] Al-Quwwatli issued a statement on behalf of the National Bloc calling on the Syrian people to contribute financially to the Palestinian effort.[92] Although the Syrians were still suffering from economic exhaustion after their fifty-day strike, they imposed a trade boycott on Palestinian Jewish products, and managed to send 4500 Syrian Lire during the first month of the strike (an amount which increased significantly in the following months).[93] Women were particularly active in demonstrations and in the fund-raising efforts, while members of the Islamic societies, especially Jam'iyyat al-Hidaiya, established a grass-roots network to collect wheat flour and other commodities.[94]

A Palestine Defence Committee, charged with coordinating the Syrian support, was first founded by Yusuf al-'Isa, a Palestinian Christian resident of Damascus and the editor of *'Alif Ba'*. After the return of Nabih al-'Azma to Syria (following the establishment of the first national government and the French amnesty), he reorganized the committee and turned it into a main centre of support for the Palestinians. To all intents and purposes, members of the committee were largely drawn from the radical Arabist circles of Damascus, the Arab Bureau, and the NAL.[95] As the strike progressed, veterans of the Syrian revolt, Islamic militants, and Arab-nationalists moved in significant numbers to Palestine, especially after the strike had developed into a violent and armed revolt. Smuggling of arms from Syria increased substantially, and Syrian experts in guerrilla warfare tactics and arms' manufacturing volunteered to train their Palestinian counterparts.[96]

Syria's strategic position in relation to Palestine, its response to the strike, and the increasing signs of its moving towards reaching an understanding with the French, precipitated deep apprehension within the ranks of the Zionist leadership and the Jewish Agency. In an attempt to contain the Syrian involvement in Palestine, leaders of the Zionist movement launched a fervent effort to accommodate the Syrian nationalists. From the end of May 1936, and for several ensuing months, Nahum Vilensky, director of the Zionist-owned Agence d'Orient, held several meetings with Abd al-Rahman al-Shahbandar, the Syrian leader and opponent of the National Bloc, as well as with Amin Sa'id, editor of *al-Rabita al-'Arabiyya*.[97] In Paris, while the Franco-Syrian negotiations were still under way, Chaim Weizmann held two meetings with the Syrians, one with Jamil Mardam and the second with the Istiqlalist, Riyad al-Sulh.[98] Mardam and al-Sulh, both consummate pragmatists, seemed to believe that the Zionists would use their influence on Leon Blum, the newly elected French prime minister (himself a Zionist Jew), to further the Syrian quest for independence. The expectations of both sides, however, failed to materialize. The Zionist moves culminated in a direct approach to the radical Arabists of the National Bloc, Shukri al-Quwwatli and Fakhri al-Barudi. In July and August 1936, Eliahu Epstein of the Jewish Agency Arab Affairs Department held three sessions with the Syrians, exploring avenues for bringing an end to the strike, and discussing the persistent question of the Arab political future and Zionism.[99]

None of these meetings bore fruit. During all the rounds of talks, and despite the differing Syrian attitudes, the negotiations stumbled on the two major blocks of the Arab–Zionist conflict: the termination of Jewish immigration to Palestine and the ending of Jewish acquisition of Palestinian land. At a defining moment during a July meeting, al-Barudi told Epstein that "not even the Prophet Muhammad, were he to rise from his grave, could convince the Arabs of Palestine to end their strike without the Jews agreeing to suspend immigration."[100] With regard to the Franco-Syrian negotiations, the Zionist leading circles concluded, despite initial disagreement, that the nationalist ascendance in Syria would further harden the Palestinian resistance to Zionism.[101] The Zionist representatives in Paris were, therefore, instructed to urge the French to limit Syrian independence.

In formulating their approach to the Palestinian question, the Syrian leaders had several considerations to weigh: first was, of course, their Arabist background and commitment; second was their aim of avoiding encroachment on Palestinian interests;[102] and third was the rising challenge of a younger breed of radical Arab nationalists and the newly emerging Islamic societies. The futility of the policy of "honourable cooperation" with the French, the deepening belief that the Arabs' salvation could be realized only through their unity, together with the moral and cultural impacts of the new age, prepared the ground for the evolution of new forces of Islamism and pan-Arabism. And here too, the Palestinian question became a powerful tributary factor in the process of political radicalization .

One of the first Islamic societies to be founded in Damascus was al-Jam'iyyat al-Gharra' in 1924. The principal force behind al-Gharra' was Shaykh Muhammad 'Ali al-Daghar (1877–1943), the son of a mercantile family and student of the Damascene reformist ulema Muhammad Jamal al-Din al-Qasimi and Badr al-Din al-Hasani.[103] Al-Gharra' embraced a cultural and educational programme, responding to French domination of Syrian education. In 1931, Jam'iyyat al-Hidaiya al-Islamiyya was also launched in Damascus by a group of ulema and Muslim moralists.[104] It was to this society that Amin al-Husayni introduced Hasan al-Banna's two emissaries in 1935. A more intellectually oriented organization was Jam'iyyat al-Tamaddun al-Islami, which appeared only a year after al-Hidaiya. Amongst its founders were the eminent reformists Shaykh Muhammad Bahjat al-Bitar, Shaykh Hasan al-Shatti and Ahmad Mazhar al-'Azma.[105] Jam'iyyat al-Tamaddun organized its own committee of support for the Palestinians in 1936. Similar Islamic societies, as well as several YMMS branches, were established during the same period in other Syrian cities, such as Aleppo's Dar al-Arqam of which the Syrian Islamist poet 'Umar Baha' al-Din al-Amiri was secretary-general. The Homs chapter of the YMMS adopted the name of Shabab Muhammad under the leadership of Abu al-Su'ud Abd al-Salam in 1934.[106] In 1945, a group of these societies came together and formed al-Ikhwan al-Muslimin of Syria,[107] for which Mustafa al-Siba'i of the Homs Shabab Muhammad became secretary-general and al-Amiri of Aleppo his deputy.

Like the Egyptian Ikhwan, these societies had rarely been involved in Syrian politics. Their entry into the political arena was the outcome of their wide involvement in the 1936 campaign of solidarity with Palestine.[108] Although their educational and cultural agenda was bound in the course of time to evolve into a political programme, it was the Palestinian strike which provided the first opportunity for this transformation. During the second phase of the Palestinian revolt, the Syrian Islamic societies became an important source of men, arms, and money for the Palestinians. Equally significant was the pressure they exerted on Jamil Mardam, the prime minister of the first nationalist government, not to restrict the freedom of the Palestinian activists and their supporters in 1937–8. Emboldened by their rising influence, the Islamic societies instigated the resignation of Jamil Mardam in 1939 over the French-proposed personal laws.[109]

The emergence of the NAL marked a turning-point in the progress of the Arab and Syrian nationalist movements in the 1930s. Established in the summer of 1933, only a year after the re-launch of the Arab Istiqlal Party in Jerusalem, the NAL was an ardently pan-Arabist organization, élitist and radically anti-imperialist, with critical views of the Syrian leadership and its approach to the questions of independence and Arab unity. The seeds of the NAL were first sown during a meeting in the autumn of 1929 in Geneva, when Farid Zayn al-Din (the young French-educated economist and Lebanese Druze), Darwish al-Miqdadi (the Palestinian graduate of the AUB and schoolteacher in Iraq), together with the Aleppine graduate of Berlin, Nafiʿ Chalabi, agreed to form a clandestine Arab-nationalist organization. Two versions of history give two different names for this organization, the Arab Liberation Society and the Arab Nationalist Bloc.[110] It seems, however, that both names were used, one for the overall organization and the other for its branch in Palestine. The main strategy of this group of young Arab nationalists was to penetrate and influence existing Arab parties and groups and form a series of frontal organizations to connect the Arab world with a network of dedicated nationalists. Following the Geneva meeting, Farid Zayn al-Din chaired a secret executive committee of the organization that consisted of Darwish al-Miqdadi, the Palestinian Arabist, Wasif Kamal, the Iraqi army officer of Syrian origin, Mahmud al-Hindi, along with the Syrians, Ahmad al-Sharabati, ʿUthman al-Sharabati, and ʿAli Abd al-Karim al-Dandashi.[111]

During those formative years, this group of young Arab nationalists had no major impact on the Arab movement. Their espousal of a more integrative, ideological and organizational outlook was, none the less, an indication of a deepening Arab crisis. Whether because of their social and cultural background, or their astounding defeat at the end of World War I, the early Arabists, even the most radical amongst them, formed their relations and their political positions on the basis of a loose and utilitarian process of socio-political compromise and negotiation. While they understood the organization of the pan-Arab movement in terms of non-binding congresses, committees, broad alliances and personal relationships, the apparent imbalance in power between the Arabs and the imperialist powers led the vast majority of them to see Arab unity as the step following, rather than preceding, national independence. For the emergent groups of young Arab nationalists, with their exclusive Western education and middle-class background, both approaches were unsatisfactory. If the Arabs were one nation, their unity should be reflected in a coherent political organization and a tightly defined political agenda. It was a vision of a new generation of Arab nationalists, the children of the failing Arab ideal, of the images of the French bombardment of Damascus, and of the British JNH policy in Palestine.

The Palestinian Arabist Wasif Kamal, whose name would frequently appear in the Palestinian and Arab-nationalist arena, was a prominent member of the newly emerging circles of Arab activists. Born in Nablus in 1907, he was educated in al-Najah National School and the AUB, and obtained a law degree from the University of London in 1930. His association with al-Miqdadi and Zayn al-Din was perhaps initiated in Europe, where the latter became widely known to the Arab students for his leading role in the Arab Student Society of Paris. After returning to Palestine, Wasif Kamal assumed a teaching post at al-Najah and threw himself into the midst of Palestine political life, without ever becoming a member of any of its main political parties.[112] Yet, in the highly charged political environment of Nablus, Wasif Kamal became a close associate of the Istiqlalists Akram Zu'aytir and 'Izzat Darwaza. When the Istiqlal Party was declared in 1932, Kamal and his fellow radical nationalists viewed it positively and worked to extend their network into its machinery.

What prompted the summer meeting of 1933 was the success of Zayn al-Din, al-Miqdadi, Kamal, and other core members of this clandestine organization, in attracting many young Arab nationalists in Palestine, Syria, Lebanon and Iraq. In addition to making links with the Istiqlal Party, they built strong ties with other Arabist organizations of a similar complexion. Among the early members in Palestine were Farid al-Sa'd, 'Izz al-Din al-Shawwa, Khlusi al-Khayri, Rashad al-Shawwa, Mamduh al-Sukhun, and Farid Ya'ish.[113] The Beirut cell included Fu'ad Mufarraj, Kazim al-Sulh, Taqii al-Din al-Sulh and 'Adil 'Usayran. In Syria, amongst others were Abd al-Razzaq al-Dandashi, George Tomah, Jubran Shamiyya, Sabri al-'Asali, Zaki al-Arsuzi, Fahmi al-Mahaiyri and Jalal al-Sayyid.[114] Strong contacts were also established with Shakib Arslan, Shukri al-Quwwatli, Fakhri al-Barudi, and Nabih al-'Azma, all of whom were regarded as uncompromising anti-imperialists, both inside and outside the National Bloc. It was in Iraq, however, where al-Miqdadi arranged a teaching job for Zayn al-Din in 1932, that the group invested some intensive effort. As a result, Siddiq Shanshal, Salim al-Na'imi, Yunis al-Sab'awi, Sadiq al-Bassam, Naji Ma'ruf, and the army officer, Salah al-Din al-Sabbagh, became at various stages associated with the network. Coextensively, Zayn al-Din, al-Miqdadi, and other Iraqi associates became involved in the founding of the pan-Arabist al-Muthanna Club.[115]

In the early summer of 1933, core members of the society concluded that their support and influence warranted the holding of a conference in which their vision of Arab unity and independence could be outlined in a political programme. The task of secretly preparing for the meeting was given to Abd al-Razzaq al-Dandashi, the Belgian-trained lawyer from Damascus[116] Attending this conference, which was held at a hotel owned by a Druze Lebanese family at Qarnaiyl on Mount Lebanon between 24 and 29 August, were approximately fifty participants, mainly from Syria, Lebanon, Palestine, and Iraq; some other Iraqi and Jordanian delegates failed to overcome difficulties of travel and visas. The Palestinians were represented by Wasif Kamal and the Istiqlalist, Akram Zu'aytir. Because the latter, as indeed many of the other participants, was unaware of the secretive core group that founded the Arab Liberation Society, his memoirs reflect the impression that the conference was organized solely to launch the NAL.[117]

The main themes of the debate at the meeting focused on Arab independence, sovereignty and unity. Aspects of Arab cultural, educational and industrial revival were discussed, and a call for non-cooperation with the imperialist administrations was firmly adopted. In a mood echoing the European nationalist scene of the interwar period, the conference called for the Arabs to assert their nationalist bond and shun the divisive social doctrines that undermine Arab heritage and unity. The conference's discourse evinced a strong sense of authoritarianism and a tendency to maximize state power. Indeed, in a distinctive departure from the Arab-Islamic traditions, it was agreed that the Arabs should not recognize linguistic, confessional, or racial minorities amongst them. For this generation of Arab nationalists, the inhabitants of Arab countries could have only one nationality and one language. This exclusive vision of "imagined community", its radical and confrontational attitudes towards the imperialist powers, was then formulated in a document that signalled the birth of the NAL.[118] The resolution to set up the NAL in Damascus, headed by the energetic Abd al-Razzaq al-Dandashi, was perhaps a reflection of the Syrian group's desire to establish a front organization in their country, where the National Bloc was largely viewed with contempt. The NAL was presumably to extend its activities into Lebanon and Jordan.

The NAL posed a serious challenge to the National Bloc, especially amongst the students and youth, yet cooperative relations were maintained with the more radical leaders of the Bloc, such as Shukri al-Quwwatli and the exiled Nabih al-'Azma.[119] In Palestine, the Arab Nationalist Bloc, of which Wasif Kamal was the most active member, also maintained close relations with the Istiqlalists and the mufti, especially after the latter adopted a more radical attitude towards the British in 1936.[120] Activists of the NAL provided the core members of the Palestine Defence Committee, particularly after it was reorganized by Nabih al-'Azma in 1937. Many of this group of Arab nationalists worked with al-Barudi in the Arab Bureau, while the crusader, Farid Zayn al-Din, became directly involved in the Palestinian strike upon his arrival in Nablus to administer al-Najah school.[121] He, and many of his Syrian and Lebanese colleagues, as well as the NAL, threw their weight behind the mufti and his Iraqi allies during the 1941 Iraqi–British war. The origins of that dramatic episode in the course of the interwar Arab movement emanated from Iraq's deep involvement with Palestine from the early days of the 1936 strike.

Iraq

One of the first manifestations of Iraq's awareness of the Palestinian question was the demonstration against a visit to Iraq by Sir Alfred Mond (Lord Melchett) on 8 February 1928. A well-known Zionist, Mond intended to negotiate with the Iraqi government a project for extending a pipeline from the Iraqi oilfields to the Mediterranean coast. News of his pro-Zionist dispositions and visit reached Baghdad through *al-Sharq al-Adna,* a magazine that was published in Cairo by the Syrian Arabist Amin Sa'id in the late 1920s.[122] Anti-Mond protests were spearheaded by al-Tadamun Club of Yusuf Zaynal and Husayn al-Rahhal, a prototype of the 1930s Iraqi radical Arab nationalist and leftist groups, and by teachers and students of Baghdad secondary school.[123] Under the auspices of Sati' al-Husri, the director of education from 1921–7, the Iraqi school education was imbued with an Arab nationalist curriculum, whose influences was augmented by an increasing number of Arab teachers in high schools and the Teachers' College. In 1928, four teachers at Baghdad secondary school were Palestinian, Lebanese, and Syrian graduates of the AUB, namely Abdullah al-Mashnuq, Anis Nassuli (Beirut), Jalal Zurayq (Ladhiqiyya) and Darwish al-Miqdadi (Tulkarem).[124] The latter would soon acquire an Iraqi nationality.

On 8 February, the day of Sir Alfred Mond's arrival in Baghdad, the students were instigated by their teachers to demonstrate against the visit. Banners carrying slogans such as "down with Balfour Declaration", "down with Zionism", and "long live the Arab nation", had been earlier prepared, while Zaynal and his associates circulated rumours that Mond's visit was a prelude to the founding of a Zionist colony in Iraq.[125] Talib Mushtaq, an ardent Arabist and the school's headmaster, persuaded the students earlier on the morning to attend their classes, but he encouraged and joined in the demonstration in the afternoon.[126] The demonstration and the ensuing clashes with the police, provoked a strong reaction from the government. Scores of students were arrested, a few were flogged, while others were expelled from Baghdad secondary school, the Teachers' College, and the Law College. Among those expelled from the Law College were Husayn Jamil and Abd al-Qadir Isma'il, who would both become founding members of al-Ahali Group in 1930. Al-Tadamun Club was closed down and Yusuf Zaynal was exiled to al-Fao, the most southern town of Iraq.[127]

The government's severe and unexpected response blew the incident out of proportion. On 10 February, Baghdadis gathered in al-Haydarkhana mosque, one of the centres of the 1920 Iraqi revolt, turning the Friday prayer into a mass support for the students.[128] During the following weeks, the demonstration surfaced as an important issue in the internal struggle for power between the moderate prime minister, Abd al-Muhsin al-Sa'dun, and his opponents, driving British officials in Baghdad to the wrong conclusion of linking the protest to the political intrigue of the ruling élite.[129] Husayn Jamil, however, asserted that the students were motivated by their own anti-Zionist feelings, and that it was he who first brought the news of Mond's visit to Yusuf Zaynal.[130] Indeed, the introduction of the Palestinian question into the Iraqi schools began in the early 1920s, when 2 November (the Balfour Declaration day) was declared an occasion for student protests and lecturing on the Palestinian dimension of Arab nationalism.

Palestinian ties with Iraq were woven gradually during the 1920s. Delegates from Jerusalem repeatedly visited Baghdad, raising funds for the renovation of al-Aqsa mosque. Yet, the Mond visit episode was to have a particularly strong impact in the wake of the Western Wall dispute. On 3 August 1929, a mass gathering was organized at al-Haydarkhana mosque, where Iraqi speakers expressed strong feelings of solidarity with the Palestinians and pointed to the British responsibility in creating the tragic situation in Palestine. An Iraqi committee for the support of Palestine was formed, chaired by Yasin al-Hashimi and which included, amongst others, Ja'far Abu al-Timman and Muzahim al-Pachachi.[131]

This was the first organized effort in the Arab lands to be undertaken on behalf of the Palestinians, and though the committee did not last, it set a precedent. While al-Hashimi's reputation as a pan-Arab leader was reinforced by his pro-Syrian and pro-Palestinian activities between 1925 and 1929,[132] the participation of Abu al-Timman in the committee was a prelude to his future alliance with al-Hashimi.

The freedom of the Iraqi movement in foreign affairs was still restricted in the 1920s by the constraints of the British mandate. This situation changed significantly after the signing of the Anglo-Iraqi treaty of 1930, which granted Iraq formal independence and secured its entry to the League of Nations two years later. The Arabs regarded the Iraqi independence as an achievement for the entire Arab movement, while the Iraqis, led by Faysal, embarked upon an intensive political effort to reclaim the Arab ideal of unity. Arab nationalism, which was perhaps envisioned by Sati' al-Husri in the 1920s as a unifying culture, was now pursued as the state ideology in Iraqi schools and colleges by the vibrant directors of education, Sami Shawkat and Muhammad Fadil al-Jamali.[133]

Like other Arab countries, Iraq reacted to the cultural and moral impact of modernization with the establishment of Islamic societies. Three chapters of the YMMS were formed in Baghdad, Basra and Mosul at the beginning of the 1930s. In Mosul, the predominantly Sunni city that produced more officers to the Ottoman military than any other Iraqi city, the YMMS attracted a group of army officers, including Fahmi Sa'id and Mahmud al-Durra, as well as the young student, Muhammad Mahmud al-Sawwaf.[134] Sa'id became the second most important member of the influential Iraqi group of Arabist officers between 1930 and 1941, while al-Durra was an assistant to the group leader, Colonel Salah al-Din al-Sabbagh. Al-Sawwaf, after graduating from al-Azhar, emerged as a founder of the Iraqi Muslim Brothers in 1943. The YMMS chapters in Iraq, being part of the loose network centred in Cairo, became frequently involved in pro-Palestinian activities.[135] In Baghdad, along with the YMMS branch, a group of Iraqi ulema and public figures set up al-Hidaiya al-Islamiyya Society on 1 January 1930, with the declared aim of "confronting atheism and propagating Islam."[136] Among the founders of al-Hidaiya were Shaykh Ibrahim al-Rawi (its president), Isma'il al-Wa'iz, Shaykh Kamal al-Din al-Ta'i (editor of *al-Hidaiya* magazine) and Hajj Nu'man al-A'zami (head of al-A'zamiyya College in Baghdad). Al-Hidaiya Society's association with Palestine was rooted in its representation by Nu'man al-A'zami in the General Islamic Congress of Jerusalem in December 1931.[137] Ever after, *al-Hidaiya* would be a powerful advocate of the Palestinian cause.[138]

The General Islamic Congress of Jerusalem nurtured the association of other Iraqi personalities with Palestine, including the radical Arabist, Sa'id al-Hajj Thabit, and the eminent Shi'i *alim*, Shaykh Muhammad Husayn al-Kashif al-Ghita'. Like many Shi'i scholars, Kashif al-Ghita' was based at al-Najaf in southern Iraq, from where he would continue his unwavering commitment to the Palestinian cause long after his involvement with the Islamic Congress. In 1933, he joined a list of senior Muslim ulema who signed the collective fatwa prohibiting the sale of Palestinian lands to the Jews. Among the leading Shi'i ulema of the 1930s, Khashif al-Ghita' was one of a few Arabs. The Shi'i religious establishment of Iraq at al-Najaf and Karbala was largely dominated by ulema of Iranian extraction, a situation that was not necessarily viewed with satisfaction by Iraqi Arabist politicians such as Yasin al-Hashimi. Upon the death of the *marji'* (the leading Shi'i religious authority), Mirza Muhammad Husayn Na'ini, in 1935, al-Hashimi (then prime minister) instructed his Shi'i supporters in al-Najaf to promote the *marji'iyyat* of Shaykh Kashif al-Ghita'.[139] This and other overtures on al-Hashimi's part, coupled with Kashif al-Ghita''s Arabist disposition, cultivated an amicable liaison between the *alim* and the prime minister. Consequently, Khashif al-Ghita' employed his religious influence in order to pacify the southern Shi'i tribes which revolted during al-Hashimi's term in office.[140] Kashif al-Ghita''s Arab orientation and engagement in Palestinian and Iraqi politics would ultimately take him to the anti-British camp of Amin al-Husayni and Rashid 'Ali al-Gaylani in 1941.

Significant as they were, the Islamic societies were neither more influential than, nor entirely segregated from, the Arabist circles of Iraq. While the Islamic sphere of Iraq was divided between Sunni and Shi'i Islam, Arabism appeared as a unifying cause, promoted by the state. In many ways, however, the two spheres were inextricably linked, since neither Islamism nor Arabism was yet expressed in exclusion of the other. And though the Anglo-Iraqi treaty contributed to a substantial liberation of the Iraqi Arab policy, it was the contentious debate over the treaty that was to draw the first lines of demarcation in the Iraqi political arena.

The Anglo-Iraqi treaty was successfully completed and signed by the government of Nuri al-Sa'id in June 1930. Nuri al-Sa'id, the father of the treaty, fought his way into parliament to guarantee its ratification against a strong opposition to the limitations that it imposed on Iraq during its prospective 25-year term. The treaty provided for two British airbases in Iraq and the movement of British military forces across Iraqi territories, and required Iraq to purchase virtually all of its military equipment from Britain. The Iraqi government was to employ a British military mission and send Iraqi officers exclusively to British military academies.[141] On the other hand, the treaty established a kind of alliance between Iraq and Britain that was seen by Nuri al-Saʿid as a shield for Iraq in times of crisis and a gateway to the League of Nations. Above all, the treaty meant the end of the mandate. Nuri's approach was, of course, supported by King Faysal, but was firmly opposed by two groups, led by the distinguished Iraqi politicians, Yasin al-Hashimi and Jaʿfar Abu al-Timman. Though both had always been regarded as radical nationalists, they were of different personalities and backgrounds.

Abu al-Timman (1885–1945), whose good education and active role in the 1920 revolt brought him to the helm of Iraqi politics, belonged to a Shiʿi merchant family of Baghdad. In the 1920s, despite hardship and distractions, he adhered to an uncompromising anti-British line, while rejecting involvement in sectarian politics.[142] After Faysal's accession to the throne, Abu al-Timman launched the National Party in 1921, which was promptly banned by the British the following year. In 1928, he revived the party with a strong leading core that included Muhammad Mahdi Kubba, the political activist of a Shiʿi merchant family, Mawlud Mukhlis, the disenchanted ex-Sharifian officer, and Saʿid al-Hajj Thabit.[143] Abu al-Timman's contribution to the pro-Palestinian movement in 1929 and his prominent standing in Iraqi politics made him a target for the scheming Arab nationalists, Farid Zayn al-Din and Akram Zuʿaytir, who were both employed in Iraq in the early 1930s.[144] However, since Abu al-Timman was increasingly drifting towards social-democratic circles, his interest in Arabism waned markedly. The Arabists were more fortunate with Muhammad Mahdi Kubba, the other leading member of the National Party.

Yasin al-Hashimi had many reasons for opposing Nuri al-Saʿid and his treaty. While al-Hashimi left the Ottoman army a decorated lieutenant general in 1920, Nuri (1888–1958) was a young officer captured by the British in Basra before joining the Sharifian army. Al-Hashimi's introverted character, decent private life, together with his religious dispositions and connections, were in deep contrast to Nuri's unscrupulous manners and unreserved demeanour.[145] They were both, however, ambitious Arabists of the first class, whose differences were manifest most in their assessment of Iraq's relations with Britain. Nuri al-Sa'id perceived politics in terms of a balance of power, which made him the model for Arab political pragmatism in the interwar era, whereas al-Hashimi's leadership was based on a well-nurtured anti-British image as well as an impeccable pan-Arab reputation. Paradoxically, despite the many differences, al-Hashimi and Sa'id maintained a liaison of a complex nature. In the context of monarchic Iraq, they functioned within the recognized constitutional framework, but were both not profoundly committed to preserving the royal system.[146] Al-Hashimi was earnestly keen to include and keep Nuri in his fateful cabinet of 1935–6,[147] in which Nuri was a foreign minister and special envoy for Palestinian affairs.

In 1930, al-Hashimi founded al-Ikha' al-Watani Party, which continued to be his political vehicle until 1935 when he decided to dissolve the party and present himself as a national rather than a factional leader. Al-Ikha's leading layer consisted of old associates of al-Hashimi together with political opponents of the 1930 treaty. Most prominent among them were: Rashid 'Ali al-Gaylani, a lawyer of a modest branch of the Gaylani ashraf of Baghdad; Naji al-Swaydi, son of the reformist *alim*, Shaykh Yusuf al-Swaydi, and a former Ottoman administrator and Iraqi prime minister; Hikmat Sulayman, an ex-Ottoman official, member of the CUP, and a brother of Mahmud Shawkat who led the anti-Hamidian *coup d'état* of 1909; and Kamil al-Chadirchi, a young radical lawyer and journalist from Baghdad.[148] In January 1931, al-Ikha' and the National Party of Ja'far Abu al-Timman formed an anti-treaty alliance.[149] Yet, after a long year of active political opposition, al-Hashimi was again rehabilitated with the regime. Faysal's skilful management of the treaty crisis led to the dismissal of Nuri al-Sa'id in November 1932, and the neutralization of al-Hashimi by involving him in the pan-Arabist schemes of 1932–3.

By March 1933, the treaty debate had receded and Rashid 'Ali al-Gaylani, supported by al-Hashimi, agreed to form his first government. A few months later, al-Gaylani found himself supervising the transfer of the crown from Faysal to his son, Ghazi. Al-Ikha's return to power put an end to the al-Hashimi–Abu al-Timman alliance and to their anti-treaty political front. Deeply depressed and unable to preserve his party's unity and steadfastness in the face of the attractions of power, Abu al-Timman resigned from the leadership of the National Party in November 1933.[150] His resignation sealed the fate of the party. Abu al-Timman, however, did not retire from politics, for his interest in social issues, and his association with a group of young Iraqis who had established *al-Ahali* newspaper in 1932, induced his participation in the founding of al-Ahali Group (Jam'iyyat al-Ahali) and its offspring, the Popular Reform Society.[151] Al-Ahali was also joined by Kamil al-Chadirchi, who similarly left the Ikha' Party after disagreeing with its pragmatic back-to-power move in 1933. What brought Abu al-Timman and al-Chadirchi into the company of Muhammad Hadid (a student of Professor Harold Laski at London University), Husayn Jamil, and Abd al-Qadir Isma'il (veterans of the 1928 protest against Sir Alfred Mond's visit), was the belief in social democracy. Al-Ahali Group was in essence a response to a situation in which problems of political instability and a precarious economy had compounded social injustice. Predictably, al-Ahali displayed no interest in the Arab-nationalist question; it opposed all governments between 1933 and 1936 and became a party to the 1936 *coup d'état* which put an end to al-Hashimi's last tenure of the premiership. Meanwhile, the Arabist members of the National Party joined forces with other active Arabists and founded al-Muthanna Club in 1935. This early bastion of Arab nationalism in Iraq deserves a closer look.

Faced with a series of short-lived governments and frequent eruptions of the southern tribes, King Ghazi finally called on Yasin al-Hashimi to assume the premiership on 17 March 1935.[152] In drawing up his cabinet, Yasin confronted what appeared then as a minor problem. For the role he played in the political intrigues that brought his party to power, Hikmat Sulayman requested the powerful portfolio of internal affairs. Al-Hashimi instead offered him the ministry of finance, but Sulayman rejected the offer, left al-Ikha', and turned his operative abilities to al-Ahali's side.[153] With Sulayman's departure, al-Hashimi's administration fell exclusively into the hands of Arabist politicians, such as Nuri al-Sa'id, Ja'far al-'Askari, Rashid 'Ali al-Gaylani, Ra'uf al-Bahrani, and Sadiq al-Bassam, while al-Hashimi's brother, General Taha, was the army Chief of Staff. Al-Hashimi's term in office represented Arabism's high point in Iraq, from whose womb a large part of the developments that led to the spring of 1941 were born.

[220]

Only a few weeks after taking office, the interior minister al-Gaylani granted two ardent Arab nationalists, the physician Sa'ib Shawkat, and Fahmi Sa'id, the army officer commanding the military police, permission to establish a literary forum under the name of al-Muthanna Club.[154] The club aimed at promoting Arabism and Arab culture in Iraq, at reviving the nationalist spirit among the young and at disseminating awareness of the Palestinian problem.[155] Sa'ib Shawkat became president of the club, and Muhammad Mahdi Kubba vice-president. Among those who occupied seats on the executive committee of al-Muthanna, or were particularly active in its functions, were: Sa'id al-Hajj Thabit; Muhammad Fadil al-Jamali; Sami Shawkat; the lawyer-journalist Yunis al-Sab'awi; his brother-in-law Siddiq Shanshal; Muhammad Hasan Salman (a physician who was employed in the ministry of education); Abd al-Majid al-Qassab; Ibrahim 'Attar Bashi; Khalid al-Hashimi; Hajj Nu'man al-'Ani; Abd al-Karim al-Arzi; Abd al-Majid Mahmud; Abd al-Muhsin al-Duri; Abd al-Razzaq al-Zahir and Dawud al-Sa'di.[156] The non-Iraqi Arab nationalists, Farid Zayn al-Din, Akram Zu'aytir, Darwish al-Miqdadi and the Syrian physician Amin Rwayha, participated in the founding of the club and assisted in maintaining its contacts with the Arab nationalist scene.

Interestingly, Lieutenant Colonel Fahmi Sa'id, who was party to an increasingly active Arabist coterie of army officers, kept a low profile. Yunis al-Sab'awi, the energetic young journalist, played a vital role in linking the officers with the club.[157] Yunis al-Sab'awi was born in Mosul to Arab parents of modest means in 1910. So harsh was his childhood that he could not finish his early schooling without the support of Ahmad al-Jalili, the local notable and leader of Mosul's National Party. His first lesson in Arabism was the Iraqi–Turkish dispute over Mosul in the mid-1920s, which inflamed the city's Arabist sentiments. In late 1928, as Mosul seemed to be too small for his ambitions, he moved to Baghdad where he was struck by the capital's vanity. Unable to sustain a regular student life with his limited means, he left his secondary education and took a teaching job at 'Ana in the heart of rural Iraq. Back in Baghdad a year later, he joined the Law School while working as a journalist for *al-Bilad* newspaper.[158] In the same year, his fervent writings and the Mosullite network in Baghdad enabled al-Sab'awi to make contact with two army officers, Salah al-Din al-Sabbagh and Fahmi Sa'id.[159]

Graduates of the Ottoman Military Academy, al-Sabbagh and Sa'id served as lieutenants in the Ottoman army until the end of World War I, after which they joined the Arab army of the Damascus government.[160] Ottoman and Damascus Arab defeats, coupled with the carving up of the Arab countries, precipitated their strong sense of resentment towards the imperialist powers and fuelled their Arabist feelings. By the late 1920s, the ineptness of Iraq's divided political élite, reflected in the short-lived and highly unstable governments, together with the pervasive British influence, pushed the energetic officers to think politically. Atatürk's success in protecting Turkey's independence and laying the foundations for its progress was an outstanding and inspiring model.

Al-Sab'awi's passionate and anti-establishment articulations, his commitment and sincerity, fascinated al-Sabbagh and his colleagues. Although al-Sab'awi was much younger than them, his access to the press and political circles as well as his cognizance of Arab and international developments provided the officers with a highly needed insight.[161] For al-Sab'awi, the army connection offered a sense of protection and support. Al-Sab'awi's first political links were with the like-minded Ja'far Abu al-Timman, but he soon turned to the Yasin al-Hashimi faction, largely because of the declining interest of Abu al-Timman in Arabism.[162] On joining al-Ikha' Party, al-Sab'awi brought with him the tacit backing of his army friends. During the murky period of political machinations in early 1935, al-Sabbagh's group of army officers, who were not permitted by law to get politically involved, worked successfully to discourage the army's interference in the tribal revolt, thereby sealing the fate of Jamil al-Madfa'i's government.[163]

Upon an unexpected setback in his preparations for a law degree, al-Sab'awi, together with his childhood friend and future brother-in-law, Siddiq Shanshal, spent the 1932–3 academic year in Damascus, concluding his law training. In the Syrian capital, he was introduced to the NAL during its early period of political evolution, becoming closely acquainted with its president, Abd al-Razzaq al-Dandashi.[164] This encounter opened al-Sab'awi's political world to the emerging trends of radical Arab nationalism, within which he felt perfectly at home. The long-lasting influence of the NAL resulted in al-Sab'awi's espousal of its ideological views. Back in Iraq, he in turn induced his army friends to join the widening ranks of Arab nationalists with which he was now connected. In the mid-1930s, al-Sabbagh and Sa'id succeeded in attracting other like-minded officers to their group. Their most prominent affiliates were Mahmud Salman and Kamil Shabib, whose similar ranks and careers united them to al-Sabbagh and Sa'id.[165] Al-Muthanna was, therefore, a child of complicated, but not always conspicuous, evolving currents in the Arab nationalist scene. Its crucial role in connecting Iraq with the wider stream of the Arab movement can be illustrated by the number and stature of distinguished Arabists who visited or lectured at the club.[166] Yet, it was the Palestinian question, more than any other issue, that came to define the club's mission.

A year after assuming office, al-Hashimi's relative success in restoring normalcy to the Iraqi domestic situation, coupled with unanticipated cooperative relations with the British embassy, increased his confidence and hopes of a long-term government. Subsequently, al-Hashimi turned to furthering the Iraqi role in the Arab arena. Against a backdrop of rising tensions in Syria and Egypt, al-Hashimi contacted Hajj Amin al-Husayni, informing him of the Iraqi intentions to revive the idea of the pan-Arab congress.[167] Less than a month later, al-Hashimi dispatched a distinguished Iraqi delegation to Palestine and Egypt. A mixture of parliamentarians, officials, and eminent public figures, this delegation included Sa'id al-Hajj Thabit, Abd al-Husayn al-Chalabi, 'Asim Chalabi, 'Ali Mahmud al-Shaykh 'Ali, Hamdi al-Pachichi, the poet Ma'ruf al-Rasafi, and the director of the Propaganda Department, Ibrahim Hilmi al-'Umar.[168] The Iraqi delegation's first stop was Nablus, where they were hosted by Akram Zu'aytir who had left Baghdad for Palestine in the summer of 1935. In Nablus, as well as later in Jerusalem and Jaffa, Sa'id al-Hajj Thabit openly incited the Palestinians to rise in a "jihad" to preserve Palestine's Arab and Islamic identity, and replied to a Palestinian appeal for help with a plain statement: "do not sit waiting the coming of an [Iraqi] expedition, you start and leave the rest [necessary support] on us."[169]

Upon returning to Iraq, Sa'id al-Hajj Thabit reactivated the Iraqi Committee for the Defence of Palestine which he and his fellow Arabists established during the 1933 Palestinian disturbances. The committee was chaired by Thabit, and included the eminent statesman and former prime minister Naji al-Swaydi, the two most active members of al-Muthanna, Muhammad Mahdi Kubba and Ibrahim 'Attar Bashi, as well as Hajj Nu'man al-'Ani of al-Hidaiya Society.[170] It established a base at al-Muthanna, attracting its most dedicated activists from amongst the supporters and members of the club and al-Hidaiya Society. When the 1936 strike erupted, the Iraqi scene was, therefore, more than any other in the Arab-Islamic landscape, set to respond.

[223]

The Iraqi Committee for the Defence of Palestine followed the general pattern of Arab political activism at the time. Fund-raising, telegrams, and collective petitions of protest to the British embassy and the League of Nations, mass gatherings, political propaganda, and press campaigns were the main features of the committee's functions.[171] In a country riddled with divisions, support for the Palestinian cause crossed ethnic and sectarian lines. Such consensus was exemplified in the composition of the delegation received by the British ambassador, Clark Kerr, in early May, when the Iraqis expressed their deep concern about the gravity of the Palestinian situation and urged a change of British policies.[172] The Iraqi solidarity with the Palestinians was not limited to the politically active circles in Baghdad. Branches of the committee were established in other Iraqi cities, as the national character of the campaign was enhanced by jihad fatwas from influential Shi'i ulema.[173] Towards the end of the strike, Iraqi emotions over Palestine reached such a point that the minister of defence, Ja'afar al-'Askari, openly called on the army to assist and donate to the Palestinian Arab brothers.[174] Yet, what was to contribute to forging a special relationship between the Iraqi and Palestinian nationalists was an Iraqi involvement of another kind.

From a strike to revolt

Violence was inherent in the Palestinian strike. After the Palestinian April attack and the ensuing Jewish reprisals, Palestinian–Jewish clashes continued unabated.[175] But following the British announcement on 18 May of a new schedule of immigration certificates for Jews, the Palestinians embraced armed struggle as a policy and on a wide scale. For the mandate government, the mountain-based clusters of armed bands became the most disturbing components of the Palestinian rebellion. Instigated at least partly by radical members of the HAC, these groups were identified by their local leaders, as each operated in a certain geographical area. Although the Qassamis, Farhan al-Sa'idi, Yusuf Abu Durra and Shaykh 'Atiyya Ahmad 'Awad, played a chief role in organizing several fighting groups, other local commanders emerged. Most prominent were Abd al-Qadir al-Husayni, son of the late nationalist leader Musa Kazim, Fakhri Abd al-Hadi, Abd al-Rahim al-Hajj Muhammad, 'Isa al-Battat, Hasan Salama, and 'Arif Abd al-Raziq.[176] Largely supplied and aided by the villagers, these bands launched a guerrilla war against British patrols, army and police stations, as well as Jewish colonies. However, inadequately trained, poorly armed and largely uncoordinated, these bands were in urgent need of Arab support.

The first shipments of arms to the Palestinian rebels were provided by Jordanian Bedouin and nationalist sources, as well as Syrian rebel circles and veterans of the Syrian revolt. More substantial supplies came from the Iraqi army camps. Issued by Salah al-Din al-Sabbagh and his fellow officers, arms and ammunition were transferred to Transjordan by members of al-Muthanna Club, with the knowledge and cooperation of the Iraqi border authorities.[177] Yasin al-Hashimi's attitudes towards the Arabist officers' activities were not clear. One may assume that the prime minister was fully aware of the army's growing links with the Palestinian revolt. His brother, General Taha al-Hashimi, army chief of staff, was particularly close to the Arabist military circle, and was undoubtedly in full knowledge of his officers' endeavour. In addition, the scope of the supply operation, involving Palestinians in Baghdad, army officers, and many political figures of al-Hashimi's own camp, was too large to escape the prime minister's attention. At any rate, in midsummer 1936, Yasin al-Hashimi's stand on the question of military aid to the Palestinians became more unequivocal.

Transjordan represented a vital link between the Iraqi army camps and the Palestinian hills. Despite pervasive British control and influence, the Jordanian nationalist circles displayed strong feelings of solidarity with the Palestinians from the early stage of the strike.[178] Tribal elements, professionals, and Syrian exiles became widely involved in sending arms and financial assistance to Palestine. Most prominent of Amman's Arabists in the mid-1930s was the Syrian lawyer 'Adil al-'Azma, a brother of the better known Arabist Nabih al-'Azma. 'Adil, a radical and widely connected Arabist who founded a Jordanian branch of the NAL, was an organizing genius.[179] His role in the Palestinian revolt soon evolved from supplying arms to participating in enlisting volunteers from all over the Arab East.

Some highly ambitious schemes for igniting a pan-Arab and anti-imperialist revolt all across *Bilad* al-Sham were in circulation within Arabist quarters during the 1930s. Such ideas might have first arisen in a discussion between the mufti and the Syrian exiled officer Fawzi al-Qawuqji in the aftermath of the 1929 Palestinian disturbances. Al-Qawuqji's strategy envisioned a liberated TransJordan, to be turned with Saudi backing into a springboard for the liberation of Syria and Palestine.[180] In the summer of 1936, the mufti and his HAC colleagues, dwelling perhaps on the never-matured schemes of 1929, decided to call upon al-Qawuqji to augment the Palestinian revolt. Conveniently, al-Qawuqji was then an instructor at the Iraqi Military Academy. This highly controversial figure of the Arab movement was born in Tripoli in 1887. Ending World War I as a young Ottoman officer, he joined the French auxiliary units in Syria, but was soon to desert and participate in the Syrian revolt of 1925–7. After the collapse of the revolt, al-Qawuqji moved to Saudi Arabia, where his unscrupulous conduct caught him in an imbroglio that led to his imprisonment by the Saudi monarch. Arabists' interventions, however, secured his release and arranged his transfer to Iraq, where he joined the Iraqi army.[181] Al-Qawuqji's erratic and adventurous style of Arabist militarism was rivalled only by an inherent urge for leadership.

In late June 1936, the HAC dispatched Mu'in al-Madi to Baghdad, where he was also joined by Salim 'Abd al-Rahman, a Palestinian Arabist *provocateur* from Tulkarem who fled to Iraq from a British arrest order.[182] Received enthusiastically in Baghdad, al-Madi approached Yasin al-Hashimi to release al-Qawuqji from the army in order that he might command an expedition of volunteers to Palestine. Al-Hashimi agreed and gave instructions to the Iraqi Red Crescent to contribute 500 Iraqi dinars towards the preparations of the expedition.[183] Deliberations over the Arab campaign, involving 'Adil al-'Azma in Amman, Yasin al-Hashimi, Sa'id Thabit, Amin Rwayha and the Iraqi army Arabist group, had actually been under way before al-Madi's arrival in Baghdad.[184] But al-Hashimi, enjoying a rare moment of smooth relations with the British, came under heavy pressure from the British embassy to stop the expedition from moving to Palestine.[185] Al-Qawuqji, however, having resigned his army commission, was no longer bound to comply with the prime minister's orders. Even before al-Qawuqji and his company left Iraq, several hundred volunteers were already arriving in Jordan or taking positions on the Palestinian hills.

Members of al-Qawuqji's expedition came from different parts of the Arab East. Among them were Iraqis, Syrians, Lebanese, Jordanians and Kurds. Volunteers from Syria were recruited by Hajj Adib Khayr, the National Bloc associate of al-Quwwatli, the NAL, the Islamic societies and the Palestine Defence Committee. All the strings led to 'Adil al-'Azma in Amman.[186] Coming from different social backgrounds, the Syrian volunteers were headed by two veterans of the 1925–7 revolt, Shaykh Muhammad al-Ashmar, a religious leader from al-Maydan quarter of Damascus, and Sa'id al-'As, the former Ottoman officer from Hama.[187] The Lebanese group was led by the Druze, Hamad Sa'ab, a notable from Shuwayfat. Other Lebanese volunteers arrived individually.[188] Scores of Druze followers of Sultan Pasha al-Atrash, leader of the Syrian revolt with whom 'Adil al-'Azma maintained strong relations, also joined the expedition. From Iraq, where Sa'id Thabit and the Palestine Defence Committee took the responsibility of recruitment, two hundred Iraqi volunteers joined the campaign, amongst whom were the former army officers, Jamil Shakir and Qasim al-Kurdi.[189] Besides 'Adil al-'Azma, the Jordanian ring included Mansur Qaddura, the Libyan director of the Arab Bank branch in Amman, Muhammad 'Ali Darwaza, brother of the Istiqlalist 'Izzat Darwaza, and the Jordanians, Abdullah Abu Qura, Qasim al-Am'ari and Hajj Khalil al-'Azizi. Notables of the Jordanian middle and northern villages in the River Jordan valley, where Amir Abdullah was not particularly popular, provided protection and guidance for crossing the river into Palestine.[190] After entering Palestine, al-Qawuqji was joined by Munir al-Rayyis, the prominent Syrian journalist, who shouldered the responsibility of establishing an intelligence and information unit.[191]

Al-Qawuqji arrived in Palestine in late August 1936.[192] Characteristically, he immediately assumed the rank of "commander-in-chief of the Arab revolt in Southern Syria".[193] Leaders of local Palestinian bands first deferred to al-Qawuqji's command,[194] but relations between al-Qawuqji and the Palestinian rebels, as well as between him and the mufti, were soon to deteriorate. Al-Qawuqji's friendly liaison with pro-Nashashibi families, such as Abd al-Hadi and Irshayd of the Jenin sub-district, raised suspicions in the mufti's circles.[195] Moreover, al-Qawuqji's appointment of Fakhri Abd al-Hadi as his deputy was not received favourably by other Palestinian military commanders (in the second stage of the revolt, Fakhri would be recruited by pro-British opponents of the revolt). Tension increased significantly after the battle of Bal'a in early September, al-Qawuqji's most successful confrontation with the British troops, where both sides exchanged recriminations over tactical mistakes during the fighting.[196] Nevertheless, cooperation between al-Qawuqji and his Palestinian counterparts was somehow maintained, and the campaign began to leave a marked impact on the military situation.

In the words of Vice-Marshal Pierce of the Royal Air Force, who was responsible for the military intelligence in Palestine during the revolt, "Rebel tactics improved and the bands showed signs of effective leadership and organization."[197] Yet, it was the campaign's disregard of the post-World War I demarcations of the Arab land which defined its position in the course of the long and persistent Arab military involvement in Palestine.

End of the strike

On 11 October 1936, Palestinian newspapers appeared with two front-page proclamations. The first was issued separately by King Ghazi of Iraq, King Abd al-'Aziz of Saudi Arabia and Amir Abdullah of Transjordan, with slightly different wording, calling on the Palestinian Arabs to end their strike and rely on "the good intentions of the British government and its desire for the realization of justice". The Arab rulers further promised that they would continue in their endeavour to help the Palestinians.[198] The second was the HAC's response to the Arab rulers' call, in which the HAC asked the people of Palestine to end their strike and resume normal life beginning the next morning. This highly uncelebrated ending to the highly dramatic six-month general strike, civil disobedience and guerrilla warfare, was the outcome of complicated negotiations between the Palestinians, leaders of the Arab states, and the British government, as well as of mounting economic, military and political burdens. Not a single demand of the strike was met by the British. Yet, implicit in the Arab intervention was a significant shift in British policy concerning the relations between the Arabs and Palestine. Not surprisingly, the HAC communiqué sounded particularly eager to underline "the great advantages emanating from the Arab rulers' mediation and support". The British policy of keeping Palestine as an affair of the mandate, at a safe distance from the rest of the Arabs, was finally yielding to the complexity of forces in the Arab world. The paradox, of course, is that where the strike failed to bring about any tangible change in the British JNH policy, it succeeded in laying the foundation for the Arabization of the Palestinian question.

The Palestinian leaders embarked on a significant effort, from an early stage of the strike, to enlist the support of the independent and semi-independent Arab states. Aware of the increasing tension in Europe and the emergence of Italy and Germany as powerful antagonists of the

Anglo-French world order, the Palestinians believed that Britain would have to reconsider its policies in Palestine if faced with strong Arab pressure.[199] What was absent from the Palestinian scheme of things was the pressing strategic imperatives that the changing international climate was creating for the British holding of Palestine. On the eve of World War II, London's view of Palestine was no longer based solely on the JNH commitments, but also on the strategic requirements for defending the empire. Indeed, officials of the Colonial Office were, perhaps subconsciously, developing a kind of Palestinian ideology in their assessment of the British position in the Middle East.[200] This would not only make British relations with the Palestinian national movement incompatible with other colonial relationships, but would also generate a certain degree of disagreement between British officials in the Arab world and their masters in London.

The first move from an Arab leader on behalf of the Palestinians came from the Saudi monarch. Upon receiving a telegram of appeal from the mufti, Ibn Sa'ud dispatched his deputy foreign minister, Yusuf Yasin (the king was officially the foreign minister), to meet Sir Andrew Ryan, the British minister in Jeddah. The two met on 29 April, when Yasin conveyed the king's strong feelings towards the Palestinian situation and the importance of his relations with Palestine, the site of "The First Qibla of Islam", for maintaining Saudi prestige in the Arab world. Ryan, whose line of response was later approved by Eden and the Colonial Office, exerted himself to the utmost to dissuade the Saudis from intervening in the Palestinian imbroglio.[201] Similar attitudes were adopted by Lampson, the British representative in Cairo, who rebuffed al-Nahhas's many offers of mediation, prior to, and after, the conclusion of the Anglo-Egyptian treaty negotiations.[202] For Lampson, it was paramount to insulate Egypt from any Arab collective action, in order to prevent "bringing her directly into Palestinian and Arab affairs which we have so far succeeded in avoiding".

Close to home was, of course, Amir Abdullah of Transjordan. In the mid-1930s, Abdullah was becoming increasingly impatient in his search to expand his domain to Palestine and Syria. In the spring of 1934, Abdullah proposed to the Zionist leaders of the Jewish Agency a plan to establish a Palestinian–Jordanian kingdom, in which the "Jewish rights" would be guaranteed.[203] His proposal was, however, rejected by the Zionists whose self-confidence was now strongly enhanced by the rising rate of Jewish emigration from Europe. Tenacious as he was, Abdullah saw in the revolt an opportunity to enter the arena through the Palestinian, and perhaps even the British, door. He began his mediation bid by inviting the HAC leaders to meet him in Amman on 1 May. However, after more than a month of intense activities, including the dispatch of two letters to the High Commissioner of Palestine (who also had jurisdiction over Transjordan), an exchange of correspondence and another meeting with 'Awni Abd al-Hadi and Jamal al-Husayni, Abdullah was firmly told by Wauchope that before any discussion of policy, violence in Palestine must first stop.[204] Abdullah's effort to elicit a British commitment to a temporary cessation of Jewish immigration was to no avail. In Iraq, Yasin al-Hashimi also met the British ambassador, Clark Kerr, and demanded an end to Jewish immigration.[205] When al-Hashimi offered to mediate between the British and the Palestinians, his offer received no encouragement from Kerr.

Neither in London nor in the Arab world were the British officials able to see the depth of the Palestinian grievances, or to anticipate how far Palestinian and Arab reactions would go. The strike was, in a sense, a new experience for the British officials in Palestine, yet, in a political setting that had been almost consistently precarious there seemed to be no particular reason for alarm. The only adjustment that the High Commissioner had to make was the offer he presented to the HAC in mid-May to appoint a Royal Commission to examine the Palestinian situation, after the violence, including the strike, had ended. Although the offer was rejected by the HAC,[206] it was still seen as necessary by the Colonial Office to organize a commission.[207] But it was not until 7 August that the commission was formed under the chairmanship of Earl Peel, a cousin of King Edward VIII, and not until November that it arrived in Palestine. The failure of the Arab states to bring about the desired change in the British position, coupled with the increasing radicalization of the Palestinian masses, resulted in the mufti's embrace of the armed struggle. Evidence abounds that from the commencement of armed activities in mid-May right until the end of June, the HAC developed no policy of armed struggle, nor were any of its members connected with the urban and/or mountain-based bands. Armed activities at this stage were largely prompted by popular initiative.[208]

The change in British policy began to develop towards the end of June. It was most fitting that suggestions for some modifications in policy should originate from the Foreign Office Eastern Department, whose view of the revolt's repercussions was relatively broader than that of other departments of Whitehall. Considering many elements in the situation, including the persistence of the Palestinian strike, the Arab response and Italy's ominous presence in Libya and Abyssinia, the Foreign Office distributed a memorandum on 20 June to other concerned departments of the government.[209] Prepared by the Eastern Department and prefaced by the foreign secretary, Anthony Eden, this document indicated that the Palestinian question was no longer "a temporary one" and was "considered by the Arabs not only in Palestine but all over the East to strike at the root of the future of the Arab people". The Foreign Office called for a "détente" in the Palestinian situation and went as far as implicitly to recommend the arrest of Jewish immigration.

Equally crucial were the views of two influential embassies in the Arab world. Before and after the release of the Foreign Office memorandum, Clark Kerr in Baghdad and Sir Miles Lampson in Cairo were expressing similar views to those adopted by their colleagues in the Eastern Department.[210] Indeed, Lampson's dispatches reflected a deepening apprehension over the strength of the strike, its wide Arab and particularly Egyptian support, the Egyptian government's evolving aspiration for a leading Arab role and, of course, the empire's strategic imperatives. By and large, the Foreign Office was coming to the conclusion that an Arab collective representation in Palestine must be acknowledged, even if this required a cessation of Jewish immigration. Yet, the Colonial Office, and certainly the cabinet, while recognizing the first point, firmly defended the continuation of Jewish immigration. This division of opinion reflected a long-standing disagreement within the British government between those who saw the British interests in the Middle East from an Arab perspective and those who disregarded the Arab wishes and embraced the Zionist project.

Towards mid-June, the Saudi king repeated his approach to the British through Hafiz Wahba, his representative in London. Cosmo Parkinson, deputy permanent under-secretary at the Colonial Office, grudgingly informed Lancelot Oliphant, his counterpart in the Foreign Office, of his department's consent to an Arab mediation.[211] Owing to the sensitivity of the Palestinian question and the issues involved, Ibn Sa'ud moved to bring the Iraqi and Yemeni monarchs on board. The Egyptian regent, Prince Muhammad 'Ali, still under the pressure of

Lampson's "insulation" policy, refrained from joining. These moves on the part of Ibn Sa'ud were again agreed to by the Colonial Office.[212] However, when the Saudi *démarche* reached a point at which the Arab rulers requested that their ally Britain agree to a temporary halt of Jewish immigration, the cabinet, against the Foreign Office's recommendation, refused.[213] By this rejection, the first round of Arab–British negotiations was brought to an end. Since the Palestinian conditions for terminating the strike were still unchanged, the Arab rulers had no choice but to suspend their mediation.

Against the backdrop of an illusive statement that the colonial secretary made to the House of Commons, Amir Abdullah returned to the scene at the end of July. Ormsby-Gore assured the House that the government contemplated no change in its policy on Palestine, but then added that regarding "the suggestion that there should be a temporary suspension of immigration while the [Peel] Commission" was carrying out its inquiry, he was "not at present in a position to make any statement as to the intention of His Majesty's Government" beyond saying that there was "no question of it being influenced by violence or attempt at intimidation".[214] Encouraged by what seemed to be a change of policy in London, as well as by the High Commissioner, who was obviously disposed towards the less-demanding amir of Transjordan, Abdullah made another approach to the HAC. Between 26 July and 5 August, he met twice with the HAC, but the discussions ended inconclusively on both occasions. Abdullah was not authorized by the High Commissioner to promise a suspension of Jewish immigration, while the mufti was not prepared to accept a solution not grounded in this demand. What was to emerge from Abdullah's mediation was a critical state of disagreement between the mufti and Raghib al-Nashashibi. During the detention of the two powerful Istiqlalist leaders, 'Awni Abd al-Hadi and his successor in the HAC, 'Izzat Darwaza, and the absence of Jamal al-Husayni in London, al-Nashashibi felt more confident to express dissent with the HAC's established position, and extend his support to Abdullah's effort.[215] Precipitating the first crack in the Palestinian unity of purpose, al-Nashashibi's shift, however, made no difference to the fate of Abdullah's initiative. Yet, inasmuch as he opened the door to the idea of a "dignified end", al-Nashashibi set a precedent that would later be embraced by other leaders when the HAC became unable to sustain the psychological or the political costs of the strike.

Another Arab attempt at mediation was set in motion by the unrelenting Iraqi foreign minister, Nuri al-Saʻid. Like Abdullah's, Nuri's initiative was not presented in a framework of joint Arab mediation.[216] Its origins lay in the persistent Iraqi effort to accomplish and lead an Arab federation. It was also called for by the intensifying support for the Palestinians in Iraq, the ongoing preparations for al-Qawuqji's campaign, and the deepening frustration of British officials in the Arab East. Nuri al-Saʻid, following in Faysal's footsteps, saw in the Palestinian revolt an opportunity to reopen the question of Arab unity. Less than two months after the outbreak of the strike, Nuri visited London and met with Rendel at the Foreign Office, where he conveyed the Iraqi official view that Jewish immigration was the main obstacle to restoring peace in Palestine. But Nuri was convinced that in the light of the British JNH policy, a political solution to the Palestinian problem required a rather extraordinary and indirect approach which went beyond the official policy of his country. Since he ascribed a great deal to Zionist influence on British policy, Nuri met Chaim Weizmann on 9 June. Nuri suggested to Weizmann that "the Zionist organization should spontaneously propose the suspension of Jewish immigration", at least during the workings of the Royal Commission of Inquiry, and accept that the Jews remain as a minority in Palestine. The final solution, in Nuri's view, should be based on the founding of an Iraqi-led Arab federation, in which the Palestinian Arabs and a sort of Jewish entity would be integrated.[217] Weizmann was either cautiously receptive to Nuri's ideas, or only expressed his objection in muted terms. At any rate, after Nuri informed the British of Weizmann's agreement, a heated debate erupted in the Zionist Organization Political Advisory Committee, forcing Weizmann to deny Nuri's version of the meeting to the British.

But Nuri's interest in the Palestinian question was not diminished in any way. In mid-August, he communicated to the British chargé d'affaires in Baghdad his desire to stop in Palestine before arriving in Turkey for a pre-planned visit.[218] It is not entirely clear whether the British embassy in Baghdad encouraged Nuri al-Saʻid to embark on his initiative, yet, in Jerusalem he was hosted at an official residence as a guest of the High Commissioner.[219] Despite his pro-Zionist views, Arthur Wauchope hoped for a political solution to the strike rather than the expected blood bath which would ensue from a full-fledged military option, and, therefore, argued for an official endorsement of Nuri's mediation. The Colonial Office, though refraining from rendering clear support for Nuri's mission, dealt with it in a matter-of-fact fashion.[220]

Nuri held several meetings with the HAC, and paid a visit to the detained leaders, where he explained his mission and listened to the Palestinian views.[221] Upon concluding the first stage of his mediation, Nuri presented the HAC with a written proposal and embarked on a private trip to Alexandria. The proposed scheme was based on two main points: an undertaking by the HAC to exert the utmost effort to end the strike, and an assurance from the Iraqi government to mediate with the British government in order to accomplish "all Palestinian Arabs' legitimate demands".[222] It appears, however, that despite its full cooperation with Nuri al-Sa'id, the HAC preferred a joint Arab role rather than a solo one by Iraq. The HAC's reluctance was further reinforced by an intervention from the newly arrived al-Qawuqji who urged the Palestinian leaders not to yield to Nuri's pressure, promising to exert all possible effort on the military front to improve the Palestinian negotiating position.[223] More decisive in ending Nuri's first initiative was his inability to promise the Palestinians the cessation of Jewish immigration.

The second stage of Nuri's mediation began in late August, when Nuri skilfully played on the apparent differences amongst the Palestinian leaders. Under tremendous pressure from Nuri, the mufti requested that the British release 'Awni Abd al-Hadi and 'Izzat Darwaza from detention to participate in the HAC's deliberations on the proposal, a request that was granted by the High Commissioner. On 30 August, the HAC informed Nuri that only a written undertaking from the Iraqi government, affirming that the Palestinian main demands would be addressed by the British, would put an end to the strike.[224] The exasperated foreign minister knew that he could not give such an undertaking. In London, Nuri's proposal received an outright rejection, as the Colonial Office saw in it a commitment to meet Arab demands before the Royal Commission began its work, as well as an implied permanent Iraqi role in Palestinian affairs.[225] Both Darwaza and Zu'aytir indicated that, despite the impasse in the talks between Nuri and the HAC, the Palestinians maintained their commitment to the negotiations for several more days.

The fatal blow to Nuri's initiative stemmed from an official letter in which the colonial secretary, Ormsby-Gore, assured Chaim Weizmann on 3 September that no promises were made on behalf of the British government regarding a halt to Jewish immigration. More damaging was

Ormsby-Gore's denial that the Iraqi mediation was in any way sanctioned by the British government.[226] The return of the uncompromising mood in Whitehall was a reflection on the one hand of Ormsby-Gore's known pro-Zionist dispositions, and on the other of the cabinet decision on 2 September to crush the revolt by sheer force. This decision entailed the arrival of new enforcements, raising the number of British troops in Palestine to 20,000 soldiers.[227] Despite its downfall, Nuri's initiative, as well as that of Abdullah, precipitated a subtle change in the HAC's position, illustrated in its readiness to negotiate an end to the strike before gaining a British ban on Jewish immigration. During the month of September, the political, military, and psychological pressures of the strike made the HAC more amenable to Arab mediation. The mufti, al-Nashashibi, and the Istiqlalist, Abd al-Hadi, all consented to ending the strike without any preconditions if the HAC was called upon to do so by the Arab rulers.[228]

Some historians of the Middle East tend to characterize resentfully Britain's grudging acceptance of the Arab intervention in the Palestinian strike as the seed of the Arabization of the Palestinian problem. Commenting on this development, G. Sheffer wrote that London's Palestinian-Arab policies in 1936 were the prelude to the construction of Arabism and Arab unity by officials of the Royal Institute of International Affairs (Chatham House).[229] In such analyses, the deliberate overlooking of the wider Arab response to the Palestinian situation is striking. The strike did indeed mark the beginning of a long and uninterrupted involvement of the Arab states in the Palestinian question. But the Arab states' role(s) in the strike was neither premeditated nor was it orchestrated. Papers of the 2 September cabinet meeting illustrate that the Saudis, as well as the Jordanians, were becoming increasingly apprehensive after the initial success of Nuri al-Sa'id. The British, on the other hand, were most of the time undecided. Both sides, the Arab and the British governments, were largely compelled to cooperate by the strong Arab popular support for the Palestinians. For the British, the primary determinant of policy was safeguarding of the empire and catering for its strategic needs. In the end, the Arab states' intervention developed along the lines of the British view, rather than of the Palestinian demands. Moreover, in November 1936, when the Iraqi and Saudi governments agreed on a united representation to the Peel Commission, Whitehall refused to admit anything other than a separate memorandum from each state.[230] London was not in any way prepared to yield to the idea of Arab unity.

NOTES

1 Zu'aytir, 1980:53–4 (entry of 16 April 1936); High Commissioner to Secretary of State for Colonies, 29 April 1936, CO 733/297/75156/II.

2 On the Qassami movement, see Lachman, 1982; Hamuda, 1985; Nafi, 1997.

3 For the British cabinet decision regarding the Legislative Council in Palestine, 19 January 1936, see CO 733/293/75102. On the Arab and Jewish responses see High Commissioner to Secretary of State for Colonies, 22 February 1936, ibid.

4 *Filastin*, 15, 19, and 22 April 1936; High Commissioner to Secretary of State for Colonies, 18 April 1936, CO 733/297/75156/II.

5 Porath, 1977: vol. 2, 159–60.

6 CID reports, 22 January 1936 and 10 March 1936, FO 371/20018, E 887 and E 1717 respectively; Zu'aytir, 1980:60.

7 Zu'aytir, ibid., 60–1; Darwaza, 1949–51: vol. 3, 122.

8 *Filastin*, 21, 23, and 25 April 1936. See also texts of telegrams from the committees of major Palestinian cities to Nablus in al-Hout (ed.), 1984:413–15.

9 *Filastin*, 26 April 1936.

10 Darwaza, 1949–51: vol. 3, 122–3.

11 Darwaza, ibid., 123. Al-Hout (1986:336), quoting Husayn al-Khalidi's unpublished memoirs, indicated that it was al-Nashashibi who first proposed the mufti's name.

12 Darwaza, ibid.; al-Hout, 1986:336; High Commissioner to Secretary of State for Colonies, 29 April 1936, CO 733/ 297/75156/II.

13 Zu'aytir, 1980:82–3 (entry of 1 May 1936). Similar demands were made in a meeting of the Arab women of Jerusalem.

14 *Filastin*, 9 and 15 May 1936.

15 On the mufti's moderate attitudes during the first days of the strike, see High Commissioner to Secretary of State for Colonies, 29 April 1936, CO 733/297/ 75156/II.

16 The speech was reported in *Filastin* (9 May 1936), and was excerpted in Zu'aytir, 1980:90–1.

17 Zu'aytir, ibid., 91.

18 Al-Sifri, 1937: vol. 2, 18.

19 High Commissioner to Secretary of State for Colonies, 6 June 1936, CO 733/ 310/75528/249.

20 Ibid.; Porath, 1977: vol. 2, 167.

21 Darwaza, 1949–51: vol. 3, 121.

22 CID reports, 6 and 21 May 1936, FO 371/20018/E 2973 and E 3490 respectively.

23 High Commissioner to Secretary of State for Colonies, 8 July 1936, CO 733/ 313/75228/37.

24 Al-Sifri, 1937: vol. 2, 28–32.

25 Ibid.; Porath, 1977: vol. 2, 172. It is maybe significant that the High Commissioner did not consider the mufti on strike, see High Commissioner to Secretary of State for Colonies, 17 June 1936, CO 733/297/7516/III. Upon receiving this report from the High Commissioner, the Secretary of State for Colonies declared the news in the House of Commons on 19 June 1936. This declaration was meant to soothe the Indian Muslims' feelings towards the situation in Palestine. However, the statement provoked a strong protest from the mufti who declared that the SMC had not been functioning since the early days of the strike (Jbara, 1985:145–6).

26 Only a few days after the beginning of the strike, the mufti wrote to Ibn Sa'ud appealing for his support against the "British Zionist policy" (Sir Andrew Ryan, Jeddah, to Antony Eden, 1 May 1936, L/P & S/12/3342/P. Z. 4107).

27 High Commissioner to Secretary of State for Colonies, 24 April 1936, CO 733/310/75528 Part I.

28 Zu'aytir, 1980:110–19.

29 The High Commissioner, however, contemplated the idea of deporting the mufti and members of the HAC as early as 18 May, but then decided not to do so, mainly to avoid possible Palestinian and Arab reactions (High Commissioner to Secretary of State for Colonies, 18 May 1936, CO 733/311/75528/6). Citing a Zionist report, Porath stated that the detention of 'Awni Abd al-Hadi was prompted by the mufti (Porath, 1977: vol. 2, 170). Porath's conclusion, however, contradicts the British official version which indicated that Abd al-Hadi's arrest was ordered by the High Commissioner because of his organizing capabilities (Kayyali, 1978:194). The British focus on the Istiqlalists can also be discerned from their decision to detain 'Izzat Darwaza who replaced Abd al-Hadi in the HAC.

30 High Commissioner to Secretary of State for Colonies, 6 June 1936, CO 733/310/75528/II.

31 High Commissioner to Secretary of State for Colonies, 20 August 1936, CO 733/257/11.

32 High Commissioner to Secretary of State for Colonies, 30 June 1936, CO 733/310/75528/II.

33 High Commissioner to Parkinson, 22 September 1936, CO 733/297/75156.

34 Cf. Porath, 1977: vol. 2, 195.

35 Aboushi, 1985:94.

36 Al-Sifri, 1937: vol. 2, 57–60, 75ff.

37 Aboushi, 1985:94–5.

38 Report of His Majesty's Government in the United Kingdom of Great Britain and Northern Ireland to the Council of League of Nations on the Administration of Palestine and Transjordan for the Year 1936, Colonial No. 129, HMSO, London 1937, p. 11. This concentration camp was erected at 'Ujat al-Hafir in the middle of the Negev desert.

39 Al-Sifri, 1937: vol. 2, 88–91.

40 Report of His Majesty's Government . . . (see n. 38), p. 14.

41 Al-Sifri, 1937: vol. 2, 108–10; Colonial Secretary's Memorandum of 10 July 1936 and Cabinet Conclusions, 52 (36), 5 July 1936, CO 733/313/75528/24.

42 According to an official memorandum written in 1947, comparing the two different policies adopted by the government of Palestine towards the 1936–9

Arab revolt and the 1945–7 Jewish revolt, it was stated that during 1936 only (the year of the strike) 314 non-terrorist Arabs were killed, while 1,337 were wounded. In the same year, 1,000 other Arabs (identified as terrorists) were killed, while the figure for the wounded was not available. Comparatively, only 37 of the security forces were killed and 206 were wounded (Cairo to the Foreign Office, Secret, 2 July 1947, FO 141/1116/ E 5918, a copy of a report from the High Commissioner for Palestine to the Secretary of State for Colonies, 14 June 1947, Memorandum on the Comparative treatment of the Arabs during the disturbances of 1936–9 and of the Jews during the disturbances of 1945 and subsequent years).

43 Ibid.
44 N. Vilensky to Sherton, 22 May 1936, CZA-S/25, 3247.
45 Al-Hout (ed.), 1984:415; Zu'aytir, 1980:75 (entry of 24 April 1936).
46 Zu'aytir, ibid., 81 (entry of 30 April 1936).
47 Darwaza, 1959: vol. I, 1937. On other manifestations of Indian support, see Zu'aytir, 1980:186, 193, 211–13.
48 *Al-Ahram*, 26 and 31 July, 18 and 25 August 1936; *al-Rabita al-'Arabiyya*, 15 July 1936.
49 *Al-Ahram*, 19 and 23 July 1936.
50 Al-Banna, n.d.: 118.
51 Gershoni, 1979:22–57; Gershoni, 1982:70–81. See also, *Jaridat al-Ikhwan al-Muslimin*, 1 Jamadi al-Akhira, AH 1352 (21 September 1933).
52 *Al-Rabita al-'Arabiyya*, first issue, 27 May 1936; Chejne, 1957:257.
53 Al-Zayyat, 1956: vol. 4, 72; Muhammad, 1982:50–1.
54 Muhammad, ibid., 22.
55 Coury, 1982: part 2, 461.
56 Ramadan, 1974:312; al-Bishri, 1980:517–25.
57 Abd al-Rahman, 1980:271–2. From July 1936, *al-Ahram* began publishing the daily schedule of Jerusalem Radio Arabic service (*al-Ahram*, 22 July 1936). On the supportive coverage of *Kawkab al-Sharq*, *al-Balagh* and *al-Jihad*, see al-Ghuri, 1973: vol. 2, 104; Mayer, 1983:45–6.
58 Qasimiyya, 1974:150–63.
59 See, for example, *al-Risala*, vol. 4, 8 June 1936, pp. 928–30; 15 June 1936, p. 989; 29 June 1936, pp. 1049–50; 27 July 1936, p. 1232; 3 August 1936, pp. 1269 and 1278; 10 August 1936, p. 1317; 24 August 1936, pp. 1363–4; 31 August 1936, p.1434; 7 September 1936, p. 1472; 14 September 1936, pp. 1512–13; 21 September 1936, p. 1551; 28 September 1936, pp. 1586–7; 5 October 1936, pp. 1628–34; 12 October 1936, p. 1671; 19 October 1936, p. 696.
60 Kelly to FO, 11 June 1936, FO 371/20035/E 3452; al-Ghuri, 1973: vol. 2, 103–4.
61 Kelly to FO, 4 June 1936, FO 371/20035/E 3483; 9 June 1936, FO 371/20035/J5232, and 11 June 1936, FO 371/20035/J 5575.
62 *Jaridat al-Ikhwan al-Muslimin*, 13 and 20 August 1935.
63 Ibid., 27 August and 5 November 1935.
64 Ibid., 19 May 1936; al-Banna, n.d.: 240–2.
65 Al-Banna, ibid.; Ministry of Interior (Cairo) to Oriental Secretary (Cairo), 17 May 1936, FO 371/20035/E 4415. On other Ikhwani activities see *Jaridat al-Ikhwan al-Muslimin*, 28 April, 26 May, and 16 June 1936.

66 *Jaridat al-Ikhwan al-Muslimin*, 2 June 1936. As a result, Abd al-Hamid Sa'id resigned his position in the National Party to dedicate more time to his activities for Palestine (*al-Ahram*, 15 and 23 July 1936). A special committee was also established, chaired by the Copt, Tawfiq Duss, to organize support within the Coptic community (Lampson to Wauchope 3 July 1936, FO 371/20035/E 4415).

67 *Al-Ahram*, 22, 27 May, and 8 October 1936.

68 Ibid., 14 June 1936; Kelly to FO, June 1936, FO 371/20035/ E 3507. What might have also contributed to al-Azhar's movement was the open letter of Shaykh al-Maraghi to the High Commissioner in Palestine, protesting the British policies (Zu'aytir, 1980:122).

69 *Jaridat al-Ikhwan al-Muslimin*, 12 October 1936. Earlier, the Egyptian police arrested a citizen distributing a leaflet, calling on the Alexandrians to rise in a *jihad* for the support of Palestine (*al-Ahram*, 12 June 1936).

70 Kelly to FO, 4, 5, 16 and 22 June 1936, FO 371/20035/E 3452, E 3483, E 3598, E 3753. The leader of the opposition Muhammad Mahmud Pasha (the Liberal Constitutionalist), spoke to British officials in Cairo of his sympathies – as an Arab – with the Palestinians (Mayer, 1983:47–8).

71 Kedourie, 1970:197–201; al-Bishri, 1980:377–8. Al-Maraghi's first term in the Shaykhdom of al-Azhar continued from 1928 to 1930, when he was forced out of office as a result of the Palace's dissatisfaction with his reform programme for al-Azhar.

72 For more details, see Charles Tripp, "Ali Mahir Pasha and the Palace in Egyptian Politics, 1936–1942: Seeking for Autocracy", Ph.D. thesis, University of London, 1984:118–21.

73 Coury, Ph.D. dissertation, 1984:518.

74 *Al-Manar*, vol. 35, 1939, pp. 1–2.

75 See a British Intelligence Assessment of the Ikhwan, written some time later, in Miles Lampson to A. Eden, 24 December 1942, FO 371/35578/J 245. Secret. Enclosure, Appendix "A". Also a memorandum by Dr J. Heyworth-Dunne, "New Political Elements in Egypt", 18 November 1943, FO 371/35539/ J 4741, in which it was argued that Abd al-Rahman 'Azzam, representing Mahir, and Ahmad al-Sukkari from the *Ikhwan*, made the relationship possible. See also Abd al-Halim, 1979: vol. 1, 147.

76 Mitchell, 1969:16; Kedourie, 1970:198.

77 *Jaridat al-Ikhwan al-Muslimin*, 13 and 14 June, 1 and 22 September 1936; al-Banna, n.d.: 252–4.

78 Sa'id, 1935: vol.1, 531–2; Darwaza, 1949–51: vol. 2, 42–3; Khoury, 1987:245–317.

79 Khoury, ibid., 424.

80 On Mardam's (1893–1960) political career, see *Man Hwa fi al-'Alam al-'Arabi, Suriyya*, 1957:578–9. A highly partisan biography, written by his daughter, is in Mardam-Bey, 1994:1–5. A brilliant discussion of his role in Syrian politics between 1920 and 1945 is in Khoury, 1987: *passim*.

81 As was relayed by his colleague, 'Awni Abd al-Hadi (Qasimiyya (ed.), 1974:16–17).

82 On Mardam's opposition to the National Bloc's 1934 resolution to call for a Syrian unity with Iraq, Palestine, and Transjordan, see al-Hashimi, 1967: vol. 1, 358.

83 On Mardam's pan-Arab activities in 1934–5, see Mackereth (Damascus) to Simon (London), 10 May 1934, FO 684/7/45; al-Hout (ed.), 1984:394; Khoury, 1987:450.

84 Khoury, ibid., 276–7. The text of the Basic Document of the Arab Bureau is in al-Hout (ed.), 1984:383–6.

85 Shukri, 1957: vol. 2, 994–6. On al-Barudi's career see *Man Hwa fi al-'Alam al-'Arabi, Suriyya*, 1957:66–7.

86 *Al-'Arab*, 16 September 1933; Zu'aytir, 1980:43–5 (entry of 20 January 1936).

87 Zu'aytir, ibid., 144–5 (entry of 27 July 1936); Darwaza, 1959: vol. 1, 133. On al-'Azma's activities during the preceding months of the strike, see Zu'aytir, ibid. 72 and 121.

88 CID (Palestine) to CO, 18 February 1936, FO 371/20018/1293; *al-Shabab*, 17 February and 2 March 1936; Quwwatli to al-'Azma, 13 March 1936, al-'Azma Papers, The Syrian Files, 4/137.

89 Farzat, 1955:131ff.; Qarqut, 1978:395–8.

90 The British consulate in Damascus expressed satisfaction over the engagement of Syrian nationalist leaders in negotiations with France, hoping that this engagement would preclude them from arousing sentiments in Syria in support of Palestine (Mackereth to High Commissioner of Palestine, 21 April 1936, FO 371/20065/2177; Ogden to Eden, 22 August, FO 371/20024/E 5495).

91 Al-Sifri, 1937: vol. 2, 64–5; Yasin, 1959:33, 219–20; Khoury, 1987:542–3.

92 Yasin, ibid.; al-Hout (ed.), 1984:413; Zu'aytir, 1980:75.

93 Al-Sifri, 1937: vol. 2, 64–5; Khoury, 1987:543.

94 Davis to FO, 9 October 1937, FO 684/10/1692; al-Quwwatli to Nabih al-'Azma, 4 June 1936, al-'Azma Papers, The Syrian Files, 4/147; al-Ghuri, 1973: vol. 2, 92; Zu'aytir, 1980:34.

95 Khoury, 1987:543. Members of the committee were: Fakhri al-Barudi; the Istiqlalist, Hajj Adib Khayr; Muhammad al-Sarraj; Fu'ad Muffarraj (a former lecturer at the American University of Beirut and member of the Arab Bureau); Fa'iz al-Khuri; Sabri al-'Asali (a former leader in the NAL); 'Afif al-Sulh; Bashir al-Shihabi; and Nabih al-'Azma as president (al-'Azma Papers, The Syrian Files, 6/383).

96 Yasin, 1959:219–20; Porath, 1977: vol. 2, 187; Zu'aytir, 1980:72 (entry of 22 April 1936).

97 "Minutes of Conversation with Dr Shahbandar and Amin eff. Said at Cairo, 21 September 1936", CZA-S25/3435.

98 "Note of Meeting of Zionist Organization Advisory Committee, London", 8 and 25 June 1936, CZA-S25/6326.

99 "Minutes of Conversation with Fakhri Bey al-Barudi at Dummar on 17 July 1936", CZA-S25/9783; "Minutes of the Meeting with the Arab Nationalist Party (the National Bloc) at Bludan on 1 August 1936", CZA-S25/10093; Political Department Diary, 10–11 August 1936, CZA-S25/443; several other reports by Eliyahu Epstein on his talks with the Syrian leaders in CZA-S25/3267.

100 For more details, see Caplan, 1986: vol. 2, 46–51; Khoury, 1987:584–92 and Porath, 1988:62–4.

101 Caplan, ibid., 49.

102 Both al-Shahbandar and al-Quwwatli were in contact with the mufti and the HAC during talks with the Zionists (Caplan, 1986: vol. 2, 46; Porath, 1988:64).

103 Reissner, 1980:50ff.; Farfur, 1987:166–8 and 289–90; al-Hafiz and Abaza, 1988: vol. 2, 586–9.

104 Al-Janhani, 1987:114; al-Banna, n.d.: 231.
105 Al-Hafiz and Abaza, 1986: vol. 2, 763–4 and 918–25; al-Tantawi, 1986:409–20.
106 Consul Gardener to Mr Eden, 10 April 1941, FO 406/79/E 2840 (Appendix); Farzat, 1955: 10; al-Husaini, 1956:75.
107 Al-Husaini, ibid.; Batatu, 1982:15–16.
108 Khoury, 1987:608–9.
109 Al-Hakim, 1983:287.
110 Khoury, 1987:401–2 (based on a conversation with Farid Zayn al-Din). Cf. al-Hout, 1986:491–6 (based mainly on an interview with Wasif Kamal).
111 Khoury, ibid., 402.
112 Al-'Awdat, 1976:543–6; Zu'aytir, 1980: 2, 3, 7, 34, 37, 40, 44 and *passim*; al-Hout, 1986:235, 242, 245, 256, 315, 334, 381.
113 Al-Hout, ibid., 492.
114 Ibid., 491; Khoury, 1987:402–3; Zu'aytir, Memoirs, *al-Hayat*, 22 June 1994.
115 Zu'aytir, ibid.; al-Hout, ibid., 494; Khoury, ibid., 403–4.
116 On Rushdi al-Jabi and Abd al-Karim al-'A'idi see *Man Hwa fi al-'Alim al-'Arabi, Suriyya*, 1957:128 and 398–9 respectively. On al-Dandashi see Khoury, 1987:406. On the Qarnaiyl meeting, see Farzat, 1955:138ff.; Qarqut, 1975:178–9.
117 Zu'aytir, Memoirs, *al-Hayat*, 22 June 1994.
118 Zu'aytir, ibid.; Consul Gardener to Mr Eden, 10 April 1941, FO 406/79/E 2840 (Appendix); Farzat, 1955:138–40.
119 On the relations between the National Bloc and the NAL during the 1930s see Khoury, 1987: 406–33.
120 Al-Hout, 1986: 495. A biography of Farid al-Sa'd is in al-'Awdat, 1976:263–4.
121 Al-Hout, ibid., 491.
122 Al-Mallah, 1980:66. Alfred Mond became president of the British Zionist Federation in the year of his visit to Iraq.
123 Batatu, 1978:398–400.
124 Al-Hasani, 1953–61: vol. 2, 84–5; al-Husri, 1966–8: vol. 1, 557–75.
125 High Commissioner (Iraq), to Secretary of State for Colonies, 9 February 1928, FO 371/13033/ E 702.
126 *Al-'Alam al-'Arabi*, 10 February 1928; Mushtaq, 1989:188–94.
127 *Al-'Alam al-'Arabi*, 16, 22, 23 February 1928; al-Husri, 1966–8: vol. 1, 13.
128 *Al-'Alam al-'Arabi*, 11 February 1928.
129 CID report (Baghdad), 15 February 1928, FO 371/13028/E 1075.
130 Jamil, 1987:204–6 and 218–19.
131 Clayton's reports (Baghdad) to CO (London), 1 and 11 September 1929, CO 730/148/68403/4 Part 1 and CO 730/149/68478/44 respectively.
132 On al-Hashimi's committee for aiding Syria during the 1925–7 revolt, see Masalha, 1991:681.
133 For a detailed analysis of the place of Arabism in the Iraqi educational system, see Simon, 1986:75–114.
134 Zu'aytir, 1980:209–10; al-Sawwaf, 1987:25 and 70.
135 Al-Sawwaf, ibid., 72–3. Hasan Rida, a lawyer and president of the YMMS chapter of Baghdad was in the Iraqi delegation at the Islamic Congress of Jerusalem in 1931 (Kupferschmidt, 1987:270).
136 Shubbar, 1990: vol. 1, 242.

137 Kupferschmidt, 1987:270
138 Zu'aytir, 1980:360 and 382; Shubbar, 1990: vol. 1, 243.
139 Al-Hashimi, 1978: vol. 2, 335.
140 Al-Hasani, 1953–61: vol. 4, 49ff.
141 Khadduri, 1951:5–6; Silverfarb, 1986:21–2.
142 Sir A. Clark Kerr to Mr Eden, 4 January 1938, FO 371/21853/E 435 (confidential, section 4, Enclosure, Report on the Leading Personalities in Iraq); al-Swaydi, 1987:113–15.
143 Batatu, 1978:295; Khadduri, 1951:31.
144 Al-Hashimi, 1978: vol. 2, 40.
145 On Nuri al-Sa'id see Kerr to Eden, 4 January 1938, FO 371/21853/E 435; Basri, 1987:126–40; al-Swaydi, 1987:83–94. For a forthright impression of the personality clash between Nuri and al-Hashimi, see al-Shabandar, 1993:128–40.
146 In 1931, supporters of al-Hashimi were openly calling for the establishment of a republic led by him (Acting High Commissioner, Baghdad, to Secretary of State for Colonies, 11 July 1931, FO 371/15324/E 715). Rumours about al-Hashimi's designs to uproot the monarchy continued to haunt him until the end of his political life in 1936 (Kerr to Eden , 23 December 1936, FO 371/20795/E 66). Similarly, Nuri's dislike of King Ghazi was the reason for Nuri's insistence in the summer of 1936 on Prime Minister al-Hashimi's removal of the king and appointment of a Regency Council to govern until the child heir reached the legal age (Kerr to Eden, 15 June 1936, FO 371/20017/133). Two years later, Nuri told an official of the British embassy in Baghdad, "We are not bound to the House of Faisal" (Peterson to Lancelot Oliphant, 31 December 1938, FO 371/21847/E 281).
147 In late 1935, al-Hashimi told the British ambassador in Baghdad that "without Nuri he clearly could not stand" (Kerr to Samuel Hoare, 6 December 1935, FO 406/73/E 7470). Again, in October 1936, Yasin refused to comply with the king's demand to remove Nuri from the cabinet (Kerr to Eden, 21 October 1936 FO 371/20013/522).
148 Brief biographies of these personalities are included in Kerr to Eden, 4 January 1938, FO 371/21853/E 435; al-Basri, 1987 and al-Swaydi, 1987. On the establishment of al-Ikha' Party see Khadduri, 1951:31.
149 Al-Hasani, 1953–61: vol. 3, 90.
150 On the first major crisis in the National Party, which led to the resignation of Sa'id al-Hajj Thabit and Mahmud al-Shaykh Ali, see al-'Alam al-'Arabi, 30 November 1932, and al-Istiqlal, 17 January 1933. On Abu al-Timman's resignation from the party see Batatu, 1978:296 and al-Mallah,1980:121–2.
151 Batatu, ibid.; 300–5; al-Chadirchi,1970:29–52.
152 The most thoughtful description of the events that led to al-Hashimi's rise to power is in Khadduri, 1951:48–55. See also Kerr to Eden, Iraq Annual Report, 1935, 31 January 1936, FO 371/20010/56; al-Hasani, 1953–61: vol. 4, 59ff.
153 Khadduri, ibid., 56.
154 Al-Istiqlal, 28 April 1935.
155 Kubba, 1965:54–7. According to the application that was presented to the interior ministry, al-Muthanna Club was committed to "disseminating the spirit of Arab nationalism, . . . preserving Arab traditions, . . . strengthening the sense of Arab manhood in the youths, and creating a new Arab culture which would integrate to the Arab heritage what is worthy in the civilization of the West", Iraqi police

file entitled *Nadi al-Muthanna bin Harithah ash-Shaibani*, entry of 2 September 1935 (quoted in Batatu, 1978:298).

156 The list of names was compiled from the following sources: Khadduri, 1951:110, 148, 159–61; Batatu: 1978:298; Zu'aytir, 1980: 9, 181, and 353; Salman, 1985:39–40; Simon, 1986:72–3; Hamdi, 1987: 230; Almond, 1993:37–8. The club membership reached 130 members, many of whom emerged later (1946–58) as founders of the Iraqi Istiqlal Party. The significant number of Iraqi Shi'i members of al-Muthanna raises doubts over Nakash's conclusion that the Shi'i of Iraq had little interest in Arab nationalism (cf. Nakash, 1994:133).

157 According to Salman (1985:39), al-Muthanna Club was effectively run from behind the scenes by a secret cell that included the army officers, Salah al-Din al-Sabbagh and Fahmi Sa'id, and Yunis al-Sab'awi, Salim Thabit, Ibrahim 'Attar Bashi and Siddiq Shanshal.

158 On al-Sab'awi's early life, see al-'Umari, 1986:13–42.

159 Batatu, 1978:457; al-Hasani, 1990:23.

160 On the careers of al-Sabbagh and Sa'id, see British embassy (Baghdad) to FO, 1 October 1940, FO 371/24562/E 22329; al-Sabbagh, 1994:31–3 (Al-Sabbagh's memoirs were first published in Damascus in 1956, the reference here is to the Rabat edition of 1994).

161 Al-'Umari, 1986:35–42 and 64–5.

162 Al-Barrak, 1987:181; al-Hasani, 1990:23.

163 Al-Swaydi, 1969:259–63; al-Sabbagh, 1994:82.

164 Al-'Umari, 1986:55–61.

165 For Salman's and Shabib's biographies see Baghdad to FO, 1 October 1940, FO 371/24562/E 22329; al-Sabbagh, 1994:31–3.

166 Including, amongst others, Sati' al-Husri, Sami Shawkat, Muhammad Ali al-Tahir, Abd al-Wahhab and Abd al-Rahman 'Azzam, and the Syrian poet, Badawi al-Jabal. See Kerr to Eden, 24 February 1936, FO 406/74/E 1173; Kubba, 1965:54–7; Cleveland, 1971:74; Coury, Ph.D. dissertation, 1984:462 and 486–7; Salman, 1985:4.

167 CID report, Periodical Appreciation Summary (PAS), 2/36, 18 February 1936, FO 371/20018/E 1293.

168 Zu'aytir, 1980:51. For the delegation's visit to Egypt see Coury, Ph.D. dissertation, 1984:381–3.

169 Al-Sifri, 1937: vol. 2, 65–6; Zu'aytir, ibid.; al-Nimr, n.d.: vol. 3:256–7; CID report, PAS, 5/36, 17 March 1936, FO 371/20018/E 1993.

170 *Al-Rabita al-'Arabiyya*, 22 July 1936; Kubba, 1965:59; al-Nimr, n.d.: vol. 3: 256; al-Sawwaf, 1987:73. On the committee's activities in 1933, in which Yunis al-Sab'awi was also involved, see *al-'Alam al-'Arabi*, 15 July 1933.

171 Kerr (Baghdad) to Eden, 4, 5, and 12 May and 17 June 1936, FO 371/20020/E 2635, E 2654, E 3399, respectively; *al-Bilad*, 28 June 1936; *al-Rabita al-'Arabiyya*, 22 July 1936; Zu'aytir, 1980:95 and 141–2.

172 The delegation, headed by Naji al-Swaydi, included Abd al-'Aziz al-Qassab, Dawud al-Sa'di, Rashid al-Khuja, Ali Mahmud al-Shaykh Ali (Sunnis), Shaykh Muhammad Rida al-Shabibi, Sayyid Abd al-Mahdi (Shi'is), and Rufa'il Butti (Christian) (Kerr to Eden, 4 May 1936, FO 371/20020/E 2653; Zu'aytir, 1980:95). On the background of the delegation's members see Kerr to Eden, 4 January 1938, FO 371/21853/E 435

173 Kubba, 1965:59; Zu'aytir, 1980:152, 173, 209–10. On the structure of the committee and its branches see *Jam'iyyat al-Difa' 'An Filastin Fi al-'Iraq, al-Nizam al-'Asasi wal-Dakili, 1937* (al-'Azma Papers, The Arab Files, 4/225).

174 *Al-Istiqlal*, 8 October 1936.

175 Al-Sifri, 1937: vol. 2, 69–89; Darwaza, 1949–51: vol. 3, 128–32.

176 Tegart Papers, "Terrorism, 1936–37", Box I, File 3/C; and, "Terrorism: General, November 1938", Box I, 3/C; Yasin, 1959:48–120.

177 Zu'aytir, 1955: 126; Salman, 1985:41; al-Sabbagh, 1994:140.

178 Al-Sifri, 1937: vol. 1, 60; Khilla, 1983:301–2.

179 On 'Adil al-'Azma's involvement with the NAL, see al-Hashimi, 1978: vol. 2, 74. On his life, see Qasimiyya (ed.), 1991:17–132 (this scattered political biography, however, is seen from the viewpoint of his relationship with his brother, Nabih al-'Azma). On his early involvement in support of the Palestinian revolt, see Khoury, 1987:546.

180 Al-Hashimi, 1967: vol. 1, 229–30; Qasimiyya (ed.), 1975: vol. 2, 9 and 22.

181 Rashid Rida to Nabih al-'Azma, 22 August 1932, al-'Azma Papers, The Syrian Files, 3/71; al-Jundi, 1960:93–4 and 553–4.

182 Batman to Eden, 25 June 1936, FO 371/20016/E 3986.

183 Al-Hashimi, 1978: vol. 2, 28–9; Qasimiyya (ed)., 1975: vol. 2, 5–12.

184 Note by 'Adil al-'Azma on al-Qawuqji's mission of August 1936, al-'Azma Papers, University of Exeter, appendix file of unclassified documents; al-Rayyis, 1976:22; Zu'aytir, 1980:147–8.

185 Al-'Azma, ibid.,; Batman to Rendel, 18 August and 30 September 1936, FO 371/20016/E 5551 and E 6507 respectively; Qasimiyya (ed.), 1975: vol. 2, 14.

186 Al-'Azma, ibid.; al-Nimr, n.d.: vol. 3: 256–8; Mackereth to FO, 15 August 1936, FO 371/20069/6709. In the meantime, al-Hashimi was channelling financial aid to the strike through the Iraqi consulate in Haifa (Zu'aytir, 1980:277).

187 Al-Jundi, 1960:561; Darwaza, 1949–51: vol. 3, 134; Nwayhid, 1981:107 and 305.

188 Al-Nimr, n.d.: vol. 3, 263; Qasimiyya (ed.), 1975: vol. 2, 10, 17, 23, 26, and 55; Zu'aytir, 1980:181 and 192.

189 Al-Nimr, ibid., 262. Jamil Shaker (as indicated by al-Nimr) is most likely Jamil al-Rawi, the former Ottoman and Sharifian officer and at one time a vice-president of the Iraqi parliament (Kerr to Eden, 4 January 1938, FO 371/21853/E 435). On al-Rawi's association with Palestine, see also Yasin al-Hashimi to Nabih al-'Azma, 1 December 1936, al-'Azma Papers, The Arab Files, 8/446.

190 Al-Nimr, ibid., 257–64.

191 Ibid., 263–4; al-Sifri, 1937: vol. 2, 146 and Porath, 1977: vol. 2, 189.

192 Darwaza, 1949–51: vol. 3, 135.

193 See al-Qawuqji's first communiqué of 28 August 1936 in al-Hout (ed.), 1984:448–9. Other communiqués, including the last (no. 20) in ibid., 449–52. See also Mahfuz, 1938:25–43.

194 When al-Qawuqji withdrew from Palestine after the end of the strike he was accompanied by the most prominent Qassami leader, Farhan al-Sa'di, who remained in Iraq until mid-1937 (Qasimiyya (ed.), 1975: vol. 2, 22; Zu'aytir, 1980:226).

195 Al-Ghuri, 1973: vol. 2, 22, 96, 118, and 219; al-Nimr, n.d.: vol. 3, 264.

196 Al-Qawuqji accused the Palestinian platoon of withdrawing before the end of battle, thereby exposing a section of the rebels' lines (Qasimiyya (ed.), 1975: vol. 2, 26; Mahfuz, 1938:38–9).

197 Peirce to Air Ministry, 15 October 1936, CO 733/317/94 (quoted in Kayyali, 1978:199).

198 *Filastin*, 11 October 1936. Ghazi's and Abdullah's texts were issued on 9 October 1936, and that of the Saudi monarch a day earlier. The British government was described as a friend in the Saudi text and as an ally in the Iraqi text, but there was no adjective to describe it in Abdullah's overcautious text (Zu'aytir, 1980:206; al-Hout (ed.), 1984:458–9).

199 See for, example, the pertinent resolutions of the HAC in *Filastin*, 27 April 1936. See also the text of the mufti's speech to the Conference of National Committees, *Filastin*, 9 May 1936. In a letter to Abd al-'Aziz al-Sa'ud, Nabih al-'Azma made a clear reference to the Saudi means, in terms of land, sea routes, and pipelines, that could influence British interests in the region (probably in August or September 1936, al-'Azma Papers, The Arab Files, 2/101).

200 Preparing Sir Harold MacMichael for his new post as High Commissioner of Palestine, the colonial secretary, W. Ormsby-Gore, wrote in a private and personal letter (MacMichael Papers, St Antony's College Middle East Centre, DS 126.2, 15 December 1937): "As I see it, we have to remain in Palestine for strategic reasons and for reasons of political prestige . . . We cannot admit that it is just like any other part of the Arab Moslem World, any more than we can admit that it is a Jewish country. Palestine is unique and of universal significance . . . We must continue to rule in Jerusalem and Bethlehem and Nazareth, and I believe we can never give up our control of Haifa and the Gulf of Akaba either to Jews or Arabs or to any other power. So Palestine is not merely a question of reconciling the conflicting aspirations of 800,000 Arabs and 400,000 Jews, but of protecting and maintaining British interests and British authorities."

201 Exchange of telegrams between Ryan and FO (30 April 1936); Rendel of the FO Middle East Department to Colonial Under-Secretary (5 May 1936); CO to Foreign Under-Secretary (8 May 1936); and FO to Ryan (7 May 1936) in CO 733/312/75528/I. See also Rose, 1972:214–15 and Porath, 1977; vol. 2, 201–2.

202 Lampson to FO, 8 July 1936, FO 371/20021/E 4257. For similar responses to al-Nahhas's overture in August see Mayer, 1983:52–3.

203 Shlaim, 1988:52–3.

204 Abdullah to High Commissioner (an Arabic text), 22 May 1936, in al-Hout (ed.), 1984:430–1; High Commissioner to Secretary of State for Colonies, 7 June 1936, CO 733/297/75156/II; Rose, 1972: 216; Porath, 1977: vol. 2, 202–3; Wilson, 1987:116.

205 Kerr to FO, 3 June 1936, FO 371/20016/E 3399.

206 Minutes of the High Commissioner's meeting with the Arab Higher Committee, 14 May 1936, CO 733/311/75528/7.

207 Statement of the Secretary of State for the Colonies to the House of Commons, 18 May 1936, Parliamentary Debates, Fifth Series, Commons, vol. 315, col. 426.

208 Yasin, 1959:34–6; al-Kayyali, 1978:193–5; Zu'aytir, 1980:107–10. See also Abu Gharbiyya (1993:67–79) in which he revealed that several armed attacks on Jewish targets in Jerusalem, during May and June, were, in fact, planned and executed by a small ring of independent Jerusalemite youths. Al-Ghuri's pro-Husayni

claims (1973: vol. 2, 82–3) that Abd al-Qadir al-Husayni, the mufti's cousin and leader of the secretive organization al-Jihad al-Muqadas, initiated the armed activities from early May 1936, are highly exaggerated. A. Q. al-Husayni emerged in September as second in command to the Syrian, Sa'id al-'As, in the Jerusalem sector. Al-'As was killed in an engagement with the British troops on 6 October 1936, while al-Husayni was seriously injured, which was the end of his activities in 1936 (Zu'aytir, 1980:201–2). However, in the second stage of the revolt, 1937–9, A. Q. al-Husayni's role was more substantial.

209 Foreign Office memorandum, 20 June 1936, FO 371/20021/E 3642. Sheffer (1974–5:59–78), predicating his analysis on a selective use of British dispatches from the Arab world and on an extremely partial and reductionist view of the Arab and international arenas, concluded that "The Arab population in the countries surrounding Palestine remained non-involved when the Palestinian Arabs launched their struggle against the British and Jews" (p. 77), and that "there was almost a complete lack of what is understood in the West as 'public opinion' or 'popular feelings' regarding that issue" (p. 78). What was more amusing than Sheffer's conclusion was the opinion expressed by the accomplished historian Y. Porath who wrote of Sheffer's "penetrating analysis" (Porath, 1977: vol. 2, 355, n. 341).

210 See, for example, Kerr's dispatches of 28 May and 17 June 1936, FO 371/19880/ E 3284 and 371/20016/E 3399 respectively, and Lampson's dispatch of 12 August 1936, FO 371/20023/E 5207. Lampson's unequivocal call for a change of policy in Palestine, including the cessation of Jewish immigration, gained him the wrath of the Colonial Office, whose secretary, W. Ormsby-Gore would describe him as "hostile . . . to the policy approved by the Cabinet", with "no knowledge of such factors as America, Poland, Geneva or the House of Commons", indicating, perhaps, changes in the international situation and sources of the Zionist pressure on the British government (Ormsby-Gore to H. MacMichael, 15 December 1937, MacMichael Papers, DS 126, 2). Lampson's position continued unchanged, even after the end of the strike; see, for example, Lampson to Eden, 17 June 1936, FO 371/19980/E 8028. Sir Archibald Clark Kerr, while in London in September 1936, also continued to express his views on the need for a change in Palestine policy, see Minutes by Clark Kerr, 23 September 1936, FO 371/20017/E 5672.

211 Parkinson (CO) to Oliphant (FO), 17 June 1936, FO 371/20012/E 3783.

212 Lampson to FO, 8 July 1936, FO 371/20021/E 4257; Parkinson to Oliphant, 26 June 1936, FO 371/20021/E 4108; Faraj, 1987:209, n. 123 (Faraj's study is the most revealing since, being based on the Iraqi Royal Archive, it shows that the Foreign Office was in fact encouraging joint Arab action).

213 CAB 52/36, 15 July 1936.

214 Parliamentary Debates, House of Commons, vol. 315, col. 416, 22 July 1936.

215 On Abdullah's initiative that ended towards mid-August 1936, see Darwaza, 1949–51: vol. 3, 138–9; Porath, 1977: vol. 2, 206–7; Wilson, 1987:117–18.

216 Darwaza, 1949–51: vol. 3, 140. The role of other Arab rulers was only hinted at by Nuri during his talks and discussions with the HAC leaders.

217 G. Rendel, Note of Talk with Nuri as-Sa'id, 9 June 1936, FO 371/20016/E 3466; Caplan, 1986: vol. II, 43–4.

218 Bateman to Eden, 17 August 1936, FO 20016/E 5201. It may be pertinent to mention that the Iraqi Royal Archive shows a continuous stream of correspondence between Iraq, Saudi Arabia, Yemen, and Transjordan during July and August 1936, which makes it perhaps safe to conclude that Nuri al-Sa'id was fully aware of the Saudi and Transjordanian failures to break the impasse (Faraj, 1987:209).

219 This, of course, boosted Nuri's image and made his mediation more credible in the Palestinians' eyes (Darwaza, 1949–51: vol. 3, 139; Zu'aytir, 1980:156).

220 Wauchope to Secretary of State for Colonies, 22 August 1936, CO 733/297/75528/I; CAB 55/36, 27 August 1936.

221 According to Zu'aytir, who participated in the meeting, Nuri al-Sa'id, the legendary figure of Arab pragmatism, allowed himself to cry when Hasan Sidqi al-Dajani appealed to the "Iraqi brothers" for support (Zu'aytir, 1980:157).

222 Zu'aytir, ibid., and 158; Darwaza, 1949–51: vol. 3, 139–40. Al-Sa'id's mediation received extensive attention from the Arab press inside and outside Palestine, *Filastin* and *al-Ahram*, 21–30 August 1936.

223 Qasimiyya (ed.), 1975: vol. 2, 22.

224 Darwaza, 1949–51: vol. 3, 139–41; Zu'aytir, 1980:157–65.

225 Porath, 1977: vol. 2, 209–10; Kayyali, 1978:198.

226 Darwaza, 1949–51: vol. 3, 141; Zu'aytir, 1980:163–4. It must be mentioned that Ormsby-Gore's association with Zionism had been firmly established since World War I (Weizmann, 1949:230, 246, 259, 261, 267–71, 290–1, and 360).

227 CAB 56/36, 2 September 1936; Cmd. 5497. The Secretary of State for the Colonies: Palestine Royal Commission, Report. London, 1937 (Peel Commission Report), p. 133.

228 High Commissioner to Secretary of State for Colonies, 12 September 1936, CO 733/314/75528/44/II. The role of the Arabs in bringing about the end of the strike was blatantly obvious. Of this, Rendel wrote to Oliphant on 13 October 1936 (FO 371/20027/E 6501) that "owing to their intervention, we may have been got out of a very nasty mess".

229 Sheffer, 1974–5:77–8. See also Rose, 1972:214–25; and Klieman, 1982:118–36.

230 Kerr to Rendel, 25 November 1936, FO 371/20029/E7647.

6

The 1936–9 revolt and the Arabization of the Palestinian question: phase 2

On 5 November 1936, only days before the arrival of the Royal (Peel) Commission of Inquiry in Jerusalem, the colonial secretary, W. G. Ormsby-Gore, announced that Jewish immigration to Palestine was not to be halted after all, and that 1,800 certificates of immigration had already been granted to Jews. In response, the HAC decided to boycott the commission.[1] This decision was communicated to the Arab rulers in Transjordan, Iraq and Saudi Arabia, accompanied by the now ritual calls for support. The Arab monarchs, consistent with their policy of pursuing the path of negotiation to the end, advised the HAC, to no avail, to rescind its decision.[2] For the first two months of the Peel Commission's operation, the Palestinian side made no representation to the commission, while the Zionists were presenting a carefully prepared case.

The decision to boycott the commission was taken hastily, with little, if any, attempt to assess the consequences of such a step or the new strategy of involving the Arab governments in the Palestinian question. Whereas the HAC was justified in reacting to the provocative announcement of the colonial secretary, its boycott of the commission was obviously unsustainable and self-destructive without the adoption of a long-term confrontation policy and the assurance of Arab backing. Unsure of its decision, the HAC dispatched a delegation, consisting of Shaykh Kamil al-Qassab, 'Awni Abd al-Hadi, 'Izzat Darwaza, and Mu'in al-Madi, to Baghdad and Riyadh to discuss the situation with the Iraqi and Saudi governments. In both countries, as well as in Syria where the Palestinians made a brief stop to sound out their allies of the National Bloc, the delegation received the same advice – that their boycott of the commission's proceedings was unwise and must be ended.[3] Upon the return of the delegation, the HAC announced a change of policy on 6 January 1937, and began presenting evidence to the Peel Commission. The Palestinian representation continued for twelve days, after which the commission returned to London where it received further testimonies from Zionist activists, British politicians and officials, and held several meetings with the prime minister and members of his cabinet. After protracted deliberations, the commission's report was finally released on 7 July 1937, and endorsed with an official statement of policy.

The central point of the commission's recommendations was the partition of Palestine. Under this scheme, a Jewish state would be established in most of the coastal belt and the fertile northern part of the country, while the Jerusalem–Bethlehem–Nazareth region, together with Lake Tiberias, would be joined together in a new mandate. The Palestinian Arabs would be allocated the rest of the country and this would be united with Transjordan in an independent state.[4] Although the partition was later disclaimed by the British government, it set a historical precedent that continued for decades to underline various internationally proposed solutions for the Palestinian problem. The recommendations of the Peel Commission represented the first clear interpretation of the JNH policy, when the British government officially adopted the policy of establishing a Jewish state in Palestine. In contrast, it denied the Palestinians their national entity and the freedom to determine their future. The Palestinian response to the proposed partition was one of outrage and deep anger.[5] Within a few months of the publication of the commission's report, a revolt of unprecedented magnitude surged throughout the country. It took almost two years of widespread destruction and bloodshed before the British government would abandon the partition scheme and yield to an Arab collective role in Palestine.

The revolt

A few weeks before the official publication of the commission's report, rumours abounded that the partition of Palestine would be its main recommendation. What seemed to give credence to this line of speculation was the increasing movement of Jordanian officials between Amman, Jerusalem and London. Apart from the Zionists, Amir Abdullah was likely to be the main beneficiary of the partitioning of Palestine. Equally suspicious was the sudden withdrawal, on 3 July, of al-Nashashibi's bloc (Raghib al-Nashashibi and Ya'qub Farraj) from the HAC. *Filastin*, a pro-opposition newspaper, explained the Nashashibi step in terms of liberation from commitments to the HAC agenda,[6] while the nationalist side saw it as a step towards the establishment of an alliance between the Nashashibis and Abdullah, in preparation for the imminent partition.

Speculation over the nature of the Peel Commission's report only exacerbated an already tense political situation. Sporadic acts of violence by Arabs and Jews never entirely ceased after the end of the strike, for arms and ammunition were still available to Jews as well as many Palestinian activists. During the days before the release of the commission's report, Arab opposition to the partition plan gave the British authorities cause to believe that only a significant pre-emptive measure would prevent the reigniting of the revolt. Subsequently, British officials in London and Jerusalem agreed on a plan to arrest the mufti and deport him from Palestine.[7] When a police force arrived at the HAC headquarters (where the mufti was presumably holding a meeting) to carry out the arrest orders on 17 July, it failed to capture him. The highly alert and elusive Palestinian leader had reportedly been informed of the police force move moments before its arrival.[8] He promptly left the HAC meeting and headed for al-Haram al-Sharif where he stayed safely, maintaining his daily contacts, until mid-October. Though the mandate authorities imposed a kind of siege on al-Haram al-Sharif, they took no measures to pursue the mufti in his refuge. The British imperial sensitivity to matters religious and fears of evoking a worldwide Muslim reaction precluded the violation of al-Haram al-Sharif's sanctity.

The entire episode was, perhaps, the result of a deeply ill-advised policy. From a political point of view, the partition scheme was certainly inapplicable without the cooperation of a credible Palestinian party. In assessing the firm opposition to the scheme, the Colonial Office assumed that liquidating the mufti would open the doors for moderate elements to take part in the process of partition.[9] The subsequent course of events would show how mistaken this assessment was. Predictably, the British decision to apprehend the mufti and sever whatever ties remained to link him to the mandate administration, removed the last constraint on his espousal of a radical course of action and provided a much needed element for making his authority and influence virtually unchallengeable.

On 26 September, Mr L. Y. Andrews, the governor of Galilee and one of the ablest district governors in Palestine at the time, together with his guard, Police Constable P. R. McWan, were shot dead in Nazareth.

Although British and Arab sources indicate that the assassins belonged to an active Qassami cell in Haifa,[10] the perpetrators were never identified with certainty. A loose Qassami network was reorganized during the few months that followed the end of the strike. Of the most prominent Qassamis, Shaykh 'Atiya Ahmad, shaykh Khalil Muhammad 'Isa and Shaykh Farhan al-Sa'di left Palestine with the withdrawing force of Fawzi al-Qawuqji in November 1936. Al-Sa'di would soon return to northern Palestine, making a base at Nuras, his own village, while 'Issa and Ahmad remained in Damascus. Aided by their Damascus-based colleagues, and the Syrian Muslim populist shaykh, Muhammad al-Ashmar (another veteran of the 1936 revolt), Farhan al-Sa'di re-established ties with the Haifan Qassami group of Yusuf Abu Durra, Husayn Hamada, Salih Abu Hishmi and Muhammad al-Salih.[11] This group was perhaps responsible for most of the attacks made on Jewish and police targets between October 1936 and September 1937. What was first to link the Qassami group to the assassination incident was the similarity between the revolver fired at Mr Andrews and the revolver used in assassinating Halim Basta, a senior Haifan police officer and an arch-enemy of the Qassamis.[12] On 30 November, the Qassami, Muhammad Naji Abu Rub, admitted to the police his participation, with two other members of Farhan al-Sa'di's band, in the killing of Andrews and his guard. However, when Abu Rub was put up for identification by a British doctor, who had seen two of the assassins, the doctor failed to identify him.[13]

Evidence implicating the northern Qassami group became available two months after the assassination incident, but no proof was found to implicate the mufti or the HAC leadership. Yet, the British response was swift and sweeping. Scores of *qadis, waqf* officials and mosque preachers were arrested within the two days following the Nazareth incident,[14] and despite the HAC condemnation of the attack, the government issued an order on 1 October banning the HAC and the national committees and declaring their activities illegal. This decision, which came after consultations between Jerusalem and London, included the removal of the mufti from the presidency of the SMC, and the arrest of the HAC leaders.[15] The Colonial Office concluded that "the immunity of the Haram could no longer be respected", and resolved to arrest the mufti as well.[16] Ya'qub al-Ghusayn, Ahmad Hilmi Abd al-Baqi, Husayn al-Khalidi and Fu'ad Saba of the HAC leadership, together with the Haifan Istiqlalist, Rashid al-Hajj Ibrahim, were deported to the Seychelles.

Jamal al-Husayni escaped arrest and fled to Syria. Other members of the HAC, who were out of the country, including 'Izzat Darwaza, 'Awni Abd al-Hadi, Abd al-Latif Salah and Alfred Rock, were banned from returning. An attempt by the government to induce Shaykh Mustafa al-Khayri or Shaykh Hasan al-Jarallah, to accept the presidency of the SMC failed. Yet, the latter agreed to join a newly formed committee, along with two British civil servants, which was entrusted with running the Muslim *waqfs*.[17] Since the SMC was not dissolved, and its remaining members were advised by the mufti not to resign, the new *waqf* committee was meant to deprive the SMC of a vital source of its power and influence. If these measures aimed at undermining the structural bases of the Palestinian national movement, the Colonial Office's assessment of the Nashashibi opposition's ability to provide an alternative seemed to be highly inflated. By dissipating the credible leadership, the mandate government was effectively creating the conditions for an uncontrollable outbreak of violence.

The arrival of an exclusive Muslim unit of the British Indian army in Palestine during the second week of October, prompted the mufti and his followers to believe that an assault on al-Haram al-Sharif was imminent. Thus, after some secret preparations had been finalized, the mufti left his residence at al-Haram al-Sharif in the early hours of 14 October for the port of Jaffa where a slow sailing-boat was awaiting his arrival.[18] His intention was to disembark at the southern Lebanese port of Sur, from where he would proceed to Damascus via Beirut. This plan was unexpectedly interrupted by a French patrol boat on the Lebanese coast. After declaring his real identity to the French, the mufti was transferred to Beirut, where a British request for his extradition was soon to be made. The French, considering the likely repercussions of such a step in the Arab and Muslim countries of their domain, decided to grant the unwelcome guest asylum. He was, however, forbidden from travelling to Damascus and his movements were restricted to the Christian-dominated Kasrwan region, where it was believed that supervision of him would be easier to arrange.[19] For the next two years, his house in the village of Dhuq Makayyil would become the main decision-making centre for the Palestinian nationalist movement.

The British official endorsement of the partition proposal, coupled with the wide-ranging reaction to the assassination incident, prepared the ground for the unleashing of the second phase of the revolt. During the first half of 1937, armed attacks were largely confined to the northern districts, the traditional stronghold of the Qassamis. After the publication of the Peel Commission's report, armed activities spread to the Jerusalem area. According to police sources, 14 cases of "terrorism" were recorded in Jerusalem in September, 10 during the first half of October, and 36 in the second half.[20] It seemed that a committee, directed by Shaykh Hasan Abu al-Sa'ud, was organizing the rebel activities in Jerusalem. Shaykh Sabri 'Abdin, the mufti of Hebron, headed another committee, charged with activating the rural areas of the district.[21] Both Abu al-Sa'ud and 'Abdin were known for their closeness to Hajj Amin al-Husayni and their radical attitudes towards the mandate and Zionism, which implies that the mufti had at least approved of their activities. After the mufti's escape to Lebanon, Shaykh Hasan Abu al-Sa'ud took refuge at al-Haram al-Sharif until his network was discovered, and subsequently broken up, by the police in January 1938.[22] Sometime later, he too escaped to Lebanon where he became one of the early Palestinian arrivals to the mufti's neighbourhood.

While the revolt was taking hold in Jerusalem, the security forces succeeded in breaking a central ring of the Qassami formations in the north by arresting Shaykh Farhan al-Sa'di and two of his aides.[23] Al-Sa'di's capture highlighted the ever unresolved tension between blood ties and national allegiance in the Palestinian setting. At the beginning of November 1937, al-Sa'di's band was suspected of murdering Rida al-'Abbushi, a young notable of the powerful 'Abbushi family of Jenin. Rida's murder seemed to have come against a background of collaboration with the British.[24] The 'Abbushis were a family known for their support of the Istiqlal Party and their nationalist role during the 1936 strike. However, the murder of their son provoked some members of the family to seek the destruction of al-Sa'di and his band. To this end, they extended their services to the district commissioner until a joint military and police force captured the elderly Qassami leader in al-Mazar village, north of Jenin.[25] Al-Sa'di was immediately presented to the military court, sentenced to death, and was subsequently hanged on 27 November.[26] His execution elicited strong feelings of indignation and rage in Palestine as well as in many Arab countries.

One of the first Palestinian leaders to meet with the mufti upon his arrival in Lebanon was the Istiqlalist, Mu'in al-Madi. Like many other Palestinian activists, al-Madi was caught up in Damascus, after attending the Bludan Conference, as a result of the British crack-down on the national movement. In their meeting, the mufti authorized al-Madi to organize and encourage band leaders who took refuge in Damascus after the end of the strike to return to Palestine.[27] By taking this action, the mufti became for the first time personally involved in directing the military side of the revolt. It was a road of no return. The first band leader to arrive in the Jenin sub-district towards the end of October was the Qassami, 'Atiya Ahmad.[28] Faced with unfriendly attitudes from the village *mukhtars* in the area, Ahmad failed to establish roots and returned to Damascus. The British pressure on the local villagers, supported by the pro-Nashashibi forces and notables, was rendering some parts of the country inhospitable for the rebels. Another attempt to establish a rebel base in northern Palestine was staged by 'Izz al-Din al-Shawwa, son of the notable Shawwa family of Gaza, in early November.[29] 'Izz al-Din al-Shawwa was an ex-district officer in the mandate administration, whose involvement with the nationalist movement prompted his flight to Damascus after the murder of L. Y. Andrews. A son of an urban notable family with no roots in the northern mountainous region, he fared no better in his mission than 'Atiya. Still, a third attempt was launched in about mid-November with the arrival of Abd al-Rahim al-Hajj Muhammad in the Jenin–Tulkarem zone of the central hills.[30] Muhammad's determination and hard work were soon to show signs of success.

Abd al-Rahim al-Hajj Muhammad (Abu Kamal) was born in the village of Dhinnaba, near Tulkarem, in 1892.[31] He belonged to al-Barqawi clan, a landowning family with a long history in the Tulkarem region.[32] Al-Hajj Muhammad received a traditional elementary education at the village *kuttab* before joining the Ottoman army during World War I. After the end of the war, he returned to Palestine, where he established himself in trade and ran the family's land possessions. Upon the outbreak of the revolt in 1936, al-Hajj Muhammad formed a rebel band in Tulkarem, emerging in August 1936 as a close aide to Fawzi al-Qawuqji.[33] It was Muhammad's strong family roots that enabled him to endure the difficulties of late 1937 and succeed in establishing a strong base with a large following in the eastern Tulkarem region. His acknowledged early success and the influence of a family with deep local roots and power were to create, paradoxically, one of the problems for the inner cohesion of the revolt.

Upon his return to Palestine, al-Hajj Muhammad contacted Muhammad Salih al-Hamad (Abu Khalid) of Silat al-Dhahir, a village of the Jenin sub-district. Al-Hamad was a dedicated Qassami rebel, widely respected for his religiosity, honesty and contribution to the 1936 revolt.[34] Until his death in September 1938, al-Hamad commanded the rebel forces east of Jenin,[35] where his young age (25 years) and tactical talents helped to turn him into one of the revolt's legends.

Soon, other bands with local leadership emerged in various parts of the country. 'Arif Abd al-Raziq (Abu Faysal), from al-Tayyiba village and another veteran of 1936, established a strong following in the hills west of Tulkarem.[36] Shaykh 'Atiya Ahmad made another comeback and successfully formed a rebel command west of Jenin city.[37] After his fall in battle, his place was filled by his aide, Yusuf Abu Durra, another Qassami. Shaykh 'Atiya was in close contact with his old comrades of the Qassami brotherhood, Khalil Muhammad 'Isa (Abu Ibrahim al-Kabir), Tawfiq al-Ibrahim (Abu Ibrahim al-Saghir) and Sulayman Abd al-Qadir Abu Hamam (Abu 'Ali), who commanded the regions of Acre, Safad, Nazareth and Tiberias, on the far northern side of Palestine. Their background, commitment and proximity to Damascus qualified them for a fundamental role in maintaining communications between the rebels in Palestine and the revolt committee in the Syrian capital.[38] Also attached to the northern command was Abdullah al-Asbah, whose participation in the post-World War I uprisings of the *mashriq* extended from the Syrian revolt of 1925–7 to the Qassami movement and the 1936 strike.[39] Like many leaders of the revolt, he was killed in an engagement with a British force, on 27 April 1938. Another important leader of the revolt was Abd al-Qadir al-Husayni.

Al-Husayni, the son of Musa Kazim and a cousin of the mufti, returned from Damascus to the Jerusalem area, where he enjoyed a strong following, in late October 1937.[40] Until the end of the revolt, al-Husayni was the undisputed leader in the Jerusalem sector, supported by Abd al-Halim al-Julani, the rebel leader in Hebron.[41] Al-Husayni's forces came to be known as the "Organization" – and sometimes the "Troops" – of the "Holy Jihad", with which Shaykh Hasan Salama, who commanded the rebels in the mid-western sector of the country (the areas of Lydda, Jaffa, and Ramla), was affiliated. Salama was an early associate of al-Husayni and was the leader of the same region during the 1936 rebellion.[42] No single leader was to emerge in the southern coastal area of Gaza, or in

Beershiba, where the open terrain made the activities of the rebel bands less sustainable. This area was mainly directed by the Jerusalem–Hebron or Lydda–Ramla commanders.

The rebels in Palestine were connected with two centres of support: the first was organized by 'Izzat Darwaza in Damascus and the second by the mufti and his closest aides in Dhuq Machayyil. Darwaza met the mufti for the first time since the latter's escape from Palestine in late November 1937. In the meeting, it was agreed that Darwaza would become the main coordinator of the revolt outside Palestine. He would also resume his responsibilities as secretary-general of the Committee for the Support of the Afflicted People in Palestine, taking charge of distributing available funds for the revolt. A Central Committee for Jihad (CCJ) was formed, comprising the mufti, 'Izzat Darwaza and the mufti's nephew and aide, Ishaq Darwish, who were joined later by Shaykh Hasan Abu al-Sa'ud.[43] Darwaza returned to Damascus where he soon established a base for the CCJ, supported by other exiled Palestinians, such as 'Izz al-Din al-Shawwa, Muhammad 'Ali Darwaza (the brother of 'Izzat) and Mu'in al-Madi. The latter, however, was ordered out of Damascus in January 1938 by the French authorities on the pretext of having an invalid passport.[44] Financial support for the revolt north of the Jerusalem–Jaffa line was the responsibility of the Damascus office, while the mufti was directly responsible for supporting Abd al-Qadir al-Husayni, Hasan Salama and the rebels in the Hebron and Gaza areas.[45]

The main external source of funds for the revolt was the Palestine Defence Committee of Damascus. In its reorganized and revitalized form, the Committee turned into a nerve-centre for the Palestinian revolt. The money collected by other Palestine Defence Committees in various Arab and Muslim countries, as well as from Arab governments, ended up at al-'Azma's office in Damascus, and was then channelled to 'Izzat Darwaza. Until late October 1938, the revolt's funds – according to the well-informed British consul in Damascus – included: £8,000 from Iraq (of which £1,000 came from the government), £3,000 from Egypt (£500 from secret government funds), and £5,000 from Syria and Lebanon.[46] A few more thousand pounds were received from Arab immigrants in South America, from Indian Muslims, and from North African countries.[47] Another source of funding was the donations sent from Saudi Arabia and other Arab and Muslim supporters to the mufti personally. These would be partly used for expenses in Lebanon, and for supporting the rebels in Jerusalem and southern Palestine as well as for the CCJ office of Damascus.[48] On average, Darwaza would distribute to the rebels about £5,000 monthly, while £1,000 would be sent by the mufti.[49] In the light of these figures, British suspicions of German and Italian aid to the revolt seem unsubstantiated.[50] The limited resources available to the Palestinians could not meet the ever increasing costs of the revolt, and finance became one of the revolt's major problems, with a drastic impact on the relations between the rebels and the populace at large.

The Office of Propaganda and Communications was another institution of the revolt to be based in Damascus. Directed by the Istiqlalist, Akram Zu'aytir, this office was part of the Arab Bureau of Fakhri al-Barudi.[51] Since the Bureau had already been active in supporting the Palestinian revolt, Zu'aytir was provided with a room and two assistants to bolster the Bureau's Palestine service. The Office of Propaganda played a vital role in disseminating the revolt's daily news, especially to the Arab countries.

An extensive network of Syrians, Lebanese, Jordanians, as well as Palestinians, emerged gradually for collecting, buying and supplying arms to the revolt. The Syrian setting of 1937–8 was relatively conducive to such activities. A nationalist government was in office, and despite the wide French influence, the Syrian political situation had become comparatively more relaxed than during the previous period of direct French rule. In early 1938, 'Adil al-'Azma, one of the most militant Arabists, was appointed director of the Syrian interior ministry. Since the Syrian gendarmerie lay within al-'Azma's jurisdiction, the border police were expected to overlook the cross-border rebel activities.[52] In addition to a group of active Palestinian exiles, such as 'Izz al-Din and Rashad al-Shawwa, 'Ali Rida al-Nahawi and Sulayman al-Husayni, the entire Arab-Islamic network of Greater Syria was virtually rallied behind the revolt. The Jordanian opposition leader Subhi Abu Ghanima, the Lebanese Abu al-Huda al-Yafi, the ubiquitous Arabists Farid Zayn al-Din and Munir al-Rayyis, and Shaykh Muhammad al-Ashmar and his followers in al-Maydan quarter of Damascus, were all involved, at one stage or another, in arming the revolt and in its logistics.[53] Guns and ammunition were purchased and transferred from as far as northern Syria, Kuwait and the Saudi desert, or supplied by the Iraqi Arabist army officers, and smuggled to Palestine via ancient routes that had existed centuries before the drawing of the new borders.[54] The Saudi monarch was approached, through his confidant Yusuf Yasin, to permit the transfer of arms which belonged to the Syrian rebels of 1925–7 and had been left in their refugee camp at al-Qarriyyat in northern Saudi Arabia. Though he initially agreed, when Muhammad 'Ali Darwaza and two other Qassamis arrived in al-Qarriyyat, they were told by the Saudi amir (governor) that the permission was rescinded after the British had apparently become aware of their mission.[55] On the other hand, an Egyptian Ikhwani role in arming the revolt was alluded to by the mufti several years later.[56] Yet, neither the British nor the Zionist sources make particular mention of such a role.

In its second phase, the revolt was exclusively led by Palestinian commanders. This, however, did not preclude Syrian, Lebanese, and especially Jordanian volunteers, from joining its ranks.[57] By mid-1938, when the British military pressure inside Palestine and restrictions on the rebels' movement across the borders became widely felt, the CCJ conspired with the Jordanian opponents of Abdullah, especially Subhi Abu Ghanima and the former army officer, Muhammad al-'Ajluni, to spread the revolt to Transjordan.[58] Although the scheme never reached the scale of extensive rebellion, it did lead to repeated armed attacks on British and Arab legion posts and patrols in northern Transjordan.[59] In April 1939, the Jordanian rebel bases in the 'Ajlun mountains were overrun in the course of a massive attack by the British army and the Arab legion.[60] Many rebels were killed, while others fled to the Syrian territories across the borders.

Palestinian rebels' activities in late 1937 and early 1938 followed the established patterns that had marked the revolt's first phase. The rebels' methods included firing at police or military patrols, attacking Jewish settlements, assassinating Jewish and British officials, or Arabs believed to be collaborators, in addition to sabotaging railways, telephone communications and the Iraq Petroleum Company pipeline (ICP).[61] But as their numbers increased and their weapons and expertise improved, the rebels became more daring in engaging the army in wide-scale confrontations. The rise in the rebels' power during 1938 was also a reflection of strong popular support. In the Galilee district, where the army was more concentrated than in any other part of the country, the district commissioner reported in February 1938: "the Arab population as a whole is in sympathy with the rebels and even the notables who have been induced to cooperate with the Government do so with considerable mental conservation."[62] During the summer and autumn of 1938, the revolt reached its peak. In August, most of the roads and many towns came under the virtual control of the rebels, while communications and transport were rendered ineffective. As a result, civil administration and management of the country were put on hold. In Nablus, a city that was run by Sulayman Tuqan, a pro-British mayor, the rebels walked the streets unhindered. Beershiba slipped out of British control from early September until late November 1938; while in the old city of Jerusalem the army had to impose a five-day siege before government authority could be restored in mid-October.[63] In the words of the High Commissioner, the ascendance of the rebels and the widening identification of the villagers with them made the movement "definitely a national one".[64] It was this triumphant spirit of a small people taking on the might of the British army which helped to lay the seeds of a Palestinian mythology in the Arab and Muslim consciousness. Under the prevailing conditions of the late 1930s, the revolt, however, could not be sustained. Elements from within, coupled with an increasingly unfavourable external situation, brought the revolt by the spring of 1939 to a state of degeneration.

Rebel leaders inside Palestine were largely of non-urban origin.[65] Though never short of courage and determination, neither their understanding of social order nor their political experience qualified them for a leading national role during a highly sensitive period. Their rise was a reflection of the urban nobility's failure to overcome its traditional reluctance to challenge symbols of power and authority, and the fragility of the middle classes. But it was also a development laden with serious flaws. Villagers' old feuds would now seek legitimation by means of patriotic euphoria, while petty ambitions for prominence would re-emerge, armed with nationalist, pan-Arabist and Islamic expressions.[66] Since the rebel leaders viewed each other as equals, local command of the revolt remained divided. None of the rebels succeeded in displaying the necessary attributes, or managed to create the conditions, for establishing an overall leadership, or even to force such leadership on the others.[67] In the event, each of the three main commanders, Abd al-Qadir al-Husayni, Abd al-Rahim al-Hajj Muhammad and 'Arif Abd al-Raziq, advanced a claim for the general command.

For all practical purposes, the CCJ was unable to exercise a definite authority over the rebels. However, as the rebels' inner divisions appeared to threaten the survival of the revolt during the summer of 1938, the CCJ exerted tremendous pressure on the local commanders to consolidate their ranks. A collective leadership, to be led by turn, was thus formed.[68] But since it was not joined by al-Husayni, and was not taken seriously by its members, the collective leadership became more of a cosmetic arrangement, unable to effect a profound change in the situation. In the late summer of 1938, the mufti and 'Izzat Darwaza attempted to recall Fawzi al-Qawuqji to take overall command of the revolt. However, deeply involved with 'Adil al-'Azma in preparations for igniting an anti-French revolt in Syria, al-Qawuqji was unable to return to Palestine.[69]

Unaware of the great risks involved in overloading the national struggle with a social dimension, several rebel leaders went to extremes in harassing Palestinian landowners and wealthy city dwellers. There is no doubt that the external assistance was never adequate,[70] for, according to various estimates, the number of rebels might well have reached 3,000 full-time fighters, 1,000 town-based elements, and 6,000 partisans, joining the bands on an irregular basis.[71] To provide for their followers, and to compensate for losses incurred in their areas as a result of British reprisals and punitive measures, rebel commanders had to make good their shortage in finance and supplies locally. But instead of relying on voluntary contributions and adjusting their needs and recruitment drives to the availability of means, many rebels infringed on private properties.[72] Moreover, a collective tax was imposed on several cities in the name of contribution to the revolt.[73] Since urban centres appeared to suffer less than the villages during the revolt's second phase, the rebels believed that it was only fair to make such demands on city dwellers.

Equally damaging to the revolt was the unleashing of a wide assassination campaign by the rebels. Some cases of assassination were certainly not objected to by the majority of people, given the euphoric nature of national uprisings and the contingency of their value systems. Such cases included collaborators and land-sale middlemen. But even here, on many occasions, the victim's family would turn into an enemy of the revolt.[74] Worse still, others were simply killed against a background of local feuds, or for standing on the wrong side of the political divide, being supporters of the opposition.[75] Incidents in the last two categories were received with disapproval by the Palestinians at large, precipitating a sense of terror in the country. Recognizing the troubled state of the revolt, the CCJ decided to attach a nationalist-intellectual advisor to each rebel commander. Wasif Kamal joined the northern command of the Qassamis; Mamduh al-Sukhun accompanied al-Hajj Muhammad; Farid Ya'ish was with 'Arif Abd al-Raziq, Dr Dawud al-Husayni was with al-Husayni, and Mustafa al-Tahir and Fayiz al-Nabulsi were with Yusuf Abu Durra.[76] Many of these intellectuals belonged to the early 1930s' secret network of Arab nationalists. This arrangement contributed to a significant improvement in the rebels' discourse and public declarations, as well as to the organization of a rebel court system.[77] But problems of the revolt lay as much with the commanders' ambitions and powers as in the conduct of individual rebels. Coupled with the highly decentralized nature of the rebel formations, this state of affairs rendered the presence of the dedicated advisors inconsequential to the ultimate course of events. On occasions, even the court system confronted the revolt with the dilemma of alienating the powerful in society or compromising with justice.[78]

The British measures of repression far surpassed those employed during the strike period. Hundreds of rebels' houses or those of their supporters were blown up, while collective fines were imposed on villages and city quarters throughout the country.[79] Thousands of rebels, members of their families, and suspects were detained in especially erected concentration camps, and many amongst them faced the death sentence that became a routine function of summary trials conducted by military courts.[80] From May 1938, the army launched a wide-scale offensive during which a village – or a group of villages – was put under siege for several days until the search for rebels and arms was completed.[81] Amounting to a virtual reoccupation of the country, this campaign was the first in a series of reconquests that within the next few years would subdue Iraq, Syria and Lebanon, and Egypt.

The British effort to crush the revolt was augmented by Palestinian as well as Jewish contributions. In contrast to the 1936 strike, the Nashashibi-dominated opposition was clearly unwilling to join the revolt. Its early withdrawal from the HAC and tacit approval of the projected partition made it averse to the whole strategy of reviving the insurgency. In mid-December 1937, Raghib al-Nashashibi contemplated the enlisting of new supporters, in preparation for a confrontation with the HAC and the nationalist forces.[82] The Zionists' reluctance to lend him the necessary finances seemed to have stalled his scheme. When the security situation deteriorated, Raghib, like some other opposition leaders, fled the country.[83] Yet, by the end of 1938, Fakhri al-Nashashibi, the most unscrupulous of all opposition figures, took heart from the British offensive and entered the fray in a highly flagrant manner. He visited several of the traditional strongholds of the opposition and contacted a wide array of alienated village heads and families, encouraging them to resist the rebel forces.[84] Fakhri's activities culminated in the forming of what was then called the "Peace Bands". Although greatly despised by the British mandate officials, Fakhri's followers were equipped by the army; financial support was extended by Amir Abdullah, and propaganda by *Filastin* in Jaffa and *'Alif Ba'* in Damascus.[85] During the last stage of the revolt, the Peace Bands worked side by side with the army, and sometimes even ahead of it,[86] terrorizing the pro-HAC villages and applying grossly felonious forms of justice on the villagers. Raghib al-Nashashibi appeared eager to dissociate himself from his cousin and right-hand man, but secretly maintained an uninterrupted liaison with him.[87] In late 1938, Sulayman Tuqan, the mayor of Nablus, returned to Palestine from his self-imposed refuge in Athens and threw his weight behind Fakhri's revolt.[88] A highly cynical aspect of this dangerous enterprise was Fakhri's repeated approaches to the mufti in Lebanon, seeking to mend fences.[89] These attempts were perhaps motivated by self-serving ambitions on the part of Fakhri for establishing his own base of leadership, in independence of his elder Raghib.

Yet, Fakhri al-Nashashibi was not the only bad omen for the revolt. In September 1938, al-Nashashibi, with the help of the British consul in Damascus, managed to recruit Fakhri Abd al-Hadi, the former deputy of Fawzi al-Qawuqji.[90] Abd al-Hadi's deteriorating moral condition during his exile in Damascus created a rift between him and the CCJ,[91] and made him thus vulnerable to enticements from Mackereth and al-Nashashibi. The recruitment of Fakhri Abd al-Hadi, a member of a notable family with a powerful base in the Jenin mountains, was drastically damaging to the revolt. No less painful was the breakaway of 'Ajaj Nwayhid, the prominent Istiqlalist, from the nationalist ranks. Although Nwayhid had impeccable nationalist and Arab-Islamic credentials, his estrangement from the mufti and his circle had been fermenting since the re-launch of al-Istiqlal Party and its mouthpiece, *al-'Arab*. From late 1937, evidence abounded of 'Ajaj's *rapprochement* and cooperation with the Nashashibi opposition.[92] In 1940, the British appointed Nwayhid a director of the Jerusalem Radio Arabic Service,[93] a position which took him into deep involvement with the British anti-Axis propaganda in Palestine.[94]

Despite the emergence of Fakhri al-Nashashibi and his accomplices as the only active political group on the Palestinian political arena after the defeat of the revolt in the summer of 1939,[95] the Nashashibi opposition would never recover from its betrayal of the revolt. Even the mufti's prolonged absence from the scene could not salvage their ever sinking fortunes.[96] Raghib spent most of the following years in Cairo Heliopolis Palace Hotel; Fakhri paid for his gambling approach to politics with his life in 1941; and two years later, Fakhri Abd al-Hadi would be killed by one of his relatives.

The Jews of Palestine were the other important force on the British side. During the revolt, the Jewish auxiliary units, attached to the British army, counted 6,000 men.[97] Despite the involvement of Zionist circles in several attacks on Arab civilians,[98] the recruitment of Jews continued unabated. Since the revolt was in essence directed against both, the British and the Jews, the British did not hesitate in strengthening military ties with the Zionists. The 1936 British policy of not disarming the Arab population without subjecting the Jews to the same measure was, thus, squarely overturned during the revolt's second phase. As a result, the Jewish colonists became heavily armed, deepening the Arab belief in British partiality.

The realities of the regional situation and the rapidly changing climate of the European powers' relations further exacerbated the revolt's predicament. Considering the unchallenged British position in Transjordan, and Amir Abdullah's view of the HAC and his interests in the partition proposal, the rebels could only helplessly watch their lifeline across the Jordan River being exceedingly squeezed. In July 1938, both banks of the Jordan were placed under one military command, while the Arab Legion, together with the British army units in Transjordan, applied severe restrictive measures on the legal and illegal movement between the two countries.[99] Jordanian acquiescence with the British demands reached its climax in July 1939 when the Jordanian forces arrested the rebel commander Yusuf Abu Durra while he was attempting to return to Palestine.[100] Abu Durra was handed over to the British authorities in Palestine, where he was executed two months later. While the rising waves of Arab nationalism provided a great source of support to the revolt, the emergence of the Arab regional states left the revolt vulnerable to the differing ties and interests of these states.

If dealing with Transjordan was largely a straightforward colonial affair, the situation in Syria was a more complex issue. Vitally important for sustaining the revolt, Syria occupied a central place in the British effort against the rebels. The 1936 Franco-Syrian treaty, which granted the Syrians a sort of independence and permitted the establishment of a national government, was never conclusively ratified by the French. Despite conceding certain spheres of power to the nationalists, the French were still largely in control. Britain was also present in Damascus, represented by the consul-general, Colonel Mackereth, the most favoured British official in Elie Kedourie's otherwise critical account of the British interwar policy in the Middle East.[101] Mackereth was skilful, well-connected and constantly kept up to date by his own network of informers. The British consul had apparently a special affinity towards the National Bloc prime minister Jamil Mardam for his pragmatic policies and mild manners.[102] Mardam's rise to power was largely the outcome of his advocacy of cooperation with the French and his successful negotiation of the 1936 treaty. But, once in office, he was faced with a number of irreconcilable problems: the French foot-dragging over the treaty; their more than agreeable attitude towards ceding the *sanjaq* of Alexandretta in northern Syria to the Turkish republic; and the challenges to his government from Syrian pan-Arabist and Islamic quarters.[103] Shukri al-Quwwatli, the most acceptable figure of the National Bloc to the Arab-Islamic and radical forces, realizing the irreparable damage inflicted on Mardam's government, resigned his cabinet post in March 1938.

From an early stage of the revolt, Mardam displayed a considerable willingness to accommodate the British demands on his government.[104] But while Mardam's government had "made furtive attempts to preserve an attitude of international rectitude in the matter of the Palestinian political refugees [the CCJ]", these attempts had been "without effect upon their activities".[105] The most important factor behind the government's impotence was the uncertainty of its political future. If Mardam was still craving to remain in power and to pursue his "honourable cooperation" with France, he would have to rely on the support of the radical Syrians who brought the nationalist rule into being in the first place. Mackereth's deep understanding of the Syrian government's dilemma did not preclude him from resorting to open threats to Mardam to deprive the Syrians of future British support in their troubled negotiations with France.[106] Mardam, whose sensitivity to the realities of power was an essential feature of his character, would thereby act in favour of the British whenever possible. In the summer of 1938, even as his government was headed towards an unstoppable decline, Mardam strongly objected to the holding of the pro-Palestine Islamic Parliamentary Congress and the Arab Women's Congress on Syrian soil.[107] This stand obliged the Palestinians and their Arab supporters to transfer the projected congresses to Cairo.

Mackereth's early reports were highly critical of the French authorities in Syria, explaining their laxity in containing the rebels' movement in terms of the traditional Anglo-French rivalry in the Middle East and the British failure to restrict the movement of Syrian rebels in Palestine in 1925. Yet, in October 1938, Mackereth had to acknowledge the French assistance against the revolt.[108] In reality, the French officials in the Levant were not particularly consistent in their response to the British demands. While some had strict concern for preserving tranquillity in Syria or were certainly Anglophobic, others were more prepared to cooperate with their British counterparts in crushing what appeared to them as a new wave of Arab radicalism.[109] Colombani, chief of the Sûreté Générale in Beirut, and Bonnet, head of the Service Spécial, the French intelligence outfit in Damascus, were notable examples of the latter group. Further pressure from London and Paris made the French more forthcoming, if not always up to the expectations of the British officials in Palestine.

In January 1938 the French authorities in Damascus banished Mu'in al-Madi, an early organizer of the revolt, to Alexandretta.[110] Two months earlier, information from French intelligence sources led to the arrest of four Syrians in Transjordan who were on their way to join the revolt.[111] Correspondence between Mackereth and Sir Charles Tegart, chief of police in Palestine, indicates that Bonnet kept his promise to provide information on the rebels' movements and the arms' trafficking through Lebanon and Syria. One of the major outcomes of this cooperation was the capture of large caches of arms and ammunition in the border village of Um Qayis by the British in April 1938, and the French seizure of 70 rifles and 20,000 rounds of ammunition at Hama in northern Syria.[112] French units kept up a steady patrol of the frontier in "loyal attempts" to stop smuggling and infiltration across it, while known pro-Palestinian activists were harassed and detained, especially in Lebanon where the French were freer to act.[113] 'Izzat Darwaza, whose activities in Damascus were largely concealed, first received a warning in the form of the cancellation of his residency permit. Later, he was subjected to a brief detention after a police raid on his house.[114] As the political tension in Europe mounted in the beginning of 1939, the French campaign intensified. Publications connected with the Palestine Defence Committee were closed down and the cooperative Syrian–Lebanese media were encouraged to attack the mufti and other leaders and supporters of the revolt.[115] Finally, in the wake of Mardam's resignation in 1939, the French apprehended a large number of Syrian nationalists, including Nabih al-'Azma and Munir al-Rayyis, followed three months later by 'Izzat Darwaza.[116] With the loss of its nerve-centre in Syria, the revolt lost all chances of recovering from the heavy military blows directed at its bases during the early months of 1939.

Simultaneous with the highly adverse conditions that enveloped the revolt within and outside Palestine were developments in the British position regarding the partition which also contributed to the waning of the Palestinian resolve. The British abandonment of the partition scheme, and the HAC participation in the Round-Table Conference, precipitated the belief that a political solution was imminent.[117] During the intervening period between the beginning of negotiations in London and the CCJ's attempt to resurrect the revolt in the summer of 1939, several rebel commanders were killed, captured, or went into exile.[118] The French dismantling of the Palestinian support formations in Damascus conclusively sealed the revolt's fate. Despite the heavy loss of life,[119] many Palestinians as well as Arabs believed that the revolt had triumphed and that Britain had after all changed its policy.

The Arab response to the partition

Two months after the release of the Peel Commission's report, the British government concluded that the partition plan was unworkable. Since the Palestinian revolt in late 1937 was not yet a pressing reality able to tip the balance, one is certainly tempted to look for other signs in the political chart to explain this development. There is little doubt that the British change of policy arose against ominous signs of the approaching war in Europe and its anticipated repercussions in the Middle East. While a marked increase in German activities in the Arab East was being recorded, more constraining for the British government was the Italian presence in Libya and Abyssinia. Yet, none of these considerations would have weighed heavily on Britain had the Arab reaction not evolved as it really did. From 1937 onwards, the British were to face an angry and antagonistic Arab opinion, deeply enraged by the deteriorating conditions in Palestine.

Soon after the 1936 strike had come to a close, the Arab political scene was to witness some important changes of marked relevance to the Palestinians, as well as to the Arab movement at large. The first was the relative increase in Egyptian freedom of movement following the conclusion of the Anglo-Egyptian treaty. The second was the rise to power of a nationalist government in Damascus, which was regarded by the Arabist circles as a firm step towards independence. No one at that early stage could anticipate that Paris would never ratify the Franco-Syrian treaty of 1936. The third major change was the Iraqi *coup d'état* of late October 1936 that resulted in the ousting of Yasin al-Hashimi's government. The inclusion of four ministers of the anti-Arabist al-Ahali Group in the newly installed government of Hikmat Sulayman raised a great deal of concern in many Arabist quarters. However, Palestinian relations with Iraq seemed to have continued largely unchanged.

Palestinian moves on the Arab arena had begun in earnest before the release of the Peel Commission's report, instigated by unfavourable news leaks from London. In February 1937 the mufti, accompanied by 'Izzat Darwaza, embarked on a religious-political visit to Saudi Arabia, aimed at performing the hajj and holding consultations with the Saudi monarch. Intent on using the opportunity to seek further Muslim support, the mufti called upon the Lebanese Istiqlalist, Riyad al-Sulh, and the Damascus-based Libyan leader Bashir al-Sa'dawi, to take charge of propaganda activities during the hajj.[120] The high political point of this mission was the meeting(s) that the group held with Ibn Sa'ud. In one version of the hajj mission, al-Sa'dawi indicated that the group attempted to impress upon Ibn Sa'ud the urgent need of the Arabs to arrive at a clear agreement on the issue of their unity.[121] The mufti and his companions stressed that in view of the situation in Palestine and other Arab countries, and the rising tension in Europe, the Arabs would not be able to secure a better deal without a united representation of their will. The king, in his customary evasive manner, expressed his despair over the Arab governments' failure to rise above their trivial rivalries, and said that Arab unity would only be realized through the peoples' striving and determination.

After the end of the hajj, the group seems to have agreed to dispatch al-Sa'dawi to the British embassy in Cairo to assess the British views. Received by Mr Smart the oriental secretary at the embassy, al-Sa'dawi presented a scheme for a gradual unity of the Arab states in Asia, developing from a cultural to a political league.[122] Being a well-known anti-Italian leader, al-Sa'dawi indicated that Britain's support for the project would substantially contribute to containing the Italian influence in the Arab lands. Otherwise, no one could guarantee that the Arabs would not opt for a "real political" agreement with the Italians. Al-Sa'dawi's proposal was given due attention by the Eastern Department of the Foreign Office, where Rendel concluded, after sounding out the British representative in the area, that the prevailing state of Arab–British relations did not call for a reconsideration of the issue involved. As Lampson accurately put it, the main question was whether His Majesty's Government was yet prepared to change its policy in Palestine. Unless that happened, Arab unity was bound to make the British position in Palestine even worse.[123]

In the other version of the hajj mission, Darwaza relayed that the meeting with Ibn Sa'ud focused mainly on the mufti's request for Saudi support in case the Royal Commission recommendations turned out to be detrimental to Palestinian rights and aspirations. Like his answer to Darwaza's similar request in late 1936, the king's reply to the mufti was noncommittal.[124] The elder and most consummate of all Arab leaders at the time was seemingly bent upon keeping his options open. Whichever of the two versions, Darwaza's or al-Sa'dawi's, was the most accurate (being in essence non-contradictory), the hajj mission highlighted two important points: first, that despite his invariably moderate approach to the Arab situation the Saudi king was still regarded by the Palestinian national leadership as its first strategic ally; and second, that the Arab option was now registering high, if not highest, on the Palestinian political scale.

Soon after, news emerged from Egypt that the regent, Prince Muhammad 'Ali, had presented the British with a scheme for solving the Palestine problem.[125] Muhammad 'Ali was a lenient and agreeable figure of the Egyptian royal family, but was not necessarily without ambitions. His proposed solution was based on the establishment of a cantonized pan-Syrian kingdom in which the Jewish community would be granted a national home in a part of Palestine.[126] Since Nuri al Sa'id, exiled by the Iraqi coup makers, was then living in Egypt, it is not unlikely that the prince's proposal was influenced by Nuri's views of Arab federation. The Egyptian version, however, was modified to leave a vacant throne to be filled, perhaps by Muhammad 'Ali himself. Within weeks of the scheme becoming known, the mufti embarked on a visit to Damascus. The election of a nationalist government in Syria made it imperative that the Palestinian and Arab situations were discussed with the Syrian leaders. The mufti was warmly received by his allies in government as well as by the Arab-Islamic quarters of Damascus. His visit was, however, cut short by the withdrawal of Raghib al-Nashashibi and his allies from the HAC,[127] and his consultations in Syria appeared, therefore, to be rather incomplete. According to Mackereth, three issues were raised during the Palestinian–Syrian meetings: Prince Muhammad 'Ali's proposal; the idea of uniting the Palestinian Istiqlal Party with its Syrian counterpart; and the convening of a pan-Arab congress.[128] Since the prince's proposal was not making any tangible progress on the British front, the issue was soon to be overtaken by events. On the other hand, Mackereth's report was not particularly clear on the idea of merging the pan-Arabist organizations in Syria and Palestine, which were closely connected anyway. As for the pan-Arab congress, which had eluded the Arab-Islamists since late 1931, its convening a few months later was to mark a high point in the course of the Arab movement.

A summary of the Peel Commission's report was broadcast to Palestinians on the evening of 7 July 1937. During the following day, a full version of the report was made available in Palestine and to Arab governments and newspapers for the British government was keen on assessing Arab reactions to the partition scheme.[129] Expressed in surprisingly mild terms, the HAC's position was outlined in two documents, a communiqué to the Palestinian people, and a telegram to the Arab rulers. It seems that a stronger version, prepared earlier by 'Izzat Darwaza, was watered down after the intervention of 'Awni Abd al-Hadi.[130] Temperamental and sometimes inconsistent, Abd al-Hadi had been shifting towards a more moderate stance since the late stages of the general strike.

The first Arab response to the partition plan and the HAC telegram came from Iraq. Hikmat Sulayman, the prime minister, communicated to the HAC Iraq's categorical rejection of the partition.[131] Sulayman's telegram, which inflamed the Palestinian public, was later reiterated in press interviews and official statements.[132] Similar views were pronounced by Sulayman's partner and main supporter, the chief of staff, Bakr Sidqi.[133] Concurrently, the Iraqi Palestine Defence Committee launched its most powerful campaign yet against the British policy and the Zionist project. Stunned by the idea of the establishment of a Jewish state in Palestine, the Iraqis organized several mass protests in Baghdad, as well as in other Iraqi cities. The campaign was augmented by a rare fatwa issued by a group of Sunni and Shi'i ulema, enjoining the Iraqis and Muslims to oppose the partition plan and regarding the support for the Palestinians as a religious duty.[134]

The Iraqi response astounded the British as much as it pleased the Palestinians. Neither in the Middle East nor in London were British officials accustomed to such a reaction from Arab officials. Many in Whitehall saw the infant kingdom of Iraq as a creation of Britain, heavily bound to London by a treaty of friendship and mutual defence. Not surprisingly, Sulayman received a fierce rebuff from the British.[135] But Sulayman's threats of resignation, implying the possibility of a military take-over in which the British would be forced to deal with the despised Bakr Sidqi, restored normalcy in relations with Britain.[136] In his analysis of the Iraqi reaction to the partition plan, Taggar explained Sulayman's motives in the context of his government's position after the resignation of Ja'far Abu al-Timman and most of the Ahali ministers in June 1937. Other important factors included Iraq's economic interests in Palestine, threatened by the allocation of Haifa (the terminal of the Iraqi oil pipeline) to the proposed Jewish state, as well as the traditional Iraqi–Saudi rivalry.[137] These considerations might well have been taken into account by Sulayman, but what was critically obvious was the Iraqi public opinion. Aware of the powerful support for Palestine in his country, Sulayman therefore indicated to the British ambassador that no government in Baghdad was able to withstand the Iraqi popular feelings on Palestine.[138] It is also pertinent that prior to the cabinet crisis of June and sometime before the declaration of the partition plan, Sulayman was informed by Grobba, the German minister in Baghdad, of the impending British proposal. Unconcerned by the fact that the Peel Commission's report was not yet officially released, the prime minister suggested that Iraq must take action against the partition in cooperation with Germany.[139] This approach, however, was overruled by Sulayman's ministers. Whatever inferences one might draw from this episode, it undoubtedly underscored the degree to which successive Iraqi rulers had come to view their country's Arab commitments.

On 11 August, Sidqi was assassinated in a plot contrived and executed by a group of army officers with whom Salah al-Din al-Sabbagh was deeply involved. Subsequently, the king dismissed Sulayman and appointed Jamil al-Madfa'i to the premiership. The new prime minister was a Sharifian officer, whose pan-Arab, pro-British and conciliatory approach made him acceptable to various political quarters.[140] Yet, Sa'id Thabit, the veteran Arab-Islamist heading the Palestine Defence Committee, was not particularly one of al-Madfa'i's admirers. Thabit accused al-Madfa'i, and rightly so, of taking part in the undermining of the late Yasin al-Hashimi's last government by inciting tribal and political elements to revolt.[141] Although Thabit had his own disagreements with al-Hashimi, he believed that his government, besides its powerful pan-Arab policy, was pulling Iraq out of the teeth of chaos and precarious politics that had plagued it since its very emergence. In the autumn of 1938, 'Izzat Darwaza arrived in Baghdad to participate in restructuring and further activating the Palestine Defence Committee. To his surprise, while al-Madfa'i expressed strong support for the Palestinians, including an open invitation to the mufti to move to Baghdad, he was adamant that he would not cooperate with Thabit. Seeing no advantage in antagonizing the prime minister, Darwaza sought to give a greater role in the committee to Naji al-Swaydi.[142] The respected president of the Bludan Congress, former primer minister and highly regarded constitutionalist, agreed.

In late 1937, Iraq was witnessing the beginnings of an unprecedented rise in the pan-Arab movement. While al-Sabbagh's army group was consolidating its position, al-Muthanna Club emerged fully recovered from the timid and uncertain times of the coup regime. King Ghazi's persistent restlessness in dealing with the British, as well as with the older politicians of his father's rule, was now expressed in pan-Arabist, popular utterances.[143] In contrast, al-Madfa'i's conciliatory policy of "drawing the curtain on the past" and his dismissal of the demands to punish Hikmat Sulayman and his accomplices brought on him the wrath of many critics,[144] while the menacing figure of Nuri al-Sa'id still loomed large on the political horizon. Never at ease when out of power, the supreme intriguer of Iraqi politics rejected all offers of cooperation made to him by al-Madfa'i.[145] Nuri's undiminished hatred of the king and Sulayman, whom he deemed responsible for the murder of his ally and brother-in-law, Ja'far al-'Askari, coupled with his yearning for power, caused the prime minister a great deal of anxiety. In view of the various forces involved, al-Madfa'i taking account of the various forces incolved and relying on his foreign minister, the pro-British Tawfiq al-Swaydi, to maintain good relations with London,[146] let the Arabist, pro-Palestinian forces loose.

In Egypt, the situation was only slightly different. Without encouragement from the Wafdi government, patterns of pro-Palestinian activity which had been established during the 1936 strike re-emerged on a wider scale.[147] The Islamic societies, most notably the Muslim Brothers and the YMMS, spearheaded the anti-partition protests with vigour and tenacity. Effecting their entry into the world of politics with success, expanding and developing a growing network of influence with several men in power, the Ikhwan revived their Palestinian campaign without hesitation.[148] In a new development, a group of 58 parliament-arians addressed the British embassy directly, protesting – though in a friendly fashion – the policies pursued in Palestine.[149] The press returned to its focus on Palestinian affairs, with opinion columns critical of the British becoming more daring and frequent.[150] *Al-Ahram*'s network of correspondents brought the Arab reactions to the partition, in Iraq, Syria and Saudi Arabia, right to the doorsteps of many Egyptian homes. Even the pro-British *al-Muqattam* found itself obliged to plead politely, in the name of the whole Egyptian nation, with the High Commissioner of Palestine, urging a change of policy.[151] The leader of the opposition, Muhammad Mahmud, telegraphed the mufti with his unequivocal support, while his colleague, Muhammad Husayn Haykal, called for al-Nahhas to present to the parliament his government's response to the Palestinian situation.[152] As they were free of the pressures of government, the Liberal Constitutionalists were noticeably more powerful in expressing their support for the Palestinians. If this support was, on the other hand, meant to inflict political damage on the ruling Wafdi government, it showed how the Palestinian question was rapidly evolving to become an integral part of Arab domestic politics.

In contrast with the popular feelings, al-Nahhas's position was largely inconsistent. While avoiding interference with the press, al-Nahhas expressed to Lampson his objection to the establishment of a Jewish state on Egyptian borders.[153] Aware of the danger emanating from such an arrangement, the Egyptian leader underscored the expansionist nature of the Zionist project and its drastic impact on the defence of Egypt, as well as on the Jewish community of Egypt. Lampson's own discomfort over partition was reflected in the moderation of his "insulating Egypt" approach. This in turn encouraged al-Nahhas to envision a more active role for himself and Egypt. Before the annual meeting of the League of Nations in September, the Egyptian prime minister approached the HAC for a full documentation of its views and opinions on the Palestinian question. Augmenting this with an Egyptian perspective, al-Nahhas prepared a cohesive document in which the Egyptian government predicated its rejection of the partition plan on the basis of history, religion, natural law and Egypt's geographical and Arab-Islamic ties with Palestine.[154] This document was to become the official guideline of the government's Palestine policy, especially for the Egyptian representative to the League of Nations. Furthermore, al-Nahhas gave instructions to the Egyptian delegation to coordinate efforts with other Arab delegates present in Geneva.[155]

At the same time, al-Nahhas was keen to inform Lampson of every step he intended to take, making sure that his government's Arab policies were approved or at least not disapproved of by the British. Conscious of the British opposition to joint Arab representation on Palestine, al-Nahhas rejected the Saudi proposal for such a scheme.[156] Similarly, he refrained from attending the Bludan Arab Congress and expressed his unwillingness to present the Palestinian cause to the world on behalf of the Arabs.[157] But sensing that his overcautious approach was perhaps offending the Palestinians, he dispatched Amin 'Uthman, his closest aide, in a reconciliatory gesture, to meet the mufti at his al-Haram al-Sharif refuge in Jerusalem.[158]

Al-Nahhas's inconsistency can be explained on different levels. First, there was the persistent affair of the British role, subtle and otherwise, in the making and unmaking of various Egyptian governments. For this, the Egyptian prime ministers would as a rule strive not to invite the wrath of their guardian angels at the British Embassy. Second, there was the perception, shared by many Egyptians, of Egypt's distinctive role and position. Although Arab ties and identity were now embraced by the majority of the ruling élite, the mood of Egypt was of leading, rather than merely participating in, Arab affairs. Al-Nahhas, as he would explicitly state, did not rule out such a role, but believed that the conditions were not yet appropriate to take it up.[159] Third, there was the government's precarious position during the second half of 1937. The split of Ahmad Mahir and Mahmud Fahmi al-Nuqrashi from the Wafd, added to al-Nahhas's deteriorating relations with the Palace, threatened the very survival of the government. By December, al-Nahhas's position had become clearly untenable, and he was subsequently dismissed by King Faruq.

The complexity that characterized the internal political fabric of Iraq, Syria and Egypt, and moulded their reactions to the partition, was largely non-existent in the case of Saudi Arabia, the other major party in the Arab political arena of the 1930s. After his triumph over the radical Islamic opposition amongst his followers in 1930, Abd al-'Aziz al-Sa'ud became the ultimate source of power in the country. His delicate and skilful manipulation of the tribal forces, his patriarchal openness and closeness to his people, together with strong support from the ulema institution, secured for him the worldly attributes of power as well as Islamic legitimacy. But the king's relations with Britain were not as simple. A veteran of exile and victory, of destitution and lordship, of Ottoman dominance and defeat, he turned into a true believer in the unavoidable need for British support and backing. In a meeting with a Palestinian delegation in December 1936, Ibn Sa'ud dwelt on the Arab weaknesses, backwardness and their urgent need to unite and recover.[160] He pointed to the many injustices perpetrated on the Arabs by the British, but did not fail to remind his guests that Britain was a world power capable of inflicting more damage and destruction. Yet, Ibn Sa'ud would not easily concede to Britain what he believed were his or his kingdom's rights.

Ibn Sa'ud was fully aware of Britain's strategic imperatives that called for his friendship, and was equally conscious of his influence and prestige, being the leader of the holiest land of Islam. Indeed, his influence was undeniably larger than the limits of his domain, as his state, independent and based on Islam, became a point of attraction for the Arab and Islamic activists. This provided Ibn Sa'ud with a group of enlightened and skilful men who served him with dedication and absolute loyalty. Prominent among them were: the Egyptian, Hafiz Wahba; the Syrian, Yusuf Yasin; the Lebanese, Fu'ad Hamza; and, at a later stage, the Libyan, Bashir al-Sa'dawi. During the 1930s, the Saudi monarch was even more fortunate to have Sir Reader Bullard as Britain's consul-general in Jeddah.[161] Bullard's experience, deep knowledge of Arabia and his ability to create an objective and rich synthesis of the past and the contingent, helped London to formulate an accurate view of the Saudi perspective and sensitivities. Not surprisingly, between his ambitions, wishes and commitments, and his fear of and need for Britain, Ibn Sa'ud balanced his action with a rigorous self-discipline. Only after World War II, when his relations with the United States were consolidated, would he change his attitude towards Britain.

Ibn Sa'ud's reaction to the partition was a reflection of his undisputed authority at home, his Arab and Islamic influence abroad and his complex relations with Britain. Besides the disagreement on Palestine, three outstanding issues were still pending between the Saudi kingdom and the British government in the summer of 1937. These were the unresolved question of the Saudi eastern borders with the British-protected Gulf sheikhdoms, Ibn Sa'ud's repeated demands for the return of the 'Aqaba and Ma'an areas of Transjordan (which had originally been part of the Hijaz), and the Italian encroachment on the Arabian peninsula. The disagreement over the Saudi borders was a chronic and protracted case that was not expected in the short term to develop into a serious dispute.[162] Similarly, though Ibn Sa'ud was repeatedly hinting at the Italians' approaches to him, their insignificant presence in Saudi Arabia and the king's mistrust of their schemes and of Mussolini's pro-Islamic policy, gave Bullard no reason to be alarmed.[163] Where the Saudis looked more justified was with regard to the more disquieting issue of 'Aqaba and Ma'an. Astonished at the British plan to offer Abdullah the projected Arab portion of Palestine, Ibn Sa'ud returned to asserting his rights over 'Aqaba and Ma'an.[164] For many in the British Foreign Office, this could only confirm the worst of their fears over what the partition plan was about to unleash.

Characteristically, Ibn Sa'ud's objections to the British policy in Palestine were phrased in a highly delicate manner.[165] He spoke to Bullard as a loyal friend of Britain, even as an inseparable part of the British world system, relentlessly pointing to the unworkability of the partition plan, the havoc it could entail and his confidence in the Palestinian determination to resist it.[166] Ibn Sa'ud's mistrust of Jews, as Jews (not merely Zionists), was a motif known to the British, but the king was able to go even further than lecturing Bullard on undesirable Jewish characteristics. In August 1937, the Sa'udi ulema issued a fatwa in which they clearly stated that no Jewish authority was permitted to prevail in a Muslim country.[167] There was little doubt that the fatwa was, explicitly or implicitly, encouraged by the king. Moreover, in a country where institutions of civil society were entirely terminated after the conquest of the Hijaz in the mid-1920s, Ibn Saʻud signalled his consent for the organization of a series of protest demonstrations and the establishment of several Palestine defence committees.[168] A central committee, headed by the pro-Saudi Hijazi notable, Muhammad Salih Nasif, was based in Mecca, the city on which hundreds of thousands of Muslims converge every year for the pilgrimage. Besides contributing to the revolt's funds, the Saudis were also suspected of supplying the rebels with arms.[169]

Arab opposition to the partition was not, however, a universal phenomenon. Expectedly, Amir Abdullah of Transjordan voiced his agreement with the partition plan. For the past few years, Abdullah had been more receptive and cooperative with Zionist leaders than any other Arab public figure. His main motivation, besides matters of finance and influence, was an unwavering ambition to extend his domain to Palestine. Despite Arab and Palestinian suspicions, Abdullah had no contribution to the development of the Peel Commission's position on partition. If any, Abdullah's role was limited to his passive allegiance to Britain. It was Reginald Coupland, Beit Professor of Colonial History at Oxford University and the Peel Commission's most cerebral and persuasive member, who perhaps played the major role in bringing the Commission to embrace partition.[170] Equally crucial were the lobbying activities of Chaim Weizmann, Moshe Sharett and David Ben-Gurion, the key Zionist leaders. Confronted with the Palestinian and Arab tenacious resistance to the JNH policy, these leaders became convinced that their only hope for realizing a Jewish state was the division of Palestine. Although they generally came to express dissatisfaction with the limits of the Jewish state envisioned in the British plan, the Zionist leaders were an active party to its formulation. As Avi Shlaim concluded, Weizmann, Sharett and Ben-Gurion

> played a greater role in crystallizing the Peel Report and its ultimate failure than they themselves were ever prepared to admit. The selection of partition in preference to establishing a legislative council with parity or cantonization; the borders of the projected states; the idea of population exchange between them, and the choice of Abdullah rather than the mufti to head the Arab state were all influenced, if only marginally, by the Zionist diplomacy.[171]

Like Churchill in 1921, the Zionists saw Abdullah as the safest neighbour to absorb the collateral calamities of the partition.

Naively assuming that partition was to be imminently implemented, Abdullah rushed to express his forthright acceptance of the plan and its terms.[172] Since the state of his relations with the Palestinian nationalist leaders was descending to the lowest of its levels, he had no illusions about the mufti's or the Istiqlalists' views of him. With his hopes pinned on the British power, his Zionist friends and the Nashashibi opposition,[173] Abdullah believed that the Palestinians would eventually come to see the merits of his position. His main argument was that, considering British policy and Zionist world influence, Palestine's union with Transjordan was the only viable course to stop the whole of Palestine from coming under Zionist control. But the winds were not blowing into his sail. The British informed him that, if enforced, the partition plan would take a long time to be achieved. His Nashashibi allies refrained from identifying with his stance,[174] while the nationalist opposition in his own country took action to demonstrate Jordanian disapproval of the partition.[175] As Abdullah was the exception, his stand contrasted with the strength of Arab rejection, so much so that he was to be severely censured by the Iraqi prime minister, his nephew King Ghazi, the Saudis, and the Arab-Islamic press all over the Arab East.[176] Sensing the strongly unfavourable repercussions of his master's dissent from the Arab consensus, Abdullah's prime minister maintained all along that his government was in tandem with the prevalent Arab view.[177] Eventually, defeated but unmoved, Abdullah issued a statement denying that he was ever prepared to comply with the partition.[178]

Separately, the three newly independent Arab states, Egypt, Iraq and Saudi Arabia, in addition to Yemen and the national government of Syria, opposed the partition.[179] The Arab collective expression of this opposition materialized on another level, the unofficial, popular level. Within two months of the British announcement of the partition proposal, ulema, politicians, populists and intelligentsia of two Arab generations gathered in the Syrian resort town of Bludan. During their meeting, the convergence of the Palestinian question with the Arab nationalist movement was demonstrated as never before. This trend was emphasized, a little more than a year later, in a series of Arab gatherings in Cairo.

The rise of Arabism

The Bludan Arab Congress was not, of course, the first to be attempted by the Arab movement during the 1930s. What made Bludan possible where the earlier attempt of the Istiqlalists had failed were some significant differences in the strategy and methods adopted in each case. The origin of many of the frustrating obstacles that the Istiqlalists encountered in 1932–3 was the connection between their project and King Faysal of Iraq. This connection rendered the Istiqlalist enterprise liable to British pressure, Zionist objections and Saudi suspicion. In 1937, the congress idea was born from within the Arab popular forces. It was not at any stage mortgaged to any Arab government, and was from its outset meant to be an anti-British, and anti-Zionist, demonstration of the Arab will. The contrast lay also in the political agenda that underpinned the two projects. While the Istiqlalist attempt was predicated on a vague vision of Arab federation, in a period when the question of Arab unity was riddled with inter-Hashemite and Syrian–Hashemite–Saudi mistrust, the principal organizers of the Bludan Congress devised a pan-Arab gathering revolving around the Palestinian problem, assuming that Arab unity could be manifested in formulating an Arab consensus on Palestine. That the successful convening of the congress was proof of this assumption should not, however, conceal the fact that its preparations, or the course of its debate, were not entirely without strains.

The idea of convening an Arab congress to discuss the Palestinian situation was first proposed by the mufti during his visit to Syria.[180] Following the release of the Peel Commission's report, the HAC contacted Nabih al-'Azma in Damascus to start preparing for the congress. A little later, Mu'in al-Madi was dispatched from Jerusalem to take part in the preparations. It is perhaps important to mention that the reaction of the Syrian government of Jamil Mardam to the partition was initially as strong as that of any other Arab government.[181] But even at that early stage, Mardam was divided between his Arabist commitments and the demands of his Syrian-nationalist constituency on the one hand, and British pressure on the other. Most probably, therefore, Nabih al-'Azma was quietly told by his colleagues in power to try to hold the congress outside Syria. This scenario was perhaps the reason for al-'Azma's prompt approaches to the Iraqi government of Hikmat Sulayman, to Ibn Sa'ud and to Mustafa al-Nahhas, asking for permission to hold the projected congress in Mecca, Baghdad or Cairo.[182] Either because of actual or anticipated British objections, the three governments declined to grant such permission. The Arabists' pressure was subsequently turned on Mardam who eventually but grudgingly relented. But to minimize the damage expected in his relations with Britain, he regarded the congress as a non-official occasion and ordered members of his cabinet not to participate in its activities.[183] In fact, none of the Arab governments would be officially represented.

Although the congress was held at short notice, close to 450 Arab respondents converged on Bludan to participate in its proceedings which continued from 8 to 10 September. The majority of the participants were Syrians, Palestinians, Lebanese and Jordanians,[184] together with 12–15 Iraqis and 6 Egyptians. Mackereth's report on the congress indicated the presence of one Saudi, without giving his name. It is doubtful whether Ibn Sa'ud could have allowed Saudi participation in the congress. Despite a widening popular support for the Palestinians in Saudi Arabia, the king's policy of insulating his people from Arab popular influences was still firmly applied. There was a noticeable presence of exiled Libyan nationalists who were becoming actively involved in pan-Arab causes. The organizers planned convening the congress in the main hall of the Bludan Grand Hotel, where only 250 people could be accommodated. But, despite the larger than expected turnout, the congress proceeded in a most orderly manner. The organization and security were entrusted to the Boy Scouts and Youth Iron Shirts of the NAL and the National Bloc, a step that was perhaps to signal the beginning of the arduous divorce between the Arab nationalist movement and the interwar Arab regimes.

By and large, the pro-British Arab circles boycotted the congress. While most of the Nashashibist leaders found it convenient to respond with sympathetic letters,[185] Amir Abdullah ordered the arrest of return-ing Jordanian members of the congress.[186] Although Abd al-Rahman al-Shahbandar, the Syrian anti-National Bloc Anglophile, was active on behalf of the Palestinian cause in Europe, he also refrained from joining.[187] But letters of support for the congress were numerous, coming from sources as diverse as the ulema of al-Azhar and the Ikhwan in Cairo and the senior Lebanese Shi'i and Sunni ulema. An important aspect of Bludan was the participation of the Greek Orthodox Bishop of Hama, Ignatius Hurayka. His anti-Zionist speech and the noticeable presence of many Arab Christian activists led Harold Beeley, a keen observer of the Arab scene in the 1930s, to note that Bludan gave "evidence of the political unity of Muslim and Christian Arabs".[188] In a similar vein, Jubran Twayni, the Lebanese Christian founder of *al-Nahar* newspaper, wrote that Bludan had directed a blow at Phoenicianism, Pharaonism and anti-Arabism.[189] What was perhaps equally indicative in the congress configuration was the strong representation of the young Arabist radicals. Compared with the Islamic Congress of Jerusalem, the last such gathering, Bludan reflected the progressively changing setting of the Arab movement. The Arab political arena appeared to be slipping from the monopoly of former Ottoman officials, officers and ulema of the urban notables. Young graduates of the American University of Beirut, and of European and Arab institutions of modern education, with modest social backgrounds, were now making their voices heard. Members of the NAL and al-Muthanna Club, and the secretive groupings of Arab nationalists, whose claim to fame was their uncompromising attitude towards the colonial powers and their adherence to an idealist vision of Arab unity, seized on the unique opportunity to press forward with their programme. But the mood, as the congress resolutions would tell, was still one of transition.

In its first session, the congress unanimously elected Naji al-Swaydi, head of the Iraqi delegation, as its chairman. Al-Swaydi was a graduate of the Istanbul Law School and an official in the Ottoman administration. His last post before the demise of the Ottoman state was the governorship of Aleppo, from which he declared his allegiance to Faysal's government of Damascus.[190] In 1920s Iraq, al-Swaydi became a minister and was prime minister for a term. Descended from a long-established family of Baghdadi ulema, his stature was based on a prominent social background, as well as on his remarkable Ottoman career. His father, Shaykh Yusuf al-Swaydi, a student of the reformist 'Alusi circles, made a distinguished contribution to the Iraqi revolt of 1920. Unlike Tawfiq, his pragmatic brother, Naji maintained strong ties with the Iraqi nationalist and pan-Arab quarters of Yasin al-Hashimi and the Palestine Defence Committee.[191] He was by no means a radical, but events of the uncertain coming times would take him on a long journey from the Bludan Congress to a tragic death in exile in Rhodesia.

Al-Swaydi's deputies were Muhammad Ali 'Alluba, Shakib Arslan (who was on a short visit) and Bishop Ignatius Hurayka. The Lebanese Istiqlalist leader Riyad al-Sulh was chosen as the congress inspector, 'Izzat Darwaza as the secretary-general and Abd al-Hamid Sa'id as the coordinator of the three special committees of political affairs, finance and propaganda. This did not mean that the younger generation of Arabists was totally devoid of influence. By constituting the bulk of the committees, the radicals left their imprint on the committee's recommendations.[192] Mackereth's memorandum on the congress, which was based entirely and exclusively on a report prepared by an informer (who did not seem to be a prominent member of the Arab nationalist circles), pointed to a radical–moderate rift within the congress.[193] The British consul regarded the resolutions adopted by the congress as a victory for the moderate viewpoint. He further indicated that, as a result of their failure, the radicals held a secret post-congress meeting at the house of Hani al-Jallad, the young militant NAL leader, where a plan for fomenting an anti-British revolt was deliberated.

While a certain degree of tension was expected between the two main blocs of members, other reports on the workings of the congress did not corroborate the assessment of Mackereth. The principal organizers of the congress were informed of the British pressure on Mardam, and were consequently inclined not to cause unwarranted problems for the Syrian government. But such considerations did not seem to have a substantive impact on the deliberations or the wide agreement by which the congress resolutions were adopted. The only recorded skirmish was the highly partisan wrangling over a proposed resolution protesting the Lebanese government's policy.[194] It is interesting that Mackereth's informer did not mention the presence of any Palestinian leader in the post-congress secret meeting except the landed notable Ya'qub al-Ghusayn, who was not particularly known for his militant outlook, for his involvement in the preparations for the revolt or for securing arms for it.[195] A meeting was, in fact, held a few hours after the conclusion of the Bludan Congress, at a coffee-house in the neighbouring town of al-Zabadani, where a group of the NAL, al-Muthanna Club, the Arab Liberation Movement and other radical Arabists from *Bilad* al-Sham and Libya gathered to discuss the idea of an Arab covenant for youth and a pan-Arab youth congress. Remarkably, the envisioned congress was to embrace not only Egypt and the Arab East, but also Yemen, Sudan and North Africa.[196] For those assembled in al-Zabadani, such as Yunis al-Sab'awi, Farid Zayn al-Din, Kazim al-Sulh, Subhi Abu Ghanima, Munir al-Rayyis, Zaki al-Arsuzi and Kamil 'Aiyad, Arab geography was now extended to its limit.

The most important of the congress's resolutions originated from the lengthy report of the political committee, which began with a historical exposition of the Palestinian question and Anglo-Arab relations since World War I.[197] Drafted with a strong political sense and careful consideration, the recommendations of the report reflected the growing self-confidence of the Arab movement. In a clear departure from the discourse of desperation and pleading, the political committee denoted that survival of Anglo-Arab friendship hinged on the realization of Arab demands, while the British insistence on the present policy would force the Arabs into new directions. The report affirmed the Arab identity of Palestine and the Arabs' responsibility in safeguarding this identity. It rejected the partition, the proposed plan for establishing a Jewish state in Palestine, and demanded the abrogation of the mandate and its pillar, the Balfour Declaration. Instead, the report called for the setting up of an Arab government in Palestine based on the Iraqi and Egyptian models, where relations with Britain could be regulated through a treaty. The point that epitomized the essence of the Arab radicals' ideal was the recommendation for turning the congress into a permanent organization. Driving the identification of the Palestinian question with the Arab nationalist movement to its logical conclusion, the report envisaged the formation of an executive committee for the permanent congress, comprising the HAC, along with representatives from other Arab countries. For the young Arabists, much more important than the emergence of Palestine support committees in various Arab countries was the organization of the Arab movement in a centralized manner.

With a few modifications, the congress approved the recommendations of the political committee, together with the reports of the economic and propaganda committees. Various means for maximizing the financial backing for the Palestinians were adopted, and a central office of propaganda was to be founded, with branches in major Arab countries, as well as in London and Geneva. The resolutions also called for a strict boycott of Jewish goods that was to be extended to British goods as well in the event of London persisting in its political enmity towards the Arabs.[198]

The Bludan Congress, important as it was in the chronicles of the Arab movement, was only the first of such collective manifestations of Arab–Palestinian rapport. In the wake of the congress, the Palestinian revolt developed into a full-scale insurgency, reverberating throughout the Arab land. During 1938, the Arab masses became less satisfied with the mere rejection of the partition. Unrestrained by what was regarded as acceptable or unacceptable in terms of the Arab governments' relations with Britain, the pro-Palestine movement emerged as an integral part of the Arab search for independence and dignity. Gradually, the Palestinian cause permeated the internal fabric of Arab politics and power relations. For the Arab masses, a government's identification with Islam and Arabism would now be largely judged on the basis of its record on Palestine. Increasingly, Arab opposition groups would employ the Palestinian sword in order to challenge the legitimacy of ruling regimes, and whenever a government's position appeared slightly uncertain, popular forces surged forward to press their own agenda.

Throughout 1938 and until the British government decided to abandon the partition plan, Ibn Sa'ud repeatedly expressed to Bullard the increasing difficulty he was facing in his attempts to restrain the ulema of Najd.[199] Signs of unease, emanating from the heart of the Saudi power base, were echoed in the quarters of Arab-Islamic opponents, as well as friends, of the Saudi regime. By choosing not to antagonize the British, the Saudi king drew criticism from the Shi'i marji' of Iraq, Muhammad Kashif al-Ghita', and, perhaps for the first time, from Hajj Amin al-Husayni and the Istiqlalist, Akram Zu'aytir.[200]

The failure of the Syrian government's policy of "honourable cooperation" was exacerbated by Mardam's equivocation on Palestine, resulting in the alienation of wider segments of the Syrian Arab and Islamic forces. Confronted with a series of protests from the ulema, Islamic societies and the nationalist opposition, Mardam resigned the premiership in February 1939,[201] in a late attempt to preserve his pan-Arab and nationalist reputation. His record in government, however, inflicted irreparable damage on his position in the Syrian nationalist movement, where he was subsequently eclipsed by the rising figure of Shukri al-Quwwatli.

In Iraq, the ascendance of the pan-Arab movement was becoming increasingly unstoppable. The return of the exiled politicians, after the collapse of the coup regime, provided the pan-Arabist army officers with the opportunity to extend their political ties even further. General Taha al-Hashimi, the highly admired former chief of staff, became the focus of the Arabist officers' allegiance.[202] Under the impact of the tragic death of his brother, Yasin, in Beirut, Taha moved closer to the Arabist circles of Syria and Palestine, a development that led him to assume the chairmanship of the Palestine Defence Committee in the summer of

1938.[203] Al-Hashimi, none the less, was a soldier with great reluctance to play the power game. Ironically, the man who emerged as al-Hashimi's and his army colleagues' candidate was Nuri al-Sa'id. Nuri had cultivated a strong pan-Arabist image by working tirelessly for Syrian independence and the Palestinian cause, thereby gaining the trust of the Arabist bloc in the army.[204] The disagreement between this evolving alliance of political and military Arabists and the premier, Jamil al-Madfa'i, stemmed initially from the latter's reluctance to punish and dismiss supporters of the coup regime. But, gradually, this disagreement developed into a solid opposition: first, for what the Arabists perceived as unwarranted concessions by the Iraqi government to Iran in the Iraqi–Iranian border treaty;[205] second, for al-Madfa'i's foot-dragging on the Syrian requests for Iraqi backing against the French and the Franco-Turkish collusion to deprive Syria of the *sanjaq* of Alexandretta;[206] and third, for al-Madfa'i's failure to match the popular expectations with regard to his government's action on the Palestinian front.[207] What made the government's Arabist credentials decline even further was King Ghazi's recasting of his image as a pan-Arab leader. In 1938, Ghazi enhanced the capacity of his private radio station at al-Zuhur Palace, obtained the rights to an international wavelength, and turned the station into a pan-Arabist voice, advocating Arab unity and Syrian and Palestinian rights.[208] Young and inexperienced as he was, Ghazi came to realize that only a pan-Arab, pro-Palestine flare would secure his popularity and preserve his position.

By the end of the year, al-Madfa'i appeared virtually isolated from the various centres of power: the Palace, the army and the masses. Demonstrations erupted in Baghdad, where the government was attacked on several aspects of its record, particularly the Palestinian issue.[209] On 24 December, the Arabist officers – in the third Iraqi coup within two years – drove al-Madfa'i out of office and forced the king to appoint Nuri al-Sa'id as the new prime minister.[210]

While the inherent instability of the state and the search for fulfilling the country's pan-Arab ideology were the principal agents for the advent of Palestine as an Iraqi domestic issue, the Palestinian problem for Egypt was the vehicle for expressing the irrepressible consciousness of its weight, power and search for a wider and leading role. Quoting the director-general of the Iraqi foreign ministry, C. J. Edmonds, the British official most acquainted with the Iraqi scene, wrote, "Pan-Arab feeling permeated the educated classes, who alone counted to an extent which no cabinet could afford to ignore . . . The leading men of Iraq had made up their minds that in the modern world of force-politics a small state of under four million inhabitants had no prospect of survival and that their only hope lay in pushing a vigorous policy aiming at pan-Arab league."[211] The struggle within the Iraqi ruling class was in a sense about the interpretation of this policy and about balancing its differing ingredients. In contrast, Egypt's espousal of the Palestinian cause evolved out of its search for a political identity and of its pursuit of an Arab and Islamic role. As this pursuit intensified, the question of Palestine advanced to the heart of the internal debate, turning into a major defining element for Egypt's Arab and changing Islamic role.

After the dismissal of the Wafdi ministry in December 1937, a new government was formed by Muhammad Mahmud, leader of the Liberal Constitutionalist Party. Mahmud headed a coalition which incorporated members from his own party and from the Sa'di Bloc, the new breakaway Wafdi faction. Although it lasted until August 1939, Mahmud's government struggled its course all the way to the end. The popular support for the Wafd was still as strong as ever, a situation that Mahmud faced unrestrainedly by rigging the elections of spring 1938 in order to secure a majority in parliament. On the other side of the power game was the Palace. With a popular young king, who was surrounded by wily and ambitious men, such as 'Ali Mahir and Shaykh Mustafa al-Maraghi, the Palace emerged as a major party in the balance of forces. Mahir's and al-Maraghi's vision revolved around the idea of reinvigorating Egypt with a strong and centralized system based on religious values and the unity of the people with their ruler. Their instrument for achieving such a vision was the cultivation of a Caliph image for Faruq.[212] The Caliph image, coupled with the desire to undermine the Wafd's popular appeal, opened the doors for the newly rising forces of the Ikhwan and Young Egypt. Either because of his own conservative background, or because of the need to adapt to the changing political scene, Mahmud embraced the Islamic populism of the new era. To enhance the Islamic credentials of the government, Mahmud appointed Muhammad Husayn Haykal, now highly noted for his Islamically-oriented writings, and Shaykh Mustafa Abd al-Raziq, the most distinguished mind of the ulema institution, as members of his cabinet.[213]

From the outbreak of the 1936 strike, Mahmud and his party repeatedly declared their support for the Palestinian struggle. In office, the prime minister was flooded with appeals from the Ikhwan, the YMMS and the powerful Shaykh al-Azhar, to intervene on behalf of the Palestinians.[214] Popular pressure took other forms, including student demonstrations and a conference of various Islamic organizations and societies at the YMMS's headquarters.[215] Even two members of Mahmud's cabinet were suspected by the British of being associated with the pro-Palestine activities.[216] The Wafd, free of the constraints of government, began to show a stronger commitment to the pro-Palestine movement.[217] In May, following the end of the general election euphoria, the distinguished Liberal Constitutionalist parliamentarian, Muhammad 'Ali 'Alluba, took a step the result of which no one could then anticipate. 'Alluba invited a group of his colleagues to his house, where they decided to form a parliamentary group for the support of Palestine.[218] And again, he presented the British embassy with a petition, signed by 160 members of both chambers of parliament.[219]

In June, 'Alluba and his group began preparations for holding a pro-Palestine, Arab-Islamic, inter-parliamentary congress.[220] 'Alluba envisaged a convention in which not only parliamentarians but also leaders of public opinion and notable personalities would participate. The idea was to open the participation to as many Arab and Islamic countries as possible. But once the British embassy realized the dimensions of 'Alluba's project, the political and diplomatic machine of Whitehall was put into top gear to impede the holding of the congress.[221] For sensing the British objection, and perhaps for fear of exposing his subjects to such unpredictable events, Ibn Sa'ud prevented the Saudi notables from joining the congress.[222] Amir Abdullah, now a main target of Arab and Muslim condemnation, followed a similar line in not dispatching a delegation.[223] The Jordanian participants were mainly exiled opposition leaders. In Egypt, although the government kept its distance from the congress, 'Alluba himself was a Liberal Constitutionalist and the 1938 parliament, under whose auspices the congress was held, was predominantly pro-government. In early August, as the Wafd announced a plan for holding a popular pro-Palestine convention, Mahmud was obliged to alter his position.[224] Not only the prime minister, but also the king would embrace the congress.

When the holding of the congress appeared to be certain, the British moved to minimize the damage anticipated to arise from it. Sir Miles Lampson made sure that 'Ali Mahir and Prince Muhammad 'Ali would use their moderating influence on ʿAlluba,[225] while pressure was being exerted by the British government on the French authorities in Lebanon to prevent the mufti from travelling to Cairo.[226] In the British view, the mufti's attendance would have inflamed the congress's debates and made their attempt to forestall its repercussions a difficult task to achieve.

On the evening of 7 October, the World Parliamentary Congress for the Defence of Palestine was opened in the vast garden of al-Lutfallah Palace in al-Jazira. An estimated 2,000 people were present at the opening session. Amongst them were the speakers of the Egyptian, Iraqi and Syrian parliaments, Bahii-al Din Barakat, Mawlud Mukhlis and Faris al-Khuri, together with distinguished delegates from their respective parliaments. In addition, there was a Lebanese parliamentary group led by Jubran Twayni, and a Palestinian delegation headed by Jamal al-Husayni. There were groups of Yemeni and Moroccan representatives, an Indian Muslim delegation led by the grand mufti, Chinese and Yugoslav Muslim delegates, Arab-Americans, and the highly visible figure of Shaykh al-Azhar.[227] ʿAlluba delivered one of the most noteworthy opening statements, in which he stressed that a Zionist state in Palestine was not only an infringement of Palestinian rights, but also detrimental to Arab, and particularly to Egypt's, security and to Egypt's leading role in the *mashriq*. Yet, the congress's significance and impact were largely experienced outside the formal sessions, in the parallel functions that touched upon a greater sphere of Egypt's political and cultural life.

In many ways, the World Parliamentary Congress epitomized the fulfilment of Egypt's embrace of its Arab-Islamic identity, and high-lighted its principal role in shaping the future of the Arab and Muslim peoples. The Arab-Islamic circles of Egypt, realizing the implications of the congress for their pursuit, grasped the moment triumphantly. A grand reception in honour of the delegates was arranged by Hamid al-Basil, the Arabist and former Wafdi leader, where Muhammad Tawfiq Diyab and Abd al-Wahhab ʿAzzam delivered the welcoming speeches. Similarly, the delegates were fêted at the Lebanese and Eastern clubs of Cairo, and at the YMMS's headquarters. On the evening of 11 October, the participants gathered in the garden of Mustafa al-Nahhas's house, as the Wafdi leader stood to declare his commitment to Palestine and the Arab cause. Responding on behalf of the Palestinians, Akram Zuʿaytir addressed al-Nahhas as the Arab leader. Later, members of the congress were received at the central office of al-Ikhwan al-Muslimin by Hasan al-Banna and an enthusiastic Ikhwani gathering.[228] The delegates were invited to lunch with the prime minister, who asserted his country's Arab ties and pointed up his government's efforts on behalf of Palestine. The Palace, too, made a point in hosting a royal tea party for the delegates at the king's summer Palace in Alexandria, where a message expressing Faruq's pleasure at the success of the congress was read out on his behalf.[229] Two days after the conclusion of the formal meeting, Mustafa al-Maraghi received the guests at al-Azhar College of 'Usul al-Din. Reflecting on his vision of Egypt's Arab and Islamic identity, al-Maraghi remarked to his guests: "He who seeks this country as an Arab will find a fulfilment of his quest and a family, and he who seeks it as a Muslim will equally be fulfilled and meet with brothers. It is therefore the fittest of all countries to link the Arab and Muslim peoples together."[230] The response to Shaykh al-Azhar's address was most appropriately presented by Faris al-Khuri, the Syrian Christian leader, whose Arabist outlook was known to be blended with strong Islamic influences.

Unlike the Bludan Congress, the Cairo parliamentary gathering fringed both the popular and the official spheres. Many of the delegates viewed their participation as an official function, and were thus committed to the interests and views of their respective governments. This consideration led to a crucial disagreement during the formulation of the congress resolutions. The Syrians proposed a resolution that called for the return of Transjordan and independent Palestine to mother Syria. To show the strength of their position, the Syrians disclosed that the proposal had the a priori approval of the mufti. The Iraqis, whose interests lay in promoting a wider framework for Arab unity, objected to the Syrian proposal. More emphatic opposition was expressed by the Egyptians, who preferred instead a resolution demanding the independence of Palestine without prematurely defining its relations with other Arab states.[231] Neither the Iraqis nor the Syrians could anticipate that Egypt's espousal of an Arab role would entail the introduction of a new vision for the Arab future. There is little doubt that, as Egypt became more involved in Arab affairs, many of its leaders began charting the Arabic strategic scope of their country. Palestine, as Harold Beeley remarked, was, after all, the "northern bastion for the Suez Canal".[232] The Egyptians, therefore, tended to ask whether, if Palestine were to become part of a larger Arab entity, it should not be linked to Egypt? In the end, it was the Egyptian proposal which carried the day.

Other resolutions adopted by the congress demanded the annulment of the Balfour Declaration, termination of Jewish immigration into Palestine, rejection of any form of partition, and the maintaining of Palestine in its entirety as an Arab country. The congress demanded the establishment of an Arab government in Palestine, an end to the mandate, a general amnesty and the repatriation of deportees and political exiles. Moreover, it adopted a resolution on the future of Arab and Muslim relations with Britain and the Jews that echoed the spirit of Bludan. It stated that if Arab demands were not met, "Arab and Muslim peoples throughout the world will be compelled to regard the attitude of the British and the Jews as inimical to them and thereby forced to reciprocate with similar attitudes."[233] Beyond the resolutions, the congress's significance lay mainly in the fact that it had convened. In the words of Ahmad Hasan al-Zayyat, the editor of *al-Risala*, the congress was a remarkable event where Arab and Muslim delegates had "gathered in one place, united in purpose, feelings, and policy".[234]

Four days after the Parliamentary Congress was concluded, Cairo became the venue for another unprecedented event in the Arab calendar: the Eastern Women's Congress. Coordinated and efficiently conducted by the Egyptian Women's Union (EWU), this meeting was inspired by Huda Sha'rawi, president of the EWU. A pioneer of the Egyptian women's movement, Sha'rawi had long been involved in the Palestinian cause. She repeatedly expressed her support for the Palestinian struggle, and called upon the prime minister, Mustafa al-Nahhas, to assume a more active role on behalf of Palestine.[235] During the strike of 1936 and after the announcement of the partition plan, the Palestinian women's societies turned to Sha'rawi for assistance and support.[236] As various Palestinian women's groups became more involved in the national protest movement, further relations were established with Arab women's organizations in Iraq, Lebanon, and Syria. Since many women activists at that time were related to male leaders of the Arab movement, the women's role in the Arab arena evolved in parallel with the rise of the Arab movement in general.

Bahira al-'Azma, wife of Nabih al-'Azma, set up a Women's Palestine Defence Committee in Damascus.[237] Subsequently, the Syrian group contacted Sha'rawi and proposed the holding of a women's congress.[238] The idea was also taken up by 'Awni Abd al-Hadi who, in consultation with Sha'rawi, enlisted the support of his fellow Istiqlalist, Akram Zu'aytir.[239] Sha'rawi's standing and the support of the pro-Palestinian Arab networks secured the participation of several women delegates from Iraq, Lebanon, Palestine and Syria, in addition to various representatives of women's associations in Egypt. When the congress convened, it was noticeable that only one of the participants arrived in the company of a male relative. Nor were any of the women veiled.[240] The other important feature stemmed from the composition of the congress, mirrored in the social, confessional and cultural backgrounds of its members. Of the 27 courageous women who gathered in the main hall of the EWU headquarters on 15–18 October 1938, there were Muslims and Christians as well as Islamists and liberals. Among them were: Zaynab al-Ghazali, president of the Young Muslim Women's Society; Sabiha, daughter of the late Yasin al-Hashimi; Furlan Mardam, Bahira al-'Azma, and Thuraiyya Munir al-Rayyis from Syria; the French-speaking Evyline Jubran Bustras and Hayat Nur Bayham from Lebanon; Tarab Abd al-Hadi, Matilda Mogannam, Rayya Jamal al-Qasim and Su'ad Fahmi al-Husayni from Palestine; and Nafisa M. A. 'Alluba, Amina Fu'ad Sultan and the editor of *al-Misriyya* magazine, Eva Habib al-Misri, from Egypt.[241] 'Aisha Abd al-Rahman, who would become one of the most prominent Arab-Islamic writers of Egypt, covered the congress proceedings for *al-Ahram*. This gathering represented a distinctive form of feminist activism in an Arab-Islamic context, in which the women's movement identified with the nationalist movement, and thus succeeded in reasserting women's role and position without antagonizing adversary forces in society.

The congress concluded with the adoption of several resolutions which echoed the most uncompromising demands of the Palestinian Arabs.[242] Sha'rawi forwarded the declaration to the British prime minister through the British embassy, with a note of congratulations for his pursuit of world peace in Munich.[243] In return, she received an acknowledgement from the embassy's oriental secretary that made no reference to the congress. Lampson, however, relayed the congress resolutions to London, which added to accumulating evidence of the changing Arab climate.

On the evening of 17 October, a reception was held for the delegates of the Women's Congress in the Cairo Palestinian Club. In the reception,

Maymna al-Qassam, daughter of 'Izz al-Din al-Qassam, spoke on behalf of the Palestinian delegation. After a moving reference to the memory of her father and his martyred followers, al-Qassam went on to chronicle the main turning-points in the history of the Arab movement. She alluded to the Arab struggle during World War I and listed the Arab martyrs of the past three decades, many of whom happened to be related to delegates present at the reception: Salim Abd al-Hadi; Ali al-Nashashibi; Amin Lutfi al-Hafiz; Shaykh Ahmad 'Arif al-Husayni; Kamil al-Budayri; Yusuf al-'Azma and Yasin al-Hashimi.[244] Blended in al-Qassam's words and idioms, was the thematic discourse of the modern Arab mythology. If the divisive circumstances of World War I, where Arabs were killed on both sides of the strife, created a psychological barrier against the Arab gratification of the self, the Palestinian revolt opened the gate for the Arab consciousness to embark on conceiving its allegorical, heroic, and tragically elated realm. Poets, littérateurs, populists, politicians and balladeers, all joined in capturing the moment out of the unfolding times, constructing in the process a figurative, linguistic parallel to the Palestinian saga.

Nations could not exist without being defended. In the revolt, therefore, the Arabs as a nation, both Muslims and Christians, came to discover the ultimate self-assertion revealed in the steadfastness of the Palestinians, in their sorrows, executed heroes and spilled blood. The blood, wrote the Egyptian, Abd al-Mun'im Khallaf, united us, Palestinians, Syrians and Iraqis, and reclaimed the glorious history from the memory of the past centuries.[245] Implicit in the mythologizing euphoria, which was readily disseminated through the modern press and advanced communications' systems, was an urge for revival and renaissance and for re-entering the world.[246] As painful and compelling as the eventful images of the revolt were to the Arab consciousness, these images were consistently and persistently re-imagined as the required price for the Arabs' "appointment with history".[247] Yet, the Arab–Palestinian mythological integrate was only a small part of a more complex process that was engendered by the revolt. While Arabism and Islamism were being inaugurated on religious, territorial, linguistic and racial bases, a Palestinian ideology emerged to become inextricably intertwined with the evolving Arab and Islamic ideological assemblies.

In the ulema's discourse and in the discourse of their counterparts in the Islamic societies, the invocation was simple, sharp and uncompromising.

No Jewish authority or power must be allowed to rise over the followers of the Straight Path, or on this very holy land of Islam. The ulema emphatically established that the land of Palestine did not belong to the Palestinians alone, but to all Muslims.[248] For the non-ulema, though Islam was not always remote from the boundaries of their ideological enterprise, Palestine was largely viewed in terms of worldly, relative configurations that had their origins in the discourse of modernity, its values and its exclusivity as well. Underlining the Arabists' view of the Palestinian question were elements of language, history and race, that united the Palestinians and the Arabs. Since the Arab world extended from the Persian Gulf to the Atlantic, Palestine was regarded as the strategic jugular vein and the binding knot of the Arabs.[249] The consequential inference of this assertion was the idea that Arab unity was contingent on the preservation of Palestine as integrally Arab, and that a Jewish state in Palestine was bound to threaten strategically its Arab neighbours. In an age when national ideals were being classified into defining and defined categories, the Arab–Zionist paradox was also related to the cultural, economic and social vitality of the Arab peoples.[250] Even the Egyptian liberal, Ahmad Lutfi al-Sayyid, would begin to see the Palestinian conflict as the main determinant of the very existence and survival of the Arabs.[251] Finally, entailed in the rise of the Palestinian ideology was the rise of the theme that has since been ingrained in the Arab mind and political world view – Palestine is the ultimate measure of the Arabs' relations with the West. Or, as Naji al-Swaydi and Nabih al-'Azma stressed in their contributions in Bludan, "in Palestine, the Arabs and Britain are reaching a crossroads".[252]

Britain, the Arabs and Palestine

The Arab reactions to the partition plan confirmed to the British government the emergence of what many in Whitehall had been trying by all means to avoid: the strengthening Arab–Palestinian bonds. Reports from the three major British outposts in the Arab world, the embassies of Jeddah, Baghdad and Cairo, were invariably projecting a grim picture of the impact of the partition proposal on Britain's position in the region.[253] Even Mackereth, with his bordering-on-racism images of the Arabs and advocacy of an anti-Arab policy, had grudgingly to admit, in his report on the Bludan Congress, to the tenacity and gravity of the rising anti-British feelings. Between July and September 1937, Rendel prepared three memoranda on the Iraqi, Egyptian and Saudi attitudes towards the Palestinian situation.[254] In November, the Foreign Office presented to the cabinet the view that the strong Palestinian and Arab opposition to the Peel Commission's report would make the partition plan impossible to implement without the use of force, an option that might result in jeopardizing British interests in the Middle East. Underlining the "organic whole" of the Arabic-speaking countries, the Foreign Office recommended that if a new commission was appointed to examine the practicality of the partition, the non-Palestinian Arab opinion should be as favourably heard as that of the non-Palestinian Jews.[255]

There is no doubt that Ormsby-Gore, the pro-Zionist colonial secretary, marshalled all possible arguments in defence of the partition policy, but eventually it was the forceful standpoint of the Foreign Office which carried the day. During the cabinet meeting of 8 December, the prime minister, Neville Chamberlain, who seemed to have been impressed by Ibn Sa'ud's approach and reasoning, sided with the foreign secretary, Antony Eden.[256] Yet, in the tradition of the empire, the partition was not to be immediately abandoned, but rather to be put to a slow death. The difference between the two courses was a long, painful year of bloody conflict.

It was one of the Peel Commission's recommendations that the technical aspects of the partition be determined by another commission. Seizing on this proposition, Chamberlain decided that the terms of reference for the new commission should be drafted in a manner that would result in the commission's recommending the unworkability of the partition plan. No clear direction to such conclusion was to be made in the terms of reference, but was rather to be intimated to the commission's chairman. Though the new policy reflected the cabinet's yielding to the Palestinian and Arab opposition to the partition, it did not entail an explicit change in the British outlook regarding Arab involvement in the Palestinian problem. For the colonial secretary, however, the writing was on the wall. Like a soldier falling on his sword, Ormsby-Gore, only few months before his resignation, wrote to the prime minister:

> Our policy always has been and must be aimed at preventing the growth of unity and solidarity in the Moslem World. We rightly

encouraged the growth of local nationalism as being the lesser danger than pan-Islamic solidarity [read, of course, pan-Arab].[257]

The setting up of a new commission of experts was decided in January 1938, and it was subsequently organized by the colonial secretary in March under the chairmanship of Sir John Woodhead (with whose name it came to be identified).[258] It arrived in Palestine on 27 April amid widespread protests in many Arab capitals, and conducted investigations until the beginning of August. As was contrived by the cabinet, the Woodhead Commission recommended the abandonment of partition. But even before the release of its report, the British government, especially the Colonial Office, was busy formulating a new approach to the Palestinian question, in which the Arab role would occupy a central place. What came to influence the forging of this approach was an array of intricate factors.

First there was an unexpected reshuffle in the British cabinet. On the one hand, Eden, the more receptive to the adoption of a new Palestinian and Arab policy, was replaced by the highly conservative Halifax in February 1938; on the other hand, Ormsby-Gore resigned from the Colonial Office in May, and was replaced by Malcolm MacDonald. While the change in the Foreign Office removed it temporarily – until the return of Eden in 1940 – from the cutting edge of shaping the British Palestinian–Arab policy, the appearance of MacDonald, free from the pro-Zionist predilections of his predecessor, opened up new avenues for the conceptualization and direction of the decision-making process at the Colonial Office. By holding numerous meetings with Arabs, Jews, and other interested parties, and paying a two-day visit to Palestine, MacDonald looked bent on developing a radical approach to the Palestinian imbroglio. Second, there was, of course, the unceasing revolt in Palestine and its Arab repercussions. Seen in the context of escalating tension in Europe and the ominous signs of a world war, where the British defence would be stretched from South-East Asia to South America, Britain became more conscious of the need to contain the Arab movement. And third, there was the rise in diplomatic and intermediary activities in the Arab–Zionist arena, from which some important ideas seem to have emerged and laid the foundations for MacDonald's evolving vision of a Palestinian solution. Of these activities two important attempts are worth noting.

One of the early British Jewish dissenting voices over the partition idea was Lord Herbert Samuel. The former High Commissioner of Palestine firmly and consistently believed that the JNH could not afford to, and should not, turn into an agent of Arab–Jewish hatred and strife. In a speech to the House of Lords on 20 July 1937, Samuel returned to his original concept of a Jewish entity (not a state) that would evolve gradually and slowly within a larger Arab framework. Calling for recognition of the Arab national movement, Samuel said, "It is a delusion to think all that is necessary is to remove the Mufti, and that then all will be well. We used to hear that kind of thing in the old days with regard to Ireland."[259] Samuel believed that, even in practical terms, the partition proposal was inapplicable, for reasons related to the geographical limitations of Palestine and for the intractable mingling of the two communities. He, therefore, proposed that Jews had to agree with subjecting immigration to the political criteria (not only the economic criteria of Churchill's doctrine of the early 1920s), and that the growth of the Jewish population in Palestine should not exceed at the end of a ten-year transitional period 40 per cent of the total population (being not more than 28–9 per cent at the time). Samuel's scheme envisaged the opening of Transjordan for Jewish immigration and the emergence of an Arab confederation within which Palestine and other Arab countries would be included. By this proposal, Samuel was trying to respond to the Arab national aspirations and furnish a milieu for mitigating Palestinian fear of the Jewish encroachment.

Though Samuel's formula provided for a strategic long-term growth of the Jewish community in Palestine, it was categorically rejected by the Zionist and pro-Zionist quarters in Britain and Palestine. Samuel, none the less, could not be easily deterred. In March 1938, as the Palestinian movement was clearly unfolding into a full-fledged revolt, Samuel embarked upon a round of active diplomacy, beginning with a visit to Egypt and Palestine. His ideas were received approvingly by Prince Muhammad 'Ali in Egypt, who had been advocating a similar scheme for the past year.[260] But when discussed with 'Awni Abd al-Hadi, the Palestinian leader raised strong objections to two key points. 'Awni argued that by proposing the rise of the Jewish proportion to 40 per cent of the total, Samuel's scheme could open the door for 400,000 more Jews to settle in Palestine. Such a substantial increase would certainly augment the Jewish quest for becoming a dominant majority.[261] By the same token, 'Awni observed that by leaving the status of Palestine at the end of the transitional period undetermined, the scheme presented no guarantees to the Palestinian aspirations for independence, or to their opposition to the establishment of a Jewish state.

Upon his arrival in Palestine, Samuel attempted to arrange a meeting with the mufti in Lebanon, but sources are unclear as to why the meeting never materialized.[262] Other mediators, however, were by then maintaining close contact with the mufti. Samuel's *démarche* crossed paths with another project that had been initiated by Albert N. Hyamson, a British Jew and former head of the Palestinian Immigration Department, and Colonel Stewart F. Newcombe, an aide to T. E. Lawrence during World War I. Newcombe, who was acquainted with many of the Sharifian officers and activists (who were then either in power or prominent national leaders), was regarded as a friend of the Arabs and was close to Arab and Palestinian lobbyists in London. Since he and Hyamson were unequivocally opposed to the idea of dividing Palestine, they joined efforts in drafting an alternative to partition. The scheme, which was submitted to the Colonial Office, was based on the idea of establishing a national communal autonomy for the Arabs and Jews to continue for a transitional period, ending with independence. During this period, Jewish immigration would be extended to Transjordan, together with Palestine, where the Jewish population on both sides of the Jordan would be allowed to grow to a maximum proportion of 50 per cent of the total.[263] With slight variations, the premises of Newcombe–Hyamson's project were essentially similar to that of Samuel, an evidence of the free trafficking of ideas between interested parties in the Palestinian problem. Furthermore, like Samuel before them, Newcombe and Hyamson also enlisted the cooperation of Nuri al-Sa'id, Dr Judah Magnes (the non-Zionist rector of the Hebrew University), and the Anglican bishop of Jerusalem, Graham-Brown.[264]

In the later months of 1937, after extensive negotiations with the Jewish Agency in London and perhaps with some Arab representatives, it became obvious that only a direct approach to the mufti could determine the chances of this undertaking. Subsequently, Nuri al-Sa'id held several meetings with the mufti and 'Izzat Darwaza in Beirut, where he emphasized that the Palestinians should be prepared to explore various venues for a solution and avoid appearing as the intransigent side. The Palestinians did agree to deal with the proposed scheme, but the mufti made two initial reservations: (a) he was not authorized to discuss or take any steps with regard to the future of Transjordan; (b) pending authority from the Arab Congress, or, alternatively, unless pressed by the Arab rulers, he could not then agree to any increase of the present number of Jews in Palestine. Indeed, although they accepted in principle the concept of a transitional period, the Palestinians proposed a new scheme, which made no mention of Transjordan, and which appeared to adhere to the Bludan resolutions regarding Jewish immigration.[265] The third paragraph of article six in the Palestinian draft reads: "During the interim period envisaged, the Arab leaders have not been authorized by Congress or by the Arab kings to agree either to further Jewish immigration or to further land sales." Added to other precedents since the successful Arab intervention to end the 1936 strike, this formulation was perhaps instrumental in developing the Colonial Office's perception that active Arab participation in the negotiations would have a moderating effect on the Palestinians.

Nuri's interlocutor on the Jewish side was Dr Magnes, who was certainly amenable to the idea of retaining the Jewish population in Palestine at a level of less than 50 per cent, but who was also aware of the ferocious objections in the Zionist wing of the Jewish Agency to such an idea. He, therefore, pressed Nuri for a compromise on the population ratio. Realizing that the Palestinian position was for the time being unchangeable, Nuri devised his own draft of the scheme, in which he skilfully phrased the article concerning the maximum limit for the Jewish population in terms of percentage rather than number, and left the relevant figure unspecified (x per cent).[266] The Palestinians, it seems, had not been informed of Nuri's proposal, but the Zionist side had been. As the Zionists became aware of the British change of mind on the partition plan, their morale ebbed low. During the uncertain times prior to the release of the Woodhead Commission's report, Magnes and Hyamson succeeded in rallying the support of non-Zionist forces in Palestine, Europe and the United States to their diplomatic effort, which further exacerbated the Zionist position. In response, the Zionists threatened Magnes into silence.[267]

Both Samuel's *démarche* and the protracted undertaking of Hyamson, Newcombe and associates, elicited a noted interest in Whitehall. On the face of it, the Colonial Office was still officially bound to partition, and thus had no reason to become unduly committed to other opinions until the Woodhead Commission's report was presented.[268] Yet, in the light of the dramatic developments in the Colonial Office's attitudes to the Palestinian question in late 1938 and early 1939, one is tempted to conclude that the non-official diplomacy of 1938 inspired many of the official policies adopted by MacDonald's team. Even the idea of an Arab–Jewish conference seems to have originated from the résumé of Hyamson's and his partners' endeavour.

The Woodhead Commission was universally boycotted by the Palestinians and the Arabs. Only Amir Abdullah made a representation to the commission amid wide condemnation from Arabs and Palestinians, including his Nashashibi allies. Abdullah submitted a twelve-point proposal for a solution based on the establishment of a united Arab kingdom that would embrace Palestine and Transjordan.[269] Abdullah's proposal – as Shlaim has observed – was designed to please all parties, the Jews, the Palestinians and the British, without neglecting his own interests.[270] For the Palestinians' sake, Abdullah abandoned his support of partition; for the Jews he proposed an autonomous region to which a reasonable degree of immigration would be permitted; and for the British he granted the continuity of the mandate for ten years, though in a milder, modified form. To the amir's great disappointment, the Woodhead Commission declined to consider his plan, on the grounds that it fell outside its terms of reference. Nor did the Colonial Office pay it much attention. Although the Jordanian option would make a grand comeback ten years later, London was not yet in the mood for entertaining Abdullah's ambitions.

The British official line of thinking began to take shape a few weeks prior to the release of the Woodhead Commission's report. In October 1938 MacDonald held consultations with representatives of various concerned departments of the government, in addition to the High Commissioner of Palestine.[271] These consultations resulted in the formulation of three key ideas: the holding of an Arab–Jewish con-ference under the supervision of the British government, to which the Arab governments should be invited in order to exercise a moderating influence on the Palestinians; the solution to be devised by the conference would include Palestinian acquiescence to a limited, yet unspecified, degree of Jewish immigration and land sales; and the Jews would remain a minority in Palestine with a certain form of political autonomy. Palestine was envisaged to join an Arab federation when such a federation was established at a later stage. Showing a particular disposition towards the concept of Arab federation, MacDonald was evidently coming to embrace the view that Palestinian consent to a political compromise could be secured only if the Palestinians' fears were mitigated in a larger Arab political entity. These ideas were subsequently presented to a cabinet committee, chaired by the prime minister and charged with outlining the solution on which the government hoped the projected conference would agree. This committee accepted in principle the results of the interdepartmental consultations.[272] In the meantime, the Woodhead Commission reported to the government its highly anticipated conclusions that the partition plan was unworkable,[273] and the whole British position was hence left to the cabinet meeting of 2 November to be wrapped up. In this decisive meeting, MacDonald defended the idea of Arab federation, but the cabinet refrained from approving this element of the new policy, though it did sanction the other elements.[274]

This was the closest that the British government came to committing itself to a policy of favouring Arab unity after the end of World War I. According to Porath it was the less-than-enthusiastic attitude of the Halifax-led Foreign Office to MacDonald which sealed the fate of the Arab federation proposal.[275] It may well have been the Foreign Office's objections that at the last minute tipped the balance against MacDonald's view, but if past instances are any guide, Britain's Arab policy had almost always been defined by its negative attitude to Arab unity. At any rate, at that important juncture in the turbulent history of British–Arab relations, the British government went even further in creating unfavourable conditions for the passing of its new policy by issuing a six-month schedule of Jewish immigration certificates, prompting a fierce reaction from the HAC.[276] Still worse was the decision to ban the mufti from taking part in the projected Arab–Jewish conference.

The new British position was published on 7 November and communicated to the public two days later.[277] In its statement, the British government announced the conclusions of the Woodhead Commission and invited "the Palestinian Arabs and of neighbouring states on the one hand, and of the Jewish Agency on the other, to confer with them as soon as possible in London regarding future policy". The statement added: "As regards the representation of the Palestinian Arabs, His Majesty's Government must reserve the right to refuse to receive those leaders whom they regard as responsible for the campaign of assassination and violence." The implication of this point was of course correctly understood by all parties concerned as indicating the mufti. The early Arab and Palestinian reactions to this statement were at best mixed.

The British statement of policy was delivered to the Iraqi foreign minister by the British counsellor in Baghdad. Tawfiq al-Swaydi's response was generally positive. He even expressed a personal opinion that there was no need for the mufti to join the proposed discussions. Yet, al-Swaydi requested that to secure the essential condition for success, "there should be a basic understanding between His Majesty's Government and the Iraqi Government on main issues before the discussions opened."[278] It was obvious that the Iraqis required some advance assurances to be given to the Arabs in terms of the British intentions before committing themselves to the conference. If these demands were indirectly implied from the Iraqi response, they were plainly stated by the Egyptians. Abd al-Fattah Yahya, the foreign minister of Mahmud's government, went even further by asking that the mufti should attend the conference, and that the British should lift the harsh punitive measures in Palestine. Supported by his prime minister, Yahya requested that the limits of the British concessions be explained to Cairo before the conference was convened.[279] In contrast, the Saudi king received the British statement with relief and satisfaction. He accepted the invitation to appoint Saudi representatives to the London meeting without questioning the exclusionary article of the statement.[280] But, on the next day, Ibn Sa'ud asked Bullard, rather reluctantly, if the British government was interested in Arab mediation for the suspension of hostilities in Palestine, or whether it would agree to announcing an amnesty and releasing the Palestinian prisoners.[281] On this occasion, London was not prepared to follow the 1936 example, for the military campaign against the revolt was still in full swing, while the British authority in many parts of Palestine, including the city of Beershiba, was not yet restored.[282]

The Palestinian public expressed satisfaction over the abandonment of partition, but resented the exclusion of the mufti. In Beirut, where opinions largely echoed the HAC's viewpoint, there was equal disappointment over the mufti's exclusion and the failure of the statement to respond to the Arab demand for the suspension of Jewish immigration. Arab radical circles made it clear that the Arabs would not sit down at a conference with Jews, nor would the revolt be halted.[283] On 15 November, the HAC issued a long communiqué outlining its response to the British statement of policy.[284] In its statement, the HAC combined its welcoming of the abandonment of the partition with an expression of regret over the long time it had taken for London to recognize its impracticability. It also appreciated the invitation of other Arab countries to the proposed London conference, but expressed its surprise that Syria and Lebanon were not invited. (The invitation did not include Transjordan either, on the grounds that these three countries were not yet independent.) The HAC denied the very existence of "Jewish rights" in Palestine, which had been referred to in the British statement, and equally rejected the possibility of an imposed solution in the event of the failure of the conference. Responding to the exclusion of the mufti, the HAC laid the blame for the ongoing violence in Palestine on British policies, and declared that it was the only representative body of the Palestinian people. Finally, the main Arab demands regarding independence, replacement of the mandate with an Anglo-Palestinian treaty, annulment of the JNH policy and stoppage of Jewish immigration, were fully stated. It was an uncompromising statement that reflected the Palestinian belief in the revolt and in the power of the pan-Arab movement. The HAC, however, did not go as far as to reject the conference proposal outright.

The preparations for the conference, which involved London, the Palestinians, and the main Arab capitals, elicited a trail of complex correspondence and moves in which two major, but also contradictory, forces became apparent. First, it was becoming clear that the Palestinian question was turning into a key Arab issue embraced by the Arab governments (with British consent). Second, it was apparent that the limited interests of the now entrenched Arab states were being consciously played out against the deepening Arab desire for unity. Ibn Sa'ud, for example, was greatly preoccupied with maintaining his special position with Britain, and not less by the role of his Hashemite rivals in Transjordan and Iraq. In the intimate atmosphere of his talks with Bullard, he would hint that if Britain "adopted a new policy requiring assistance and called in someone else [i.e. Abdullah] rather than their loyal friend and supporter Ibn Sa'ud, he would be aggrieved". His aim was not only to confine Abdullah within the boundaries of his arid and poor emirate, but also to remind the British that if a king was needed for Palestine, he was always prepared to offer one of his sons.[285] To illustrate his unwavering friendship to the British, Ibn-Sa'ud telegraphed Cairo and Baghdad pressing for a quick and unconditional response when the Egyptian and Iraqi replies seemed to be delayed.[286]

The Iraqi approach, reflecting the intensified public pressure on al-Madfa'i's last days in office, was rather more concrete. Ten days after Tawfiq al-Swaydi had conveyed his initial impressions to the British counsellor, the Iraqi government presented a comprehensive *aide-mémoire* to the British embassy.[287] The memorandum indicated that if the method of the conference was to offer real hope of success, the following measures should be taken before formal discussions were opened in London: there should be a truce in Palestine; Jewish immigration certificates should be suspended; effective representation of recognized Arab and Palestinian leaders must be assured; and invitations should be extended to Lebanon and Syria. Iraq also said that a careful preliminary study must be conducted and agreement in principle must be reached about the proportions of the Arab and Jewish populations of Palestine. While it was not explicitly stated, the Iraqi participation was conditional on the British response to these demands. However, London was determined not to accommodate preconditions from any of the invitees, nor was it willing to reveal the delicate aspects of its evolving concept of the solution. Halifax, therefore, instructed his ambassador in Baghdad to inform the Iraqis to that effect and to press them instead for a prompt acceptance of participation in the conference.[288] The Iraqi government communicated its formal assent on 28 November, but never relented in its effort to obtain some further concessions from London.[289] Nuri al-Sa'id, who, with army support, had replaced al-Madfa'i, moved once again to test the British nerve. In a meeting with Peterson on 27 December, Nuri expressed the view that the JNH would be fulfilled "if in addition to 400,000 Jews resident in Palestine, other Jews were free to visit Palestine even for a prolonged period, but without acquiring Palestinian nationality".[290] He further argued, to British chagrin, that the Palestinian delegation should be allowed to visit Lebanon to meet with the mufti before travelling to London.

While Britain was not prepared to budge from its stance on the major issues, Iraqi as well as other Arab pressure succeeded in securing to the HAC the right of naming its own delegates. The process of forming the Palestinian delegation became central to the diplomatic manœuvering immediately after the mufti's exclusion was announced. Other HAC members were not excluded by the British. However, London made it clear to the Arab governments that it regarded the HAC as only a faction amongst others, and that it would only accept a Palestinian delegation representing the Palestinian people and not the HAC. It also indicated that it favoured an effective moderate presence within the delegation.[291] The HAC, supported by the rebel leaders, was bent upon excluding the opposition, insisting on its own authority to represent the Palestinians. The mufti made a skilful move by informing Ibn Sa'ud and Muhammad Mahmud that he would agree with whatever list of delegates they proposed.[292] Negotiations on this issue between Saudi Arabia, Egypt, and the British government were uncoordinated until Halifax had to instruct Bullard that Ibn Sa'ud should first consult with the Egyptian government.[293] Lack of Arab coordination notwithstanding, the negotiations over the Palestinian delegation brought up the names of Husayn al-Khalidi, Ya'qub al-Ghusayn and Ahmad Hilmi as possible delegates. Since they were still exiled in the Seychelles, the Arabs demanded that all exiles there must be freed. The British complied with the request.[294] Further Arab interventions with London and Paris secured their entry to Lebanon, where the HAC held a meeting of all its members on 13 January 1939, the first such meeting since the autumn of 1937.

Mackereth's report of 19 January 1939 has been for long the main source available on the deliberations and trends of opinion expressed in the HAC meeting. According to Mackereth, the discussions were "stormy" and revealed a deep divide amongst the Palestinian leaders.[295] The moderates included the Seychelles group, in addition to 'Awni Abd al-Hadi, while the hard-liners were 'Izzat Darwaza, Jamal al-Husayni and Alfred Rock. Musa al-'Alami and 'Izzat Tannus were identified as "on the fence" moderates. The lines of division were defined by two key issues: the fate of the revolt, and the London conference. The moderates condemned the degeneration of the revolt into terrorism and banditry, called for its end, and favoured unconditional participation in the proposed conference. In contrast, the hard-liners argued for non-participation, but "when forced to cede on this point, sought to obtain such preconditions as would make the outcome of the conference hopeless from the start". At the core of their agenda was the continuation of the revolt. On close examination, Mackereth's report seems to raise a few questions. If the hard-liners, who were the dominant group before the arrival of the Seychelles' exiles, had opposed joining the conference, the mufti would not have been involved in extensive negotiations with Arab governments over the formation of the Palestinian delegation. Another problem was the reportedly large number of people attending the HAC meeting, when in fact 'Izzat Tannus, Musa al-'Alami and Rashid al-Hajj Ibrahim were not even members of the HAC.

'Izzat Darwaza, the keen chronicler of the Palestinian interwar history and a prominent member of the HAC at the time, painted a different picture of the meeting. He wrote of the triumphant spirit that pervaded the deliberations and mentioned nothing about a rift over the revolt or the participation in the London conference.[296] Despite the fact that the mufti had doubts about naming 'Awni Abd al-Hadi to the delegation because of his widely known inconsistency and penchant for risky compromises, this issue never surfaced during the meeting. The mufti finally agreed to include Abd al-Hadi, especially after Amin al-Tamimi, the radical member of the SMC, was added to the delegation. The HAC members were not only united in their support of the revolt, but also in their resolve to adhere to the HAC as the sole representative of the Palestinians. Abd al-Hadi unreservedly censured the opposition, while Ya'qub al-Ghusayn and Ahmad Hilmi of the Seychelles' group emerged as the most radical in their advocacy of restricting the representation in the conference to members of the HAC. The meeting concluded with agreement on formation of the Palestinian delegation from within and outside the HAC; the delegates included Jamal al-Husayni, head of the delegation, Fu'ad Saba, its secretary, together with 'Awni Abd al-Hadi, Amin al-Tamimi, Musa al-'Alami, Husayn al-Khalidi, George Antonius, Alfred Rock and Y'aqub al-Ghusayn as members.[297] Ahmad Hilmi on account of illness, and Darwaza on account of his involvement with the revolt's affairs, stayed behind. Abd al-Latif Salah did not join the delegation, protesting that he was not directly invited by the British government.[298] However, this list of delegates did not include any of the Nashashibi opposition whose representation was emphatically demanded by the British. This issue was dealt with by all Arab representatives in the Cairo meeting that was held prior to the London conference.

Against a background of lack of coordination between the Arab governments, and despite the intrigues of 'Ali Mahir which resulted in him being precluded from heading the Egyptian delegation to London, Muhammad Mahmud demonstrated some powerful qualities of leadership. Reflecting on Egypt's quest to assert its Arab position, he expressed regrets that the conference was to be held in London rather than in Cairo.[299] At the same time, the Egyptian prime minister moved to establish a united Arab front at the conference. Steering official Egypt to a leading Arab role for the first time, Mahmud proposed that all Arab delegates should meet in Cairo to establish a unified Arab position before departing for London.[300] The meeting, the first of its kind, was consequently held between 17 and 21 January 1939, under the chairmanship of Mahmud.[301] In the face of continued British pressure to include the Nashashibi opposition in the Palestinian delegation, Nuri al-Sa'id, Fu'ad Hamza, Jamal al-Husayni and Amin 'Uthman flew to Lebanon to resolve the issue in consultation with the mufti. Under such Arab pressure, the mufti agreed that the opposition should be represented by Nimr al-Nabulsi and Ya'qub Farraj.[302] Raghib al-Nashashibi, who was still in Cairo, rejected the mufti's offer and demanded equal representation with the HAC. The situation was further complicated when al-Nabulsi announced that he would travel to London only on behalf of the HAC and not the opposition, while Farraj declined the invitation, ostensibly on grounds of ill health.[303] Despite the fact that the entire HAC leadership was now out of the country, the decline of the revolt and the success of Fakhri al-Nashashibi in recruiting a sizeable following, the political influence of the HAC in Palestine was still overwhelming. Except for a handful of hard-core elements who dared challenge the political will of the HAC, the opposition was effectively in disarray. In the end, the question of the opposition's representation was resolved only two days after the London conference was officially inaugurated, where the colonial secretary persuaded the Arabs and Palestinians to include Raghib al-Nashashibi and Ya'qub Farraj in the Palestinian delegation. The humiliation that al-Nashashibi and Farraj had suffered deeply affected them, and their contribution to the conference was thus negligible.

A more decisive outcome of the Arab deliberations in Cairo was the agreement on the strategy to be followed during the conference. Amongst those present in Cairo were powerful and high-profile leaders like Nuri al-Sa'id, 'Ali Mahir, Amir Faysal and Fu'ad Hamza, whose perceptions of a solution for the Palestinian question were not always compatible. It was perhaps because of strong popular pressure, or because of the rampant sense of optimism that the British were finally recognizing the gravity of their Palestine policy, that the Arabs agreed that the Palestinians would have the final say in the conference.[304] The Cairo meeting resolved that no proposal or suggestion would be approved or rejected by the Arab governments unless the Palestinian delegation gave its assent. This decision amounted to a total undermining of MacDonald's calculations that the Arab participation would have a moderating effect on the Palestinian side.

The London Conference was opened by Neville Chamberlain on 7 February 1939, and continued until 17 March. During its long and arduous proceedings, the Arabs declined to confer with the Zionist delegation directly, although direct encounters were held outside the formal sessions. The British, therefore, played the main role in formulating the issues of negotiation and the proposals for their solutions.[305] During the thirtieth session of 15 March, MacDonald presented the conference with a package of suggestions that he described as final in substance but not necessarily in form. Throughout the conference, the Arab delegates showed more flexibility than either the Palestinians or the Zionists. In the end, however, the Arabs deferred to the Palestinian viewpoint. On 17 March, amid angry Arab and Zionist reactions and recriminations, the conference ended without an agreement. Further attempts by Mahmud to bring the Palestinian and British positions closer failed conclusively.[306] Consequently, the British government decided unilaterally to propose a solution, which was then released on 17 May in the form of a statement of policy or White Paper.[307]

The White Paper stated that the British government now declared "unequivocally" that it was not part of their policy that Palestine should become a Zionist state". Jewish immigration to Palestine was limited to a total of 75,000 people during the ensuing five years, beginning in April 1939. No further immigration was permitted unless the Palestinian Arabs agreed to it. What emerged as the most contentious provisions of the White Paper for the Palestinians were the White Paper articles denoting the constitutional arrangement. It was indicated that the objective of the British government was to establish within ten years an independent Palestinian state, tied to Britain by a treaty which would guarantee British interests in the area. During these ten years, Palestine would continue to be ruled by the mandate authority, where the Palestinians (Arabs and Jews proportionately) would be gradually placed in charge of departments, advised by British officials. After five years, the drafting of a constitution would be considered by the British government. However, independence was not guaranteed even after the transitional ten-year period, but was rather conditional on the improvement of Arab–Jewish relations to a degree such as "would make good government possible". If the relations between the two sides did not improve, the postponement of independence would therefore be considered through consultation with representatives of the people of Palestine (both Arabs and Jews), the Council of the League of Nations, and the neighbouring Arab states.

The policy outlined in the White Paper was immediately rejected by both principal parties, the HAC and the Jewish Agency. While criticism was directed at various aspects of the proposed solution, at the core of the ensuing disagreement were the implications of the constitutional arrangements. As Harold Beeley insightfully observed,[308] "Whereas the mandate acknowledged the status of the Jewish nation as a whole in relation to Palestine and had accorded no recognition to the Arabs as a people, the White Paper exactly reversed those positions." From the Arab perspective, none the less, the White Paper appeared to put a premium on Jewish non-cooperation, enabling the Jewish community at the end of ten years of each subsequent probation, "to create a situation in which the mandatory [power] would decline to relinquish its control". In Arab eyes, Beeley maintained, the wording of the White Paper was a mere camouflage for a Jewish veto on the establishment of an independent Palestinian state. Considering Zionist influence in the British parliament and public life, and its visible bearing on American decision-making, at a time when the British began to look towards Washington for support in the event of European war, the White Paper appeared as the most equitable deal offered to the Arabs by Britain. However, given the British attitude during the following months, one is inclined to conclude that the White Paper was never really meant to be fully implemented. In words that were tinged with irony, Lord Samuel described the White Paper as the policy of granting "each side . . . a veto on the aspirations of the other in order to induce both to become friends".[309] In Palestine, however, there was much at stake in terms of history, nationalism and religion, to be reconciled with the contradictions of the White Paper.

During the deliberations of the Cabinet Special Committee on Palestine before the convening of the London Conference, it was made clear that the independence of Palestine was a highly remote possibility. The new policy presented in the White Paper, and the allowances that Britain ostensibly furnished to the Arab countries, were essentially meant to safeguard vital British interests in the Middle East. The colonial secretary, who knew that the mufti would be a major obstacle in the way of such a half-baked solution, issued what seemed to be an uncalled-for order excluding him indefinitely from Palestine.[310] By communicating this order only one day before the publication of the White Paper, Britain guaranteed that the mufti would either reject the proposed solution, or vacate the Palestinian political arena once and for all.

Eventually, the White Paper did prove to be disastrous for the Palestinian national movement. In the wake of the HAC's rejection of the White Paper, both 'Awni Abd al-Hadi and Ya'qub al-Ghusayn dissented and initiated contacts with the British, offering cooperation in exchange for minor clarifications of policy, which the British would never provide.[311] Even Jamal al-Husayni (together with Musa al-'Alami) sounded unsure of the HAC's decision which he himself had signed.[312] 'Izzat Darwaza believed that the decision reflected the judgment of the Palestinian people, but other evidence indicated that the Palestinian feelings were more of puzzlement and bewilderment.[313] Attempts to revive the revolt were to no avail and Darwaza, the coordinator of such efforts, was later arrested by the French mandate authority in Syria.

On the release of the White Paper, Egypt, Iraq and Saudi Arabia declared their disagreement with its constitutional provisions and recommended that the Palestinians should not accept it.[314] This position, of course, emboldened the HAC's resolve. The most vociferous reaction came from none other than Nuri al-Sa'id, the pro-British and pragmatic Iraqi prime minister. Nuri's radical attitude reflected perhaps the attitude of the pan-Arabist circles inside as well as outside the Iraqi army, whose support he was then enjoying. But he also might have thought that the British position could still be changed since the gulf between it and the Arab stance was not, in terms of practical diplomacy, unbridgeable. In his search for an exit, 'Awni Abd al-Hadi told a British official in Egypt, "it was impossible for him or any other leader to return to Palestine and cooperate with the Government so long as the declaration of the Arab states against the White Paper remains unmodified." 'Awni believed that the Arab governments of Egypt, Iraq and Saudi Arabia were prepared to shift their stance to support the White Paper and direct the Palestinian people to do so if they were given "some plausible pretext" in the form of a statement from MacDonald interpreting the questionable aspects of the document. Ibn Sa'ud appeared disposed to make such an appeal to the Palestinians and even Nuri, "the nigger in the woodpile", could be brought into line.[315] The problem, of course, was that Britain had no intention of issuing any such interpretation of the White Paper.

Muhammad Mahmud soon fell ill and had to cede his position to 'Ali Mahir, who, although prepared to support the White Paper, made no effort at that early stage of his premiership to intervene against the mufti. As soon as the pressure of the revolt subsided, the Saudis equally held back. In July and again in August, Nuri met the mufti in Lebanon where at one point other members of the HAC joined in. According to Nuri, whose unscrupulous manner of reporting will always pose a dilemma for a student of history, the mufti showed greater flexibility. He demanded that the British relax the punitive measures in Palestine and release the Palestinian prisoners. There was no question of his return to Palestine and, considering that peace was being restored, the mufti asked for clarification of the ambiguities in the White Paper, including the question of transfer of power to the Palestinians at the departmental level. The other point that seemed to indicate a change of attitude was the mufti's preparedness to come out in support of the British war effort if his demands were met with a reconciliatory response by Britain.[316] Nuri reported this to the British ambassador, Basil Newton, but did not mention it in his conversation with Taha al-Hashimi, his ally and defence minister.

Britain, however, persisted in showing no interest in going beyond the terms of the White Paper, neither in form nor in substance. Even the White Paper was soon to be discarded. Towards the autumn of 1939, the mufti began to suspect an Anglo-French collusion against him. The outbreak of World War II consolidated Anglo-French relations far beyond minor issues such as the freedom or safety of the mufti. It was as early as the spring of 1939 that the mufti seems to have tried to leave Lebanon for Egypt, Iraq or Saudi Arabia, but was blocked by the British.[317] On 13 October, exactly two years after his escape from Palestine, he slipped out in the darkness of the night from his home in Dhuq Makayyil, to be driven through Damascus and the Syrian–Iraqi desert to Baghdad.[318] Mahmud Salman, a former comrade of his in the Ottoman army and now a senior Iraqi officer and associate of Salah al-Din al-Sabbagh, was perhaps the one who encouraged the mufti to embark upon such a dramatic passage to Iraq.[319] The revolt was over.

NOTES

1 *Filastin*, 8 November 1936; Peel Commission Report, 1937:102–3.
2 Darwaza, 1949–51: vol. 3, 150–3; al-Hout (ed.), 1984:461–2; Faraj, 1987:212–14. For the British praise of the Saudi position see Rendel's minute, 9 December 1936, FO 371/20029/E 7669.
3 Darwaza, ibid., 153–4. A more vivid description of Darwaza's and Abd al-Hadi's reflections on their mission to Iraq and Saudi Arabia is included in Zu'aytir, 1980:255–6. The HAC's compliance was published in *Filastin*, 7 January 1937.
4 Peel Commission Report, 1937, pp. 381–2. Cabinet Minutes, 30 June and 5 July 1937, Cab 27/37 and 28/37 respectively.
5 High Commissioner to Secretary of State for Colonies, 5 August 1937, CO 733/351/75718/6.
6 *Filastin*, 6 July 1936; Darwaza, 1949–51: vol. 3, 156–7; Zu'aytir, 1980:293–4. More details on the period between 30 June and 7 July 1937 are in al-Ghuri; 1973: vol. 2, 133–6.
7 Secretary of State for Colonies to High Commissioner, 14 July 1937, CO 733/326/75023/4, and the latter to Parkinson, 19 July 1937, CO 733/322/75156/1.
8 High Commissioner to Secretary of State for Colonies, 19 July 1937, CO 733/352/75718/9; Darwaza, 1949–51: vol. 3, 181; al-Ghuri, 1973: vol. 2, 140–1; Zu'aytir, 1980:305–6.
9 Raghib al-Nashashibi and Ya'qub Farraj seem to have intimated to the High Commissioner their preparedness to accept the partition plan (High Commissioner to Parkinson, 14 July 1937, CO 733/332/75156/1, and a copy in FO 371/20811/54566). However, as the universal rejection of the partition became evident, the Nashashibi party issued a statement denouncing the plan and Raghib gave a press interview to that effect (*Filastin*, 27 July 1937).
10 O.A.G. to Secretary of State for Colonies, 5 October 1937, CO 733/332/75156/I; Yasin, 1959:64
11 Undated report on the Qassamis (most likely of late 1937), Tegart Papers, Box I, file 3/C. Financial aid to al-Sa'di was provided by Rasim al-Khalidi, a high-ranking Palestinian employee of the mandate government. See statement of Diab ibn Abdul Hamid Fahoum of Nazareth, 19 January 1938, CID Headquarters, Tegart Papers, ibid.
12 Headquarters, the Palestine Police Force, Jerusalem, to D.I.G. (CID) 29 September 1937, Tegart Papers, Box I, file 3/C.
13 Statement of Mohamed Niji Abu Rub, 30 November 1937, and report entitled "Terrorism, 1936–1937", pp. 14–15, Tegart Papers, ibid.
14 O.A.G. to the Secretary of State for Colonies, 5 October 1937, CO 733/333/75156/23; Darwaza, 1949–51: vol. 3, 187–8.
15 Note of Conference at the Colonial Office, 28 September 1937, CO 733/332/75156/I; O.A.G. to Secretary of State for Colonies, 1 October 1937 and Chief Secretary of the Government, Jerusalem, to Secretary of State for Colonies, 5 October 1937, CO 733/332/75156.
16 Shuckburgh to Battershill (O.A.G.), 4 October 1937, CO 733/332/75156/I.
17 O.A.G. to Secretary of State for Colonies, 13 October 1937, CO 733/332/75023; Darwaza, 1993: vol. 3, 47 (entry of 10 October 1937), and 70–1.
18 Al-Ghuri, 1937: vol. 2, 154–8; Mardini, 1986:101–4.

19 *Filastin* (Bulletin), Beirut, no. 74, May 1967, pp. 9–11; Jbara, 1985:164–5.
20 "Terrorism, 1936–1937", Tegart Papers, Box I, file 3/C, p. 18.
21 Ibid., pp. 18–20; Statement of Mohamed ibn Mustafa el-Masakhar, CID Headquarters, Jerusalem, 22 January 1938, ibid., Box I, file 3/C.
22 "Terrorism, 1936–1937", ibid., p. 21; Statement of Atiyeh Awad of Hammam el- Ain, 21 January 1938, CID Headquarters, ibid., Box I, File 3/C.
23 *Filastin*, 23 November 1937.
24 Rida al-'Abbushi was in reality collaborating with the British against al-Sa'di's band ("Terrorism", Tegart Papers, *op. cit.*, p. 11).
25 Ibid., p. 12. A few days after al-Sa'di's arrest, the Istiqlalists, Fahmi and Shawqi al-'Abbushi, arrived in Damascus to meet 'Izzat Darwaza, who was then directing the Jihad Committee. Both of them denied their family's involvement in the incident (Darwaza, 1993: vol. 3, 127). Porath (1977: vol. 2, 257) mistakenly indicted the Irshayd family rather than the 'Abbushis.
26 *Filastin*, 25 and 28 November 1937; Zu'aytir, 1980:340–1. Like the three martyrs of 1930, Farhan al-Sa'di was immortalized in Palestinian mythology by the verses of the Palestinian poet, Abu Salma.
27 This particular episode was revealed in Darwaza's memoirs which were published posthumously (Darwaza, 1993: vol. 3, 88–9.) Though Darwaza was a prolific chronicler of Palestinian history, this volume of his papers contains a great deal of previously unknown or misunderstood details on the second phase of the Palestinian revolt.
28 "Note on Recent Terrorist Activity in the Samaria Division", 24 December 1937, Tegart Papers, Box II, file 3, p. 2; Statement of Haj Said Abdulla of Zera'in, 20 January 1938, Tegart Papers, Box I, file 3/C.
29 "Note on Recent Terrorist Activity", ibid., p. 3.
30 "Terrorism" *op. cit.*, p. 4.
31 'Auda, 1984:71.
32 Al-Nimr, 1975:325 and 359–61; Scholch, 1988:264–6.
33 'Auda, 1984:72–5.
34 *Filastin* (Bulletin), no. 44, October 1964; Hamuda, 1985:107.
35 Darwaza, 1949–51: vol. 3, 212.
36 Report, Gangs, Northern Sector (undated; most likely summer 1938), Tegart Papers, Box II, file 3.
37 "Terrorism, 1936–37", Tegart Papers, Box I, file 316, p. 4.
38 Darwaza, 1949–51, vol. 3, 212; "Note on Recent Terrorist Activity in the Samaria Division", 24 December 1937, Tegart Papers, Box II, file 3, p. 5.
39 *Filastin* (Bulletin), nos. 65 and 66, July and August 1966; District Commissioner, Galilee and Acre District to Inspector General of Police, 28 February 1938, Tegart Papers, Box II, file 3.
40 Arab Rebel Documents, by Kenneth Waring (possibly autumn of 1938), Tegart Papers, Box II, file 4; al-Ghuri, 1973: vol. 2, 162–3.
41 Yasin, 1959:165–6. Al-Julani emerged as leader of the Hebron area after the army killed on 9 May 1938 'Isa al-Batat, who led an early rebel band in the area. See "Terrorism, 1936–37", Tegart Papers, *op. cit.*, p. 4.
42 Darwaza, 1949–51: vol. 3, 212; al-Ghuri, 1973: vol. 2, 53 and 84.
43 Darwaza, 1993: vol. 3, 112–13. In an earlier version, Darwaza indicated that Munif al-Husayni (in Lebanon) and Mu'in al-Madi in Damascus were also

members of the CCJ (Darwaza, 1949–51: vol. 3, 209). The British District Police Headquarters (Nablus) report of 22 December 1937 was not particularly accurate in naming members of the CCJ since it indicated people such as Fakhri Abd al-Hadi and Jamal al-Husayni, both of whom never joined the CCJ at any stage of its work (the report is in Tegart Papers, Box II, file 3).

44 Zu'aytir, 1980:346. Al-Madi moved to Alexandretta where he lived with his wife until he joined the mufti in Baghdad in late 1939.

45 Darwaza, 1993: vol. 3: 121.

46 Col. Mackereth (Damascus) to Sir Charles A. Tegart (Chief of Palestine Police, Jerusalem), 27 October 1938, Tegart Papers, Box III, file 5; Halifax to Phipps, 28 June 1938, FO 406/76/E 3577.

47 Ibid.; Nabih al-'Azma to the committees of Arab Immigrants, 20 February 1939, Al-'Azma Papers, Arab Files, Appendix A. On London's effort to pursue fund sources in South America, see: Mr Baggallay's Minute, 30 September 1939, FO 371/23195/E 6735; Mackereth to FO, 2 November 1939, FO 371/23195/E 7381; Mackereth to FO, 8 December 1939, FO 371/23915/E 7381. On the Indian Muslims' support see Extract from Report of the Director, Intelligence Bureau, Home Department, Government of India, 6 August 1938, CO 733/369/5; India Office to CO, 25 August 1938, CO 733/369/5 (a copy of P & L S 741/38).

48 Bullard to Halifax, 10 June 1938, FO 406/76/E 1237; Darwaza, 1993: vol. 3, 121.

49 Ibid., 123.

50 See n. 46.

51 Zu'aytir, 1980:332 and 335.

52 News of 'Adil al-'Azma's appointment was received with horror by the British officials in Palestine (Tegart's report on a visit to Syria and Lebanon, 12 February 1938, Tegart Papers, Box III, file 5).

53 Mackereth to Eden, 18 October 1937, FO 684/10/2207; Mackereth to Tegart, 27 October 1938, Tegart Papers, Box III, file 5; Tegart's report on a visit to Syria, 12 February 1938, Tegart Papers, Box III, file 5; Darwaza, 1993: vol. 3, 118–19.

54 Tegart's report, ibid.; Terrorism, General, April 1938, Tegart Papers, Box I, file 3/C; Report by the Secret Agent R, 3 February 1938, and Letter from Mackereth, 11 April 1938, Tegart Papers, Box III, file 5; Zu'aytir, 1980:363; Wilson, 1987:125.

55 Darwaza, 1993: vol. 3, 119–20.

56 The mufti's statement was given in defence of the Ikhwan during their mass trial of 1950 (Abd al-Halim, 1981:230). See also Mitchell, 1969:55.

57 The early units of A. R. al-Hajj Muhammad consisted mainly of Syrian rebels ("Note on Recent Terrorist Activity in the Samaria Division", 24 December 1937, Tegart Papers, Box II, file 3). Estimates of the number of Jordanians who joined the revolt varied from 50 to 250 (Yasin, 1959:219 and Wilson, 1987:125). Although the contribution of the Syrian Druze was markedly less than it had been during the 1936 strike (Porath, 1977: vol. 2, 271–3), their Lebanese counterparts, especially followers of Hamad Sa'b, were still noticeably active in supporting the revolt (al-Nahar, 24 March, 2 December 1937 and 16, 17 and 23 August 1938).

58 Darwaza, 1993: vol. 3, 120–1.

59 *Report by His Majesty's Government in the United Kingdom of Great Britain and Northern Ireland to the Council of the League of Nations on the Administration of*

Palestine and Trans-Jordan for the Year 1938, Colonial No. 166, London, 1939, pp. 309–403. A number of reports from the Jordanian rebels on their operations were published in al-Hout (ed.), 1984:645–6.

60 Glubb, 1948:235–8; Khilla, 1983:304–5.

61 "Terrorist Crimes", 1 October 1937 to 30 April 1938, Tegart Papers, Box II, file 3.

62 District Commissioner, Galilee District, to Tegart, 28 February 1938, Tegart Papers, Box II, file 3.

63 Lesch, 1973:38; Porath, 1977: vol. 2, 237–8. A fascinating and vivid eye-witness account of the period was recorded by the teacher of English at Bir Zait school, H. M. Wilson, in her "School Year in Palestine, 1938–1939", St Antony's College Middle East Centre, University of Oxford.

64 High Commissioner to Secretary of State for Colonies, 2 September 1938, Tegart Papers, Box I, file 5.

65 On A. R. al-Hajj Muhammad see n. 31. On other commanders, see List of Principal Arab Gang Leaders, Tegart Papers, Box I, file 3/B.

66 'Arif Abd al-Raziq, who would not recognize the leadership of A. R. al-Hajj Muhammad, signed his declarations with *al-Mutawakil 'ala Allah* (the one whose reliance is on God), regarding his command as the "General Command of the Revolution Army in Southern Syria". 'Arif Abd al-Raziq, in turn, issued his declarations in the name of the "Higher Command of the Palestine Revolution's Army", and signed as the "Servant of his Religion and Country". Throughout the upheaval, the rebels' declarations would repeatedly invoke the early Islamic conquests and Salah al-Din al-Ayyiubi's victory in the Crusades. For many examples, see al-Hout (ed.), 1984:479–519.

67 Darwaza, 1949–51: vol. 3, 211–12.

68 Ibid., 213. Porath (1977: vol. 2, 245) confirms that A. Q. al-Husayni and the Jerusalem area did not join the General Command. It is clear from various rebel declarations, from August 1938 onwards, that the agreed name for the united command was Diwan al-Thawra al-'Arabiyya fi Filastin (The Headquarters of the Arab Revolt in Palestine). See al-Hout (ed.), 1984:514ff.

69 Darwaza, 1949–51: vol. 3, 211; Zu'aytir, 1980:443–4. Most revealing of al-Qawuqji's secret planning at the time is his letter to Nabih al-'Azma, 25 August 1938, al-'Azma Papers, Arab Files, 8/459.

70 Only 4,000 Palestine pounds would be distributed monthly to the different rebel commands from Damascus. Additional 1,000 Palestine pounds were sent monthly from the mufti in Lebanon. See Darwaza, 1993: vol. 3, 123. It is, however, pertinent that Darwaza's figures covered the period between November 1937 to May 1938. In September 1938, Darwaza would express to 'Awni Abd al-Hadi in Cairo the dire need of the revolt for financial support (al-Hout, 1986:381).

71 Yasin, 1959:42; Porath, 1977: vol. 2, 247–8.

72 On such incidents see: al-Nimr, 1975: vol. 4, 20–1; Darwaza, 1993, vol. 3, 752–4 and 785–6. See also Miss H. M. Wilson, "School Year in Palestine, 1938–1939", St Antony's College Middle East Centre, University of Oxford, pp. 16 and 21. On the rebel commanders' attempt to curb this phenomenon see the proclamation of 12 December 1938 in al-Hout (ed.), 1984:523.

73 Harold Macmichael (High Commissioner) to Malcolm MacDonald (Secretary of State for Colonies), 16 January 1939, FO 371/23243/472 (a copy); al-Nimr, 1975: vol. 4, 21.

74 A few members of the powerful 'Abbushi family of Jenin would turn into informers for the police, following the killing of Rida 'Abbushi ("Terrorism, 1936–1937", Tegart Papers, Box I, file 3/C, pp. 11–12). Following the assassination of Mustafa Abu Shaqra, the notable from 'Asira village of Nablus, his relative Muhammad Abd al-Hadi Abu Shaqra led the army to the rebels' meeting at Dir Ghassana, where the prominent Qassami leader, Muhammad al-Salih, would be killed in September 1938 (al-Nimr, 1975: vol. 4, 19.)

75 The most tragic incident of this kind was the assassination of Hasan Sidqi al-Dajani, a confused pro-Nashashibi figure, who had earlier contributed to the spread of the 1936 strike, while his wife was participating in the Arab Women's Conference in Cairo (entry of 13 October 1938, Zu'aytir, 1980:472–3). In December 1938, both Shaykh Sa'id al-Khatib and Shaykh Abd al-Rahman al-Bitawi were assassinated, apparently by rebels (High Commissioner to Secretary of State for Colonies, 16 January 1939, FO 371/23243/SF/472/38; Darwaza, 1993: vol. 3, 793) merely for being suspected of anti-revolt activities. See also the report of Kenneth Waring of *The Times*, 18 January 1939; Report by GOC, 26 December 1938, Tegart Papers, Box II, file 4.

76 Porath, 1977: vol. 2, 258; Zu'aytir, 1980:441 (entry of 31 August 1938); Darwaza, 1993: vol. 3, 115.

77 The advisors' mark on the revolt's language can be discerned from studying the rebel proclamations before and after the arrival of the advisors in the summer of 1938. On the revolt's court see Porath, 1977: vol. 2, 248.

78 One startling example of this dilemma was recorded by Miss H. M. Wilson in her "School Year in Palestine, 1938–1939", ibid., pp. 11 and 27–8. In this case the rebel judge was caught between the right of a poor villager and the wrong of his opponent, a member of the prominent Nasir family of Bir Zait.

79 High Commissioner to Secretary of State for Colonies, 5 September 1938, CO 733/368/75156/23/I; Darwaza: 1949–51: vol. 3, 200–7.

80 The official figure for total executions during 1937–9 was given at 110, and for the number of detained suspects at 12,622 Palestinians (R. I. Campbell, Cairo, to FO, 5 July 1947, FO 141/1116/E 5918). Darwaza (1949–51: vol. 3, 201) put the total number of executions at 146.

81 Instructions by His Excellency the High Commissioner, 18 May 1938, Tegart Papers, Box II, file 3.

82 Porath, 1977: vol. 2, 251.

83 CID to Inspector General, Interview with Suleiman Bey Toukan, 29 April 1938, Tegart Papers, Box I, file 3/C; al-Nimr, 1975: vol. 4, 14; Nashashibi, 1990:104.

84 High Commissioner to Secretary of State for Colonies, 16 January 1939, FO 371/23243/SF/472/38, provides an exclusive coverage of Fakhri's activities during the later period of 1938. Fakhri's move might have also been partially prompted by 'Arif Abd al-Raziq's proclamation of the rebels' determination to kill him (al-Hout, 1986:204).

85 On Abdullah's and the army's support see Porath, 1977: vol. 2, 252 and 256. On the support of *Filastin* and *'Alif Ba'* see Zu'aytir, 1980:502 and Darwaza: 1993: vol. 3, 786.

86 Miss H. M. Wilson, "School Year in Palestine", ibid., 63–4 and 71ff.

87 Writing of Fakhri's denunciation of the mufti, Raghib stated (*The Times*, 19 November 1938) that it "absolutely disagrees with my personal opinion or the

opinion and principles of the National Defence Party, of which I have the honour to be president". On the secret contacts between the two Nashashibis, which culminated in the appointment of Fakhri as secretary of the National Defence Party on 24 January 1939, see al-Hout, 1986:388.

88 Al-Nimr, 1975: vol. 4, 20–1.

89 Darwaza:1993: vol. 3, 223 (entry of 6 February 1938).

90 Porath, 1977: vol. 2, 252–3.

91 'Awni Abd al-Hadi to Nabih al-'Azma, 5 October 1938, al-'Azma Papers, Arab Files, 9/572; Zu'aytir, 1980:516–17; Darwaza:1993: vol. 3, 754–5.

92 Darwaza, ibid., 95, 110 and 196.

93 Nwayhid, 1993:256–8ff.

94 *Filastin*, 20 December 1943.

95 'Arif al-'Arif, in his "Gaza Diaries, 1939–1940", painted a vivid picture of the pathetic political scene during 1938 and early 1940, as Fakhri al-Nashashibi was the only active figure in the country (St Antony's College Middle East Centre, University of Oxford).

96 On 2 September 1938, the High Commissioner wrote to the Secretary of State for Colonies, "When one has excepted the Mufti and his staff, there are no Arab representative leaders, except rebel leaders in the hills. The very name of moderate has become a term of abuse . . .", Telegram no. 517, Tegart Papers, Box I, file 5. On 27 February 1939, the High Commissioner wrote again to his Secretary of State of the collapse of the Nashashibi-dominated Palestine Defence Party (FO 371/23243/SF/80/39).

97 *Report by His Majesty's Government to the League of Nations for the Year 1938*, p. 22.

98 *Al-Sirat al-Mustaqim*, 31 May and 30 July 1938; *al-Ahram*, 20, 25, and 26 June 1939. On the growing formations of Jewish paramilitary troops see Periodical Assessment Summary (P.A.S.) of 26 July and 28 September 1936, Nos. 13/36 and 16/36 respectively, FO 371/20018/E 5142 and E 6608 respectively.

99 *Report by His Majesty's Government to the League of Nations for the Year 1938*, p. 301–2.

100 *Filastin*, 26 July 1939; Yasin, 1959:164.

101 Kedourie, 1982:108.

102 See, for example, Mackereth's reports on Syrian personalities, 6 May 1937, FO 371/20849/2142, and FO 406/76/E1405.

103 For excellent details see Khoury, 1987:494–514 and 555–6.

104 Mackereth to Eden, 5 May 1937, FO 371/20850/25759.

105 Mackereth to Sir Charles Tegart, 27 October 1938, no. 2159/2207/2, Tegart Papers, Box III, file 5.

106 Mackereth to Eden, 18 October 1937, FO 684/10/2207.

107 Mackereth to Sir Charles Tegart (n. 105 above).

108 Mackereth's early views of the French attitude are in his dispatch to Eden, 18 October 1937 (n. 106 above).

109 Sir Charles Tegart's report on his visit to Damascus and Beirut, 12 February 1938, Tegart Papers, Box III, file 5.

110 Zu'aytir, 1980:346.

111 See n. 106.

112 Copy of extract of letter dated 11 April 1938 from Col. G. Mackereth, British Consul, Damascus, Tegart Papers, Box III, file 5. See also an earlier telegram from Mackereth to Tegart, 14 February 1938, in ibid.

113 *Al-Nahar*, 16, 17 and 23 August 1938. The anti-revolt policy was strongly supported by the Lebanese pro-French president, Emile Idah (Zu'aytir, 1980:293); see also Halifax to Phipps, 5 July 1938, FO 406/76/E 3841 and Enclosure.

114 Darwaza, 1993: vol. 3, 720–1 and 820–1. Darwaza's aides, Rashad and Izz al-Din al-Shawwa, together with several Syrian, Lebanese and Jordanian activists, were arrested by the French on 5 May 1938 (ibid., 355–6). Akram Zu'aytir was also ordered out of Syria on 21 November 1938 (Zu'aytir, 1980:518–20).

115 Ibid., 833; Mackereth to Baxter, 2 January 1939, FO 684/12/2746; Mackereth to High Commissioner (Jerusalem), 10 January 1939, FO 684/12/542.

116 Mackereth to Baxter, 13 April 1939, FO 371/23276/2996; Mackereth to Halifax, 28 October 1939, FO 371/23195/E 7381; Darwaza, 1993: vol. 3, 819–20.

117 Zu'aytir, 1980:576 (entry of 29 February 1939).

118 GHQ (Palestine) to War Office, 14 April 1939, CO 733/398/4 (H. P. 739); Mackereth to FO, 14 April 1939, CO 733/398/4 (no. 24); Yasin, 1959:157–8; Zu'aytir, 1980:522 and 587–9; Darwaza, 1993: vol. 3, 268, 275, 281 and 365.

119 Out of slightly less than a million Palestinian Arabs, 1,791 were killed and 3,388 wounded from amongst the ordinary people (excluding the rebels) as a result of actions by the security forces; 2,150 rebels were killed between 1936 and 1938 (no figures were available for the year 1939 which witnessed a high number of rebel casualties, and no figures for the total number of wounded rebels were available either). See the report of Sir R. I. Campbell to the FO, 5 July 1947, FO 141/1116/5918. It is doubtful whether the number of Palestinians killed by Palestinians was ever known.

120 Darwaza, 1993; vol. 2, 372–3.

121 Shukri, 1957: vol. 2, 998–9.

122 Lampson to Eden, 8 April 1937, FO 371/20806/E 2158. Al-Sa'dawi, however, presented the project on his own behalf together with Riyad al-Sulh, Hashim al-Atasi and other Arabists without indicating the mufti's name.

123 Ibid.; Mackereth to Eden, 26 May 1937, FO 371/20807/E3054, and minutes by the Eastern Department officials.

124 Darwaza, 1993: vol. 2, 294–6. On the king's similar response to the Palestinians in December 1936, see ibid. 359. Bullard's report on the mufti's hajj mission is in his dispatch to Eden, 4 March 1937, FO 371/20839/E 1639.

125 *Al-Muqattam*, 28 June 1937.

126 The scheme presented by Muhammad Ali is in Cairo's dispatch of 11 May 1937, FO 371/20806/E 2920.

127 Khoury, 1987:553; Darwaza, 1993: vol. 2, 416–17.

128 Mackereth to Eden, 7 August 1937, FO 371/20786/E 4719.

129 Zu'aytir, 1980:294–5.

130 *Filastin*, 9 July 1938; Darwaza, 1993: vol. 2, 423.

131 *Filastin*, 1 July 1937; Clark Kerr to Eden, 12 July 1937, CO 733/352/75718/12 (a copy).

132 *Filastin*, 12 July 1937; *al-Ahram*, 15 July 1937. On 15 July, Sulayman expressed to Dr Grubba, the German envoy in Baghdad, the hope that the Germans would

do everything in their power to frustrate the partition plan (Hirszowicz, 1966:34). See also the Iraqi foreign minister's memorandum in Scott's dispatch from Baghdad, 6 August 1937, FO 371-20811/E 4579.

133 *Al-Ahram*, 22 July 1937.

134 *Al-Istiqlal*, 11 and 12 July 1937; *al-Ahram*, 16 and 24 July 1937; Clark Kerr to Eden, 17 July 1937, FO 371/20809/E 4129; Amin Rwayha to Nabih al-'Azma, 18 July 1937, al-'Azma Papers, Palestine Files, Appendix 2/84. Rendel's memorandum "Palestine: Iraqi Attitude", 13 September 1937, FO 371/20813/E5392.

135 Cabinet Minutes, 21 July 1937, CAB 31/37. See also the sharp criticism of Iraq by Ormsby-Gore, the colonial secretary, in his statement to the House of Commons, FO 371/20809/E 4150.

136 Clark Kerr's dispatch on Sulayman's threats to resign, 17 July 1937, FO 371/20809/E 2128.

137 Taggar, 1978:195–213.

138 Clark Kerr to Eden, 17 July 1937, FO 371/20809/E 4128.

139 Al-Hashimi, 1967: vol. 1, 219.

140 On al-Madfa'i, see Clark Kerr to Eden, 4 January 1938, FO 406/76/E 435.

141 Sa'id Thabit to Nabih al-'Azma, 1 June 1936, al-'Azma Papers, Arab Files, 4/201.

142 Darwaza to Nabih al-'Azma (Baghdad, n.d.), al-'Azma Papers, Palestine Files, 10/169; Darwaza, 1993: vol. 3, 38, 46, 50, 63 and 65–6.

143 C. J. Edmonds, "Political Situation in Iraq", Enclosure, Peterson to Baxter, 6 July 1938, FO 371/21846/E 4417.

144 Clark Kerr to Eden, 10 January 1938, FO 406/76/E 172; Morgan to Eden, 8 February 1938, FO 406/76/E 1010; al-Hashimi, 1967: vol. 1, 253–61; Mushtaq, 1989:285.

145 Scott to Eden, 23 September 1937, FO 371/20796/E 5730; Kelly (Cairo) to Eden, 1 October 1937, FO 371/20796/E 5840; Batatu, 1978:339.

146 Tawfiq al-Swaydi's "tact and moderation" in his approach to the Palestinian question was always appreciated by the British (Clark Kerr to Eden, 4 January 1938, FO 406/76/E 435). One of his first assignments as the foreign minister of al-Madfa'i's government was to represent Iraq in the League of Nations' annual meeting where he delivered a powerful speech on behalf of the Palestinians (*al-Ahram*, 21 September 1937). However, during an informal discussion with the British delegation, he expressed his support for a solution of the Palestinian problem based on cantonization (Minutes by Rendel, 11 September 1937, FO 371/20813/E 5392). None the less, al-Swaydi made it clear that this was a personal opinion, not necessarily shared by his government. On his return to Baghdad, when he presented his proposal to Darwaza, the latter told him that unless the percentage of the Jewish population was considered and the Jewish immigration stopped, even cantonization would not be accepted (Darwaza, 1993: vol. 3, 48–50).

147 Lampson to High Commissioner of Palestine, 12 July 1937, FO 371/20809/E4077; Lampson to High Commissioner of Palestine, 9 December 1937, FO 371/20819/E 6568; Rendel's memorandum "Palestine: Egyptian Attitude", 13 July 1937, FO 371/20809/E 4162; Sayigh, 1959:242–3.

148 *Jaridat al-Ikhwan al-Muslimin*, 16 July 1937. In October 1937, the Ikhwan led a demonstration of about 5,000 people to Abdin Palace, protesting the partition. *En route*, the demonstrators clashed with the police (ibid., 15 October 1937).

149 Petition to the British ambassador in Cairo, 21 November 1937, Enclosure in Lampson to Eden, 4 January 1938, FO 406/76/E 443.

150 See for example, *al-Risala*, 5 and 26 July, 16 August, and 11 October 1937; *al-Siyasa*, 17 and 24 July, 7 and 14 August and 16 and 23 October 1937; *al-Rabita al-'Arabiyya*, 4, 11, 19 and 24 August 1937.

151 See an extract from *al-Muqattam*, 14 October 1937, and Lampson's comments in Enclosure of Lampson to Eden, 3 January 1938, FO 406/76/E23.

152 *Al-Rabita al-'Arabiyya*, 21 July 1937. On Haykal's blunt questioning of the government's policy see *al-Ahram*, 14 July 1937. Al-Nahhas's statement to the parliament is in *al-Ahram*, 21 July 1937.

153 Lampson to Eden, 25 July 1937, FO 371/20810/E4320.

154 On al-Nahhas's contact with the HAC, see Darwaza, 1993: vol. 2, 500–1 (entry of 25 August 1937). On the Egyptian memorandum of policy see Kelly's dispatch of 6 September 1937, FO 371/20813/E 5246.

155 Al-Swaydi, 1969:277.

156 See Lampson's dispatches of 25 and 27 July 1937, FO 371/20810/E 4320 and E 4370 respectively, and the FO's appreciative response in FO 371/2081/E 4668. Moreover, before answering Haykal's question in the parliament, al-Nahhas contacted Lampson for advice (Lampson to Eden, 15 July 1937, FO 371/20808/E 4051).

157 Mayer, 1983:73.

158 *Al-Ahram,* 19 and 20 September 1937.

159 Kelly to Eden, 6 September 1937, FO 371/2031/E 5246.

160 See a vivid account of Ibn Sa'ud's style of governing, and a full account of his meetings with the Palestinian delegation in late December 1936 in Darwaza, 1993: vol. 2, 552–9. The classic sources on the rise of Abd al-Aziz's leadership and the founding of Saudi Arabia are Wahbah, 1964 and Philby, 1928 and 1930.

161 Bullard was a consul-general in Jeddah during the decisive years of 1923–5 and a minister plenipotentiary there between 1936 and 1939. His fascinating autobiography *The Camels Must Go* was published in 1961. Hodgkin (ed.), 1993, is a selection of his most interesting letters and dispatches during his two terms of service in Jeddah.

162 On 19 December 1937, Bullard received a friendly memorandum from Fu'ad Hamza stating the Saudi readiness to open negotiations with Britain on the border issue (Enclosure in Bullard to Eden, 28 December 1937, FO 406/75/E 439). The dispute would explode only in 1952 when the Saudis occupied the Buraimi Oasis of Abu Dhabi. After their expulsion by the British, Saudi–British diplomatic relations remained suspended for seven years. However, it is pertinent that in 1952 Saudi Arabia was no longer dependent on British financial support, and Saudi–American relations were steadily on the rise.

163 Bullard began to be seriously alerted to the Italians' intrusions when they presented Ibn Sa'ud with a gift of six aeroplanes in November 1936 (Hodgkin (ed.), 1993:119–20). The gift, of course, entailed the possible training of Saudi pilots by the Italians. Throughout 1937, Italian activities caused constant nuisance to the British. Yet, by December, Bullard reported to London that during a long conversation with the king, he noticed that "whereas in March it had seemed amusing to Ibn Sa'ud that Mussolini should wave the sword of Islam, he now expressed astonishment at the extent to which, despite the notoriously ill-treatment

of the Arabs in Libya, Mussolini had been accepted by the Arabs as their champion" (Bullard to Eden, 1 January 1938, FO 406/76/E 661, Jedda Report for December 1937, Enclosure).The Italian influence in Yemen was none the less extensive, as the Saudi envoy, Bashir al-Sa'dawi, observed (Shukri, 1957: vol. 1, 1013–14). But the Saudi king was certainly unhappy about the situation in Yemen (Bullard's Jedda Report, ibid.).

164 Rendel's memorandum on "Palestine: Saudi Attitude", 14 July 1937, FO 371/20809/E 4063; Bullard to Eden, 10 July 1937, FO 371/20808/E 3885.

165 Several months before the publication of the partition plan, Ibn Sa'ud was unceasingly presenting the FO with Arab demands, enveloped in friendly gestures towards Britain. See, for example, his memorandum of 6 February 1937, which was handed over to the FO by Hafiz Wahba, in FO 371/20804/E774. On 25 March, Ibn Sa'ud conveyed to Bullard his appreciation of the Palestine government's leniency towards the abrogation of some death sentences on a few Palestinians (Bullard to Eden, 25 March 1937, FO 371/20805/E 1696). A few days later, the king presented the FO with a memorandum disputing the British interpretation of the Balfour Declaration (Bullard to Eden, 28 March 1937, FO 371/20805/E1707). Despite warnings from Rendel, who was visiting Saudi Arabia, to stay away from the Palestinian entanglement, the king, who met him on 12 and 18 March 1937, made certain that he realized that the Palestinian question was the most important factor in his dealings with Britain. He was absolutely determined to preserve close and friendly relations with the British government, yet had no choice but to support the Palestinians (Rendel's Report in FO 371/20805/E 2012).

166 On 6 September 1937, Ibn Sa'ud, after voicing his unwavering rejection of the partition plan, said "we did not wish to increase the many difficulties with which the British Government is faced, by protesting publicly against the partition of Palestine, or declaring our condemnation or disapproval of it, but were content to state our remarks and express our views to our friend, the British Government, directly, in a private manner, in the belief that it will favourably accept what we have expressed in all frankness and sincerity" (Included in Cabinet Minutes, 19 November 1937, CAB 24/37). In December 1937, Bullard reported that the king's position on Palestine "was not violent or even reproachful", but that he was "very anxious about his own position as being dependent on that of His Majesty's Government". Bullard continued: "He said more than once, as he has said before, that while he objected to partition as an Arab and a Moslem, he objected to it also because he felt it would be ruinous to His Majesty's Government and therefore dangerous to him." (Hodgkin (ed.), 1993:178). Again, a month later, Ibn Sa'ud expressed to Bullard that "if sufficient force were used Arabs of Palestine might acquiesce in partition for the present, but sooner or later, probably at a moment when His Majesty's Government were gravely embarrassed, they would break out. They would never recognize that Jews have any right to sovereignty over any part of Palestine. Nor would any other Arabs." (Bullard to Eden, 17 January 1938, FO 406/76/E 326). Finally, the king presented Bullard with a comprehensive memorandum in which the Saudi views on the partition and the whole question of Palestine were deployed in full details and, as has always been, with extremely friendly manner (Bullard to Eden, 25 January 1938, FO 406/76/E 973, Enclosure 1 and 2).

167 *Al-Ahram*, 11 August 1937. See also Rendel to Secretary of State, 29 September 1937, CO 733/352/75718/19 (a copy).
168 *Al-Ahram*, 21 July and 22 August 1937; *Filastin*, 22, 23 July 1937, *al-Jami'a al-Islamiyya*, 1 September 1937. Muhammad Salih Nasif to Nabih al-'Azma, 14 September 1937, al-'Azma Papers, Palestine Files, 12/312; Thabit Abd al-Nur (the Iraqi consul in Jedda) to Nabih al-'Azma, 7 June 1938, al-'Azma Papers, Palestine Files, 8/474.
169 *Al-Ahram*, 29 August 1937; Bullard to Eden, 6 June 1938, FO 406/76/E 3791; Bullard to Eden, 10 June 1938, FO 406/76/E 1237.
170 Shlaim, 1988:57.
171 Ibid., 58.
172 Report by the High Commissioner on an interview with Abdullah, 10 July 1937, FO 371/20811/E 4556; *al-Ahram*, 10 July 1937; Letter from Abdullah to High Commissioner of Palestine, 25 July 1937, CO 733/350/75718/2.
173 Amid rumours that the Peel Commission was to recommend a partition of Palestine, Abdullah, who was *en route* to attend the coronation ceremonies in London, was received lavishly by the Nashashibi opposition in Palestine (*Filastin*, 24, 26 and 28 April 1937). The Husayni camp boycotted the reception.
174 Porath, 1977: vol. 2, 230.
175 *Al-Shabab*, 21 and 28 July 1937; Darwaza, 1993: vol. 2, 442.
176 *Al-Ahram*, 15 July 1937. Also texts of violent attacks on Abdullah by the Baghdad daily *al-Difa'* of 16 and 21 July 1937 (al-'Azma Papers, Arab Files, 1/18); Faraj, 1987:216. Wilson (1987:124) remarked that in the summer of 1937, Abdullah stood alone in the Arab world. "So extreme was his sense of isolation that he sent Muhammad al-Unsi to Jerusalem to make sure that the Jewish Agency did not desert him as well, to deal with other, more popular Arab leaders."
177 *Filastin*, 24 July 1937.
178 *Filastin*, 27 July 1937.
179 On the Yemeni reaction see *al-Ahram*, 29 August 1937 and the long telegraph of protest sent by the minister of foreign affairs of the Yemen to Viscount Halifax on 20 April 1938, FO 406/76/E 2311. On Lebanon see *al-Shabab*, 1 and 5 September and 27 October 1937. On Tunisia, see *al-Shabab*, 20 October 1937. On Algeria, see *al-Shabab*, 23 August and 6 October 1937, and on the Moroccan reaction, see *al-Shabab*, 18 August and 25 August to 1 September and 3 and 17 November 1937. Echoes of protest were also sounded by Muslims in India (*al-Ahram*, 26 September 1937), and Nigeria (al-'Azma Papers, Palestine Files, 12/311), and in the Arab immigrant community of Detroit (al-'Azma Papers, Palestine Files, 10/167).
180 Mackereth to Eden, 15 September 1937, FO 371/20814/E 5515. This detailed report on the congress was first revealed by Kedourie (1982:107–25). Mackereth's view of the congress was entirely based on the report of an informant, whose seemingly undistinguished position made his assessment not entirely free of errors. Other sources on the Bludan Congress include: Muffarraj, 1937; Beeley, 1938:552–3; Zu'aytir, 1980:315–27; Darwaza, 1993: vol. 3, 7–17. Al-'Azma Papers, Palestine Files, Appendix, 39–44 and files 11 and 12 contain a great many of the congress's original documents.
181 *Filastin*, 21 July 1937; Amin al-Husayni to Nabih al-'Azma, 22 July 1937, al-'Azma Papers, Palestine Files, 10/55.

182 Scott (Baghdad) to Eden, 13 August 1937, FO 371/20812/E 4799; Bullard to Eden, 18 December 1937, FO 406/76/E 196; Shukri, 1957:999–1001.

183 Mackereth's report, *op. cit.*

184 Al-'Azma Papers, Palestine Files, 12/267; Muffaraj, 1937:24 and 29–34; Darwaza, 1993: vol. 3, 8.

185 The congress idea was first attacked by *Filastin* (27 August 1937), the pro-opposition newspaper. Later, when the congress convened, Raghib al-Nashashibi and other opposition leaders sent telegrams of support (Zu'aytir, 1980:322). It is worth noting that invitations to the congress were sent to Palestinian leaders of all political complexions.

186 *Al-Shabab*, 13 October 1937.

187 Al-Shahbandar to al-'Azma, 4 September 1937, al-'Azma Papers, Palestine Files, 12/322. A similar attitude was expressed by Nuri al-Sa'id (Daghir to al-'Azma, 30 August 1937, ibid., Syrian Files, 5/268).

188 Beeley, 1941: vol. 1, 441.

189 *Al-Nahar*, 12 September 1937.

190 Al-Swaydi, 1969:48; Basri, 1987:114–17.

191 Kerr to Eden, 4 January 1938, FO 406/76/ E 435.

192 On the structure of the congress and its committees see Mackereth's report, *op. cit.*; al-'Azma Papers, Palestine Files, 12/267.

193 Mackereth's report, *op. cit.*

194 Darwaza, 1993: vol. 3, 8 and 10.

195 Annexe 6, Mackereth's report, *op. cit.*

196 Zu'aytir, 1980:225–6.

197 The text of the political committee's report is in al-'Azma Papers, Palestine Files, 12/371. An English translation is in Annexe 2, Mackereth's report, *op. cit.*

198 The final resolutions of the congress were included in Muffarraj, 1937:143.

199 Bullard to Eden, 17 January 1938, FO 406/76/ E 326; Bullard to Halifax, 6 June 1938, FO 406/76/ E 3791 and Enclosure 2.

200 On Kashif al-Ghita''s statement against Ibn Sa'ud and Amir Abdullah, see Darwaza, 1993: vol. 3, 798–9. On the mufti's criticism, see al-Hashimi, 1967: vol. 1, 289–90. On Zu'aytir's position see Zu'aytir, 1980:436–7.

201 See, for example, details of the Ulema Congress that was organized in Damascus by the Ulema Society from 6–8 September 1938 in al-Hafiz and Abaza, 1986: vol. 2, 665–6. For the deterioration in Mardam's position, leading to his resignation in February 1939, see Khoury, 1987:575–7.

202 Al-Hashimi, 1967: vol. 1, 253–61.

203 Houstoun-Boswall to Halifax, 10 August 1938, FO 406/76/ E 4786.

204 Al-Hashimi, 1967: vol. 1, 259 and 290; al-Sabbagh, 1994:133.

205 Peterson to Halifax, 30 March 1938, FO 406/76/E 2014.

206 Nabih al-'Azma (Baghdad) to Jamil Mardam, 10 July 1938, al-'Azma Papers, Syrian Files, 18/107; al-Hashimi, 1967: vol. 1, 279–80.

207 On the Arabist officers' bitter view of al-Madfa'i's policy towards Palestine see al-Sabbagh, 1994:87. See also al-Hashimi, 1967: vol. 1, 226, 243, 283, and 287. On the rise of pro-Palestinian pan-Arabist activities in Iraq during 1938 and the ambivalent attitude of al-Madfa'i's government, see Houstoun-Boswall to Halifax, 29 August 1938, FO 406/76/E5394 and the enclosure of Edmonds to the first, 22 August 1938; Houstoun-Boswall to Halifax, 1, 2, 10, and 24

August, 14 September 1938, FO 406/76/E 4536, E 4550, E 4736, E 4506, E 5479 respectively.

208 Khadduri, 1951:138; Faraj, 1987, 220–1.

209 Peterson to Halifax, 16 November 1938, FO 406/ 76/ E7060; Peterson to Halifax, 16 December 1938, FO 406/ 76/ E7632. On the role of al-Sab'awi, the associate of the Arabist officers, in organizing the demonstration, see al-Hashimi, 1967: vol. 1, 292.

210 Peterson to Halifax, 25 December 1938, FO 406/76/7755.

211 C. J. Edmonds, "Note on the Present Orientation of pan-Arab policy in Iraq", 23 August 1938, Enclosure in Houstoun-Boswall to Halifax, 29 August 1938, FO 406/76/E 5393.

212 Lampson to Eden, 17 February 1938, FO 406/76/E 1114; Lampson to Halifax, 22 April, 1938, FO 406/76/E 2504. *Al-Risala* (15 November 1937) would consequently focus on Faruq's attendance of the religious sermons of Shaykh al-Azhar during the holy month of Ramadan. A few months later, *al-Risala* (13 March 1938) would describe the king as *Amir al-Mu'minin*. For the Ikhwani support of the king see Mahmud, 1979: vol. 1, 147–8; and for the support of Misr al-Fatat see Jankowski, 1975:35–6.

213 For an exalting response from the Arab-Islamic circles to the appointment of Haykal and Abd al-Raziq, see Ahmad Hasan al-Zayyat's editorial in *al-Risala*, 2 May 1938. For the Ikhwan's positive attitude towards Mahmud's ministry see Mahmud, 1979: vol. 1, 145–6.

214 *Al-Risala*, 22 August 1938; *al-Rabita al-'Arabiyya*. 4 and 11 May 1938; *al-Ahram*, 19 August 1938; Bateman to Halifax, 23 August 1938, FO 406/76/5015.

215 Lampson to Halifax, 28 April and 17 May 1938, FO 371/218751/E 2462 and 21877/E 3172 respectively and *al-Rabita al-'Arabiyya*, 4 May 1938.

216 Mayer, 1983:87.

217 *Filastin*, 4 and 20 July 1938; *al-Rabita al-'Arabiyya*, 13 and 27 July 1938.

218 *Al-Ahram*, 30 May 1938.

219 *Filastin*, 3 July 1938; 'Alluba's Petition, 25 June 1938, Enclosure of FO 371/ 21878/E 4257.

220 M. A. 'Alluba (Cairo) to Faris al-Khuri (Damascus), 13 June 1938, and Faris al-Khuri to Nabih al-'Azma, 20 June 1938, al-'Azma Papers, Palestine Files, 15/450.

221 Halifax to Bateman, 4 August 1938, FO 406/76/E 5652.

222 Trott to Halifax, 26 September 1938, FO 406/76/E 5655.

223 Beeley, 1941:441–2.

224 On the Wafd's planning for a mass conference in solidarity with Palestine, see As'ad Daghir (Cairo) to Nabih al-'Azma, 3 August 1938, al-'Azma Papers, Arab Files, 8/425. For Mahmud's early decision to keep at a distance from the congress, see Bateman to Halifax, 7 September 1938, FO 371/21880/E 5238. On his change of attitude, giving various justifications, see Lampson to Halifax, 6 and 9 October 1938, FO 371/21881/E5844 and E 5895 respectively.

225 Lampson to Halifax, 5 October 1938, FO 371/21881/ E 5816.

226 Halifax to Furlonge (Beirut), 21 September 1938, FO 406/76/ E 5551.

227 *Al-Ahram*, 8 and 9 October 1938; Zu'aytir, 1980:462–3.

228 *Al-Ahram*, 9 and 12 October 1938.

229 Lampson to Halifax, 14 October 1938, FO 371/21881/ E6179; *al-Ahram*, 14 October 1938.

230 *Al-Ahram*, 15 October 1938; Zuʻyatir, 1980:474–5.
231 Beeley, 1941:441–2.
232 Ibid., 441.
233 Lampson to Halifax, 20 October 1938, FO 406/76/E 6209, and Enclosures 1 and 2; *al-Ahram*, 12 October 1938.
234 *Al-Risala*, 10 October 1938. See also Lampson to Halifax, 24 October 1938, FO 406/76/E 6508.
235 *Al-Marʼa al-ʻArabiyya wa Qadiyyat Filastin*, 1938:13–17.
236 Mogannam, 1937:81; Lampson to Eden, 17 July 1937, FO 371/20809/E 4206.
237 Bahira al-ʻAzma to the Society of Women's Union, Beirut, May 1938, al-ʻAzma Papers, Palestine Files, 14/415.
238 Mackereth to Halifax, 17 June 1938, FO 371/21877/ E 4049; *al-Marʼa al-ʻArabiyya wa Qadiyyat Filastin,* 1938:18.
239 Qasimiyya (ed.), 1974:99.
240 For a vivid description of the congress, see Zuʻaytir, 1980:476–92.
241 For a list of participants, see al-ʻAzma Papers, Palestine Files, 14/422. Documents 413–41 of file 14 provide other information on the congress. See also Zuʻaytir, 1980:472ff.
242 *Al-Ahram*, 19 October 1938; Lampson to Halifax, FO 406/76/E 6209; al-ʻAzma Papers, Palestine Files, 14/431.
243 Lampson to Halifax, 21 October 1938, FO 371/21881/E 6302.
244 Zuʻaytir, 1980:484–5.
245 *Al-Risala*, 5 October 1936 and 19 September 1938. See also the Iraqi Christian teacher, Mary Abd al-Masih Wazir, *al-Marʼa al-ʻArabiyya, op. cit.,* 128–30.
246 "The rise of the Arabs and Muslims for rescuing Palestine has revealed a new life . . . The awakening of the Arabs is not like other races' awakening; in their earliest awakening [the Arabs] possessed the earth and the sky" (Ahmad Hasan al-Zayyat, *al-Risala*, 10 October 1938). See also the article of the Syrian, Majid al-ʼAtasi, in the same issue.
247 Opening the Eastern Women's Congress, Huda Shaʻrawi said, "the Arab nation will restore its glory, God willing, and the blaze of civilization will shine for its sky. Perhaps the tragedies and sacrifices are carrying a lesson for us and a promise of propitious conclusion" (*al-Marʼa al-ʻArabiyya, op. cit.,* 46–7).
248 See, for example, the statements of: the Iraqi ulema (Houstoun-Boswell to Halifax, 10 August 1938, FO 406/76/E 4787); the Saudis (*al-Ahram*, 11 August 1937); the Egyptians (Bateman to Halifax, 23 August 1938, FO 406/76/E 5015 and Enclosure); and the Syrians (Darwaza, 1993: vol. 3, 674). See also Hasan al-Banna, *Jaridat al-Ikhwan al-Muslimin*, 19 May, 16 June, and 8 September 1936.
249 These themes were emphasized: by ʻAlluba in his speeches to the Bludan Congress (Mackereth's dispatch, 15 September 1937, FO 371/20814/E 5515), and to the Parliamentary Congress (*al-Ahram*, 9 October 1938); by Riyad al-Sulh in Bludan; by Faris al-Khuri in the Parliamentary Congress; and by several writers and populists (*al-Risala*, 7 February, 23 and 30 May, 1 August 1938; *al-Rabita al-ʻArabiyya,* 11 August 1937).
250 *Jaridat al-Ikhwan al-Muslimin*, 11 August 1936; *al-Siyasa*, 17 July 1937; *al-Risala*, 2 and 9 August 1937.

251 Qasimiyya (ed.), 1974:100.

252 Mackereth, dispatch of 15 September 1937, FO 371/20814/E 5515; al-'Azma Papers, Palestine Files, 12.

253 Bullard (24 June 1938, FO 406/76/E 440) commented on the gloomy impact that the news broadcasts of the London Arabic service, regarding the execution of an Arab in Palestine, had left on the Saudi king and a group of his subjects. He said: "Not that I question the wisdom and honesty of telling the world . . . that an Arab has been hanged. Only one cannot expect the Arabs to receive the news with pleasure or even with indifference. Nor can one explain away their feelings by calling them pan-Arabs, which is almost becoming a term of abuse. It is true, as I said to the King, that Arabs are not punished for their politics, but it is not easy to find a convincing reply to the King's question, whether the crimes for which the British were hanging and imprisoning Arabs in Palestine would have been committed had it not been for the policy adopted by His Majesty's Government."

Houstoun-Boswell in Baghdad reported (6 September 1938, FO 406/76/E 5473): "It would, of course, be a mistake to attribute the Government's policy [of moderation and restraint] to any fundamental difference between the views of ministers and those of the man in the street. The ministers hate Zionism as much as the most forceful members of the Palestine Defence League and the nationalist clubs, and they share with the rest of Iraq a fervent desire to save Palestine from Jewish domination."

Perhaps the most telling were Lampson's dispatches. On the eve of the Parliamentary Congress, Lampson said that not a soul was still friendly to Britain in Egypt, and that the Palestinian question was alienating the Arab, and much of the Muslim, world from Britain (10 October 1938, FO 371/2188/E 5925). After the congress, Lampson wrote of Palestine becoming the nerve-centre of the Muslim world, a development that through the congress augmented the "sense of unity existing between the Arab countries, both in the particular aspect of opposition to the policy of his Majesty's Government in Palestine and in the more general aspect of Muslim cooperation against Western encroachment" (24 October 1938, FO 406/76/E 6508).

254 Rendel's memoranda on: "Palestine: Egyptian Attitude", 13 July 1937, FO 371/20809/E 4162; "Palestine: Saudi Attitude", 14 July 1937, FO 371/20809/E 4063; "Palestine: Iraqi Attitude", 13 September 1937, FO 371/20813/E 5392.

255 Rendel's memorandum, 3 November 1937, FO 371/20819/E 6470.

256 Cabinet Minutes, CAB 46/37, 8 December 1937.

257 Ormsby-Gore to Chamberlain, 9 January 1938, FO 371/21862/E 559; see also Taggar, 1978:108.

258 The decision regarding the appointment of the Technical Commission was announced in Cmd. 5634. Policy in Palestine, The Colonial Office, Great Britain, London, January 1938.

259 Parliamentary Debates, House of Lords, vol. 106, 1936–7, cols. 599–674, 20 July 1937.

260 Lampson to Cadogan, 31 March 1938, FO 371/21875/E 2098.

261 Samuel to Ormsby-Gore, 7 April 1938, FO 371/21876/E 2668 and ibid.

262 Darwaza, 1993: vol. 3, 262 (entry of 9 March 1938).

263 Hyamson's memorandum, 11 October 1937, CO 733/333/75156/33; Hyamson to Parkinson, 21 November 1937, ibid.

264 On the extensive involvement of these personalities in the arduous negotiations that involved the mufti and the HAC in Lebanon, some non-Zionist circles in Palestine and the Iraqi and British governments, see Caplan, 1986: vol. 2, 78–84. A first-hand view was provided by Darwaza (1993: vol. 3, 227, 242, 262–3, 326–7, 508 and 516–17).

265 Enclosure 2, Hyamson to Parkinson, 8 August 1938, FO 406/76/E5008. The Palestinian draft was dated 12 January 1938.

266 Enclosure 3 in ibid., dated 6 February 1938.

267 Caplan, 1986: vol. 2, 83–4.

268 On the Colonial Office's final reaction to Samuel's proposal see Shuckburgh to Oliphant, 18 July 1938, FO 371/21878/E 4324. On its similar response to Newcombe-Hyamson's project see Parkinson to Hyamson, 19 August 1938, FO 406/76/E 5008.

269 Enclosure of High Commissioner to Secretary of State for Colonies, 11 June 1938, FO 371/21885/E 3866. On the Arab critical reaction to Abdullah's scheme see *Filastin*, 28 May 1938; *al-Difa'*, 29 May 1938; al-'Azma Papers, Palestine Files, 15/449 and Abdullah, 1978:86–90.

270 Shlaim, 1988:65.

271 Minutes in FO 371/21864/E 6217.

272 Minutes in FO 371/21865/E 6379; see also Porath, 1986:111–12.

273 Cmd. 5854. Palestine Partition Commission Report, Colonial Office, Great Britain, London, October 1938.

274 Cabinet Minutes, CAB 52/38, 2 November 1938.

275 Porath, 1986:112–14.

276 See the HAC's communiqué, 6 November 1936 (al-Hout (ed.), 1984:514–16).

277 Palestine: Statement by His Majesty's Government in the United Kingdom, 7 November 1938, FO 406/76/E 6506.

278 Peterson to Halifax, 9 November 1938, FO 406/76/E 6604. See also Peterson's initial assessment in Peterson to Halifax, 31 October 1938, FO 406/76/E 6805.

279 Bateman to Halifax, 18 November 1938 FO 371/21866/E 6871.

280 Bullard to Halifax, 11 November 1938, FO 406/76/E 6805.

281 Bullard to Halifax, 12 November 1938, FO 406/76/E 6702.

282 Halifax to Bullard, 14 November 1938, FO 406/76/E 6702, and Halifax to Bullard, 21 November 1938, ibid., E 6831.

283 Havard (Beirut) to High Commissioner (Jerusalem), 11 November 1938, FO 406/76/E 6699.

284 Consul-General, Beirut, to Halifax, 16 November 1938, FO 406/76/E 6818. Consul-General, Beirut, to Halifax, 16 November 1938, ibid., E 6907, and Enclosures (Statement by the Higher Arab Committee, published by the Beirut Press on 16 November 1938).

285 Bullard to Halifax, 16 November 1938, FO 406/76/E 6860; Bullard to Halifax, 17 November 1938, ibid., E 6831; Bullard to Halifax, 17 November 1938, ibid., E 6831; Bullard to Halifax, 22 November 1938, ibid., E 6961; Bullard to Halifax, 27 November 1938, ibid., E 7126; Bullard to Halifax, 28 November 1938, ibid., E 7624. According to Nuri al-Sa'id, Fu'ad Hamza, the Saudi deputy

foreign minister, who joined Amir Faysal in the Saudi delegation to the London conference (7 February to 17 March 1939), continued to press the British for considering Faysal as a future king for Palestine (al-Hashimi, 1967: vol. 1, 313).

286 Bullard to Halifax, 24 November 1938, FO 406/76/E 6802.

287 Peterson to Halifax, 19 November 1938, FO 406/76/E 6875; Peterson to Halifax, 19 November 1938, ibid., E 7067, and Enclosures.

288 Halifax to Peterson, 23 November 1938, FO 406/76/E 6875; Peterson to Halifax, 26 November 1938, FO 406/76/E 7105.

289 Peterson to Halifax, 26 November 1938, FO 406/76/E 7158.

290 Peterson to Halifax, 27 December 1938, FO 406/76/E 7189.

291 Halifax to Bullard, 21 November 1938, FO 406/76/E 6831; Halifax to Peterson, 23 November 1938, FO 406/76/E 6875.

292 Bullard to Halifax, 25 December 1938, FO 406/76/E 7448; Lampson to Halifax, 15 December 1938, FO 371/21868/E 7577.

293 Halifax to Bullard, 9 December 1938, FO 406/76/E 7314.

294 MacDonald's memorandum, 18 January 1939, CAB 1/39.

295 Mackereth to High Commissioner for Palestine, 17 January 1939, CO 733/408/15 (a copy of E 689).

296 Darwaza, 1993: vol. 3, 800–3.

297 *Filastin*, 16 January 1939.

298 Porath, 1977: vol. 2, 282–3.

299 Bateman to Halifax, 15 November 1938, FO 371/21884/E 6812.

300 Bullard to Halifax, 20 December 1938, FO 406/76/E 7677.

301 *Al-Rabita al-'Arabiyya*, 25 January 1939.

302 Lampson to Halifax, 23 January 1939, FO 371/23220/E 631.

303 High Commissioner to Secretary of State for Colonies, 27 February 1939, FO 371/23243/SF/80/39; *Filastin*, 1 February 1939.

304 *Filastin*, 27 January 1939; Lampson to Halifax, 6 February 1939, FO 371/23222/E 978; Darwaza, 1949–51: vol. 3, 240–1.

305 Records of the London Conference are included in FO 371/23224 to 23230. See also an analysis of the conference, from a Zionist perspective, in Cohen, 1973:571–96, and a thoroughly objective view in Beeley, 1941:447–58.

306 *Filastin*, 26 March and 10 May 1939; Beeley, 1941:458–9.

307 Cmd. 6019. Great Britain: Statement of Policy Presented by the Secretary of State for the Colonies to Parliament, London, 1939.

308 Beeley, 1941:462. See also the HAC communiqué of 30 May 1939 in al-Hout (ed.), 1984:648–53.

309 Parliamentary Debates, House of Lords, vol. 113, col. 104, 23 May 1939.

310 Secretary of State for Colonies to High Commissioner, 16 May 1939, CO 733/398/4/75156/13.

311 Lampson to FO, 3, 13, and 18 June 1939, and High Commissioner to Parkinson, 14 July 1939, CO 733/408/15/75872/30. The Nashashibis also supported the White Paper (*Filastin*, 1 June 1939).

312 Phipps (Paris) to FO, 26 May 1939, CO 733/408/14/75872/30.

313 Darwaza (Damascus) to Zu'aytir (Baghdad), 22 May 1939, in al-Hout (ed.), 1984:647–8. A different perspective of the Arab public opinion was provided by Miss H. M. Wilson, the British School Teacher in Palestine in her "School Year in

Palestine', 1938–1939", p. 68 (St Antony's College Middle East Centre, University of Oxford). See also High Commissioner to Secretary of State for Colonies, 8 June and 21 July 1939, CO 733/398/14/75156.

314 For Mahmud's reaction, see Lampson's dispatch, 18 May 1939, FO 371/23235/E 3673. On Nuri's position, see Newton's dispatches of 4 and 5 July 1939, FO 371/23238/E 4929 and 23211/E 6095 respectively and *Filastin*, 23 May 1939. See also Darwaza, 1949-51: vol. 3, 245.

315 Bennet (Alexander) to FO, 29 July 1939, CO 733/408/15/75872.

316 Newton to Halifax, 15 September 1939, FO 371/23240/E 6505. Cf. al-Hashimi, 1967: vol. 1, 311 and 313.

317 Mackereth to Jerusalem, 14 April 1939, and Lampson to FO, 9 May 1939, CO 733/398/4/75156; Houstoun-Boswell to FO, 6 May 1939, FO 371/23234/E 3349.

318 When the British discovered the mufti's escape, they first suspected that he would go to Egypt. One day after he reached Baghdad, the counsellor general in Beirut managed to compile a dramatic version of the escape story. The High Commissioner in Palestine, despite the *esprit de corps* that now united Britain with France, suspected a French hand. See Lampson to Ali Mahir Pasha, 15 October 1939; Havard to FO, 16 October 1939; High Commissioner to Secretary of State for Colonies, 21 October 1939; CO 733/398/4/57156. Before departing, the mufti left a letter of gratitude and apology to the French High Commissioner of Syria and Lebanon, Monsieur Puaux (text in ibid.). The mufti's version of his escape is told in Zu'aytir, 1980:608–10.

319 Shabib, 1981:48.

7

A defeat in Iraq:
the decline of Arab-Islamists

The mufti's unannounced arrival in Baghdad took many of the Iraqi politicians by surprise. But given the country's highly charged pan-Arabist and pro-Palestinian climate, he was none the less warmly welcomed. His role in the Iraqi and Arab national movement during the fateful 17 months he spent in Baghdad has long been celebrated, condemned, and highlighted.[1] The unfolding events, however, showed that the mufti's stay in Iraq was from the start thrown open to all possibilities. If the Iraqi state had been more stable, or the British government (under Churchill) been more receptive to the fulfilment of its own policy in Palestine or to the idea of Arab unity, and if it had not been an occasion of world war, the mufti's stay in Iraq would have become perhaps much less eventful than it turned out to be.

Being the prominent Arab and Palestinian leader, the mufti was widely honoured by official and popular circles and by the Iraqi press.[2] He became a familiar face on official occasions, was hosted by the government at a house on al-Zahawi Avenue near the royal court and was given a monthly stipend. For several months, he evidently kept his promise not to intervene in Iraqi internal affairs.[3] Yet, the political animal in him and the very nature of internal power relations, were soon to draw him into the heat of the Iraqi political entanglement. The prime minister, Nuri al-Sa'id, who was still on friendly terms with the mufti but not particularly fond of his increasing anti-British radicalism, first suggested that he settle in Kirkuk in northern Iraq to avoid irritating the British or becoming a cause of constraint in their relations with Iraq.[4] But realizing the popular enthusiasm with which the mufti was received, Nuri was soon to abandon this scheme, and began to seek some openings in the mufti's relations with Britain. A few days after the mufti's arrival, the Iraqi foreign minister relayed to the British ambassador, Sir Basil Newton, that "He [the mufti] accepted the fact that Arab countries must support the cause of democratic states in the present war and gave the undertaking that while in Iraq he would not engage in any political activities (anti-British as it sounded)."[5] Moreover, Nuri pressed the mufti to make "a pronouncement of his abhorrence of Nazism" in order to reduce the implacable enmity between him and the British.

Characteristically, Nuri believed that in politics there were no absolutes, including the British ban on the mufti. Being a friend of both sides, he proposed to reconcile the mufti with the British government on the basis of immediate implementation of the White Paper. Yet, even such a reconciliation was, from the British perspective, out of the question. For the British, the mufti was now becoming an incorrigible, and above all a defeated, leader. Hence, Lacy Baggallay, the Foreign Office's hawk in the Eastern Department, would write to the British ambassador in Iraq, that only by making absolutely clear to the mufti's supporters and opponents alike that his return to Palestine was in no way contemplated would "HM's Government be able to break his influence". Baggallay also intended to request the mufti's extradition from Iraq but was wisely advised by the embassy in Baghdad not to do so.[6] Yet, after two months of enjoying Iraqi hospitality, the mufti was reported to be looking for other avenues to resume his political enterprise. In agreement with Shukri al-Quwwatli, the mufti seems to have been preparing for the formation of a pan-Arab committee, centred in Riyadh, to work for the independence of Palestine and Syria. But the project, as well as the mufti's attempt to visit Saudi Arabia, were rejected by the Saudi king.[7] Perhaps aware of the ongoing deliberations in London for an Arab federation under his rule, Ibn Saud began to see the mufti as nothing but a "nuisance".

During the next few months, the mufti emerged as a main party to the dramatic developments that led Iraq into war with Britain. The war and Iraq's subsequent defeat amplified the crisis of the Arab interwar generation and their inability to respond effectively to the demanding conditions of their time. What became markedly apparent by the beginning of the 1940s, was the breakup of the Arab dominant political forces into two broadly defined blocs: those who believed that Arab progress and unity were inescapably linked to the prospect of reaching an understanding with Western powers, especially Britain; and those who perceived the Arab revival in terms of challenging Western domination. The defeat of the Palestinian revolt, the failure of Mardam's "honourable cooperation" with France in Syria, followed by the flagrant dismissal of 'Ali Mahir and his ministerial partners by Lampson in Cairo, provided the Arab confrontationists with ample evidence to validate their stance. Yet, it was in Iraq, rather than anywhere else in the Arab world, that the Arab rupture with Britain was to occur. Three key factors seem to have contributed to this rupture: the precarious political situation in Iraq and its troubled relations with Britain; the deepening Palestinian and Arab crisis; and the role of the Axis powers.

The Iraqi dimension

If instability had been a malignant feature of the Iraqi state since its inception in the early 1920s,[8] it was Nuri al-Sa'id's ministry of December 1938 which prepared the ground for the outburst of 1941. Nuri replaced al-Madfa'i with the support of the army, represented by seven Arabist officers, including Husayn Fawzi, the chief of staff, Amin al-'Umari, the commander of the first division, and his associate, 'Aziz Yamulki, together with the more closely linked group of Salah al-Din al-Sabbagh, Fahmi Sa'id, Mahmud Salman, and Kamil Shabib. The seven officers, who were effectively in full control of the army, had been earlier cultivated by Nuri with the help of Taha al-Hashimi. By any standard of Iraqi politics, Nuri's government was based on a powerful cabinet that included, amongst others, Taha al-Hashimi for defence, Rustum Haydar for finance and Naji Shawkat for the interior, and was later augmented by 'Ali Jawdat al-'Ayyubi for foreign affairs. It also lasted for more than a year, during which Nuri might have been able to achieve a considerable level of stability, end the military intervention in politics, and restore the constitutional legitimacy of the state. Instead, he did exactly the contrary.

In a meeting, held after Nuri's ascendance to the premiership, Nuri, al-Hashimi, and Haydar decided formally to involve the army in the major issues of government.[9] Nuri's objective was not, of course, to share power in acknowledgment of the officers' support, but rather to liquidate his political opponents. Unable to forgive the leaders of the 1936 coup for forcing him into exile and murdering his brother-in-law and ally, Ja'far al-'Askari, or King Ghazi for supporting the coup, Nuri became obsessed with bringing retribution on Hikmat Sulayman, the prime minister following the *coup d'état* in 1936 as well as the king. What incensed Nuri even further was the return of Sulayman to the political arena through the strengthening of his relations with the Palace.[10] On 6 March 1939, Nuri announced the uncovering of a conspiracy to assassinate the king and the prime minister in which he accused Hikmat Sulayman and many other accessories to the 1936 coup.[11] Nuri's military court found Sulayman guilty and sentenced him to death. But, since it was clear that the entire affair was concocted by the prime minister, and following the forceful intervention of several ministers and politicians, as well as of the British ambassador, the sentence was commuted to five years' imprisonment.[12] Nuri's thirst for revenge was, however, unquenchable. There then occurred one of the most controversial events in Iraq's modern political history: on the morning of 4 April 1939 the government of Nuri declared the death of King Ghazi from injuries sustained in a car accident the previous night.[13]

Amid the rising nationalist, anti-British sentiments, the Iraqi public did not accept the accident story and many pointed instead to the involvement of the British.[14] Demonstrations erupted all over the country, encouraged – according to the British advisor of the interior ministry – by Naji Shawkat, the radical minister of the interior. In Mosul, angry crowds invaded the British consulate and murdered the consul-general, Monck Mason.[15] Nuri responded to the unexpected developments by dismissing Shawkat and moving quickly to tackle the constitutional consequences of the king's death.[16]

The questions that surrounded Ghazi's death will perhaps continue to haunt historians of modern Iraq for several years to come. As early as December 1938, the British ambassador wrote graphically of Nuri's intentions to dispose of certain friends and accessories of the king, and Ghazi himself.[17] But though Peterson, approved by London, did not support the idea of dethroning Ghazi, considering the political and constitutional risks involved, anti-British provocations emanating from the king's circles, reached unprecedented levels during the few months prior to his death. Besides allowing fervent pro-Palestinian and pro-Syrian broadcasts on his own radio station, Ghazi encouraged Kuwaiti nationalists to rise against their pro-British ruler, calling for the return of Kuwait to mother Iraq.[18] At a certain stage, he gave orders to the army to prepare to invade the Emirate, but was overruled by the deputy prime minister (Nuri being absent in London).[19] From Nuri's perspective, two moves on the part of the king were perhaps crucial in determining his fate. The first was the appointment, while Nuri was still out of the country, of

Rashid 'Ali al-Gaylani as chief of the royal diwan, which was done without consulting the cabinet.[20] Al-Gaylani was a strong rival of Nuri, though not necessarily yet an opponent, who had his own channels to the army, especially the chief of staff. The second was Ghazi's initiation of contacts with the four colonels, al-Sabbagh and his coterie,[21] which, if developed into an alliance, would have become fatal to Nuri's position. Notwithstanding the reality of Ghazi's death, it was the impact that it left on the state's image which mattered. What followed was even more detrimental.

Since the heir to the throne was still a child, many of the leading Iraqi politicians believed that the regency must be entrusted to Amir Zaiyd, Ghazi's uncle and an experienced diplomat, or to a council of eminent Hashemites and politicians. The prime minister, however, opted for Abd al-Ilah, a cousin of the deceased king and his brother-in-law, who had been long cultivated by Nuri. On the basis of what was widely believed to be a fraudulent affidavit by Ghazi's widow, Queen 'Aliya, Nuri announced that the appointment of Abd al-Ilah was in fulfilment of the late king's will.[22] Nuri introduced the young regent to his army friends, to whom Abd al-Ilah avowed his friendship and faithfulness.[23] Once again, in that critical moment of transition, the army sided with Nuri. But while Nuri was consolidating his power, his and the state's integrity were being questioned by the people.

When Britain declared war on Germany on 3 September, the British ambassador, invoking the Anglo-Iraqi treaty, requested that Iraq sever its diplomatic relations with Germany. Impressed by the German triumphant revival, Iraqi public opinion was definitely unconcerned with Britain's war effort. During the cabinet meeting, as well as that of the high defence council, Nuri proposed the declaration of war on the British side, a measure uncalled for by the treaty.[24] When his proposal was rejected, he suggested that one or two Iraqi brigades should be dispatched to join the British defence of Egypt on the western Saharan front. This proposal was also turned down, and Nuri was subsequently granted a limited mandate to terminate Iraqi–German relations, a step that was clearly not favoured by the Iraqi people. A few weeks after the departure of the German mission, Nuri, instead of deporting the German nationals who stayed behind, handed them over to the British to be detained as prisoners of war. Nuri's overenthusiasm to demonstrate his British loyalty, outraged the people and parliament alike.[25] It is doubtful whether Nuri could have embarked on such a risky venture without the backing of the army.

By the beginning of 1940, the government was reaching the end of its life, but Nuri, true to himself, would not cede power without a dramatic exit. On 18 January, a former police constable fired at the finance minister, Muhammad Rustum Haydar, while he was leaving his office.[26] Haydar, a confidant of the royal family and widely regarded as the brain behind the government, died in hospital a few days later. A former member of al-Fatat and a functionary of Faysal's Damascus government, Haydar was a moderate with pro-British inclinations. Although he belonged to a prominent Lebanese Shi'i family,[27] his assassination was evidently a result of personal rather than sectarian animosity. Hence, considering the apolitical nature of the incident, the justice minister decided that the case should be tried before a criminal civil court. The prime minister, however, insisted that the killer be sent to a military tribunal. Furthermore, after a confidential meeting with Nuri, the assassin made the claim that Subhi Najib and Ibrahim Kamal, two of the prime minister's opponents and former ministers in the government of Jamil al-Madfa'i, were accessories to the crime. Many inside and outside the cabinet suspected that these claims were contrived by the prime minister.[28] Nuri could no longer maintain the inner cohesion of the cabinet, and had thus no alternative but to present his resignation.

The regent accepted the resignation on 20 February 1940, and upon a suggestion of Nuri, his political mentor, called on Rashid 'Ali al-Gaylani to take office, hoping that Nuri would become the foreign minister of the new government and Taha al-Hashimi its defence minister. With his unblemished and nationalist image, al-Gaylani was in fact sought after as a cover for a pro-British, unpopular foreign policy during the critical years of war.[29] When news of the projected government reached the army, the group of seven split into two blocs. Husayn Fawzi, the chief of staff, Amin al-'Umari and 'Aziz Yamulki objected to the inclusion of Nuri and al-Hashimi in the cabinet, and to prove the seriousness of their objection, they put their troops on alert. Infuriated by Fawzi's demands, the four other influential officers, whose principal loyalty was to al-Hashimi, decided to resist their chief of staff.[30] On the night of 21 February, the army troops in the Baghdad military region were divided into two opposing sides: the first at al-Washwash military camp and the second at al-Rashid. Conscious of the tragic consequences of a confrontation, and that his side was the least likely to win, Husayn Fawzi backed down. In the meantime, al-Gaylani rejected the offer presented to him, declaring to the regent that the mess created by Nuri should be cleared by no one but Nuri. In the light of these developments, Abd al-Ilah had no choice but to re-nominate Nuri to form the government. But Nuri's highly untenable position could not sustain his government in office for more than five weeks. In the event, Fawzi, al-ʿUmari, and Yamulki were dismissed and the bloc of four colonels, known now in British and Iraqi circles as the "Golden Square", emerged as the most powerful "political" arbitrator in the country.

It is unclear why Fawzi and his followers opposed Nuri and al-Hashimi. One explanation was that, besides their personal dislike of Nuri and their growing intolerance of al-Hashimi's influence with al-Sabbagh and his associates, their move was also encouraged by the mufti.[31] At the heart of this explanation was the assumption that the mufti had already resolved to approach the Germans and was, therefore, keen to preclude Nuri, with his impeccable Britishness, from occupying the influential post of foreign minister. Amin al-ʿUmari was also an old friend and Ottoman army comrade of the mufti. This theory, logical as it sounds, has at least one important flaw: had the mufti been an accomplice in Fawzi's mutiny, his involvement would not have escaped Nuri's attention and would certainly have resulted in the deterioration of their relations; in contrast, immediately after the end of the February crisis, the mufti was called upon by Nuri to support his eleventh-hour attempt to re-establish the state's integrity by proposing some fundamental constitutional and political reforms.[32] If one was to disregard the idea of his collusion with Fawzi, the mufti's entry into the Iraqi political entanglement would appear to have been initiated by none other than Nuri.

Upon the resignation of Nuri on 28 March 1940, the mufti was again asked to help facilitate the transition of government to Rashid ʿAli al-Gaylani. A strong and amicable understanding was evolving between them since the spontaneously warm reception that al-Gaylani afforded to the mufti in October 1939. Their relations might have also been augmented by mutual, though disproportionate, distrust of the British. To ensure the success of his friend, the mufti arranged a meeting between al-Gaylani and the four colonels, during which the mufti's Islamic and Arabist moral authority was employed to the full for the sake of establishing trust between the two parties.[33] Confident of the army's support, al-Gaylani formed a powerful and highly representative government, involving Naji al-Swaydi, Naji Shawkat, Nuri al-Saʿid, Taha al-Hashimi, Sadiq al-Bassam

[335]

and Ra'uf al-Bahrani. But though this government was the first since Sidqi's coup of October 1936 to reach power in a constitutional and relatively peaceful climate, it occasioned a period during which the state's legitimacy was substantially undermined by years of internal strife, *coups* and counter-*coups*, and the unscrupulous manners in which Nuri al-Sa'id conducted the affairs of Iraq. It also coincided with rise of the "Golden Square", unchallenged inside the army and in alliance with al-Gaylani and the mufti.

Two extremist views have dominated the studies of the four colonels' role in Iraqi politics. One was a romantically drawn picture of an idealist military group, pan-Arabist and Iraqi nationalist, that fell victim to an unholy alliance of profligate politicians and the British imperialist arrogance.[34] The tragic death of the four officers, and the subsequent publishing of al-Sabbagh's memoirs in 1956, reinforced the mythical perception of their contribution to the Arab movement. The other view, which was at least partially derived from the British diplomatic correspondence of the period, portrayed the colonels as a rabid radical group which constituted a fifth column for the German grand designs in the Arab East. This perspective is fittingly represented by Reeva Simon's study, *Iraq Between the Two World Wars*. In her overenthusiastic theorizing, Simon argued that Germanophilia was a deep-seated trait of the Iraqi military, rooted in the Ottoman–German alliance during World War I and the German influence in the Ottoman army.[35] German militarism and nationalist spirit were therefore ingrained in the Iraqi army as they were in the state education and propaganda. Both views are highly and largely non-historical.

It is an undisputed fact that the officers held pan-Arabist convictions, tempered with an Islamic outlook.[36] But their Arabism was not particularly unique in the Iraqi political climate of the late 1930s. As Mustafa al-'Umari, the justice minister, once said to C. J. Edmonds: "The leading men of Iraq had made up their minds that in this modern world of force-politics a small state of under 4 million inhabitants had no prospect of survival, and their only hope lay in pushing a vigorous policy aiming at a pan-Arab League."[37] The four colonels were after all children of an era where ideas were greatly influenced by the Arab-Islamic reform movement. Their world was shaped by the modernization epoch, technological developments, the discourse of progress and the belief in the power of the state. It is doubtful whether they ever had a close acquaintance with German officers during World War I, since they were rather young Ottoman lieutenants who had little to do with the high-ranking German advisors. What is certain is that throughout their military careers in Iraq until the outbreak of war with Britain in May 1941, none of the four colonels took part, or became involved, in initiating relations with the Germans. In 1940–1, contacts with the Axis powers were handled by the mufti and the government, while the officers were mainly at the receiving end of this political imbroglio. If the Ottoman experience had any bearing, it would have been more apparent in the political attitude of Jamil al-Madfaʿi, ʿAli Jawdat al-ʾAyyubi, Mawlud Mukhlis, Taha al-Hashimi, Arshad al-ʿUmari, Nur al-Din Mahmud and Ismaʿil Namiq, who were senior to al-Sabbagh and his friends in the Ottoman army and proved to be either strongly pro-British, or at least suspicious of the German enterprise.[38]

The idealistic image of the "Golden Square" is equally fictitious. In many respects, the four colonels were soldiers-turned-politicians. During their alliance with Nuri al-Saʿid, they were fully aware of, and sometimes actively participating in, his plots to silence opponents, the cover-up of his possible involvement in the "murder" of Ghazi, and his contrivance to install Abd al-Ilah as regent. They made no objection to the termination of relations with Germany in 1939, were witness to Nuri's attempt to declare war on the British side, participated in the elimination of their Arabist chief of staff and other army colleagues for their opposition to Nuri, and accepted the trying of Rustum Haydar's case in a military tribunal, against the will of the justice minister.[39] In the end, what became blatantly obvious was the destructive effect of their involvement in politics on the morale of their troops, and the consequent neglect on the part of the senior officers of their military duties, a situation that contributed to Iraqi's total defeat in May 1941.

Until the crucial meeting in which the mufti introduced al-Gaylani to the four colonels, the association between them and the mufti was not yet consummated. They admired and respected his Arab nationalist role and position, but, like him, could not anticipate his involvement in Iraqi political affairs. Yet, Yunis al-Sabʿawi, the officers' close friend, was a frequent visitor to the mufti's house.[40] After the ascendance of al-Gaylani to power, relations between the officers, the mufti and the prime minister developed rapidly, placing Rashid ʿAli al-Gaylani in the forefront of the events that led to the May 1941 war. In the background and complex character of al-Gaylani lay a significant number of the ingredients which came to delineate the route to that war.

Rashid 'Ali al-Gaylani was born in 1892 to a family distantly related to *naqib al-ashraf*.[41] The Gaylanis claimed descent from the founder of al-Gaylaniyya Sufi *tariqa* and were thus guardians of its immense *waqf* in Baghdad. But Rashid's immediate family was not among the privileged Gaylanis, since his grandfather lost the position of *naqib al-ashraf* in the nineteenth century. While a minister in Yasin al-Hashimi's government of 1935–6, Rashid 'Ali enforced his guardianship on the Gaylaniyya *waqf* through the power and influence of his position. From the highly religious environment of his childhood, al-Gaylani moved to the Law School. His graduation from there in 1914 entitled him to join the Ottoman *waqf* bureaucracy. After the Ottoman withdrawal from Mosul, where he was last posted, he returned to Baghdad where he practised and taught law until he was appointed judge in the Court of Appeal at the age of twenty-seven.[42] His début in politics coincided with his appointment as minister of justice in Yasin al-Hashimi's first government. He then joined al-Hashimi in founding al-'Ikha' al-Watani Party, becoming one of its most prominent leaders. After several years in opposition, he formed his first government in 1933 with the encouragement and backing of Yasin al-Hashimi. Al-Gaylani, like his late ally al-Hashimi, was not particularly friendly towards the British, but when in office he maintained good working relations with British officials and advisors.

Tawfiq al-Swaydi, a political opponent of al-Gaylani, wrote of his conservative attitude, traditionalism, support for law and order and preference for a system based on the leadership of a just guiding ruler rather than on democracy.[43] In a British biography of him, his term as a judge in the court of appeal was noted positively.[44] Yet, in a disparaging report, written at the end of February 1941, C. J. Edmonds described al-Gaylani as a reckless, obstinate and unscrupulous politician "who would set fire to the bazaars in order to steal a handkerchief under cover of the smoke".[45] This image was, of course, the result of the turbulent times of early 1941 as British officials in Iraq recalled al-Gaylani's adventurous and conspiratorial activities with the tribal forces, as well as his support for the military crushing of the Assyrian revolt in 1933. But reckless, obstinate and unscrupulous as he may have been, al-Gaylani demonstrated on more than one occasion the political acumen of a skilful Iraqi ruler. After the sudden death of King Faysal in 1933, which created a difficult and unprecedented experience for an infant state, he conducted a smooth transition of the crown.[46] Again, after the resignation of Nuri in late March 1940, al-Gaylani's awareness of the unstable conditions of the country made him request that the leading politicians agree in writing to render their support to his government and give him the freedom to restore unity and confidence in state and country.[47] His request was approvingly accepted.

During the first few months of al-Gaylani's ministry, his effort to quell the anti-British press, and his orders to the security service to keep watch on Palestinian and Syrian refugees and to check their activities, was appreciated by the British embassy.[48] But, soon the climate began to change. Upon the entry of Italy into the war on 10 June 1940, the British ambassador, Newton, requested that Iraq break off diplomatic ties with Italy. The Iraqi government met the next day and agreed by a majority vote not to take a hasty decision in this regard.[49] This position was further upheld by the high defence council. It may be important to note that the Iraqi reluctance to cut off relations with Italy did not amount to a complete rupture with Britain, nor was it an indication of a premeditation to do so.

Undoubtedly, the spectacular German advances in Europe during the previous months played a crucial role in determining the Iraqi attitudes, but until then al-Gaylani was not in contact with the Germans and no plans existed on his part for the initiation of such contacts. The majority of the cabinet, except Nuri al-Sa'id and Amin Zaki, believed that despite Nuri's precedent of September 1939 (when relations with Germany were terminated) the Anglo-Iraqi treaty did not oblige Iraq to sever diplomatic ties with countries at war with Britain. To emphasize its commitment to provisions of the treaty, the Iraqi government agreed to the British request regarding the passage of British troops. The other reason for the strengthening Iraqi neutrality was the uncertainty of the regional situation. In mid-1940, the Iraqis were not particularly sure which side Turkey, their powerful neighbour, was going to take, and the implications of its decision for the future of Syria in the event of a French defeat.[50] Awaiting the elucidation of these questions, many leading Iraqis envied the great benefits that Turkey's neutrality was reaping in terms of good relations with Germany and British financial and military aid.

In the context of Iraqi–British relations, the disagreement over the breaking of diplomatic ties with Italy came on top of several other outstanding issues. Most notable was the chronic Iraqi complaint of not being adequately supplied with needed arms by Britain. This issue reached a critical stage upon Britain's declaration of war on Germany. While British armaments continued to reach Turkey and Greece, Britain, motivated by more pressing needs elsewhere or intending to use weapon supplies as a political lever to check the Iraqi support of the Palestinians, ceased the shipping of arms to Iraq.[51] The Iraqis were advised by Britain to seek the required weapons from the United States, yet the British government declined to make United States' dollars available to the Iraqi treasury.[52] Since the Anglo-American "Lend-Lease" arrangement – whereby the US Congress could tend or lease defence items, etc to any country vital to US defence – was largely based on Britain's inability to pay for American supplies, Churchill believed that furnishing Iraq with dollars would compromise his position with the Americans. The war brought other strains in the relations between Iraq and Britain. One source of friction concerned the handling of the Iraqi oil, for Britain unilaterally decided to increase its pumping to Haifa, on account of the disruption of shipping lanes in the Mediterranean. Another concerned Iraqi contacts with Japan for the marketing of dates, Iraq's main agricultural produce, which Britain had refused to buy.

Although Newton considered the policies adopted by al-Gaylani's government to be "irritable and dangerous", he could not recommend forcing his resignation "unless he were to oppose coming of British troops or for any other reason the situation became critical".[53] But since the Iraqi government had already accepted allowing passage to British troops, the ambassador had to agree with the assurances of a friend such as Nuri who said that al-Gaylani's seemingly irritating policies did not necessarily reflect "bad faith and ill-will towards the British alliance". What was more assuring was the British confidence in the loyalty of Nuri, the regent, and the chief political leader outside the cabinet, Jamil al-Madfaʿi. Despite his flirtation with the German option, Nuri in particular was moving even closer to the British side. When the high defence council was called to discuss the British demand for severing diplomatic relations with Italy, Nuri recommended that Colonel al-Sabbagh should be invited to the meeting, although he was not a member. Al-Sabbagh's support of the prime minister during the council meeting made Nuri realize that he had lost the army card.[54] Conscious of the unpopularity of his views among the masses, Nuri became almost totally dependent on the British.

In August, the Jordanian Arab Legion arrested two Palestinians at the Iraqi–Jordanian border while they were attempting to enter Transjordan without passports. One of the captured men was found to be in possession of documents that referred to hidden arms' caches in Palestine, in addition to Iraqi military training manuals. Later, they admitted to having received training at al-Rashid military camp, a stronghold of the "Golden Square".[55] Although no evidence existed of the prime minister's involvement in his officers' pro-Palestinian activities, this incident marked a turning-point in the relations between al-Gaylani and the British. In September, C. J. Edmonds discovered that the Iraqi government was seeking the resumption of telegraphic services with Germany and Italy through Tehran. Another troublesome issue came up two months later when the prime minister pardoned the Mosullites convicted of the killing of the British consul-general in the disturbances that followed the death of King Ghazi.[56] With his deeply entrenched social and political background, al-Gaylani was not necessarily pursuing a radically nationalist policy, but was most likely seeking popularity at a time when Arab anti-imperialist feelings were running high. The breaking-point arrived when London received some evidence of Iraqi–German contacts.[57] These contacts were conceived and initiated by the justice minister, Naji Shawkat, with the encouragement of the mufti. Although approved by al-Gaylani, these contacts were merely exploratory in nature and proved to be inconclusive. Neither before Shawkat's approach to the Germans nor after did al-Gaylani plan for a confrontation with the British. His grievous mistake, however, was not to terminate negotiations with the Germans as soon as they proved unproductive, or to bring the issue to public knowledge and let his policy be judged by the people and parliament. But a believer in the guidance of a just ruler would not need to do so!

Rather than adhering to their traditional method of indirect interference, the British adopted a bluntly explicit approach to the situation in an attempt to oust al-Gaylani's government. Newton made a request to the regent for the dismissal of the prime minister. When it became apparent that Abd al-Ilah was unable to effect this, Newton took the matter up directly with al-Gaylani, telling him that the British government had lost confidence in his leadership.[58] By setting a precedent in approving Lampson's removal of 'Ali Mahir in June 1940, the British war cabinet had indicated that it was in the business of clearing the Middle Eastern theatre of unfavourable regimes. But al-Gaylani, backed by army and radical elements inside and outside his cabinet, refused to step down. In mid-December, Nuri al Sa'id presented a memorandum to the cabinet, underlining his disagreement with its foreign policy; thereafter he stopped attending cabinet meetings.[59] Al-Gaylani was also subjected to British-instigated pressure from the American minister in Baghdad, the Saudi monarch, Abd al-'Aziz al-Sa'ud, and the Egyptian prime minister, Husayn Sirri.[60] In the meantime, several attempts were made by Taha al-Hashimi to mediate a compromise allowing for the replacement of the controversial cabinet ministers, or the appointment of a new prime minister, acceptable to the army, the regent, the British and al-Gaylani altogether. Such mediation was to no avail. The British direct intervention provoked strong nationalist reactions, brought the polarization of the Iraqi political scene to the surface and made the removal of al-Gaylani and maintaining stability more difficult than it should have been.

In late January 1941, the regent left Baghdad for al-Diwaniyya, headquarters of the Fourth Division.[61] While mediation efforts continued, Abd al-Ilah began soliciting the support of local governors and senior army officers outside Baghdad for the overthrow of al-Gaylani. The forces loyal to the prime minister were put on alert, while Nuri, backed by al-Madfa'i and the Shi'i leader, Sayyid Abd al-Mahdi, succeeded in rousing the parliament against the government.[62] Since the regent would not agree to dissolve the parliament, and many members of the cabinet as well as the four colonels sought to avoid a bloody confrontation, al-Gaylani presented his resignation.[63] In consultation with Sayyid Muhammad al-Sadr, leader of the upper house and a wise and conciliatory figure, the regent called upon Taha al-Hashimi to form a new government.[64] Taha's closeness to the colonels secured the backing of the army and postponed the crisis to another day.

Taha's government lasted from the beginning of February until 2 April, during which time he was torn between ensuring Iraq's neutrality in the war, satisfying the British demands, and avoiding presenting the officers with reason to interfere in governmental affairs. His position was so impossible that it was soon to become untenable. The new cabinet was largely made up of traditional and pro-British elements, including Tawfiq al-Swaydi for foreign affairs.[65] Although contacts with the Germans were firmly terminated by Taha, London was still not satisfied.

On 12 February, Taha received Colonel William Donavan, the special envoy of the American president. Donavan informed the Iraqi prime minister of the American government's unreserved backing of Britain's war effort, and its determination to ensure its victory. He expressed his hope that Iraq would follow the same policy, implying that American assistance to Iraq was contingent on Iraqi cooperation with the British.[66] Concurrently, London halted the supply of all military spare parts to Iraq and made it absolutely clear that it would not furnish the Iraqi treasury with American dollars.[67] The major British requirements from the government of Taha al-Hashimi were spelled out by Winston Churchill to Sir Kinahan Cornwallis, in preparation for his succession to Newton as His Majesty's ambassador to Iraq, as follows:[68]

> 1. The breaking off of diplomatic relations with Italy. 2. The cessation of all intrigues with the Axis powers and Japan. 3. The proper guidance by the Government of public opinion on the subject of Anglo-Iraqi relations. 4. Elimination from politics of hostile military elements. 5. The encouragement of Palestine political refugees to return to their homes and the removal from official posts, especially in education, of men who are well-known for their openly expressed hostility towards Great Britain. 6. The effective control of the Mufti's activities.

These requirements were again conveyed in terse terms by Anthony Eden (who had been back at the Foreign Office since December 1940) to the Iraqi foreign minister, Tawfiq al-Swaydi,[69] when they met in Cairo on 6 March. Such requirements were obviously beyond the capacity of a reconciliatory figure like al-Hashimi to meet, and, if implemented, were certain to exacerbate the Iraqi political situation even further. But Churchill, at that critical time of the war, would see Iraq only in terms of the European war situation not in terms of the complex reality of Iraq itself.

In the face of this tremendous pressure, Taha realized that he had reached a crossroads. He invited the senior army officers to a meeting in his house and told them that Iraq had no choice but to agree to the British requests.[70] On 26 March, Taha ordered Kamil Shabib, commander of the Baghdad-based first division, to exchange his position with that of Ibrahim al-Rawi of the Diwaniyya-based fourth division. He further instructed Salah al-Din al-Sabbagh, commander of the third division, to transfer his headquarters from Baghdad to Jallula'.[71] The four colonels, sensing the approaching danger, decided, after deliberating with their allies, the mufti, al-Gaylani, Naji Shawkat and Yunis al-Sab'awi, not to comply with the orders of Taha al-Hashimi. On the evening of 1 April, they moved to establish their control in the capital city of Baghdad. Al-Hashimi was politely told that the only way out of the crisis was to cooperate with al-Gaylani, or he must resign. While the prime minister sat to write his letter of resignation, the regent was quietly leaving his Palace on his way out of Baghdad.[72]

What the colonels feared was in fact real. In the last week of March, the regent proposed to the British to "turn out" al-Hashimi's government if it did not comply with the British demands. In order to succeed in his move, he requested the backing of the British. But aware of the difficulties surrounding such a scheme in terms of military preparations, Newton argued against prompt action.[73] The ambassador believed that the British Middle East Command would not be able to spare a sizeable military contingent to be stationed in Iraq. His view, however, was overruled by none other than the British commander-in-chief Middle East. On 30 March, Britain's Middle East command recommended that action should be taken in Iraq "to bring about change in Government or at least rupture with Italy without delay".[74] The removal of the Italians from Baghdad was seen as particularly urgent in view of Syria's fall to the French Vichy government. It was also underlined that the carrying out of "forward policy" in Iraq must be aimed at checking the mufti's activities and the development of anti-British feelings in the Iraqi army. The British military mistakenly believed that the regent enjoyed strong political support inside the cabinet and among leading Iraqi politicians, and that he "could count on Shiah support against [the] army whereas army clique dare not risk sectarian split". On the next day, the Chief-of-Staff Committee met in London to discuss the line of action to be recommended in the light of various dispatches from Baghdad and Cairo.[75] It concluded, "a forward policy in Iraq was now desirable with the object of causing a rupture with Italy and of upsetting the extremist clique, which included the Mufti and the Golden Square." The committee agreed that the occasion was opportune, but the timing of action and the methods to be employed were to be left to the people on the spot. Since the new British ambassador, Cornwallis, was expected in Iraq on 1 April, the general feeling in London was to give him a few days before a specific set of measures could be described. The coup of 2 April in Baghdad put a halt to this line of planning.

The Arab-Palestinian dimension

The precarious political situation of late 1930s' Iraq was paralleled by Arab and Palestinian confusion and uncertainty with regard to Arab unity and the future of Palestine and Syria. Several hundred Palestinian political refugees preceded, or followed, the mufti to Iraq. Known revolt organizers, rebels and pan-Arab activists, such as Akram Zu'aytir, 'Arif Abd al-Raziq, Wasif Kamal, Mamduh al-Sukhun, Abd al-Qadir al-Husayni, Rasim al-Khalidi, Dawud al-Husayni, 'Izz al-Din al-Shawwa and many others, were received with open arms by the Iraqi Arabists in the military and civil institutions of the government, where they found prompt employment.[76] Their influence on education and the mass media added a new element to the volatile Iraqi situation. After the French crack-down on the Syrian nationalists in the spring of 1939, many Syrian pan-Arabists followed their Palestinian counterparts to Iraq.[77] The assassination of Abd al-Rahman al-Shahbandar in July 1940 brought another wave of Syrian nationalists to Iraq, headed by Jamil Mardam and Sa'd-Allah al-Jabiri.[78] But Arab convergence on Iraq and the turning of the Iraqi capital into a centre for Arab activities could not liberate the Arab movement from bewilderment and disorientation. The failings of the past two decades were now giving rise to more radical, élitist, and detached conceptualizations of Arabism, conflicting projects for Arab unity, divided positions on the future of Palestine and uncertainty with regard to relations with Britain and the Axis powers.

A few months after the initial Arab rejection of the British Palestinian policy, the governments of Egypt (under 'Ali Mahir), and of Iraq (under Nuri al-Sa'id) looked more prepared to deal with Britain on the basis of the White Paper. Nuri exerted unrelenting pressure on the mufti to declare his support for the allies in exchange for some pro-Arab clarifications of the White Paper. Upon the outbreak of World War II, the Iraqi premier embarked on a frantic effort to bring about a joint Arab position on Palestine as well as on the issue of Arab unity. Three basic assumptions underlined Nuri's motivation for this enterprise. The first was his belief that the war, and Britain's need for Arab support, offered a unique opportunity for the extraction of substantial concessions from London.[79] The second was Baghdad's increasing apprehension of a German-supported Iranian attack on Iraq, or a Turkish invasion of Syria, especially if the French were defeated or forced to evacuate forces from Syria.[80] The third was the widening opposition of the Arab radical forces in Iraq to Nuri's pro-British policy.

In November 1939, Nuri visited Cairo where he discussed with Mahir the idea of a joint Arab appeal to the British government, and the conclusion of a treaty of alliance between Egypt and Iraq.[81] Nuri envisaged the appeal as calling for a general amnesty in Palestine, the return of the mufti to Jerusalem, and a speedy implementation of article ten of the White Paper, whereby a gradual empowerment of the Palestinians would conclude with independence after a transitional period. Mahir, on the other hand, cared little for the mufti. Besides favouring the White Paper, Mahir was also disposed to agree with the opinions of 'Awni Abd al-Hadi, who was becoming an outspoken critic of the mufti. Equally important to the Egyptian premier was to arrest the deterioration of his relations with Sir Miles Lampson over the latter's demand for Egypt to declare war on Germany, a step that Mahir's government was not prepared to take. In order to prove his moderation to Lampson and to illustrate Egypt's leading Arab role, Mahir proposed a less comprehensive formula for the joint appeal, according to which the Palestinians would be asked to cooperate with Britain in return for a general amnesty (with no reference to the mufti's return) and the lifting of punitive measures.[82] Although the two premiers could not reach an agreement on the substance of the proposed statement, and Mahir subsequently failed to enlist Saudi backing for his position, he went ahead and issued the appeal.[83] The British responded by reintroducing civil courts in Palestine and permitting a selected number of political exiles to return, a response too limited to create an opening in the Palestinian deadlock.

The first attempt at formulating a united Arab position was obviously a failure. What aggravated this failure was Mahir's noncommittal approach to Nuri's treaty of alliance between Egypt and Iraq.[84] The irony, of course, was in the wide gap between the Arab perception of Mahir's government and the reality. Under Mahir, Egypt was ruled by a cabinet that included M. A. 'Alluba and Abd al-Rahman 'Azzam, the well-established Arab-Islamists, 'Aziz al-Misri, the Ottoman Arabist officer and founder of al-'Ahad, and Muhammad Salih Harb, the new president of the YMMS and former pro-Ottoman army officer. Besides maintaining a high Arab-Islamic profile in his cabinet, Mahir had strong ties with the Palace, the Ikhwan, the YMMS and Young Egypt. The Arab-Islamic image of this government, which encouraged Nuri to seek an alliance with Egypt, was eventually to lead to Mahir being forced out of office by Sir Miles Lampson when the Egyptian government stopped short of declaring war on the Axis.[85] But Mahir, like most of the Egyptian prime ministers before him, was divided between his pursuit of a leading Arab role, and the need to accommodate the British demands. Only after being ousted in June 1940 would Mahir turn into a fervent crusader for Arab coordination.

The difficulties that were to face the Arab nationalist movement at those crucial times stemmed also from the unexpected change in the British government, which resulted in the formation of a new cabinet, headed by Churchill, in May 1940. Neither on Arab unity nor on the Palestine question was Churchill prepared to respond to Arab wishes. On Arab unity, Churchill was committed to the policy ironed out by the Foreign Office in September 1939. Since the issue was raised repeatedly by Nuri al-Sa'id, Sir Herbert Samuel and the Palestinian delegation to the London Conference, in connection with forging a solution for the Palestinian entanglement, Lacy Baggallay of the Foreign Office Eastern Department made it his task to prepare a detailed memorandum on Arab unity. In this memorandum, Baggallay admitted that most of the present boundaries of the Arab countries – except those of Egypt and, to a lesser extent, Iraq – were not inherently permanent. He also noted the historical, cultural, political and economic developments that strengthened the movement for Arab federation. But following in the footsteps of Rendel, Baggallay listed several elements that hindered the realization of Arab unity: Arab rivalries; the French opposition; the Turkish latent ambitions in Syria and northern Iraq, and, more importantly, the interests of Britain. In order to safeguard its lines of communication and oil supply, Britain saw that its position in the Arab world would be more secure if it had to deal with several small and weak states rather than with a unified state. In conclusion, Baggallay suggested a rather complex, but safe approach for dealing with the issue of Arab unity. He first stressed that, even if the other obstacles were cleared, Britain should not encourage or promote Arab unity. Yet, in the light of the growing movement for Arab federation, Britain should not actively oppose such a movement either, but should declare that the initiation of Arab federation "should and must come from the Arabs themselves". Baggallay also indicated that if Britain was to face a situation in which Arab unity became an unavoidable option, it "should ensure that the ensuing federation or union was friendly to Great Britain".[86]

Because of the outbreak of war, Baggallay's memorandum was not presented to the war cabinet, but was printed and distributed to various concerned departments and outposts. Since no fundamental challenge was directed at its arguments, this memorandum became, in effect, the guiding light of British official policy on Arab unity until Eden's too-little, too-late statement at the Mansion House on 29 May 1941. The problem, however, was that less than three months before Eden's speech and while the situation in Iraq was clearly deteriorating towards an Arab–British confrontation, Churchill instructed his newly appointed ambassador in Iraq to adhere literally to the ambivalent terms of Baggallay's memorandum.[87] On the Palestinian question, Churchill was even more inflexible. He was a firm supporter of the Zionist movement, and was strongly in favour of the idea of establishing a Jewish state in Palestine. His dislike of the White Paper was intense; he believed firmly that Britain should neither respond to the Arab demands for clarifications of the White Paper nor try to carry its policies to their logical end. For Churchill, the Arabs would understand only the language of force, and Britain's position in the Arab world could be secured only by British victories on the battle fronts, not diplomacy and concessions.[88] These views were highly instrumental in bringing the Arab–British disagreement on Palestine to breaking-point, especially after the abrupt termination of the controversial Newcombe mission in August 1940.

Colonel Stewart Newcombe, the British friend of the Arabs, reached Iraq in July 1940. His mission was conceived by Lord Lloyd, a prominent orientalist, former high commissioner in Egypt and the colonial secretary of the war cabinet. Lloyd, a less inflexible figure, with different views on the Arabs and Palestine, became aware of the Arab pressure, supported by Britain's main representatives in the Middle East, for a change of policy on Palestine. Eager to confront the Germans' successful exploitation of the Palestinian question, Lloyd decided to dispatch Newcombe to Baghdad to explore unofficially areas of understanding with the mufti.[89] Negotiations between Newcombe and the Baghdad-based Palestinians, with the active involvement of Nuri al-Sa'id, reached a point where Jamal al-Husayni initialled an agreement on the White Paper which implicitly indicated Jamal's acquiescence to the mufti's exclusion. Though the mufti first responded to the agreement with anger, he later yielded to the position taken by Jamal. At this critical stage, Newcombe was ordered back to Cairo, leaving behind an impression amongst the Palestinians and the

Iraqis that an understanding had been reached.[90] During the negotiations with Newcombe, Nuri committed the Iraqi government to declaring war on the Axis powers and dispatching one or two Iraqi divisions to join the British war effort in Egypt, after a final agreement on Palestine had been reached. In August, Nuri visited Egypt to present General Wavell with his proposal and conclude talks with British officials in Cairo.[91] To his astonishment, he found that Newcombe's mission had been terminated.[92] It was clearly the decision of Churchill not to reactivate the White Paper. Nuri's return to Iraq empty-handed was regarded by the mufti and the Iraqi pan-Arabists as the ultimate validation of their distrust of Britain.

Yet, the hardening British attitude was going side by side with Arab ineptitude and confusion, embedded in divisions of the ruling élite and the regional state's tendency to preserve its own entity. At the outbreak of war, the Arab movement for unity was infused with a strong sense of urgency. But while the existence of the Arabs as a political whole had not been questioned by any of the political schools in the later Ottoman empire, "the division of the post-war settlement called it in question".[93] This divided reality was now expressed in Arab official policies, and in the political attitudes of pan-Arabist leaders.

Having been rebuffed by the Woodhead Commission, Amir Abdullah turned his sights on Syria, the other element in his unrepressed dream for expanding his rule. Since Abdullah was aware of the republican, pro-Saudi, and anti-Hashemite sentiments in the National Bloc, he focused on enlisting the support of Abd al-Rahman al-Shahbandar and of the restive but powerful Druze leaders of Jabal Huran.[94] With the death of King Ghazi in 1939, the fall of the National Bloc government and the defeat of the Palestinian revolt, Abdullah's position looked stronger than ever. But to gain the Syrian throne he still had other obstacles to overcome. His support in Syria was never adequate to counterbalance the National Bloc and the large anti-Hashemite camp, nor was it so compelling as to make him a serious candidate in the eyes of the French. Similarly, Abdullah failed to attract British backing for his scheme, for the British were not prepared to contemplate such a radical change in the regional balance; nor could they see the wisdom of antagonizing the French to entertain Abdullah's ambitions.[95]

Moreover, Abdullah's Syrian scheme faced strong opposition from both the Iraqi and Saudi governments. The Saudi position was as firm as ever in its resistance to any attempt by Abdullah to extend his rule beyond the borders of Transjordan.[96] On the other hand, the return of Nuri to power reactivated the quest for an Arab federation, led by Iraq and embracing Syria in the larger sense. Nuri presented his project during the London Conference on Palestine in March 1939, when he again tried to impress upon the British officials how the emergence of the Arab federation would lead to a solution to the Palestinian entanglement.[97] The deterioration of the Syrian political situation during 1939 encouraged Nuri to renew his efforts in Syria, especially as the Syrian question was eliciting a strong reaction from the Iraqi Arabist circles and the people at large.[98] To avoid an inevitable collision with Abdullah, Nuri endeavoured to induce him to call off his activities in Syria and focus instead on a Jordanian–Palestinian unity, offering to bring about a reconciliation between him and the mufti.[99] Nuri pointed to the damage that the Iraqi–Jordanian rivalry could inflict on the Syrian and Arab future, but Abdullah was in no mood to concur with Nuri's advice.

While the outbreak of the war gave more incentives to both Nuri and Abdullah to intensify their efforts in Syria, another enterprise was being launched by the mufti and other radical pan-Arab circles. Sources are not particularly clear on the exact nature of the secretive activities and networking of the pan-Arabists during that period. Yet, it is perhaps safe to conclude that an attempt at creating a pan-Arab organization was under way from the late 1930s onwards. Upon his arrival in Iraq, the mufti was involved with Shukri al-Quwwatli in the formation of a pan-Arab committee to coordinate the struggle for independence in Syria and Palestine. The efforts in this direction seem to have continued in 1940, since sources close to the mufti indicate that a pan-Arab organization (Hizb al-'Umma al-'Arabiyya or Party of the Arab Nation) was in existence in 1940, led by the mufti.[100] This party was perhaps a front for a much deeper endeavour for the creation of a pan-Arab organized body. The development of the mufti's anti-imperialist attitude, especially after his escape from Jerusalem, attracted to his side many of the enterprising pan-Arab activists, such as Wasif Kamal, Munir al-Rayyis, Kazim al-Sulh and Yunis al-Sab'awi. This group had been extensively involved in underground pan-Arab networking since the early 1930s, and in the founding of the NAL in 1933. The principal scheme of the new generation of pan-Arabists was to infiltrate existing Arab nationalist organizations and work secretly from within towards linking the Arab political arena. Gradually, however, they seem to have come to realize that Arab political divisions were much deeper than they had earlier perceived.

Sometime in 1937 a group of Palestinian, Syrian, and Lebanese pan-Arabists, including Muhammad ʿAli Hamada, Hani al-Sulh, ʿAdil ʿUsayran, Kazim and Taqii al-Din al-Sulh (Lebanon), Wasif Kamal, Mamduh al-Sukhun and Farid Yaʿish (Palestine), Qustantin Zurayq, Farid Zayn al-Din, Fuʾad Mufarraj, Munir al-Rayyis, Fahmi al-Mahaiyri, Abd al-Rahman al-Jukhdar, Musalam al-Hafiz and Saʿid Fattah al-Imam (Syria), met in Beirut. Out of their discussion, the Arab Nationalist Party (al-Hizb al-Qawmi al-ʿArabi), a secretive pan-Arab organization, was launched.[101] It was decided that the party would be led by a committee comprising Kazim al-Sulh, Zayn al-Din, Kamal, Zurayq and Mufarraj. The party's founders renewed their contacts with their Iraqi pan-Arabist acquaintances and succeeded in recruiting Yunis al-Sabʿawi, Siddiq Shanshal, Muhammad Hasan Salman and Musa al-Shabandar, together with the four colonels. While the organization expanded to Transjordan, it attracted new members in Palestine and Syria. One of the latter group was the lawyer Jalal al-Sayyid,[102] scion of a powerful family in the eastern Syrian city of Dayr al-Zur, who emerged in 1942 as one of the early founders of the Baʿth Party. With the Arab defeat of 1948, the circles of the Arab Nationalist Party became the fertile soil from which the Arab Nationalist Movement (Harakat al-Qawmyyin al-ʿArab) would grow.

It appears that, in 1940, this group of young radicals was looking for a figurehead to guide it towards the formation of a pan-Arabist organization, a role that the mufti looked highly suited for.[103] How successful the mufti and the radical pan-Arabists were in their organizational project is difficult to determine. In the face of Arab inter-state rivalries and the fixedness of the imperialist system, the aspiration for a pan-Arabist organization, forcing its way towards Arab unity, was vastly ambitious. What the mufti and his young radical associates were involved in was principally a movement of opposition forces. Apart from Iraq, where the scheme attracted some of the most powerful elements, the Arab ruling classes showed no interest in resorting to a radical pan-Arabist course. Although Arabism was now the dominant ideology for the majority of the Arabs on both sides of the power divide, the ruling forces were still largely faithful to their relations with the Western powers. It was on

London and Paris that their hopes were pinned for the achievement of Arab unity, a unity that the ruler saw as a means to augment and expand his domains and preserve his powers.

Beyond the meeting of the young radicals with elements of the old guard, such as Hajj Amin al-Husayni and Rashid 'Ali al-Gaylani, there was another set of paradoxes. One was related to the socio-political complex which underlined their sense of mission and set the limits for their political actions. For the older Arab-Islamists, with their notable and Ottoman background, power was understood mainly in its local, regional terms; while for the young pan-Arabists, with their exclusive vision of Arabism and modest social origins, Arab unity was embraced with determination, idealism and uncompromised devotion. If the radical anti-imperialist politics was, for that small faction of pan-Arabist notables, rather contingent, for the newly emerging generation it was a constituent part of its ideological formation. These inherent tensions coloured the rise of radical pan-Arabism with frustration, desperation and failure to develop a coherent agenda, features that characterized most of the pan-Arabist attempt to present some answers to the questions of Syria, Palestine and Arab unity.

The Syrian nationalists, led now by Shukri al-Quwwatli, remnants of the NAL, and the Arab Club (al-Nadi al-'Arabi), a newly-founded pan-Arabist forum in Damascus, maintained various levels of contact with the mufti and the active pan-Arabists in Baghdad.[104] But whether they were all party to the mufti's endeavour for forming a pan-Arab organization is unclear. The murder of Abd al-Rahman al-Shahbandar was perhaps an indication of the level of coordination, as well as of the frustration, that shaped the relations between Damascus and Baghdad. In June 1940, against the background of his intensifying challenge to the National Bloc and the conspicuous promotion of Abdullah's scheme in Syria, al-Shahbandar was assassinated in Damascus. Although the assassins were apprehended, the French authorities suspected a wider plot involving leaders of the National Bloc.[105] The latter were eventually cleared of complicity, but close associates of al-Shahbandar, especially his brother-in-law, Nazih al Mu'ayyad al-'Azm, claimed that the plot to assassinate their leader was hatched in Baghdad under the supervision of the mufti and in coordination with Mardam and al-Quwwatli in Damascus.[106] This claim was clearly accepted by the British officials in Syria.

In the political climate of 1940, al-Shahbandar was considered the strongest and most credible link in the evolving alliance that embraced his party, Amir Abdullah and the Nashashibists of Palestine. Besides its bearing on the local nationalist rivalry in Syria, his elimination was, therefore, a severe blow to Abdullah and his shaky schemes to establish Syrian unity under his throne. In any event, al-Shahbandar's assassination marked the beginning of a period of deep political polarization in the Arab arena. Echoing the Palestinian and Iraqi internal divisions, leaders of al-Shahbandar's party approached the British officials in Syria for financial assistance, offering to cooperate in combating the influence of al-Quwwatli and the mufti and their pro-Axis propaganda.[107] Even within the National Bloc, Mardam and Sa'd-Allah al-Jabri dissociated themselves from al-Quwwatli, the mufti and the Iraqi pan-Arabists, and moved to assert a moderate, pro-British image.[108] Beyond this chaotic loss of direction was a more damaging feature of the pan-Arabist politics – the lack of a coherent agenda.

Concurrent with the arrest of the Iraqi-trained Palestinian group at the Iraqi–Jordanian border Syrian elements were reportedly being recruited in preparation for the resumption of the Palestinian revolt.[109] Further indications of the same activities could also be discerned in some intercepted correspondence between Emile al-Ghuri, the pro-mufti Palestinian leader resident in Cairo, and Baghdad.[110] Behind these moves was the mufti's belief that, despite the collapse of the Palestinian movement, the Arab strategy should begin with a Palestinian uprising against the British. From Palestine, the pan-Arab revolt should then spread to Transjordan and Syria, culminating with Arab liberation and unity. This view was evidently in disagreement with that of the majority of other pan-Arabists in Iraq.

Upon the fall of France in June 1940 the Syrian leader, 'Adil al-'Azma, the Iraqi defence minister, Taha al-Hashimi, and the Syrian, Fawzi al-Qawuqji, called for the igniting of a Syrian revolt backed by Iraq, with the view of forcing the independence of Syria and Iraqi–Syrian unity. The influential Iraqi army officers, led by Salah al-Din al-Sabbagh, were also prepared to back this project.[111] Since the French administration in Syria was now turned to the Vichy government, the political conditions were considered favourable for Arab action. The British military in the Middle East, which looked with deep apprehension at the inability of the Vichy authorities to check German activities in Syria, was expected to welcome such a scheme. And even if the British objected, it was thought unlikely that they would take action to stop it. According to al-Gaylani, the British ambassador in Baghdad repeatedly hinted at an active Iraqi role in Syria.[112] Although never translated into an official policy by the war cabinet, an Iraqi intervention in Syria was a matter of deliberation in London right until after the outbreak of hostilities between Iraq and Britain.[113] It was envisaged that the involvement of Iraq in Syria would simultaneously secure Palestine (the most likely host of the British Middle East Command in the event of withdrawal from Egypt), and satisfy the Iraqi quest for Arab unity.

However, unable to discern the implications of an active Iraqi role in Syria and the potential emergence of Iraqi–Syrian unity, the mufti rejected the "Syria first" idea. Furthermore, the mufti used his influence to turn Salah al-Din al-Sabbagh and the army officers, whose opinion was the most decisive factor in the discussions, against the project.[114] Viewed simply, this attitude on the part of the mufti could be explained in the context of his by then incurable distrust of the British or of his growing relations with the Axis powers. But neither explanation offers a satisfactory answer. In the summer of 1940 hopes were not completely lost of arriving at an agreement with the British, while no tangible results had yet arisen from the Arab contacts with the Axis. A more convincing explanation is that the mufti, in his blind focusing on the Palestinian situation, believed that the Syrian option would entail British–Iraqi understanding and that this might consequently lead to Iraq deserting the Palestinians or the shelving of the Palestine question. Although totally immersed in pan-Arab politics, the mufti failed to realize the eventual bearing that an Iraqi–Syrian unity might have on the future of Palestine.

The disagreement over Syria was exacerbated by wider Arab disagreement over Arab unity. Sometime prior to the arrival of Colonel Newcombe in Baghdad in July 1940 the Iraqi minister in Egypt, Tahsin al-'Askari, was approached by 'Ali Mahir, 'Azzam and 'Alluba (leaders of the deposed Egyptian government) with the idea of convening a pan-Arab conference to forge a united Arab view towards the Axis powers.[115] This idea received a favourable response in Iraq, especially from the anti-British quarters, and was turned into a main press item with the encouragement of al-Gaylani and al-Hashimi.[116] Nuri al Sa'id, conscious of the great risks emanating from Mahir's proposal, reformulated the conference idea into a project for discussing the whole issue of Arab unity. His vision, as it was defined to C. J. Edmonds, was based on the establishment of an Arab confederation, embracing Iraq, Transjordan, Palestine and, if possible, Saudi Arabia. In practical terms, Nuri conceived a closer union between these countries to be achieved in the following manner:[117]

> a. Extension of the Anglo-Iraqi alliance include Transjordan, Palestine and, if King Abdul Aziz agreed, Saudiya. b. Removal of all customs barriers for produce and manufactures. c. Unified Public Instruction (without prejudice to Jewish cultural autonomy in Palestine). d. Unified currency with currency notes in the name of the confederation. e. Common system of military training. f. Development of inter-State communications by coordinated programme, and so on.

In addition to his expectation of British backing, Nuri assumed that the White Paper could be promptly implemented to allow for gradual transfer of power to the Palestinians. He confirmed to Edmonds that the mufti and the entire Palestinian leadership were now in agreement with the White Paper, including its provisions for a JNH. To illustrate the advantages that his proposal would carry for the Jews of Palestine, the Iraqi foreign minister indicated that the Jews were poised to gain most from the abolition of internal customs' barriers. Nuri expressed the view that he, as well as the Iraqi government, believed that, once circumstances allowed it, Syria would also join the confederation. As the Iraqis were still deliberating their policy towards Syria, one idea emerged that the Syrians should proceed unilaterally with the formation of a nationalist government, in or outside Syria, supported by Iraq.

Nuri's project was more modest than the vision of Arab unity had ever been. It struck a careful balance between the existing reality and the aspirations for unity, representing perhaps a psychological retreat in the face of the regional state. However, together with the Arab conference idea, Nuri's proposal was given the cold shoulder by London. He was informed of Britain's adherence to its existing policy in Palestine, the official line being that a full implementation of the White Paper could be attended to only at the end of the war, and that Britain had no intention of playing an active role in bringing about an Arab confederation. The question of Arab unity, Halifax reiterated, was a matter for the main Arab governments to agree upon.[118] Abdullah's rejection of Palestinian–Jordanian unity with Iraq had already been voiced. The Saudis, cautious as they had always been, initiated an exchange of correspondence with the British to ascertain their position on the Iraqi initiative. Once they realized that Nuri lacked British support, they vigorously attacked both his proposal for Arab unity and the idea of an Arab conference, declaring that the Arab future was for Britain to decide when the war was over.[119]

In Egypt, where Nuri anticipated that the Egyptian participation in the projected Arab conference would lend powerful moral support to his scheme, he was rebuffed by the new premier, Hasan Sabri.[120] The fate of his predecessor taught Sabri not to venture into areas not particularly close to the British heart. Nuri was told, to the enormous pleasure of Lampson, that Egypt was no longer interested in Arab affairs but was ready to extend its technical expertise for developing the irrigation system in Iraq. By the end of September 1940 the scheme was totally off the Arab political agenda. During al-Hashimi's short term in office, the issues of Palestine and Arab unity were again raised by the Iraqi premier with the British ambassador, but the tone was rather casual.[121] All sides were by then fully aware of their respective positions.

Under these conditions of nationalist failures, strategic confusion and political deadlock, an Arab anti-British alliance was to emerge from the convergence of Arab nationalist groupings of the young radicals and a group of Arab-Islamist leaders with a notable and Ottoman background. Despite ideological differences and social disparity, Arab-Islamic leaders such as al-Gaylani, al-Quwwatli, al-Husayni, Naji al-Swaydi and Naji Shawkat, were joined by al-Sab'awi, Wasif Kamal, the NAL and Arab Nationalist Movement activists. While the radical Arab nationalists were mainly of middle-class background and were new arrivals to the Arab arena, lacking the mass following and a state apparatus, their alliance with the anti-imperialist elements of the Arab-Islamic old guard seemed to provide them with power, influence and legitimacy. For both, the West was no longer seen in terms of the early reformists' admiration, fascination and synthetic view, but rather in the shadow of imperialist atrocities, domination and collusion with the Zionist project. Yet, unable to resolve the dilemma of defining the West's limits and position with regard to the Arab present, the Arab radicals brought themselves to believe that the West could be defeated by another West, and that the Axis powers could become safer and more just allies than the dominant imperialists. This development, which brought Arab internal divisions to an unprecedented low, reflected the overwhelming desperation that enveloped the Arab interwar generation in its last attempt to account for the collapsing world and shattered aspirations that it had espoused.

The Arabs and the Axis powers

The development of Arab relations with the Axis powers was in many respects the result of the deterioration of the Arab ideological and political views of the West rather than the evolution of a positive Arab view of the Axis. Germany was, of course, an ally of the Ottoman state during World War I, but only a few Arabists were still recalling this alliance with special sentiments in the 1930s. Amongst those who came to be known for their pro-German views were Shakib Arslan, who returned to exile in Switzerland after a short sojourn in Syria in 1937, as well as 'Aziz 'Ali al-Misri and Muhammad Salih Harb, ministers of 'Ali Mahir's deposed government. Al-Misri was a senior officer in the Ottoman army until 1915 and his fascination with Germany was essentially of military origin. This fascination, however, posed no hindrance to the cultivation of amicable relations between him and the British when he was briefly appointed by Sharif Husayn to command forces of the Arab revolt, or later during his military career in Egypt.[122] Salih Harb was a pro-Ottoman officer in the Egyptian border guards who defected to the Ottoman side in the Libyan liberated zone during World War I.[123] Upon the deterioration of relations between Mahir and the British, both Harb and al-Misri seemed predisposed to develop a pro-German outlook based on the belief that a German victory would lead to the freeing of Egypt from British domination. Arslan was perhaps a different case. Germany was Arslan's first place of exile after the Ottoman defeat, where he and his idol, Anwar Pasha, established ties with German Foreign Office officials.[124] But these ties were of little, if any, relevance to the Arab interwar movement, first because they were of marginal importance to German politics, and second because of the absence of a German Arab policy, even after the Nazis' rise to power.

Arab expressions of admiration for the German model of the 1930s were equally limited to a small circle of Arab intellectuals.[125] For these Arabists, it was the efficiency of the Nazi state, its ability to liberate Germany from the constraints of the Versailles Peace Treaty and to salvage the German spirit from the defeat and chaotic times of the 1920s, that had the greatest positive impact. The new Arab intellectuals, reacting to the endemic political instability of the Arab states, tended to believe that Arab resurgence and progress could be accomplished only through the reassertion of state power. Also related to the internalization of the German model by some Arab intellectuals was the rise of the exclusivist vision of Arab nationalism. Implicit in the over-Arabization of Arabism was a fanatical affirmation of an imagined absolute loyalty to the Arab *umma*, which reflected the increasing suspicion on the part of the Arab radicals of the non-Arab minorities. The pan-Arabist celebration of the Iraqi military's suppression of the Assyrian revolt in 1933 signalled the beginning of a trend that reached its climax in the Ba'th Party's covenant whereby founders of the party envisaged the expulsion of non-Arab minorities if they proved disloyal to the Arab nation.[126] But the Arab ideological scene was too complex to be translated in terms of fascination with German nationalism and the state model. Despite their deepening opposition to the imperialist powers, the new Arab intellectuals were by and large more exposed to Franco-British culture and political thought than to their German counterparts. What came to make a difference was the convergence of the Italo-German political encroachment, spearheaded by an aggressive propaganda campaign, and the deepening of Arab nationalist anti-imperialist and anti-Zionist feelings.

To be sure, Italian penetration of the Arab world preceded German interest by several years. A late entrant to the arena, Italy first expressed its ambition to join the imperialist club in a body of literature, journals and imperialist cultural societies.[127] In its search for a share in the economic spoils of imperialism and for national aggrandizement, Fascist Italy saw itself as the reincarnation of the Roman empire and the inheritor of its domain.[128] Not surprisingly, the Mediterranean world would become the primary target of the Italian imperialist enterprise. In September 1930 Italy's campaign to consolidate and expand its domination of Libya reached a dramatic point with the capture of Shaykh 'Umar al-Mukhtar, the Libyan resistance leader. The subsequent execution of al-Mukhtar and widespread Italian atrocities in Libya generated strong Arab and Islamic reactions. One of the most active Arabists in the anti-Italian movement was Shakib Arslan.[129] Yet, a few years later, Arslan's desperate search for a Western ally would lead into an astonishing shift in his views of Italy.

From the beginning of the 1930s, the Italians adopted a visible Arab-Islamic policy, aimed at dislodging their main European opponents from the Mediterranean basin. *L'Italia Musulman* was a policy of "peaceful" and cheap expansion that envisioned an empire built with the support and consent of the Mediterranean peoples, Arabs and Muslims. Inaugurating this novel imperialist approach, the Italian king paid a visit to Egypt in 1933, which was meant to signal Italy's friendship and respect for the Arabs and Muslims.[130] In the following year, the Italian foreign ministry marked the advent of wireless-broadcasting power by launching the Arabic service of Radio Bari.[131] The main themes of Radio Bari's propaganda were the glorification of modern Italy, support of the Arab national struggle against the French and the British, and the highlighting of Italy's preparedness to assist the Arab liberation movement. In late 1934 and early 1935, Rome was the venue for an Italian-backed Eastern Student Conference, through which Mussolini's government sought to penetrate and orchestrate Muslim and Arab nationalist youth movements. This classic game of imperialist rivalry attracted the attention of a few Arab-Islamic activists, most notably Shakib Arslan and his aide and friend, Ihsan al-Jabiri. In a widely resonating and highly controversial move, Arslan and al-Jabiri met Mussolini in February 1934.[132] Faced with angry reactions from the Libyan nationalists and pro-British Arab circles, Arslan justified his step in terms of attempting to improve conditions in Libya and enlist Italian support for the Arab national struggle.

Although Arslan's reply to his critics was not particularly convincing, the Italian option was beginning to look more appealing for certain Arabs after the failure of Britain and the League of Nations in stopping the Italian conquest of Abyssinia in 1935–6. In these conditions, secret contacts were initiated between Hajj Amin al-Husayni and the Italian consul in Jerusalem in 1937, prior to the mufti's escape to Lebanon.[133] Another Arab leader who was suspected of establishing links with the Italians was the leader of the Ikhwan, Hasan al-Banna.[134] Yet, the expediency and pragmatism which shaped some Arabs' view of Italy could not conceal the reality of Italy's threats to the Arab world. The Italian forces were after all still occupying Libya and Abyssinia, while their ambitions in Egypt and Tunisia, together with their penetration of Yemen and approaches to Saudi Arabia, were becoming too ominously conspicuous to be ignored. It was, therefore, to Germany that the Arab nationalists would look in their search for a Western ally in the struggle against the West. Primarily, attempts at reaching out to Germany stemmed from the deepening Arab concern at the rapid increase of German Jewish immigration to Palestine.

Shortly after the Nazis' rise to power in Germany, the mufti twice met Heinrich Wolf, the German consul in Jerusalem, in March and April 1933. The mufti spoke approvingly of the Nazis' Jewish policies, particularly of the anti-Jewish boycott in Germany. Yet, especially in the second meeting, the mufti, along with other Palestinian personalities present at the meeting, tried to impress upon the German consul the Palestinian demand for the termination of Jewish emigration from Germany to Palestine.[135] The mufti's approach to Wolf was probably motivated by the mixed feelings that Nazi Germany elicited amongst the Palestinians. The Nazis, on the one hand, were known for their anti-Jewish ideology; on the other hand, however, their ascendance led to a significant increase in German Jewish immigration to Palestine. Germany was not yet seen as a world power, nor as a possible anti-British ally. In 1933, and well until after the outbreak of the Palestinian general strike in April 1936, the mufti's relations with the British mandate authorities were still fairly normal. At any rate, the mufti's approach to Wolf was of no avail.

The Nazi racist ideology, coupled with a foreign policy based on the strategy of seeking an understanding with Britain, made the Nazi regime largely disinterested in Arab affairs. Indeed, Hitler's Germany saw its vital sphere of interest to be in the Soviet and East European steppes rather than the Arab East. This German disinterest in the Arab question was translated into a German pro-Zionist policy, leading to the signing of the *Haavara* (Transfer) agreement of August 1933 with the Zionists, which regulated and facilitated Jewish emigration from Germany to Palestine and gave the Zionists a monopoly over German–Palestinian trade,[136] and in September 1936 into an understanding between Hitler and Mussolini which granted the Italians a free hand in the Mediterranean basin and the Arab world.[137] No significant change would be effected in German Arab policy until the summer of 1938.

Following the conflagration of the Palestinian general strike in 1936, the Arab chamber of commerce in Jerusalem submitted a petition to the German consul, urging a revision of the *Haavara* agreement and the opening of German trade to the Arabs. In view of the Palestinian strike and the Arab nationalist attempts to impose an economic boycott on the Jews, the Palestinian petition warned that the continuation of the Zionist monopoly of trade with Germany would result in a Palestinian boycott of German goods.[138] But despite the support rendered to the

Palestinian petition by Consul Döhle, Berlin made no move to revise the terms of the *Haavara* agreement.

Intermittently, Berlin was to come under pressure from German diplomats in the Arab world, who were witnessing the increasing radicalization of the Arab political scene and what appeared to be an opportunity for Germany to acquire a foothold in a region totally dominated by the British and the French. One highly active member of the German diplomatic corps in the Arab East was Fritz Grobba, the minister in Baghdad. An Arabic-speaking career diplomat with "Lawrencian dreams", Grobba was posted to Iraq in 1932. After being briefly called to Germany in 1935, Grobba returned to Iraq brainwashed, with apparent commitment to the Nazi enterprise.[139] His egalitarian demeanour and fondness of the Arab East, together with the dedicated support of a charming and energetic wife, attracted to his receptions Iraqis of various backgrounds – politicians, journalists, bureaucrats and army officers.

In January 1937, a Palestinian delegation including 'Izzat Darwaza, Mu'in al-Madi and 'Awni Abd al-Hadi met Grobba in Baghdad.[140] The Palestinians appealed once more for the cessation of German Jewish immigration to Palestine and requested German backing for their national struggle and the establishment of an Arab state in Palestine. Grobba responded by pointing out that the issue of Jewish immigration was now being reconsidered in Berlin, but he could not commit his government to more than moral support for the Palestinians. During the following months, Grobba was repeatedly approached by Hikmat Sulayman, the Iraqi prime minister, as well as by Yusuf Yasin, the Saudi deputy foreign minister, who reiterated the Palestinian demands.[141] Concurrently, Döhle, the German consul in Jerusalem, presented Berlin with a situation assessment that raised alarm over the projected British plan for establishing a Jewish state in Palestine.[142] Clearly sympathetic to the Palestinian side of the conflict, Döhle critically questioned the 1933 German agreement with the Zionists.

The Germans became aware of the British plan for founding a Jewish state in Palestine at least one month before the official declaration of the Peel Commission's report in July 1937. Coupled with their realization of the enormous impact that the Palestinian question was leaving on Arab opinion, this development led to the crystallization of a new German position on Palestine. In a memorandum reflecting Nazi animosity to world Jewry rather than a real shift in attitude to the Arab cause, the German foreign minister expressed an unequivocal objection to the establishment of a Jewish state in Palestine, mainly because such a state, while lacking the capacity to provide a home for all Jews, would provide a new centre of power for world Jewry.[143] As it was in the German national interest to keep the Jewish forces dispersed, the strengthening of the Arab world was envisioned as a balancing factor to the increasing influence of international Jewry. Designed to be publicized in the Arab world, the new German position encouraged the mufti to meet with Consul Döhle to propose the dispatch of a personal envoy to Germany to discuss the German–Arab and Islamic interests in full.[144] Döhle, aware of his government's adherence to a policy of non-intervention in Arab–British relations, was not receptive. Unable to see the fine line between the inherent Nazi obsession with the Jewish question and the real existence of a German Arab policy, the mufti's proposal marked the first step in a long, convoluted itinerary that would take him all the way to Berlin. Yet, the mufti's friendly approach to Döhle, like his meeting with the Italian consul, came after the outbreak of the Palestinian revolt and in a period of drastic deterioration in Anglo-Arab relations.

After escaping the British crack-down in Lebanon in October 1937, the mufti resumed his attempts to establish links with Berlin. The man he chose to carry out this task was Sa'id Abd al-Fattah al-Imam, an active Syrian Arab nationalist. Al-Imam was trained as a dentist in Germany where he grew to admire, and in certain ways identify with, the German nationalist ideal. Upon returning to Syria, he founded the Arab Club of Damascus, a radical pan-Arabist forum which was regarded by British officials as a pro-Nazi organization.[145] Al-Imam reached Germany in November 1937, and presented to German officials an Arab proposal demanding German propaganda and political and financial support for the Arab movement in exchange for Arab efforts to develop trade with Germany, the creation of a pro-German atmosphere in the Arab world, cooperation in the struggle against the spread of communism, continuation of violent activities in the French-occupied Arab region, etc.[146] Besides the fact that the views of the two sides were incompatible, the Germans were not yet prepared to take a practical step in the Arab direction, since German Arab policy was still constrained by the policy of reassuring the Italians while avoiding a rupture with the British. The Nazi attitude towards the Palestinian question at the time can be gauged from Hitler's intervention in the debate that had been raging between various German agencies over the *Haavara* agreement and German Jewish emigration. Confident of the failure of the partition plan and the British abandonment of the idea of establishing a Jewish state in Palestine, Hitler reaffirmed, in January 1938, Germany's commitment to the continuation of Jewish emigration from Germany to Palestine and to the *Haavara* agreement.[147]

Tension in Europe began to intensify from the early months of 1938, first after the German annexation of Austria, and then over Germany's clear intentions towards Czechoslovakia. German–British relations did not develop as Berlin had wished, and Britain continued to oppose German hegemony in Europe. Bracing themselves for a possible confrontation with Britain, the Germans became more interested in encouraging instability in the British empire, and their policy towards Palestine was thus modified, but only slightly. Abwehr, the German counter-intelligence service, whose Admiral Canaris had met the mufti secretly in Beirut earlier in 1938, began extending financial help to the mufti in August of the same year, and seems to have unsuccessfully attempted to smuggle arms to the Palestinian rebels.[148] One is, however, tempted to believe that German support had no marked impact on the course of the Palestinian revolt, since the revolt had already been approaching its high point before the German entry into the arena. Where the Germans were really leaving their impact was on the course of Jewish emigration to Palestine. Throughout 1938 and until the outbreak of World War II, the Gestapo and other German agencies cooperated with, assisted and encouraged Zionist agents in Germany and Austria, in order to speed up the emigration of German Jews and secure their entry to Palestine by legal as well as illegal means.[149] In the gap that separated the policy of extending support to the Palestinians from encouraging the Jewish influx into Palestine lay neither a belief in the Arab cause nor in Jewish rights, but rather German imperialist interests in their most refined and immoral form.

Concurrently, negotiations were proceeding between Germany and Saudi Arabia over a Saudi request to purchase German weapons and the German wish to establish diplomatic ties with the Saudis. Like most of the Arab political class, the Saudi monarch was conscious of the power changes in the European arena. In late 1937, perhaps because of his dissatisfaction with the quality and quantity of arms supplied by the British, or as a means of establishing relations with the German government, Ibn Sa'ud authorized Yusuf Yasin, who was on a visit to Baghdad, to approach the agents of the firm of Otto Wolf for the purchase of 1,500 German-made rifles.[150] Similar requests were made by Khalid al-Hud al-Qarqanni and Fu'ad Hamza, the king's advisors, during their separate visits to Berlin in early and mid-1938.[151] In both visits, the Saudi envoys broadened the discussion with their German interlocutors to cover other areas of possible German assistance to the Saudi state. Although not entirely explicit, Hamza gave an indication of the Saudi interest in establishing diplomatic ties with Berlin.

Ibn Sa'ud was not particularly a favourite of Nazi Germany. His close relations with Britain and what the Germans saw as his insincerity in his dealings with the Palestinian question weighed heavily against the adoption of a pro-Saudi policy by Germany. In addition, the Germans feared that such a policy would incur the wrath of the British and the Italians who regarded Saudi Arabia as part of their sphere of influence. However, as the ominous signs of war loomed large over Europe in late 1938, Germany became more interested in accommodating the Saudis. It was estimated in Berlin that the Saudi government would take a neutral position in the event of a world war, and that Saudi Arabia would thus be an appropriate retreat for the German representative in Baghdad.[152] Consequently, Grobba was instructed to make an exploratory visit to Saudi Arabia, a journey he undertook on 17 January 1939. During his stay in Jeddah, Grobba became aware of the evident Saudi distrust of the Italians which became even more apparent after the Saudi government expelled the Italian air mission in February 1939. The positive impressions that Grobba got from his meetings with Ibn Sa'ud and his advisors strengthened his belief in the need for an Arab policy for Germany.[153] But, mainly for fear of the British reaction, neither the German government nor Ibn Sa'ud were yet prepared to go the last mile.

Hamza, al-Qarqanni and Yasin were certainly closely connected with the wider Arab-Islamic interwar arena. Their allegiance to Ibn Sa'ud could not have precluded them from discussing developments in Saudi–German relations with other Arab-Islamic figures such as the mufti of Jerusalem. In reality, German policy towards the Arab movement was still largely unchanged, though the German signals were becoming too frequent to be ignored. On 28 April 1939, Hitler made a sharp attack on the Western powers' presence in the Arab world during a speech delivered to the Reichstag, singling out British policies in Palestine for his most violent expressions.[154] Although the speech came in the context of the Anglo-German propaganda war in Europe, Hitler's remarks had an electrifying effect on Arab opinion in general and the Palestinians in particular. Equally effective was the launching of Berlin Radio's Arabic service, of which the British–Zionist alliance was the most favourite target.[155] The perception of a positively changing German Arab policy was reinforced by the warm reception that Hitler granted to Khalid al-Qarqanni when he visited Berlin in June 1939, and Germany's belated approval of the Saudi request for arms.[156] The agreed deal, however, was never concluded because of the outbreak of war a few months later.[157] By the year's end, Germany's unchallenged incursions into Europe had precipitated an image of German invincibility in the Arab world. The German victories in the early stages of the war strengthened this image and seemed to turn the Arab nationalist vision of a West against the West into reality. Yet, despite the widely circulated belief of an Arab scramble towards, and unreserved embrace of, the Nazis, the Arab approaches to Germany after the outbreak of war were cautious and highly pragmatic.

In a strongly worded letter to Nuri al-Sa'id, the Iraqi prime minister, Shakib Arslan, who was regarded as the most fervent pro-German Arab, wrote in late 1939 of his unequivocal preference for Arab neutrality.[158] While still uncompromising in his condemnation of the Western powers, Arslan believed that the Arabs had no particular interest in siding with Germany. The mufti, too, was circumspect in his assessment of the Arab approach to the war situation. His position was, however, more pragmatically defined and less decided on preserving neutrality than that of Arslan. According to Salah al-Din al-Sabbagh, the mufti believed that:[159]

> 1. The Arabs, especially the Iraqis, while continuing to accommodate the British within the limits of the Anglo-Iraqi treaty, should avoid antagonizing the Axis. 2. The Iraqi army must be properly equipped and not be driven into unnecessary adventures. 3. The Arab forces should avoid entering the war and preserve their strength from being bled for the sake of Britain's victory. The victory of Britain is not in the Arabs' interest, for Britain would turn against the Arabs as she had done after World War I. 4. If Russia, Japan and Italy joined the war on the German side, and their armies were subsequently to reach Egypt and Iran, all the Arab countries must declare revolt against the British and their allies.

Although uncommitted to the Axis, what this analysis lacked was a serious evaluation of the dangers that the Arabs might face if Germany emerged as the victorious side in the war, especially when the Third Reich was evolving, at least in Europe, as a typical imperialist power.

By mid-summer 1940, the Iraqi government of Rashid 'Ali al-Gaylani was struggling to cope with the increasing deterioration of Anglo-Iraqi relations, and the deepening Iraqi and Arab internal divisions. Together with the unexpected fall of France, the Italian entry into the war and fears of Turkish ambitions in northern Syria and Iraq led Baghdad to take a secret decision to establish contacts with the Axis powers. The Italian diplomatic mission was still functioning in Iraq, but the Arab target was Germany rather than Italy. The first initiative in that direction came from Naji Shawkat, al-Gaylani's minister of justice.

Muhammad Naji Shawkat (1893–1980) was born to an Arabized family of Turkish and Caucasian origins in the Iraqi town of al-Kut where his father was stationed as provincial governor.[160] At the time when he finished his school education in Baghdad, his father was elected to the Ottoman parliament of 1909, which provided Shawkat with the opportunity to join the Ottoman Law School in Istanbul. Subsequently he became the assistant general prosecutor in the Iraqi city of al-Hila. When World War I broke out he interrupted his legal career and joined the Ottoman army as a reserve officer. After two years of involvement in the Ottoman military defence of Iraq, Shawkat was captured by the advancing British troops in March 1917. He was subsequently taken to a British Indian prison camp where he, like many other detained Arab officers, was offered the choice of joining the Arab revolt, an offer he promptly accepted.

In Faysal's government in Damascus, Shawkat was appointed a legal advisor to Yasin al-Hashimi's *Diwan al-Shura*, the infant military command of the Arab government. After the French occupation of Syria he returned to Iraq, where he took an administrative post until he was chosen for his first ministerial position in 1928. In 1932, Shawkat was called on by Faysal to head a non-partisan government that was intended to clear the political congestion which accompanied the signing of the Anglo-Iraqi treaty. Faced with strong opposition from within the Iraqi political establishment and the anti-treaty campaign, Shawkat's government could not last for more than five months. Thereafter, he was appointed as a representative of Iraq in Ankara where he cultivated strong relations with the Turkish ruling circles and developed a sense of admiration for modern Turkey. Shortly after his return to government in 1938, he was forced to resign from the ministry of interior by Nuri al Sa'id over allegations of his involvement with the anti-British demonstrations that followed the suspicious death of King Ghazi. Shawkat was a late arrival on the Arab nationalist scene. Compared with his brother, Dr Sami Shawkat, the ardent Arab nationalist and co-founder of al-Muthanna Club, Naji was a statesman with little ideological concern. He was not exposed to European cultural influences, nor was he known for his interest in international affairs. In Iraq of the interwar period, his expertise was largely limited to affairs of local government. A typical ex-Ottoman Arabist and Iraqi nationalist, Shawkat saw no reason why Iraq should continue to be controlled and managed by the British. However, he was rather inadequately endowed, politically and intellectually, to provide a strategic judgment on the direction of the Iraqi state in the critical time of war.

In June 1940, the government of Rashid 'Ali al-Gaylani decided to send an Iraqi delegation, consisting of Nuri al-Sa'id and Naji Shawkat, to assess Turkey's position on the war.[161] Prior to his departure, and without consulting the cabinet, Shawkat suggested to al-Gaylani the idea of holding confidential talks with the German representative in Turkey. Having obtained the consent of the prime minister, Shawkat discussed the idea with the mufti who provided him with a letter of introduction to von Papen, the German minister in Ankara.[162] The letter, in which the mufti congratulated Hitler on his latest victories, urged the German leader to begin addressing the Arab question.[163] Meant to endow Shawkat with a pan-Arab status, rather than a limited Iraqi representation, the letter was signed on behalf of the HAC. This indicated that the mufti's efforts towards establishing an organized pan-Arab body had not taken shape by the summer of 1940. Two months later, the mufti's envoy in Berlin would make a different claim.

A week after their arrival in Ankara, Nuri al-Sa'id returned to Baghdad, while Shawkat proceeded to Istanbul, where he met von Papen on 5 July 1940. Shawkat, presenting the Arab case, inquired about the German views on the Palestinian and Syrian questions and urged Germany to show its support for the independence of Syria.[164] In his reply, von Papen made no secret of his government's lack of interest in Arab affairs, nor of the fact that Germany had recognized the Arab world as a part of the Italian sphere of influence. Shawkat expressed the Arabs' distrust of Italy and their determination to liberate their countries from Western imperialism, alluding to the possibility of Iraq's siding with Germany at the opportune time. The discussions also covered the resumption of diplomatic ties between Iraq and Germany and Shawkat's request for an Italo-German declaration on Arab independence and unity.

A similar request for a declaration was made by Rashid 'Ali al-Gaylani to Luigi Gabrielli, the Italian minister in Baghdad. The Italian response was delivered to al-Gaylani in a confidential letter that said:[165]

> His Excellency Count Ciano, the Italian Minister for Foreign Affairs, has instructed me to inform Your Excellency that coherently with the policy so far followed Italy aims at ensuring the complete independence and territorial integrity of Syria and the Lebanon as well as of Iraq and the countries under British mandate. In consequence Italy will oppose any eventual British or Turkish pretensions for territorial occupation whether in Syria, Lebanon or Iraq.

This statement seems not to have been carefully deliberated in the Italian foreign ministry to the extent that, a few months later, an Italian official would find it difficult to recall having issued it. Although phrased in an assertive manner with regard to the Arab East, the statement was meant to conceal Italy's ambitions in Egypt and North Africa.

Shawkat reported his mission to al-Gaylani, Naji al-Swaydi, Taha al-Hashimi and the mufti (but not to Nuri al-Sa'id). Reflecting the dominant feelings in Baghdad, they all approved the line that Shawkat followed in his talks with von Papen. At this juncture, as the Axis advances appeared unstoppable, even Nuri al-Sa'id made a reluctant attempt to contact the Germans.[166] However, it seems that realizing how difficult it was for such a staunch friend of the British as himself to change course, he stopped short of actually doing so. The mufti, capitalizing on Shawkat's mission, decided to send a special envoy to Berlin. This time his choice was 'Usman Kamal Haddad, a young Arab activist from the northern Lebanese city of Tripoli. Haddad's mission was clearly agreed upon between the mufti and the Iraqi prime minister who provided Haddad with an Iraqi passport carrying an alias.[167] Haddad, who stayed in Berlin from late August until mid-October 1940, presented himself to Grobba and other senior functionaries of the German Foreign Office as a representative of the Arab leadership. He reported to his German interlocutors the formation of an Arab coordination committee led by the mufti and including: al-Gaylani, Naji Shawkat, Naji al-Swaydi, the Golden Square colonels and Yunis al-Sab'awi (Iraq); Shukri al-Quwwatli and Zaki al-Khatib (Syria); Yusuf Yasin and Khalid al-Qarqanni (Saudi Arabia).[168] Although a much smaller Arab committee would later be established, it is doubtful whether Haddad's report reflected an existing reality. The only organized pan-Arabist body at the time was the Arab Nationalist Party of the radical Arab intellectuals who were still lesser-known young activists than those on the list of prominent names provided by Haddad. It is most likely that, by reporting the existence of such a leading Arab committee, Haddad was trying to impress upon the Germans the representative nature of his mission.

The main aim of Haddad's talks in Germany was to obtain an Axis declaration in line with the Arab aspirations which he outlined as follows:

> 1. Recognition of the independence of the Arab countries, particularly those under French and British control. 2. Recognition of the Arabs' right to unite their countries. 3. Recognition of the Arabs' right to solve the Jewish problem in Palestine in a manner that conforms to the national interest of the Arabs. 4. An assertion to the effect that the Axis powers had no imperialist designs with respect to Egypt and the Sudan.[169]

Haddad elaborated that the term "Arab countries" covered the North African countries as well as countries of the Arab East. From the Arab side, Haddad proposed that the projected Axis declaration would be met with the resumption of diplomatic ties between Iraq and Germany, granting the Axis powers a favourable position in the Iraqi oil industry, and the resumption of the anti-British revolt in Palestine and Transjordan, for which Haddad requested German logistic and financial support. Concurrently, the same issues were being discussed by von Papen and Naji Shawkat, as the latter returned to Istanbul in September for a second meeting with the German minister.[170]

The Germans, highly interested in the prospects of an anti-British Arab revolt and beginning to doubt the wisdom of allowing Italy exclusive postwar influence in the Middle East, appeared willing to accommodate the Arab demands, a position that was not acceptable to the Italians. Both, however, were not prepared, in the light of their commitments to Vichy France, to support the Arab demands for full Syrian independence or Syrian–Iraqi unity.[171] It was not until 21 October that the Axis powers finalized a common declaration that read as follows:[172]

> Germany (Italy) which has always been animated by sentiments of friendship for the Arabs and cherishes the wish that they may prosper and be happy, and assume a place among the peoples of the earth in accordance with their historic and natural importance, has always watched with interest the struggles of the Arab countries to achieve their independence. In their effort to obtain this goal, the Arab countries can count upon Germany's (Italy's) full sympathy. In making this statement Germany (Italy) finds itself in full accord with her Italian (German) ally.

This declaration was delivered to Haddad and Shawkat and broadcast on Radio Bari and Radio Berlin Arabic services, although it was not published in the Axis print media until December. The declaration was received with disappointment in the Arab camp, where it was seen as inadequate for clarifying the ambiguity of the Axis powers' position on the Arab question.[173] But the Arab leaders in Baghdad had by then gone too far in their project to change direction. In the atmosphere of crisis that enveloped Iraqi politics in late 1940, many were prepared to exonerate the Germans and lay the blame for the hindering of Arab–Axis understanding at the Italians' door.

By December, as relations between al-Gaylani and the British deteriorated to a point of no return, the Iraqi prime minister made a formal request through the Italian minister in Baghdad for German weapons and military supplies.[174] Only days before the fall of al-Gaylani's government at the end of January 1941, Haddad was sent back to Berlin, carrying a letter and a new draft declaration from the mufti to Hitler.[175] The mufti's *démarche*, underlining the mutual Arab–German concerns, focused on the Arabs' animosity to Britain and their determination to revolt at the proper time against its domination of the Arab world. It also outlined in full detail the Arab political demands with little, but important, difference from the earlier Arab draft declaration of summer 1940. While demanding unequivocal recognition of the independence of Arab countries occupied by Britain (Palestine, Transjordan, Oman, Kuwait, etc.), the new draft declaration was less emphatic in regard to Syria and Lebanon. Instead of making the independence of Syria central to the Arab agenda, the mufti's draft was phrased to provide for the least binding commitments from the Axis powers over the future of the French-occupied regions, at a time when Syrian independence was the most obvious test of Axis' intentions towards the Arab world. The French administration in Syria supported the Vichy government immediately after the fall of France, and Germany, if willing, was in a powerful position to affect a French reconsideration of the Syrian question. Similarly, while the draft demanded recognition of Egypt's and Sudan's independence, it made no mention of the other North African countries.

Clearly, if a collective Arab committee did exist at the time, it had no role in formulating the mufti's *démarche*, since the independence of Syria was certainly not suggested as a point of compromise by any of the active Arab parties. What seemed to underline the accommodating approach to the German backing of Vichy France and the not-so-secret Italian ambitions in North Africa was a desperate desire on the part of the mufti to enlist German support. The radical Arabists, driven by their animosity to Britain, pursued the German option with little debate over the political or ideological costs involved in such an approach.

The Italians, after the failure of their offensive against Greece and Egypt, were reduced to a much weaker position in terms of their alliance with Germany. Subsequently, the Germans became more interested in interfering directly in the Mediterranean basin. These developments, however, left little impact on the German attitude towards the Arab question. The German response to Haddad's second visit was delivered in a confidential note – not a declaration – to the mufti from Weizsäcker, the German Secretary of State. Issued in early April 1941, the warmly worded letter promised a prompt delivery of military supplies to Iraq, but did not offer any substantial addition to the Italo-German declaration.[176] In contrast to its specificity in underlining the Arab–German agreement against their common enemies, the British and the Jews, the German letter contained only a general statement with regard to the recognition of the Arab countries' independence. Neither the question of Arab unity, nor the particular issues of Egypt and the Sudan were alluded to. On this occasion, the German letter raised no questions, even within the inner circle of the radical Arabists. As the political crisis in Iraq was reaching a climax, it was German military aid which occupied the minds of the mufti and his partners in the Iraqi government of national defence.

War and defeat

At the end of February 1941, only a month before al-Gaylani and his adherents seized power, a secret meeting was held in the mufti's house on al-Zahawi Avenue. In addition to the mufti, this meeting was attended by Colonels Salah al-Din al-Sabbagh, Fahmi Sa'id and Mahmud Salman; Yunis al Sab'awi; Naji Shawkat and al-Gaylani. This group of Arab leaders agreed to work together, liberated from selfishness and personal ambitions, for the salvation of the Arab countries.[177] Regarding their association as a higher committee for the Arab movement, they also agreed on electing the mufti as its leader. According to Naji Shawkat, meetings of this group functioned as the leading committee for a larger Arab political party and for deciding major affairs of the Iraqi government as well. In their memoirs, Shawkat, al-Sabbagh and the mufti implied that the formation of this committee was the culmination of an ongoing project for the establishment of a pan-Arab organization, but made no mention of other leading members from Syria or Saudi Arabia as Haddad alluded to earlier in his report to the Germans. Shukri al-Quwwatli, Zaki al-Khatib, Khalid al-Qarqanni and Yusuf Yasin might have been contacted by the mufti in relation to the establishment of a pan-Arab organization, but no evidence is available to suggest that they were conscious of the emergence of the Baghdad committee or that they were subordinate to the policies adopted by its members.

Without severing his relations with the Axis representatives in Syria, al-Quwwatli was by early 1941 actively involved in cultivating popular agitation against the Vichy authorities.[178] Al-Quwwatli's activities were not necessarily in agreement with the mufti's strategy, in which a Syrian revolt was seen to serve the British interests. The allegiance of al-Qarqanni and Yasin was, on the other hand, to Ibn Sa'ud who possessed the ultimate authority in Saudi Arabia. Thus, whether al-Qarqanni and Yasin were, or were not, associated with the mufti's pan-Arabist formations, was largely inconsequential to the determination of Saudi policy. The leading members of the Baghdad committee saw themselves as representatives of the Arab movement and as the standard-bearers of the Arab enterprise for independence and unity. In their dealings with the Axis powers, as well as in their challenge to the British, they were no longer acting on behalf of Iraq or Palestine, but for the Arab nation at large.

The immediate results of the 2 April coup were perhaps surprising to most of the parties involved in the Iraqi situation. For al-Gaylani and his coterie, the regent's escape was certainly an unanticipated development. Having no illusions about taking on the military might of Britain, al-Gaylani began the impossible task of legitimizing his rule, constitutionally and diplomatically. His twofold task was to reconcile the British and fulfil the nationalist and pan-Arabist expectations of his adherents. Since no German military aid had been received, nor even seemed to be arriving, and the Axis armies were still too distant to be able to interfere in the event of an Iraqi war, the Arabist committee of Baghdad decided to consolidate its grip on power, clear the Iraqi political arena of pro-British elements, and work to strengthen the Iraqi army.[179] This strategy was certainly in line with al-Gaylani's political instincts. Although highly ambitious, pan-Arabist and never comfortable with the British influence in Iraq, he was essentially a statesman with strong notable origins. His late arrival in Arab radical politics made him a major player in a game that seemed to be leading beyond the wildest dreams of his imagination.

Al-Gaylani's first step was to reconstruct the constitutional appearance of his regime by filling the vacuum that was created by the escape of Abd al-Ilah, and forming a credible government. Against the wishes of the "Golden Square", al-Gaylani called for a joint parliamentary meeting of the lower and upper houses on 10 April. Upon a suggestion from Naji al-Swaydi, the country's formidable constitutionalist mind, the session declared that the escape of Abd al-Ilah was an abdication of responsibilities, and subsequently resolved to appoint Sharif Sharaf, a little-known Hashemite figure, as the new regent.[180] Following this step, al-Gaylani was confirmed as prime minister, with full constitutional powers to form his cabinet. By including Naji al-Swaydi and Naji Shawkat, two former prime ministers, as ministers of finance and defence respectively, al-Gaylani reinforced the foundations of his regime. Yet, the cabinet was largely dominated by pan-Arabist and radical elements.[181] Out of its eight members, two ministers (Naji Shawkat and Musa al-Shabandar), were regarded by the British as pro-German, while two others (Yunis al-Sab'awi and 'Ali Mahmud al-Shaykh 'Ali) were described as known anti-British agitators. Two other ministers, Muhammad Salman and Ra'uf al-Bahrani, were also closely associated with the pan-Arabist al-Muthanna Club.

The British, too, were surprised by the coup, more perhaps by its timing than its mere occurrence. Since the war cabinet was not yet resolved on a specific course of action in Iraq, the rise of the Arab nationalists to power forced a reconsideration of the whole situation. The first British assessment was formulated by Cornwallis, the new ambassador in Baghdad. The British envoy, writing three days after the coup, described three possible courses open to his government:[182] "1. Restore the situation by armed intervention, 2. To inform Rashid 'Ali that they will have no official relations with his regime and to squeeze him as much as possible, 3. To recognize the regime of Rashid 'Ali." Dismissing the third option as unthinkable, Cornwallis expressed his preference for the ousting of al-Gaylani's regime by force, if the necessary troops could be spared. While London agreed with ruling out official recognition of al-Gaylani, it was left to General Wavell, commander-in-chief Middle East, to decide on the possibility of military action. Cornwallis, an uncompromising imperialist and cunning operator who had been well acquainted with the Iraqi scene since his earlier service in the Iraqi interior ministry, was the driving force behind the military solution.

Pressed with the requirements of the defence of Egypt and Palestine, as well as the escalating tension in the Mediterranean, Wavell could not afford to launch a full-fledged military operation in Iraq. Nor was he disposed to wait for the uncertain results of political pressure to squeeze al-Gaylani out of office. In view of the predictable consolidation of al-Gaylani's regime and the possibility of a German military intervention, Wavell recommended a large air demonstration, staged with aircraft available at the Habbaniyya airbase, to rally support for the regent and activate latent opinion in his favour.[183] Wavell also recommended that Amir Abdullah, the elder of the Hashemite family, should declare his backing for the regent and be allowed to contact and enlist the support of Iraqi tribes on the grounds of protecting the interests of the young king. If the situation remained fluid enough, Wavell indicated, the deployment of a battalion by air and a brigade by sea to Basra could be considered. Wavell's predictions proved to be only partly correct. The government of al-Gaylani was consolidating and gaining power by the day. The Iraqi parliamentary approval of the regime coupled with the mass support demonstrated by the Iraqi people convinced Cornwallis that without full use of force neither political pressure nor Wavell's air demonstration would restore the situation, since the regent was too weak and unpopular to effect the emergence of credible opposition.[184]

On 12 April, the ambassador was informed of the war cabinet's decision to dispatch troops from India to Basra.[185] According to instructions, Cornwallis was to delay notifying the Iraqi government of the troops' arrival as long as possible, in order not to allow the Iraqis enough time to prepare for resisting the landing if they decided to resort to such action. To secure the safety of the arriving troops, Cornwallis played his cards in a highly skilful manner.

Following his escape from Baghdad, the regent took refuge aboard a British battleship docked at Basra. His contacts with Iraqi military officials and tribal leaders, were becoming a source of irritation for the Iraqi government. Seeking to create a better atmosphere for his relations with al-Gaylani, Cornwallis ordered the removal of Abd al-Ilah from Iraqi waters to Jerusalem.[186] The second reconciliatory measure was to stop the British radio attacks on al-Gaylani and his adherents. This was followed by playing the recognition card. Formally, Cornwallis' had not yet presented his credentials to Sharif Sharaf, indicating British refusal to recognize the regime and the new regent. Considering the strong financial and economic ties between Iraq and Britain, and Britain's influence on other Arab countries, recognition by Britain became one of al-Gaylani's most urgently sought goals. On 16 April, only one day before the troops' arrival, Cornwallis held a decisive meeting with al-Gaylani, where he waved the recognition card without really surrendering it, in order to obtain the Iraqi premier's full consent to the landing of the troops at Basra.[187] Here again, al-Gaylani's action was motivated by the notable, the statesman in him, rather than the rebel. He gained power on an Arab nationalist and anti-British agenda, but only British recognition would give him the ultimate legitimacy and the sense of triumph that he eagerly desired. In the event, al-Gaylani's consent caused deep apprehension amongst the army commanders.

While no attempt was made to challenge the landing of the troops at Basra, the army commanders responded by drafting a list of requests for the government to present to Cornwallis.[188] The Iraqi military demanded that the British troops should be moved through to Palestine at once; other troops should not arrive until after the departure of the present force; in future more notice should be given; and troops should arrive in such a manner that they could pass through quickly. Al-Gaylani also sent Cornwallis a message indicating that the Iraqi government considered it important that "at no time should there be any large concentration of

British troops in the country". Although these requests were in conformity with the terms of the Anglo-Iraqi treaty, neither Cornwallis nor the war cabinet had the intention of responding to the Iraqi demands. Seen from the military viewpoint,[189] the British landing at Basra was to secure lines of communication to Turkey through Iraq (which assumed greater importance because of German air superiority in the Aegean Sea), to enable the British forces to establish an air reinforcement route to the Middle East via Basra, and to be in a position to secure Iraqi oil or at least to deny it to the enemy if necessary. For Cornwallis, the aim was to create a situation conducive to the ousting of al-Gaylani and his supporters. He would thus warn London that:[190]

> Retention of a large force at Basra without opening lines of communication will be quickly turned to our disadvantage. If we are to establish our position more firmly and safeguard our strategic and other interests throughout Iraq we must show the flag here. Baghdad is hub of Iraq.

The Chiefs of Staff Committee did contemplate moving the troops to the Habbaniyya airbase, some fifty miles west of Baghdad, but not until the situation in Basra was secured. On 24 April, with no serious Iraqi challenge in sight, troops arrived in Hubbaniyya and the airbase was subsequently reinforced.[191] Located within easy reach of Baghdad, the airbase posed a higher threat to the Iraqi government's ability to defend itself than Basra. Yet, it appeared that despite Cornwallis' preference for an active policy against al-Gaylani, what motivated the decision to airlift the troops to Habbaniyya was the base's vulnerability to a possible German intervention. Coupled with the Iraqis' realization that the arriving British force was not proceeding to Palestine after all, this step exacerbated Iraqi–British relations even further. The Anglo-Iraqi treaty provided for no reinforcement of the two British airbases in Iraq without consultation with the Iraqi government. Unsurprisingly, the Iraqis regarded the latest British provocation as a flagrant infringement of their national sovereignty, and as an indication of British scheming against the nationalist government. But since Britain was determined to protect its position in Iraq, while the Arabist leaders were viewing it more as an enemy than an ally, the semantic disagreement over the Anglo-Iraqi treaty was rather irrelevant to the course of events.

On 28 April, the Iraqi government was faced with another short notice from Cornwallis, announcing the impending arrival of additional troops at Basra. Deeply alarmed at the prospects of the British build-up, al-Gaylani refused permission. However, despite Iraqi opposition, three ships carrying more troops and military equipment docked the following day in Basra for disembarkation.[192] Concurrently, preparations for the evacuation of British civilians from Iraq began in earnest on orders from the British ambassador. For the "Golden Square", no further evidence was needed to convince them that the British strike they always feared was imminent. As a result, Colonel Fahmi Sa'id led a significant force of the Iraqi army into the vicinity of the Habbaniyya airbase. Initially, the Iraqi army informed the British commander of the base of no hostile intentions, attributing the deployment of their forces to regular military manœuvring. Soon, Baghdad was inundated with rumours to the effect that more British troops were advancing towards Iraq from Transjordan, while the Iraqi commanders decided to restrict the movements of the British military outside Habbaniyya.[193] Although the idea of overrunning the Habbaniyya base was discussed by the four colonels and the rest of the Arabist leaders in Baghdad, no orders were issued from the Iraqi chief of staff (who was on friendly terms with the "Golden Square") to that effect.[194] At any rate, fearing an Iraqi attack that might result in substantial destruction of the base, the British decided to take the initiative. In the early light of 2 May, the Iraqi positions in the Habbaniyya sector were heavily bombarded.[195]

Interestingly, three days after the outbreak of war, General Wavell sent an angry dispatch to the War Office, expressing his grave doubts over the ability of the British force at Habbaniyya to resist an Iraqi offensive. Wavell, considering that the prolongation of fighting in Iraq would seriously endanger the defence of Palestine and Egypt, urged in the strongest possible terms for a settlement to be negotiated as soon as possible.[196] By then, however, the Defence Committee of the war cabinet had embarked on a new course for the Iraqi operation. Wavell was thus informed that developments in Iraq provided "an excellent chance for restoring the situation by bold action, if it is not delayed".[197] Churchill's uncompromising approach to the Arab question was this time reinforced by the opinions of a hawkish ambassador in Baghdad.

Both sides of the conflict seemed to have overestimated the German commitment to the Arab cause, as well as the German ability to maintain a worldwide war machine. By the early months of 1941, World War II was largely turning into a British–German war in which the interruption of British lines of communication and supply was a central goal for the German strategists. Hence, the deterioration in British–Arab relations in Iraq must have been a welcome development for the Germans. In reality, the German response to the evolving events in Iraq was significantly slow and unfocused. At the conclusion of his second visit to Berlin (February 1941), Haddad received German agreement for the supply of arms to Iraq, but such supplies were not delivered, even after the return of al-Gaylani to power at the beginning of April. On 10 April, the two Axis powers communicated their sympathy to al-Gaylani through the Italian minister in Baghdad, but warned at the same time against resisting Britain with arms until the balance of forces offered a chance of success, adding that they were preparing active military and financial aid to reach Iraq as soon as the transportation difficulties were solved.[198] After the landing of British troops in Basra, both al-Gaylani and the mufti approached the Italian envoy for urgent military support. Despite the fact that they were fully aware of the British knowledge of al-Gaylani's relations with them, the Germans had developed no plans for military intervention or for maintaining a line of supply to the Iraqis. The Italian legation in Baghdad realized that the arriving British troops were in fact preparing to remain in Iraq, but even this assessment could not elicit prompt reaction from the Germans. It was strange – as Hirszowicz noted – that some Nazi leaders were still entertaining the hope that the Iraqi government would manage to defer a clash with Britain.[199] With their involvement in several large-scale operations in Crete, Greece and the Balkans, while preparing for their attack on the Soviet Union, the Germans were not able to grasp the rapid pace at which the Iraqi situation was developing, nor did they regard the Arab question as high on their agenda.

It was only on 10 April that Ribbentrop, the German foreign minister, obtained Hitler's agreement to the supply of arms to Iraq, and it was not until 23 May (a few days before the Iraqi collapse) that Hitler issued directive 30 which made supplying the "Arab liberation movement" a part of the German world strategy.[200] Between the two dates, the Germans struggled slowly and indecisively to overcome obstacles of transportation to Iraq. The first German military shipment (15,500 rifles, 200 machine-guns, 4 field-guns calibre 7.5, with ammunition) reached Mosul from Aleppo on 13 May, after Vichy France had agreed to the supplying of Iraq through Syria.[201] Arriving too late to be introduced to an army mainly equipped by Britain, these arms were of little use to the Iraqis. It was rather the German air support which Iraq was in desperate need of, especially after the spectacular success of the British air force of Habbaniyya in destroying the inexperienced Iraqi air force.[202] But the German aeroplanes did not participate in the fighting until 13 May, almost a week after the Iraqi siege of Habbaniyya was broken.[203] Because of the damage that several German airplanes suffered during landings on the Syrian airfields and the unfavourable effect of the Iraqi environment on the wear and tear of the planes, the German air assistance had little or no impact on the course of war. In this regard, the situation was not helped either by the shortage of Iraqi fuel for the aeroplanes.

In many respects, the Iraqi–British war and the subsequent defeat of Iraq marked the beginning of the end for the Arab interwar movement. Firstly, it revealed the utter inability of the pan-Arabist military, which came to occupy centre stage of the Iraqi and Arab nationalist movement from the mid-1930s, to defend their country. Although the military aspects of the war are beyond the scope of this study, it is perhaps pertinent to mention that notwithstanding the German failure to render necessary and timely support for the Arab side, the Iraqi military conduct of the war was dismally ineffective. Until the last days of fighting, forces on the Iraqi side outnumbered the British forces by a high proportion.[204] The rise in the water-level of the Tigris, flooding and Iraqi disruption of the Basra–Baghdad railway, confined the British troops in Basra to the southern corner of the country. Fahmi Sa'id, with 9,000 troops under his command, failed conclusively to defeat the much smaller British contingent at Habbaniyya. Although the British were significantly helped by air superiority, this superiority was at least partly achieved by the failure of the Iraqi air force, led by none other than Colonel Mahmud Salman, to avoid early destruction by the British. Kamil Shabib, the other Golden Square colonel, deserted his position on the western front, leaving the Iraqi lines in total disarray.[205] The British expedition, advancing from Transjordan, was thus presented with an easy access to the Habbaniyya airbase and subsequently to Baghdad.

As early as 8 April, the Iraqi minister in Ankara, under orders from al-Gaylani, appealed to the Turkish government to mediate between Iraq and Britain.[206] Turkey was a partner of Iraq in the Sa'dabad Pact, and, as a neutral country, was deeply concerned over the preservation of peace in Iraq, with which it shared long borders as well as a recurring Kurdish problem. The Turkish response to the Iraqi appeal reflected a sense of urgency upon the outbreak of fighting, and more so after the arrival of Naji Shawkat in Ankara on a mission to expedite the Turkish mediation.[207] Viewing the internal developments in Iraq as of a purely nationalist nature in which Britain had no right to intervene, the Turkish government presented the two belligerent parties with a proposed solution that provided for the safeguard of Iraqi sovereignty while fully implementing the Anglo-Iraqi treaty. The ambiguous terms of the treaty were given reasonably fair explanations.[208] While the British, now intent on restoring the *status quo ante*, rejected the Turkish proposal, the Iraqi response never reached the Turkish government. Until 16 May, when Shawkat decided to return to Baghdad, the Iraqi government was unable to reach an agreement on the Turkish proposal.[209] Conscious of the army's retreat in the Habbaniyya sector, the ineffectiveness of German assistance and Germany's involvement in the Balkans, Shawkat and al-Gaylani preferred acceptance of the Turkish solution. In contrast, al-Sabbagh, supported by al-Sab'awi, was still entertaining the hope that the Germans would lead a strong force into Syria, immediately after the fall of Greece. "No negotiations without the departure of the occupying troops," declared al-Sabbagh.

The incidence of this fundamental disagreement virtually paralysed the leading pan-Arabist committee. On 21 May, the demoralized Shawkat left Iraq for Turkey, accompanied by his wife and the prime minister's wife, who was also his relative. Within the next few days, other ministers and high-ranking officials fled the country to Turkey or Iran. By the end of the month, even before the end of fighting or the fall of Baghdad, the four colonels were on their way out of Iraq, followed by the mufti and Rashid 'Ali al-Gaylani. Characteristically, it was Yunis al-Sab'awi, the young radical Arab nationalist, who stayed behind, desperately determined to organize last-stand popular resistance.[210]

The second effect of the Iraqi–British dispute on the Arab interwar movement was to bring the inner differences of the interwar Arabists into open conflict. The Iraqi politicians who fled the country and joined with the regent and the British side were no less Arabist than those who adhered to al-Gaylani and the mufti. Nuri al-Sa'id, 'Ali Jawdat and Jamil al-Madfa'i, were all Sharifian officers with strong roots in al-'Ahd Society.

During the crisis, Nuri turned into an enthusiastic advisor for the British campaign.[211] No less committed to defeating the government of national defence, Jamil al-Madfa'i was designated the first prime minister of the post-Gaylani era, returning to Iraq in a British military aeroplane that landed at the Habbaniyya base.[212] Most revealing of the Arabist divisions were the attitudes of Tawfiq al-Swaydi. A founder of al-Fatat and member of the Arab Paris Conference of 1913, Tawfiq al-Swaydi was most uncompromising in inviting British military intervention. On 6 April, he told Cornwallis that "boycotting the Government of National Defence by leading politicians would not defeat Rashid Ali". He took the line that only force could now do this, Cornwallis said.[213] Ironically, Naji al-Swaydi, one of the most prominent ministers of the government of national defence, was the older brother of Tawfiq. The disintegration of the Iraqi ruling class was in many respects the culmination of a wider Arab political breakup that began with the bloody conflict between the Palestinian rebels and the Nashashibi opposition in the closing months of the 1936–9 revolt, and continued with the assassination of Abd al-Rahman al-Shahbandar in Syria.

Thirdly, the Iraqi–British war was also an occasion for the manifestation of the divided will of the post-World War I Arab regional states, a reality that had long been overlooked by Arab nationalist leaders and groupings. The Egyptian government, led by Husayn Sirri, assured the British that it had no intention of recognizing al-Gaylani's regime.[214] Sirri's concerns for Iraq took the form of an ambivalent telegram to Baghdad, in which he pointed to the strengthening of fraternal ties between Egypt and Iraq and expressed his wish to see the end of disagreement and the return of normalcy in relations between Iraq and Britain.[215] The response of Amir Abdullah and his government took a different track. Partly because of his unrepressed ambition to expand his domain beyond the Emirate of Transjordan and partly because of the British desire to give their invasion of Iraq an Arab face, Abdullah became totally involved in the British operation. Defying Jordanian popular support of the Iraqi insurgency, Abdullah decided to join the British expedition that originated from Haifa. Units of the Arab Legion and the Jordanian Border Guards were thus attached to the British force.[216] As they reached the Iraqi–Jordanian border crossing, a mutiny within the ranks of the Guards led to their exclusion,[217] but units of the Arab Legion, led by Major Glubb, continued all the way to Habbaniyya.

Ibn Sa'ud was a different case altogether. With the Iraqi government of national defence, Ibn Sa'ud had a unique chance to establish a healthy and sound relationship with Iraq. The Gaylanis of Baghdad had once provided the father of Abd al-'Aziz al-Sa'ud with refuge and protection during his exile from Najd in the late nineteenth century.[218] More important, perhaps, was al-Gaylani's role in improving Iraqi–Saudi relations in 1940, especially with regard to the tribal problems that involved the two countries.[219] Besides the ties which connected the mufti with the Saudis, Ibn Sa'ud also knew Colonel Salah al-Din al-Sabbagh. In 1939, al-Sabbagh made a successful visit to Saudi Arabia, during which he initialled a protocol of military cooperation with the Saudi government. The positive image of the new regime was reinforced by the positive political changes that it brought about. It was a regime that diminished the grip on Iraq of the Hashemites, whose power and influence had always been a major preoccupation for the Saudis, and removed Nuri al-Sa'id, the most untrustworthy Arab politician in the eyes of the Saudi monarch. Therefore, it was not particularly surprising that the Arabists of Baghdad should expect support from Ibn Sa'ud.

In the beginning, the Saudi monarch was careful not to endorse the British views of al-Gaylani.[220] If the British distrust of al-Gaylani stemmed mainly from their suspicions of his German links, the Saudis, too, had been temporizing with Germany. But early in 1941 Ibn Sa'ud seems to have returned to a neutral position coloured with his traditional friendship with Britain. The Italian failure in the Western Desert and East Africa, coupled with Britain's reassertion of its naval control in the Red Sea, were important factors in the readjustment of Saudi policy. Under these conditions, the Saudis faced the outbreak of the Iraqi–British war with a pragmatic approach, largely devoid of their common expressions of Arab and Islamic solidarity. Despite constant British pressure, the Saudis made no public condemnation of al-Gaylani or his adherents. Simultaneously, they rejected the Iraqi demands for assistance. On 5 May, the Iraqi government decided to send Naji al-Swaydi to Saudi Arabia, hoping to secure financial aid as well as the employment of Saudi influence among the Jordanian tribes to interrupt the line of communication between Transjordan and Iraq.[221] In Riyadh, al-Swaydi made a strong appeal to the Saudi monarch, referring to the Iraqi–Saudi treaties of 1931 and 1936, as well as to the Arab values of brotherhood and solidarity. The treaties, however, were too loosely phrased to impose any obligations on the Saudi government. Ibn Sa'ud did express his sympathy with the Iraqis, but the essence of his position was typically displayed by the invocation of a short and direct analogy. "Son!", the king said to Naji al-Swaydi, "living next to a satisfied and content lion is better than living next to a hungry eagle."[222]

Yet, beyond the failure of the Arab-Islamist interwar generation, its inner conflict and ineptitude and the disunity of regional states, the Iraqi spring of 1941 was turning into a focal point for the Arab masses and popular forces. Baghdad was crowded with Palestinian and Syrian volunteers, a number of whom did actually participate in the fighting, especially on the western front. Many others were still arriving across the Syrian–Iraqi borders when Baghdad was declared fallen.[223] Most interesting was the impact that the events of Iraq had on two political groupings, one in Egypt and the other in Syria.

For a group of nationalist, anti-British young army officers in Egypt, 'Aziz al-Misri emerged as a national hero after the British forced his dismissal from the command of the army. Upon the outbreak of hostilities in Iraq, al-Misri prepared himself to join the Iraqi insurgency. Al-Misri was a pan-Arabist of a special style who was considered a spiritual father of many Iraqi ex-Ottoman officers; his moves were coordinated with his young army supporters as well as with some members of the Young Egypt Party.[224] The Egyptian officers were so captivated by the events in Iraq that Jamal Abd al-Nasser, a member of the group, sent a message of support to Muhammad Salman, a minister of al-Gaylani's government who was being hospitalized in Beirut during the war.[225] Al-Misri's preparations, however, seem to have been interrupted by the sudden collapse of the Iraqi government of national defence. But, shortly afterwards, al-Misri and his army supporters began planning for a revolt in Egypt, for which he established some secret links with the Germans. In the event, al-Misri was advised by the Germans to move from Egypt into a country controlled by the Axis powers. Helped by Anwar al-Sadat and Abd al-Mun'im Abd al-Ra'uf of the army group, al-Misri made an unsuccessful attempt to fly to Libya.[226] The plot was aborted, but the small group of al-Misri's army supporters would later grow to become the most influential network of nationalist officers in the Egyptian army. This group, known as the Free Officers, would eventually take power on 23 July 1952.

In Damascus, a different but no less significant development was simultaneously taking shape. An important vehicle for Syrian support to the Iraqi insurgency was the Iraq Defence Committee of the veteran Arabist, Nabih al-'Azma.[227] Parallel to al-'Azma's, another solidarity group under the name of the Iraq Support Society was also established in the Syrian capital. This society was founded as a forum to combine the efforts of Michel 'Aflaq and Salah al-Din al-Bitar, the Syrian Arab nationalist intellectuals, and their like-minded colleagues in the circle of Zaki al-'Arsuzi, a former leader of the NAL and radical Arab nationalist ideologue.[228] The society's involvement with the Syrian mass movement in solidarity with Iraq consolidated relations between its two founding groups, leading two years later to the emergence of the formative organization of the Arab Ba'th Party.

Against the rise and defeat of Iraq, a new era of Arab nationalism was in the making.

NOTES

1   See, for example, Waters, 1942; Pearlman, 1947; Schechtman, 1965; Khadduri, 1951; Silverfarb, 1986; Simon, 1986; Mattar, 1988; Elpeleg, 1993.
2   Newton to Halifax, 24 and 29 October 1939, CO 733/398/4/75156; al-Hasani; 1990:62.
3   Newton to Halifax, 20 January 1940, FO 406/78/E500.
4   Shabib, 1981:48.
5   Newton to FO, 18 October 1939, CO 733/398/4/75156, and Newton to Baggallay, 2 November 1939, ibid.
6   Baggallay to Downie, 28 October 1939; Newton to Halifax, 13 November 1939; Baggallay to Newton, 13 December 1939, ibid.
7   Trott (Jeddah), 9 and 16 December 1939, ibid.; al-Hashimi, 1967: vol. 1, 312–13.
8   Lukitz (1995) is in many respects the most complete and comprehensive study of the factors and aspects of Iraq's instability during the monarchic era. It, however, fails to pinpoint the other side of Iraq, namely the powerful forces that prevented its disintegration in the face of recurrent internal and external centrifugal crises.
9   Al-Sabbagh, 1994:115.
10 C. J. Edmonds, "Political Situation in Iraq", Enclosure, Peterson to Baxter, 6 July 1938, FO 371/21846/E 4417.
11 Peterson to Halifax, 30 March 1939, FO 371/23201/E 2749; Peterson, 1950:143.
12 Khadduri, 1951:135–6; al-Hashimi, 1967: vol. 1, 303; al-Durra, 1969:100.
13 Al-Hasani, 1953–67: vol. 5, 75–6.
14 Longrigg, 1954:276; al-Husri, 1966–8: vol. 2, 586.
15 British Embassy (Baghdad) to FO, 11 April 1939, FO 371/23201/E 2820; al-Hasani, 1953–67: vol. 5, 76.
16 Houstoun-Boswall to FO, 16 April 1939, FO 371/23201/E 2549.

17 Peterson to FO, 11 January 1939, FO 371/23200/E 448; Peterson to Oliphant, 31 December 1938, FO 371/23207/E 281; Peterson to FO, 11 January 1939, FO 371/23200/E 448.

18 *Al-Istiqlal*, 17 and 19 February 1939; Peterson, 1950:150; Kubba, 1965:95; al-Durra, 1969:101.

19 Al-Hashimi, 1967: vol. 1, 300; Shawkat, 1974:358.

20 *Al-Istiqlal*, 20 January and 1 March 1939; British Embassy (Baghdad) to FO, 25 January 1939, FO 371/23200/E 938.

21 Peterson to FO, 22 February 1939, FO 371/20200/E 1399; al-Sabbagh, 1994:111.

22 Khadduri, 1951:139; Longrigg, 1954:277; al-Hasani, 1953–67: vol. 5, 76; al-Swaydi, 1969:326–7; al-Hashimi, 1978: vol. 2, 77.

23 Al-Hashimi, 1967: vol. 1, 304–5; al-Sabbagh, 1994:116–20.

24 Newton to Halifax, 20 January 1940, FO 406/78/E 500; al-Hasani, 1953–67: vol. 5, 91–2; al-Durra, 1969:140–1.

25 Khadduri, 1951:142–4.

26 Newton to FO, 3 April 1940, FO 371/24558/E 1725; Yaghi, 1974:42–3.

27 Clark Kerr to Eden, 4 January 1938, FO 371/21853/E 435; Basri, 1987:193–201.

28 Khadduri, 1951:144–6; al-Hashimi, 1967: vol. 1, 321–4.

29 Be'eri, 1970:28–30.

30 Al-Hashimi, 1967: vol. 1, 326–5; al-Durra, 1969: 111–12.

31 Al-Hasani, 1990:49.

32 Al-Hashimi, 1967: vol. 1, 335–6; Mardini, 1986:128–9.

33 Al-Sabbagh, 1994:165–6.

34 See, for example: Yaghi, 1974; al-Barrak, 1987; al-Hasani, 1990.

35 Simon, 1986:7–43.

36 Al-Sabbagh, 1994: 16–21 and 35–42.

37 C. J. Edmonds, "Note on the Present Orientation of pan-Arab Policy in Iraq", 23 August 1938, Enclosure in Houstoun-Boswall to Halifax, 29 August 1938, FO 406/76/E 5393.

38 For their biographies see: Clark Kerr to Eden, 4 January 1938, FO 371/21853/E 435; Basri, 1987: *passim*; al-Swaydi, 1987: *passim*; al-Sabbagh, 1994:30–3.

39 Al-Sabbagh's memoirs (1994), despite their emotional tone and heavy leaning on the side of self-justification, are a testimony to these facts.

40 Salman, 1985:38.

41 Basri, 1987:146–53.

42 Ibid.

43 Al-Swaydi, 1987:111.

44 Clark Kerr to Eden, 4 January 1938, FO 371/21853/E 435.

45 Edmonds to Newton, 15 February 1941, Enclosure in Newton to Eden, 27 February 1941, FO 406/79/E 1317.

46 Humphrys to FO, 9 September 1933, FO 371/16924/E 5295; al-Hasani, 1953–67: vol. 3, 323–5.

47 Khadduri, 1951:153–4; Rashid 'Ali al-Gaylani, memoirs, *Akhir Sa'a*, 27 February 1957.

48 Newton to Halifax, 16 May 1940, FO 406/78/E 2022; Newton to Halifax, 27 May 1940, FO 406/78/E 2095.

49 FO to Newton, 16 June 1940, FO 371/24561/E 2128; Newton to FO, 18 June 1940, FO 371/24561/E 2128; al-Hasani, 1953–67: vol. 5, 149–59.

50 Newton to Halifax, 5 June 1940, FO 406/78/E 2280.
51 Newton to FO, 15 June 1939, FO 371/23216/E 4475; War Office (WO) to FO, 24 November 1939, FO 371/23207/E 7738; FO to Newton, 13 February 1941, FO 371/27061/E 405; WO to FO, 15 January 1940, FO 371/24551/E 246.
52 Churchill to Cornwallis, 11 March 1941, FO 406/79/E 795.
53 Newton to Halifax, 8 July 1940, FO 406/78/E 2228.
54 Be'eri, 1970:32.
55 High Commissioner to CO, 7 August 1940, FO 406/77/E 2355; Halifax to Newton, 14 August 1940, FO 406/78/E 2355.
56 Edmonds to Newton, 15 February 1941, Enclosure in Newton to Eden, 27 February 1941, FO 371/27063/E 1317.
57 FO to Newton, 14 November 1940, FO 371/24558/E 2905.
58 Newton to FO, 2 January 1941, FO 371/27061/E 58; Newton to Eden, 17 January 1941, FO 406/79/E 653; Khadduri, 1951:201.
59 Newton to Eden, 2 January 1941, FO 371/27061/E 376; Shawkat, 1974:425.
60 H. Sirri's letter to al-Gaylani of 28 December 1940 and al-Gaylani's reply of 3 January 1941 are included in Lampson to FO, 17 January 1941, FO 371/27061/223. For the Saudi correspondence with al-Gaylani, see Stonehewer-Bird (Jeddah) to FO, 22 January 1941, FO 371/27061/E 84.
61 Newton to FO, 30 January 1941, FO 371/27061/E 320; HQ RAF, Middle East to Air Ministry, 31 January 1941, FO 371/27061/X. 7138.
62 Edmonds to Rashid Ali, 27 January 1941, Enclosure in Newton to FO, 3 February 1941, FO 371/27062/E 815. Also, Edmond's report, 15 February 1941 (note 45).
63 Newton to FO, 27, 29 and 31 January 1941, FO 371/27061/E 320.
64 Al-Hasani, 1953–67: vol. 5, 183–5; al-Hashimi, 1967: vol. 1, 387.
65 Edmonds to Newton, 1 April 1941, Enclosure in Cornwallis to Eden, 6 April 1941, FO 371/27067/E 1806.
66 Knabenshue's minute, 12 February 1941, FO 371/27098/E 780.
67 FO to Newton, 13 February 1941, FO 371/27061/E 405; Churchill to Cornwallis, 11 March 1941, FO 406/79/E 795.
68 Churchill to Cornwallis, 11 March 1941, FO 406/79/E 694, especially the Enclosure.
69 Minute of conversation between Eden and al-Swaydi, 7 March 1941, FO 371/27092/E 1477; FO to Newton, 24 March 1941, FO 371/27062/E 1075. In his memoirs (al-Swaydi, 1969:36–9), Tawfiq al-Swaydi was highly economical with the truth when he wrote of his meeting with Eden. Al-Swaydi's version dwelled mainly on what he was supposed to have said to Eden with little of Eden's side of the conversation.
70 Al-Hashimi, 1967: vol. 1, 413; al-Sabbagh, 1994:254–6.
71 Newton to FO, 31 March 1941, FO 371/27062/E 1246; al-Hashimi, 1967: vol. 1, 413–19.
72 Newton to FO, 2 April 1941, FO 371/27062/E 1251 and E 1244; Cornwallis to FO, 3 and 4 April 1941, FO 371/27062/E 1255 and E 1265 respectively.
73 Newton to FO, 21 March 1941, FO 371/27062/E 1075; Newton to FO, 28 March 1941, FO 371/27062/E 1154.
74 Commander-in-chief, Middle East, to the War Office, 30 March 1941, FO 371/27062/E 1154, Annex 1.

75 Minute of the Chiefs of Staff Committee, War Cabinet, 31 March 1941, CAB. 208/41, ibid.

76 Newton to Halifax, 20 January 1940, FO 406/78/E 500; Zuʻaytir, 1980: 611–12.

77 Mackereth to Baxter, 27 September 1939, FO 371/23277/E 7298; Gardener to Eden, 10 April 1941, FO 406/79/E 2840; Newton to Halifax, 16 May 1940, FO 406/78/E 2022; Thorpe, 1971:80.

78 Memorandum by R. A. Beaumont, Enclosure in Gardener to FO, 11 January 1941, FO 371/27330/E 655.

79 Al-Hashimi, 1967:315.

80 Bullard (Tehran) to Halifax, 29 May 1940, FO 406/78/E 1642; Newton to Halifax, 31 May 1940, FO 406/78/E 1642; al-Hashimi, 1967:348.

81 Lampson to FO, 20 November 1939, FO 371/23241/E 7726; Bullard (Jeddah) to Halifax, 30 November 1939, FO 371/23241/E 7768.

82 Lampson to FO, 10 September and 1 November 1939, FO 371/23240/E 6529 and 23241/E 7318 respectively.

83 Lampson to FO, 24 April 1940, FO 371/24566/E 1829.

84 Newton to FO, 8 December 1939, FO 371/23242/E 7886.

85 On the dismissal of Mahir's government, see Ramadan, 1970:60–81; Coury, Ph.D. dissertation, 1984: 466–77ff.; Abdel Nasser, 1994:38–62.

86 Baggallay's memorandum, 28 September 1939, FO 371/23239/E 6357; Porath, 1980:36–50.

87 Churchill to Cornwallis, 11 March 1941, FO 406/79/E 694. See also Newton to Halifax, 31 August 1940, FO 406/78/E 2572.

88 Ibid.; Churchill, Note on Palestine, 28 April 1943, FO 371/35034/E 2742.

89 Lloyd to High Commissioner (Jerusalem), 22 June 1940, FO 371/24549/E 2152; Furlonge, 1969:127–8.

90 Newton to Eden, 17 January 1941, FO 406/79/E 653; *Al-Maktab al-ʻArabi, Mushkilat Filastin*, vol. 2, 1946, pp. 63–4; Amin al-Husayni to Abd al-Razzaq al-Hasani, 17 January 1970, in al-Hasani, 1990:63.

91 Newton to FO, 3 August 1940, FO 371/24549/E 2283; al-Hasani, ibid.

92 Halifax to Newton, 20 August 1940, FO 406/78/E 2283 (Nos. 284 and 285); Edmonds to Newton, 10 October 1940, FO 371/24561/E 2997.

93 Hourani, 1962:293.

94 Porath, 1986:28–9; Khoury, 1987:587–8.

95 Baxter to Shuckburgh, 17 July 1939, FO 371/23280/E 4826; Moody to General Barker, 24 August 1939, ibid., E 7365.

96 Trott to Halifax, 22 August 1939, FO 371/23271/E 6447; Newton to Halifax, 19 July 1940, FO 406/78/E 2027.

97 Porath, 1986:44.

98 Al-Hashimi, 1967: vol. 1, 310–12.

99 Kirkbride to High Commissioner (Palestine), 9 April 1940, Enclosure in High Commissioner to Shuckburgh, 11 April 1940, FO 371/24569/E 1626.

100 Al-Hout, 1986:449 (quoting Rasim al-Khalidi). Cf. Hirszowicz, 1966:260–6.

101 Al-Rayyis, 1969: vol. 1, 103–9; al-Sayyid, 1973:25–7. Although it was presumably an underground organization, the Arab Nationalist Party was detected by British officials in Damascus. Its programme was described as containing "the usual wild and unpractical ideas of pan-Arabism" and was thought to be supported by the Germans. See Consul Gardener (Damascus) to Eden, 10 April 1941, FO 406/79/E 2840.

102 Al-Hout, 1986:491–4.
103 Although the activists of the Arab Nationalist Party became close to the mufti, identified with his political line, and placed their networking experience at his service, they did not disclose their secret organization to him (ibid., 493).
104 Gardener to Eden, 10 April 1941, FO 406/79/E 2840. It must be mentioned that Dr Sa'id Abd al-Fattah al-Imam was one of the founders of the Arab Nationalist Party, and since he briefly studied in Germany (dentistry), he seems to have been an accessory to the mufti's early contacts with Germany. See al-Rayyis, 1969: vol. 1, 103–9; Khoury, 1987:564–6.
105 Gardener to FO, 8 October 1940, FO 406/78/E 2365; Gardener to FO, 25 February 1941, FO 371/27330/E 655.
106 Gardener to FO, 11 January 1941, FO 371/27330/E 172.
107 Gardener to FO, 7 March 1941, FO 371/27330/E 1835.
108 Newton to FO, 23 December 1940 and 16 March 1941, FO 371/27330/E 169 and E 1036 respectively.
109 Gardener to Halifax, 5 September 1940, FO 406/78/E 2604. According to this report, the Bloc was of the view of creating revolt in Syria rather than in Palestine.
110 Extracts from M.E.I.C. Censorship Summary, No. 45, 2–10 September 1940, and Daily Intelligence Summary, No. 312, 14 September 1940, CO 733/427/8.
111 Al-Hashimi, 1967: vol. 1, 363; al-Sabbagh, 1994:130–1. Al-Quwwatli appears to have been also of this view, see Gardener to FO, 5 September 1940 and 8 April 1941, FO 406/78/E 2604 and FO 371/27330/E 1412 respectively.
112 Al-Hasani, 1990:68.
113 The idea of Iraqi intervention in Syria was first raised during negotiations with Colonel Newcombe in August 1940 (Edmonds to Newton, 10 October 1940, FO 371/24561/E 2997). It was again raised during the meeting of the War Cabinet Defence Committee on 8 May 1941, but was considered by Churchill too late to be implemented in the light of the outbreak of hostilities in Iraq (Porath, 1986:246).
114 Al-Hashimi, 1978: vol. 2, 74–5.
115 Edmonds to Newcombe, 31 July 1940, Enclosure in Newton to Halifax, 3 August 1940, FO 406/78/E 2283; Lampson to Halifax 20 and 25 August 1940, FO 406/78/E 2474 and E 2511 respectively.
116 Newton to Halifax, 1 August 1940, FO 406/78/E 2027.
117 Edmonds to Newton, 31 July 1940, FO 406/78/E 2283.
118 Halifax to Newton, 4 and 20 August 1940, FO 406/78/E 2027 and E 2289 respectively; Newton to Halifax, 31 August 1940, FO 406/78/E 2572.
119 Stonehewer-Bird to Halifax, 16 August, 2 and 7 September 1940, FO 406/78/E 2432, E 2594 and E 2620 respectively; Halifax to Stonehewer-Bird, 22 August 1940, FO 406/78/E 2432.
120 Lampson to Halifax, 25 August 1940, FO 406/78/E 2511.
121 Newton to FO, 5 and 8 February 1941, FO 371/27061/E 385 and E 405 respectively; al-Hashimi, 1967: vol. 1, 398–401.
122 Be'eri, 1970:41–9; Khadduri, 1973:140–63; Coury, Ph.D. dissertation, 1984:472–5.
123 A full discussion of this episode in Harb's career is provided by Stoddard, Ph.D. dissertation, 1963:93–101, and 206–7.
124 Al-Sharabasi, 1978:37; Grobba, 1967:270; Cleveland, 1985:40–3 and 139–44.

125 For the Nazi influences on the early Ba'thist formations see *Nidal al-Ba'th*, 1963: vol. 1, 169. Beginning on 21 October 1933, Yunis al-Sab'awi introduced what might have been the first Arab translation of Hitler's *Mein Kampf* in a series of articles in the Iraqi daily *al-'Alam al-'Arabi* (al-'Umari, 1986:41). For other Arab positive views of Nazi Germany in the mid-1930s, see Nicosia, 1980:355.

126 On the radical Arabists' celebration of the Iraqi suppression of the Assyrian revolt see Zu'aytir, 1994: vol. 1, 581–3. For the Ba'th Party's views of the non-Arab minorities see al-Sayyid, 1973:205.

127 Miège, 1968:137–9.

128 Ibid., 130–1; Villari, 1956:71.

129 *Al-Fath*, 21 Dhu al-Qa'da and 19 Dhu al-Hijja AH 1349; Muhafiza, 1985:456; Cleveland, 1985:100.

130 Bessis, 1981:89–90; Muhafiza, 1985:453.

131 Grange, 1974:166–9.

132 Miège, 1968:170. On the Arabist protests over Arslan's *rapprochement* with the Italians see Muhafiza, 1985:457 and Cleveland, 1985:146–8. Arslan's defence appeared in *al-Jami'a al-'Arabiyya*, 9 May 1935, and in Arslan, 1937:760–2, 764–6 and 791–2.

133 Statement of Mohamed ibn Mustafa el-Masakhar, 22 January 1938, Tegart Papers, Box I, file 3/C.

134 Lampson to Eden, 24 December 1942, FO 371/35578/J245 (Enclosure, Appendix A).

135 Porath, 1977: vol. 2, 76; Nicosia, 1985:85–6. In this case, not only was Germany disinterested in supporting the Palestinian Arabs but Wolf himself was strongly pro-Zionist.

136 On the Nazi–Zionist cooperation that continued from 1933 until the eve of World War II see Hirszowicz, 1966:26; Polkehn, 1976:54–82; Black, 1984; Nicosia, 1985:27–84, 143–67.

137 Bessis, 198 :330.

138 Nicosia, 1985:129.

139 Kerr to Eden, 4 January 1938, FO 406/76/E 436.

140 Melka, 1969:221.

141 Grobba's reports of 17 July and 9 November 1937, Documents on German Foreign Policy: 1918–1945, Washington, United States Government Printing Office (hereafter DGFP), Series D, vol. V, pp. 756–7 and 769–72 respectively.

142 Melka, 1969:221–2.

143 Neurath's memorandum, 1 June 1937, DGFP, Series D, vol. V, pp. 746–7. Neurath's position had obviously its origin in Hitler's *Mein Kampf* (1939:447–8).

144 Dohle's report, 15 July 1937, DGFP, Series D, vol. V, pp. 755–6.

145 Gardener to Eden, 10 April 1941, FO 406/79/E 2840; *Man Hum fi al-'Alam al-'Arabi, volume 1, Suriyya*, 1957:53.

146 A memorandum by the Propaganda Ministry, 14 December 1937, DGFP, Series D, vol. V, pp. 778–9.

147 Nicosia, 1985:141.

148 Abshagen, 1956:208; Nicosia, 1985:185–6.

149 Kimche and Kimche, 1954:15–38ff.; Avriel, 1975:28–42ff.; Nicosia, 1985:159–63.

150 Hirszowicz, 1966:47.

151 Ibid., 48; Minutes by Hentig, 27 August 1938, DGFP, Series D, vol. V, pp. 789–91.

152 Hentig to Ribbentrop, 22 May 1939, DGFP, Series D, vol. VI, pp. 555–6.
153 Grobba's report and Enclosure, 18 February 1939, DGFP, Series D, vol. V, pp. 800–10.
154 Baynes (ed.) 1942:1648.
155 Translation from Munich Latest News, 22 March 1939, Tegart Papers, Box IV, file 5; Baker, 1942:102–7.
156 Minutes by Hentig, 20 June 1939, DGFP, Series D, vol. VI, pp. 743–4. For repercussions of this meeting see Muhafiza, 1985:335–6.
157 According to Nicosia (1985:190), the Germans might never have intended to deliver the agreed weapons deal since the Saudis did not conceal the fact that in a situation of war they would certainly take the British side.
158 A full translation of Arslan's letter (Geneva, 17 November 1939) to Nuri al-Sa'id is included in Newton to Halifax, 27 December 1939, FO 371/24546/E 41.
159 Al-Sabbagh, 1994:131.
160 The following brief assessment of Shawkat is based on Kerr to Eden, 4 January 1938, FO 371/21853/E 435; Basri, 1987:141–5; al-Swaydi, 1987:124–6.
161 Halifax to Newton, 5 June 1940, FO 406/78/E 2063; al-Hashimi, 1967: vol. 1, 347.
162 Khadduri, 1960 (revised edn):178–9.
163 An English translation of the letter is in DGFP, Series D, vol. X, pp. 143–4.
164 Von Papen's report, 6 July 1940, ibid., 141–3 and Woermann's note, 21 July 1940, ibid., 261–2. Shawkat's side of his mission in Turkey is in Shawkat, 1974:392–400.
165 An English text (seems to be the original text that was delivered to the Iraqi government) of the letter, dated 7 July 1940, is in Haddad, 1950:22.
166 Khadduri, 1962:328–36. Khadduri's conclusions of Nuri's flirtation with the Germans have recently been supported by the published memoirs of Musa al-Shabandar, a senior official in the Iraqi foreign ministry at the time, and later the foreign minister of the 1941 coup government. See al-Shabandar, 1993:246.
167 Haddad, 1950:24–7ff.
168 Grobba's note, 27 August 1940, DGFP, Series D, vol. X, pp. 556–9.
169 Haddad, 1950:29–31. The English text of Haddad's draft declaration (DGFP, Series D, vol. X, pp. 559–60) refers to the recognition of the Arab countries' right to solve the problem of the Jews living in Palestine or elsewhere in the Arab world "in a manner that conforms to the national and ethnic interests of the Arabs and to the solution of the Jewish question in the countries of Germany and Italy". This formulation does not only appear differently in Haddad's version (Haddad, ibid.) but seems also to disagree with the draft declaration that Shawkat presented to von Papen in Turkey during their meeting in September 1940. Shawkat's version is in fact identical to Haddad's with regard to the particular point of the Jewish question (al-Hasani, 1990:95–6).
170 It was this meeting between Shawkat and von Papen which came to be discovered by the British and subsequently to precipitate the first British doubts about al-Gaylani's government (Edmonds to Newton, 3 February 1941, Enclosure of Newton to Baxter, 10 February 1941, FO 371/27062/E 815).
171 Haddad, 1950:37–49; Hirszowicz, 1966:86–90.
172 DGFP, Series D, vol. X, pp. 320–1. A shorter version is included in "Declaration made by German Government on 21 October 1940, concerning the Arab Policy

of the Axis Powers", FO 406/78/E 2837. The Arabic text as was broadcast on the Italian and German radios is in al-Durra, 1969:146–7.

173 Experiencing a sense of frustration, Arslan said that the Arabs should not "rely on official declarations and promises" (Haddad, 1950:58). For other expressions of the Arab disappointment see Hirszowicz, 1966:92–4; and al-Hasani, 1990:97.

174 Woermann's report, 9 December 1940, DGFP, Series D, vol. XI, pp. 829–31.

175 For the letter's text see DGFP, ibid., pp. 1151–5. The letter was written in French, dated 20 January 1941 and addressed to "His Excellency, Führer of Greater Germany, Adolf Hitler, Berlin". For Haddad's version of his second mission to Germany see Haddad, 1950:85–97. For the new Arab draft declaration see Hirszowicz, 1966:109–11.

176 Text of Weizsacker's letter, 8 April 1941, DGFP, Series D, vol. XII, pp. 488–90. The Arabic text is in Haddad, 1950:106–8.

177 Haddad, 1950:83–4; al-Durra, 1969:87–8. See also in this regard the mufti's letter to Naji Shawkat (28 September 1942) and Shawkat's reply (30 September 1942) in Shawkat, 1974:540–2. A similar version of this meeting was described in al-Sabbagh, 1994:267.

178 Gardener to FO, 8 April and 4 May 1941, FO 371/27330/E 1412 and E 1955 respectively.

179 Shawkat, 1974:434.

180 Proceedings of (the Iraqi) Parliament, 10 April 1941, FO 371/27069/E 2214; Cornwallis to FO, 11 April 1941, FO 371/27064/E 1409.

181 Cornwallis to FO, 12 April 1941, FO 371/27064/E 1443 and E 1438.

182 Cornwallis to FO, 5 April 1941, FO 371/27062/E 1292; FO to Cairo, 7 April 1941, FO 371/27062/E 1292.

183 Commander-in-chief, Middle East to the War Office, 7 and 10 April 1941, FO 371/27063/E 1359 and E 1385 respectively.

184 Cornwallis to FO, 9 and 11 April 1941, FO 371/27063/E 1386 and 27064/E 1410 respectively. The Air Force Intelligence reported rising support for al-Gaylani throughout Iraq, AHQ, Iraq to RAF, ME, 11 April 1941, FO 371/27064/E 1431.

185 War Cabinet, Chiefs of Staff Committee, Minutes of Meeting held on 12 April 1941, FO 371/27064/E 1457.

186 Cornwallis to FO, 14 April 1941, FO 371/27064/E 1478; FO to Cornwallis, 15 April 1941, FO 371/27064/E 1450.

187 Cornwallis to FO, 15 April 1941, FO 371/27065/E 1507, and 16 April 1941, ibid., E 1521, E 1523 and particularly E 1524.

188 Cornwallis to FO, 18 April 1941, Annex II of the Minutes of the War Cabinet, Chiefs of Committee of 20 April 1941, FO 371/27066/E 1623.

189 The War Office to Commander-in-chief, Middle East, 4 May 1941, FO 371/27069/E 2104.

190 Cornwallis to FO, 18 April 1941, FO 371/27066/E 1623 (Annex III).

191 AHQ Iraq to RAF, HQ Middle East, 24 April 1941, FO 371/27065/E 1592.

192 Cornwallis to FO, 28 and 29 April 1941, FO 371/27067/E 1782 and E 1790 respectively; GOC, Basra to Commander-in-chief, India, 29 April 1941, FO 371/27067/E 1905; al-Hasani, 1990:242.

193 AHQ Iraq to RAF, HQ, Middle East, 30 April 1941, FO 371/27067/E 1802; same to same, 1 May 1941, FO 371/27067/E 1616; Cornwallis to FO, 30 April 1941, FO 371/27067/E 1817.

194 Haddad, 1950:110; al-Durra, 1969:260; al-Hasani, 1990:239–40.
195 The RAF, HQ, Middle East (in Cairo) gave the Commanding Officer at Habbaniyya (who was coordinating with Cornwallis) the option of giving the Iraqis an ultimatum before attacking their forces (RAF, HQ, Middle East to AOC Iraq, 1 May 1941, FO 371/27067/E 1851). The British military in Iraq, as well as Cornwallis, preferred to give no such ultimatum. Instead, a statement with vicious attacks on al-Gaylani and the "Golden Square" was distributed to the Iraqi people by Cornwallis and was repeated by the BBC and Jerusalem Radio (English text is in Lampson to FO, 2 May 1941, FO 371/27067/E 1893; Arabic text is in al-Hasani, 1990:243–7). It is clear that even before the outbreak of war, Cornwallis had in his mind the destruction of al-Gaylani's government and not the defence of Habbaniyya. See, for example, Cornwallis to FO, 1 May 1941, FO 371/27067/E 1876 and E 1884.
196 Commander-in-chief, Middle East to the War Office, 5 May 1941, FO 371/27069/E 2109.
197 The War Office, Chiefs of Staff, to Commander-in-chief, Middle East, 6 May 1941, FO 371/27068/E 2051.
198 Hirszowicz, 1966:145.
199 Ibid., 146.
200 The English text of directive 30 is in DGFP, Series D, vol. XII, pp. 862–4. On the slow German move to supply Iraq with arms, and the problems of transportation see: Hirszowicz, ibid., pp. 147–64; Muhafiza, 1985:360–72.
201 "Report of the German Mission in Syria from May 9th to July 11th, 1941, drawn up by Rohn for Ribbentrop", Special train Westfaleu, July 30th, 1941, DGFP, Series D, vol. XIII, pp. 237–65.
202 See Haddad's version of al-Sabbagh's panicking pleas for German air support on 6 May 1941 (Haddad: 1950:112–13).
203 Playfair, 1956: vol. 2, 188; Silverfarb, 1986:133.
204 At the outbreak of hostilities, the Iraqi army totalled 45,000 men of whom a force of 9,000 men, equipped with one Field Artillery Brigade and two anti-aircraft/anti-tank battalions, encircled Habbaniyya. One Infantry Brigade was stationed in Ramadi to block a possible British advance from Transjordan, and was reinforced by another battalion at Falluja to serve the same purpose (al-Durra, 1969:268–9). The British force at Habbaniyya was composed of 1,000 RAF personnel and about 2,000 servicemen, reinforced by 500 British and Indian troops flown up from Basra (Playfair, 1956: vol. 2, 189). On 16 May, 2,000 British troops from Palestine and British-led troops from the Arab legion arrived at the base (Silverfarb, 1986:132). Al-Sabbagh (1994:303) wrote of the Iraqi troops on the Habbaniyya front dominating the British force by ten to one.
205 Haddad, 1950:115–16; al-Hashimi, 1967: vol. 1, 449; al-Sabbagh, 1994:304. Hamdi (1987) provides a detailed and highly accurate study of the military aspects of the Iraqi–British conflict, especially pp. 107–64.
206 Knatchbull Hugessen (Ankara) to FO, 8 April 1941, FO 371/27063/E 1363.
207 The Turkish proposal was officially presented to the two sides on 3 May 1941 (Ankara to FO, 3 May 1941, FO 371/27067/E 1907). On 6 May, Eden made a statement to the House of Commons in which he responded to the Turkish offer by stating, "our position is as follows: The first requisite is the withdrawal of troops from Habbaniyyah and cessation of hostilities against His Majesty's Forces in Iraq.

When this has been done and fighting between Allied nations has in consequence ceased, His Majesty's Government are prepared to discuss the fulfilment of their Treaty rights . . ." (Extract from House of Commons Debates, 6 May 1941, FO 371/27068/E 2093). Eden's lenient statement was in fact a bluff, for, two days earlier, Churchill informed Wavell that mediation was not acceptable (Churchill, 1950: vol. 3, 227). At any rate, the Turks interpreted Eden's statement as a diplomatic go-ahead for their initiative. The arrival of Shawkat in Ankara on 8 May endowed the Turkish mediation with a credible chance of success (Ankara to FO, 9 May 1941, FO 371/27068/E 2083).

208 Ankara to FO, 9 May 1941, FO 371/27068/E 2085; Ankara to FO, 14 May 1941, FO 371/27069/E 2245.

209 Haddad, 1950:120–1; al-Hasani, 1990:269–71. Haddad indicated that the mufti was in favour of the Turkish proposal whereas al-Hasani wrote of the mufti's opposition to the proposal. The split in al-Gaylani's cabinet became known to the British from mid-May (MICE, Military Intelligence Center, Middle East, to AOC Iraq, 14 May 1941, FO 371/27070/E 2300).

210 Haddad, 1950:123–30; Yaghi, 1974:178–9; al-Hasani, 1990:273.

211 From Palestine to CO, 6 April 1941; Downie to Baxter, 7 April 1941, FO 371/27063/E 1384.

212 Although the government of al-Madfa'i was not announced until 2 June 1941 (al-Hashimi, 1967: vol. 1, 455), his premiership was envisaged by Cornwallis on 1 May (Cornwallis to Jerusalem, 1 May 1941, FO 371/27067/E 1884). After the outbreak of hostilities, al-Madfa'i asked if he could join Glubb and the Arab Legion's units advancing to Iraq with the British Palestine expedition (High Commissioner, Palestine, to Secretary of State for Colonies, 8 May 1941, FO 371/27069/E 2112).

213 Cornwallis to FO, 6 April 1941, FO 371/27063/E 1306.

214 Cornwallis to FO, 9 April 1941, FO 371/27064/E 1448; Lampson to FO, 21 April 1941, FO 371/27066/E 1643. On 13 April 1941, Prince Muhammad Ali and Husayn Sirri spoke to Amir Abdullah by telephone, expressing anxiety lest developments in Iraq should cause similar moves elsewhere and offering him the use of the Egyptian broadcasting service for messages to the people of Iraq (Officer Administering the Government, Palestine, to Secretary of State for Colonies, 15 April 1941, FO 371/27065/E 1570).

215 *Al-Ahram*, 5 May 1941. The text of the Egyptian message to al-Gaylani was in fact approved in advance by the British, see Lampson to FO, 3 May 1941, FO 371/27068/E 1920.

216 Glubb, 1957:258–9ff. Besides his difficulties with Jordanian public opinion, Abdullah was having some in-house troubles with his son and heir apparent Prince Talal who seemed to oppose his father's siding with the British against the Iraqi insurgency (High Commissioner, Palestine, to Secretary of State for Colonies, 8 May 1941, FO 371/27069/E 2119).

217 Cabinet Office, Historical Section, Official War Histories, Narrations (Military): Formation of Habforce: The Move to Iraqi Frontier, The Recovery of Rutbah, CAB 44/122, 8 May 1941.

218 Basri, 1987:148. See also Newton's correct analysis of Ibn Sa'ud's attitudes towards al-Gaylani in Newton to FO, 4 January 1941, FO 371/27061/E 84.

219 Al-Sabbagh, 1994:200–1.

220 Stonehewer-Bird (Jeddah) to FO, 29 December 1940 and 22 January 1941, FO 371/27061/E 000 and E 84 respectively; FO to Stonehewer-Bird, 10 January 1941, FO 371/27061/E 1. In mid-April 1941, Ibn Sa'ud did in fact contemplate recognizing al-Gaylani's government (Stonehewer-Bird to FO, 16 April 1941, FO 371/27065/E 1580).

221 On al-Swaydi's visit to Saudi Arabia, see Stonehewer-Bird to FO, 8, 14, 18, and 19 May 1941, FO 371/27069/E 2121, E 2235, 27070/E 2376 and E 2387 respectively.

222 Al-Hasani, 1990:276. See also Stonehewer-Bird to FO, 18 May 1941, FO 371/27070/E 2331.

223 Haddad, 1950:19. A vivid description of the role of non-Iraqi Arabists in the Iraqi insurgency is provided by Zu'aytir, 1994: vol. 2, 7–52.

224 El-Sadat, 1957:38–42; Mitchell, 1969:25. Mustafa al-Wakil, one of Young Egypt's leaders, had already been living in Baghdad since November 1940, and was closely linked to the mufti and involved in the Iraqi insurgency (Jankowski, 1975:83–5).

225 Al-Rayyis, 1977: vol. 1, 11; Salman, 1985:85. In his message to Salman, Abd al-Nasser wrote, "we are a group of free officers who wish to join the Iraqi national revolution to serve our Arab nation and its nationalist goals . . ." According to Salman, Nasser's letter was carried to him by the Iraqi consul in Cairo.

226 Hirszowicz, 1966:152; Be'eri, 1970:45–6.

227 Al-'Azma Papers, Arab Files, 5/310 (A declaration to the Syrian people on the establishment of a central committee for the support of Iraq, May 1931).

228 Al-Sayyid, 1973:15 and 39–40; Dandashli, 1979:34.

8

Conclusion

———

The emergence of the Arab-Islamic reform movement in the late nineteenth century under the impact of Islamic revivalist thought, the Western challenge and the programme of modernization, marked a new era in the history of Islam and the Arabs. With the breakdown of Islamic cultural autonomy, a composite world view was brought about, in which the boundaries between the self and the other overlapped. By incorporating Western themes of progress, rationalism and constitutionalism into the Islamic discourse, the modern Arab-Muslim intellectual developed an eclectic and pragmatic sense of the world. Yet, faced with the power of the despotic state and the tenacious resistance of traditional Islamic circles to the unfolding of modern times, the Arab-Islamic reformists embraced an Arabist agenda. Arabism was the political expression of the struggle for legitimacy, in which the Arab-Islamic reformists represented the minority voice. Their rise to prominence and their domination over Arab culture and politics coincided with the demise of the Ottoman state. This rise, however, carried with it the first failure of the Arab movement, one that continued to haunt Arab nationalism for decades to come. Inasmuch as it reflected an assertion of the Arab self-view, the triumph of Arabism and its bold alliance with the British during World War I ultimately inaugurated an Arab entity without a state, a nation without unity.

The versatility and resources of the Arab interwar generation were certainly beyond doubt. A broad coalition of reformist ulema, notables, graduates of modern Ottoman and European schools, bureaucrats and army officers, they came to represent a continuation of the past as well as the spirit of the present at the same time. Although they were generally an élitist group that was not yet familiar or entirely comfortable with the mass movements, their popular channels were most of the time carefully and tactfully maintained by a balancing act of employing the traditional power of the *a'yan* class and reflecting aspirations and demands of the people. Their achievements were no less impressive. Faced with the disintegration of the Ottoman order, they succeeded with relative ease and avoidance of grave civil tribulations in reconstituting the Arab entity and expressing a fairly defined Arab national voice. The Arab-Islamists' achievements were equally manifested in their transcendence of the Arabist–Ottomanist divide of the war years, establishment of an extensive Arab-Islamic network and reaffirmation of the Islamic dimension of the Arab struggle through a series of pan-Islamic congresses. It was in this subtle and purposeful movement of people, organizational expansion of Arab and Islamic associations and societies and the prompt emergence of support and solidarity committees, that the international legality of the mandate system was challenged. This challenge would certainly become more apparent in the course of the Arab–Zionist confrontation in Palestine.

Following the demise of the Damascus Arab government, no single issue would help turn Arabism into a mass movement like the Palestinian question. Whether because of the alien nature of the Zionist project, the dangers emanating from the increasing power of the Zionists, or the Palestinians' active promotion of their cause, Palestine became a major unifying force of the Arabs. Both Arabism and the Palestinian question were products of the turbulent times of the late nineteenth century and of the declining fortunes of Islamdom in the face of Western encroachment. Together they became the driving force, as well as a compelling challenge, for a whole generation of Arab intellectuals and political élite. The involvement of pan-Arab activists from one country in the affairs of another Arab country was still generally acceptable, and, in some cases, even welcomed. But only in Palestine were the Arab common feelings and their united will expressed in such intensity and determination, beginning with the Arab reaction to the Western Wall dispute and the powerful demonstration of the General Islamic Congress of Jerusalem and moving on to the political and military pan-Arab participation in the 1936–9 revolt.

While the Arab scene during the interwar period was riddled with irrepressible tension between the old and new, the Palestinian question engendered strong responses from almost all segments of Arab society – centres of modern and traditional education, the ulema and the intelligentsia, the press, the Islamic societies, the novel political parties and the tribal formations. It was this intensifying popular support for the Palestinians on the one hand, and the geopolitical implications of the Zionist project for the vision of Arab unity on the other hand, which was to bring the Arab regional states into Palestine. For its early achievement of independence and its permanent quest for Arab unity, Iraq was the first to enter the fray. But, soon enough, both Saudi Arabia and Egypt were to follow. By the late 1930s, neither ideologically nor politically could Arabism continue to exist without the Palestinian question.

The rise of Arabism, with its Islamic complexion, as a frame of reference for Arab culture and politics, provided the Arabs with the basis for constructing a new consensus to replace the Ottoman Sultanic order. This consensus, however, never fully crystallized. One important reason for this failure was the inherent weakness of the Arab-Islamic trend. Neither as a ruling class nor as an opposition force were the Arab-Islamists – notable and non-notable alike – able to rise to the task of leading their people. Burdened by a long history of local and factional allegiances, while lacking the traditions, etiquette and responsiveness demanded for a leading national role, the Arab interwar generation could not fully overcome the challenges of its times. Internal rivalries were too deeply ingrained between the Husaynis and the Nashashibis, the Shahbandars and the Quwwatlis, the Sa'ids and the Gaylanis, and the Palace and the Wafd, for a cohesive and effective post-Ottoman Arab leadership to emerge. On a pan-Arab level, although the Arab regional state was, in many respects, a recent phenomenon that had largely reflected imperialist designs, rather than Arab wishes, it moved very rapidly to define its borders and enforce its entity. Increasing identification of a divided political class with the regional state further exacerbated the Arab situation. The Hashemite, Saudi and Egyptian royal competition, coupled with the growing Syrian and Palestinian nationalist ambitions, would thus be legitimated in terms of the geopolitical interests of the newly constructed entities of Iraq, Transjordan, Saudi Arabia and Egypt. Leading groups of the Arab interwar generation did not, of course, abandon the Arab-Islamic pursuit of unity. Rather, Arab unity came more and more to imply the regional state's ambition and its inherent tendency to self-affirmation and domination.

Yet, the Arab crisis was not entirely of intrinsic origins. It was equally a reflection of the adverse conditions emanating from the objective situation. Arabism evolved at a time when European imperialism was reaching the zenith of its power and when imperialist expansion was calling for more expansion. In one sense, the imperialist challenge, including the Zionist project in Palestine, infused the Arab movement with vigour and vitality. For, if Arabism was primarily predicated on its opposition to the late Ottoman state, its opposition to imperialism added further validation to its existence. In another sense, however, the imperialist penetrating impact and pressures were much greater than the Arab interwar generation could withstand. Imperialist interests were decisive in preserving and safeguarding the Arab order of the post-World War I era, of which the regional state was the backbone. Such interests precluded a peaceful development of a united Arab system, or alternatively the emergence of a dominant Arab power capable of enforcing a Prussian model of national unity. In the end, while Palestine was turning into the *cause célèbre* of Arab unity, Arab divisions placed the Arab movement at a grave disadvantage in Palestine.

To be sure, the Arab confrontation with the imperialist regime left a deep impact on the ideological and political configuration of the Arab movement as a whole. The Arab-Islamists' reactive, eclectic and fissionary approach to the West, which was concomitantly their enemy and partner, contributed to the Arab failure to define a cohesive position *vis-à-vis* the imperialist powers. Compounded by a series of set-backs in the struggle for independence, the Arab arena was finally disrupted. This disruption not only ushered in the age of radicalization, but also inspired the breakup of the synthetic, eclectic heritage of the Arab-Islamic reform movement. Arabism thereafter tended to reassert its being by re-creating the Arab self-view in a more exclusive manner, laying the seeds for the conflictual split of Islamism and Arab nationalism. Simultaneously, the Arab movement, miscalculating its own strengths and weaknesses, as well as those of the imperialist powers, while desperately seeking to bond with the wrong ally, headed for a major defeat in the early 1940s.

There is little doubt that only the British, amongst all the imperialist powers, seemed to possess a cohesive and defined Arab policy. The problem, of course, is that this policy proved to be the wrong one, not only from the Arab perspective, but perhaps equally from the standpoint of British interests in the Arab world. By the late 1920s, it became abundantly clear that the JNH policy was virtually running out of control. Earlier assumptions in London that the JNH could be created through peaceful means, and that it did not necessarily entail the establishment of a Jewish state in Palestine, proved to be too simplistic and highly unthoughtful. While the Palestinians showed fierce resistance to the Zionist project, the Zionists were clearly intent on establishing a Jewish state. On several occasions, none the less, a certain level of Arab unity could have contained the Palestinian conflict. The British government, however, was more apprehensive over the strategic implications of Arab unity than it was over the growing Zionist boldness and aggressiveness. Influential circles in London were not only blindly pro-Zionist, but also tended not to take the Arab aspirations for unity seriously. This approach to the Arab question was ultimately to inflict as much damage on the British and the Western standing in the Arab world as it did on the Arab future.

In the aftermath of World War II, it was the rationale of compromise that underlined the policies of the Arab regional state towards Arab unity. When the Arabs finally succeeded in laying down the basis of a pan-Arab system, which the Arab League was meant to be, the emerging system fell short of Arab aspirations. In other words, the Arab movement's defeat in the early 1940s implied the defeat of the Arab unity enterprise as was sought by the Arab interwar generation. Not surprisingly, the provisions of cooperation and coordination that the Arab League Charter promised were curtailed by firm guarantees of the regional state's entity as it existed in the wake of World War I. The demise of the Arab interwar generation was completed by the resounding defeat in Palestine in 1948, in which the Arab states lost whatever remained of their claim for legitimacy. Their existence would thereafter be marked by an intensifying degree of violence in the rulers' relations with the ruled, a violence that was reinforced by the nationalist-Islamist strife, the continuous Arab–Israeli encounter and the contentious relationship between the Arabs and the West. Despite its profound imprint on the modern Arab world, the fate of the reformists' project was effectively sealed.

If the propositions presented in this study are right, there seem to be still some unanswered questions concerning the political history of the Arab movement in the interwar period. First, there is the ever thorny issue of the Arab rupture with Istanbul after the outbreak of World War I. A careful re-examination of the moves and attitudes of the Damascus-based Arabists and the itinerary of Amir Faysal, especially the timing of his decisive meeting with al-Fatat leaders in 1915, might shed more light on the direct role that Jamal Pasha's repressive policies in Syria played in severing the last ties between Istanbul and the Arab movement, as well as in providing the moral pretext for the Arab revolt.

Secondly, in the light of the deterioration in the position of the civil society in many Arab countries after World War II, students of the modern

Middle East seem to overlook the fact that the Arab cities, especially in the *mashriq*, abounded with cultural, political and philanthropic activities during the interwar period. The quick explanation for this contrast in the fortunes of the Arab civil forces between the colonial and the post-colonial eras is that the imperialist administrations were more tolerant and less repressive than the nationalist governments. Although this was perhaps true in certain cases, it does not provide a satisfactorily comprehensive and cohesive answer to such a complex phenomenon. A more attentive approach may lie in a closer investigation of the social impact of the modernization programmes of the Ottoman, imperialist and nationalist regimes, and the popular responses to them.

Third, there is the issue of Arab–Zionist contacts during the interwar period. Recent studies of Arab–Zionist relations (most notably, Caplan's *Futile Diplomacy*) seem to suggest that the Arab leaders developed a dual and contradictory attitude to the Zionist project: while they were prepared in secret meetings to accommodate the Zionist wishes, they were more hostile and belligerent in public, either for reasons of popular pressure or internal rivalries. The initial problem in studying early Arab–Zionist diplomacy is largely a problem of perception. After a series of bloody Arab–Israeli confrontations, many seemed to overlook the fact that official and non-official Arab–Zionist contacts and discussions were not entirely unusual at the time. A careful re-evaluation of these contacts is likely to show a universal pattern, where a genuine disagreement on the nature of the JNH and Jewish immigration was the real cause behind their failure, rather than the seemingly presupposed theory of dual approach.

Finally, there is the issue of the Islamic–Arab nationalist conflict of the post-World War II Arab world. Dividing Arab politics and culture since the Ikhwani–Nasserite confrontation of 1954, this conflict was neither inherent nor as inevitable as it might have appeared. Perhaps more research on the social, political and cultural transformation of the dominant Arab forces and of the ruling élite after World War II is needed before a better understanding of this highly destructive Arab phenomenon can be achieved.

Bibliography

Archives

Public Record Office, United Kingdom:
    Cabinet Papers (CAB)
    Colonial Office Papers: CO537,732 and 733.
    Foreign Office Papers: FO 141, 195, 371, 406, 684 and 882.

India Office, United Kingdom:
    L/P&S series.

Arab Studies Society, Jerusalem:
    Publications and Other Documents of the Supreme Muslim Council
    and the Palestinian Political Parties in the 1920s and 1930s.

Al-Azhar, Cairo:
    File of the Caliphate Congress.

Central Zionist Archive, Jerusalem (CZA):
    S25 series.

United States Government Printing Office, Washington:
    Documents on German Foreign Policy, 1918–1945 (DGFP).

Private Papers

George Antonius Papers (St Antony's College Middle East Centre, University of Oxford).
'Arif al-'Arif: Amman Diaries, 1926–8, and Gaza Diaries, 1939–40 (St Antony's College Middle East Centre, University of Oxford).
Nazih al-Mu'ayyad al-'Azm Papers (Centre for National Historical Documents, Special Section, Damascus).
Nabih and 'Adil al-'Azma Papers (University of Exeter Library, Exeter).
Mir Basri Private Papers on Iraqi Personalities (in his possession in London).
Gilbert Clayton Papers (University of Durham Library, Durham).
Alan Cunningham Papers (St Antony's College Middle East Centre, University of Oxford).

[401]

'Abbas Hilmi Papers (University of Durham Library, Durham).

Harry Luke Diaries (St Antony's College Middle East Centre, University of Oxford).

Harold MacMichael Papers (St Antony's College Middle East Centre, University of Oxford).

Najdat F. Safwat Private Papers on Iraqi Personalities (in his possession in London).

Khalil al-Sakakini: Diaries, 1918–20 (a copy obtained from Hala al-Sakakini).

Abd al-Rahman al-Shahbandar Papers (Centre for National Historical Documents, Special Section, Damascus).

Sir Charles Tegart Papers (St Antony's College Middle East Centre, University of Oxford).

Miss H. M. Wilson, *School Year in Palestine, 1938–1939* (a manuscript; St Antony's College Middle East Centre, University of Oxford).

Reginald Wingate Papers (University of Durham Library, Durham).

Akram Zu'aytar Papers (Institute of Palestine Studies, Beirut).

Newspapers, magazines and other periodicals

Egypt, Cairo

al-Ahram

Akhir Sa'a

al-Balagh

al-Fath

al-Hilal

Jaridat al-Ikhwan al-Muslimin

al-Jihad

Kawkab al-Sharq

Majallat al-Shubban al-Muslimin

al-Manar

al-Mu'ayyad

al-Muqattam

al-Muqtataf

Nur al-Islam

al-Rabita al-'Arabiyya

al-Rabita al-Sharqiyya

al-Risala
al-Shabab
al-Shura
al-Siyasa
al-Ustadh
al-Zahra'

Britain, London
The Jewish Chronicle
The Times

France, Paris
Le Monde Diplomatique
Revue du Monde Musulman
al-'Urwat al-Wuthqa

The Hijaz, Mecca
al-Qibla (the Sharifian organ)
Umm al-Qura (the Saudi organ)

Iraq, Baghdad
al-'Alam al-'Arabi
al-Bilad
al-Difa'
al-Istiqlal

Lebanon, Beirut
Filastin (Bulletin of the High Arab Committee)
al-Hayat (published in London since 1988)
al-Mufid
al-Nahar
al-Thawra al-Filastiniyya

Palestine
al-'Arab (Jerusalem)
Filastin (Jaffa)
al-Jami'a al-'Arabiyya (Jerusalem)
al-Jami'a al-Islamiyya (Jaffa)

al-Karmil (Haifa)
The Palestine Post (Jerusalem)
al-Sirat al-Mustaqim (Jaffa)
al-Yarmuk (Haifa)

Syria, Damascus
al-Muqtabas

Official publications

United Kingdom:
"Personalities of South Syria: I. South Palestine, February 1917. II. Trans-Jordan, April 1917. III. North Palestine", May 1917. Prepared by the Arab Bureau, Cairo, Government Press (a copy is in Reginald Wingate Papers, University of Durham Library, 206/5).

Report and General Abstract of the Census of 1922, Palestine. Compiled by T. B. Barron, Superintendent of the Census, Jerusalem, 1923.

Cmd. 3229: The Western or Wailing Wall in Jerusalem. Memorandum by the Secretary of State (The White Papers of 1928), London, November 1928.

Cmd. 3530: Report of the Commission on the Palestine Disturbances of August 1929 (The Show Commission Report), London, March 1930.

Cmd. 3582: Palestine, Statement of Policy with Regard to British Policy (The White Papers on Show Commission Report), London, 1930.

Colonial Office: Report of the Commission Appointed by His Majesty's Government with the Approval of the Council of the League of Nations to Determine the Rights and Claims of Moslems and Jews in Connection with the Western or Wailing Wall at Jerusalem, London, 1930.

Cmd. 3686: Palestine, Report on Immigration, Land Settlement and Development. Sir John Hope Simpson, London, October 1930.

Cmd. 3692: Palestine, Statment of Policy by his Majesty's Government in the United Kingdom (The Passfield White Paper), London, October 1930.

Colonial Office: Middle East No. 39, Palestine: Letter from the Prime Minister to Dr Ch. Weizmann, 13 February 1931.

Cmd. 5479: The Secretary of State for the Colonies, Palestine Royal Commission Report (The Peel Commission Report), London, July 1937.

Cmd. 5634: Policy in Palestine, The Colonial Office, London, January 1938.

Cmd. 5854: Palestine Partition Commission Report (The Woodhead Report), London, November 1938.

Cmd. 5957: Correspondence between Sir Henry McMahon and the Sherif Hussein of Mecca, July 1915–March 1916, London, 1939.

Cmd. 5964: Statement Made on Behalf of His Majesty's Government During the Year 1918 in Regard to the Future Status of Certain Parts of the Ottoman Empire, London, 1939.

Cmd. 5974: Report of a Committee Set Up to Consider Certain Correspondence between Sir Henry McMahon and the Sherif of Mecca in 1915 and 1916, London, 1939.

Cmd. 6019: Palestine: A Statement of Policy (The White Papers of May 1939), London, May 1939.

Report by His Majesty's Government in the United Kingdom of Great Britain and Northern Ireland to the Council of the League of Nations on the Adminstration of Palestine and Trans-Jordan for the Year 1937, London, 1937.

Report by His Majesty's Government in the United Kingdom of Great Britain and Northern Ireland to the Council of the League of Nations on the Adminstration of Palestine and Trans-Jordan for the Year 1937, London, 1938.

Report by His Majesty's Government in the United Kingdom of Great Britain and Northern Ireland to the Council of the League of Nations on the Adminstration of Palestine and Trans-Jordan for the Year 1936, London, 1939.

Chief Secretary: A Survey of Palestine, 3 vols., Palestine Government, Department of Statistics, Government Printer, Jerusalem, 1946.

Playfair, Major-General I.S.O., History of the Second World War, United Kingdom Military Series: The Mediterranean and the Middle East, Vol. 2: The Germans Come to the Help of Their Ally, London, HMSO, 1941.

Hansard's Parliamentary Debates: House of Lords and House of Commons, 1936–41.

Unpublished Ph.D. theses

Azzam, Abd al-Rahman (1995), "Abd al-Rahman 'Azzam and the Formation of the Arab League", Oxford University.

Coury, Ralph Moses (1984), "Abd al-Rahman 'Azzam and the Development of Egyptian Arab Nationalism", Princeton University.

Gross, Max L. (1979), "Ottoman Rule in the Province of Damascus, 1860–1909", Georgetown University.

Harran, Tag E. A. M. (1969), "Turkish–Syrian Relations in the Ottoman Constitutional Period, 1908–1914", University of London.

Kayali, Hasan (1988), "Arabs and Young Turks: Turkish–Arab Relations in the Second Constitutional Period of the Ottoman Empire, 1908–1918", Harvard University.

Marr, Phebe Ann (1967), "Yasin al-Hashimi: The Rise and Fall of a Nationalist: A Study of the Nationalist Leadership in Iraq", Harvard University.

Ruded, Ruth Michal (1984), "Tradition and Change in Syria During the Last Decades of Ottoman Rule: The Urban Elite of Damascus, Aleppo, Homs and Hama, 1876–1918", University of Denver.

Stoddard, Philip Hendrick (1963), "The Ottoman Government and the Arabs, 1911 to 1918: A Preliminary Study of the Teskilat-I-Mhususa", Princeton University.

Tripp, Charles (1984), "Ali Mahir Pasha and the Palace in Egyptian Politics, 1936–1942: Seeking for Autocracy", University of London.

Articles

Abir, Mordechai (1975), "Local Leadership and Early Reforms in Palestine 1800–34" in Moshe Ma'oz (ed.), *Studies on Palestine During the Ottoman Period*, Jerusalem, Magnes Press, pp. 284–310.

Abu Manneh, Butrus (1978), "The rise of the Sanjak of Jerusalem in the Late 19th Century" in Gabriel Ben-Dar (ed.), *The Palestinians and the Middle East Conflict*, Ramat Gan, Turtledove Publishing, pp. 21–32.

—(1979), "Sultan Abdelhamid II and Shaikh Abulhuda al-Sayyadi", *Middle Eastern Studies*, 15 (1979):131–54.

—(1986), "The Husaynis: The Rise of a Notable Family in 18th Century

Palestine" in Daviv Kushner (ed.), *Palestine in the Late Ottoman Period: Political, Social and Economic Transformation*, Jerusalem and Leiden, Yad Izhak Ben Zvi and E. J. Brill, pp. 93–108.

—(1990), "The Sultan and Bureaucracy: The Anti-Tanzimat Concepts of Grand Vizier Mahmud Nedim Pasa", *International Journal of Middle East Studies*, 22 (1990):257–74.

Abu Lughod, Ibrahim (1973), "Educating a Community in Exile: The Palestinian Experience", *Journal of Palestine Studies*, 2 (1973):94–111.

Abu Lughod, Janet L. (1971), "The Demographic Transformation of Palestine" in Ibrahim Abu Lughod (ed.), *The Transformation of Palestine: Essays on the Origin and Development of the Arab–Israeli Conflict*, Evanston, North Western University Press, pp. 139–56.

al-Adhami, Muhammad Muzafar (1990), "al-'itijahat al-fikriyya wa 'atharuha 'ala 'intikhabat majlis al-mab'uthan fi al-'Iraq, 1908–1914" in Abdeljalil Temimi (ed.), *al-Hayat al-fikriyya fi al-wilayat al-'Arabiyya Athna' al-'ahd al-'uthmani*, Tunisia, Centre d'Etudes et de Recherches Ottomanes, Morisques, de Documentation et d'Information, Zaghwan, pp. 69–81.

Akarli, Engin D. (1986), "Abdelhamid II's Attempts to Integrate Arabs into the Ottoman System" in David Kushner (ed.), *Palestine in the Late Ottoman Period: Political, Social and Economic Transformation*, Leiden, E. J. Brill, pp. 74–89.

Baer, Gabriel (1977), "Popular Revolt in Ottoman Cairo", *Der Islam*, 54 (1977):213–42.

—(1896), "Jerusalem's Families of Notable and Waqf in the Early 19th Century" in David Kushner (ed.), *Palestine in the Late Ottoman Period: Political, Social and Economic Transformation*, Leiden, E. J. Brill, pp. 109–22.

al-Bakhit, Mohammad 'Adnan (1990), "Ramla in the Hijra Tenth Century/the Sixteenth Century", *Dirasat: A Journal of the Jordanian University*, Series A, 17,1 (1990).

Barbir, Karl K. (1988), "Getting and Spending in Eighteenth Century Damascus: Wealth at Three Social Levels" in Abdeljalil Temimi (ed.), *La Vie Sociale dans les Provinces Arabes à L'Epoque Ottomane,* vol. 3, Zaghwan, Tunisia, Centre d'Etudes et de Recherches Ottomanes, Morisques, de Documentation et d'Information, pp. 63–76.

Batuta, Hanna (1982), "Syria's Muslim Brethren", *MERIP Report*, 12, 110 (1982):12–20.

Bayat, Fadil Mahdi (1990), "al-Ta'lim fi al-'Iraq fi al-'ahd al-'uthmani: Dirasa Tarikhiyya fi Daw' al-Salnamat al-'Uthmaniyya" in Abdeljalil Temimi (ed.), *al-Hayat al-fikriyya fi al-wilayat al-'arabiyya athna' al-'ahd al-'uthmani*, Zaghwan, Tunisia, Centre d'Etudes et de Recherches Ottomanes, Morisques, de Documentation et d'Information, pp. 109–43.

Beeley, Harold (1941), "The Mediterranean" in Arnold J. Toynbee (ed.), *Survey of International Affairs*, 1938, vol. 1, London, Oxford University Press, pp. 414–92.

Bowden, Tom (1975), "The Politics of Arab Rebellion in Palestine, 1936–1939", *Middle Eastern Studies*, 2 (1975):147–74.

Brown, L. Carl (1964), "Stages in the Process of Changes" in Charles Micaud (ed.), *Tunisia: The Politics of Modernization*, London, Pall Mall Press.

Buchanan, J. R. (1922), "Moslem Education in Syria", *The Muslim World*, 12 (1922):395–406.

al-Buhayri, Marwan (1980), "al-Sadirat al-zira'iyya li-mutasarifiyyat al-Quds al-Sharif, 1885–1914", *Samid al-Iqtisadi*, 22 (1980):3–22.

Burke III, Edmund (1973), "A Comparative View of French Native Policy in Morocco and Syria, 1912–1925", *Middle Eastern Studies*, 9 (1973):175–86.

Chejne, Anwar G. (1957), "Egyptian Attitudes Towards Pan-Arabism", *Middle East Journal*, 2 (1957):253–68.

Chevallier, Dominique (1968), "Western Development and Eastern Crisis in the Nineteenth Century: Syria Confronted with the European Economy" in W. R. Polk and R. L. Chambers (eds.), *Beginings of Modernization in the Middle East*, Chicago, The University of Chicago Press, pp. 205–22.

Cohen, Michael J. (1973), "Appeasement in the Middle East: The British White Paper on Palestine, May 1939", *Historical Journal*, 16, 3 (1973):571–96.

Commins, David (1986), "Religious Reformers and Arabists in Damascus, 1885–1914", *International Journal of Middle East Studies*, 18 (1986):405–25.

Coury, Ralph M. (1982), "Who Invented Egyptian Arab Nationalism?", *International Journal of Middle East Studies*, 14 (1982):249–81 and 459–79.

—(1992), "Egyptians in Jerusalem: Their Role in the General Islamic Conference of 1931", *The Muslim World*, 82, 1–2 (1992):37–54.

Cunningham, Alan (1968), "Stratford Canning and the Tanzimat" in W. R. Polk and R. L. Chambers (eds.), *Beginnings of Modernization in the Middle East*, Chicago, The University of Chicago Press, pp. 245–66.

Davidson, Rodric H. (1961), "Westernized Education in Ottoman Turkey", *Middle East Journal*, 15, 3 (1961):289–301.

—(1968), "The Advent of the Principle of Representation in the Government of the Ottoman Empire" in W. R. Polk and R. L. Chambers (eds.), *Beginnings of Modernization in the Middle East*, Chicago, The University of Chicago Press, pp. 93–108.

Dawn, C. Ernest (1988), "The Formation of Pan-Arab Ideology in the Interwar Years", *International Journal of Middle East Studies*, 20 (1988):67–91.

—(1991), "The Origins of Arab Nationalism" in Rashid al-Khalidi *et al.* (eds.), *The Origins of Arab Nationalism*, New York, Columbia University Press, pp. 3–30.

Farah, Caesar (1976), "Protestantism and British Diplomacy in Syria", *International Journal of Middle East Studies*, 7 (1976):321–44.

Firestone, Ya'kov (1975), "Crop-Sharing Economics in Mandatory Palestine", *Middle Eastern Studies*, 2 (1975):3–23.

Firro, Kais (1990), "Silk and Agrarian Changes in Lebanon, 1860–1914", *International Journal of Middle East Studies*, 22 (1990):151–69.

Gelvin, James L. (1994), "The Social Origins of Popular Nationalism in Syria: Evidence for a New Framework", *International Journal of Middle East Studies*, 26 (1994):645–61.

Gershoni, Israel (1979), "Arabization of Islam: The Egyptian Salafiyya and the Rise of Arabism in Pre-Revolutionary Egypt", *Asian and African Studies*, 13 (1979):22–57.

—(1982), "The Emergence of Pan-Nationalism in Egypt: Pan-Islamism and Pan-Arabism in the 1930s", *Asian and African Studies*, 16 (1982):59–94.

Ghunaym, Adil Hasan (1972), "Thawrat al-Shaykh 'Izz al-Din al-Qassam", *Shu'un Filastiniyya*, 6 (1972):181–92.

—(1973), "al-Mu'tamar al-islami al-'am, 1931", *Shu'un Filastiniyya*, 22 (1973):119–35.

Gibb, H. A. R (1935), "The Islamic Congress at Jerusalem in December 1931" in Arnold Toynbee (ed.), *Survey of International Affairs*, 1934, London, Oxford University Press, pp. 99–109.

Goldschmidt, Jr., Arthur (1968), "The Egyptian Nationalist Party: 1892–1919" in P. M. Holt (ed.), *Political and Social Change in Modern Egypt*, London, Oxford University Press, pp. 308–33.

Grange, Daniel J. (1974), "Structure et Techniques d'une Propagande: Les Emissions Arabes de Radio Bari", *Relations Internationales*, 2 (1974):165–85.

Haddad, Mahmud (1994), "The Rise of Arab Nationalism Reconsidered", *International Journal of Middle East Studies*, 26 (1994):201–22.

Hagopian, Edward and A. B. Zahlan (1974), "Palestine's Arab Population: The Demography of the Palestinians", *Journal of Palestine Studies*, 13, 4 (1974):32–73.

Hamada, Husayn 'Umar (1986), "Jawanib min hayat al-Shaykh 'Izz al-Din al-Qassam", *Waqa'i' Filastiniyya*, 1, 2 (1986):51–82.

Haim, Sylvia G. (1954), "Alfieri and Al-Kawakibi", *Oriente Moderno*, 34 (1954):231–4

Hallaj, Mohammad (1980), "The Mission of Palestinian Higher Education", *Journal of Palestine Studies*, 9, 4 (1980):75–95.

Heyd, Uriel (1961), "The Ottoman Ulema and Westernization in the Times of Selim III and Mahmoud II", *Scripta Hierosolymitana*, 9 (1961):63–96.

Hobsbawm, Eric (1992), "Inventing Traditions" in E. Hobsbawm and T. Ranger (eds.), *The Invention of Tradition*, Cambridge University Press, Cambridge, pp. 1–14.

Hourani, Albert (1968), "Ottoman Reform and the Politics of Notables" in W. R. Polk and R. L. Chambers (eds.), *Beginnings of Modernization in the Middle East*, Chicago, The University of Chicago Press, pp. 41–68.

al-Hout, Bayan N. (1979), "The Palestinian Political Elite During the Mandate Period", *Journal of Palestine Studies*, 9 (1979):85–111.

Husry, Khaldun S. (1975), "King Faysal I and Arab Unity, 1930–33", *Journal of Contemporary History*, 10 (1975):323–40.

Inalcik, Halil (1964), "Tanzimatin Uygulanmasi Ve Sosgal Tepkileri", *Belleten*, 28, 112 (1964):660–71.

Issawi, Charles (1970), "Middle East Economic Development, 1815–1914: The General and the Specific" in M. A. Cook (ed.),

Studies in the Economic History of the Middle East, London, Oxford University Press, pp. 395–411.

al-Janhani, al-Habib (1987), "al-Sahwa al-islamiyya fi Bilad al-Sham: Mithal Suriyya" in *Nadwat al-haraka al-islamiyya fi al-watan al-'Arabi*, Beirut, Markaz Dirasat al-Wahda al-'Arabiyya, pp. 105–54.

Jankowski, James (1980), "Egyptian Response to the Palestine Problem in the Interwar Period", *International Journal of Middle East Studies*, 12 (1980):1–38.

—(1981), "The Government of Egypt and the Palestinian Question, 1936–1939", *Middle Eastern Studies*, 17 (1981):427–53.

Kampffmeyer, G. (1932), "Egypt and Western Asia" in H. A. R. Gibb (ed.), *Whither Islam?*, London, Victor Gollancz Ltd., pp. 99–170.

Karpat, Kemal (1968), "The Land Regime, Social Structure and Modernization in the Ottoman Empire" in W. R. Polk and R. L. Chambers (eds.), *Beginnings of Modernization in the Middle East*, Chicago, The University of Chicago Press, pp. 69–90.

Kautsky, John H. (1967), "An Essay in the Politics of Development" in J. H. Kautsky (ed.), *Political Change in Underdeveloped Countries, Nationalism and Communism*, London and New York, John Wiley and Sons, pp. 3–122.

Kawtharani, Wajih (1988), "al-Ulama wa turuq al-sufiyya wal-tanzim al-hirafi: mu'tayat men tarikh al-sulta wal-mujtama' fi Wilayat Suriyya" in Abdeljalil Temimi (ed.), *al-Hayat al-'ijtima'iyya fi al-wilayat al-'arabiyya athna' al-'ahd al-'uthmani*, Zaghwan, Tunisia, Centre d'Etudes et de Recherches Ottomanes, Morisques, de Documentation et d'Information, pp. 619–30.

Kayali, Hasan (1995), "Elections and the Electoral Process in the Ottoman Empire, 1876–1919", *International Journal of Middle East Studies*, 27 (1995):265–86.

Kedourie, Elie (1982), "The Bludan Congress on Palestine, September 1937", *Middle Eastern Studies*, 17 (January 1981):107–25.

Khaddouri, Majid (1962), "General Nuri's Flirtation with the Axis Powers", *Middle East Journal*, 16 (1962):328–36.

—(1965), "Aziz Ali al-Misri and the Arab Nationalist Movement" in Albert Hourani (ed.), *St Antony's Papers 17: Middle East Affairs 4*, London, Oxford University Press.

Khalaf, Ali Husayn (1982), "Tajrubat 'Izz al-Din al-Qassam: Madrasat Jami' al-'Istiqlal, 1922–1935", *Shu'un Filastiniyya*, 126 (1982):84–104.

Khalidi, Rashid (1981), "Abd al-Ghani al-'Uraisi and al-Mufid: The Press and Arab Nationalism before 1914" in Marwan R. Buheiry (ed.), *Intellectual Life in the Arab East, 1890–1939*, Beirut, Centre for Arab and Middle East Studies, American University of Beirut, pp. 38–61.

—(1984), "The 1912 Election Campaign in the Cities of Bilad al-Sham", *International Journal of Middle East Studies*, 16 (1984):461–74.

—(1991), "Ottomanism and Arabism in Syria Before 1914: A Reassessment" in Rashid Khalidi *et al.* (eds.), *The Origins of Arab Nationalism*, New York, Columbia University Press, pp. 50–69.

—(1994), "Ottoman Notables in Jerusalem: Nationalism and Other Options", *The Muslim World*, 84 (1994):1–18.

Khoury, Philip S. (1981), "Factionalism Among Syria Nationalists During the French Mandate", *International Journal of Middle East Studies*, 13 (1981):441–69.

Kliemen, Aaron S. (1982), "The Arab States and Palestine" in Elie Kedourie and Sylvia G. Haim (eds.), *Zionism and Arabism in Palestine and Israel*, London, Frank Cass, pp. 118–36.

Kramer, Martin (1982), "Shaykh Maraghi's Mission to the Hijaz, 1925", *Asian and African Studies*, 16 (1982):121–36.

Kupferschmidt, Uri M. (1986), "A Note on the Muslim Religious Hierarchy towards the End of the Ottoman Period" in David Kushner (ed.), *Palestine in the Late Ottoman Period: Political, Social and Economic Transformation*, Leiden, E. J. Brill, pp. 123–9.

Lachman, Shai (1982), "Arab Rebellion and Terrorism in Palestine 1929–39: The Case of Shaykh Izz al-Din al-Qassam and his Movement" in Elie Kedourie and Sylvia G. Haim (eds.), *Zionism and Arabism in Palestine and Israel*, London, Frank Cass, pp. 52–99.

Lamance, Henry (1899), "al-Yahud fi Filastin wa musta'maratuhum", *al-Mashriq*, 2 (1899):1088–94.

Lesch, Ann Mosely (1973), "The Palestine Arab Nationalist Movement under the Mandate" in William B. Quandt *et al.* (eds.), *The Politics of Palestinian Nationalism*, Berkeley, Los Angeles and London, University of California Press, pp. 5–42.

Lewis, Bernard (1992), "Rethinking the Middle East", *Foreign Affairs*, (Fall 1992):99–119.

Mandel, Neville J. (1965), "Turks, Arabs and Jewish Immigration into Palestine, 1982–1914" in Albert Hourani (ed.), *St Antony's Papers 17: Middle Eastern Affairs 4*, London, Oxford University Press.

Manna, Adil (1983), "Cultural Relations Between Egyptian and Jerusalem Ulema in the Early Nineteenth Century", *Asian and African Studies*, 17 (1983):139–52.

Mardin, Serif (1969), "Power, Civil Society and Culture in the Ottoman Empire", *Comparative Studies in Society and History*, 2, 3 (1969):258–81.

Matuz, Josef (1982), "The Nature and Stages of Ottoman Feudalism", *Asian and African Studies*, 16 (1982):281–92.

Mayer, Thomas (1982), "Egypt and the General Islamic Conference in Jerusalem in 1931", *Middle Eastern Studies*, 18 (1982):311–22.

—(1984), "Dreamers and Opportunists: 'Abbas Hilmi's Peace Initiative in Palestine, 1930–1931" in Amon Cohen and Gabriel Baer (eds.), *Egypt and Palestine: A Millennium of Association (868–1948)*, New York, St Martin's Press, pp. 284–98.

Melka, R. (1969), "Nazi Germany and the Palestine Question", *Middle Eastern Studies*, 5, 3 (1969):221–33

Miller, Joyce Laverty (1977), "The Syrian Revolt", *International Journal of Middle East Studies*, 8 (1977):545–63.

Mousa Suleiman (1978), "A Matter of Principle: King Hussein of the Hijaz and the Arabs of Palestine", *International Journal of Middle East Studies*, 9 (1978):183–94.

Mouton, Marie-Renée (1979), "Le Congrès Syro-Palestinien de Genève, 1921", *Relations Internationales*, 19 (1979):313–28.

Nafi, Basheer M. (1997), "Shaykh 'Izz al-Din al-Qassam: A Reformist and a Rebel Leader", *Journal of Islamic Studies*, 8, 2 (1997):185–215.

Nashif, Taysir (1977), "Palestinian Arab and Jewish Leadership in the Mandate Period", *Journal of Palestine Studies*, 9, 1(1977):113–21.

Nevo, Josef (1984), "Al-Hajj Amin and the British in World War II", *Middle Eastern Studies*, 20 (1984):3–16.

Nicosia, Francis (1980), "Arab Nationalists and National Socialist Germany, 1933–1939: Ideological and Strategic Incompatibility", *International Journal of Middle East Studies*, 12 (1980):351–72.

Nielson, Alfred (1932), "The International Islamic Conference at Jerusalem", *The Muslim World*, 22 (1932):340–54.

—(1935), "Islam in Palestine", *The Muslim World*, 25 (1935):354–8.

Ochsenwald, William L. (1976), "Arab Muslims and the Palestine Problem", *The Muslim World*, 66 (1976):287–96.

Polkehn, Klaus (1976), "The Secret Contacts: Zionist–Nazi Relations, 1933–1941", *Journal of Palestine Studies*, 5, 19 & 20 (1976):54–82.

Porath, Yehoshua (1971), "Al-Hajj Amin al-Husayni, Mufti of Jerusalem: His Rise to Power and the Consolidation of His Position", *Asian and African Studies*, 7 (1971):121–56.

—(1972), "The Palestinians and the Negotiations for the British–Hijazi Treaty, 1920–1925", *Asian and African Studies*, 8, 1 (1972):20–48.

—(1975), "The Political Awakening of the Palestinians Arabs and Their Leadership Towards the End of the Ottoman Period" in Moshe Ma'oz (ed.), *Studies on Palestine During the Ottoman Period*, Jerusalem, The Hebrew University Institute of Asian and African Studies, pp. 351–81.

—(1980), "Britain and Arab Unity (Document)", *Jerusalem Quarterly*, 15 (1980):36–50.

Qasimiyya, Khayriyya (1974), "Muhammad Ali al-Tahir: qalam Filastin fi Misr", *Shu'un Filastiniyya*, 39 (1974):150–63.

Rabab'a, Ahmad (1980), "al-Sina'a fi Filastin fi al-'usur al haditha" in *al-Mu'tamar al-dawli al-thalith li-tarikh Bilad al-Sham*, vol. 2, Amman, The Jordanian University, pp. 158–91.

Ramadan, Abd al-'Azim (1970), "al-Diblumasiyya al-misriyya athna' al-harb al-'alamiyya al-thaniyya", *al-Siyasa al-Duwaliyya*, 22 (1970):60–81.

Ro'i Ya'cov (1980), "The Zionist Attitudes to the Arabs, 1908–1914", *Middle Eastern Studies*, 4 (1968):198–242.

Rose, N. (1972), "The Arab Rulers and Palestine, 1936: The British Reaction", *Journal of Modern History*, 44, 2 (1972):214–25.

Rosen, Minna (1984), "The Naqib al-Ashraf Rebellion in Jerusalem and its Repercussions on the City's Dhimmis", *Asian and African Studies*, 18 (1984):249–70.

Schleifer, S. Abdullah (1979), "The Life and Thought of 'Izz al-Din al-Qassam", *The Islamic Quarterly*, 23, 2 (1979):61–81.

Schölch, Alexander (1981), "The Economic Development of Palestine, 1856–1882", *Journal of Palestine Studies*, 10, 3 (1981):35–58.

—(1982), "European Penetration and Economic Development of Palestine, 1856–1882" in Roger Owen (ed.), *Studies in the Economic and Social History of Palestine in the Nineteenth and Twentieth Centuries*, London, The Macmillan Press, pp. 10–88.

—(1985), "The Demographic Development of Palestine, 1850–1882", *International Journal of Middle East Studies*, 17 (1985):485–505.

—(1989), "Jerusalem in the Nineteenth Century" in K. J. Asali (ed.), *Jerusalem in History*, Buckhurst Hill, Scorpion Publishing, pp. 228–48.

Seikaly, Samir (1991), "Shukri al-'Asali: A Case Study of a Political Activist" in Rashid Khalidi *et al.* (eds.), *The Origins of Arab Nationalism*, New York, Columbia University Press, pp. 73–96.

Shahin, Emad Eldin (1989), "Muhammad Rashid Rida's Perspectives on the West as Reflected in al-Manar", *The Muslim World*, 78 (1989):113–32.

Shamir, Shimon (1968), "The Modernization of Syria: Problems and Solutions in the Early Period of Abdulhamid" in W. R. Polk and R. L. Chambers (eds.), *Beginnings of Modernization in the Middle East*, Chicago, The University of Chicago Press, pp. 351–81.

—(1975), "The Impact of Western Ideas on Traditional Society in Ottoman Palestine" in Moshe Ma'oz (ed.), *Studies on Palestine During the Ottoman Period*, Jerusalem, The Hebrew University Institute of Asian and African Studies, pp. 507–14.

Shaw, Stanford J. (1968), "Some Aspects of the Aims and Achievements of the Nineteenth-Century Ottoman Reformers" in W. R. Polk and R. L. Chambers (eds.), *Beginnings of Modernization in the Middle East*, Chicago, The University of Chicago Press, pp. 29–39.

—(1978), "The Ottoman Census System and Population, 1831–1914", *International Journal of Middle East Studies*, 9 (1978):325–38.

Sheffer, Gabriel (1974–5), "The Involvement of Arab States in the Palestine Conflict and British–Arab Relationships Before World War II", *Asian and African Studies*, 10 (1974–5):59–78.

Shils, Edwards (1960), "The Intellectuals in the Political Development of the New States", *World Politics*, 12 (1960):329–68.

Smith, Charles (1973), "The Crisis of Orientalism: The Shift of Egyptian Intellectuals to Islamic Subjects in the 1930s", *International Journal of Middle East Studies*, 4 (1973):382–410.

Swedenburg, Ted (1988), "The Role of the Palestinian Peasantry in the Great Revolt, 1936–1939" in Edmund Burke III and Ira M. Lapidus (eds.), *Islam, Politics and Social Movements*, I. B. Tauris & Co. Ltd., London, pp. 169–203.

Taggar, Y. (1978), "The Iraqi Reaction to the Partition Plan for Palestine, 1937" in Gabriel Ben-Dor (ed.), *The Palestinians and the*

Middle East Conflict, Ramat Gan and London, Turtledove Publishing, pp. 195–213.

Tarabein, Ahmad (1991), "Abd al-Hamid al-Zahrawi: The Career and Thought of an Arab Nationalist" in Rashid Khalidi *et al.* (eds.), *The Origins of Arab Nationalism*, New York, Columbia University Press, pp. 97–119.

Tauber, Eliezer (1995) "Rashid Rida's Political Attitudes During World War I", *The Muslim World*, 85, 1–2 (1995):107–21.

Thorpe, James A. (1971), "The United States and the 1940–1941 Anglo-Iraqi Crisis: American Policy in Transition", *Middle East Journal*, 25 (1971):79–89.

Tignor, R. L. (1977), "Bank Misr and Foreign Capitalism", *International Journal of Middle East Studies*, 8 (1977):161–81.

al-'Umar, Faruq Salih (1983), "Min watha'iq al-balat al-malaki al-iraqi: awraq al-qunsuliyya al-'iraqiyya fi Haifa" in *al-Mu'tamar al-dawli al-thalith li-tarikh Bilad al-Sham*, vol. 3, Amman and Irbid, The Jordanian University and al-Yarmuk University, pp. 497–512.

Weinstock, Nathan (1973), "The Impact of Zionist Colonization on Palestinian Arab Society Before 1948", *Journal of Palestine Studies*, 2, 2 (1973):49–63.

Zaharaddin, M. S. (1979), "Wahhabism and its Influence Outside Arabia", *The Islamic Quarterly*, 23 (1979):146–57.

Books

Abd al-Halim, Mahmud (1979), *al-Ikhwan al-Muslimun, ahdath sana'at al-tarikh: ru'iya min al-dakhil*, Cairo, Dar al-Da'wa lil-Tiba'a wal-Nashr wal-Tawzi'.

Abd al-Rahman, 'Awatif (1980), *Misr wa Filastin*, Kuwait, al-Majlis al-Watani lil-Thaqafa wal-Funun wal-Adab.

Abd al-Raziq, Ali (1925), *al-Islam wa 'usul al-hukm*, Cairo, Matba'at Misr.

Abdel Nasser, Hoda Gamal (1994), *Britain and the Egyptian Nationalist Movement 1936–1952*, Reading, Ithaca Press.

Abduh, Muhammad (1902), *al-Islam wal-nasraniyya ma' al-'ilm wal-madaniyya*, Cairo, Matba'at al-Manar.

—(AH 1327), *al-Islam wal-rad 'ala muntaqidih*, Cairo, Matba'at al-Manar.

—(1971), *Risalat al-tawhid*, 4th edn, Cairo, Dar al-Ma'arif.

—(1972–4), *al-A'mal al-kamila*, ed. Muhammad 'Amara, 6 vols., Beirut, al-Mu'assassa al-'Arabiyya lil-Dirasat wal-Nashr.

Abdullah, King of Transjordan (1978), *My Memoirs Completed: 'al-Takmilah'*, London, Longman.

Abshagen, Karl Heinz (1956), *Canaris,* tr. Alan Houghton Brodrick, London, Hutchinson.

Abu Gharbia, Bahjat (1993), *Fi khidam al-nidal al-'arabi al-filastini: mudhakkirat 1916–1949*, Beirut, Institute of Palestine Studies.

Abu al-Nasr, 'Umar, Ibrahim Najm and Amin 'Aql (1936), *Jihad Filastin al-'arabiyya: fusul tabhath fi tarikh al-qadiyya al-filastiniyya wa ma tara' 'alaiyha min tatawur wa tahawul munth al-nidal al-'arabi al-awwal hata al-thawra al-hadira*, Jaffa, n.p.

al-Afghani, Jamal al-Din (1979–81), *al-A'mal al-kamila*, ed. Muhammad 'Amara, 2 vols., Beirut, al-Mu'assassa al-'Arabiyya lil-Dirasat wal-Nashr.

'Aflaq, Michel (1959), *Fi sabil al-Ba'th*, Beirut, Dar al-Tali'a.

Ahmad, Feroz (1969), *The Young Turks: The Committee of Union and Progress in Turkish Politics 1908–1914*, Oxford, Oxford University Press.

Ahmad, Jamal M. (1960), *The Intellectual Origins of Egyptian Nationalism*, London, Oxford University Press.

'Akam, Abd al-Amir (1986), *Tarikh Hizb al-Istiqlal al-'Iraqi, 1946–1958*, Baghdad, Wizarat al-Thaqafa wal-I'lam.

'Alluba, Muhammad Ali (1964), *Filastin wal-damir al-insani*, Cairo, Dar al-Hilal.

Almond, Harry J. (1993), *Iraqi Statesman: A portrait of Muhammad Fadhel Jamali*, London, Grosvenor Books.

Alter, Peter (1989), *Nationalism*, London, Edward Arnold.

al-'Alusi, Mahmud Shukri (AH 1314), *Bulugh al-'irab fi ahwal al-'Arab*, 3 vols., Baghdad, Dar al-Salam.

'Amara, Muhammad (1967), *al-'Uruba fil-'asr al-hadith*, Cairo, Dar al-Kitab al-'Arabi.

Amery, Julian (1951), *The Life of Joseph Chamberlain*, vol. 4 (the first three volumes were written by J. L. Garvin), London, Macmillan.

Amin, Ahmad (1979), *Zu'ama' al-islah fi al-'asr al-hadith*, 4th edn, Cairo, Maktabat al-Nahda al-Misriyya.

Amin, Qasim (1911), *al-Mar'a al-jadida*, 2nd edn, Cairo, Matba'at al-Sha'b.

—(1941), *Tahrir al-mar'a*, 2nd edn, Cairo, Ros al-Yusuf Press.

Anderson, Benedict (1991), *Imagined Communities*, revised edn, London and New York, Verso.

Anonymous (As'ad Daghir) (1916), *Ahad a'da' al-jam'iyyat al-'arabiyya: thawrat al-'Arab, muqadimatuha, asbabuha, nata'ijuha*, Cairo, Matba'at al-Muqattam.

Antonius, George (1969), *The Arab Awakening: The Story of the Arab National Movement*, Beirut, Librairie du Liban.

al-'Arif, 'Arif (1943), *Tarikh Ghazza*, Jerusalem, Dar al-'Aytam al-Islamiyya.

—(1961), *al-Mufassal fi tarikh al-Quds*, Jerusalem, Maktabat al-Andalus.

'Arif, Jamil (1977), *Abd al-Rahman 'Azzam, safahat min al-mudhkkirat al-sirriyya li-'awwal amin 'am lil Jami'a al-'Arabiyya*, Cairo, al-Maktab al-Misri al-Hadith.

Arslan, Shakib (1913), *Bayan lil-umma al-'arabiyya 'an hizb al-la markaziyya*, Cairo, Matba'at al-'Adl.

—(1937), *al-Sayyid Rashid Rida wa Ikha' arba'in sana*, Damascus, Ibn Zaydun Press.

—(n.d.), *al-Nahda al-'arabiyya fi al-'asr al-hadir*, Damascus, Jaridat al-Jazira.

—(1941), *'Urwat al-ittihad bayn ahl al-jihad* (a collection of essays), Buenos Aires, Jaridat al-'Alam al-'Arabi.

—(1969), *Sira dhatiyya*, Beirut, Dar al-Tali'a.

al-Asad, Nasir al-Din (1970), *Muhammad Ruhi al-Khalidi*, Cairo, Ma'had al-Buhuth wal-Dirasat al-'Uliya.

al-Asali, Kamil Jamil (1986), *Turath Filastin fi kitabat Abdullah Mukhlis*, Amman, Dar al-Kamil and Samid Publications.

al-'Athari, Muhammad Bahjat (AH 1345), *A'lam al-'Iraq*, Cairo, al-Matba'a al-Salafiyya.

—(1958), *Mahmud Shukri al-'Alusi wa ara'whu al-lughawiyya*, Cairo, Ma'had al-Buhuth wal-Dirasat al-'Uliya.

'Auda, Ziyad (1984), *Abd al-Rahim al-Hajj Muhammad: batal wa thawra*, al-Zarqa, al-Wakala al-'Arabiyya.

Avriel, Ehud (1975), *Open the Gate*, New York, Atheneum.

'Awad, Abd al-Aziz Muhammad (1969), *al-'Idara al-'uthmaniyya fi wilayat Suriyya*, 1864–1914, Cairo, Dar al-Ma'arif.

al-'Awdat, Ya'qub (1976), *Min a'lam al-fikr wal-adab fi Filastin*, Amman, Jam'iyyat 'Ummal al-Matabi' al-Ta'awiniyya.

al-A'zami, Ahmad 'Izzat (1931–4), *al-Qadiyya al-'arabiyya*, 6 vols., Baghdad, Matba'at al-Sha'ab.

al-'Azm, Haqqi (1912), *Haqa'iq 'an al-intikhabat al-niyabiyya fi al-'Iraq wa Suriyya wa Filastin*, Cairo, Matba'at al-Akhbar.

al-'Azm, Rafiq (AH 1344), *Majmu'at athar Rafiq Bey al-'Azm* (ed.) Uthman al-'Azm, Cairo, Matba'at al-Manar.

'Azouri, Najib (1978), *Yaqzat al-umma al-arabiyya*, ed. and tr. from the 1905 French edn by Ahmad Milhim, Beirut, al-Mu'assassa al-'Arabiyya lil-Dirasat wal-Nashr.

al-'Azzawi, 'Abbas (1955–6), *Tarikh al-'Iraq bayn 'ihtilalayn*, vols. 7 and 8, Baghdad, Sharikat al-Tijara wal-Tiba'a.

—(1958), *Dhikra Abi al-Thana' al-'Alusi*, Baghdad, Sharikat al-Tijara wal-Tiba'.

Badawi, M. A. Zaki (1976), *The Reformers of Egypt*, London, Croom Helm.

Badran, Nabil (1969), *al-Ta'lim wal-tahdith fi al-mujtama' al-'arabi al-filastini*, Beirut, Palestine Liberation Organization Research Centre.

Baker, Randall (1979), *King Husain and the Kingdom of Hejaz*, Cambridge, The Oleander Press.

Baker, Robert L. (1942), *Oil, Blood and Sand*, New York, D. Appleton Century Company.

al-Banna, Hasan (1979), *Majmu'at rasa'il al-Imam al-Shahid Hasan al-Banna*, Beirut, al-Mu'assassa al-Islamiyya lil-Tiba'a wal-Sahafa wal-Nashr.

—(n.d.), *Mudhakkirat al-da'awa wal-da'iyya*, Cairo, Dar al-Tawzi' wal-Nashr al-Islamiyya.

al-Baqir, Muhammad and Muhammad Kurd Ali (1916), *al-Ba'tha al-'ilmiyya ila dar al-khilafa al-islamiyya*, Beirut, al-Matba'a al-'Imiyya.

Barnes, J. B. (1986), *An Introduction to Religious Foundations in the Ottoman Empire*, Leiden, E. J. Brill.

al-Barrak, Fadil (1987), *Dawr al-jaysh al-'iraqi fi hukumat al-difa' al-watani wal-harb ma' baritaniya 'am 1941*, Beirut, al-Dar al-'Arabiyya lil-Mawsu'at.

al-Barudi, Fakhri (1951), *Mudhakkirat al-Barudi*, 2 vols., Beirut, Dar al-Hayat.

Basri, Mir (1971), *A'lam al-yaqza al-fikriyya fi al-'Iraq al-hadith*, Baghdad, Wizarat al-I'lam.

—(1987), *A'lam al-siyasa fi al-'Iraq al-hadith*, London, Riad El-Rayyes Books.

al-Bassam, Abdallah bin Abd al-Rahman bin Salih (AH 1398), *'Ulama' Najd khilal sitat qurun*, vol. 1, Mecca, Matba'at al-Nahda al-Haditha.

Batuta, Hanna (1978), *The Old Social Classes and the Revolutionary Movements of Iraq: A Study of Iraq's Old Landed and Commercial Classes and of its Communists, Bathists and Free Officers*, Princeton, N. J., Princeton University Press.

Bayham, Muhammad Jamil (1950), *Qawafil al-'uruba wa mawakibuha khilal al-'usur*, vol. 2, Beirut, Dar al-Kashaf.

Baynes, Norman H. (ed.) (1942), *The Speeches of Adolf Hitler: April 1922–August 1939*, London, Oxford University Press.

Be'eri, Eliezer (1970), *Army Officers in Arab Politics and Society*, New York, Praeger.

Bentwich, Norman and Helen Bentwich (1965), *Mandate Memoirs: 1918–1948*, London, The Hogarth Press.

Berkes, Niyazi (1964), *The Development of Secularism in Turkey*, Montreal, McGill University Press.

Bessis, Juliette (1981), *La Méditerrannée Fasciste, l'Italie Mussolinienne et la Tunisie*, Paris, Editions Karthala, Publications de la Sorbonne.

Birdwood, Lord (1959), *Nuri as-Said: A Study in Arab Leadership*, London, Cassell.

Birru, Tawfiq (1991), *al-'Arab wal-Turk fi al-'ahd al-dusturi al-uthmani, 1908–1914*, 2nd edn, Damascus, Dar Tlas.

al-Bishri, Tariq (1972), *al-Haraka al-siyasiyya fi Misr min 1945–1952*, Cairo, Dar al-Kitab al-'Arabi.

al-Bitar, Abd al-Raziq (1961–3), *Hilyat al-bashar fi tarikh al-qarn al-thalith 'ashar*, ed. Muhammad Bahjat al-Bitar, 3 vols., Damascus, Majma' al-Lugha al-'Arabiyya.

al-Bitar, Salah and Michel 'Aflaq (1944), *al-Qawmiyya al-'arabiyya wa mawqifuha min al-shyu'iyya*, Damascus, Maktab al-Ba'th al-'Arabi.

Black, Edwen (1984), *The Transfer Agreement: The Untold Story of the Secret Pact between the Third Reich and Jewish Palestine*, New York, Macmillan.

Blumberg, Arnold (1985), *Zion Before Zionism, 1838–1880*, Syracuse, N. Y., Syracuse University Press.

Blunt, Wilfrid Scawen (1919), *My Diaries, 1888–1914*, 2 vols., London, Martin Secker.

Bonne, Alfred (1948), *State and Economics in the Middle East: A Society in Transition*, London, Kegan Paul.

Breasted, James Henry (1916), *Ancient Times: A History of the Early World: An Introduction to the Study of Ancient History and the Career of Early Man*, Boston, Ginn, tr. into Arabic by Dawud Qurban as: *Al-'Usur al-qadima: nahwa tamhid li-dars al-tarikh al-qadim wa a'mal al-insan al-awwal*, Beirut, al-Matba'a al-Amrikaniyya, 1926).

al-Bu'ayni, Hasan Amin (1993), *Duruz Suriyya wa Lubnan fi 'ahd al-intidab al-faransi, 1920–1943*, Beirut, al-Markaz al-'Arabi lil-Abhath wal-Tawthiq.

Burgoyne, Michael Hamilton and D. S. Richards (1987), *Mamluk Jerusalem: An Architectural Study*, London, World of Islam Festival Trust.

Cachia, Pierre (1990), *An Overview of Modern Arabic Literature*, Edinburgh, Edinburgh University Press.

Caplan, Neil (1983), *Futile Diplomacy*, 2 vols., London, Frank Cass.

al-Chadirchi, Kamil (1970) *Mudhakkirat Kamil al-Chadirchi wa tarikh al-Hizb al-Watani al-Dimuqrati*, Beirut, Dar al-Tali'a.

Churchill, Winston S. (1950), *The Second World War: vol. 3, The Grand Alliance*, Boston, Houghton Mifflin.

Cleveland, William L. (1971), *The Making of an Arab Nationalist: Ottomanism and Arabism in the Life and Thought of Sati' al-Husri*, Princeton, N. J., Princeton University Press.

—(1985), *Islam Against the West: Shakib Arslan and the Campaign for Islamic Nationalism*, Austin, Texas University Press.

Cohen, Amnon (1989), *Economic Life in Ottoman Jerusalem*, Cambridge, Cambridge University Press.

Cohen, Israel (1946), *The Zionist Movement*, New York, Zionist Organization of America.

Commins, David Dean (1990), *Islamic Reform: Politics and Social Change in Late Ottoman Syria*, Oxford and New York, Oxford University Press.

Coulson, N. J. (1964), *A History of Islamic Law*, Edinburgh, Edinburgh University Press.

Cromer, Lord (1908), *Modern Egypt*, 2 vols., London, Macmillan and Co.

al-Dabbagh, Mustafa Murad (1965), *Biladuna Filastin*, vol. 1, Beirut, Dar al-Tali'a.

Daghir, As'ad (n.d.), *Mudhakkirati 'ala hamish al-qadiyya al-'arabiyya*, Cairo, n.p.

Daghir, Yusuf As'ad (1978), *Qamus al-sahafa al-lubnaniyya 1825–1974*, Beirut, Manshurat al-Jami'a al-Lubnaniyya.

Dandashli, Mustafa (1979), *Hizb al-Ba'th al-'Arabi al-'Ishtiraki, 1940–1963*, Beirut, n. p.

Darwaza, Muhammad 'Izzat (1949–51), *Hawl al-haraka al-'arabiyya al-haditha*, 6 vols., Sidon, al-Maktaba al-'Asriyya.

—(1959), *al-Qadiyya al-filastiniyya fi mukhtalaf marahiliha*, 2 vols., Sidon, al-Maktaba al-'Asriyya.

—(1971), *Nash'at al-haraka al-'arabiyya al-haditha*, Sidon, al-Maktaba al-'Asriyya.

—(1984–6), *Mi'at 'am filastiniyya: mudhakkirat wa tasjilat*, 2 vols., Damascus, al-Jam'iyya al-Filastiniyya lil-Tarikh wal-'Athar and al-Markaz al-Jughrafi al-Filastini.

—(1993), *Mudhakkirat 1884–1887*, 6 vols., Beirut, Dar al-Gharb al-Islami.

Davidson, Roderic H. (1963), *Reform in the Ottoman Empire: 1856–1876*, Princeton, N. J., Princeton University Press.

—(1989), *Turkey: A Short History*, 2nd edn, Hutington, The Eothen Press.

—(1990), *Essays in Ottoman and Turkish History 1774–1923: The Impact of the West*, Austin, University of Texas Press.

Dawn, Ernest C. (1973), *From Ottomanism to Arabism: Essays on the Origins of Arab Nationalism*, Urbana, University of Illinois Press.

Dugdale, Blanche E. C. (1937), *Arthur James Balfour, First Earl Balfour*, 2 vols., New York, Putman.

al-Duri, Abd al-'Aziz (1986), *al-Takwin al-tarikhi lil-umma al-'arabiyya: dirasa fi hawiya wal-wa'i*, Beirut, Markaz Dirasat al-Wahda al-'Arabiyya.

al-Durra, Mahmud (1969), *al-Harb al-'iraqiyya al-baritaniyya 1941*, Beirut, Dar al-Tali'a.

al-Dastur, (AH 1301) tr. Nufal Affandi Ni'mat Allah Nufal, Beirut, al-Matba'a al-Adabiyya.

Elpeleg, Zvi (1993), *The Grand Mufti, Haj Amin al-Husaini, Founder of the Palestinian National Movement*, tr. David Harry and ed. Shmuel Himelstein, London, Frank Cass.

Faraj, Lutfi Ja'far (1987), *al-Malik Ghazi*, Baghdad, Maktabat al-Yaqza al-'Arabiyya.

Farfur, Muhammad Abd al-Latif Salih (1987), *A'lam Dimashq fi al- qarn al-rabi' 'ashar al-hijri*, Damascus, Dar al-Mallah and Dar Hassan.

Farzat, Muhammad Harb (1955), *al-Hayat al-hizbiyya fi Suriyya*, Damascus, Dar al-Ruwwad.

al-Fatwa al-khatira bi sha'n bay' al-ard lil-sahyuniyyin, Jerusalem, Dar al-Aytam al-Islamiyya, 1935.

Faydi, Sulayman (1952), *Fi ghamrat al-nidal: mudhakkirat*, Baghdad, printed by Abd al-Hamid Sulayman.

Findley, Carter V. (1980), *Bureaucratic Reform in the Ottoman Empire: The Sublime Porte, 1789–1922*, Princeton, N.J., Princeton University Press.

Finn, Elizabeth Ann (1866), *Home in the Holy Land: A Tale Illustrating Customs and Incidents in Modern Jerusalem*, London, N. Nisbet.

Foucault, Michel (1977), *Discipline and Punish*, New York, Vintage.

—(1980), *Power/Knowledge: Selected Interviews and Other Writings, 1972–1977* (tr. and ed. Colin Gordon), New York, Pantheon Books.

Furlonge, Geoffrey (1969), *Palestine is My Country: The Story of Musa Alami*, London, John Murray.

Gellner, Ernest (1983), *Nations and Nationalism*, Ithaca, Cornell University Press.

—(1987), *Culture, Identity, and Politics*, Cambridge, Cambridge University Press.

—(1992), *Postmodernism, Reason and Religion*, London, Routledge.

Gerber, Haim (1987), *The Social Origins of the Modern Middle East*, London, Mansell Publishing Ltd.

Gershoni, Israel and James P. Jankowski (1986), *Egypt, Islam and the Arabs: The Search for Egyptian Nationhood, 1900–1930*, Oxford, Oxford University Press.

al-Ghazzi, Najm al-Din (1979), *al-Kawakib al-sa'ira fi a'yan al-mi'a al-'ashira*, 3 vols., ed. Gebra'il Jabur, Beirut, Dar al-Afaq al-Jadida.

Ghunaym, Adil Hasan (1980), *al-Haraka al-wataniyya al-filastiniyya min thawrat 1936 hata al-harb al-'alamiyya al-thaniya*, Cairo, Maktabat al-Khanji.

al-Ghuri, Emile (1972 and 1973), *Filastin 'abr sitin 'aman*, vols. 1 and 2, Beirut, Dar al-Nahar.

al-Ghusayn, Fa'iz (1956), *Mudhakkirat 'an al-thawra al-'arabiyya*, Damascus, Matba'at al-Taraqqi.

Gibb, Hamilton A. R. (1962), *Studies on the Civilization of Islam*, Boston, Beacon Press.

Gibb Hamilton A. R. and Harold Bowen (1950–7), *Islamic Society and the West: A Study of the Impact of Western Civilization on Moslem Culture in the Near East*, 2 vols., London, Oxford University Press.

Glubb, Sir John Bagot (1948), *The Story of the Arab Legion*, London, Hodder and Stoughton.

—(1957), *A Soldier with the Arabs*, London, Hodder and Stoughton.

Granot, A (1952), *The Land System in Palestine: History and Structure*, London, Eyre and Spottiswoode.

Greenfeld, Liah (1992), *Nationalism: Five Roads to Modernity*, Cambridge, Mass., Harvard University Press.

Grobba, Fritz (1967), *Männer and Mächte im Orient: 25 Jahre Diplomatischer Tätigkeit im Orient*, Göttingen, Musterschmitt.

Ha-Am, Achad (1922), *Ten Essays on Zionism and Judaism*, tr. Leon Simon, London, George Routledge and Sons.

Haddad, 'Uthman Kamal (1950), *Harakat Rashid 'Ali al-Kaylani*, Sidon, al-Maktaba al-'Asriyya.

al-Hafiz, Muhammad M. and Nizar Abaza (1986), *Tarikh 'ulama' Dimashq fi al-qarn al-rabi' 'ashar al-hijri*, 2 vols.; (vol. 3 was published in 1991), Damascus, Dar al-Fikr.

Haim, Sylvia G. (1962), *Arab Nationalism: An Anthology*, Berkeley and Los Angeles, University of California Press.

al-Hakim, Hasan (1985), *Abd al-Rahman al-Shahbandar: Hayatuh wa Jihaduh*, Beirut, al-Dar al-Mutahida lil-Nashr.

al-Hakim, Yusuf (1966), *Dhikraiyat al-Hakim: Suriyya wal-'ahd al-'uthmani*, Beirut, al-Matba'a al-Khathulikiyya.

—(1982), *Suriyya fi al-'ahd al-faysali*, Beirut, Dar al-Nahar.

—(1983), *Suriyya wal-intidab al-faransi*, Beirut, Dar al-Nahar lil-Nashr.

Hamada, Muhammad 'Umar (1988–91), *A'lam Filastin*, 3 vols., Damascus, Dar Qutayba.

Hamdi, Walid, M. S. (1987), *Rashid Ali al-Gailani: The Nationalist Movement in Iraq, 1939–1941*, London, Darf Publishers.

Hamuda, Samih (1985), *al-Wa'i wal-thawra: dirasa fi hayat wa jihad al-Shaykh 'Izz al-Din al-Qassam, 1882–1935*, Jerusalem, Jam'iyyat al-Dirasat al-'Arabiyya.

Hanioglu, M. Sukru (1995), *The Young Turks in Opposition*, Oxford and New York, Oxford University Press.

Hanna, Abdullah (1987), *Min al-'itijahat al-fikriyya fi Suriyya wa Lubnan*, Damascus, al-Ahali lil-Tiba'a wal-Nashr wal-Tawzi'.

—(1989), *Abd al-Rahman al-Shahbandar, 1879–1940*, Damascus, al-Ahali lil-Tiba'a wal-Nashr wal-Tawzi'.

Hasan, Muhammad Abd al-Ghani (1968), *Tarajim 'arabiyya*, Cairo, Dar al-Kitab al-'Arabi.

al-Hasani Abd al-Razzaq (1953–67), *Tarikh al-wizarat al-'iraqiyya*, 10 vols., Sidon, Matba'at al-'Irfan.

—(1990), *al-'Asrar al-khafiyya fi harakat al-sana 1941 al-taharruriyya*, Baghdad, Dar al-Shu'un al-Thaqfiyya al-'Ama.

Hasasyan, Manadil (1987), *al-Sira' al-siyasi dakhil al-haraka al-wataniyya al-filastiniyya*, Jerusalem, Dar al-Bayadir.

al-Hashimi, Taha (1967), *Mudhakkirat Taha al-Hashimi: vol. 1: 1919–1943* (ed. Khaldun S. al-Husry), Beirut, Dar al-Tali'a.

—(1978), *Mudhakkirat Taha al-Hashimi, vol. 2: 1942–1955* (ed. Khaldun S. al-Husry), Beirut, Dar al-Tali'a.

Haykal, Muhammad Husayn (1935), *Hayat Muhammad*, Cairo, Matba'at Misr.

—(1937), *Fi manzal al-wahi*, Cairo, Maktabat al-Nahda al-Misriyya.

—(1951), *Mudhakkirat fi al-siyasa al-misriyya*, vol. 1, Cairo, Maktabat al-Nahda al-Misriyya.

Haykal, Yusuf (1943), *Nahwa al-wahda al-'arabiyya*, Cairo, Dar al-Ma'arif.

Heyd, Uriel (1960), *Ottoman Documents on Palestine: 1552–1615*, Oxford, The Clarendon Press.

Hirszowicz, Lukasz (1966), *The Third Reich and the Arab East*, London, Routledge and Kegan Paul.

Hitler, Adolf (1939), *Mein Kampf*, New York, Reynal and Hitchcock.

al-Hizb al-'Arabi al-Filastini (1935), *al-Qanun al-'asasi, al-qanun al-dakhili*, Jerusalem, n.p.

al-Hizb al-Hur al-Filastini (1927), *Dusturuh wa nizamuh al-dakhili*, Jaffa, Matba 'at Filastin al-Jadida.

hizb al-Istiqlal al-'Arabi (1932), *Bayanuh wa qanunuh*, Jerusalem, Matba'at al-'Arab.

Hodder, Edwin (1886), *Life and Works of Seventh Earl of Shaftesbury*, 3 vols., London, Cassell.

Hodgson, Marshal G. S. (1974), *The Venture of Islam*, 3 vols., Chicago, The University of Chicago Press.

Hodgkin, E. C. (ed.) (1993), *Two Kings in Arabia: Sir Reader Bullard's Letters from Jeddah*, Reading, Ithaca Press.

Hopwood, Derek (1969), *The Russian Presence in Syria and Palestine 1843–1914*, Oxford, The Clarendon Press.

Hourani, Albert (1962), *Arabic Thought in the Liberal Age 1798–1939*, Oxford, Oxford University Press.

—(1981), *The Emergence of the Modern Middle East*, Oxford, Macmillan and St Antony's College, University of Oxford.

al-Hout, Bayan N. (ed.) (1984), *Watha'iq al-haraka al-wataniyya al-filastiniyya 1918–1939: Min Awraq Akram Zu'aytir*, Beirut, Institute of Palestine Studies.

—(1986), *al-Qiyadat wal-mu'assassat al-siyasiyya fi Filastin, 1917–1948*, Beirut, Institute of Palestine Studies.

—(1987), *al-Shaykh al-Mujahid 'Izz al-Din al-Qassam fi tarikh Filastin*, Beirut, Dar al-Istiqlal lil-Dirasat wal-Nashr.

Howard, Harry N. (1963), *The King–Crane Commission*, Beirut, Khayat.

Hukm al-Islam fi qadiyat Filastin: fatawa shar'iyya khatira, Beirut, Al-Haiy'a al-'Arabiyya al-'Ulya li Filastin, AH 1396.

Hurewitz, J. C. (1956), *Diplomacy in the Near and Middle East: Documentary Record: 1535–1914*, vol. 1, Princeton, N. J., D. Van Nostrand Company.

—(1976), *The Struggle for Palestine*, New York, Schocken Books.

Husaini, Ishak Musa (1956), *The Moslem Brothers: The Greatest of Modern Islamic Movements*, Beirut, Khayat.

Husayn, Ahmad (1936), *'Imani*, Cairo, Matba'at al-Ragha'ib.

—(1971), *Nisf qarn min al-'aruba wa qadiyyat Filastin*, Sidon, al-Maktaba al-'Asriyya.

Husayn, Muhammad Muhammad (1970), *al-'Itijahat al-wataniyya fi al-adab al-mu'asir*, 2 vols., Beirut, Dar al-Irshad.

Husayn, Taha (1938), *Mustaqbal al-thaqafa fi Misr*, Cairo, Dar al-Ma'arif.

al-Husayni, Muhammad Amin (1954), *Haqa'iq 'an qadiyat Filastin*, Cairo, Maktab al-Hay'a al- 'Arabiyya al-'Uliya.

al-Husayni, Muhammad Yunis (1946), *al-Tatawur al-'ijtima'i wal-'iqtisadi fi Filatin*, Jaffa, Maktabat al-Tahir Ikhwan.

al-Husri, Sati' (1956), *Nushu' al-fikra al-qawmiyya*, Beirut, Dar al-Itihad.

—(1960), *al-Bilad al-'arabiyya wal-dawla al-'uthmaniyya*, Beirut, Dar al-'Ilm lil-Malayin.

—(1966–8), *Mudhakkirati fi al-'Iraq*, 2 vols., Beirut, Dar al-Tali'a.

Ibn Bishr, 'Uthman bin Abdullah (1971), *'Unwan al-majd fi tarikh Najd*, ed. A. al-Shaykh, 2 vols., Riyadh, Wizarat al-Ma'arif bil-Mamlaka al-'Arabiyya al-Sa'udiyya.

Ibn Ghannam, Husayn (1985), *Tarikh Najd*, ed. Nasir al-Din al-Asad, Beirut, Dar al-Shuruq.

Ibn al-Husayn, Abdullah (1973), *al-Athar al-kamila lil-malik Abdullah ibn al-Husayn*, Beirut, al-Dar al-Mutahida lil-Nashr.

Ibn Kathir, Abu al-Fida' al-Hafiz al-Dimashqi (1985), *al-Bidaya wal-nihaya*, 7 vols., ed. Ahamd Abu Milhim *et al.*, Beirut, Dar al-Kutub al-'Ilmiyya.

Inalcik, Halil (1973), *The Ottoman Empire: The Classical Age, 1300–1600*, tr. Norman Itzkowitz and Colin Imber, London, Weidenfeld and Nicholson.

Issawi, Charles (1980), *The Economic History of Turkey, 1800–1914*, Chicago, University of Chicago Press.

—(1981), *The Arab World's Legacy*, Princeton, N. J., The Darwin Press.

Issawi, Charles (ed.) (1966), *The Economic History of The Middle East, 1900–1914*, Chicago, University of Chicago Press.

al-Jabarti, Abd al-Rahman (1904–5), *'Aja'ib al-'athar fi al-tarajim wal-'akhbar*, 4 vols., Cairo, Bulaq Press.

Jamal Pasha, Ahmad (1923), *Mudhakkirat Jamal Pasha*, tr. Ahmad Shukri, Cairo, Dar al-Hilal.

al-Jamil, Saiyar (1989), *al-'Uthmaniyun wa takwin al-'Arab al-hadith*, Beirut, Mu'assassat al-Abhath al-'Arabiyya.

Jankowski, James (1975), *Egypt's Young Rebels: "Young Egypt", 1933–1952*, Stanford, California, Hover Institute Press, Stanford University.

Jannaway, Frank G. (1914), *Palestine and the Jews; or the Zionist Movement, an Evidence that the Messiah will soon appear in Jerusalem to Rule the Whole World Therefrom*, Birmingham, C. C. Walker.

Jarvis, Major C. S. (1942), *Arab Command: The Biography of Lieutenant Colonel F. W. Peake Pasha*, London, Hutchinson Company Ltd.

Jbara, Taysir (1985), *Palestinian Leader: Hajj Amin al-Husayni, Mufti of Jerusalem*, Princeton, N. J., The Kingston Press.

Jum'a, Badi' Muhammad (1980), *al-Shah 'Abbas al-Kabir*, Beirut, Dar al-Nahda al-'Arabiyya.

al-Jundi, Abd al-Halim (1978), *al-Imam Muhammad bin Abd al-Wahhab aw intisar al-madhhab al-salafi*, Cairo, Dar al-Ma'arif.

al-Jundi, Adham (1960), *Tarikh al-thawrat al-suriyya fi 'ahd al-'intidab al-faransi*, Damascus, Matba'at al-Itihad.

al-Jundi, Anwar (1963), *al-Sahafa al-siyasiyya fi Misr*, Cairo, Matba'at al-Risala.

al-Jundi, Sami (1969), *al-Ba'th*, Beirut, Dar al-Nahar.

Kabha, Mustafa Dauwd (1988), *Thawrat 1936 al-kubra: dawafi'uha wa in'ikasatuha*, Nazareth, Maktabat al-Qabas.

Kahala, 'Umar Rida (1957), *Mu'jam al-mu'alifin*, 15 vols., Beirut, Dar 'Ihya' al-Turath.

Karpat, Kemal H. (1985), *Ottoman Population, 1830–1914: Demographic and Social Characteristics*, Madison, Wisconsin, The University of Wisconsin Press.

al-Kawakibi, Abd al-Rahman (1899), *Umm al-qura*, Cairo, Jaridat al-'Arab.

—(1901), *Taba'i' al-'istibdad*, Cairo, Dar al-Ma'arif.

Kawtharani, Wajih (1980), *Bilad al-Sham, al-sukkan, al-'iqtisad wal-siyasa al-faransiyya fi matla' al-qarn al-'ishrin*, Beirut, Ma'had al-'Inma' al-'Arabi.

—(1986), *al-'Itijahat al-'ijtima'iyya wal-siyasiyya fi Jabal Lubnan wal-Mashriq al-'arabi: min al-mutasarrifiya al-'uthmaniyya 'ila dawlat Lubnan al-kabir*, Beirut, Manshurat Bahsun al-Thaqafiyya.

—(1988), *al-Sulta wal-mujtama' wal-'amal wal-'amal al-siyasi: min tarikh al-wilaya al-'uthmaniyya fi bilad al-Sham*, Beirut, Markaz Dirasat al-Wahda al-'Arabiyya.

Kayyali, Abd al-Rahman (1946), *Mudhakkirat: vol. 1: al-marahil fi al-intidab al-Faransi wa nidaluna al-watani; vol. 2: al-Jihad al-siyasi*, Aleppo, Matba'at al-Dad and al-Maktaba al-'Asriyya respectively.

Kayyali, Abd al-Wahab (1978), *Palestine: A Modern History*, London, Croom Helm.

—(ed.) (1988), *Watha'iq al-muqawama al-filastiniyya al-'arabiyya did al-'ihtilal al-baritani wal-sahyuniyya, 1918–1939*, Beirut, Institute of Palestine Studies.

Keddie, Nikki (1968), *An Islamic Response to Imperialism: Political and Religious Writings of Sayyid Jamal al-Din al-Afghani*, Berkeley and Los Angeles, University of California Press.

—(1972), *Sayyid Jamal al-Din "al-Afghani"*, Berkeley and Los Angeles, University of California Press.

—(ed.) (1972), *Scholars, Saints and Sufis*, Berkeley and Los Angeles, University of California Press.

Kedourie, Elie (1956), *England and the Middle East: The Destruction of the Ottoman Empire, 1914–1917*, London, Bowes and Bowes.

—(1966), *Al-Afghani and Abduh: An Essay on Religious Unbelief and Political Activism in Modern Islam*, London, Frank Cass.

—(1970), *The Chatham House Version and Other Middle Eastern Studies*, New York, Praeger Publishers.

—(1974), *Arabic Political Memoirs and Other Studies*, London, Frank Cass.

—(1976), *In the Anglo-Arab Labyrinth: The McMahon–Husayn Correspondence and its Interpretation, 1914–1939*, Cambridge, Cambridge University Press.

Khadduri, Majid (1951), *Independent Iraq: A Study in Iraqi Politics since 1932*, London, Oxford University Press.

—(1960), *Independent Iraq, 1932–1958: A Study in Iraqi Politics*, London, Oxford University Press.

—(1973), *Arab Contemporaries: The Role of Personalities in Politics*, Baltimore and London, The John Hopkins University Press.

Khadduri, Majid and Herbert J. Liebesny (eds.) (1956), *Law in the Middle East vol. 1: Origin and Development of Islamic Law*, Washington, D.C., Middle East Institute.

al-Khafash, Husni Salih (1973), *Mudhakkirat hawl tarikh al-haraka al-'ummaliyya al-'arabiyya al-filastiniyya*, Beirut, Markaz al-Abhath (the Palestine Liberation Organization Research Centre).

Khalaf, Issa (1991), *Politics in Palestine: Arab Factionalism and Social Disintegration 1939–1948*, Albany, State University of New York.

Khalidi, Rashid Ismail (1980), *British Policy Towards Syria and Palestine 1906–1914: A Study of the Antecedents of the Hussein–McMahon Correspondence, the Sykes–Picot Agreement, and the Balfour Declaration*, Oxford, The Middle East Centre, St Antony's College and Ithaca Press.

al-Khalidi, Ruhi (AH 1326), *'Asbab al-inqilab al-'uthmani*, Cairo, Matba'at al-Manar.

al-Khatib, 'Adnan (1971), *al-Shaykh Tahir al-Jaza'iri ra'id al-nahda al-'ilmiyya fi bilad al-Sham*, Cairo, Ma'had al-Buhuth wal-Dirasat al-'Arabiyya.

al-Khatib, Muhammad Kamil (ed.) (1993), *Mudhakkirat wa khutab al-doktor Abd al-Rahman al-Shahbandar: al-a'mal al-kamila*, vol. 4, Damascus, Wizarat al-Thaqafa.

al-Khatib, Muhib al-Din (AH 1344/1925), *'Ittijah al-mawjat al-bashariyya fi Jazirat al-'Arab*, Cairo, al-Matba'a al-Salafiyya.

—(1959), *al-Doctor Salah al-Din al-Qasimi, AH 1305–1334: safahat min tarikh al-nahdha al-'arabiyya fi awa'il al-qarn al-'ishrin*, Cairo, al-Matba'a al-Salafiyya.

—(1979), *Hayatuh bi-Qalamih*, Damascus, Jam'iyyat al-Tamadun al-'Islami.

al-Khatib, Muhib al-Din (ed.) (1913), *al-Mu'tamar al-'arabi al-awal al-mun'aqid fi al-qa'at al-kubra lil-Jam'iyya al-Jughrafiyya bi Shari' San Jirman bi Paris, 18–23 Huzayran 1913*, Cairo, al-Lajna al-'Ulya li-Hizb al-Lamarkaziyya.

al-Khatib, Nimr (1967), *Ahdath al-nakba aw nakbat Filastin*, Beirut, Dar Maktabat al-Haya.

Khilla, Kamil Mahmud (1974), *Filastin wal-'intidab al-baritani, 1922–1939*, Beirut, Markaz al-Abhath (The Palestine Liberation Organization Research Centre).

—(1983), *al-Tatawur al-siyasi li-Sharq al-Ardun, 1921–1948*, Tripoli, Libya, al-Munsha'a al-'Ama lil-Nashr wal-Tawzi' wal-I'lam.

Khoury, Philip S. (1983), *Urban Notables and Arab Nationalism: The Politics of Damascus 1860–1920*, London and New York, Cambridge University Press.

—(1987), *Syria and the French Mandate: The Politics of Arab Nationalism, 1920–1945*, Princeton N.J., Princeton University Press

Khoury, Yusuf (1976), *al-Sahafa al-'arabiyya fi Filastin, 1876–1948*, Beirut, Mu'assassat al-Dirasat al-Filastiniyya.

al-Khutba al-tarikhiyya allati alqaha fi al-jalsa al-thaniya 'ashra min jalasat al-Mu'tamar al-Islami al-'Am: Samahat al-'Allama al-Jalil al-Imam al-Huja al-Mujtahid al-Shaykh Muhammad al-Husayn al-Kashif al-Ghita' yawm al-ithnayn 4 Sha'ban sanat 1350, Jerusalem, Dar al-Aytam al-Islamiyya Press, 1932.

Kimche, Jon, and Kimche, David (1954), *The Secret Roads: The Illegal Migration of a People, 1938–1948*, London, Secker and Warburg.

Kimmerling, Baruch and Joel S. Migdal (1993), *Palestinians: The Making of a People*, Cambridge, Mass., Harvard University Press

Kisch, Frederick H. (1938), *Palestine Diaries*, London, Victor Gollancz.

Klieman, A. (1970), *Foundations of British Policy in the Arab World: The Cairo Conference of 1921*, Baltimore, John Hopkins University Press.

Kohn, Hans (1944), *The Idea of Nationalism: A Study in Its Origin and Background*, New York, The Macmillan Company.

Kramer, Martin (1986), *Islam Assembled: The Advent of the Muslim Congresses*, New York, Columbia University Press.

Kubba, Muhammad Mahdi (1965), *Mudhakkirati fi samim al-ahdath, 1918–1958*, Beirut, Dar al-Tali'a.

Kupferschmidt, Uri M. (1987), *The Supreme Muslim Council: Islam Under the British Mandate for Palestine*, Leiden, E. J. Brill.

Kurd-Ali, Muhammad (1948–9), *Mudhakkirat*, 3 vols., Damascus, Matba'at al-Taraqqi.

—(1980), *Al-Mu'asirun*, ed. Muhammad al-Misri, Damascus, Majma' al-Lugha al-'Arabiyya.

—(1983), *Khitat al-Sham*, 6 vols., Damascus, Maktabat al-Nuri.

Landau, Jacob (1990), *The Politics of Pan-Islamism: Ideology and Organization*, Oxford, The Clarendon Press.

Laoust, Henri (1938), *Essai sur les doctrines sociales et politiques de Taki-d-Din b. Taimiya*, Le Caire, Institut Français d'Archéologie.

Lapidus, Ira M. (1967), *Muslim Cities in the Later Middle Ages*, Cambridge, Mass., Harvard University Press

—(1988), *A History of Islamic Societies*, Cambridge and New York, Cambridge University Press.

Lapierre, Jean (1936), *Le Mandat Français en Syrie*, Paris, Recueil Sirey.

Laqueur, Walter (1961), *Communism and Nationalism in the Middle East*, London, Routledge and Kegan Paul.

—(1976), *A History of Zionism*, New York, Schocken Books.

Lesch, Ann Mosley (1979), *Arab Politics in Palestine, 1917–1939: The Transition of a Nationalist Movement*, Ithaca and London, Cornell University Press.

Leslie, Shane (1923), *Mark Sykes: His Life and Letters*, London, Cassell.

Lewis, Bernard (1950), *The Arabs in History*, London, Hutchinson's University Library.

—(1961), *The Emergence of Modern Turkey*, London, Oxford University Press.

Longrigg, S. H. (1954), *Iraq 1900–1950*, London, Oxford University Press.

Luckas, John (1990), *Confessions of an Original Sinner*, New York, Ticknor and Fields.

Lukitz, Liora (1995), *Iraq: The Search for National Identity*, London, Frank Cass.

al-Maghrabi, Abd al-Qadir (1948), *Jamal al-Din al-Afghani: Dhikrayat wa Ahdath*, Cairo, Dar al-Ma'arif.

al-Mahbuba, Ja'far al-Shaykh Baqir (1986), *Madi al-Najaf wa hadiruhu*, 2 vols., Beirut, Dar al-Adwa'.

Mahfuz, Khadir al-'Ali (1938), *Tahta rayat al-Qawuqji*, Damascus, Matba'at Babil.

al-Makhzumi, Muhammad Pasha (1931), *Khatirat Jamal al-Din al-Afghani al-Husayni*, Beirut, al-Matba'a al-'Ilmiyya.

al-Maktab al-'Arabi (1946), *Mushkilat Filastin*, vol. 2, Jerusalem, Matba'at Bayt al-Maqdis.

al-Mallah, Abd al-Ghani (1980), *Tarikh al-haraka al-dimuqratiyya fi al-'Iraq*, Beirut, al-Mu'assassa al-'Arabiyya lil-Dirasat wal-Nashr.

Man hum fi al-'alam al-'arabi, vol. 1, Suriyya, Damascus, Maktab al-Dirasat al-Suriyya wal- 'Arabiyya, 1957.

Mandel, Neville (1976), *The Arabs and Zionism Before World War I*, Berkeley, University of California Press.

Manna', Adil (1986), *A'lam Filastin fi awakhir al-'ahd al-'uthmani: 1800–1918*, Jerusalem, Jam'iyyat al-Dirasat al-'Arabiyya.

Ma'oz, Moshe (1968), *Ottoman Reform in Syria and Palestine, 1840–1861: The Impact of the Tanzimat on Politics and Society*, Oxford, Oxford University Press.

Mardam Bey, Khalil (1971), *A'yan al-Qarn al-Thalith 'Ashar fi al-Fikr wal-Siyasa wal-'Ijtima'*, Beirut, Lajnat al-Turath al-'Arabi.

Mardam-Bey, Salma (1994), *Syria's Quest for Independence, 1939–1945*, Reading, Ithaca Press.

Mardin, Serif (1962), *The Genesis of Young Ottoman Thought*, Princeton, N. J., Princeton University Press.

Mardini, Zuhayr (1977), *Alf Yawm ma' al-Hajj Amin*, Sidon, Dar al-'Irfan.

—(1986), *Filastin wal-Hajj Amin al-Husayni*, Beirut, Dar 'Iqra'.

Marsot, Afaf Lutfi al-Sayyid (1984), *Egypt in the Reign of Muhammad Ali*, Cambridge, Cambridge University Press.

al-Matba'i, Hamid (1988), *Muhammad Bahjat al-'Athari*, Baghdad, Wizarat al-I'lam al-'Iraqiyya.

Mattar, Philip (1988), *The Mufti of Jerusalem: Al-Hajj Amin al-Husayni and the Palestinian National Movement*, New York, Columbia University Press.

Mayer, Thomas (1983), *Egypt and the Palestine Question, 1936–1945*, Berlin, Klaus Schwarz Verlag.

Messick, Brinkley (1993), *The Calligraphic State: Textual Domination and History in a Muslim Society*, Berkeley and Los Angeles, University of California Press.

Miège, Jon Louis (1968), *L'Impérialisme colonial Italian de 1870 à nos jours*, Paris, Société d'Edition et d'Enseignement Supérieur.

Migdal, Joel S. (ed.) (1980), *Palestinian Society and Politics*, Princeton, N. J., Princeton University Press

al-Miqdadi, Darwish (1932), *Tarikh al-'Umma al-'Arabiyya*, Baghdad, Matba'at Baghdad.

al-Misri, Ibrahim al-Sayyid 'Isa (1936), *Majma' al-'Athar al-'Arabiyya*, Damascus, Matba'at ibn Zaydun.

Mitchell, Richard P. (1969), *The Society of the Muslim Brothers*, London, Oxford University Press.

Mogannam, Matiel (1937), *The Arab Woman and the Palestine Problem*, London, H. Joseph.

Mousa, Suleiman (1970), *Al-Haraka al-'Arabiyya: Sirat al-Marhala al-'Awla lil-Nahda al-'Arabiyya, 1908–1924*, Beirut, Dar al-Nahar.

al-Mu'alim, Walid (1988), *Suriyya:1916–1946*, Damascus, Dar Tlas.

Mufarraj, Fu'ad Khalil (1937), *al-Mu'tamar al-'Arabi al-Qawmi fi Bludan*, Damascus, al-Maktab al-'Arabi al-Qawmi lil-Di'aya wal Nashr.

al-Muhafiza, Ali (1985), *Mawqif Faransa wa Italiya min al-Wahda al-'Arabiyya, 1919–1945*, Beirut, Markaz Dirasat al-Wahda al-'Arabiyya.

—(1987), *Al-Haraka al-Fikriyya fi 'Asr al-Nahda fi Filastin wal-'Urdun*, Beirut, al-Ahliyya lil-Nashr wal-Tawzi'.

al-Muhibi, Muhammad Amin bin Fadl-Allah (n.d.), *Khulasat al-'Athar fi A'yan al-Qarn al-Hadi 'Ashar*, 4 vols., Beirut, Maktabat Khayat.

Mujahid, Zaki Muhammad (1950), *Al-A'lam al-Shariayya fi al-Ma'at al-Rabi 'at 'Ashrat al-Hijriyya.*, 2 vols., Cairo, Maktabat al-Mujahid.

al-Muradi, Muhammad Khalil (1874–83), *Silk al-Durar fi A'yan al-Qarn al-Thani 'Ashar*, 4 vols., Cairo, Bulaq Press (vol. 1 was in fact published in Istanbul; the whole book was reprinted by al-Muthanna Press in Baghdad).

Mushtaq, Talip (1989), *Awraq Ayami, 1900–1958*, Baghdad, al-Dar al-'Arabiyya lil-Tiba'a.

Muslih, Muhammad Y. (1988), *The Origins of Palestinian Nationalism*, New York, Columbia University Press.

Mustafa, Ahmad Abd al-Rahim (1973), *Tatawur al-Fikr al-Siyasi fi Misr al-Haditha*, Cairo, Ma'had al-Dirasat al-'Arabiyya.

al-Mu'tamar al-Nisa'i al-Sharqi (1938), *al-Mar'a al-arabiyya wa qadiyyat Filastin*, Cairo, The Egyptian Women's Union.

al-Mu'tamar al-Suri al-Filastini, Cairo, Matba'at al-Manar, 1922.

al-Nabulsi, Abd al-Ghani (1989), *al-Haqiqa wal-majaz fi rihlat Bilad al-Sham wal-Hijaz*, ed. Riyad Abd al-Hamid Murad, Damascus, Dar al-Ma'rifa.

Nairn, Tom (1977), *The Break-up of Britain*, London, New Left Books.

Nakash, Yitzhak (1994), *The Shiis of Iraq*, Princeton, N. J., Princeton University Press

Nakhleh, Khalid and Elia Zureik (eds.) (1980), *The Sociology of the Palestinians*, New York, St Martin's Press.

al-Nashashibi, Is'af (AH 1342), *Qalbun 'arabi wa 'aqlun urubbi*, Jerusalem, al-Maktaba al-Salafiyya.

al-Nashashibi, Nasser al-Din (1990), *Jerusalem's Other Voice: Ragheb Nashashibi and Moderation in Palestinian Politics: 1920–1948*, Exeter, Ithaca Press.

Nassar, Najib al-Khuri (1911), *al-Sahyuniyya: tarikhuha, gharaduha wa ahdafuha, mulakhasa min al-Incyklubidiya al-Yahudiyya*, Haifa, Matba'at al-Karmil, .

Nazmi, Wamid Jamal 'Umar (1984), *al-Judhur al-siyasiyya wal-fikriyya wal-'ijtima'iyya lil-haraka al-qawmiyya al-'arabiyya (al-'istiqlaliyya) fi al-'Iraq*, Beirut, Markaz Dirasat al-Wahda al-'Arabiyy.

Nicosia, Francis R. (1985), *The Third Reich and the Palestinian Question*, London, I. B. Tauris & Co. Ltd.

Nidal al-Ba'th, al-qutr al-Suri, 1943–1949: min ma'rakat al-'istilal 'ila nakbat Filastin wal-'inqilab al-'askari al-'awal, vol. 1, Beirut, Dar al-Tali'a, 1963.

al-Nimr, Ihsan (1961), *Tarikh Jabal Nablus wal-Balqa': ahwal 'ahd al-iqta'*, vol. 2, Nablus, Matba'at al-Nasr al-Tijariyya.

—(1975), *Tarikh Jabal Nablus wal-Balqa'*, vol. 1, 2nd edn, Nablus, Matba'at Jam'iyyat 'Umal al-Matabi' al-Ta'awuniyya.

—(n.d.), *Tarikh Jabal Nablus wal-Balqa': 'ahd tatbiq al-nuzum al-haditha*, vol. 3, Nablus, Matba'at Jam'iyyat 'Umal al-Matabi' al-Ta'awuniyya.

—(1975), *Tarikh Jabal Nablus wal-Balqa': Ahwal al-mi'at sana al-madiyya*, vol. 4, Nablus, Matba'at Jam'iyyat 'Umal al-Matabi' al-Ta'awuniyya.

Nwayhid, 'Ajaj (1981), *Rijal min Filastin*, Beirut, Manshurat Filastin al-Muhtala.

—(1993), *Sittun 'aman ma' al-qafila al-'arabiyya*, ed. Bayan N. al-Hout, Beirut, Dar al-Istiqlal.

Ohannah, Yuval A. (1981), *The Internal Struggle Within the Palestinian Movement 1929–1939*, Tel-Aviv, Shiloah Centre for Middle Eastern and African Studies.

Oliphant, Laurence (1880), *The Land of Gilead*, Edinburgh and London, William Blackwood & Sons.

Owen, Roger (1969), *Cotton and the Egyptian Economy 1820–1914*, Oxford, Oxford University Press.

—(1981), *The Middle East in the World Economy 1800–1914*, London and New York, Methuen.

—(ed.) (1982), *Studies in the Economic and Social History of Palestine in the Nineteenth and Twentieth Centuries*, Oxford, The Macmillan Press.

Pearlman, Maurice (1947), *Mufti of Jerusalem: The Story of Haj Amin el-Husseini*, London, Victor Gollancz.

Peters Rudolph (1979), *Islam and Colonialism: The Doctrine of Jihad in Modern History*, The Hague, Mouton Publishers.

Peterson, Sir Maurice (1950), *Both Sides of the Curtain*, London, Constable.

Philby, H. St John B. (1928), *Arabia of the Wahhabis*, London, Constable.

—(1930), *Arabia*, London, Benn.

—(1955), *Saudi Arabia* (second impression), London, Ernest Benn Ltd.

Pinsker, Leo (1932), *Auto-Emancipation*, ed. A. S. Eban, London, Federation of Zionist Youth.

Porath, Y. (1974), *The Emergence of the Palestine National Movement, 1918–1929*, vol. 1, London, Frank Cass.

—(1977), *The Palestinian Arab National Movement, 1929–1939*, vol. 2, London, Frank Cass.

—(1986), *In Search of Arab Unity, 1930–1945*, London, Frank Cass.

Qadri, Ahmad (1956), *Mudhakkirati 'an al-thawra al-'arabiyya al-kubra*, Damascus, Matabi' ibn Zaydun.

al-Qa'id al-'Am lil-Jaysh al-Rabi' (Ahmad Jamal Pasha) (AH 1334), *'Idahat 'an al-masa'il al-siyasiyya alati jara tadqiquha bi-diwan al-harb al-'urfi al-mutashakil bi-Aleyh*, Istanbul, Matba'at Tanin.

Qal'aji, Qadri (1967), *Jil al-fida': qisat al-thawra al-kubra wa nahdat al-'Arab*, Beirut, Dar al-Katib al-'Arabi.

Qarqut, Dhuqan (1975), *Tatawur al-haraka al-wataniyya fi Suriyya*, Beirut, Dar al-Tali'a.

—(1978), *al-Mashriq al-'arabi fi muwajahat al-isti'mar*, Cairo, al-Hay'a al-'Ama lil-Kitab.

Qasim, Abd al-Sattar (1984), *al-Shaykh al-Mujahid 'Izz al-Din al-Qassam*, Beirut, Dar al-Umma.

al-Qasimi, Jamal al-Din (1965), *Mudhakkirat*, ed. Zafir al-Qasimi, Damascus, Maktabat Atlas.

al-Qasimi, Zafir (1965), *Jamal al-Din al-Qasimi wa 'asruhu*, Damascus, Matba'at al-Hashimiyya.

Qasimiyya, Khayriyya (1973), *al-Nashat al-sahyuni fi al-sharq al-'arabi wa sadah, 1908-1918*, Beirut, The Palestine Liberation Organization Research Centre.

—(1982), *al-Hukuma al-'arabiyya fi Dimashq bayn 1918–1920*, Beirut, al-Mu'assassa al-'Arabiyya lil Dirasat wal-Nashr.

—(ed.) (1974), *'Awni Abd al-Hadi: 'awraq khassa*, Beirut, The Palestine Liberation Organization Research Centre.

—(ed.) (1975), *Filastin fi mudhakkirat Fawzi al-Qawuji, 1936–1948*, Beirut, Dar al-Quds.

—(ed.) (1991), *al-Ra'il al-'Arabi al-Awal: hayat wa-awraq Nabih wa 'Adil al-'Azma*, London, Riad El-Rayyes Books.

al-Qassab, Muhammad Kamil and Muhammad 'Izz al-Din al-Qassam (AH 1344/AD 1925), *al-Naqd wal-bayan fi daf' awham khayzaran*, Damascus, Matba'at al-Taraqqi.

al-Qaysi, Sami Abd al-Hafiz (1975), *Yasin al-Hashimi wa dawruh fi al-siyasa al-'iraqiyya bayn 'ami 1922-1936*, vol. 1, Basra, Matba'at Hadad.

Rabbath, Edmond (1937), *Unité Syrienne et devenir arabe*, Paris, Librairie Marcel Rivière.

Ramadan, Abd al-'Azim (n.d.), *Tatawur al-haraka al-wataniyya fi Misr, vol. 1, 1918–1936*, Cairo, Dar al-Kitab al-'Arabi.

—(1974), *Tatawur al-haraka al-wataniyya fi Misr: 1937–1948*, vol. 2, Beirut, al-Watan al-'Arabi.

Ramsaur, E. I. (1957), *The Young Turks: Prelude to the Revolution of 1908*, Princeton, N. J., Princeton University Press.

al-Rayyis, Munir (1969), *al-Kitab al-dhahabi lil-thawrat al-wataniyya fi al-Mashriq al-'Arabi*, vol. 1, Beirut, Dar al-Tali'a.

—(1976), *al-Kitab al-dhahabi lil-thawrat al-wataniyya fi al-Mashriq al-'Arabi: thawrat Filastin*, Damascus, 'Alif Ba' Press.

Reissner, Johannes (1980), *Ideologie und Politik der Muslimbruder Syriens*, Freiburg, Klaus Schwarz Verlag.

Repp, R. C. (1986), *The Mufti of Istanbul: A study in the Development of the Ottoman Learned Hierarchy*, London, Ithaca Press.

Rida, Muhammad Rashid (1906–31), *Tarikh al-'Ustadh al-'Imam*, 4 vols., Cairo, Matba'at al-Manar.

—(AH 1344/AD 1925), *al-Khilafa*, Cairo, Matba'at al-Manar.

—(AH 1341/AD 1922), *al-Wahhabiyyun wal-Hijaz*, Cairo, Matba'at al-Manar.

Rihani, Amin (1967), *The Fate of Palestine*, Beirut, Rihani Publishing House.

Roy, Olivier (1994), *The Failure of Political Islam* (tr. Carol Volk), Cambridge, Mass., Harvard University.

al-Sabbagh, Salah al-Din (1994), *Fursan al-'uruba: mudhakkirat al-Shahid Salah al-Din al-Sabbagh* (new edn, ed. Samir al-Sa'idi), Rabat, Tanit lil-Nashr.

Sachar, Howard M.(1982), *A History of Israel from the Rise of Zionism to Our Time*, New York, Alfred A. Knopf.

El-Sadat, Anwar (1957), *Revolt on the Nile* (tr. Thomas Graham), New York, John Day Company.

Safran, Nadav (1961), *Egypt in Search of Political Community*, Cambridge, Mass., Harvard University Press.

Sa'id, Amin Muhammad (1934), *al-Thawra al-'arabiyya al-kubra*, Cairo, Matba'at 'Isa al-Babi al-Halabi.

—(AH 1395), *Sirat al-'Imam al-Shaykh Muhammad bin Abd al-Wahhab*, Riyadh, Darat al-Malik Abd al-'Aziz.

al-Sa'idi, Abd al-Mut'al (1962), *al-Mujadidun fi al-Islam min al-qarn al-awal 'ila al-rabi' 'ashar, 100–1370 AH*, 2nd edn, Cairo, Maktabat al-'Adab wa Matba'atuha.

al-Sakikini, Khalil (1925), *Filastin ba'd al-harb al-kubra*, vol. 1, Jerusalem, Matba'at Bayt al-Maqdis.

—(1955), *Kadha ana ya duniya* (a shorter version of al-Sakakini's diaries, ed. Hala al-Sakakini), Jerusalem, al-Matba'a al-Tijariyya.

Salam, Salim Ali (1982), *Mudhakkirat Salim Ali Salam, 1868–1938, ma' dirasa lil-'ilaqat al-firansiyya al-lubnaniyya* (ed. Hassan Ali Hallaq), Beirut, al-Dar al-Jami'iyya.

Salih, Muhsin Muhammad (1988), *al-Tayyar al-islami fi Filastin wa 'atharuh fi harakat al-jihad, 1917–1948*, Kuwait, Maktabat al-Falah.

Salman, Muhammad Hasan (1985), *Safahat min hayat Muhammad Hasan Salman*, Beirut, al-Dar al-'Arabiyya lil-Mawsu'at.

al-Samara'i, Yunis al-Shaykh Ibrahim (1982), *Tarikh 'ulama' Baghdad fi al-qarn al-rabi' 'ashar al-Hijri*, Baghdad, Wizarat al-Awqaf.

al-Sawwaf, Muhammad M. (1987), *Min sijil dhikrayati*, Cairo, Dar al-I'tisam.

Sayigh, Anis (1959), *Tatawur al-fikra al-'arabiyya fi Misr*, Beirut, Matba'at Haykal al-Gharib.

—(1966), *al-Hashimiyun wal-thawra al-'arabiyya al-kubra*, Beirut, Dar al-Tali'a.

al-Sayyid, Jalal (1973), *Hizb al-Ba'th al-'Arabi*, Beirut, Dar al-Nahar.

Schechtman, Joseph B. (1965) *The Mufti and the Fuehrer: The Rise and Fall of Haj Amin al-Huseini*, New York, Thomas Yoseloff.

Seton-Watson, Hugh (1977), *Nations and States*, Boulder, Colo., Westview Press.

al-Shabandar, Musa (1993), *Dhikrayat Baghdadiyya: al-'Iraq bayn al-ihtilal wal-istiqlal*, London, Riad El-Rayyes Books.

Shabib, Mahmud (1981), *Safahat matwiyya min tarikh al-'Iraq*, Beirut, al-Mu'assassa al-'Arabiyya lil- Dirasat wal-Nashr.

Shafiq, Ahmad (n.d.), *Mudhakkirati fi nisf qarn*, vol. 3, Cairo, Dar Majallati.

al-Shahbandar, Abd al-Rahman (1967), *Mudhakkirat al-Doktor Abd al-Rahman al-Shahbandar*, Beirut, Dar al-'Irshad.

al-Sharabasi, Ahmad (1963), *Amir al-bayan: Shakib Arslan*, vol. 2, Cairo, Dar al-Kitab al-'Arabi.

—(1978), *Shakib Arslan da'iyyat al-'uruba wal-Islam*, Beirut, Dar al-Jil.

Sharabi, Hisham (1970), *Arab Intellectuals and the West: The Formative Years, 1875–1914*, Baltimore and London, The John Hopkins University Press.

al-Sharif, Mahir (1985), *Tarikh Filastin al-'iqtisadi-al-'ijtima'i*, Beirut, Dar Ibn Khaldun.

Sharif, Regina (1983), *Non-Jewish Zionism: Its Roots in Western History*, London, Zed Press.

Shaw, Stanford J. (1962), *Ottoman Egypt in the Eighteenth Century*, Cambridge, Mass., Harvard University Press.

—(1971), *Between Old and New: The Ottoman Empire Under Selim III, 1789–1807*, Cambridge, Mass., Harvard University Press

—(1976), *History of the Ottoman Empire and Modern Turkey*, vol. 1, Cambridge, Cambridge University Press.

Shaw, Stanford J. and Ezel K. Shaw (1977*), History of the Ottoman Empire and Modern Turkey*, vol. 2, Cambridge, Cambridge University Press.

Shawkat, Naji (1975), *Sira wa dhikrayat thamanin 'aman, 1894–1974*, Baghdad, Matba'at Sulayman al-A'zami.

Shayyal, Jamal al-Din (1951), *Tarikh al-tarjama wal-haraka al-thaqafiyya fi 'asr Muhammad Ali*, Cairo, Dar al-Fikr al-Arabi.

al-Shihabi, Mustafa (1959), *Muhadarat 'an al-qawmiyya al-'arabiyya*, Cairo, Ma'had al-Dirasat al-'Arabiyya al-'Aliya.

Shimoni, Ya'cov (1956), *The Arabs of Palestine*, New Haven, Conn., Human Relations Area Files.

Shlaim, Avi (1988), *Collusion Across the Jordan: King Abdullah, the Zionist Movement, and the Partition of Palestine*, Oxford, Clarendon Press.

Shubbar, Hasan (1990), *Tarikh al-'Iraq al-siyasi al-mu'asir; al-tarikh al-islami 1900–1957*, vol. 2, Beirut, Dar al-Muntada lil-Nashr.

Shukri, Muhammad Fu'ad (1957), *Milad dawlat Libya al-haditha: watha'iq tahriruha wa istiqlaluha*, 2 vols., Cairo, Matba'at al-'I'timad.

al-Shuqayri, Ahmad (1969), *Arba'un 'aman fi al-hayat al-'arabiyya wal-dawaliyya*, Beirut, Dar al-Nahar.

al-Sifri, 'Isa (1937), *Filastin al-'arabiyya bayn al-intidab wal-sahyuniyya*, 2 vols., Jaffa, Matba'at Maktab Filastin al-Jadida.

Silverfarb, Daniel (1986), *Britain's Informal Empire in the Middle East: A Case Study of Iraq, 1929–1941*, New York and Oxford, Oxford University Press.

Simon, Reeva S. (1986), *Iraq between the Two World Wars: The Creation and Implementation of a National Ideology*, New York, Columbia University Press.

Smith, Charles D. (1992), *Palestine and the Arab–Israeli Conflict*, New York, St. Martin's Press.

Smith, Pamela Ann (1992), *Palestine and the Palestinians 1876–1983*, New York, St Martin's Press.

Stein, Kenneth W. (1984), *The Land Question in Palestine, 1917–1939*, Chapel Hill, N.C., University of North Carolina Press.

Stein, Leonard (1925), *Zionism*, London, E. Denim Ltd.

—(1961), *The Balfour Declaration*, London, Vallentine, Mitchell.

Storrs, Ronald (1945), *Orientations* (Definitive edn), London, Nicholson and Watson.

al-Swaydi, Tawfiq (1969), *Mudhakkirati: nisf qarn min tarikh al-'Iraq wal-qadiyya al-'arabiyya*, Beirut, Dar al-Kitab al-'Arabi.

—(1987), *Wujuh 'iraqiyya 'abr al-tarikh*, London, Riad El-Rayyes Books.

Tahbub, Fa'iq Hamdi (1982), *al-Haraka al-'umaliyya wal-naqabiyya fi Filastin, 1920–1948*, Kuwait, Kazima lil-Nashr wal-Tarjama wal-Tawzi'.

al-Tahir, Muhammad Ali (1932), *Nazarat al-shura*, Cairo, Matba'at al-Shura.

—(1950), *Mu'taqal al-Hucksteb*, Cairo, al-Matba'a al-'Alamiyya.

Tajir, Jack (n.d.), *Harakat al-tarjama fi Misr khilal al-qarn al-tasi' 'ashr*, Cairo, Dar al-Ma'arif.

al-Takriti, Shakir Ali (ed.) (1990), *al-'Asira raqam 93: mudhakkirat Madiha al-Salman*, Baghdad, Dar Wasit lil-Nashr.

al-Tamimi, Muhammad Rafiq and Muhammad Bahjat (AH 1335), *Wilayat Beirut*, 2 vols., Beirut, Matba'at al-'Iqbal.

Tantawi, Ali (1986), *Rijal min al-tarikh*, Jeddah, Dar al-Manara.

Tauber, Eliezer (1993), *The Emergence of the Arab Movements*, London, Frank Cass.

Taymur, Ahmad (1967), *A'lam al-fikr al-islami fi al-'asr al-hadith*, Cairo, Lajnat Nashr al-Mu'alafat al-Taymuriyya.

al-Tha'alibi, Abd al-'Aziz (1988), *Khalfiyyat al-mu'tamar al-'islami bil-Quds, 1931*, Beirut, Dar al-Gharb al-'Islami.

Tibawi, Abd al-Latif (1928), *al-Tasawuf al-islami al-'arabi: bahth fi tatawur al-fikr al-'arabi*, Cairo, Dar al-'Usur lil-Tab' wal-Nashr.

—(1956), *Arab Education in Mandatory Palestine*, London, Luzac and Co.

—(1961), *British Interests in Palestine*, Cairo, Oxford University Press.

—(1966), *American Interests in Syria, 1800–1901: A Study of Educational, Literary and Religious Works*, Oxford, Clarendon Press.

—(1969), *A Modern History of Syria, Including Lebanon and Palestine*, London, Macmillan.

—(1977), *Anglo-Arab Relations and the Question of Palestine, 1914–1921*, London, Luzac and Co.

—(1978), *The Islamic Pious Foundations in Jerusalem*, London, The Islamic Cultural Centre.

—(1985), *Dirasat islamiyya wa 'arabiyya*, London, The Islamic Cultural Centre.

Tibi, Bassam (1990), *Arab Nationalism: A Critical Enquiry*, ed. and tr. Marion Farouk-Sluglett and Peter Sluglett, New York, St Martin's Press.

Toynbee, Arnold J. (ed.) (1927), *Survey of International Affairs 1925, volume 1: The Islamic World Since the Peace Conference*, London, Oxford University Press.

Trimingham, J. Spencer (1971), *The Sufi Orders in Islam*, Oxford, The Clarendon Press.

Tuchman, Barbara W. (1982), *Bible and Sword: How the British Came to Palestine*, London, Macmillan.

Tuqan, Qadri Hafiz (1946), *Bayn al-'ilm wal-adab*, Jerusalem, Maktabat Filastin al-'Ilmiyya.

al-'Umari, Khayri (1986), *Yunis al-Sab'awi: sirat siyasi 'isami*, Baghdad, Dar al-Shu'un al-Thaqafiyya al-'Ama.

al-'Umari Muhammad Amin (1924–5), *Tarikh muqadirat al-Iraq al-siyasiyya*, 3 vols., Baghdad, al-Maktaba al-'Asriyya.

al-'Uthaymin, Abdullah al-Salih (1984), *Tarikh al-Mamlaka al-'Arabiyya al-Sa'udiyya*, vol. 1, Riyadh, Matabi' al-Sharif.

Verete, Mayir (1992), *From Palmerston to Balfour: Collected Essays of Mayir Verete*, ed. Norman Rose, London, Frank Cass.

Villari, Luigi (1956), *Italian Foreign Policy Under Mussolini*, New York, Devin-Adair Co.

Voll, John Obert (1982), *Islam: Continuity and Change in the Modern World*, Boulder, Colo., Westview Press.

Wahbah, Hafiz (1964), *Arabian Days*, London, Barker.

Walters, Moshe P. (1942), *The Mufti Over the Middle East*, London, Barber [Moshe Walters is the pen-name for Maurice Pearlman].

Wasserstein, Bernard (1991), *The British in Palestine*, Oxford, Basil Blackwell.

Weber, Eugen (1976), *Peasants into Frenchmen: The Modernization of Rural France, 1870–1914*, Stanford, Stanford University Press.

Webster, Sir Charles (1951), *The Foreign Policy of Palmerston, 1830–1841*, London, Bell.

Weizmann, Chaim (1949), *Trial and Error: The Autobiography of Chaim Weizmann*, London, Hamish Hamilton.

Westrate, Bruce (1992), *The Arab Bureau: British Policy in the Middle East, 1916–1920*, University Park, Pennsylvania, The Pennsylvania State University.

Whitehead, Alfred N. (1979), *Process and Reality*, New York, The Free Press.

Wilson, Mary C. (1987), *King Abdullah, Britain and the Making of Jordan*, Cambridge, Cambridge University Press.

Yaghi, Abd al-Rahman (1968), *Hayat al-adab al-filastini al-hadith min awal al-nahda Hata al-nakba*, Beirut, al-Maktab al-Tijari lil-Tiba'a wal-Nashr wal-Tawzi'.

Yaghi, Isma'il Ahamd (1974), *Harakat Rashid 'Ali al-Gaylani: dirasa fi tatawur al-haraka al-wataniyya al-'iraqiyya*, Beirut, Dar al-Tali'a.

Yapp, M. E. (1991), *The Making of the Modern Near East, 1792–1923* (5th impression), London, Longman.

Yasin, Abd al-Qadir (1981), *Kifah al-sha'b al-filastini hata al-'am 1948*, Beirut, al-Mu'assassa al-'Arabiyya lil-Dirasat wal-Nashr.

Yasin, Subhi (1959), *al-Thawra al-'arabiyya al-kubra fi Filastin, 1936–1939*, (Cairo), Dar al-Hana lil-Tiba'a.

—(1964), *Nazariyat al-'amal li-istirdad Filastin*, Cairo, Dar al-Ma'rifa.

al-Yasini, Ayman (1987), *al-Din wal-dawla fi al-Mamlaka al-'Arabiyya al-Sa'udia*, London, Dar al-Saqi.

Yehosha'a, Ya'aqoub (1974), *Tarikh al-sahafa al-'arabiyya fi Filastin fi al-'ahd al-'uthmani, 1908–1918*, Jerusalem, Matba'at al-Ma'arif.

al-Zahrawi, Abd al-Hamid (1960), *al-Fiqh wal-tasawuf*, Cairo, al-Maktab al-Fanni lil Nashr (first published in Cairo at al-Matba'a al-'Uthmaniyya in 1901).

—(1962), *al-'Irth al-fikri lil-muslih al-'ijtima'i Abd al-Hamid al-Zahrawi*, ed. Jawdat al-Rikabi and Jamil Sultan, Damascus, al-Majlis al-A'la li-Ri'ayat al-Funun wal-Adab wal-'Ulum al-'Ijtima'iyya.

Zeine, Zeine N. (1960), *The Struggle for Arab Independence: Western Diplomacy and the Rise and Fall of Faisal's Kingdom in Syria*, Beirut, Khayat.

—(1973), *The Emergence of Arab Nationalism with a Background Study of Arab–Turkish Relations in the Near East* (3rd edn), New York, Caravan Books.

Ziadeh, Nicola A. (1953), *Urban Life in Syria Under the Early Mamluks*, Westport, Conn., Greenwood Press.

al-Zirikli, Khayr al-Din (1925), *'Aman fi Amman*, Cairo, Maktabat al-'Arab.

—(1989), *al-A'lam* (8th edn), 8 vols., Beirut, Dar al-'Ilm lil-Malayin.

Zu'aytar, Akram (1980), *al-Haraka al-wataniyya al-filastiniyya, 1935–1939*, Beirut, Mu'assassat al-Dirasat al-Filastiniyya.

—(1994), *Min mudhakkirat Akram Zu'aytar*, 2 vols., Beirut, al-Mu'assassa al-Arabiyya lil-Dirasat wal-Nashr.

Index

Abbas Hilmi   37, 48, 125–6
Abd al-Baqi, Ahmad Hilmi
    194, 252
Abd al-Hadi, Amin   54, 115
Abd al-Hadi, 'Awni   35, 38,
    104, 120–1, 147, 160, 163,
    164, 165, 166, 230, 232,
    234, 235, 291, 296–7, 305,
    309, 346, 361
    Higher Arab Committee
    194, 197, 234, 249, 253,
    270, 304
    Istiqlalist Party foundation
    172
Abd al-Hadi, Fakhri   224,
    227, 263, 264
Abd al-Hadi, Salim al-Ahmad
    42, 51
Abd al-Hamid   5, 17–18,
    29–30
    1909 counter coup   27
    deposition in CUP coup   23
    Jewish immigration policy
    59
    opposition to rule   23
    oppressive policies   19, 20
    pan-Islamic policies   18, 19
Abd al-Ilah   333, 334, 335,
    337, 341, 342, 344, 373, 375
Abd al-Nasser, Jamal   383
Abd al-Qadir, Muhii al-Din
    39
Abd al-Raziq, Ali   99, 157,
    158
Abd al-Raziq, 'Arif (Abu Faysal)
    224, 256, 260, 262, 345
Abd al-Raziq, Mustafa   157,
    286
'Abdin, Sabri   197, 254

'Abduh, Muhammad   15, 17,
    18, 22, 30, 52, 67, 112, 151
Abdullah   48, 56, 71, 96,
    104, 140, 146–7, 152, 153,
    173, 228, 229–30, 232,
    235, 250, 251, 263, 264,
    277, 278, 280, 287, 299,
    302, 349–50, 353, 355,
    374, 381
Abu al-Sa'ud, Hasan   110,
    254, 257
Abu al-Timman, Ja'far   167,
    215, 216, 218, 219, 220,
    271
Abu Durra, Yusuf   224, 252,
    256, 262, 264
Abu Ghanima, Subhi   258,
    259, 282
'Affula peasant evictions   58
al-Afghani, Jamal al-Din   5,
    15, 17, 18, 52
Agence d'Orient   208
al-Ahali Group   215, 220,
    268, 271
al-Ahali newspaper   220
al-'Ahd   23, 38–9, 47, 51, 53,
    141, 144, 167, 346, 380
Ahmad, 'Atiya   252, 255, 256
al-Ahram   37, 112, 166, 201,
    273, 291
al-Rabita al-'Arabiyya   200
al-'Alami, Musa   304, 305,
    309
Alexander II assassination   57
Ali, Muhammad   102, 106,
    109, 204, 223, 231, 269,
    286, 287, 296, 373
Ali, Shawkat   100, 102, 106,
    107, 108, 109–10, 112,

    115, 116, 117, 118, 121,
    122, 124, 160
'Alif Ba'   208, 263
Allenby   56, 101
Alliance Musulmane
    Internationale   125
Alliance Universelle Israélite
    57
Allied Supreme Council   56,
    145
'Alluba, Muhammad Ali   109,
    114, 115, 118, 120, 124,
    125, 158, 204, 281, 291,
    346, 354
    World Parliametary Congress
    for the Defence of Palestine
    287, 288
al-'Alusi, Mahmud Shukri
    15, 51, 52, 53, 120
Amman   115, 146, 147, 225
'Amun, Iskander   42, 43, 61,
    142
Anderson, Benedict   6, 7, 11
Andrews, L. Y.   251, 252, 255
Anglo-American "Lend-Lease"
    arrangement   340
Anglo-Egyptian treaty   202,
    229, 268
Anglo-French Boundary
    Convention (1923)   56
Anglo-Iraqi treaty (1930)
    153, 164, 176, 177, 216,
    217–18, 333, 339, 366,
    376, 380
al-'Ani, Nu'man   221, 223
Anwar Pasha   159, 357
al-Aqsa mosque
    General Congress of Jerusalem
    agenda   108, 120

General Congress of Jerusalem
opening session 117
Restoration fund 101, 154,
158, 215
Western Wall (al-Buraq;
Wailing Wall) disputes
94–5, 156, 160, 162, 207,
215, 396
Arab Bureau (al-Maktab
al-'Arabi) 206, 207, 214,
258
Arab Bureau for Research and
Information see Arab
Bureau (al-Maktab
al-'Arabi)
Arab Club (al-Nadi al-'Arabi)
68, 69, 90, 93, 142, 352,
362
Arab Congress 43, 44, 61
Arab League 117, 181, 399
role of Egypt 154
Arab League Society (Jam'iat
al-Jami'a al-'Arabiya) 37,
48
Arab Legion 264
Arab Liberation Society 211,
213, 282
Arab Nationalist Bloc 211
Arab Nationalist movement
(Harakat al-Qawmyyin
al-'Arab) 351, 356
Arab Nationalist Party (al-Hizb
al-Qawmi al-'Arabi) 351,
352
Arab notables 1
in Abd al-Hamid
administration 18–19
Arabist support 51, 54–5
in "big stick elections" (1912)
39
al-Fatat opposition in
Damascus 141
post-Hamidian CUP support
24
Syrian Arab-Islamic reformists
21
urban élite 10–11, 50, 51, 56
see also a'yan class
Arab Renaissance Society
(Jam'iat al-Nahda
al-'Arabia) 22
Arab Revolt 48, 50, 51, 53,
143, 144, 154, 366, 399

Arab Student Society of Paris
212
Arab unity 191, 211, 279
Amin al-Husayn's project
268–9
British attitudes 175,
179–81, 269, 293, 294–5,
299–300, 347–8, 355
differences during
Iraqi–British War 380–1
Ghazi's support 285
Hasan al-Banna's views
161, 162
Palestinian Question consensus
279
World War II 345, 347,
349, 350–2, 353–7
see also Pan-Arabism
Arab-Islamic reformists 1, 10,
11, 163, 395, 398
anti-despotism 17, 20
Arab Caliphate project 8
Arabic language 7–8, 30
1908 coup support 23
CUP support 23, 27
evolution towards nationalism
15–16, 17, 18, 21
invocation of pristine Islam
9, 17
origins of Arabism 5–6, 9,
15, 51, 52, 55
Ottoman bond 52–3
in Palestine 67
print media utilization 8
regional centres of activity
15
rifts following 1912 elections
40
Western influences 15
Arab–Jewish conference 299,
300–9
Arab–Jewish Conference White
Paper 307–9, 345, 346,
355
Churchill's view 348, 349
Egyptian response 309,
345, 346
Higher Arab Committee
(HAC) response 308,
309
Iraqi response 309, 345
Jewish Agency response
308

Newcombe mission to Iraq
348–9
Saudi response 309, 310,
356
Arab–Ottoman Brotherhood
Society (Jam'iat al-'Ikha'
al-'Arabi al-'Uthmani)
25–6, 27–8
Arab–Zionist entente 60–1,
62
Arabic language 6, 7–8, 17,
18, 19, 22, 28, 46, 55, 151,
162, 213
Arabism 5, 6, 7–8, 15–23,
51, 55, 139–81, 395
interwar Egypt 156–7,
200–1
North African Arabs 163–4
opposition 51–2
origins 5–6, 9, 15, 50, 52,
55
in Palestine 67
relation to regional state
12, 397, 399
response to fall of Damascus
government 146
response to Zionist project
60, 397
Wafd Party support 156
al-'Arif, 'Arif 35, 70, 71, 72,
153
Arslan, 'Adil 51, 151, 165, 174
Arslan, Shakib 40, 44, 50,
52, 98, 103, 107, 118, 125,
149, 150–1, 156, 159, 165,
212, 281, 357, 358, 359,
365, 109
Arab unity ideal 164
support for Faysal 169
Syrian Revolt fund-raising
152
al-Arsuzi, Zaki 212, 282, 384
al-As'ad, Kamil 39, 49
al-'Asali, Shukri 21, 36, 37,
39, 45, 51
Ashkenazim 57
al-Ashmar, Muhammad 227,
252, 258
'Asir province dispute 158
al-'Askari, Ja'far 220, 224, 273
Association of Car Owners and
Drivers 195
Assyrian revolt 358

al-Atasi, Hashim   145, 205, 206, 207
Atatürk   222
al-'Athari, Muhammad Bahjat   120, 163
Australian troops   56
Axis powers   356, 357–71
a'yan class   40, 49
  anti-Arabists   51
  Husayni–Nashashibi rivalry   89, 93–4
  land appropriation   63
  sources of power   63–4
  strength of Arabist support   55
  see also Arab notables
al-'Ayyubi, Ali Jawdat   166, 331
al-A'zami, Nu'man   216, 217
al-Azhar   98, 99, 100, 101, 111, 112, 113
  support for Bludan conference   280
  support for General Strike   203
al-Azhar, Shaykh   204, 205, 287, 288, 289
al-'Azm, Haqqi   42, 61
al-'Azm, Muhammad Fawzi   39, 44, 50, 51
al-'Azm, Nazih al-Mu'ayyad   151, 352
al-'Azm, Rafiq   20–1, 23, 27, 42, 51, 52, 61, 142
al-'Azm, Shafiq al-Mu'ayyad   25, 26, 27, 37
al-'Azma, 'Adil   151, 163, 225, 226, 227, 257, 258, 353
al-'Azma, Bahira   290, 291
al-'Azma, Nabih   118, 125, 126, 147, 151, 158, 163, 171–2, 174, 207, 208, 212, 213, 214, 267, 279, 384
'Azzam, Abd al-Rahman   114, 117, 118, 119, 121–2, 156, 164, 204, 345, 354

Baggalley, Lacy   330, 347, 348
Baghdad
  anti-Mond demonstrations   214–15
  Arab-Islamic reform movements   15, 16

"big stick elections" (1912)   39
  educational provision   28, 46, 214
  General Congress of Jerusalem opposition   115
Baghdad congress committee   167, 174, 175
al-Bahrani, Ra'uf   220, 336, 373
al-Bakri, Nasib   140, 146
Bal'a confrontation   227
al-Balagh   156, 202
Balfour   58, 62, 72
Balfour Declaration (1917)   58, 62, 69, 71, 92
  demands for annulment   149, 150, 152, 283, 290
Balkan War   40, 41, 45
al-Banna, Hasan   161–2, 202, 203, 204, 289, 359
Barakat, Bahii-al Din   156, 288
al-Barudi, Fakhri   206, 209, 212, 214, 258
Bashi, Ibrahim 'Attar   221, 223
al-Basil, Hamad   156, 203, 288
Basra Reform Society   41, 42, 43
al-Bassam, Sadiq   212, 220, 335
Ba'th Party   351, 358, 384
Beeley, Harold   280–1, 289, 308
Beirut
  Arab nationalist repression by Jamal Pasha   49
  "big stick elections" (1912)   39
  CUP opposition   37
  educational provision   28, 46
  al-Fatat activities   38
  Nationalist Action League (NAL)   212
Beirut Reform Society (Jam'iyyat Beirut al-'Islahiyya)   41, 42, 43, 45
Ben-Gurion, David   277
"Big stick elections" (1912)   39–40
al-Bilad   221

Bilad al-Sham   18, 282
Biluim activists   57
al-Bitar, Abd al-Razzaq   15, 21
Bitar land posessions   64
al-Bitar, Salah al-Din   384
"Black Letter"   105, 108
Bludan Arab Conference   274, 278–83, 293, 298
Blum, Leon   208
Bols   71
Bonnet   266
Brodetsky   111, 178
Bullard, Reader   275–6, 284, 301, 302
al-Buraq *see* al-Aqsa mosque
Bureau for National Propaganda (Maktab al-Di'aya wal-Nashr)   206

Cairo
  anti-British demonstrations   192–3
  Arab-Islamic reform movements   15, 16
  Colonial Office Conference   146
  CUP opposition   37
  Ottoman Decentralization Party formation   41–2
  pan-Arab congress project support   170
  pan-Islamic (Caliphate) congress (1926)   98–101, 113
Cairo Arabists
  Arab Revolt support   50
  interwar period   148–9
  move to Damascus   142, 143, 144
  schism   151
  Zionist contacts   150
Caliphate   95, 99–100
  abolition   96
  Fu'ad's claim   98
  Husayn's claim   96–8, 143
  opposition   20, 21
Caliphate Movement of India   100, 103, 106, 107, 111
Caliphate question   8, 16, 20, 101–2, 107, 108, 191
  General Islamic Congress of Jerusalem   107, 108, 110–11, 112, 113

Central Committee for Jihad
(CCJ)   257, 258, 259,
260–1, 267
Centralization policies   16,
33
Arabism as response   50
CUP post-Hamidian policy
26, 30
educational aspects   8
see also Ottoman
modernization/centralization
programme (tanzimat)
al-Chadirchi, Kamil   219, 220
Chamberlain, Neville   58,
294, 307
Chancellor, John   104, 105,
165
Churchill, Winston   146,
278, 329, 340, 343, 347,
348, 349, 377
Colombani   266
Colonial Office Cairo
Conference   146
Committee for the Support of
the Afflicted People in
Palestine   257
Committee of Union and
Progress (CUP)
anti-Abd al-Hamid coup
(1908)   23, 67
Arab opposition   25–6,
31–2, 34, 36–7, 39
Arab reconciliation   45–6
Arab–Turkish conflicts   24
Arabist support   23, 26–7
"big stick elections" (1912)
39–40
bureaucratic reorganization
31, 36
central committee   25, 26,
34
1909 counter coup   23,
27–8
despotic tendencies   34–5,
39–40
Egyptian allies   154
guild system abolition   65
oppressive policies   16, 28
organizational deficiencies
24–5, 34
parliamentary party   25
parliametray elections (1908)
26

post-Hamidian policies
23–4, 26, 30
pro-Zionist stigmatization
25, 36
1912 relinquishment of power
40
response to First Arab
Congress   44–5
return to power   43, 45–6
Turkish biases   31, 55
Congress of the Palestine
Muslim Nation   115
Cornwallis, Kinahan   343,
374, 375, 376, 377, 381
Criminal Investigation
Department (CID)
pan-Islamism reports
107

Daghir, As'ad   142, 144, 151,
165, 166, 167, 201
al-Dajani, 'Arif   68, 69
Dajani family social position
63, 64
al-Dajani, Hasan Sidqi   195,
197
al-Dajani, Raghib   89, 115
Damascus   15, 16, 21–2, 26,
27, 28–9, 37, 38, 39, 42,
56, 71, 140, 141, 142, 209,
213, 253, 265
Damascus Arab Army   168
Damascus Arab government
21–2, 41, 48–9, 56, 68, 71,
140–5, 206, 396, 399
al-Dandashi, Abd al-Razzaq
212, 213, 222
al-Dandashi, 'Ali Abd al-Karim
211
Dar al-Arqam   210
Dar al-'Ulum   161
Darwaza, 'Izzat   70, 106, 126,
140, 146, 160, 165, 172,
212, 232, 234, 249, 253,
257–8, 261, 266–7, 268,
269, 270, 272, 281, 297,
304, 305, 309, 361
Darwaza, Muhammad Ali
227, 257, 259
Dawn   50, 51, 52
decentralization   20, 52
al-Afghani's views   17
Arabist views   34

Entente Libéral programme
37
post-Hamidian CUP policy
24
Democratic Party   142
detention centres   198
Dohle   361, 362
Druze revolt   32
al-Durra   216

Eastern Student Conference
359
Eastern Women's Congress
266, 290–3
resolutions   291
Eden, Antony   229, 231, 294,
295, 343, 348
Edmonds, C. J.   285, 336,
338, 341, 355
education   8, 12, 50
Arabist groups   51
CUP policies   26, 46
interwar Iraq   214
language issues   17–18, 28,
29–30, 46
Ottoman Education Law
(1869)   28
in Palestine   64, 66
tamzimat reforms   17
ulema families   64
Egyptian nationalism   153,
154
Misr al-Fatat   201
Wafdi support   156
Egyptian revolt (1919)   154
Egyptian Women's Union
(EWU)   290
support for General Strike
203
Egyptian–British treaty   200
Egyptian–Iraqi treaty of alliance
346
Entente Libéral (Party of
Freedom and Concord)
37–8, 40, 41
Shawkat assassination plot
45
Enver   25, 42–3, 45
European influences   15, 24,
55
Abd al-Hamid's responses
18, 19
al-Afghani's views   17

concepts of nationhood   9,
   20
societal change in Palestine
   65, 66
European products boycott
   107–8

Farraj, Ya'qub   194, 306
Faruq   204, 275, 286, 289
al-Faruqi, Sulayman al-Tajj
   60
al-Fatat   23, 45, 46–7, 69,
   140, 167
   al-'Ahd Syrian group
      opposition   141
   Cairo Arabist group
      opposition   144
   Damascus Arab government
      involvement   140–1
   Damascus notables opposition
      141
   Damascus recruitment drive
      141, 144
   dissatisfaction with CUP
      reforms   45
   educational background   51
   Faysal's recruitment   49,
      140, 399
   First World War support for
      Ottoman cause   46–7
   formation   38
   King–Crane Commission
      reception   70
   leading bureau   140, 146
   Ottoman military repression in
      Syria   49
   Palestinian activists   70
   First Arab Congress   43
   CUP response   44–5
   Paris-based activities   43
   repression by Jamal Pasha
      49
   al-Taqadum (Progress)
      influence   142
al-Fath   148, 157, 161, 200
Fawzi, Husayn   331, 334, 335
Faysal   48–9, 53–4, 56, 62,
   71, 97, 140–1, 144, 145,
   146, 147, 164, 166,
   168–70, 173, 174, 175,
   177, 178–9, 216, 218, 219,
   278, 338, 366, 399
Faysal–Clemenceau treaty   145

Faysal–Weizmann agreement
   62, 70
Ferraj, Ya'qub   69, 250
Filastin   44, 59, 250–1, 263
Fiqhi schools   9
First Palestinian Arab Congress
   69, 70
French mandate   56
   Syria   145
Fu'ad   101, 111, 177, 204
   al-Aqsa mosque restoration
      fund donations   154
   Caliphate ambitions   98,
      99, 112, 155
   mufti of Jerusalem meeting
      154
   relations with Britain   154

Gaylani family   338, 382, 397
al-Gaylani, Rashid 'Ali   219,
   220, 221, 333, 334, 335,
   337–9, 340, 341–2, 343,
   352, 354, 356, 366, 367,
   368, 369, 370, 382
   Iraqi–British war (1941)
      372–4, 376, 377, 379, 380
Gaza a'yan land ownership   64
General Islamic Congress of
   Jerusalem (1931)   94, 95,
   101, 103, 163, 164, 207,
   396
   agenda   110, 119
   Caliphate question   107,
      108, 110–11, 112, 113
   demise   124–7
   Egyptian opposition   111,
      112–14, 116
   executive committee for
      permanent congress   118,
      125, 126, 171
   final resolutions   120, 121,
      122, 123
   funding   124, 125
   Hashemite opposition
      115–16
   impact   123–4
   international response   116
   Islamic University project
      109, 110, 111, 113, 122–3,
      124
   meeting at Abd al-Hadi's
      house   163–4
   origins of idea   106

Palestinian delegation   101
Palestinian opposition
   114–15
   participants   114, 115, 117,
      118, 119–20, 217
   planning background   104–9
   preparation   109–16
   preparatory committee
      110, 115
   proceedings   117–23
   religious propagation and
      guidance committee report
      122
   Western Wall question   94,
      108, 110, 120
   Zionist opposition
      110–11
General strike see Palestinian
   General Strike; Syrian
   national strike
'Geographic Palestine'   67
Gershoni   153
al-Ghalayini, Mustafa   122,
   163
Ghazi   219, 220, 228, 272,
   285
   death   332–3, 337, 349,
      367
al-Ghita', Muhammad Husayn
   al-Kashif   119, 217, 284
al-Ghuri, Emile   201, 353
al-Ghusayn, Ya'qub   194,
   252, 282, 304, 305, 309
"Golden square" colonels
   335, 336, 337, 341, 342,
   343–4, 351, 353, 354, 369,
   373, 377, 379, 380
Gouraud, Henri   145
Greater Syrian state project
   143–4
Greek Orthodox support for
   Bludan conference   280
Grobba, Fritz   271, 361, 364,
   368
Guild system abolition   65

Haavara agreement   360, 361,
   363
Haddad, 'Usman Kamal
   368–9, 370, 378
al-Hafiz, Isma'il   102, 110
Hajj Congress   97–8
al-Hakim, Hasan   147, 151

Halifax   295, 300, 303, 304, 355

Hamada, Khalil   31

Hammad, Tawfiq   54, 149

Hamza, Fu'ad   275, 306, 364

Hananu, Ibrahim   169, 206

al-Haram al-Sharif
    burial of Muhammad Ali   106
    Hasan Abu al-Sa'ud sanctuary   254
    mufti of Jerusalem sanctuary   253
    restoration   92, 104

Harb, Muhammad Salih   346, 357

Harb, Tal'at   155, 156

Hashemite–Saudi rivalry   152, 173–4

al-Hashimi, Taha   38, 220, 225, 284, 331, 334, 335, 342–4, 353, 354, 356, 368

al-Hashimi, Yasin   38, 47, 53, 120, 140, 166, 167–8, 170, 173, 174, 175, 215, 216, 217, 218–19, 220, 223, 225, 226, 230, 268, 272, 284, 338, 366

Hassuna, Hasan   108

Haydar, Ali   31, 48

Haydar, Rustum   46, 170, 331, 334, 337

Haydar, Sa'id   140, 146

Haykal, Muhammad Husayn   156, 158, 273, 286

Hebrew University inauguration   101

Hebron a'yan land ownership   63

al-Hidaya magazine   216, 217

al-Hidaya al-Islamiyya Society   157
    Iraqi group   216–17, 223

Higher Arab Committee (HAC)   194, 195, 262, 270, 300, 367
    Arab-Jewish conference participation   301–2, 303, 304–5
    White Paper rejection   308, 309

Bludan Arab Congress   279, 283

deportation of members   252–3

Palestinian revolt   224, 226, 228, 230, 232, 234, 235

Peel Commission
    evidence   249–50
    initial boycott   249
    response to report   270
    Round-Table Conference participation 267

al-Hihyawi   122

Hijaz
    ashraf rulers   47–8
    British assurances   143
    educational facilities   29
    Egyptian contacts   155
    ports blockade   48
    Saudi seige   147, 155

Hijaz railway   48, 62, 102, 118, 119

al-Hilal   157

Hilmi, Ahmad   115, 119, 172, 304, 305

Hitler   362, 363, 364–5, 367, 370, 378

Hizb al-Istiqlal (Independence Party)   141

Hizb al-Ittihad al-Suri (Syrian Union Party)   142, 143–4, 146

al-Hizb al-Qawmi al'-Arabi (Arab Nationalist Party)   351, 352

Hizb al-'Umma al-'Arabiyya (Party of the Arab Nation)   350

al-Hizb al-Watani al-Suri (Syrian National Party)   141

Hochberg, Sami   61

Hope-Simpson, John   104, 105

Hourani, Albert   10

al-Hout, Bayan   64, 65

Humphreys, Francis   176, 177, 178–9

Hurayka, Ignatius   280, 281

Husayn   33, 44, 47–8, 96, 99, 142, 143, 144, 152
    Arab Revolt   48, 50, 143
    British contacts   48, 49
    Caliphate aspirations   96–8, 143, 152

al-Husayni, Abd al-Qadir   224, 256, 257, 260, 262, 345

al-Husayni, Amin (mufti of Jerusalem)   70, 71, 72, 89, 90–5, 101, 102, 104, 106, 108, 109, 110, 113, 114, 115, 116, 117, 118, 121, 123, 124, 125, 126, 127, 152, 154, 158, 164–5, 170, 171, 172, 194–5, 196, 197, 198, 199, 200–1, 210, 213–24, 230, 232, 234, 235, 251, 252, 253, 254–5, 257, 258, 263, 268–9, 270, 279, 284, 288, 297–8, 300, 301, 302, 303, 304, 305, 306, 309, 310, 329–30, 335, 336, 337, 341, 343, 344, 345, 346, 348, 349, 350, 351, 352, 353, 354, 359, 360, 362, 363, 365, 367, 368, 369, 370–1, 372, 380

al-Husayni, Dawud   262, 345

al-Husayni family   63, 68, 69, 89, 91, 93, 397

al-Husayni, Husayn   55

al-Husayni, Jamal   101, 104, 160, 194, 230, 232, 253, 288, 304, 305, 306, 309, 348

al-Husayni, Musa Kazim   68, 71, 72, 89, 92, 93, 104, 150

al-Husayni, Sa'id   37, 39, 46

Husayni–Nashashibi rivalry   89, 93–4

al-Husri, Sati'   52, 140, 214, 216

Hyamson, Albert N.   297, 298, 299

Ibn al-Rashid   33

Ibn Rifada revolt   173, 174

Ibn Sa'ud   100, 102, 103, 116, 148, 168, 275, 279, 372
    Arab congress project response   174
    Arab-Jewish conference   301, 304
    'Asir province dispute   158
    Bludah conference response   280
    British relations   275–6, 301, 302–3

Faysal meeting (1930)   164
German relations   363, 364
al-Husayni (mufti of
    Jerusalem) contacts
    268–9, 330
Iraqi relations   170, 342
Iraqi–British War response
    382–3
Palestinian revolt mediation
    228, 229, 231–2
Peel report response   276–7,
    284
Syrian nationalist contacts
    170
World Parliametary Congress
    for the Defence of Palestine
    response   287
Ibrahim, Abdurrahman Hajj
    54
Ibrahim, Rashid al-Hajj   160,
    172, 193, 252, 305
al-'Ikha' al-Watani Party   219,
    220, 222, 338
al-Ikhwan al-Muslimun see
    Muslim Brotherhood
al-Imam, Sa'id Abd al-Fattah
    351, 362
Independence Party (Hizb
    al-Istiqlal)   141
India
    Caliphate Movement   100,
        103, 106, 107, 111
    support for General Strike
        199
al-Inkilizi, Abd al-Wahhab
    21, 40, 45, 51
International Committee on the
    Western Wall   104, 106,
    108, 121
Iqbal, Muhammad   118, 122
Iraq Defence Committee   384
Iraq Support Society   384
Iraqi National Party   218, 219
Iraqi-British war (1941)   214,
    330, 338, 372–84
    Arab volunteers   383
    background   329–32
    British troop movements
        374–5, 377
    Egyptian responses   381,
        383
    German military aid   370,
        371, 378–9

German response   377–8
    ineffectiveness of Iraqi
        defences   379
    Iraqi Arabist divisions
        380–1
    outbreak   377
    Saudi responses   382–3
    Syrian support   383–4
    Turkish mediation   379–80
Iraqi-Iranian border treaty   285
'Isa, Khalil Muhammad (Abu
    Ibrahim al-Kabir)   252,
    256
Islamic Parliamentary Congress
    266
Islamic reform movement   5,
    15, 19, 51, 151
    Arab political movement
        opposition   52
    Arabism origins   52
Islamic societies
    Damascus   209
    Egypt   273
    Iraq   216–17
    support for Palestinian general
        strike   210
Islamic University project
    108, 109, 110, 111, 113,
    122–3, 124
Islamism   5
Isma'il, Abd al-Qadir   215, 220
Istiqlal Party/Istiqlalists   115,
    118, 147, 150, 151, 152,
    164, 270, 279
    goals   172
    National Bloc membership
        205–6
    Nationalist Action League
        (NAL) links 212
    opposition   172–3
    Palestinian   170–3
    Palestinian General Strike
        support   201
    Palestinian revolt support
        194
    pan-Arabic congress project see
        pan-Arabic congress project
    relations with Amin al-Husayni
        170, 171, 172
    Syro-Palestinian Congress
        (1921) participation   149
L'Italia Musulman   359
al-Ittihad al-'Uthmani   37

al-Jabiri, Ihsan   165, 359
al-Jabiri, Nafi'   35, 39
al-Jabiri, Sa'd-Allah   345, 353
al-Jabri, Ihsan   150
Jaffa
    anti-Zionist demonstrations
        (1920)   71
    a'yan land ownership   64
    General Strike   195, 198
    Jewish-Arab clashes   192,
        193
    Muslim-Christian Association
        (MCA)   68
    Young Muslim Men's Society
        (YMMS) 160
Jahid, Husayn   30–1
Jama'iyya Muhammadiyya
    (Muhammadan Society)
    27
al-Jamaili, Fadil   216, 221
Jamal Pasha   48–9, 55, 399
    contacts with Faysal   53
    repression of Arab nationalists
        23, 36, 42, 49, 52
    Suez Canal attack   49
al-Jami'a al-'Arabiyya   106
Jam'iyyat al-Da'wa wal-'Irshad
    (Society for Proselytizing
    and Guidance)   37
Jam'iyyat al-'Ikha' al-'Arabi
    al-'Uthmani (Arab-Ottoman
    Brotherhood Society)
    25–6, 27–8
Jam'iyyat al-Jami'a al-'Arabiyya
    (Arab League Society)
    37, 48
Jam'iyyat al-Nahda al-'Arabiyya
    (Arab Renaissance Society)
    22
Jamil, Husayn   215, 220
al-Jam'iyyat al-Gharra'   209
Jam'iyyat al-Hidaiya al-Islamiyya
    209–10
    support for General Strike
        203, 208
Jam'iyyat al-Rabita al-'Arabiyya
    (Arab Bond Society)   200
Jam'iyyat al-Rabita al-Sharqiyya
    (Eastern Bond Society)
    157–8, 159
Jam'iyyat al-Shura
    al-'Uthmaniyya (Ottoman
    Consultative Society)   23

Jam'iyyat al-Tamaddun al-Islami
210
Jam'iyyat Beirut al-'Islahiyya
(Beirut Reform Society)
41, 42, 43, 45
Jankowski 153
Jaridat al-Ikhwan al-Muslimin
200
Jawish, Abd al-'Aziz 44, 52,
154, 159
al-Jaza'iri, Muhammad Sa'id
118–19
al-Jaza'iri, Salim 21, 38
al-Jaza'iri, Tahir 15, 21, 29,
36, 51, 149
Jenin *a'yan* land ownership 63
Jerusalem 28, 49, 55, 56, 59,
63, 64, 66, 67, 68, 69, 71,
91, 101, 108, 109, 160, 170
Jerusalem Radio Arabic Service
264
Jewish Agency
Arab-Jewish conference White
Paper rejection 308
response to Syrian involvement
in general strike 208
Jewish auxiliary units 264
Jewish immigration 57–9,
104, 150, 169, 193, 209,
224, 233, 249, 300, 400
Arabist responses 60
Bludan Congress resolution
283, 298
British policy following
Palestinian revolt 231,
232, 234
demands for cessation during
Palestinian revolt 230,
231, 232, 234, 290
demands for cessation
preparatory to Arab-Jewish
conference 302, 303
following Nazis' rise to power
359, 360, 361, 363
following response to Passfield
White Paper 106, 171
limitation following
Arab-Jewish conference
307
Newcombe-Hyamson project
297
Ottoman government policy
59

Samuel's formula 296
Jewish land sales 58, 59, 60,
68, 121, 209
Egyptian responses 156
Passfield White Paper
104–5
Jewish National Home policy
92, 93, 105, 124, 150, 156,
169, 175, 176, 178, 180,
181, 228, 229, 269, 296,
398, 400
Arab-Jewish conference White
Paper responses 355
Bludan Congress resolution
283
Churchill's support 348
Peel Commission
recommendations 250,
277
Jewish products boycott 207,
283, 360
Jewish state 57, 58, 62, 63,
398
Jewish Telegraphic Agency
report 110, 111
Jewish-Arab violent clashes 95,
192, 193, 224, 251–2, 254
al-Jihad 202
"Junior Circle" 21–2

Kamal, Mustafa 95, 96, 125
Kamal, Wasif 193, 211–12,
213, 250, 262, 345, 351,
356
Kamil Pasha 40, 41, 42
deposition 34–5, 43
al-Karmi, Sa'id 42, 51, 67
al-Karmil 37, 44, 59
al-Kashkul 117
Kautsky, John H. 18
al-Kawakibi, Abd al-Rahman
19, 22, 30
Kawkab al-Sharq 156, 202
Kelly, David 203
Kerr, Clark 224, 230, 231
al-Khadra, Subhi 165, 172
Khalidi family 55, 63, 64
al-Khalidi, Husayn 193, 194,
195, 252, 304, 305
al-Khalidi, Musa 55
al-Khalidi, Nazif 62
al-Khalidi, Ruhi 36, 40, 52,
66, 67

al-Khalidi, Yusuf Diya 65–6
al-Khalil, Abd al-Karim 22,
36, 45, 46, 49, 119
al-Khatib, Muhib al-Din 22,
23, 42, 51, 52, 104, 142,
144, 148, 151, 159
al-Fath 200
influence on al-Banna 161,
162
Khoury 50
al-Khuri, Faris 21, 174, 288,
289
King-Crane Commission 70
Kitchener 48
Kubba, Muhammad Mahdi
218, 221, 223
Kurd-Ali, Muhammad 21,
37, 50, 51
Kuwait 332

al-Lajna al-'Uliya li-Ighathat
Mankubi Filastin 203
Lampson, Miles 229, 231,
232, 256, 269, 273, 274,
287, 291, 331, 341, 346,
347
Land laws 63
Land ownership 64
Language issues
CUP post-Hamidian policy
26, 28
education 17–18, 28,
29–30, 46
Entente Libéral policies 38
Nationalist Action League
(NAL) policy 213
Ottoman Decentralization
Party policies 42
League of Nations 150, 153,
158, 216, 218, 274, 308,
359
Lebanese Christians 41, 43
support for Bludan conference
281
Lebanese Muslim Council 122
Liberal Constitutionalist Party
99, 114, 155, 156, 201,
273, 286
Liberal Union (Osmanli Ahrar
Firkasi) 25
Libya
Italian atrocities 121, 358
Italian imperialism 358, 359

refugees   117
Libyan nationalists
  Bludan conference
    participation   280
  Eastern Bond backing   158
Literary Forum (al-Muntada
  al-Adabi)   23, 35–6, 68,
  93
Lloyd   348
Lloyd George   58, 62, 72
Local Arab states   11, 12
Local nationalism (*wataniyya*)
  16, 19
Lorraine, Percy   177
Luckas   2
Lutfallah, Amir Michel   142,
  144, 148, 149, 151, 152, 157
Lynch Brothers   32

MacDonald, Malcolm   295,
  299, 300, 307, 308, 309
MacDonald, Ramsay   104, 105
McDonnell, Michael   198
Mackereth   263, 265–6, 270,
  280, 282, 293, 304
al-Madfa'i, Jamil   166, 222,
  272, 273, 285, 303, 331,
  340, 342, 380, 381
al-Madi, Mu'in   226, 249,
  254–5, 257, 266, 279, 361
  Istiqlalist Party foundation
  172
Madina   29, 50
  Hijaz railway project   48
Magazine of the Muslim World
  120
al-Maghribi, Abd al-Qadir
  50, 52
Magnes, Judah   297, 298
al-Mahaiyri, Fahmi   212, 351
Mahir, Ali   204, 205, 286,
  287, 305, 306, 310, 331,
  345, 346–7, 354
Mahmud, Muhammad   273,
  286, 304, 305–6, 310
Majallat al-Hidaiya al-Islaimyya
  200
Majallat al-Rabita al-Sharqiyya
  158
Majallat al-Shubban al-Muslimin
  200
al-Makhzumi, Muhammad
  25, 44

Maktab 'Anbar   21, 28–9
al-Maktaba al Salafiyya   161
al-Manar   19, 20, 59, 143,
  157, 158, 161, 200
  CUP opposition   37
  relaunch   204
al-Maraghi, Muhammad
  Mustafa   99, 112, 155,
  204, 286, 289
Mardam, Jamil   38, 146, 169,
  174–5, 206, 207, 208, 210,
  265–6, 267, 279, 280, 282,
  284, 330, 345, 352, 353
Mecca
  educational facilities   29
  Hijaz railway project   48
  Islamic reform society   19
  Muslim World Congress
    (1926)   102–3, 116
merchants   65
Mesopotamia
  British mandate   56
  river transport project   32
Midhat Pasha   16, 18, 29
al-Miqdadi, Darwish   210,
  211, 212, 214, 221
Misr al-Fatat (Young Egypt)
  201, 205
al-Misri, Aziz Ali   23, 38, 39,
  53, 157, 346, 357, 383
al-Misriyya   291
Moderate Liberal Party   35, 37
Mond, Alfred   214
Morocco
  national movement   158
  support for General Strike
    199
al-Mu'ayyad   22
Mufarraj, Fu'ad   212, 351
al-Mufid   37, 38
Mufti of Jerusalem *see*
  al-Husayni, Amin
Muhammad, Abd al-Rahim
  al-Hajj   224, 255, 256,
  260, 262
Muhammadan Society (Jama'ia
  Muhamadia)   27
Mukhlis, Mawlud   166, 218,
  288
Mukhtar Pasha   40, 41
al-Muntada al-Adabi (Literary
  Forum)   23, 35–6, 68, 93
al-Muqattam   37, 61, 201, 273

al-Muqtabas   22, 37, 112
al-Muqtataf   22
Muslim Brotherhood (al-Ikhwan
  al-Muslimum)   127, 157,
  200, 273, 289
  Egyptian group   286
  foundation   160–1
  Iraqi group   216
  Islamic principles   162
  Nasserite confrontation   400
  Palestinian Question
    involvement   162–3
  political activism   204, 205,
    273
  support for Bludan conference
    280
  support for General Strike
    202–3, 205
  Syrian group   210
Muslim World Congress (1926)
  102–3, 116
Muslim World Congress (1949)
  127
Muslim-Christian Association
  (MCA)   68
  First Palestinian Arab Congress
  69
Mussolini   359, 360
al-Muthanna Club   212, 220,
  221, 223, 225, 272, 367, 373
  Bludan conference
    participation   281, 282
al-Muzaffar, Abd al-Qadir
  97, 110, 119, 158

Nablus   68
  a'yan land ownership   63
  1931 conference   107–8
  local national committee
    193
  strength of Arabist support
    54
  Young Muslim Men's Society
    (YMMS)   160
al-Nadi al-Watani (National
  Club)   41
al-Nadi al'-Arabi (Arab Club)
  68, 69, 90, 93, 142, 352,
  362
al-Nahar   281
al-Nahhas, Mustafa   114, 117,
  174, 202, 203, 204, 229,
  273–5, 279, 288, 289

al-Najjar, Salim   61
al-Naqib, Talib   26, 27, 37,
   39, 41, 46, 51
al-Nashashibi, Fakhri
   114–15, 263, 264, 306
Nashashibi family   63, 68, 69,
   89, 93, 114, 115, 196, 253,
   280, 397
   Abdullah political allies
      153, 232, 251, 263, 278
   inclusion in Arab-Jewish
      conference delegation
      305, 306
   Palestinian revolt opposition
      262–3, 264
   al-Shahbandar alliance   152
   Zionist contacts   94, 114,
      115
al-Nashashibi, Raghib   68, 71,
   72, 89, 93, 104, 115, 193,
   194, 195, 232, 235, 250,
   262–3, 264, 270, 306
Nassar, Najib   59, 60
National Bloc   205–6, 207,
   213, 249, 265, 280, 349,
   352, 353
   Nationalist Action League
      (NAL) relations   213–14
   Zionist approaches   208–9
National Club (al-Nadi
   al-Watani)   41
Nationalist Action League (NAL)
   207, 208, 210–13, 222,
   280, 350, 352, 356
   Bludan conference
      participation   281, 282
   Mount Lebanon conference
      212–13
   National Bloc relations
      213–14
Nationhood concept   6–7, 8
al-Natur, Tawfiq   38, 140
Newcombe, Stewart F.   297,
   298, 348, 354
Newton, Basil   310, 329, 339,
   340, 341, 344
North African Arabs
   Arabism   163–4
   General Islamic Congress of
      Jerusalem participation
      163
Nwayhid, 'Ajaj   102, 110,
   165, 172, 201, 263–4

Occupied Enemy Territory
   Administration (OETA)
   71
   anti-Zionist sympathies   72
Office of Propaganda and
   Communications   258
Oliphant, Lancelot   177, 231
Organization of the Islamic
   Conference (1969)   127
Ormsby-Gore, W. G.   232,
   234, 235, 249, 294–5
Osmanli Ahrar Firkasi (Liberal
   Union)   25
Ottoman Administrative
   Decentralization Party
   23, 41–2, 43, 142
   First Arab Congress   43, 44,
      45
   First World War support   47
Ottoman bond   16, 18, 34,
   40, 44
   Arab-Islamic reformists   52
   dissolution   47–72
   relation to Islam   52
Ottoman Consultative Society
   (Jam'iyyat al-Shura
   al-'Uthmaniyya)   23
Ottoman Decentralization Party
   Arab Congress invovlement
      43, 44
   Damascus government
      involvement   140
   formation   41–2
   policies   42
   response to Zionist project
      60
Ottoman Education Law (1869)
   28
Ottoman modernization/
   centralization programme
   (tanzimat)   15, 16–18,
      29, 30, 400
   language issues in education
      29–30
   opposition   16–17
Ottoman Patriotic Party   60

Palestinian Arab Executive
   89, 92, 93, 170
   a'yan rivalry   94
   British relations   92, 93
   negotiations with British
      Labour Government   104

recognition of Husayn as
   Caliph   97
Syro-Palestinian Congress
   (1921) participation
   149, 150
Palestinian Arab League   60
Palestinian Christians   64
Palestinian Committee in Cairo
   149
Palestinian Defence Committee
   208, 214, 226, 267
   Iraq   223, 224, 227, 271,
      272, 284–5
   Palestinian revolt funding
      257
   Saudi Arabia   277
Palestinian General Strike
   193–7
   Arab leaders' mediations
      228, 229
   Arab women's movement
      support   290
   Arab–Islamic support
      199–200
   Egyptian support   199,
      200–5, 286–7
   end   228–36
   escalation towards revolt
      224–8
   Iraqi support   214–24
   punitive British response
      198–9
   Syrian support   205–14
Palestinian Istiqlal Party
   170–3
Palestinian National Congress
   72
   a'yan rivalry   94
Palestinian nationalism   16,
   44, 63–72
   Husayni–Nashashibi rivalry
      89
Palestinian partition proposal
   250, 253
   abandonment   267, 284,
      294–5, 300–2
   Arab response   267–78,
      293
   Bludan Congress resolution
      283
   British Jewish dissent
      296–8
   Egyptian reactions   273–5

Iraqi reaction 270–2
reaction in Palestine 250–1, 268
see also Peel Report
Palestinian Question 12
absence from First Arab Congress agenda 44, 61
Arab leaders mediation 235, 249
British policy following Palestinian revolt 231, 235
Churchill's view 348
convergence with Arab political movement 278, 283, 284, 293, 396
Egyptian interwar attitudes 155, 156, 269
Faysal's proposals 168–9, 175
General Islamic Congress of Jerusalem impact 123–4
Muhammad Ali's proposals 269–70
Muslim Brotherhood (al-Ikhwan al-Muslimum) attitudes 162–3
Nazi attitude 362–3
Royal Commission 230
united Arab position following outbreak of World War II 345, 346
Palestinian revolt 191–236, 249–310, 346, 396
Palestinian "terrorism" 251–2, 254, 261–2
Pan-Arab congress project 163, 270, 279
Baghdad congress committee 167
British opposition 177–8, 279
decline 173–81
executive committee 165
Faysal's Syrian–Iraqi union agenda 169, 173, 177
Iraqi support 166–7, 168–70, 223
preparations 165, 166, 170
proposed transfer to Jerusalem 179
Saudi opposition 174, 279

Second World War project 354–6
Zionist opposition 178, 279
pan-Arabism 11, 16, 145, 176
Iraq 153, 217, 220, 223, 272–3, 284–6, 372
Muslim Brotherhood attitudes 162
National Bloc 205–6
Nationalist Action League (NAL) 210
revival 163–5
Rida'a views 142–3, 144
pan-Islamic conventions 98, 99–103, 396
pan-Islamism 5, 18, 19, 20, 23, 89–127, 161, 162, 191
interwar Egypt 157
Palestinian Criminal Investigation Department (CID) reports 107
pan-Islamic conventions 98, 99–103
rebirth 95–103
relation to Palestinian Question 123–4
rebirth 95–103
relation to Palestinian Question 123–4
Paris
Arab Congress 43
al-Fatat activities 38, 43
Peace Conference (1919) 56, 69–70
Parkinson, Cosmo 231
Parliamentary elections 1908 26, 27
"big stick elections" (1912) 39
October 1912 (incomplete) 40–1
April 1914 46, 61
opposition to Zionism 61
Party of the Arab Nation (Hizb al-'Umma al-'Arabiyya) 350
Passfield White Paper 104–5
"Peace Bands" 263
Peel Commission 105, 230, 232, 235, 249–50, 251, 267, 268, 269, 270, 277

Higher Arab Committee boycott 249
Higher Arab Committee evidence 249–50
Palestinian response 250, 270
Woodhead commission 294–5
Zionists evidence 249, 250, 277
Peel Report 250
British responses to Arab reaction 294
Egyptian response 273–5, 278
German response 361–2
Iraqi response 270–2, 278
Saudi response 276–7, 278, 284
support from Abdullah 277–8
Syrian response 278, 279
Yemen response 278
see also Palestinian partition proposal
People's Party 120
Petah Tikva incident 58, 192
Peterson 303, 332
Political Islam 1
Popular Reform Society 220
Publishing activities 8, 19, 66

Qadri, Ahmad 35, 38, 53, 140, 146
al-Qarqanni, Khalid al-Hud 364, 365, 369, 372
al-Qasimi, Jamal al-Din 15, 51
al-Qasimi, Salah al-Din 21, 22
al-Qassab, Kamil 47, 51, 122, 142, 143, 144, 146, 147, 174, 249
al-Qassam, 'Izz al-Din 160, 192
al-Qassamis 207, 224, 252, 254, 255, 256, 262
al-Qawuqji, Fawzi 225–6, 234, 255, 261, 353
Palestinian revolt military expedition 226–7, 233
Qur'an 6, 9, 15, 28, 30
al-Quwwatli, Shukri 21, 118, 140, 146, 147, 148, 151,

152, 169, 199, 205–6, 207,
209, 212, 213, 265, 284,
330, 350, 352, 353, 356,
369, 372

al-Rabita al-'Arabiyya 208
Radio Bari Arabic Services
359, 370
Radio Berlin Arabic Services
365, 370
Radio Jerusalem Arabic Service
264
al-Rasafi, Ma'ruf 40, 44, 50,
52, 223
al-Rawi, Ibrahim 216, 343
al-Rayyis, Munir 227, 258,
267, 282, 291, 350, 351
Regional Arab states 11–12
Religious reform 19, 20, 36–7
Rendel, G. W. 179, 180,
233, 269, 294, 347
Ribbentrop 378
Rida, Rashid 39, 45, 51, 52,
67, 99, 107, 115, 125, 126,
144, 148, 149
Amin al-Husayni relationship
165
Arab League Society 48
Arab–Islamic reformist ideas
15, 18, 19, 30, 36–7, 90
Arslan friendship 151
al-Banna influence 161, 162
Committee of Union and
Progress (CUP) support
26–7
Faysal support 169
First World War support 46
General Islamic Congress of
Jerusalem 117, 121, 122
Jam'iyyat al-Rabita
al-Sharqiyya (Eastern Bond
Society) 157, 158
al-Manar 59, 200
Muslim World Congress
(1926) 102, 103
Ottoman Administrative
Decentralization Party
42
Ottoman Consultative Society
23
pan-Arab congress project
support 163, 165, 170,
174

political development
142–3
School of Islamic learning
project 36, 37
Syrian Congress presidency
145
Young Muslim Men's Society
(YMMS) 159
al-Rikabi, Rida 140, 145
al-Risala 200, 201, 290
Riza, Ahmad 16, 25, 28
Rock, Alfred 104, 194, 253,
304, 305
Round-Table Conference 267
Rushdiyya schools 29, 30
Russia 57
Rwayha, Amin 221, 226
Ryan, Andrew 229

Saba, Fu'ad 252, 305
al-Sab'awi, Yunis 212, 221,
222, 282, 337, 343, 350,
351, 356, 369, 372, 373,
380
al-Sabbagh, Salah al-Din
212, 216, 221–2, 225, 272,
331, 333, 335, 336, 340,
343, 353, 354, 365, 372,
380, 382
Sa'dabad Pact 379
al-Sadat, Anwar 383
al-Sa'dawi, Bashir 163, 206,
268, 269, 275
Sa'di Bloc 286
al-Sa'di, Farhan 224, 252, 254
Sadiq Bey 37, 45
Sa'id, Abd al-Hamid 104,
109, 113, 117–18, 122,
158, 159, 203, 281
Sa'id, Abd al-Hamidi 114,
115
Sa'id, Amin 156, 208
Sa'id, Fahmi 216, 221–2,
331, 372, 377, 379
al-Sa'id, Hafiz 39, 42
Sa'id land possessions 64
al-Sa'id, Nuri 53, 164, 166,
176–7, 217–19, 220,
269–70, 272–3, 285, 297,
303, 306, 309, 310,
329–30, 335, 336, 340,
342, 367
al-'Ahd membership 38

concepts of Arab Unity
354–6
Iraqi premiership 331–4,
335, 345, 346, 348, 349,
350, 367
Iraqi–British War 380, 381
Palestinian revolt resolution
mediation 233–5
al-Sa'ids 397
Salah, Abd al-Latif 193, 194,
253, 305
Salama, Hasan 224, 256, 257
Salman, Mahmud 222, 310,
331, 372, 379
Salman, Muhammad Hasan
221, 351, 373, 383
Samuel, Herbert 72, 91, 101,
169, 296–7, 298, 308, 347
Saudi congress of the Muslim
world 101–2
al-Sayyid, Jalal 212, 351
School of Islamic learning
36, 37
Second International Missionary
Conference protests 94
Secret Intelligence Service (SIS)
reports 96
"Senior Circle" 21, 22
al-Sha'b 117
al-Shabab 201
Shabab Muhammad 210
al-Shabandar, Musa 351, 373
Shabib, Kamil 222, 331, 343,
379
al-Shahbandar, Abd al-Rahman
21, 142, 143, 144, 145,
146, 149, 151–2, 169, 208,
280, 345, 349, 352, 353
al-Shahbandars 397
al-Sham'a, Rushdi 25, 26, 35,
37, 39, 51
Shamil, Sa'id 121, 125
Shanshal, Siddiq 212, 221,
222, 351
al-Shanti, Muhammad 42, 60
Sharabi, Hisham 50
Sharaf, Sharif 373, 375
Sha'rawi, Huda 290, 291
Sharett, Moshe 277
Shari'a law 19, 33, 99, 162,
196
Sharifian officers 53, 272,
380

al-'Ahd membership   38
    in Arab Revolt   53, 218
al-Sharq al-Adna   214
Shatwan, Yusuf   26, 50
Shawkat, Mahmud   23, 45,
    219
Shawkat, Naji   331, 332, 335,
    341, 343, 356, 366–7, 368,
    369, 370, 372, 373, 380
Shawkat, Sami   216, 221, 367
al-Shawwa family   54–5, 64
al-Shawwa, 'Izz al-Din   212,
    255, 257, 258, 345
al-Shawwa, Rashad   212,
    258
Shihab al-Din   15
al-Shihabi, 'Arif   22, 47, 49,
    51
Shi'i revolt   217
Shils, Edward   6
Shlaim, Avi   277
Shukri, Hasan   195, 196
al-Shuqayri, As'ad   44, 46, 50,
    51, 52, 67, 101
al-Shura   149, 157, 201
Sidqi, Bakr   271, 272
Sidqi, Isma'il   111–12, 113,
    114, 117, 118, 177
Simon, Reeva   336
Sirri, Husayn   342, 381
al-Siyasa   155, 156, 158
Societal change   63–5
Society for Guarding al-Aqsa
    and the Sacred Islamic
    Places   94, 95
Society for Proselytizing and
    Guidance (Jam'iyyat
    al-Da'wa wal-'Irshad)   37
Sokolow, Nahum   61, 62
Standing Official Sub-Committee
    on the Middle East of the
    Committee of Imperial
    Defence   176
Storrs, Ronald   48, 93
al-Subahi, Muhammad   117,
    118
Suez Canal   161, 289
Sufi *tariqas*   9
al-Sukhun, Mamduh   212,
    262, 345, 351
Sulayman, Hikmat   219, 220,
    268, 270, 271, 272–3, 279,
    331–2, 361

al-Sulh, Kazim   212, 282,
    350, 351
al-Sulh, Rida   39, 49
al-Sulh, Riyad   118, 121, 123,
    125, 126, 208, 268, 281
al-Sulh, Taqii al-Din   212,
    351
Sunna (Prophet's traditions)
    6, 9, 15
Supreme Muslim Council
    (SMC)   91–2, 94, 95, 96,
    108, 110, 171, 196, 253
    al-Haram al-Sharif restoration
    104
    recognition of Husayn as
    Caliph   97
al-Swaydi, Naji   46, 223, 272,
    281, 335, 356, 368, 369,
    373, 381, 382, 383
al-Swaydi, Tawfiq   38, 43,
    273, 301, 338, 342, 343,
    381
al-Swaydi, Yusuf   219, 281
Sykes, Mark   58
Sykes–Picot agreement   53,
    56, 143
Syrian Arabists   20–1, 43, 140
    Arab Congress support   43,
    44
    Arab Revolt support   50
    CUP support   27
    "Junior Circle"   21–2
    move to Cairo   40
    Ottoman outlook   23
    repression by Jamal Pasha
    23, 49
    Saudi contacts   147–8, 152
    "Senior Circle"   21, 22
Syrian Congress   145
Syrian Islamic societies
    209–10
    support for Palestinian general
    strike   210
Syrian National Party (al-Hizb
    al-Watani al-Suri)   141
Syrian national strike   193, 207
Syrian nationalism   18, 206,
    207, 208, 209
Syrian revolt   102, 117,
    151–2, 169, 205, 207, 226
    Eastern Bond backing   158
    Second World War project
    353

Wafd response   156
Syrian Union Party   (Hizb
    al-Ittihad al-Suri)   142,
    143–4, 146
    Cairo group   148, 149
    Syro-Palestinian Congress
    (1921) participation   149
Syrian-Iraqi union   169, 173,
    175–6, 178, 179, 350, 353,
    354, 370
Syro-Palestinian Congress
    (1921)   149
    resolutions   149, 150

Taba'i' al-'Istibdad   19–20
al-Tabatba'i, Diya' al-Din
    118, 123, 124, 125–6
al-Tadamun Club   214, 215
al-Taftazani, Muhammad
    al-Ghanimi   109, 118,
    122, 157
Taggar   271
al-Tahir, Muhammad Ali
    117, 119, 121, 148–9, 151,
    156, 201, 262
Tal'at   25, 33, 36, 44
al-Tamimi, Abd al-Hadi   55
al-Tamimi, Amin   46, 110,
    147
al-Tamimi family   55
al-Tamimi, Rafiq   35, 38, 51,
    70, 140, 146, 305
Tanin   30, 31
Tannus, 'Izzat   304, 305
Tanzimat see Ottoman
    modernization/centralization
    programme
al-Taqadum (Progress)   142
Tasawuf   15
al-Tha'alibi, Abd al-'Aziz   50,
    52, 98, 106, 107, 109, 110,
    112, 113, 114, 120, 125,
    199
Thabit, Sa'id   120, 166, 167,
    217, 218, 221, 223, 226,
    227, 272
al-Thaghir   122
Tlay', Rashid   147, 152
Tourism   65
Tripolitania invasion   31, 34,
    38, 40
Tulkarem *a'yan* land ownership
    63

Tunisia
national movement   158
support for General Strike
199
Tunisian Dustur Party   98
Tuqan, Haydar   46, 54
Tuqan, Sulayman   193, 260,
263
Turkification policies   30,
31
Turkish language   18, 26, 27,
39
in education   28, 30
Turkish nationalism   29–30
Tusun, 'Umar   99, 101, 155,
157, 160, 202
Twayni, Jubran   281, 288

Ulema   1, 18, 55, 63
in Abd al-Hamid
administration   18–19
anti-British protests   197
Arabist support   51, 67
Bludan conference support
280
Caliphate issue   98, 100–1
decline in influence   64
fatwa against Jewish authority
in Muslim countries
276–7, 292–3
al-Husayni leadership in
Palestine   92
influence on educational
policy   28, 30
Islamic reformists   15
Jewish land sales prohibition
217
land ownership   64
Palestinian general strike
support   203, 224
Palestinian partition rejection
271, 284
Syrian Arab-Islamic reformists
21
see also Arab notables (élite)
Ulema Solidarity Society
203
al-'Umari, Amin   331, 334,
335
Umma   19, 45, 60, 119, 124,
162, 358
al-'Uraysi, abd al-Ghani   38,
43, 49, 51, 119

Urban Arab notables (élite)
10–11, 50, 51, 56, 63
Arabist support   51
Urban growth   41
Urban Jews in Palestine   58
USA
Iraqi arms sales   340
Iraqi relations   342, 343
King-Crane Commission
70
'Usayran, 'Adil   212, 351
'Uthman, Amin   274, 306

von Papen   367, 368

Wafd   99, 156, 201, 286, 397
Arab congress project
involvement   174
Egyptian–British treaty   200
Jerusalem Congress
representation   114, 117
Palestinian support   287
response to Syrian revolt
156
World Parliamentary Congress
for the Defence of Palestine
support   287, 288
Wahba, Hafiz   164, 231, 275
Wahhabi movement   102,
122, 148
Wali   47
Waqf   8
Wauchope, Arthur G.   106,
165, 171, 177, 179, 230,
233
Wavell   349, 374, 377
Weizmann, Chaim   62, 105,
208, 234, 277
meeting with Nuri al Sa'id
233
Western Wall Commission
104, 106, 108, 121, 158
Western Wall disputes see
al-Aqsa mosque
wilayat law   48
Wolf, Heinrich   360
Wolf, Otto   364
Women's Palestine Defence
Committee   290
Woodhead commission
294–5, 298, 299, 300, 349
Woodhead, John   295
wool-knitting trade   65

World Parliametary Congress for
the Defence of Palestine
287–90
British opposition   287,
288
preparation   287
resolutions   289–90
World War I   56, 395
implications for Zionist
project   62
outbreak   46
support for Ottoman cause
46–7
World War II   333, 340, 349,
399

Yahya, Abd al-Fattah   301
Ya'ish, Farid   212, 262, 351
Yamulki, 'Aziz   331, 334, 335
Yasin, Yusuf   147, 148, 229,
259, 275, 361, 364, 369,
372
Yemen
'Asir province dispute   158
Ottoman Consultative Society
(Jam'iyyat al-Shura
al-'Uthmaniyya)   23
rejection of Palestinian
partition proposal   278
Yemen campaign   32–3
Young Egypt Society   157,
286
Young Muslim Men's Society
(YMMS)   104, 108, 114,
118, 120, 157, 158, 159,
199, 273
Arab-Islamic orientation
159, 160
Iraqi branches   216
Palestinian branches
159–60
publications   200
support for General Strike
202, 203, 287
Young Muslim Women's Society
291
Young Ottoman movement
16
suppression   17
Young Turks   21, 23
Yugoslavia   116
al-Yusuf, Abd al-Rahman   39,
43, 50, 51

Zaghlul, Saʻd   99, 156
al-Zahra   148
al-Zahrawi, Abd al-Hamid
    20, 21, 39, 42, 45, 51
Zaki, Ahmad   157, 158
al-Zawahiri, al-Ahmadi   112,
    114
Zayn al-Din, Farid   210, 211,
    212, 214, 218, 221, 282,
    351
Zaynal, Yusuf   214, 215
al-Zayyat, Ahmad Hasan
    200, 290
Zionist Commission in Palestine
    72, 92
Zionist Congress (1897)   57
Zionist Organization   57, 233
Zionist products boycott   121
Zionist project   16, 34, 36,
    44, 56, 57–63, 68, 70, 72,

89, 156, 231, 348, 398–9,
    400
Zionist–Unionist collusion
    60
Zionists
    Abdullah contacts   153
    Arab–Jewish conference
        307
    Arabist contact during First
        Arab Congress   44, 61
    Baghdad Arabic conference
        opposition   178
    Cairo Arabist contacts   150
    General Islamic Congress of
        Jerusalem opposition
        110–11
    Haavara agreement with Nazis
        360, 361, 363
    al-Nashashibi family contacts
        94, 114, 115

Passfield White Paper response
    105
Peel Commission
    representation   249, 250,
    277
religious ambitions in Palestine
    120
response to alternatives to
    partition   296, 298
Shawkat Ali contacts   111
Syrian approaches during
    general strike   208–9
al-Zirikli, Khayr al-Din   147,
    165
Zuʻaytar, Akram   172, 193,
    197, 199, 212, 213, 218,
    221, 223, 234, 258, 284,
    288–9, 291, 345